MISSOURI GENEALOGICAL RECORDS & ABSTRACTS

VOLUME 1: 1766 – 1839

By

Sherida K. Eddlemon

HERITAGE BOOKS, INC.

Copyright 1990 By

Sherida K. Eddlemon

Surname Index By Marlene Towle

Other Titles By the Author:

Genealogical Abstracts from Tennessee Newspapers
1791 - 1808

Genealogical Abstracts from Tennessee Newspapers
1803 - 1812

Dickson County, Tennessee, Marriage Records
1817 - 1879

Morgan County, Missouri, Marriage Records
1833 - 1893

Published 1990 By

HERITAGE BOOKS, INC.
1540E Pointer Ridge Place, Bowie, Maryland 20716
(301)-390-7709

ISBN 1-55613-315-4

A Complete Catalog Listing Hundreds of Titles on
History, Genealogy & Americana
Free on Request

ACKNOWLEDGMENTS

My sincere thanks to the staffs of the Boonslick Regional Library, Sedalia, Missouri; The Missouri State Archives, Jefferson City, Missouri; and Memphis State University, Memphis, Tennessee for their helpful assistance during my research trips to their facilities. I also appreciate the continued encouragement of my parents, Amelia and Nelson Eddlemon, in support of my genealogical writing endeavors.

DEDICATION

This book is dedicated to the memory of my elusive French ancestor, Achille Godin (Gaudin), who died between 1812 and 1818. He left his widow, Marguerite (Margaret) James, and children living near the mouth of the Arkansas River and the Mississippi several miles below Arkansas Post; but not a footstep to show from whence he came. The search for information about these French ancestors continues.

PREFACE

The white man came early to Missouri. Spanish and French explorers were pushing deep into this virgin territory long before the English settlers thought about crossing the Smoky Mountains into Tennessee and Kentucky. The Spanish explorer Hernando De Soto first laid eyes on the Mississippi River in 1534. After De Soto's death during his expedition to explore the lands west of the Mississippi River, his successor Luis de Moscoso traveled in the area now known as Arkansas. Two French explorers, Marquette and Joilet, traveled through the Arkansas River country and pushed northward to discover the Missouri River in 1673.

But the region was still Indian country until 1682 when La Salle claimed the Mississippi Valley for France. He named the region Louisiana in honor of his King, Louis XIV. The French explorer Henry de Tonty made a settlement in 1686 that was later to be known as Arkansas Post.

Pierre le Moyne, Sieur d'Iberville, established a royal Louisiana colony in 1699 known now as Ocean Springs, Miss. Farther north French priests established the Mission of St. Francis Xavier in 1700 at the mouth of the Des Peres River.

In 1732, settlers from the area now Illinois made the first permanent settlement at Ste. Genevieve, Missouri. Civilization began to develop quickly. In 1764 Auguste Chouteau and Pierre Laclede Liguest established St. Louis. John Dodge settled in Ste. Genevieve followed three years later by Israel Dodge. Missouri no longer belonged to just the Indians, French and Spanish. By 1795 American settlements flourished along the Femme Osage Creek in St. Charles County.

In 1762 France gave this land called "Louisiana" to Spain. The Spanish gave it back to France in 1800 and three years later in 1803 France sold the area to the United States in what became known as the Louisiana Purchase. In 1804 St. Louis became the capital of the District of Louisiana. Missouri was proclaimed a territory separate from Louisiana in 1812 and became the 24th state in 1821.

This switching from France to Spain then back to France and later to the United States makes researching an early ancestor in Missouri or Arkansas extremely difficult. Even after the Louisiana Purchase the area was briefly part of the territories of Orleans and Indiana. Later the region known as the Territory of Illinois was formed. It was actually six years after the purchase from France that the Missouri Territory was formed.

Not only did the settlers of Missouri, Northern Arkansas, West Tennessee and Southern Illinois have to struggle with the common problems of Indians, isolation, weather and illness, but settlers of the time period of 1811 to 1812 were faced with one more terrifying experience -- that of earthquakes. The earthquakes were so severe at one time the Mississippi River flowed backwards for over an hour and formed Reelfoot Lake in Tennessee. Some stayed and toughed it out and others left to find land that did not move.

When the Louisiana Purchase was made some of the French wanted to be considered truly American. They anglicized their names. Example: Celestine Mitchell became known as Sarah Mitchel and Achille Godin became Ashel Gordon..

Also the French used the practice of "dit" names or aliases. The early French would assume the name of a place or even another family name as a form of identity. The English or Americans did not understand this practice so the early records might be under either name or even shortened in later generations. Example: Nicholas Caillot dit Lachance. The records could be under Caillot or Lachance or even Chance. Both surnames are indexed in this volume.

All names appear as they were written on the records including abbreviations of given names. No attempt has been made to make corrections in spelling. Cemetery listings include only information on those people born before 1840 and who died before 1900.

In some instances it was necessary to use abbreviations which are primarily used in tax lists. They are as follows:

```
    I   - Newspaper issue date      UM   - Unmarried
    JP  - Justice of the peace      agt  - Agent
    L   - Livestock                 P    - Poll Tax
    a   - acres                     W    - Watch
    T   - Tanyard                   LD   - Land
    M   - Mill                      D    - Distillery
    OC  - Original Claimant.
```

Example: Joshua Alexander, L, 221 a., OC. John Smith.

Joshua Alexander was taxed on livestock, has 221 acres and John Smith was the original claimant to the land. Each entry is separated by a semi-colon.

This volume is a collection of records from that hazy period of 1766 to 1839 which is often puzzling to the Missouri/Arkansas researcher. These records were chosen to help fill the gap created by the lack of a 1810 and 1820 census and to pinpoint an ancestor to a specific locality.

I have yet to find my elusive French ancestor Achilles Godin/Gaudin in these records. I wish you luck in finding yours within these pages.

DATES TO REMEMBER

1541	The Spanish explorer Hernando De Soto first saw the Mississippi River.
1586	The Lost Colony was unsuccessfully attempted on Roanoke Island.
1607	Settlement at Jamestown.
1620	The ship "Mayflower" arrived at Plymouth, Mass.
1673	Marquette and Joliet, French explorers, discovered the Missouri River.
1682	Robert Cavelier de La Salle claimed the Mississippi Valley for France. He named the region LOUISIANA.
1700	The Mission of St. Francis Xavier was established by French priests on the present site of St. Louis.
	The orginal Arkansas Post was abandoned.
1722	A new settlement was formed at Arkansas Post.
1732	Settlers from what is now Illinois established a settlement at Ste. Genevieve, Missouri.
1763	French and Indian War ended. The Louisiana Teritory was given to Spain.
	France gave Canada to the British.
1764	Pierre Laclede Liguest and Auguste Chouteau settled St. Louis.
1776	Declaration of Independence was adopted.
1787	John Dodge, an American, settled in Ste. Genevieve.
1790	Israel Dodge, an American, followed John Dodge to Ste. Genevieve.
1799	Daniel Boone moved to St. Charles County.
1800	Spain gave up the Louisiana Territory to France.

1803	France sold the Louisiana Territory to the United States.
1804	Two territories were formed out of the Louisiana Purchase. 1. Territory of Orleans, District of Louisiana 2. Territory of Indiana
1805	Territory of Louisiana was formed.
1809	Out of the Territory of Louisiana the Territory of Illinois was formed.
1811/12	The severe earthquake tremors known as the "New Madrid Earthquakes" that formed Reelfoot Lake in Tennessee.
1812	Part of the Territory of Louisiana became the Territory of Missouri.
1813	County of Arkansas was formed out of the Territory of Missouri.
1818	Missouri asked to be admitted into the Union.
1819	The Territory of Arkansas was formed.
1821	Missouri became the 24th state.
1837	Missouri gained six northwestern counties with the Platte Purchase.

TABLE OF CONTENTS

Page

BARRY COUNTY
FOUNDED 1835 FROM GREENE COUNTY

Marriage Reccords - 1837 to 1839 224

BENTON COUNTY
FOUNDED 1835 FROM PETTIS AND ST. CLAIR COUNTIES

Animal Marks and Brands - 1839 146
Marriage Records - 1839 191

BOONE COUNTY
FOUNDED 1820 FROM HOWARD COUNTY

Tax List - 1821 3
Delinquent Tax List - 1825 37
Animal Marks and Brands - 1826 - 1839 43
Tax List - 1825 52
Delinquent Tax List - 1830 176
Estrays from the "Missouri Independent" 237

CALLAWAY COUNTY
FOUNDED 1820 FROM MONTGOMERY COUNTY

Non-Resident Tax List List - 1823 142
Receipts and Expenditures - January 14, 1823 143
Delinquent Tax List - 1830 185
Estrays from the "Missouri Intelligencer" 230

CAPE GIRARDEAU COUNTY
FOUNDED 1812

Spanish Census - 1803 125
Tax List - 1822 170
Estrays from the "Missouri Gazette" 181
Licenses - December 8, 1821 185

CHARITON COUNTY
FOUNDED 1820 FROM HOWARD COUNTY

Delinquent Tax List - 1825 38
Tax List - 1821 46
Delinquent Tax List - 1830 143

Chariton County Continued

Letters at the Post Office - January 28, 1823 149
Tax List - 1827 151
Delinquent Tax List - 1829 166

CLAY COUNTY
FOUNDED 1822 FROM RAY COUNTY

Delinquent Tax List - 1825 7

COLE COUNTY
FOUNDED 1820 FROM COOPER COUNTY

Delinquent Tax List 40
Estrays from the "Missouri Intelligencer" 229

COOPER COUNTY
FOUNDED 1818 FROM HOWARD COUNTY

Delinquent Tax List - 1834 52
Delinquent Tax List - 1835 73
Tax List - 1819 92
Delinquent Tax List - 1826 150
Delinquent Tax List - 1827 151
Estrays from the "Missouri Intelligencer" 233

FRANKLIN COUNTY
FOUNDED 1818 FROM ST. LOUIS COUNTY

Tax List - 1820 71
Letters at the Post Office 142
Delinquent Tax List - 1830 149
Letters at the Post Office 174
Estrays from the "Missouri Gazette" 186
Marriage Records - 1819 - 1839 192
Estrays from the "Beacon" 227

GASCONADE COUNTY
FOUNDED 1820 FROM FRANKLIN COUNTY

Delinquent Tax List - 1826 151
Delinquent Tax List - 1828 177
Estrays from the "Beacon" 227

HENRY COUNTY
FOUNDED 1834 FROM LAFAYETTE COUNTY

Bethel Baptist Church Cemetery 146

Henry County Continued

Bear Creek Cemetery 157
(No Name) Cemetery, Tebo Township 162

HOWARD COUNTY
FOUNDED 1816 FROM ST. CHARLES AND ST. LOUIS COUNTIES

Territorial Tax List - 1817 1
Delinquent Tax List - 1823 7
Delinquent Tax List - 1824 38
Licenses - November 2, 1816 149
Delinquent Tax List - 1830 150
Licenses - November 26, 1822 181
Petitioners - December 23, 1819 188

JEFFERSON COUNTY
FOUNDED 1818 FROM STE. GENEVIEVE AND ST. LOUIS COUNTIES

Delinquent Tax List - 1830 154

JOHNSON COUNTY
FOUNDED 1834 FROM LAFAYETTE COUNTY

Delinquent Tax List - 1838 143
Delinquent Tax List - 1836 162
Brethren Cemetery 174
Hocker Cemetery 177
Licenses - 1836 228

OLD LAWRENCE COUNTY
FOUNDED 1815 FROM NEW MADRID: ABOLISHED 1818

Delinquent Tax List - 1818 1
Estrays from the "Missouri Gazette" 191

LINCOLN COUNTY
FOUNDED 1818 FROM ST. CHARLES COUNTY

Delinquent Tax List - 1835 93
Delinquent Tax List - 1830 185
Licenses - July 8, 1820 227
Estrays from the "Beacon" 227

MACON COUNTY
FOUNDED 1837 FROM RANDOLPH COUNTY

Animal Marks and Brands - 1837 - 1839 152
Marriage Records - 1837 - 1839 190

MARION COUNTY
FOUNDED 1822 FROM RALLS COUNTY

Tax List - 1827 7

MONITEAU COUNTY
FOUNDED 1845 FROM COLE AND MORGAN COUNTIES

Advent United Church of Christ Cemetery 228
German Methodist Church Cemetery 232

MONTGOMERY COUNTY
FOUNDED 1818 FROM ST. CHARLES COUNTY

Tax List - 1819 112
Tax List - 1823 204

NEW MADRID COUNTY
FOUNDED 1812

Delinquent Tax List - 1830   92
Spanish Census - 1797 107
Oaths of Allegiance - 1793 - 1795 138
Licenses - February 15, 1817 185

OSAGE COUNTY
FOUNDED 1841 FROM GASCONADE COUNTY

Old St. Joseph Cemetery 155

PERRY COUNTY
FOUNDED 1820 FROM STE. GENEVIEVE COUNTY

Delinquent Tax List - 1830 138

PIKE COUNTY
FOUNDED 1818 FROM ST. CHARLES COUNTY

Licenses 185
Delinquent Tax List - 1830 191
Delinquent Tax List - 1829 233

PLATTE COUNTY
FOUNDED 1838 FROM THE PLATTE PURCHASE

Personal Property Tax List - 1839 120
Marriage Records - 1838 - 1839 215

RALLS COUNTY
FOUNDED 1820 FROM PIKE COUNTY

Delinquent Tax List - 1830	59
Delinquent Tax List - 1826	162
Licenses - December 6, 1821	177
Estrays from the "Missouri Intelligencer"	229

RANDOLPH COUNTY
FOUNDED 1829 FROM CHARITON COUNTY

Delinquent Tax List - 1830	149
Estrays from the "Missouri Intelligencer"	233

RAY COUNTY
FOUNDED 1820 FROM HOWARD COUNTY

Tax List - 1821	38
Receipts and Expenditures	148
Tax List - 1830	148
Delinquent Tax List - 1836	228

ST. CHARLES COUNTY
FOUNDED 1812

Tax List - 1836	8
Petitioners - Academy St. Charles - 1817	99
Petitioners - Establishment of Post Office	141
Delinquent Tax List - 1830	151
Tax List - 1817	157
Estrays from the "Missouri Republican"	187

ST. FRANCOIS COUNTY
FOUNDED 1821 FROM JEFFERSON, STE. GENEVIEVE, AND WASHINGTON COUNTIES

Tax List - 1830	94
Marriages in the Deeds - 1819 - 1835	167
Delinquent Tax List - 1830	176

ST. LOUIS COUNTY
FOUNDED 1812

Mortgages executed under Spain - 1766 - 1804	40
Petitioners - Establishment of Post Office - 1818	106
Militia - 1780	114
Delinquent Tax List - 1830	150
Marriage Contracts in the Deeds - 1766 - 1804	163
Dissolved Partnerships from the "Missouri Republican"	176

St. Louis County Continued

Licenses - May 29, 1822	181
Wills and Testaments executed under Spain	185
Estrays from the "Missouri Gazette"	206
Petitioners - Carondelet - January 8, 1817	232
Spanish Census - 1791	234

STE. GENEVIEVE COUNTY
FOUNDED 1812

Tax List - 1805	1
Slave Bills of Sale - 1766 - 1827	48
Land Concessions - 1766 - 1804	57
Litigations	99
Delinquent Tax List - 1830	106
Petitioners - March 10, 1818	124
Licenses - August 13, 1819	150
Estrays from the "Missouri Gazette"	225
Notes, Bonds and Obligations	74

WASHINGTON COUNTY
FOUNDED 1813 FROM STE. GENEVIEVE COUNTY

Delinquent Tax List - 1830	99
Members of the Grand Jury - August 20, 1819	166

STATE WIDE
FIRST FRENCH SETTLEMENT 1700; TERRITORY 1812; STATE 1821

French and Spanish Land Grants	60
Military Bounty Land - War of 1812	76
Pardon Papers, Secretary of State 1837 1839	94
Spanish Patriotic War Contributions - 1799	97
Petitioners - New Madrid Land Titles	119
Memorials Gov. Wilkinson - 1805	129
Nathan Boone's Company - July 13, 1812	160
Steamboat Disaster Victims	166
Supporters for the Louisiana Academy	216
Runaway Spouses, Slaves, and Bad Debts	217

Ste. Genevieve County, Missouri, Tax List, 1805

Charles Archambra, Ezekiel Abel, Ami Buich, John Bork, Squire Boldua, Vital Beauman, L'Guierme Beauonouis, Baptiste Becket, sen., Madame Ls. Boldene, Vital St. James Beauvai, Louis Carrot, Francis Cimins, Pasquale Dutchimendy, Jo. Doublenay, Mos. Deluquerre, Widow Valle, Grael Dodge, Jn. Baptiste Fortuna, Henry Govers, Jo. Govers, Michel Gevero, Louis Govero, Etienne Govero, Robt. Hinkson, Ross James, Mde. Kormes, J. W. Lafleur, Pierre Leveal, Madame Lachance, Jaque Labeau, Nicholas Reusau, Nicholas Laplant, Madame Loels, Jn. Baptiste Martan, Jaque Mirra, Grabriel Lachance, Madam Moro, Baptiste Moro, Mn. J. Maxwell, Francis Olgie, Joseph Pratt, Pierre Obachon, Jn. Baptiste Prater, Aken Pagel, N. Reusau, Julien Rattan, Mesami P. Roben, Pierre Souval, Jn. Baptiste Turmure, Nicholas Tamau, Jp. Tesero, Nicholas Vieman, Moses Austin, Jn. Baptiste Valle, Anthony Brent, Francois Burrice, Lewis Biuat, Tobias Butler, Joseph Beckel, Barthw. Beauvais, Bapiste Becket, junr., Js. St. James Beauvai, Akin Bolduc, Anthony Cere, Anthony Duclous, D. Defour, Baptiste Duqier, Anthony Dulcound, Doct. Elliott, Walton Farnsvack, Andrew Henry, Madame Gironard, Henry Gale, Madam Huberdeau, Francis James, Janot Larochal, Baptiste Larouge, Harry Lohua, Joseph Lafluer, Francis Lafluer, Louis Laclere, Madame Lafluer, Madame Lassame, Joseph Lachance, Harry Morris, John Price, Francis Morrell, Bazelle Manuel, Perran Missla, Paul Polett, Augustus Obuchon, Anthony Obachon, Madam Pasont, Jn. Baptiste Tamu, Pierre Rangie, Pierre Robert, Peter Strickland, Widow Toniech, Louis Tredeau.

Lawrence County, Missouri, Delinquent Tax List, 1818, St. Louis, Enquirer, March 31, 1819.

Baton Staton, John Givens, John Gragg, Baldwin Robinson, Felix Taylor, John Tidwell, Benjamin Crow, William Thomson, William P. Morrison, James Duncan, John M'Call, John Hobs, Chrisley Harness, Charles Bradshaw, John Hudgens, Charles Gallaher, William Garret, Benjamin Piburn, George Gordon, Jester Cox, Rice Gullet, William Duncan, Thomas Wagnor, John Bradbury, Thomas M'Glocklin, Elisha Norman, Even Horrow, Jacob Cragg, Jonathan Hubble, William Tucker, Thomas Ferrel, William Fowler, Isaac Foster, Aaron Hughes, Peter Carpenter, John Cooke, Moses Moore, James Brannon, Benedict White, Baranabas Norman, James Bato, Ichabud Hublec, Amis Evans, Isaac Balmore, John Clayton, Jonathan Thackum, Jacob Rudder.

Howard County, Missouri, Territorial Tax List, 1817.

John Adams, James Alexander, William Allen, Price Arnold, Michael Atterberry, Robert Austin, Aquilla Barnes, William Bicknell, John Barnes, David Barnett, jr., Joseph Bays, Seth Botts, Robert Bennom, Taylor Berry, Joseph Bradley, Benjamin

(Howard County, Missouri Continued)
Cooper, James Brock, Robert Brown, Willian Brown, William Brown (sic), James Burleson, Gray Bynum, George Carson, Edmund Carter, Peter Chouteau, James Cockrell, Stephen Cole, senr., Middleton Anderson, John Copeland, John Davis, John Elliott, James Creason, Levin Cropper, Isaac Drake, Daniel Durben, William Estes, John Ferrill, George Foster, George Foster, John Hutchinson, Hiram Fugitt, Humphrey Gibson, Jefferson Fulcher, Reuben Gentry, Samuel Hinch, dec., John Grayum, Harmon Gregg, Joseph Hamilton, Thomas Hardeman, John Heath, Anthony Head, Joseph Hiatt, Thomas Hickman, Absalom Huff, Uriah Hinch, Samuel Hodges, William Howard, Parthenia and Saml. Gibbs, admn., Thomas Gray, John Berry, William Hunt (sic), Thomas Adams, James Allcorn, Joseph Austin, John Browley, James Anderson, Amos Ashecraft, Robert Barclay, John Hines, James Barnes (sic), Joshua Barton, Shadrick Barnes, George Bellas, James Benson, William Berry, Austin Blocker, David Bozer, Joseph Brasher, Perry Brock, Isaac Clark, James Carter, Samuel Brown, Thomas Burris, William Calvert, William Caton, Lindsay Carson, Hannah Cole, Joseph Cooley, Benjamin Cooper, jr., Hiram Craig, George Crump, Peter Doolin, Daniel Dugan, Braxton Cooper, dec., Robert and Ruth Cooper, adm., Henry Earthman, Silas Enyard, Benjamin Estill, Henry Geyer, David Fletcher, James L. Foster, Melida Figitt, Edward Good, Richard Fulkerson, Robert Fowler, dec., Jas. Fowler, adm., Duff Green, Moses Hallet, John Hancock, James Harris, Gaven Head, John Hensley, Moses Hiatt, Josiah Higgins, John Doxey, Thomas Holliday, James Howell, William Hughes, Theodore Hunt, Marquis Stephenson, dc., Aspah Hubbard and Nancy Stephenson, admn., William Hunt (sic), William E. Aikmon, John Allen, Jesse Ashecraft, Peter Austin, Abraham Barnes, Humphrey Best, James Barnes (sic), David Barnett, William Baxter, Jonathan Benedict, Wm. Smit, Leon Bradley, Judson Brasher, James Cole, James Brown, David Bryant, Walter Burris, William Campbell, William Carson, George Cathey, William Chambers, John B. N. Smith, William Cleton, Perrin Cooley, George Cooper, Peter Creason, Abner Davis, Sally Duncan, John Earthman, Freeman Foster, Henry Estes, Andrew Evans, John Foster, Hahn Hassel, William Fraser, Nancy Figitt, Josiah Gennings, Samuel Gibbs, Rebeccah Gregg, Robert Hancock, William Hays, Robert Heath, William Hensley, Absalom Hicks, Michael Hinch, Jacob Magard, Daniel Hodges, Nathan Holloway, Thomas Hubbard, Thomas Todd, John Hutchinson, George Hutton, George Jackson, Levi Turner, Andrew Johnson (sic), Andrew Johnson (sic), David Kinkead, William Johnson (sic), William Johnson (sic), Moses Langley, William Livingston, Robert Marquis, John McClure, Archibald Woods, John McDowell, Thomas McMahan (sic), David McQuitty, Thomas McMahan (sic), Thomas Mitchell, David McGee, Soloman Mordica, Edward McDaniel, John Mayes, James Mahan, William

(Howard County, Missouri Continued)
Nash, Jacob Ish, David Jones (sic), Levi Jones, James Pipes, Wm. Kincheloe (sic), Wm. Kincheloe, David Jones (sic), John Munro, James Lamm, Jeremiah Leaky, James Long, William Jack, William Job, Thomas Keany, William Lamm, Asa Morgan, Henry Lightfoot, James Mackey, Randolph March, David McClain, Ira Nash, Susanna Mullens, William Monro (sic), Henry Peslay, John W. Pettigrew, Robert Poage, John Pursley, John Warden, Abraham Reece, Jesse Richardson, John Roberts, Gillead Rupe, Labert Scott, Abraham Shelly, Charles Simmons, Joseph Smith, Robert Steel, James Thorp, Daniel Tilmon, Enich Turner, Adam Woods, Philip Trammell, Samuel Turley, Thomas Vaughn, James Turner (sic), Benjamin Weeden, William Welch, Robert Wolcup, Ezekial Williams, Alexander Wood, Anderson Woods, Benjamin Young, Daniel Munro, sr., William Moro (sic), William Pipes, Thomas Pharris, Nicholas Proctor, Daniel Rawls, Elisha Todd, Silas Richardson, William Reece, Wm. Robertson, Jesse Wood, James Turner (sic), John Turner (sic), Philip Turner, John Neely, Luke Patrick, Tarlton Whitlock, John Savage, William Wolfskill, Benjamin Weaver, James Turner (sic), Jacob Yows, Joseph Wolfskill, William Ridgeway, Jacob McFarland, Andrew Smith, Lewis Scott, John Silvers, David Smelsor, Joel Shaw, Reuben Smith, John Stephenson, Isaac Thompson, David Ward, Francis Travis, Stephen Turley, John Wallace, Henry Weeden, William Warden, Urian Williams, James McMahan, John Welch, William Monroe, Eneas Morgan, Thomas Noble, William Taylor, David McClain, Samuel Perry, John Pharris, Hezekiah Purdon, Coledon Williams, Richard Winscot, Patrick Woods, William Silvers, John Turner (sic), William Savage, Robert Thompson, Smith Turner, Edward Turner, David Trotter, Lewis Richards, Elias Rector.

Boone County, Missouri, Tax List, 1821.
Joshua Alexander, L, 221 a.; John Anderson, L; Jeremiah Bizewell, L, 320 a.; David Austin, L; Ann Barnes, L, 320 a.; Peter Austin, L, 270 a.; Thomas Anderson, L, 316 a.; William Bledsoe, L, 80 a.; T. Beazley and R. Estes, L; Abner Davis, L, 160 a.; Little James Barnes, L, 320 a.; Thomas Berry, L; Thomas Bizwell, L; Henry Barnes, L, 80 a.; Elam Boler, L; Alexander Collins, L, 160 a.; William Callahan, L, 320 a.; John S. Barnes, L; Jonathan Barker, L, 160 a.; Roland Cave, sen., L, 687 a.; Joshua Barks, L, 190 a.; Stephen Bruner, L; Isam Belcher, L, 92 a.; John Belcher, sr., L, 92 a.; William Barnes, L, 160 a.; Levi Bennet, L; David Buile, L; Benjamin Collin, L, 100 a.; John Belcher, jr., L, 160 a.; Henry Cave, L, 1076 a.; Robert Bauley, L 160 a.; Peter Bass, L, 4150 a.; Josiah Bounds, L, 80 a.; Adam S. Barnett, L; James Adams, L; Alex. Buttermilk, L; John Blackburn, L, 160 a.; John Barnes, L, 400 a.; William Berry, L, 160 a.; David Crump, L, 80 a.;

(Boone County, Missouri Continued)

Alex. Buttermilk, L; Neddy Balinger, L, 300 a.; Benjiman F. Green, L, 160 a.; Hugh Briant, L; Peter Creason, L, 160 a.; Archibald Ballard, L, 160 a.; John Boid, L, 160 a.; Samuel Bucknold, L, 280 a.; Big James Barnes, L, 165 a.; Richland Cave, jr., L, 1012, a.; Aquilla Barnes, L, 360 a.; Hubbard Brink, L, 320 a.; Henry Callew, L, 160 a.; Lawrence Bass, L; Robert Cochran, L, 800 a.; John Christain, L; Dan Cainey, L; Henry Collin, L; Jesse Coffer, L, 450 a.; Robert Austin, L; Dennis Callahan, L, 480 a.; Thomas Carson, L, 50 a.; Samuel Caldwell, L, 160 a.; John Collen, sen., L, 160 a.; Jonathan Bidicks, L, 80 a.; James Cunnigham, L, 1617 a.; Willis Boos, L, 160 a.; John Austin, L, 610 a.; Isham Austin, L; William G. Berry, L; John Cook, L, 160 a.; Sarah Beston, L; William Boon, L, 400 a.; John Berry, L, 160 a.; Anthony Bledsoe, L; Benjamin Burdine, L; Joseph Austin, L, 160 a.; Littleberry Wice, L, 160 a.; Edmund Biddick, L; James Beatie, L; Joseph Burnett, L, 80 a.; Moses Ballolew, L, 240 a.; Samuel Beatie, L, 216 a.; Austin Bledsoe, L, 92 a.; John Beokits, L; John Burnett, L, 480 a.; Gaven Bledsoe, L; Betty Burdine, L; John Coastraul, L, 528 a.; Wilkes Burleston, L, 160 a.; William Canfield, L, 460 a.; Isaac Bledsoe, L, 198 a.; Jrd. Nash, L, 1126 a.; Isham Belcher, L, 272 a.; Jacob Bittle, L, 92 a.; George T. Boyez, L, 218 a.; Jesse Boid, L, 176 a.; Elizabeth Barnes, L; Richard Barnes, L; Philip Barger, L, 60 a.; Jesse Blackburn, L, 222 a.; Bazwell Brown, L; Stephen Chapman, L; Huram Briant, L, 160 a.; Robert Callew, L, 160 a.; William Douglas, L, 340 a.; John Collet, L; Hugh Chalten, L; George Crump, L, 211, a.; John Creason, L, 160 a.; Lucy Collin, L; Elijah Creason, L; Peyton Collin, L; Burton Cave, L; Samuel Davis, L; 160 a.; Lewis Collin, L, 160 a.; John Dillon, L; Samuel Clocker, L, 160 a; Jesse B. Dale, L; James Dixen, L; 30 a.; John Davis, L, 320 a.; James Davis, L, 326 a.; Henry C. Davis, L, 320 a.; Isaac Davis, jr., L; John Douglas, L; Thomas Elison, L; Alex. Elingtom, L; Peter Ellis, L, 480 a.; Thomas Edmunson, L, 80 a.; Pursley Edwards, L, 400 a.; Caleb Fenton, L, 630 a.; Benjamin Furgusin, L; Joshua Freeman, L, 120 a.; Jefferson Fulcher, L. 326 a.; John Grey, L; Richland Fulkerson, L, 160 a.; John Fuegit, L, 160 a.; Hugh Glenn, L; John M. Fowler, L; Lewis French, L; Thomas Hart, L, 80 a.; Peter Foutain, L, 800 a.; John Graves, L, 200 a.; Ichabod A. Hisick, L; Robert Goodsin, L, 80 a.; Joshua Gillam, L; John Harrison, L, 320 a.; Thomas Gray, L; Peter Hendrick, L; John Hesson, L, 160 a.; Agnez Head, L, 160 a.; Jeremiah Hall, L; Nicholas Gentry, L, 160 a; James Guthery, L, 180 a.; William Gavsten, L, 320 a.; Matthew Graves, L, 320 a.; James Harris, L, 480 a.; James Gorforth, L, 160 a.; Calten Hein, L; James Harrison, L, 160 a.; Charles Haddick, L; William Heusley, L; Michael Halten, L, 80 a.; Isaac Hush, L; Samuel Hillard, L;

(Boone County, Missouri Continued)
William Header, L, 190 a.; Charles Hughes, L, 320 a.; Jesse Harris, Jr., L, 160 a.; Rueben Holton, L, 480 a.; Benjamin Estell, L; Anthony Hoosley, L, 104 a.; Charles B. Hutson, L, 160 a.; Abram T. Hatfield, L, 160 a.; Adam Ficus, L; Andrew Hendricks, L, 80 a.; David Hubbard, L, 160 a.; Wm. Hall, L, 326 a.; David Haldaine, L; Benjamin Dale, L, 160 a.; Bledsoe Davis, L; Hugh Davis, L; Anthony P. Davis, L; John Gray, L, 190 a.; James Dusky, L; Isaac Davis, sr., L, 480 a.; Thomas Duley, L, 400 a.; John Ethell, L, 160 a.; Rueben Elliott, L; Andrew C. Estes, L, 160 a.; James Ethell, L, 160 a.; Elijah Foster, L, 160 a.; David Finley, L; James Fainen, L, 162 a.; John Freeman, L, 120 a.; John Finney, L; Seward Gray, L; Wm. Havensteader, L; James Fisher, L, 240 a.; James Faubash, L, 160 a.; Hugh French, L, 640 a.; Michael Glass, L; Jonathan Grayson, L; Mark Goodhugh, L, 80 a.; William Graham, L; John Graham, L; Boutty Gentry, L, 320 a.; Silas Heinler, L; David Hodges, L, 480 a.; William Gleen, L, 480 a.; Nathan Glasow, L, 245 a.; Daniel Goddes, L; Jessee Grayson, L, 1626 a.; Wm. Harrington, L, 80 a.; Richard Gentry, L; William Holten, L; Samuel Hodges, L, 480 a.; Thos. Holidah, L, 160 a.; Michael Hugh, L, 160 a.; Higgerson Harris, L; Jesse Harris, L; Jacob Havedstocker, L; Jacob Hosivinger, L; George Howel, L; John Hardeman, L, 622 a.; Joseph Hickmin, L; Noah Payne, L; John Hickermin, L; John Hickburn, L, 470 a.; Renard Pigg, L; Isam Payne, L; Overton Harris, L, 478 a.; James Hens, L; Robert Hinkston, L, 160 a.; David Hubbard (sic), L, 800 a.; Samuel Jamisen, L; Charles Hazeling, L; Absolem Hicks, L, 519 a.; Levi Jones, L; William Jones, sen., L, 320 a.; Harry James, L, 240 a.; David Jackson, L, 217 a.; Peyson Jamison, L; M. Kirkland, L, 160 a.; Christopher James, L, 160 a.; William Kelly, L, 60 a.; Robert Jones, L; Benjamin Kelly, L; Richard Lawrence, L; Jefferson Kilegore, L, 160 a.; Jesse Keunon, L, 320 a.; Jesse Kirkland, L, 160 a.; S. Mathias, L; Elizabeth M'Coy, L; Nicholas Kavenaugh, L, 320 a.; Alexander Ogin, L; William Levitz, L, 1065 a.; David Lamphir, L; John Mays, L; Charles Langford, L, 160 a.; Polly Laughlin, L, 160 a.; Tyne Martin, L, 949 a.; Andrew M'Quitz, L, 480 a.; John Yates, L; Benjn. Netheuhead, L, T, 320 a.; Shedrick Mosley, L; Addison M'Pherson, L, 80 a.; James Mays, sen., L, 160 a.; Absalom Locksford, L; John M'Tricle, L, 1578 a.; William Pisser, L; Nicholas M'Cuestion, L, 100 a.; Charles M'Intire, L; Joseph C. M'Kay, L, 246 a.; Archibald M'Neal, L; Walter M'Kay, L; Ang. Manney, L, 640 a.; Thomas M'Dow, L, 560 a.; Joel Hens, L, 80 a.; John Nealey, L, 226 a.; John Payne, sen., L; John Newton, L. 166 a.; Miner Neal, L, 160 a.; Jesse Philips, L; William Pisser, L; Nancy Procter, L, 160 a.; William Payne, L; Jahier (sic) Parks, L; John Philips, L, 222 a.; William Noulson, L; Jesse Perkins, L, 160 a.; John Patten, L, 92 a.;

(Boone County, Missouri Continued)
Jesse Perkins, L, 160 a.; Thomas Patten, L, 80 a.; William Jones, jr., L, 160 a.; Wm. L. Hughston, L, 320 a.; Harrison Jamison, L, 893 a.; David Inard, L, 160 a.; Thomas Jones, L; Lewis Jones, L; Zachariah Jackson, L; Jesse Lewis. L; Robert M' Dow, L, 160 a.; John Jamisin, L, 88 a.; Moses James, L, 160 a.; Tyne H. Jones, L, 160 a.; Hiram Kirkwood, L, 137 a.; Thomas Korrow, L, 160 a.; Davis Kirkland, L, 320 a.; William Levitz, L, 300 a.; George Lowery, L, 240 a.; Daniel M'Swain, L, 160 a.; Henry Casley, L, 160 a.; George Payne, L, 240 a.; David M'Quitz, L, 311 a.; Stephen Mitchell, L, 160 a.; Jacob M'Bride, L, 175 a.; John M'Daniel, L, 320 a.; John Ogin, L, 229 a.; William Lewis, L; William Lyson, L; Samuel Pace, L; Thomas Lipscomb, L; Samuel Nutting, L, 166 a.; John M'Carty, L; Lucy marcus, L, 107 a.; John M'Kensie, L, 160 a.; John G. Philips, L, 227 a.; Charles M'Dow, L, 320 a.; James M. Moss, L, 2560 a.; Joseph M'Daniel, L, 158 a.; Thomas Mansfield, L, 160 a.; William Mitchell, L, 160 a.; Hiram Philips, L; Hugh Patten, L; Oliver Parker, L; Francis M'Daniel, L; Augustus Thrall, L, 300 a.; John Poaque, L; Stephen Wilkes, L; Lewis Smith, L; Silas Richardson, L, 230 a.; William Rice, L; John Read, L, 328 a.; William Ryan, L, 160 a.; Nathaniel Teaque, L, 218 a.; Patterson Russell, L, 160 a.; James Ross, L; John Sullins, L, 560 a.; Weyman Ruddell, L; Lewis Telen, L; Zadic Riggs, jr., L, 151 a.; James Ready, L; William Ross, L; Hugh Silan, L, 80 a.; William Russell, L; Redin Riggs, L; Joseph Simpson, L; William Ridgivary, L, 875 a.; Mary Richards, L; Roger N. Todd, L, 1120 a.; Nathan Russel, jr., L; Markam Stephenson, L; William Rowland, L, 160 a.; Thomas Tood, L; Benjamin Scrivner, L, 80 a.; William Ramsey, jr., L, 160 a.; Nathan Roberts, L, 160 a.; George Seaton, L, 160 a.; Milford Stephens, L; William Sims, L, 440 a.; William Stone, L; John Simmons, L; Jesse Samuel, L, 480 a.; Peter Slice, L, 160 a.; Edward Sullins, L, 160 a.; Newberry Stockson, L; William D. Young, L; John Turner, sen., L, 951 a.; Peter I. Tubble, L; Wm. I. Smith, L, 235 a.; Nathan Russell, L, 160 a.; England Sonoss, L, 640 a.; Simpson Wilhill, L, 240 a.; John Wood, L, 160 a.; Sussanah Smith, L; Thomas Tuttle, L, 320 a.; Robert Wakefield, jr., L; John D. Stokes, L; Charles Vanuesur, L; William Tally, L, 160 a.; James Tayler, L, 80 a.; Benjamin Young, L, 160 a.; Bengn. Sanderson, L; John Stowe, L; Elijah Tayler, L, 85 a.; John Tuttle, L; Jesse Talla, L; George B. Wilcox, L; Esgard Tipton, L, 80 a.; John Walker, L; William Simmons, L, 160 a.; Davis Turner, sen., L, 320 a.; William Ramsay, L, 400 a.; James Rezelsseur, L; Richard Talbert, L, 160 a.; John Vaughn, L, 160 a.; John Stack, L, 160 a.; John Rowland, L, 160 a.; James Richards, L, 75 a.; Daniel Tolson, L; Parson Riddle, L; Silas Riggs, L, 180 a.; Thomas Rowland, L; Adam C. Rabaum, L; John Wakefield, L; Absolum Roulson, L;

(Boone County, Missouri Continued)
Mason Moss, L, 180 a.; William Orear, L; John Pidgeon, L; David Richfield, L, 160 a.; John May Willingham, L, 199 a.; John M'Gill, L, 160 a.; William Shields, L, 320 a.; Zadoc Riggs, sen., L; John Stephenson, L, 360 a.; Alfred Windson, L; Samuel Riggs, L, 320 a.; Nathan Turner, L, 120 a.; Samuel Shiver, L; Jesse Richardson, L, 320 a.; Isham B. Seaton, L; Stephen Strode, L; Josiah Short, L, 160 a.; James Sowell, L; Lanier Scriviner, L, 80 a.; Elijah Stephens, L, 160 a.; John D. Turner, L, 160 a.; Larsen Tinley, L, 160 a.; Henry Smith, L, 160 a.; Nancy Sappington, L; Elias Sims, L, 250 a.; Riley Slocum, L, 160 a.; Smith Turner, L, 160 a; Thomas Tipton, L; William Smith, L, 80 a.; John Thorton, L, 640 a.; Benjamin White, L, 160 a.; Wm. Timberlick, L; Fielden Milton, L; Wm. Stucklin, L; Bilson Tuttle, L, 312 a.; Isaac Willingham, L, 80 a.; Foster Sappington, L; Lewis Turner, L, 160 a.; Joseph Taylor, L; Henry Winkfield, L; Richard Winscott, L, 250 a.; John Ward, jr., L, 60 a.; Thomas Thompson, L, 800 a.; James Winn, L, 160 a.; David C. Wilsarfield, L; Michael Woods, L, 480 a.; William Wright, L, 1664 a.; James Wiseman, L; Vance Woodland, L, 160 a.; Andrew Woods, L, 160 a.; Noah Wilcox, L, 320 a.; Thomas Williams, L, 160 a.; Rbt. S. Walkouse, L, 145 a.; William Winagrin, L, 160 a.; John Walkup, L, 160 a.; Jacob Michertower, L, 160 a.; Peter Wright, L, 352 a.; John Williams, L, 160 a.; George Williams, L; John Williams, L, 160 a.; Abram Winscott, L, 160 a.; Benjn. Williams, L; John Will, L, 320 a.; John Winagram, jr., L; Geo. Mibertower, L; Lazarus Wilcox, L, 810 a.; Wm. S. Wayne, L, 320 a.

<u>Clay County, Missouri, Delinquent Tax List, 1825, Missouri Intelligencer, February 1, 1826.</u>
Tilman Clark, Edward B. Hall, John Hensley, Page Stanley, Michael Tiohall.

<u>Howard County, Missouri, Delinquent Tax List, 1823, Missouri Intelligencer, September 4, 1824.</u>
Isreal Arterberry, William Burke, Muke Box, James Caine, William Bagwell, Joseph Casteel, Wm. Cogdale, Charles Hays, Simeon Coy, Nathan Culp, Jonathan Culp, William Dosier, John Stevens, Abram Goodwin, Charles D. Hill, Michail Hinch, Tice Ham, George W. Hardin, Charles Hays, James Hawkins, Benjamin Irvin, Joshua Lamme, James Mason, jr., Nily Martin, Richard Mitchell, John Muncus, Thomas M'Caferty, Joseph Morgan, jr., Jesse Patterson, Josiah Shockley, Dodson H. Tharp, Samuel Thorton.

<u>Marion County, Missouri, Tax List, 1827.</u>
Thomas Armstrong, Richard Bruce, Littleton Bradley, John Gash, Moses Gentry, William Blakey, John Howell, John Lear,

(Marion County, Missouri Continued)

William B. Brown, Abraham Bird, Daniel Bradley, Carrol Moss, Squire Bozarth, Elijah Baxter, Willis Boulware, Henry Lane, Mordecai Boulware, John Bozarth, senr., William Bourne, sr., Benjamin Bowls, Moses D. Bales, Archibald Brant, Bannister Gregory, William Carson, George Calvert, Mary Conway, Joseph Culbertson, David Clark, Edward Carey, Samuel Conway, Isaac Forman, William Duncan, Shadrack Davis, Obadiah Dickerson, William Eastin, William Forman, Benjamin Frye, Isaac Forman, Joshua Feazle, Zachariah Feagan, John Finley, Barton Fields, William Fisher, Abraham K. Frye, Jonathan Flemming, William Gash, Richard Bruer, adm. of Charles Markle, dec., Benjamin Forman, James Gardner, Joshua Gentry, Jesse Gentry, Moses Gentry, Martin Gash, sen., Martin Gash, jr., William Garner, Joseph D. Gash, jr., Joseph D. Gash, sr. John Garner, Joseph Huffman, Abraham Huntsberry, Michael B. Heather, Hugh Henry, William Henry, Thomas Hannon, Elijah Haden, James Kendrick, Obadiah Dickerson, guard. infant heirs of Peton Matson, John Longmire, Robert Irvine, Richard W. Jones, Victor M. Lewis, Valentine S. Lewis, jr., Marshal Kelly, Christopher Keiser, Samuel M. King, James Laytham, Charles Lake, James Miller, William W. Lewis, Burgess Lake, William Landers, Benjamin J. Lewis, Ballard Lake, Thomas Lewis, Thomas J. Lewis, Benjamin Means, Aaron Lewis, jr., Thomas Lake, Jasper W. Lewis, John Maxwell, Patrick Magee, William McRae, Samuel Morton, Joshua Morris, George McDaniel, James F. Mahan, Robert Masterson, John McFall, Eli Merrill, James Muldro, William McReynolds, Jacob Matthews, Samuel Maxwell, John Moss, James McWilliams, Thomas Marlin, Matthew Moss, William J. McElroy, Zepheniah Robnet, John Muldrow, sr. and Samuel Muldrow, Thomas Newell, John McWilliams; William Massie, Henry Matthews, John Rush, John Parmer, William Pritchard, Ezekial Parrish, John Smith, Edmund Rutter, John Randal, Felix G. Rutter, Susannah Rush, Gabriel Rush, William Ritchey, Elijah Rice, Hugh W. Shannon, Burdit Sams, Hawkins Smith, sr., Charles Smith, Elijah Stap, Alexander Shannon, Ellis Schofield, Henry Settles, Green Lee Sams, Elijah Stapp, guard. of Preston and Darwin Stapp, John Verbryck, Jeremiah Strode, George See, sr., Benjamin Thomas, James Thomas, John F. Thrasher, Charles L. Turner, Jeremiah Taylor, Joseph Trotter, George Turner, Gabriel Turner, John B. White, Stephen F. Thrasher, Jeptha Thurman, Edward White, Lewis Vanlandingham, Meshak Vanlandingham, William Whaley, Richard Van Carnop, Edward Whaley, Clement White, Evan Ward, James Whaley, John White.

St. Charles County, Missouri, Tax List, 1836.

Reputed Owner	Acres	Original Claimant
Henry Abington	210	S.W. Allen and U. Witt
John Allen	138	R. B. Allen

(St. Charles County, Missouri Continued)

Reputed Owner	Acres	Original Claimant
Samuel Abington	210	S.W. Allen and U. Witt
Lea Abington	210	"
John Abington	210	"
Henry Abington	210	"
Jas. H. Alexander's heirs	212	John Walker
Jas. H. Alexander's heirs	25	Jos. H. Alexander
Samuel Audrain	212	Baptist Chartran
Samuel Audrain	680	Jos. Beaucham
Peter G. Audrain	680	"
James H. Audrain	680	"
Julien Abare	680	"
William Aclare	680	"
Adolphus Aklemauct	680	"
Joseph Aubury	680	"
Ferdinand Ahart	60	St. Chas. Commissioners
Joseph J. Allen	138	R. B. Allen
Peter F. Audrain	138	"
Thomas Amos	138	"
Joseph Appleton	138	"
James Ashley	138	"
Peter Ahart	138	"
Robert B. Allen	160	Preston McRoberts
Robert B. Allen	---	Robert B. Allen
Robert L. Allen	---	Elizabeth M. Allen
Robert L. Allen	---	Mirree Walker
Robert L. Allen	---	Smith W. Allen
Robert L. Allen	---	R. L. Allen
Rachael Allen	---	"
Lucy A. and Susan M. Allen	80	Pines H. Shelton
William S. Allen	80	"
William L. Anderson	80	"
John Adams	80	"
John Adams	80	Anselam Leopold
Samuel Aldridge	80	"
Solomon Alkire	161	Isaac Darst
Solomon Alkire	28	Solomon Alvener
Jesse Alkire	85	Jas. Clay
Edward Bates	255	Peter Zumalt
Edward Bates	224	David H. Marcum
Femer Buffrey	144	---- Delure
Jane Brown	144	"
Josephus Brown	377	John McCoy
Moses Bigalow	170	John Crow
Moses Bigalow	99	William Marshal
Hyram Boyd	99	"
Ruthe Boyd	142	Ruthe Boyd

(St. Charles County, Missouri Continued)

Reputed Owner	Acres	Original Claimant
Ruthe Boyd	179	Bosmer Clifton
Ruthe Boyd	151	Alexander S. Sherley
Elijah Boyd's heirs	100	Benjamin Jones
Amos Burdyne	100	"
William Burdyne	100	"
Amos Burdyne, junr.	100	"
James Burdyne	100	"
Daniel Baldridge, senr.	6	Daniel Baldridge
Daniel Baldridge, senr.	51	Freland Rose
Daniel Baldridge, senr.	434	Daniel Baldridge
John Baldridge	200	"
Josiah Baldridge	200	"
Icim Butcher	200	"
Thomas Black	200	"
John Black, junr.	200	"
James F. Baugh	200	"
Carry A. Boyd	120	William S. Lacey
Nancy Banks	120	"
Dabney Bass	120	"
John Bass	120	"
James Baldridge	528	James Baldridge
Wm. H. Baldridge	136	"
Melkia Baldridge	136	"
Isadore Bernard	70	Laurent Derocher
Timothy Bruin	24	St. Chas. Commissioners
Jacob Bosah	20	"
James G. Bayley	28	Tuscint Cerre
James G. Bayley	118	St. Chas. Commissioners
Carr Bayley's heirs	63	"
Albert Benadict	63	"
Charles Brantine	63	"
Baptist Brusier	63	"
Francis Brusier	189	"
Louis Barada	63	"
Benjamin Bladwin	123	"
Michael Bellond	63	"
Joria Brady	63	"
Leonard Beddow	63	"
Elisha Bluster	63	"
Louis Boshma	63	"
Tuscint Brunell	2	"
John Bruin	2	"
John M. Bayley	2	"
Baptist Burdo	2	"
Henry Bangs	2	"
Josia Ball	2	"
Walter Bowles	127	Abraham Keathley

(St. Charles County, Missouri)

Reputed Owner	Acres	Original Claimant
Leao Bowles	2	St. Chas. Commissioners
James Bowles	127	Abraham Keathley
D. F. G. Browning	127	"
Ettienne Bernard's heirs	20	Paleja Laberdie
Ettienne Bernard's heirs	133	Louis Jannett
Ettienne Bernard's heirs	152	Lorren Derouchy
Hypolite Bernard	136	Pal--- Laberdie
Hypolite Bernard	56	Maryan Violett
Christain Barnes	85	Noel Hebert
David Bedler	85	"
George Boswell	85	"
John Beverley	85	"
Sophara Brown	40	Silas Massey
Patterson Bernard	40	"
Randolph Biggs' heirs	216	R. Biggs
Dert. Bakerbread	216	R. Biggs
Andrew Boshman	40	St. Chas. Commissioners
Silvest. Baradie	120	"
Antwine Baradie	240	"
Mary Best	170	H. Crosby
Mary Best	80	James Piper
Stephen Best	80	"
Thomas Bernum	80	"
Peter Barrier	80	"
Acan Bevaman	80	Francis Socie
Isadore Boyer	34	"
David Boshett	160	St. Chas. Commissioners
Harmon Boshett's heirs	60	"
John Boshett	60	"
Phillip Baker	100	"
Sebastin Bobbinrath	100	"
Joseph Berthol	120	"
Modest Blaxen	60	"
Hermon Blackforth	60	"
Michael Boile	60	"
John Baldridge, sr.	159	John Baldridge
Wilson Baldridge	159	"
Daniel Baldridge, the son of John Baldridge	159	"
Robert Baldridge	114	Robert Baldridge
Robert Baldridge	164	William Crow
Alexander Baldridge	81	Robert Baldridge
Robert Bayley	81	Melkia Baldrdige
John Bernard	276	William Crow
James Bernard	276	"
Marshal Bird	276	"
Evin Baldridge	276	"

(St. Charles County, Missouri Continued)

Reputed Owner	Acres	Original Claimant
Nathan Boon	600	Nathan Boon
Thomas C. Batt	50	Jacob Zumalt
Thomas C. Batt	998	N. B. Tucker
Squire Boon	198	Thomas Smith
Sydner S. Boon	198	"
R. B. Brumfield	200	Daniel Boon
R. B. Brumfield	340	James Davis
Squire Boone	340	"
James Bryant	64	William Haynes
Washington Bryant	64	"
Weston Bryant	64	"
Haden Boon	100	Thomas Smith
Henry Bender	100	"
Even Bruin	90	Christian Woolf
Jacob Burkenmaster	90	"
Frederick Bush	90	"
Jane Butcher	90	"
Bazil Butcher's heirs	90	"
Jacob Bush	90	"
Joseph Baugh	167	Joseph Baugh
Joseph Baugh	80	John M. Taylor
Benjamin Baugh	80	"
Henry Bendick	80	"
John Buckley	2	Leonard Harold
John Benner	2	"
Elija Bryant	150	Jeremia Clay
James Bryan	312	Jonathan Bryan
Jonathan Bryan	385	David Edwards
Adolph Blackman	386	"
Charles Bleamer	44	Jas. Clay
John P. Blucher	44	"
Detreck and Augustus Barra	100	Addam Martin
Frederick Beurbon	100	On Femme Osage
Henry Beurbon	100	Addam Martin
William H. H. Carter	---	
Jacob Comegys	170	John Baker, Sr.
Jacob Comegys	43	George Collier
Jonathan Comegys	42	John Baker, sr.
Jonathan Comegys	56	Jonathan Comegys
William Collins	56	"
Mary Coons	56	"
Thomas Chinn	56	"
B. T. Coalter	80	Samuel Wells
Charles Cheely	80	"
Hancy Custer	80	"
Robert Cheely	80	"
Thomas P. Copes	320	Jos. Voiszard

(St. Charles County, Missouri Continued)

Reputed Owner	Acres	Original Claimant
Thomas P. Copes	340	L. Laburn
Thomas P. Copes	216	St. Chas. Commissioners
Wm. Christy, jr.	216	A. Janis
Wm. Christy, jr.	216	Nicholas Janis
Wm. Christy, jr.	432	Ant. Teabeau
Wm. Christy, jr. guardian of		
S. P. Elisa Christy	216	"
James Carrol's heirs	216	"
William Carter	74	St. Chas. Commissioners
William M. Campbell	81	"
Robert A. Cummins	214	Samuel Lewis
Cummins, Goodrich & Long	---	St. Chas. Commissioners
Alax. B. Campbell	160	"
Baptist Cota	160	"
Acan Canell's heirs	160	"
Walter M. Charleswort	340	Antoine Janis
Thomas M. Cunningham	340	"
John D. Coalter	113	"
Wm. M. Christy	20	"
James Carr	240	James Carr
James Carr	80	Absolem Keathley
Benjamin Comegys	185	Sulvenis Cottle
Alecta Cottle	185	"
Jos. Chairmuer	185	"
John Chairmuer	185	"
Andrew Courtermach	185	"
Rebecca Coons	340	Nicholas Coons
William Coons	170	Wm. McConnel
Felix Coons	---	Robert Spencer, guardian
Nicholas Coons	340	Wm. McConnell
Nicholas Coons	170	Nicholas Coons
Nicholas Coons' heirs	170	Wm. McConnell
Nicholas Coons' heirs	51	Nicholas Coons
Warren Cottle's heirs	992	Warren Cottle
Warren Cottle's heirs	127	Nathan Simons
Lorenzo Cottle	127	"
Lewis Crow	320	Lewis Crow
Alonzo Cottle	320	"
Louis Chanchillar's heirs	45	Ant. Janis
Louis Chanchillar's heirs	45	Ant. Pricot
Louis Chanchillar, jr.	45	"
Pleasant Cayey	160	St. Chas. Commissioners
Louis Corbono	52	"
Mary Champaign	34	Collen McLoad
Archibald Caldwell	170	L. Laburne
Louis Clarmo	340	"
Francis Clarmo	170	"

(St. Charles County, Missouri Continued)

Reputed Owner	Acres	Original Claimant
Joseph Cader	170	L. Laburne
Michael Cader	170	"
A. H. Carutherathers	170	"
Edith Cararthers	170	"
George Crow	170	"
Pier Cornoirer	34	Jacques Clamorgin
Pier Cornoirer	34	Pier Cornoirer
Pier Cornoirer	56	Maryan Violett
Pier Cornoirer	53	Jos. Beauchamp
Luther Cole's heirs	120	St. Chas. Commissioners
Ann Cole's heirs	77	"
Andrew Cole	77	"
Charles Cole	77	"
Samuel Clark	20	"
Hiram Cole	87	"
William Clough	87	"
William Craig, sr.	480	William Craig
William Craig, jr.	480	"
Johnathan Craig	480	"
Isaac Craig	480	"
George Cauchrun	255	Daniel McCoy
James Campbell	255	"
Charles G. Campbell	255	"
William Coshow	156	William Coshow
William Coshow	161	Daniel Boon
William Coshow	258	Timothy Kibbay
William Coshow	170	Hugh McGlaughlin
William Coshow	30	William Hayes
John B. Calaway's heirs	459	F. Calaway
John H. Castlio	80	John H. Castlio
John H. Castlio	134	Andrew Zumalt
J. H. Castilio and Boon Calaway	57	Noah Zumalt
J. H. Castilio and Boon Calaway	112	Andrew Zumalt
Therese Calaway	106	Godfrey Kroh
Thomas Calaway	87	Jeremia Groshon
Thomas Calaway	106	Godfrey Kroh
Wm. B. Calaway	106	"
Wm. B. Calaway	87	Jeremia Groshen
Edwin Curle	87	"
Curle & D. K. Pitman	87	"
Samuel Cunningham	87	"
Jesse Cox	204	Richard Taylor
Samuel Courtney's heirs	204	Thos. D. Stephenson
Jonathan Crow	204	"
Daniel Crow	204	"

(St. Charles County, Missouri Continued)

Reputed Owner	Acres	Original Claimant
Elizabeth Crow	340	Henry Crow
David Crow	340	"
Thomas Cunningham	340	"
Nancy H. Clay	133	James Clay
Eley Clay's heirs	108	"
Nancy Clay	299	"
Robert Callerson	299	"
James Callerson	299	"
Ann Callerson	299	"
Absolem Callerson's heirs	299	"
William Cunningham	299	"
John D. Clopton	299	"
Cyrus Carter	299	"
Alaxander Chambers	80	Alax. Chambers
Joseph Cannon	80	Joseph Cannon
Phillip Cannon	80	"
Christopher Carter	50	Barner Thornhill
James Carter	50	"
George Corley	50	James A. Coiles
Henry Cox	50	"
Joseph Cheeley	50	"
Sulvenis Cottle's heirs	260	Sulveener Cottle, sen.
Sulvenis Cottle's heirs	44	Isaac Cottle
Frederick Dubet	44	"
Henry Dubet	44	"
Thadeus G. Dulin	44	"
Charles Deufau	44	"
Thomas Dumore	40	St. Chas. Commissioners
Pattrice Dophine	40	"
Alexa Dophine	40	"
Stephen Decamp	60	"
Edmond Davis' heirs	160	Wm. Wilkerson
Edmond Davis' heirs	80	Herrod Wilkerson
Edmond Davis' heirs	80	Edmund Davis
Therren H. Davis	80	"
Isaac Davis	80	"
Frederick Davis	80	"
Lyada Dorsay	80	"
Joshua Dotson's heirs	85	Joshua Dotson
David H. Darst	408	David Darst, sr.
Isaac Darst	112	David H. Darst, jr.
George Deaster	112	"
Christopher Deaster	112	"
Samuel Drummons	112	"
Mellon Drummons' heirs	112	"
William L. Deirice	96	Jeremia Clay
Henry Dickhoust	23	"

(St. Charles County, Missouri Continued)

Reputed Owner	Acres	Original Claimants
John Davis	23	Jeremia Clay
Nathaniel Day	23	"
Nighton Day	23	"
Jefferson Dyre	100	Lewis Crow
James Drummons	100	"
Harrison Drummons	100	"
Mary L. Duquette	85	Jos. Beauchamp
Mary L. Duquette	42	Clermont Misty
Mary L. Duquette	40	Peter Pallenda
Mary L. Duquette	40	----- Quinnell
Mary L. Duquette	40	Jos. Lamarch
Mary L. Duquette	40	Francis Dorlac
Mary L. Duquette	40	Baptist Bruxie
Mary L. Duquette	72	M. L. Duquette
Mary L. Duquette	34	Baptist Lamarch
Mary L. Duquette	43	Paul Corvoirser
A. T. Douglass	43	"
John H. Dennis	43	"
Michael Deraway	43	"
Joseph Deraway	43	"
August Dorlac	43	"
Baptiste Dorlac's heirs	34	Baptist Dorlac
William Dotson	132	Samuel Clay
Joshua Dotson's heirs	56	William Haws
Charles Denny, sr.	266	John Cook
Charles Denny, sr.	170	Maryan Violett
Charles Denny, sr.	90	Louis Jannett
Charles Denny, sr.	90	Absolem Keathley
Charles Denny, jr.	90	"
Ann G. Durfey	90	"
Jefferson Drake	227	"
George Deer	102	Pier Chouteau
Jacko Dubaugh	51	Ant. Janie
Acan Dubeaugh	119	"
St. Croix Deroughy	80	St. Chas. Commissioners
Cefrey Debeaugh	40	"
James W. Drury	40	"
Andrew Davidson	40	"
Afreu David (free colored)	40	"
Walter Dillin	40	"
Anton Earnes	40	"
Rufus Easton's heirs	34	Edward Hamsted
Jacob Eversall	34	"
Samuel Emery	34	"
E. R. Eversall	34	"
Benjamin Eaton	34	"
James D. Earl	80	St. Chas. Commissioners

(St. Charles County, Missouri Continued)

Reputed Owner	Acres	Original Claimant
William Elclosh	80	St. Chas. Commissioners
Benjamin Emouron, sr.	80	"
William Echart	269	"
Wm. Echart, G. Collier, Ira Moor and ---- Baradie	---	Steam Mill Co.
Sydney Ensaw	40	St. Chas. Commissioners
Martin Emarine	40	"
Noil Saint Ebau	40	"
John C. Evens	32	Julien Roy
John C. Evens	102	Charles Roy
Daniel Edling	102	"
Elisha Ellett	102	"
William C. Edwards	102	"
Henry Edwards	102	"
Edward S. Eaves	189	Christopher Zumalt
Anthony Ernes	189	"
Gustavus Eulenstine	189	"
John Fetter	189	"
Edward Ford	189	"
Rolf Flaugherty	162	Rolf Flaugherty
George B. Fant	102	"
Noble Furline	102	"
Nancy Fisher	145	John Zumalt
Hutchens B. Ferrel	145	"
Frederich Ferrell	84	St. Chas. Commissioners
Bernhart Fetter	84	"
Wm. N. Fulkerson	20	"
Wm. N. Fulkerson	20	E. Bernard and Jos. Lofton
Joshua Fine	3	St. Chas. Commissioners
Joseph Ficett	3	"
Jos. Flaugherty's heirs	85	Jos. Flaugherty
Stephen Frazure	42	St. Chas. Commissioners
Mary Ford	90	"
John Fraynoth	90	"
Joseph Flair	90	"
Andrew Fox	90	"
Michael Fetch	90	"
Benjamin Feckly	90	"
Joseph Farter's heirs	40	Silas Massey
Daniel Fisher	40	"
Joseph Flare	40	"
John Farmer	40	Mathew Farmer's heirs
Mary Farmer	40	"
L. C. Fullington	40	"
Mary Foushee	40	"
Samuel B. Farmer	40	"

(St. Charles County, Missouri Continued)

Reputed Owner	Acres	Original Claimant
William France	40	Mathew Farmer's heirs
John Frazure	200	John Watkins
David Frazure	200	Geo. Bonham
David Frazure	79	John Watkins
Thomas Frazure	79	"
Martin Frazure	79	"
Henry Faderhouse	79	"
Nicholas Fisher	425	John Lindsay
Isaac Fulkerson's heirs	340	Henry McGlaughlin
Isaac Fulkerson's heirs	70	Isaac Vanbibber
Isaac Fulkerson's heirs	83	Joshua Dotson
William Forman	83	"
Joseph Fare	83	"
Ferdinand Focke	83	"
Bial Farnesworth	340	Ira Cottle
Alden Farnsworth	340	"
Wm. Farnsworth's heirs	150	Isaac Cottle
Benjamin P. Ferrel	150	"
Mary Ferrel	150	"
Joseph Flare	150	"
Adolph Fagenburner	150	"
Joseph Farnax	150	"
Tobitha Fulton's heirs	77	St. Chas. Commissioners
Joshua Fine	77	"
Herrod Grover	77	"
Adolph Griseau	77	"
Elija W. Gutheridge	175	John McMitchel
Elija W. Gutheridge	25	John Belloncourt
Hemon Garlich	25	"
Earnst Golternart	25	"
John Gill	54	Milton Lewis
John Gill	183	P. J. F. Gill
John Gill	40	Christopher Hutchen
Robert Gutherie	30	Christopher Zumwalt
Elizabeth Groce	160	Benjamin Jones
David Groce	160	Solomon Zumalt
Isaac Groce	160	"
Lewis Groce	160	"
Elija R. Goodrich	34	St. Chas. Commissioners
Louis Garman	68	"
Beriah Graham	62	"
Thomas Glenday	170	Nicholas Tarart
George N. Gata	190	George Gata, sr.
John Gata, sr.	190	"
John Gata, sr.	76	John Gata
John Gata, junr.	76	"
Isadore Gardner	76	"

(St. Charles County, Missouri Continued)

Reputed Owner	Acres	Original Claimant
John B. Garvin	59	St. Chas. Commissioners
Alaxander Garvin's heirs	85	Ant. Barada
Peter Grace	85	Ant. Barada
Battest Gascou	30	St. Chas. Commissioners
Carter Griffin	87	Isaac Follis
Sinclear Griffin	170	"
Asa Griffin	435	L. Laburne
Asa Griffin	112	Jas. Swift
Daniel Griffith	204	Peter Lewis
Daniel Griffith	272	L. Laburne
Daniel Griffith	340	Samuel Griffith
Daniel Griffith	87	Michael Reanney
Daniel Griffith	340	Francis Dequett
Daniel Griffith	313	Daniel Griffith
Daniel Griffith	240	"
Joseph Graviene's heirs	11	Baptist Lacrosse
Joseph Graviene's heirs	28	Solomon Pettit
Joseph Graviene's heirs	11	Joseph Guinnard
Joseph Ginnard	34	Abraham Dumond
Alex Ginnard	34	"
Louis Ginnard	34	"
Louis Godfrey	34	"
Clerma Griffay	34	"
George Grady	40	St. Chas. Commissioners
Modest Gardheafair	40	"
Squire Green	110	Francis Dequett
Joshua Grimes	110	"
Grimes, Cambel & Orrick	110	"
Thomas Gilmore	640	Angus Gillis
Thomas Gilmore	87	Thomas Gilmore
John Gilmore	87	"
Samuel Glass	72	Malkice Baldridge
T. P. Grantham	72	"
William Gordon	72	"
Samuel Givens	131	John Creech
Daniel Grimes	131	"
James Green, jr.	156	James Green, jr.
John Green	170	"
James Goodrich	255	Elisha Goodrich
Phileo Gillett	108	Peter Teauqe
Leonard Gillett	108	"
John Griffin	108	"
Joel Griffin	108	"
Conrad Griffin	108	"
Ambrose Griggs	100	John Watkins
Benjamin Howel	276	John Peuget
Daniel Hunt	276	"

(St. Charles County, Missouri Continued)

Reputed Owner	Acres	Original Claimant
Larkin Howel	220	Thomas Howel
Alonzo A. Howel	299	"
Pizaro Howel, sr.	70	"
Charles Hutcheson	80	Cornelius Comegys
Johnas Heald	80	"
George W. Hoffman	80	"
Richard Harless	80	"
A. C. Hilbert	80	"
John Hunnwell	80	"
Joseph Hall	80	"
Lorenzo B. Holmes	80	"
Ellen Holmes	5	St. Chas. Commissioners
Samuel Holmes	40	"
John C. Hancock	40	"
Henry Hartman	40	"
John H. Housen	40	"
Samuel Howlin	80	"
Conrad Hunn	80	Noil Ant. Prior
Martin Hunn	80	"
John Hook	80	"
Andrew Hawley	80	"
Joseph Hunn	50	Pier Chouteau
George Headerick	50	"
Joseph Headerick	80	Travis Biggs
Nathaniel Heald's heirs	382	Jacob Zumalt
Nathaniel Heald's heirs	34	Joseph Gerard
Nathaniel Heald's heirs	102	Pier Cornoiren
Nathaniel Heald's heirs	80	Nathan Heald
Rebecca Heald	80	"
Monty Hunt	307	St. Chas. Commissioners
Samuel Heart	307	"
Silvest Honory	307	"
Maddan Francis Honory	307	"
Tesent Honory	307	"
Louis Honory	307	"
Harmon Holdra	307	"
Stephen Hulkey	307	"
Harmon Holdraugh	80	"
Henry Hickman	60	"
Francis Hostetor	60	St. Chas. Commissioners
Francis Hunn	160	Francis Hunn
Henry Harless	160	"
Edward Harless	160	"
John Howel	421	John Howel
James Howel	350	Francis Howel
Thomas Howel	743	Thomas Howel
Thomas Howel	150	Christopher Zumalt

(St. Charles County, Missouri Continued)

Reputed Owner	Acres	Original Claimant
Zorado Hutcherson	120	Arend Rutgers
Zorado Hutcherson	30	John Welden
Aaron Hutchens	130	Arend Rutgers
Thonas Hopkins	130	"
Joseph Hanes' heirs	186	Samuel Clay
Joseph Hanes' heirs	170	Jos. Hanes
Jane Hanes	170	"
Daniel Hayes	213	Daniel Hayes
Daniel Hayes	75	Phillip Miller
Daniel Hayes	80	Daniel Hays
Francis Howel	104	Francis Howel, jr.
Ftancis Howel	217	Francis Howel
Lewis Howel	50	Isaac Weldon
Lewis Howel	136	Francis Howel. sr.
Greenbury Hutchens	409	John Aelden
Christopher Hutchens	150	Milton Lewis
A. G. Hutchens	150	"
George Huffman	640	George Huffman
R. C. Hendrick	640	"
Peter Huffman	640	Son of Geo. Huffman
J. Huffman	640	"
Peter Huffman	175	Peter Huffman
Peter Huffman	85	Arend Rutgers
John Huffman	80	Peter Huffman
George Huffman	80	Son of Peter Huffman
Francis Hillencamp	50	Wyett P. Woodrough
Charles Haupt	50	"
Jonas Hurcules	50	"
Obed Holesclaw	50	"
G. W. Hutcheson's heirs	127	John Walker
Benjamin F. Howel	127	"
Christian Hostetor's heirs	425	Francis Hostetor
Heirock Heartman	425	"
Henry Helman	425	"
Henry L. Harney	425	"
Addam Harness	425	"
A. D. Harmon	60	St. Chas. Commissioners
Leonard Harold	195	L. Harold
Conrad Hosper	80	James Frazier
William A. Lewis	80	Leonard Harold
Benjamin Hancock	212	John Crow
Charles Helfrech	212	"
John M. Helfrech	212	"
John Johnson	212	"
Hill H. Jarvey	212	"
Antwine Janie, jr.	212	Ant. Janis
Antwine Janie, jr.	67	St. Chas. Commissioners

(St. Charles County, Missouri Continued)

Reputed Owner	Acres	Original Claimant
Ant. Janis' heirs	134	Ant. Janis
Nicholas Janis	24	"
Elisha Jorden	5	St. Chas. Commissioners
Joseph Jott	5	"
Solomon Jinkins	5	"
William Jackson	5	"
Jonathan Jones	136	Baptist Bellond
Daniel Ilor	88	Noil Hebert
Almenda Inman	88	"
Eliah Jinkins	88	"
Levi Johnson's heirs	85	Isaac Follis
Levi Johnson's heirs	288	L. Laburne
Easter Johnson	288	"
Joseph John	288	"
James Johns	134	St. Chas. Commissioners
Evans Johnson	234	L. Laburne
John Johnson	234	"
Charles M. Johnson	234	"
August Juney	123	A. J. Jurney
George B. Johnson	123	"
John H. Johnson	123	"
Baker Johnson	40	Green James
Daniel Inman	135	Isaac Darat
Bayley W. Johnson	135	"
Stephen Ilor	100	Henry Stefenson
Joseph Jurney	169	James Jurney
Joseph Jurney	85	Thomas Caulk
Ann Icenhour	85	"
Jarvis Johnson	85	"
William King's heirs By Roden Renner	240	William King
James Kirbin	240	"
Jacob Kibler	40	St. Chas. Commissioners
David Knott	152	"
Charles Krettzer	3	Maurice Mechant
Osbern Knott's heirs	3	"
William Knott	200	St. Chas. Commissioners
Samuel Keathley	276	S. Keathley
Samuel Keathley	27	Randolph Biggs
Simon Keathley	34	Tuscint Ceerce
Simon Keathley	51	James Morrison
Obedia Keathley	51	"
Daniel Keathley	51	"
Frederick and Earnst Kayser	340	Ferdinand H. Crosby
John King	340	"
Wallace Kirkpatrick	34	Bazel Picard
Wallace Kirkpatrick	80	Wallis Kirkpatrick

(St. Charles County, Missouri Continued)

Reputed Owner	Acres	Original Claimant
James Kidwill	68	Pier Palarda
John Kase	80	St. Chas. Commissioners
John H. Krumkey	40	"
Arnold Kackel	40	"
Conner Kelley	272	"
Thomas H. Kelly	40	Noah Zumwalt
Thomas H. Kelly	10	Melkice Baldridge
Thomas H. Kelly	58	Thomas H. Kelley
Isaac Keathley,. Nathaniel Keathley, Isaac Keathley	172	Michael Crow
Daniel Keathley	172	"
William R. Keathley	172	"
Nathaniel Keathley	172	"
Isaac Keathley	172	"
Frederich Keathley	172	"
Absalem Keathley	160	Absalem Keathley
William Kinnard	80	"
Henry Krichbam	80	Michael Grator
Andrew Kray	80	"
Lewis, Edward and Paul Kray	80	"
Peter Krag	80	"
Richard B. Kibble	80	"
Leonhard Keashler	80	"
Godfried Kassel	80	"
Julien Kruise	150	James Vanbiber
Frederich Kruise	150	"
Abrech Krust	150	"
Jonathan Kunze	150	"
John and Ferdinand Kosk	150	"
John Keller, sr.	150	"
John Keller, jr.	150	"
David Keller	150	"
James Keller	150	"
Thomas Langford	150	"
Evens Lamasters	141	James Flaugherty
Benjamin Lamasters	282	"
Benjamin Lamasters	170	Thomas Caulk
William C. Lyndsay	184	Wm. C. Lyndsay
Milton Lewis	99	Milton Lewis
Pier Lora	20	St. Chas. Commissioners
Antwine Lattrail	20	"
Henry C. Lyndsay	2	"
John B. Lagenes	2	"
John Lilley	281	"
Barbary Lovering	20	"
Thomas Lyndsay, jr.	45	Francis Duquett
Charles Ludolf	11	"

(St. Charles County, Misouri Continued)

Reputed Owner	Acres	Original Claimant
George Lynch	11	Francis Duquett
William Low	640	David Conrod
J. C. Lackland	640	"
John Lasarge	640	"
Joseph Larver's heirs	640	"
Louis Leebo	640	John B. Leebo
Louis Lorce	1	St. Chas. Commissioners
James W. Long	1	"
John T. Long	41	"
Joseph Long	40	"
Landen Lyndsay	40	"
Henry Loclor	40	"
Jeramice Lollar	40	"
John Laphsen	40	"
James Lyndsay, sr.	100	Francis Duquett
James Lyndsay, sr.	34	Francis Corbono
James Lyndsay, sr.	34	Timothy Kibbey
James Lyndsay, jr.	68	August Fent
James Lyndsay, jr.	34	Joseph Tayon
Thomas Lyndsay, sr.	240	Francis Duquett
Thomas Lyndsay, sr.	380	Michael Rybolt
Thomas Lyndsay, sr.	160	Louis Baber
Thomas Lyndsay, sr.	45	Nicholas Lafourett
Thomas Lyndsay, sr.	68	Charles Tayon
Thomas Lyndsay, sr.	34	Alex. Cota
Thomas Lyndsay, sr.	34	Charles Cardinal
Thomas Lyndsay, sr.	34	Pier Rauden
Gabriel Lattrail	90	Joseph Langlois
John Lavac	30	St. Chas. Commissioners
Joseph Lamarch	20	"
Charles Lurton	85	Ant. Barada
Francis Lodie	170	"
Eliett Lusby	170	"
Ant. Laduque	170	"
Thirrese Louiso	170	"
Charles Lefress	85	"
Napoleion F. Lasier	34	Francis Socier
Alxa. Laferve	86	Mathew Socier
August Lafevere	34	Baptist Pujol
Louis Lacroix	34	"
Ambrose Labo	34	"
Francis Laclear	34	August Clarmont
Francis Laclear	25	Solomon Pettit
Antwine Laclear	25	"
Garrart Lanford	25	"
Alex. Lafan, jr.	25	"
Andrew Lafarge	68	Simon Lafarge

(St. Charles County, MIssouri Continued)

Reputed Owner	Acres	Original Claimant
Joseph Lature	12	August Lafane
Thomas Lord	12	"
William Luckett	12	"
James Lewis	80	Samuel Johnson
David Lynch	80	"
Green Logan's heirs	160	Green Logan
William C. Logan	80	William C. Logan
Cambel Langford	80	"
Allen B. Lucus	80	"
V. M. Lewis	80	"
Henrie Logmyer	80	"
Waller C. Maupin	80	"
Charles D. May	80	"
Pinkney M. May	80	"
John McClenney	80	"
Micaja McClenney	240	William Keathley
David McGowin	80	"
Preston McRoberts	80	"
John McRoberts	80	"
Nathan Mason's heirs	100	Walker Wright
Nathan Mason's heirs	80	John M. Faulkner
John McConnel	640	John McConnel
John McConnel	532	Peter Teungo
Charles P. May	80	John Castello
Charles P. May	20	William Keathley
Charles P. May	364	Allen Walker
Charles P. May	95	R. B. Allen
Charles P. May	240	Preston McRoberts
Charles P. May	160	Pines H. Shelton
Charles P. May	180	Andrew S. Woods
Edward P. Mathews	180	"
John McNutt	160	Christopher Zumalt
James McClenney	80	Samuel Givens
Charles Maychett	80	St. Chas. Commissioners
James Maychett	20	"
G. B. Maschaney	20	"
Robert McClure's heirs	603	James Kerr
Robert McClure	137	Robert McClure
Alexander McDonnel	90	St. Chas. Commissioners
Seth Millington's heirs	176	Charles Tayon
Seth Millington's heirs	4	Charles Valley
Jeremia Millington	120	St. Chas. Commissioners
Sophia McClure	80	"
David McCauslin	40	"
A. W. McKinney	4	"
William Mileu	60	"
Louis Myre	60	"

(St. Charles County, Missouri Continued)

Reputed Owner	Acres	Original Claimant
John Moore	60	St. Chas. Commissioners
John C. Moore	60	"
George W. Miller	60	"
Gabriel Marlow	60	"
Henry Marshall	6	"
Elisha McClenlland	6	"
Joseph Martinno	6	"
James McCourt	6	"
John C. Middleburger	85	Worre Gilbert
Francis Moletoe	85	"
James Morrisson	44	Isadre Savory
James Morrisson	44	Baptist Belland
James Morrisson	34	Jaques Malett
James Morrisson	34	Anne Buett
James Morrisson	120	Benjamin Rogers
Jas. and Jesse Morrison	68	Francis Lafrance
Jas. and Jesse Morrison	34	---- Clermont
Jas. and Jesse Morrison	51	---- Lafranchin
Jas. and Jesse Morrison	34	John Baptist
Jas. and Jesse Morrison	68	Joseph Lorene
Jas. and Jesse Morrison	51	Pier Palardu
Jas. and Jesse Morrison	34	Ant. Gokie
Jas. and Jesse Morrison	850	Francis Socier
Jas. and Jesse Morrison	68	Francis Howard
Jas. and Jesse Morrison	34	---- Conder
John M. McMillen	216	Arend Rutgers
Joseph Marr	128	St. Chas. Commissioners
Baptist McDonnel	128	"
Elija Mallerson	149	"
Elija Mallerson	80	Jas. Mitchel
Elija Mallerson	185	E. Patterson
Stephen McCatee	85	John Wealty
Francis Mascheda	85	"
Timothy McCoy	100	Henry Stephenson
Gasper Miacal	100	"
William McClay	86	Wm. and David McClay
William McClay	100	John Cool
Ignatus Milles	100	"
Thomas W. Mozee	100	"
Henry Meddendorf	100	"
Elonis S. Meginnes	100	"
John Manley	20	St. Chas. COmmissioners
Robert Mcurvine	20	"
John McClane	20	"
Francis Moginzo	68	Francis Moginzo
Archibald McCoskey	25	Charles Ebert
Archibald McCoskey	30	---- Lafarge

(St. Charles County, Missouri Continued)

Reputed Owner	Acres	Original Claimant
Peter Martinno	21	Abraham Dumond
Charles Martinno's heirs	33	Bazel Pecard
Charles Martinno's heirs	8	Louis Pujol
Charles Martinno's heirs	32	Abraham Dumond
Francis Martinno	26	"
Francis Martinno	15	Bazel Pecard
John F. McNight	80	John F. McNight
J. F. and D. G. McNight	200	Worner Gilbert
J. F. and D. G. McNight	398	L. Laburne
Joseph A. McNight	102	"
Acan Marice	102	"
Phillip Martin	120	St. Chas. Commissioners
Laurence Mclamee	120	"
Jacob Miller	46	"
James M. McKay	46	"
John G. McKay	46	"
Aaron McWaters	254	David Edwards
Edward McWaters	254	"
Wilford McWaters	254	"
Hugh McWaters	254	"
George Myres	672	Henry Zumalt
George Myres	5	John McCoy
James Majores	5	"
James R. Mcdermont	200	John Little
William McCoy	205	William McCoy
Milton McRoberts	240	Milton McRoberts
Sarah McRoberts	229	Geo. W. Zimmereman
Harrison McRoberts	202	"
James L. Martin	67	Walker Wright
John Mathews	276	Mattrou Lewis
James and Phineas Mathews	276	"
William Morris	62	Phillip Miller
Benjamin Morris	84	"
Lasarez McFall	152	Biol Farnesworth
George Myres	152	"
Charles McFarris	152	"
Zacaria Moore	152	"
James D. Moore	152	"
Thomas J. Marshall	152	"
Zerelda McCutchen	152	"
Robert Miller	151	"
Frederick Myres	151	"
John Myres	151	"
Fleming Miller	157	Fleming Miller
Mary Mason	85	Thomas Caulk
James McConnel	85	"
William S. McClearney	80	Wm. S. McClearny

(St. Charles County, Missouri Continued)

Reputed Owner	Acres	Original Claimant
William S. McClearny	3	N. B. Tucker
Travis Murphey	3	"
J. L. McCutchens' heirs	221	David Darst, jr.
J. L. McCutchens' heirs	28	"
Christian R. Miller	80	Dedn. Iman
Christain R. Miller	40	John Bellor
Mary Moordock	40	"
Alexander Moordock's heirs	47	Geo. Bingham
Alexander Moordock's heirs	342	John Bell Winant
Alexander Moordock's heirs	278	Alexander Murdock
George Moordock	56	"
James Moordock	56	"
William Morris	56	"
Walter T. McCutchen	56	"
John Moordock	56	"
Edward Morris	116	Edward Morris
Robert Moordock	80	James Mordock
Robert Moordock	93	George Baughan
Justice Muhnn	152	M. Miclenna
John Mabe	152	"
Custavus Martilo	160	H. A. H. Russel
Custavus Martilo	145	Charles Palmer
Frederick Martilo	145	"
Ludwig Meyer	80	Henry Zumwalt
Charles Myer	80	"
Julies Malenkott	80	"
Garner J. Medcalf	80	"
Francis Noval	34	Bazel Pecard
Joseph Noval	34	"
Chesley M. Noell	34	"
John Nipp	34	"
John Naylor	247	Jacob Zumalt
John Naylor	138	John Naylor
Thomas Naylor	138	"
Martin Noarth	138	"
John Oliver	340	William Sturd
John Ottin	340	"
Phillip Orrich	340	"
Joseph Ongee	54	Pattrice Rove
Ezra Overall	34	"
Cambel Orrick	34	"
John Orrick	68	St. Chas. Commissioners
Benj. and John Orrick	68	"
Benjamin Orrick	68	"
John Overstreet	68	"
Louis Obeshon	68	"
W. D. Orrick	68	"

(St. Charles County, Missouri Continued)

Reputed Owner	Acres	Original Claimant
William L. Overall	297	L. Laburne
William L. Overall	572	James Swift
William L. Overall	142	Louis Leboure
Wilson L. Overall	1041	"
Wilson L. Overall	463	James Swift
Nathaniel Overall's heirs	26	Baptist Lacroix
Nathaniel Overall's heirs	78	Solomon Pettit
Nathaniel Overall's heirs	45	Joseph Ginnard
Nathaniel Overall's heirs	45	Julien Roy
Nathaniel Overall's heirs	45	Bazel Pecard
Nathaniel Overall's heirs	170	Thomas Guinn
Nathaniel Overall's heirs	17	Abraham Dumond
Aaron Osgood	21	Baptist Lacroix
L. E. Powel	200	St. Chas. Commissioners
Joseph Patri	40	"
Harden Poe	40	"
Farris Patterson	40	"
P. P. Patchen	40	"
Frederich Prior	40	"
Holmere J. Pokern	420	"
Noriel John Prior	40	"
John Phelphes	40	"
Samuel Pearce	40	"
William H. Prince	40	"
Joseph Perrow	49	"
S. W. Perrow	49	"
Peter Pallarda	8	"
Bazel Pallarda	8	"
Antwine Pallarda	54	"
Peter Pallarda, jr.	17	"
Bazel Poinsalate	18	John Bernard
Louis Pujet	18	"
Montgomery Perry	77	Isaac Follis
Montgomery Perry	18	James Piper
Louis Pujol	254	Isaac Follis
Louis Pujol	56	August Lafevre
Mary Pujol	56	"
Noil Ant. Preor	56	"
Charles Peck	20	St. Chas. Commissioners
Frederick Price	84	Danl. Keathley
William Preston	480	John B. Chandiller
William Preston	640	Daniel Keathley
William Preston	340	John Tayon
William Preston	24	George Cauthren
George Price	552	Conrod E. Price
Augustus Price	552	"
Jacob Price	552	"

(St. Charles County, Missouri Continued)

Reputed Owner	Acres	Original Claimant
George R. Pittis	142	George R. Pittes
Richard B. Pitman	142	"
James Patten	152	Jas. and Samuel Steel
George Pitzer's heirs	179	John Jurney
George Pitzer's heirs	212	Francis Smith
D. K. Pitman	128	N. Simonds
D. K. Pitman	340	George Huffman
D. K. Pitman	44	D. P. Pitman
William Portzey	44	"
James Patterson	44	"
Samuel G. Pullem	209	Michael Crow
Micheal Price	290	Isaac Welden
William Petty	290	"
George Power	290	John Pettey
William Price	290	"
Henry Porter	290	"
Thomas Pearce, jr.	290	"
Henry Pritchet	290	"
WIlliam Pearce	290	"
Thomas Pence, sr.	320	Peter Power
John Rochester	80	George Collins
Hollem Rice	10	St. Chas. Commissioners
S. W. Rice	3	"
John Rashaw	3	"
Antwine Reynold	68	Pier Rubardu
John Readman	68	"
Welcome A. Robbins	85	H. Crosbey
Welcome A. Robbins	85	E. Patterson
Welcome A. Robbins	111	St. Chas. Commissioners
Lucy Readman	60	"
George Readman's heirs	100	"
Isaac Robertson's heirs	85	Pier Chouteau
Thomas J. Robbins	85	E. Patterson
Thomas J. Robbins	32	James Swift
Thomas J. Robbins	20	James Mitchel
Frederick M. Robbins	85	E. Patterson
Frederick Robbins	42	H. Crosby
Thadeus E. Robbins	85	E. Patterson
Thadeus E. Robbins	85	Warren Gilbert
Thadeus E. Robbins	32	James Swift
Simeon Rice	200	St. Chas. Commissioners
Hollen Rice	18	"
Moses B. Robbins	42	H. Crosbey
Moses B. Robbins	85	E. Patterson
Moses B. Robbins	87	Micheal Reanney
Moses B. Robbins	92	James Piper

(St. Charles County, Missouri Continued)

Reputed Owner	Acres	Original Claimants
Moses B. Robbins	100	Warner Gilbert
Cinthie Richey	85	Antwine Barada
Burrel Reeves	85	"
Pattrice Roy	14	Julien Roy
Louis Renjstoft	14	"
Thomas Redman	14	"
John Rosseau	14	"
Joel Rassor	14	"
Francis Reynolds	14	"
Francis Rosseau, sr.'s heirs	14	"
Joseph Rosseau	14	"
Julien Roy	14	"
Martin Reeder and Anton Bovaushecter	14	"
Nicholas Rice	60	St. Chas. Commissioners
Joel Richards	60	"
Jacob Rouce	60	"
Frederick Rouvenbergach	60	"
Frederick Ringo	80	Jacob Zumwalt
Erasmus Rupard	80	"
Frederick A. Rexroad	80	"
Daniel Rennard	80	"
George Reeder	80	"
John D. Readhorst	101	James Clay
Frederick Readman	101	"
John Remmons	101	"
Henry Ringo	101	"
Lawrence Ross' heirs	160	Benjamin Jones
Noiles Scough's heirs	260	Michael Rybolt
Daniel Smith	320	John A. Smith
John Smith's heirs	320	"
John A. Smithe	320	"
Peter Shomaker's heirs	30	St. Chas. Commissioners
Erasmus Simpson	160	A. Chambers
Erasmus Simpson	80	E. Simpson
William H. H. Simpson	80	"
James W. Simpson	80	"
George Spires	80	Feline Scott
George Spires	80	George Spires
Foster B. Simpson	80	"
Joseph Scott	80	Joseph Scott
Jeremia Suliven	80	"
David Suliven	80	"
Felix Scott	80	F. Scott
George Scott	80	"
Presley Scott	80	"
Daniel Shevil	80	"

(St. Charles County, Missouri Continued)

Reputed Owner	Acres	Original Claimant
George Shannon	30	Martin Bovett
George Shannon	273	St. Chas. Commissioners
George S. Spencer	150	Robert Spencer
Elizabeth Scott	428	John Scott
Andrew Stupp	428	"
Samuel Slator	428	"
James N. Shelton	160	Henry Zumwalt
Volentine Smith	57	St. Chas. Commissioners
Josie C. Shinn	57	"
Samuel Shaw's heirs	57	"
P. A. Stockslager	57	"
Thomas P. Scott	57	"
Since (Free colored woman)	57	"
Robert Samuels	47	"
Elen Sutee	47	"
Francis Sterer	11	"
Chancey Shepherd	34	"
George Sibley	34	A. Buett
George Sibley	34	Louis Blanchett
George Sibley	68	John Cook
George Sibley	68	Nicholas Coons
George Sibley	34	A. Valley
Robert A. Spencer, jr.	34	"
Joseph Snyder	34	"
Anthony Steelsmith	34	"
Thomas Spalding	34	"
John Sturd	68	August Fectueau
George Spencer's heirs	212	George Spencer
Sarah Spencer	212	"
William and Joseph Spencer	212	"
Son of Robert Spencer	87	"
Ferdinand Sack	87	Michael Keenney
John B. St. Louis	87	"
George Stump	87	"
John Spain	87	"
John Smelser	210	L. Labeaume
Robert Seagraves	210	"
Mathew Socier	34	Mathew Socier
Mary Socier	68	Francis Socier
Battist Socier	34	Mathew Socier
George Swenderman	60	St. Chas. Commissioners
George Strother	60	"
Francis Socier	180	"
Joseph Sumner	68	Michael Lasage
Joseph Sumner	68	Joseph Crow
Joseph Sumner	68	Mathew Socier
Joseph Sumner	68	Charles Boyer

(St. Charles County, Missouri Continued)

Reputed Owner	Acres	Original Claimant
Joseph Sumner	68	Ettanier Pappin
George Smelser's heirs	423	L. Laburne
John Sumner's heirs	59	Ettania Laforge
Frederich Shaver	160	St. Chas. Commissioners
John H. Shroer	42	"
Madden Swenderman	40	"
Phillip Snyder	50	"
John F. Smemure	60	"
Randolph B. Smith	152	Allen Walker
Nancy Smith	74	"
Robert Spencer, sr.	640	R. Spencer
Robert Spencer, sr.	23	Antwine Janis
Robert Spencer, sr.	212	Loren Derouchey
Robert Spencer, sr.	682	G. R. Spencer
Robert Spencer, sr.	382	Michael Rybolt
Robert Spencer, sr.	136	Widow Labodee
Robert Spencer, sr.	135	Louis Jarrett
Robert Spencer, sr.	3	Robert Spencer
Pines H. Shelton	330	P. H. Shelton
James Sylva	640	James Bayly
Dennis Sylva	640	"
Curthbert Stump	640	"
Reuben Scidmore	640	"
John Stump	135	Isaac Vanbibber
Miles Stump	135	"
Abraham Shobe	1010	Daniel Boon
James Smithe	510	"
John Sturd	510	"
Christopher Saupe	510	"
Francis Sturd	90	Perry Brown
Francis Sturd	37	A. Zumwalt
Elias C. Sturd	37	A. Zumwalt
Elias C. Sturd	80	Perry Brown
William Stuard	80	"
Joseph Swathercup	117	Christian Woolf
Joseph Swathercup	117	A. Duchman
Addam Stephen	117	"
Addam Sheleer	117	"
Andrew Stultsmith	117	"
David Scott's heirs	117	"
Tho. D. Stephenson	195	Godfrey Krah
John Smith	162	John Smith
Phillip Spanhouse	162	"
Charles Spanhouse	162	"
William J. Sampson	90	Henry Steel
William J. Sampson	15	John Bell
William J. Sampson	60	Jas. Mitchel

(St. Charles County, Missouri Continued)

Reputed Owner	Acres	Original Claimant
William J. Sampson	223	John Watkins
John Sack	223	"
Jeremia Shaver	223	"
Addam Stinemiller	223	"
Herman Stroukhoff	223	"
John G. Seipes	223	"
William Shearman	223	"
Frederick Schultz	223	"
Andrew Schultz	223	"
Frederick Schultz	293	"
Louis Schultz	293	"
Andrew Schultz	293	"
Vicenot Scoobark	293	"
R. E. Taylor	80	B. Rogers
R. E. Taylor	40	Richard Taylor
Jesse Thomas	184	Louis Crow
David Thomas	184	"
James P. Thomas	220	Benjamin Jones
Leo Twyman	660	"
Samuel Taylor	8	Daniel Colgen
William Turner	40	St. Chas. Commissioners
Antwine Teabo	40	"
Henry Tipcer	40	"
Joseph Tayon	40	"
Joseph Teabo	40	"
Paul Turnley	255	Christian Dornnay
Paul Turnley	110	Noel Hebert
Joseph Turnley	110	"
Therrese Turnbeau	110	"
Peter Tritley	8	Ant. Janis
John Tritley	8	"
JOhn P. Tritley	56	Maryan Violett
Roger Towers	56	"
Pier Tayon	56	"
Francis Tayon	56	"
Joseph Tisdale	56	"
Henry Tisscart	56	"
Thomas J, Travis	56	"
John M. Taylor's heirs	385	Thomas Smith
John M. Taylor's heirs	13	George Pursley
Nancy Taylor	13	"
George Tobbe	13	"
Ira E. Tatum	13	"
Washington Taylor	13	George Piersley
Washington Taylor	125	Phillip Miller
William Taylor	55	"
Benjamin Timberlake	223	Flanders Calaway

(St. Charles County, Missouri Continued)

Reputed Owner	Acres	Original Claimant
Benj. Teater, sr.	69	Christian Wolf
John Teater	69	"
Adam Tengeldene	69	"
Andrew Tagart	69	"
James Tagart	89	Elisha Goodrich
James Tagart	85	Jas. Green
James Tagart	157	John Jurney
James Tagart	185	Jas. Green, sr.
R. A. Tagart	185	"
Richard Tagart	196	"
Abner Tagart	196	"
William Teater	196	"
Reuben Teater's heirs	214	Jonathan Rucen
John Thornhill	214	"
Mary Thornhill	214	"
Reuben Thornhill's heirs	80	R. Thornhill
Waddy Thompson	80	"
Jonathan Thomas	320	Peter Power
Sarah Taylor	---	Richard Taylor
Francis Taylor's heirs	240	"
George A. Upshaw	240	"
Charles H. Vanquinbuin	50	Louis Jarrett
Charles H. Vanquinbuin	34	Louis Daberg
John Vermyer	76	St. Chas. Commissioners
Stephen Vermyer	76	"
Francis Viont	136	Charles Tayon
Samuel Vanburkeler	100	Henry Stephenson
William Vanburkeler	320	"
William Vanburkeler	85	Isaac Hostetor
Joseph Voisard	320	Joseph Voisard
John Voisard	320	"
George S. Vincent	320	"
Charles Vansperker	83	L. Harold
Henry Velmyer	83	"
Henry Velmyer	80	Robert B. Woolfork
Robert B. Woolfork	159	Norman Woolfork
B. Wray	159	"
John C. Wray	159	"
Archibald Watson's heirs	68	Louis Barada
Mary Watson	68	"
Thomas S. Williams	170	Ant. Barada
Samuel S. Watson	252	St. Chas. Commissioners
Benjamin F. Walker	80	Alexander Givens
Reuben C. Wiett	80	"
George W. Wattes	276	Mattrou Lewis
Anthony B. Wattes	100	George Pursley
Christian Woolf	100	"

(St. Charles County, Missouri Continued)

Reputed Owner	Acres	Original Claimant
Augustus Walche	100	George Pursley
John Wetmore	100	"
James Watson	100	"
Z. T. Woolfolk	240	Benjamin Rogers
Z. T. Woolfolk	40	Richard Taylor
Nicholas Willson	40	"
Samuel Welles	40	"
Joseph Wallace's heirs	85	Noil Hebert
Samuel Welles' heirs	480	Christopher Zumwalt
Sydney S. Woodes	163	James Herr
John S. Whittle	163	"
Charles Welde	163	"
Joseph Wise	163	"
Lorrence Wetmore	163	"
A. D. Watson	163	"
Andrew A. Willson	171	St. Chas. Commissioners
Jacob D. Williams' heirs	2	"
Benjamin R. Wardlow	17	"
B. and Lackham Wardlow	17	Syeans Will
Jacob White	30	Francis Socier
Jacob White	30	Charles Valley
H. W. Wardlaw	225	St. Chas. Commissioners
Preston Welot	110	Pier Chouteau
Conrad Welot	110	"
Peter Wenzel	18	John Bernard
Hiram Welles	18	"
Henry Wensenvickles	75	St. Chas. Commissioners
R. A. Woolfolk	160	William Cruiz
Warren Walker	160	"
Gordon H. Wallace	160	"
Joseph Word	160	"
John Wolf	216	Christian Wolf
Thomas L. Wood's heirs	216	"
John S. Wyatt	140	John Littlejohn
William Woolton's heirs	34	Louis Chanchiller
William Woolton's heirs	34	John Bisonett
William Woolton's heirs	34	Gabriel Cerre
Samuel Wells' heirs	77	Samuel Wells
George Yardley	77	"
Hiram Young	77	"
Joseph Yardley	160	John B. Chanciller
Joseph Yardley	80	William Yardley
William Yardley	80	William Yardley
Benjamin Young	36	St. Chas. Commissioners
Riley Yokum	36	"
Frederick Yardley	36	"
Stephen Yarnel	36	"

(St. Charles County, Missouri Continued)

Reputed Owner	Acres	Original Claimant
John Yarnel's heirs	80	John Yarnel
Elizabeth Yarnel	80	"
Oglesbe Young	80	"
----- Yager	60	"
Amos Yarnold	2	"
Emile Young	2	"
Andrew Zumalt	170	A. Zumalt
Samuel Zumalt	170	"
Jonathan Zumalt	206	Addam Zumalt
Solomon Zumalt	307	"
Gabriel Zumalt	320	"
Gabriel Zumalt	74	Perry Brown
John Zumalt	74	"
George C. Zumalt	74	"
George Zumalt's heirs	302	Timothy Kibby
George Zumalt's heirs	68	George Zumalt
Jacob Zumalt	31	Timothy Kibbey
William Zumalt	348	John McMitchell
William Zumalt	66	Timothy Kibbey
William Zeddies	66	"

Boone County, Missouri, Delinquent Tax List, 1824, Missouri Intelligencer, February 22, 1825, Vol. 5, No. 25

Delinquent taxpayers, per Samuel Wright: William Bledso, George Abit, John R. Bechetts, Jesse R. Barnett, Littlebury Witt, Sampson Bledso, George T. Boyce, Elias Bishop, Thomas Biswell, John Barton, Wiley Bagwell, Robert Barber, Daniel Crump, Jesse Corlew, John Creason, sr., Joseph Crump, jr., Thomas Dobson, Baylor Davis, John Dobson, John Faucy, Edward Fountain, John H. Evans, John M. Fowler, Mary Grayson, John Goodro, Jonathan Grayum, Peter Hart, Charles Halten, James Hun, John Huntsuckersen, John B. Halten, Arthur Hun, William Hunsicker, Jacob Hooberry, Hightower Hachney, Benjamin Irvin, Rueben Hall, Joseph W. Holt, John Y. Hodget, Peter Hendrix, Benjamin Kelly, John Kelso, James King, jr., William Lewis, Littleton Lunsford, John Lemmon, David Lynch, jr., Margaret Laughlin, John Lvich, jr., David Montooth, Soloman Mordicai, James Mathews, John McCarty, James McCarty, John H. Martin, Isaac Moody, Thomas B. Malcum, Ezekiel McCarty, John Pente, Joseph McNutt, George Moore, Gideon P. Norman, Elijah Owins, John Phillips, Archibald Patterson, William Perkins, Thomas Patten, David Parent, Henry Phillips, John Pente, Thomas L. Shaw, Miner Perry, Phillip Russel, John Ross, sr., Samuel B. Tribble, John Ross, jr., Isaac Reader, Parker Shedicar, John Smith, jr., Thomas L. Shaw, Elijah Tate, Isaac Tethum, Henry Winfield, George Winterbower, William Ward, William White, James Weathers, Samuel Wicjersham, John Wood, David Wilson.

Howard County, Missouri, Delinquent Tax List, No Year Given, Missouri Intelligencer, December 14, 1824, Vol. 6, No. 14.

Delinquent taxpayers, per John Harvey, col.:Andrew Burns, 640 a., Geo. Bollinger, agt.;Henry Beafield, 531 a.; Robert Burkett, 558 a.; Morgan Burns, 160 a.; Wm. H. Brooks, 80 a.; Wm. Bisswell, 47 a.; Wm. Cumins' heirs, 85 a.; Wm. Edwards, 510 a.; Robert D. Dawson, 160 a.; Abraham Goodin, lot; Wm. S. Hatch, 57 a.; Justin Hazel, lot; Wm. S. Hatch, 57 a.; Wm. Moldy, 80 a.; Moses Hiatt, 160 a.; Burton Lawless, lot; Noah Martin, lot; Peter A. Laforge, 640 a.; Robert Wash, 150 a.; Henry Lightfoot, 80 a.; Sterling Nucklus, lot;Chas. Simmons, 160 a.; Middle Anderson, 160 a.; Abbot Hancock, 160 a.

Chariton County, Missouri,Delinquent Tax List,1825, Missouri Intelligencer, December 9, 1825, Vol. 7, No. 12.

Delinquent taxpayers, per: F. A. Bradford, William Mott, Nicholas Dysart, William Donohoe, Stephen Donohoe, William Fleetwood, Isaac Earl, John Field, Jacob Hold, T. D. Looney, Sabrette Johnson, William Redcock, Daniel Redman, Archibald Taggart, Edmond Swinny, Alexander Trent.

Ray County, Missouri, Tax List, 1821.

William Adkins, UM; Joshua Adams; Martin Adams, UM; Isaac Allen, UM; Richard Adams; Abraham Allen, UM; John Allen, UM; William Adams; Wiatt Adkins, jr., UM; John Allen; Alexander Bogart, UM; William Adkins; Pleasant Adams; Hugh Brown; John A. Bartleson, UM; Howard Averett, Thorton V. Allen, UM; John Crowley; Wiatt Adkins, sr.; James Buckridge; Humphrey Best; James W. Black, UM; William Beaty; Stephen Brewer, UM; James Brown, UM; Jeremiah Burns; Stephen Baxter; William L. Black, UM; Joseph Brown; Thomas Brewer; John Baitman, UM; William Black; James Buchanan; Henry Brewer; Joseph Cox; Kemp Cary; William Creason; Jonas Casner; Pharis Clevenger, UM; Thomas Campbell; John Collier, UM; Elisha Camron; John Carell; John Clevenger; Benjamin Cornelius; Rensselaer Clark; John Dean; Richard Clevenger; Samuel Crowley; James Carell; John Evans; Thomas Crowley; Dickson Clack, UM; Samuel Clevenger; Abraham Creek; James Crowley; Jeremiah Crowley; Jefferson Cary, UM; John Cornelius; Nathaniel Cary; Samuel Crowley; John Dobson; Joseph Crockett; Abraham Coots; Jonathan Camron; Wm. Grooms; Levy Fields; James Collins, UM; Zachariah Clevenger; Daniel Duvaul; David Crocket; John Crowley; Norman Davis; Cornelius Gilliam; James Dagley; William Davis; John Davis, UM; Thomas Edwards; John Davis, UM; John Edwards; Peter Estes; Benjamin Fields; William Elliott, UM; Henry Estes; Thomas Estes; John Gilliam; John Elliott; Travis Finley; Joseph Fowler; Timothy Bancroft, UM; Ebenezer Fields; Thomas Frost; Stephen Fields, UM; Thomas Fields; John Fields, sr.; John Ferrens, UM; Jesse Fletcher; Joseph Fields; David Fletcher; Moses Fletcher, UM;

(Ray County, Missouri Continued)
Jesse Gilliam, Francis Grooms, UM; Abraham Grooms; Alexander Newman, UM; Joseph Gauge; Baley George; Benjamin Gragg; John Owens; Henry Gragg; Joseph Gill; Peter Irons; Tho. Inglish; Thomas Hixson and Andrew Hixton; James Hill, UM; John Huff; James Hiatt; William Hall; Elisha Hall; John Harris; Harlow Hinston, UM; Uriah Huffman, UM; Wm. Henderson, jr., UM; John Hodge, UM; Ezekiel Huffman; Davis Homes; John Hutchings, UM; Smith Hutchings; Moses Hutchings, UM; James Gillmore; Foushe Garner; Jesse Hill; Alexander Hill; George Jeffers; Eldridge Potter; James James; Thomas Jacks, UM; John Keeny; Benjamin Sampson, sr.; James Lyon; Patrick Lany; John Livingston; Ahi Smith; Isaac B. Lance, UM; John Lincoln, UM; John Ledgewood; William Lanehart, UM; Malachi Liles; Richard Linville; James Lamm; William L. Smith, UM; William Richards, UM; William B. Martin; Samuel Livingston; David Liles; Isaac Lowthian; John McGaugh; William Martin, UM; William Liles; Jonathan Ligget; Abraham Linville;Aaron Linville; Joshua Lamm; John McCroskie and Andrew McCroskrie; Zadoc Martin, jr; Edmond Murray; John S. Malott; Calvin Stephens, UM; David Montgomery, UM; Edward Morris; Thomas Sollars, UM; Sebron J. Miller; Andrew Pogue, UM; William Monroe; Zadoc Martin, sr; William Millsaps; John Scott, UM; William Miller; Thomas Monroe; Jesse Mann; Andrew Moor; Isaac McCroskrie; Isaac Martin; Henry Morgan, UM; Hugh Porter, UM; Samuel Magill, UM; Daniel McCray; Charles McGee; William Malotte, UM; Richard Munkers; Theoderick Mayberry; Francis Meguire; Blake Masingill; Benjamin Munkirs; William Osborn; James W. McClellan; Redman Munkirs; William Officer; William Stanley, UM; Larkin Stanley, UM; Edward Roberts, UM; David McElwee; David Magill; James Munkirs; Samuel Oliphant; Jacob McCoy, UM; David Nutting; John Nichols, UM; Nicholas Roberts; Robert Nicholson; Thomas Officer; John Richy; Jonas Roberts; John Proffit; William Prine; Hannah Peebly; Samuel Prewit; Thomas Peebly, UM: Robert Pierce; Christopher Stone; Robert Pritchet; Edward Piburn; Joseph Porter, UM; Mayberry Splawn; Andrew Pogue, UM; Dowdle Rowland, Russel Reynolds; Andrew Russel; Absalom Reed; Lewis Richards; Jonathan Reed, UM; James Reynolds; George Rowland; Timothy Riggs; Humphrey Smith; Aaron Roberts; William Rollims; Mathew Rowland; Jacob Riffe; John Riffe; Samuel Roberts; Peter Rightsman; Benjamin Sampson; John Rightsman; John Renfroe; John Stone; William Shaw, UM; John Shields and William Shields; William Shelton; Andrew Robertson; Sabert Sollars; William Scott; Mrs. Polly Smith; John Stanley; James Stanley; Elisha Sollars; Charles Scott; Jacob Snowden; Daniel Shackleford; Elijah Smith, UM; Terah Smith; Wilson Spicer; James Snowden; Jacob Tarwaters; Jesse Tevault; James Telford; George Taylor, UM; Alexander Williams; William Turner; John Thompson, UM; Abner Vickery; Winant Vanderpool, sr.; John Turner; William Turnage; Thomas

(Ray County, Missouri Continued)
Willson; Winant Vanderpool, jr.; John Trotter, UM; Littleton West; Medders Vanderpool, UM; John Thornton, UM; John Woods; Eppe Tillery, UM; Hardin Vickery, UM; Samuel Vasser; William Morgan, UM; Enos Vaughn; John Vanderpool; Hugh Valandingham; Chesley Woodard; Alexander Willard; George Wills, UM; Joseph Woods; Francis Williams, UM; James B. Wills; James Willhyte; William Wiggins; Benedick Welldon, UM; James Wills; Abraham Whitson; Nehemiah Woolsey; Samuel Williams, UM; Rich. Hill; James Williams; Tarlton Whitlock; Noah Wollsey, UM; Joseph Wells; John Willson, UM; Joseph Hutchings, UM.

Cole County, Missouri, Delinquent Tax List, 1831, Jeffersonian Republican, December 31, 1831.

Thomas C. Burch, William Brookshire, Walter Burris, James Clendennen, William Birdsong, Benjamin Clark, Michael Soane, Abraham Crabtree, James Clendennen, Mathew Clendennen, John Denson, Jepthah Duncan, Levi Ellis, John Frame, Philip Hale, Thomas Furguson, John Hostey, Charles Hebbert, David Harman, E. M. Holden, William King, Joshua Lendrum, Greenvil Moore, Robert Luster, John Landrum, Royal Messersmith, James Riggs, Handy Medlin, John Nidever, Levi Oneal, John Tooms, Jas. L. Pool, Daniel Prine, Samuel Richardson, Peter Swezy, Thomas Smith, Samuel Salisbury, Patrick Ward, William Rogers, Hugh Dillon.

St. Louis County, Missouri, Mortgages Executed Under The Spanish Government, 1766 - 1804.

Peter Berger to Francois Laboun, 1766; Louis Honore Tesson to Francois Duchoriquet, 1767; Fran. Marie Touloze to Pierre Montardy, 1767; J. Honore & Denoyers to Eugene Posevie, 1767; Pierre Laclede Liquest to Jean Datchevict, 1767; T. Pierre & Blondeau to Laclede & Bernard, 1767; Laclede Liquist to Louis Vivat, 1767; Pierre Piquirres to Pierre Montardy, 1767; Paul Liq---- to Antoine Sans Lowey, 1768; Michel Rolet dit Beroude to Lambert, 1768; Eugene Pouare to Dateherut, 1768; Bazete Deneyers to Pierre Montardy, 1768; Bapt. Densquette Bauche to Pierre Montardy, 1768; Antoine Hubert to Louis Chamart, 1768; M--te J. B--hers to L. Lambert, 1768; ---- to Perrault Houault, 1768; ----- to Pierre Lambrement, 1768; L. Beau---- to P. Poupel, 1768; ---quest to Peole Belestre, 1768; Pierre Lafvere dit Barron to Antoine Hubert, Joseph --- to Francois Durey, 1768; Phillip Laflame to Joseph Legond, 1768; Joseph Labress to Paul Legrand, 1768; Rene Buet to Joseph Legond, 1768; Nicholas Boyer to Jean Comparios, 1768; Jean Peron dit Bouche to Pierre Montardy, 1768; Louis Latrave to Pevault, 1768; Martin Baron to Luis Dubrieiel, 1768; Madam Hebert to Heirs of Guelliame Bizet, 1772; Benito Vasquez to Heirs of Guelliame Bizet, 1772; Joseph Conand to Antoine de Oro, 1773,

(St. Louis County, Missouri Continued)
Nicholas Bouchenu to Benito Vasquer, 1773; Jean Lamontagvie to Pierre Pery, 1773; Pierre Baron to Joseph Legond, 1773; Pierre Gadobert to Jean B. Sarpy, 1773; Alexis Cotte to Marie Louis Lotte, 1774; Barsatou to Dubruit, 1773; Antoine Rolet dit Laderoute to Joseph Legonet, 1773; Joseph Labuqiere to Antoine Benard, 1774; Antoine Morin to Joseph Legon, 1773; Montardy to Joseph Legond, 1773; Noel Langlois to Joseph Legond, 1774; Michel Lamy to Martin Duvalde, 1774; Nicholas Barsaloux to Benito Vazquez, 1774; Pierre Montardy to Martin Duvalde, 1775; George Blin to Joseph Legond, 1774; Guillaume Hebert dit Lecomte to Joseph Paul, 1773; Joseph Hasselin to J. M. Gauyet dit Beliste, 1776; Jn. Bte. Martigny to Martin Duvalde, 1777; Charles Bizet to Pierre Laclede, 1776; Joseph Hebert to Martin Duvalde, 1775; Jean Bte. Provenche to Jos. Labrosse, 1781; Louis Vachard and wife to Laclede, 1776; J. Bte. Malveau to Louis Marchoteau, 1779; Alexander Langlois dit Rondeau to Martin Duvalde, Louis Honore Tesson to Bernard Lanthe, 1780; Pierre Montardy to Martin Duvalde, 1777; Jean Bte. Duchine Perrialt to Jacques Voise, 1781; Francois Cotte to Jean Lalle, 1783; Auguste Chouteau to Louis Marchoteau, 1778; Godefroy de Lindot to Joseph M. Papin, 1781; Josephte Farrot to Joseph Hortez, 1781; Louis Robert, jr. to Antoine Vincent, 1782; Joseph Lami and Joseph Papin to Benito Vasque, 1782; Joseph Rivar to Papin and Vasques, 1782; Joseph Guillot to Guillaume Hebert dit Lecomte, 1782; Joseph Charbrant to Louis Robert, 1782; Clement Ditor to Frances Cachol, 1783; Pierre Bissonet to Papin and Vasques, 1782; Pierre Bissonet to Benitz Vasques, 1783; Louis Robert to Augustus Chouteau, 1783; Jo. M. Tayo and wife to Jn. P. Chouteau, 1783; Joseph Hortes and wife to Silvestre Labbadie, 1783; Louis Honore to Auguston Dubue, 1784; Louis Boury to Auguste Chouteau, 1784; Jn. Bte. Truteau to Louis Perrault, 1784; Jacques Clamorgan Laconta to Jn. Bonaventure Collett, 1784; Francois Cailhol and wife to Antoine Vincent, 1785; Pierre Zuemel to Joseph Robidoux, 1786; Francois Leberge to Auguste Chouteau, 1785; Francois Dorlac to Auguste Chouteau, 1785; Gasper Robieu to Deroselliers, 1786; Thomas Taylor (Tyler) to Gabriel Cerre, 1786; Joseph Labrosse to Austin Dubuc, 1785; Claude Duclo to Gabriel Cerre, 1786; Jo. Charles Bois to Lauvent Durocher, 1786; Auguste Dubue to Simon Dubardo, 1786; Joseph Ferret to Joseph Molard, 1787; Joseph Molard to Claude Mercier, 1787; Laurent Durocher to Ch. Tayson and L. Dechamp, 1787; Andre Tagot to Auguste Chouteau, 1788; Francois Fleuri dit Grehier to Guillaume Hebert Lecomte, 1788; Louis Robert to Antoine Vincent, 1788; Louis Chevallier to Joseph Taillon, 1789; Jn. B. Delille to Gabriel Cerre, 1789; Joseph Robidoux to Jacques Noise dit Cabbe, 1789; Etienne Papin to Gabriel Cerre, 1789; Francois Deleuviere to Gabriel Cerre, 1789; Jn. Bt. Lalande

(St. Louis County, Missouri Continued)
to Pierre Pellebierd, minor heirs, 1789; Baptiste Lapierre to Charles Lanquinet, 1789; Austin Roque and wife to Joseph Mainville, 1789; Thomas Taylor (Tyler) to Jacques Clamorgan, 1789; Genevieve Caloire to Eulaleu Pollet, 1789; Nicolas Gais to Jacques Clamorgan, 1792; Nicholas Lavigne to Pierre Pery, 1789; Louis Beaudouin and wife to Sanquinet V. Robidou, 1789; Jean and Joseph Martigny to Guillme Hebert Lecomte, 1789; Jn. Bt. Gresar to Silvestre Sarpy, 1790; Pierre Gueret Dumon to Jacques Clamorgan, 1789; Auguste Chouteau to Manuel Perez, 1792; Matharon Bouvet to Jacques Clamorgan, 1791; Baptiste Lenecal to Jean Thomas Ubalde, 1792; Jacques Noise dit Labbe to Silvestre Sarpy, John Countz to Jacques Clamorgan, 1790; Antoine Barada to Auguste Chouteau, 1790; Joseph Pungembre to Philip Fine, 1793; Joseph M. Papin to Auguste Chouteau, 1796; Joseph Beaudoin to Guillaume Hebert Lecomte, 1793; Jn. Bte. Dufau to Jn. Bte. Laurin, 1790; Antoine Roy to Joseph Brazeau, 1797; Pierre Perry to J. and T. Sarpy, 1794; Joseph Vachard to Jacques Clamorgan, 1793; Joseph Molard to Jacques Clamorgan, 1794; Jacques Clamorgan to Antoine Janis, 1797; Marie Jeanette (free negro) to Charles Lanquenet, 1790; Jean Bte. Truteau and wife to Auguste Chouteau, 1792; Jacob Lans to Vincent Bouis, 1798; Charles Delille and wife to Gabriel Cerre, 1796; Louis Chevalier to Auguste Chouteau, 1797; Paul Guierre to Clamorgan Lousel, 1798; Regis Loiset to Gregoire Tarpy, 1797; Andre Landveville to Joseph Brazeau, 1797; John Hildebrand to Joseph Hunder, 1800; Alexis Lalande and wife to Jacques Clamorgan, 1789; Henry M'Laughlin to Clamorgan, 1798; William Griffin to Loise Clamorgan, 1798; Jacob Lanse to Loise Clamorgan, 1798; Elias Metz to Jacques Clamorgan, 1798; Antoine Dejarlais to Loisel Clamorgan, 1798; William Clark to Gregouire Sarply, 1798; John Whitesides to Jacques Clamorgan, 1798; John Whitesides to Loisel Clamorgan, 1798; John James to Loisel Clamorgan, 1798; Louis Labeaume to Lenon Trudeau, 1799; Marie to her children, 1799; Francois Lacombe to Joseph Robidou, 1799; Joseph Gutarre to Auguste Chouteau, 1798; Antoine Barada to Antoine V. Bouis, 1799; Pierre Didier to Pierre Tagnon, 1799; Baptiste Dellile to Lennon Trudeau, 1799; Chrisley Romine to Loisel Clamorgan, 1798; Mathurin Bouvet to Charles Gratiot, 1799; Antoine Vachard to Gregoir Larpy, 1799; Ezekiel Crosby to Louis Labraume, 1798; Musich William to Loisel Clamorgan, 1798; Noel Laiserait to Miville, Louis Boissy to Auguste Chouteau, 1800; James M'Daniel to Hezekiah Land, 1799; Tenon Trudeau to the children of J. B. Trudeau, 1798; Lois Boissy to Gregoire Sarpy, 1799; Pierre Didier to Pierre Tagnon, 1799; William Clark to Gregoire to Sarply, 1803; Benito Vasques to Louis Coignard, 1802; Bazeki Hebert Desmet to Vincent Bouis, 1800; Etienne Papin and wife to Peter Chouteau, 1801; Paul Promau to Augte. Choteau, 1804;

(St. Louis County, Missouri Continued)
William Musick to Charles Gratcot, 1801; Hypolite Bolon to Joseph Robidou, 1801; James M'Donald to Samuel Duncan, 1801; Benito Vasques to Antoine Roy, 1801;John Gates to Francis M. Benoist, 1802; Hyacinthe Dehetre to Antoine Jouland, 1802; Ausgustin Trudell to Gregoire Sarpy, 1803; Antoine Dejarlais to Antoine V. Bouis, 1803; Joseph Beaudirum to Chouteau and Lanqiunet, 1803; Elias Herrington to Peter Chouteau, 1803; Louis Dehebre to Louis Jos. Vincennes, 1803; Manuel Lisa to M. Villars, 1803; Ira Nash to Patrick Lee, 1803; Andrew Park to Jacques Clamorgan, 1803; John P. Cabann to Widow Labbie, 1803; Joseph Calvary to Joseph F. Germain, 1803; John Land to Jacques Clamorgan, 1804; Paul Promau to Ate. Chouteau, 1804; Paul Primau and wife to Chouteau and Rankin, 1804; Jn. Bte. Truteau's children to Lenon Trudeau, 1799; Jean Bte. Duplauy to Auguste Chouteau, 1800; Jacques Godefroy to Augt. Chouteau, 1804.

Boone County, Missouri, Marks and Brands, 1826 - 1839.

Name	Date Recorded
John Ethell	January 9, 1826
David B. Rowland	January 18, 1826
James McClelland	January 23, 1826
Abraham Winscott	January 26, 1826
Thomas Beazley	January 26, 1826
Jacob McBride	January 31, 1826
John Roberts	January 31, 1826
Samuel Cardwell	January 31, 1826
James Roberts	January 31, 1826
William Lientz	February 7, 1826
Winfield Alford	February 7, 1826
Nathan Glasgow	February 13, 1826
Peter Bass	February 18, 1826
Joseph Nesbit	February 27, 1826
Martin Baker	March 15, 1826
Robert W. Morris	May 18, 1826
Addison McPheeter	May 19, 1826
John Fortney	May 25, 1826
Robert Baker	May 28, 1826
Thomas Stricklin	September 11, 1826
Sinclair Kirtley	September 23, 1826
Hector Shock	September 23, 1826
John Douglass	October 9, 1826
Willie West	January 1, 1827
Jesse Vinsen	January 12, 1827
Caleb Fenton	January 22, 1827
Henry Cave, jr.	January 22, 1827
James Harrison	April 7, 1827
Charles Haddock	May 30, 1827

(Boone County, Missouri Continued)

Name	Dated Recorded
Heritage Cheaney	July 24, 1827
Richard Cave	July 28, 1827
Martin Lawless	October 15, 1827
William Rowland	November 24, 1827
Elias Sims	November 29, 1827
Isaac Alford	December 5, 1827
James Callaway	December 11, 1827
Hardeman Stone	February 4, 1828
Squire B. Sappington	February 4, 1828
Thomas Owen	February 4, 1828
Jesse Murphy	February 25, 1828
John Robnett, sr.	June 2, 1828
Stephen Wilhite	June 23, 1828
Granville L. Branham	July 4, 1828
William M. Baker	October 11, 1828
Thomas Turner	November 24, 1828
John H. Keath	December 9, 1828
Robert Cockran	December 31, 1828
Eppa Elliott	January 19, 1829
John Graham	January 20, 1829
William Cockran	February 4, 1829
John G. Cockran	February 4, 1829
Edmond McQueen	February 18, 1829
Newman B. Starke	January 1, 1830
John Green Halph	May 4, 1830
John H. Baker	May 10, 1830
Robert Wilburn	December 24, 1830
Higgason Harris	January 1, 1831
David L. Lamme	January 13, 1831
Robert Teeter	January 21, 1831
Allen Coats	January 22, 1831
Henry Coats	January 22, 1831
John Barnes	March 17, 1831
John Mathew	March 17, 1831
Young B. Hicks	May 2, 1831
Moses Baker	May 2, 1831
Philander Finley	July 11, 1831
Robert Johnston	July 14, 1831
David N. Cophen	September 14, 1831
Lemuel B. Larcy	January 18, 1831
William Y. Hitt	March 3, 1832
James Arnold	September 24, 1832
Eli E. Bass	November 27, 1832
John C. Sullins	December 19, 1832
James Bowling	January 28, 1833
Adam Fickes	May 6, 1833
Thomas Stone	June 17, 1833

(Boone County, Missouri Continued)

Name	Date Recorded
Isaac Stone	November 23, 1833
John Crestwaite	November 23, 1833
Michael Stip	December 14, 1833
Willliam Risk	March 4, 1834
David Gordon	June 17, 1834
James W. Moss	June 17, 1834
Joseph W. Hickam	June 17, 1834
Michael Woods	June 17, 1834
John W. Dawson	October 29, 1834
Benjamin Turner	November 19, 1834
John Corlen	January 16, 1835
Hirm Beasley	August 8, 1835
Jacob Hern	September 28, 1835
John C. Phillips	September 24, 1835
Joseph Carpenter	April 4, 1836
George Northcut	June 1, 1836
Charles Burke	June 8, 1836
Enoch C. Crear	October 22, 1836
Richard Bondurant	November 10, 1836
Thornton Huffman	January 22, 1837
Macon Purcell	January 31, 1837
Barnett Dickerson	March 7, 1837
John L. Jones	July 15, 1837
Buford Stide	July 15, 1837
William Slavin	July 15, 1837
Phillip Barnes	July 15, 1837
David Prowell	July 15, 1837
James Rummons	July 15, 1837
William H. Stapleton	November 6, 1837
Randolph Sims	November 7, 1837
Alexander E. Ellington	June 22, 1838
Robert F. Gibbs	March 8, 1838
Edmond B. Griffey	May 12, 1838
William Berry	May 21, 1838
Nathaniel Ridgeway	October 27, 1838
John Cleman	December 11, 1838
John N. Slack	December 18, 1838
William Shock	December 22, 1838
James Kelly	February 22, 1839
Eskeil Hickman	March 23, 1839
James N. Downy	April 1, 1839
Levi Park	April 2, 1839
William H. Dunn	April 3, 1839
Henry H. Ready	July 16, 1839
Peyton Griggs	August 5, 1839
David H. Sims	August 8, 1839
James G. Lewis	September 23, 1839

(Boone County, Missouri Continued)

Name	Dated Recorded
Samuel Hock	September 23, 1839
John Gay	September 31, 1839
James Kelly	October 31, 1839

Chariton County, Missouri, Tax List, 1821.

Daniel Ashby, L, W; Benjamin Ashby, L;Thomas Anderson, L; Thomas Adams, L, LD; John M. Bell, L; Josiah Brown, L; Jesse Brown, L; Pleasant Browder, L, LD; Elizabeth Beaty, L; John Barnett, LD; Thomas Brooks, W; Thomas Botts, L, LD; Fredrick W. Bainbeck, L, W; Joseph Brewer, LD, L, P; John Ball, L, W, LD; Frederick Bradford, L, LD, W; Thomas Binns, L; Benjamin Bolls, LD; Elias Bishop, P, W; David Bailie, L; Seth Botts, L, LD; William Bolls, LD; Greenbury Boswell, L, LD; Taylor Berry, LD, OC. G. Hunot; James H. Benson, LD; Charles Baker, L, LD; Joseph M. Baker, L, LD; Nathaniel Butler, L; Charles Baker, sr., L, LD; Joshua Botts, L; William Baker, W; James Barnes, L, LD; Phillip Barnes, LD; James Baty, L, LD; George Burcheart, L, LD; Nicholas T. Burcheartt, LD;Thomas Bradley, L, LD; May Burton, L, LD; Baylor Banks, L, LD, W; Abram Beck of St. Louis, LD; Henry H. Bradford, LD, L, W; William Cap, L; Henry H. Bradford, L, LD, W; Leonard Brassfield, L, LD; Joseph Cockrell, L, LD; James Cockrell, L, LD; William Cox, LD, OC. James Nesbee; William Cox, LD, OC. Jacob Ostrader; James Collins, L, LD; William Claybrook, L; Saml. Campbell, L, LD; William Curnett, L; Henry Clark, L; Reuben Clark, L; Jesse Clark, L; Benjamin Cross, L, LD, W; Hiram Craig and Charles Simmons, LD; William Crawford, L, LD; Jesse Cates, L; Andrew Clark, L, LD; Edward B. Cabell, L, LD; John Cates, L, LD; William Cabeenm, LD; Alfred Coats, L, P, W; Frederick Cogdale, L; Charles W. Carter, LD; Saml. Carpenter, L; John Doxey, L; Houston Cross, LD, OC. James West,OC. John Backus, OC. Patrick Colley, OC. James Andrews, OC. Patrick Robinson, OC. William Forbes, OC. John Nookly, OC. Wm. Thomas, OC. Wm. Akerman; Wilson Davis, LD; Stephen Donohoe, L,·LD, W; Robert Dunlap, L, LD; James Dunlap, P, W; John Drummond, L; James Drummond, L; James Dinwiddy, L; Lawon Dunnington , L, LD; James Dysert, L, LD, W; Wilson Davis, L; Stephen Donohoe, L, LD, W; Robert Dunlap, L, LD; James Dunlap, P, W; James Davis, L, LD, W; Robertson Daniel, L, LD, W; John Dunlap, L; Henry Dunn, L; John Dysert, P; Jesse Drake, L, LD, W; David H. Denny, L, LD, P; James L, LD; William Duston, L, P; James Erickson, L, LD, M, D; Samuel Davis, L, LD, W; Robert Erwin, L; William Drinkard, L, LD; John Erwin, L;Cyrus Edwards, LD; Perrigrine Erickson, L, LD; Finis Ewing, L; William Elliot, L, LD; Benjamin F. Edwards, L; William Fort, L, P; Anderson Foster, L, P; Samuel Forest, L, LD; James Fowler, L, LD, P, W; James Forrest, L, LD; James Furgerson, L, P;Jas. Head, L;

(Chariton County, Missouri Continued)
Dabney Findley, LD; William Findley, LD;John P. Findley, LD; William Fields, LD; Benjamin L. Fox, L; Simon Foot, P; John Farrar, P; Anthony Farrar, L; Edward Fleetwood, P, W; Edward and William Fleetwood, L, LD; Gentry Floid, LD; David Floid, L, LD; Edward Farr, L, LD; Thomas P. Gage, L, P; Duff Green, L, LD, P, W; Willis M. Green, L, P; Duff Green and Jeremiah Conner, L;Duff Green, James H. Benson, and James Hickman, L; John Graves, L, P, W; John Gaither, L, W, M, D;Mary Gaither, L, W; Abram Gross, LD, L; Thomas Gorham, LD, L; Nathan Hunt, L, LD, P; Thomas Griffin, LD; David Hunt, L; Andrew Harris, L; Joseph HUghes, L, LD; Christian Hoozer, L, LD, OC. Hugh Burney; Archibald Hix, P; Richard, P; Allen Hoskins, P; John Holeman, L, LD, P, W; Ira Hedden, P; Henry Hickman, L; John House, P; Thomas Hardwin, L; William Heronamus, L; Anthony Head, L, LD; Thomas Herrington, L, LD; Moses Hadley, L; John Harris, L; Wright Hill, L, LD; Joseph Holeman, L;Susan Knox, L, LD; James Herriford, L, LD; Josiah Humphrey, L; William Herrington, L, LD; John Humphrey, L, P; Benjamin Harris, L; Edwin T. Hickman, L, LD; Samuel Humphreys, L, LD; Abel Lee, L, LD; Thomas Jackman, L, P; William Jones, L, LD; William Lammer, LD; Thomas Joice, LD, OC. George Stranger, OC. Elias Rector, OC. Wm. Kincheloe; Andrew King, L;Moses King, LD, L; Walter Kendrick, L; Asa Kirby, LD, P; David Kirby, L; James Leeper, L; John Kirby, L; Francis Kirby, L, LD;Joel King, L; Henry Lewis, LD, L; Thomas Lock, LD, L, P;Abram Lock, L, LD; David Love, L, LD; Peter Lyon, P;Thomas D. Loney, L, W; Jas. C. Morrison, L, OC. James Robinson, OC. Rich. Bell, OC. Leah Alexander, OC. Miles Northern, George Stern, OC. James Wall, OC. Jesse Lackeners, OC. Wm. Clark, OC. Jas. Burson,OC. Tho. Smith; John Morrow, L; John Moore, P; Nathan Marsh, L; John Morse, L, LD; John McDaniel, L; Wm. Monroe, L, LD, W; Clark McCalister, L, LD; William Martin, L; James McGee, L; Martin Morgan, L; David Morgan, L; Stephen B. Munn, LD; John Moore, L, LD; David McCollum, L; Richard Mobly, L, LD; John Sears, L, LD; Sterling Morgan, L, LD; James W. Moss, LD; Ignatius Mattox, L, P; Epraim Moore, L, P, W; John Moore and Ephraim Moore, LD; Joseph Jones Monroe, L, P; Thomas Patterson, LD; Daniel McKellar, L; Jacob Mason, sr., L; Jacob Mason, L, LD; Chas. McClain, L, LD; James Mason, jr., L, LD, P;Mark Noble, L, LD; Powel Ownby, L; Jesse Owens, L;Peterson Parks, L, LD; James Parks, L, LD; Edward Peascock, LD, Fredrick Pulse, LD; Joshua Potter, L, LD; Jesse Rowland, L; Samuel Riggs, L; Wm. Riggs, L; James Ross, LD, L, W; William Ragan, L; Collin C. Stoneman, L, LD; Josiah Rogers, L; Charles Simmons, LD; John Splawn, L; Samuel Stanfield, L; Joseph Sears, W;Hardy Sears, L, LD; Blandy Smith, L; Abram Sportsman, L; William Slayter, P; James Semple, L, LD; Ivison Sears, L; Jeremiah Thomas, L, LD; Ferriba Stone, L, LD; Champion Turpin, L;Martin Wheat,W;

(Chariton County, Missouri Continued)
Elias Sales, L; Daniel Tilman, L; Alexander Trent, L; Talton Turner, L, LD; John Thorton, LD; Levi Taylor, L, LD, P;Rich. B. Thorton, P; C. Tiffany, LD, L, P, W; Richardson Terril,P; John J. Turner, LD, L; John Tooley, LD, L; James Tooley, LD, L; Isaac Taylor, P; Jacob Vanderson, P; Saml. Williams, L, LD; Joseph Vance, L; Addison Webster, W; Richard Woodson, L, LD, W; Thomas Watson, L, LD; James Wells, LD; Josiah Watson, L, LD; Lewis White, LD, L, P; James Woodson, L; Adam Wilson, L, LD; John Wiggenton, P; Joseph Woodfolk, LD; John Wilson, L; Silas Walwood, L, P; John Williams, L; Philip Welden, LD, L; John Weldon, LD, L; Henry Wilkerson, LD, L;James Berryman of New York, LD; Stephen Bess, LD; Brackston Cooper, LD;John Dulay, LD; David R. Drake, LD; Capt. Desha, L; Gentry Floid, LD; Jonathan T. Findley, LD; Harmon Gragg, LD;Daniel Riggs. L; John L. Findley and Elias Rector, LD; Dervell Hubbard, L; Charles L.Hempstead, LD; Judge Hardwin, LD; Hugh Lackey, LD; James Heckman, LD; Richard A. Maupin, LD; Ephraim Moseby and John Morris, LD; Thomas Patterson, LD; John Smart, LD; John L. Setton, LD; Benjamin R. Pierce, LD; Thomas Time, LD; Coly Tramel, LD; Richard Steel, LD; John H. Smith, LD; Richard G. Williams, LD; William Ward, LD; John Tharp, LD, OC. Micajah Burnett, OC. Isaac Meeker, OC. Hugh Barney.

Ste. Genevieve County, Missouri, Slave Bills of Sale, 1766 to 1827.

Seller	Buyer	Slaves	Year
Joseph Niberville	Louis Vivat	3	1766
Michel Placet	Charles Marois	1	1766
---- Robinet	Frois. Chauvin dit Joveneuse	1	1767
Mrs. Alary	Francois Valle	1	1770
Gabriel Caillot dit Lachance	Francois Valle	2	1799
Henry Carpentier	Charles Beauvais	2	1774
Gabriel Cerre	Etienne Bolduc	2.	1792
Etienne Deninelle	Simon Rubardeau	1	1801
Israel Dodge	Chas. Deluziere	1	1794
Thomas Ferguson	Mrs. Peyroux	2	1798
Joseph Gauvraux	Michelle Placette	1	1796
J. Baptiste Gendron	Francois Moreau	1	1792
Mrs. Mitchel Antata	Jacques Clamorgan	1	1791
Harrison Boyd	Simon Hubardeau	1	1800
Carlos Valle	Louis Bolduc	1	1778
Widow Louis Trudeau	Trope Ricard	1	1776
William Shannon	Samuel D. Dixon	5	1827
John Price	David Mackay	1	1801
William Sullivan	Guillaume Girouard	1	1800
Widow Francois Moro	Manuel Lisa	1	1801

(Ste. Genevieve County Continued)

Seller	Buyer	Slaves	Year
Simon Hubardeau	Jn. Bte. Placette	1	1798
---- Jussaume dit St. Pierre	Charles Beauvais	1	1774
Pierre Menard	Pierre Cabanne	1	1801
Francois Moraux	Regis Lasource and wife	1	1782
Israel Dodge	Geo. A. Hamilton	1	1797
Antoine Duclos	Jn. Bte. Pratte	1	1777
Walter Fenwick	Pre. Chas. Delassus	1	1804
Pierre Gibault	Louis Bolduc	1	1784
Guillaume Girouard	Ve. M. Bourguignon	1	1777
William Griffin	F. Detchemendy	1	1798
Simon Hurardeau	Louis Bolduc	1	1777
Nicholas Caillot dit Lachance	Louis Baugi	1	1786
Jean Datchurut	Jn. Bte. Morel	1	1786
Carlos Valle	F. Valle (his father)	1	1777
Benjamin Spencer	Guillaume Girouard	3	1797
Mrs. Peyroux	----- Dubourg	1	1800
Michel Placet	Lois Bolduc	1	1781
Pierre Chevallier	Jn. Bte. Janis	1	1798
John Coffe	Paschall Detchmendy	1	1798
Joseph Doulton	John Burke	1	1796
Michel Antaya and wife	Louis Lorimer	1	1789
Robert Broustee, dec.	Delassus Deluziere	1	1799
Gerard Barsaloux	---- Hortiz	1	1789
Solomon White	Auguste Aubuchon	4	1784
Simon Hubardeau	Guillaume Girouard	2	1801
Gabriel Lachance	Bonadventure Collell	1	1789
Jean Bapt. Laffont	L. Deloriers	1	1789
Samuel Martin	Jn. Bte. Laffont	1	1784
Jacques Noize	Francois Valle	1	1789
Louis Labeaume	Thos. Riardon	1	1801
Andre Deguire	Pierre Vivat	1	1798
Israel Dodge	David Rhorer	1	1799
Widow Francois Duchouquet	Emanuel Escalera	1	1774
Widow John Duff	Neal Hornbeck	1	1800
Parfait Dufour	J. Clamorgan	1	1801
Walter Fenwick	Israel Dodge	1	1790
Pierre Gibault	Antonio de Oro	1	1784
Guillaume Girouard	Etienne Parent	1	1798
Pierre Chevallier	Henri Peyroux	1	1790
Jean Cons	John Edgar	1	1793
Andre Price	Moses Austin	1	1801
Harry Simpson	Mme. Peyroux	1	1799

(Ste. Genevieve County, Missouri Countinued)

Seller	Buyer	Slaves	Year
Carlos Valle	Bazile Valle	1	1784
Francois Vigo	Louis Bolduc	1	1782
Pierre Viviat	Joseph Vasseur	1	1804
Israel Dodge	Jacque de St. Vrain	1	1799
Daniel Fagot	Pre. Pre. Gadobert	1	1770
Guillaume Girouard	Joseph Le Valleau	1	1799
William Griffin	Jacques Manuel	3	1798
Simon Hubardeau	Trope Ricard	1	1791
Auguste Aubuchon	Chas. A. D. Delassus	1	1787
Jean Bapt. Beauvais	Auguste Chouteau	1	1789
Jacques Clamorgan	Simon Hubardeau	1	1791
Jean Bte. Bequet	Jos. Lalumandiere	1	1785
Antoine Renaud	Joseph Segond	1	1768
John Price	Widow Lalumandiere	3	1799
William Scott	Louis Lorimer	1	1778
Harry Simpson	Mme. Peyroux	1	1799
---- St. Albin	Mrs. Charles Charlesville	2	1788
Benjamin Spencer	Guillaume Girouard	3	1797
Philippe Rocheblave	Guill. Hebert dit LaComte	1	1775
Widow Louis Trudeau	Emilien Yosti	1	1777
Carlos Valle	Francois Valle	1	1776
Widow Louis Villard	Jean Price	2	1801
Nathaniel Williams	John Dodge	1	1788
Simon Hubardeau	Jn. Bte. Placette	1	1801
Thomas Hutchings	Jean Laffont	1	1780
James Jenkins	Trope Ricar	1	1803
Wd. Antoine Lachance	Fremon de Luziere	1	1799
Jacques Maxwell	Joseph Placi	4	1800
William Mackintosh	Henri Peyroux	5	1804
Israel Dodge	Moses Austin	1	1803
James Farel	William Curran	1	1799
Guillaume Girouard	Pierre Viriat	1	1800
Vance Lusk	John Price	1	1801
Alexandre Levrard	Louis Lasource	1	1777
Catherine McLean	Jacques Maxwell	2	1894
Francois Moraux	Regus Lasouece and wife	1	1783
Jean Baptiste Motard	Emilien Yosti	1	1776
Guillaume Girouard	Joseph Perrilliard	1	1802
Pierre Grammont	Sylvestre Labbie	1	1776
Idrael Dodge	Bernard Pratte	1	1794
Auguste Aubuchon	Francois Valle	1	1802
Honore Ardouin	Trope Ricard	1	1787
Francois Bernier	Jn. Bte. Sarpy	1	1784
Jacques Clamorgan	Louis Bolduc	2	1786

(Ste. Genevieve County, Missouri Continued)

Seller	Buyer	Slaves	Year
Jacques Clamorgan	Louis Bolduc	2	1786
John Coffe	Guil. Girouard	2	1798
Joseph Doulton	Joseph Pratte	1	1797
Francois Valle	Martin Duralde	1	1778
Thomas Theobald	John Pride	1	1798
Simon Hubardeau	Francois Aubuchon	1	1798
Widow Israel Dodge	Francois de Rouin	3	1804
Ant. Duclos and Jos. Deselle	Joseph St. Aubin	1	1776
William Fugat	Louis Bolduc	1	1800
Francois Guelle and wife	Jean Laffont	1	1782
George Hamilton	Leonard Hamilton	1	1799
Simon Hubardeau	----- Poitou	1	1768
Gabriel Caillot dit Lachance	Etienne Parent	1	1786
William Cowan	Jn. Bte. Pratte	1	1800
Andrew Price	J. Clamorgan	1	1801
Jean Baptiste Valle	Jacques Clamorgan	1	1791
Thomas Riardon	Guillaume Girouard	1	1808
Euphrasie Vilard Price	J. Clamorgan	2	1801
William Morrison	Jean Price	3	1798
Mrs. Peyroux	Pierre Menard	1	1798
Jn. Bte. Pratte and wife, Ther. Billeron	Benito Vasques	1	1782
Jacques Clamorgan	Jean Bte. Pratte	1	1792
John McLean	Solomon White	2	1781
Joseph Langellier and wife, Eliz. Billeron	Joseph St. Aubin	1	1786
Joseph Langlois	Chas. Sanguinet	1	1785
Jean Batiste Laffont	Francois Menard	3	1792
Antoine Lacourse	J. Bte. Laffont	2	1784
Louis Lalumandiere's heirs	Henri Bourguignon	1	1788
Walter Fenwick	Guill. Girouard	1	1797
Jean Baptiste Valle	Simon Hubardeau	1	1801
Jean Baptiste Valle	Bernard Pratte	1	1791
John Hamilton	John Hawkins	1	1800
J. Bte. Gendron and wife	Nicholas Janis	1	1792
John Dodge	Francois Valle	3	1789
Francois Valle	Jn. Bte. Pratte	1	1791
Widow Francois Moro	Manuel Lisa	1	1801
Mrs. Ant. Louvien dit D'Amour	Antoine Lachance	1	1798
Manuel Lisa	Michel Plante	1	1803

Cooper County, Missouri, Delinquent Tax List, 1834.

Name	Comments
James Burney	Gone to Clay County
Isam Akins	Cannot locate
Staunton Brannan	"
Cooper Bennett	Insolvent
James Kirkpatrick	Gone to Morgan County
Joseph D. Jones	Dead
Robt. Boyl	Cannot locate
Elijah Bates	Gone to Texas
John F. Ritter	Dead
Allin McCrery	Cannot locate
James Liles	"
Henderson Bates	Gone to Cole County
Isaac Davis	Cannot locate
John Thompson	Gone to Kentucky
George W. Boyd	Gone to Virginia
Jonathan Carpenter	Gone to Morgan County
Joshua Dean	Cannot locate
Joseph Ellison	Gone to Saline
Jane Stanly	Gone to Salt River
Alva Caldwell	Gone to Morgan County
John Greenstreet	Cannot locate
William Hawkins	Gone to Boone County
Thomas G. Thompson	Cannot locate
Thompson B. Coram	Gone to Clay County
Isaac Cook	Cannot locate
Daniel Redman	Gone to Morgan County
Sandford Coram	Cannot locate
William Donalson	Insolvent
Eli Berman	Gone to Cole County
James Murphy	Cannot locate
William Dillard	Gone to Texas
Newell Johnson	Dead
John Deakin	Gone to Morgan County
John C. Rochester	Gone to Osage
James Morrison	Gone to Salt River
Joseph Dillard	Gone to Texas
Thomas Goin	Cannot locate
Wiley Jones	Gone to Kentucky
James Douglas	Cannot locate
Jonathan Reavis	Gone to Santa Fe
John Woolf	Cannot locate
John M. Doyl	Gone eastward
Elijah Mullins	Gone to Saline County
Nathan Mullins	Gone to Saline County'

Boone County, Missouri, Tax List, 1825
  Benjamin J. Adcock; Henry A. Anderson, OC. S. Beaty; Joel

(Boone County, Missouri Continued)
Austin; Thomas Agin; Josiah Austin; Benjamin Austin; William Abraham; John Austin, OC. S. Beaty; Hugh Alford;James Adair; Peter Austin, OC. S. Beaty; Josiah Austin; Lewis Anthony, A. Cobs; Robert Austin, Jn. Thompson; Richard Alexabder; Robert Askins; Isaac Alford; James Adams; John Anderson; Elijah C. Allen; Thomas Anderson; Will. R. Anderson; James N. Benett; Enoch Bathcer, OC. Jo. M. Adinson; Shaderick Barnes; William A. Betes; Cushon Blevins; Thomas B--rks; James Brooks; James Borger; Henry Borger; John Bullard; David Brinnagan; John Bryd; Big James Barnes, OC. D. Hubbard; Jane Boyd; Francis Buford; Gasper Barger, OC. T. Tuttle; Martha Bullard; James Baners; Jesse Blackburn; Stephen Bruner; Laurance Bass, OC. P. Bass; John Baker; Hutchons Barkett, OC. J. Perkins; Wm. Barnes; John Berry, William Campbell; Robert Barclay, OC. P. Ellis; John Barnes, OC. --- Madick; John A. Brady; Anthony Bledsoe; Joseph Bennet, OC. T. Hatten; Levi Bennett, OC. Jn. Bennett; Isaac Bledsoe; John R. Beckett; Edward Ballinger; Jesse R. Barnett; Nancy Barnes; Tyree Berry;Jonathan Barton; Herbet Bovick; Joshua Brown; Meredith Brown; Charles Burns; Robert Baker, OC. J. Edwards; Elias Baugh; Benjamin Bazus; Josiah Bates, OC. --- Bass; Peter Bass, N. Langham; Samuel Van Buckaloe; Jacob Bettle; Aquilla Bamisco; Thomas Beazly; William Burk; Will. Berry; Moses Batterton; Amos Bucker; Wm. Bair; Isaac Belcher; John Belcher, jr.; John Belcher;John H. Baker; Amos Barnes; Jeremiah Biswell; Henry Barny; Abraham Bargor; Charles Buchannon, OC. Geo. Siston;Larkin Buchannon; Joseph Brown, OC. A. Hicks; Ephraim Brink; John Brink;Rueben D. Black; Herbet L. Brink; Benjamin Bryan; Richard Barnes; John Barton; Lemuel Batterton; Rawson Batterton; Rich. Bibb; Hiram Bryant, OC. Wm. Ramsay; John Barnett;William I. Burch; Philip Barnes; Squire Bradly; Baswell Brown; John Burnett; Joseph Blevins; Milton Berry; Samuel Beaty; John Batteston; Allen Ball; Philip Barger; Richard Barnes; John Boyd; Thomas G. Berry; Joseph Crump; Fielding Curtis, OC. Thos. Bryant; Fielding Curtis, OC. Wm. Ramsey; John Crump; Joseph Crump; John Creason, P. Creason; Patrick Crump; Joseph Crump; John Curry, OC. OC. R. Lowell; Anderson Crump; Thomas Creason, OC. Jno. Walsh; Dennis Callahan, OC. A. Woods; John Calvin; James Cunningham; James Creason; Walter Creason; Jeremiah Calvin, OC. J. Calvin; John Coleman, OC. I. Creason; James Calloway; Boyd Calvin; Boyd Calvin, jr.; Graham Calvin; Wm. Crouch; Peyton Colier; Lewis Collins; James Collins; Bartell Collins; William B. Curry; Richard Cave, jr.;Catherine Cave, OC. Thos. Dolley; William Cave; Richard Cave; John Cave; Wm. Cooley; Bejn. Chisum; Samuel Crickett, OC. A. Gay; Alexander Calvin; Hugh Crockett; Thomas Coley; Henry Cave; Henry Cave, jr.; Howell Carter; Robert Corlew; Adam Christain; Elizabeth Coyl; John Corlew; John Corlew, jr.; John Collet;Simon Coyl;

(Boone County, Missouri Continued)
William Corlew; Hiram Crews; George Cussing; Robt. Coleman;
Stratten Coleman; Adn. W. Cochran, dec.; Robt. Cockran; Wm.
Callahan, OC. S. Galliam; John Cockran; John Crew; Hezekiah
Charles; Lewis Clarkin; Thomas Copler; David Copler, OC. T.
Perry; John Copeland; John Cook; Peter Creason; James Davis;
Garland Clemens; Thomas Coppeage; Simon Coppeage;John Davis;
Thomas Cheers; Peter Carney; Thomas W. Conyers; James Davis;
William Dozer, OC. Wm. Manson; Goslbard Davis; Joseph Davis;
Hugh Douagh, jr., OC. E. Walker; Audrain Davis; Hugh Davis;
Briscoe Davis; John Deavingport; Isaac Davis, sr.; Benajmin
Davis, OC. B. Reaves; Isaac Davis, jr.; Hugh Davis; William
H. Dunn; Amos Davis; Baylor Davis; James Dusky;John Douglas;
Hugh B. Douglass; Hoss Davis; Wm. Douglas, OC. Nelson; Jesse
B. Dale, OC. D. Todd; Samuel Davis; Josiah Dejanatt; Samuel
Davis; Alexander Douglass; Bengn. Dale, OC. B. F. Gavin; Wm.
Eaton; John Dodd, OC. W. Thurston; Elijah Dale, OC. R. Dale;
Michael Daley; Benjamin Davis; Robert Dale; John Dillon; Wm.
Glen; Richard Estes; Peter Ellis; Bjn. Estell, OC. I Estell;
Joseph Esham; Presley Edwards; Will Early; Jeremiah Elsten;
John Evans; James Ethell; Ricgard Estes; John Evins; Thomas
Edmondson; John East; James Ethell; Pleasant Evans; Persena
Eastin; Alexr. Ellison; Alxr. H. Ellington; Rueben Elliott;
John Ethell; Benjn. Ehtell; George Engleheart; Eppy Elliot;
Ambross Estes; John Forice; Philander Findley; Philip Flahe;
John Falkner; Capt. John Gordon; Hue Finch, OC. W. D. Ewing;
Peter Fountain, OC. Ag. Camery, OC. J. Frinke; John Fevier,
OC. J. Conley; Joseph Fountain; James Fowler; Robert Fowler;
Caleb Featon, OC. J. Gayian; Jefferson Filcher; John T. Far;
Benjamin Furgson; Joshua Fuechan; John Freeman; Elijah Fale,
OC. Austin Black; Thomas Fleming; David Furley; James Fokes;
Abram N. Foley; William Grisham; Joseph H. Goodin, OC. Jacob
Little; Hank W. Goodhue; Samuel Garner, OC. A. Barnes;Thomas
Grant, OC. R. Cave; Hank W. Goodhue; John Green; Wm. Green;
Thomas Grant, OC. R. Cave; Samuel Garner, OC. A. Barnes; Wm.
Goslin, OC. J. Grayson; Nathan Glasgow, OC. J. Adams; Allen
Glasgow; Benjamin Gentry; Zachariah Gentry;Abram Grindstaff;
Michael Grindstaff; Nicholas Gentry; Henry Gentry; Benjamin
Goodin, OC. J. Fugat; Robert Goodin; Amos Goodin;E. Hubbard;
Samuel Galaway; Richard Gorten; Bartell Gentry; James Gooth;
Bartell Gentry; Joshua Gillium; Elizabeth Gentry; Nicholas
Gentry; John Gray; William Goustz; William Graham; Alexander
Goldin; Richard Goldin; Robt. Good; David Grant; Tho. Gray;
John Grant, OC. D. King; David Grant, jr.;George Grant; John
Grayson; John Gray; Briant Hahn, OC. J. W. Bass; Archibald
Halock, OC. J. C. F. Barnett; Daniel Hubbard, OC. E. Elston;
Robert Hinkeson; Robert Houston; John Hickam; David Hickman,
H. C. S. Tuttle; George Hume; Mathew Harry; Charles Haddock,
OC. R. Cave; Andrew Hana, OC. J. Williams;Hightower Hickney;

(Boone County, Missouri Continued)
James Harmon; Erwin Hannon; L. Houston; John B. Harton; John Hughs, OC. J. W. Thorp, OC. J. Morris; James Henderson; Jas. Henderson; Jacob Hooking; Will Hill; Young E. Hicks, OC. G. Colier; Elizabeth Hicks; Absalom Hicks, OC. J. Hicks; James Hicks; Thomas Hinson; William Hall, OC. A. Daniel; William Y. Hite, OC. W. Scott; Allen Hughes; Hue Harryman;Wm. Lynes; John Harryman; Josiah Halten; Rueben Halton; John Haskins; Richard Hudson; Wilks Hawkes; Charles Hughes, OC. S. Wilson; David Higgs; Howard Higgs; William Hesoughbrough; David R. Harris; Sedick Hudson; Tyne Hayes; Allen Home; Clayton Home; Moses Head; George Holmes; Furgeson Hutson; John Hardy; John Happer; James Hardin; Roland Hutson; W. P. John Hudson; Wm. Ham; George Harrish; Tyice Hams, jr.; Thomas Hark; Soleman R. Ketchum; Jacob Hensinger; George Hush; Agnes Head; James Harnes; J. B. Howard; Charles Hardin, OC. T. Turner; Samuel Jameison; Christopher Jones; Tyree R. Jones; Ryhan Jameison; Elijah Jackson; Isaac T. Jeffery; James Jones; Geo. Jenston; George Jewell, OC. A. Woods; Samuel Justin; James Jennings; Royal Jennings; Zachariah Jackson; William Jones; Thomas G. Jones; William Jones; Big William Jones; David Jackson; John Kelly; William Jones, OC. J. Ferguson, OC. A. Smith; Leroy Jones; John B. Jones; William Jewell, OC. J. M. Williams, OC. W. Paynes; Mosias Jones; John Jamieson; William Keeton; Hiram Kiruman; John G. Keloe;James Kitley; John Kennan,OC.R. Cave; Jane Kavenaugh; Thomas Kennan; John Kennan; Benjamin Kelly; Thomas Keeler; James King, sr.; James King, jr.; John W. Kisor, OC. J. Grayison; Daniel King; Joseph Kinkaid; John Kinkaid; William Kinkaid; Lewis Kinkaid; David Kinkaid; John Koyle; Hatcher Kinkaid; Austin Kilgore; Islam Kilgore;Thomas Kilgore; William Kelly; James Ketchum; William Lynes, OC. J. Adams; John Leman; Roland Lanham; Samuel Lankin;Harry Lynes; Stiart Lewis; Polly Lylia; Hiram Little; Robert Lemman; Ira Lewis, OC. J. Hiram; David Lynch; John Lynch; James Lynch; William Long, OC. --- Richardson; Jesse Long; John Lissler. Samue; Leonard; Sistura Lansford; James S. Long,OC. B. Dale; John Larkins; Joseph Little; Martin Lawles; Bird Lawles; Wm. S. Leamar; Charles Laughlin; Daniel Larkins;George Lawrence, OC. M. Burch; James Laughlin; William Lyntx; William Martin; James Moss; Leroy M'Guire; Joseph M'Daniel; William Mullins; Thomas M'Clain; John Manpin; Thomas Manpin;John M'Dow; James M'Clelland, OC. T. Dooly, OC. J. C. Moss; Robert M'Dow; John Moody; Samuel Martin; Adison M'Pheters, OC. A. Woods; Walter Macey; Andrew M'Haus; Joseph G. M'Cay; John M'Clintock;W. E. Matthews, OC. N. Rusell; Turner, M'Baird; John M'Kinsey; Wm. Man; John Mayo; James Maney; Rudolph March; Wm. Martin; John M'Micle; Jacob M'Bird, OC. J. Morgan; Warner Morris; Thomas Bird; David M'Adams; And. Maney; Jose Murphey; Samuel Mars, OC. W. Adams; Stephen Mars; Enoch M'Kinney;Stephen M'Kinney;

(Boone County, Missouri Continued)
James Mays; Ezekiel M'Carty; Soloman Mordica;Sarah M'Daniel;
Samuel M'Daniel; James Martin; David M'Gee; John M'Mullin;
Michael M'Mullin; Aaron M'Mullin; John M'Carty;John B. Mick;
James M'Carty; James Mays, sr.; William Minten; John Miner;
Benjamin Mathstead; David M'Guide; George M'Guitty; Anderson
M'Guitty; David M'Guitty; William Mitchel; Stephen Michel;
Bral (sic) M'Gee, OC. T. Halton; Absalom M'Daniel; Smallwood
V. Noland; Tyree Martin; John Moss; James Miller;Mason Moss,
OC. J. Newbaugh; James W. Moss; George M'Farland; William J.
Rees; Joseph Nesht; James P. Nichols; Ira P. Nash; Wm. Orr;
Isaac Newland; John O. Nolen; James Nichols; Miner Neal; Wm.
Seaper; David W. Kinkaid, agt. John Nealy; Daniel Neal; Adam
Nichols; Samuel Nullins; Robt. Nichels; Jeptha Osborn; Jesse
H. Pairy; William Ogan; Anthony Ousley; John Ogan; Ballinger
Payne; Noah Payne, OC. E. Edison; Thomas Phillips; Nathaniel
Pearson; George Phillips; Hiram Phillips, OC. R. Cave; James
Pearson; Renard Peg, OC. Jn. Krauss; William Pearson; Joseph
Pusington, OC. W. Hinch; Joseph R. Prate; John parker; Mann
Page; John Phillips, jr.; Samuel Pace; Nancy Proctor; David
Parat; John Phillips, sr.; James Phillips; John Potts; John
Reed, Jonathan Pace; Andrew Reairs; Jese Richardson; James
Richards; Harkin Richardson; Silas Richardson, Samuel Ross;
Patterson Russell; Henry Robinson; Thomas Riddle;Elias Sims;
James Riddle; Joel Riddle; James Reaves; James Richardson;
Mary Stroad; Jacob Stroad, OC. R. Heath; Wm. Sims; Jeremiah
Spencer; Perry Spencer, OC. Thom. Binkston;Green Sappington;
James Shelton; Foster Sappington; Nancy Sappington; Tarlton
Sims; James Sims; John Sappington; Asa Stone, OC. W. Samuel;
Elijah Stephens; Isham B. Sectser; James Sullinger,OC. J. W.
Moss; James H. Sullens; John Shell; Cumberland Shell, OC. R.
Shell; Jacob Stadler; William Smith, OC. A. Teler; William
Smith; Gurard Sappington; Jacob Shoats; Edward Sullens; John
Sullens; Edward Sullens adm. of Micajah; Nancy Shock; David
Shock; Amy Shock; Riley Solcum, OC. W. Lientz; Moses Solcie;
William Stolen; Charles Slice; Peter Slice; Will Singmond;
Samuel Searcy; Hardman Stove; Joseph Simpson; John Silvers;
Samuel Riggs; Gasper Roland; Marriot Richards; James Ready;
Samuel Rice; John Rage; Wilkins Razy; James Rice; Wm. Ross;
Joseph Rusell; William Ridgerove, OC. J. Barnes;John Roland;
Enoch Ridgway; Kirbery Rogers; William Robards;Zadock Riggs,
OC. I. Hicks; Nathan Robards; James Robards; William Roland;
John Robards, OC. Saml. Minott; Silas Riggs,OC. I. Farnharm;
James C. Redmind, OC. I. Reabon Riggs; Thomas Roland; Jones
Reaves; William Ryan, OC. Geo. Soctin; Adam C. Rayburn; Mark
Reairs, OC. W. Barnes; Edwin Reairs; Andrew Polk; Wm. Risk;
M'Cana Precel, OC. David M'Lane; John Puden; William Payne;
James Payne, OC. Jn. Williams; John Payne; Isiah Payne; John
Payne; Ellen R. Phillips; William Phillips; William Pulliam;

(Boone County, Missouri Continued)
Oliver Parker; Henry Pullen; Henry Paely; John G. Phillips;
William Pise; Frederick Potts; William Pulliam, jr.; William
Patton; Dabney Patten; Jenack Park; David Rice;Zadock Riggs;
Aaron Rutherford; William J. Ramsay; David Ruse, OC. William
Smith; William Rusell; Absalom Renfroe, OC. E. Sterns; Hugh
Silvers; John Stack; William Silver; David Slasa; Cornelius
Short; Josiah Short; John Stephenson; John Short; Wm. Smith;
Hume Sturgeon; Peter Smith; William G. Smith; Andrew Spence;
Wilson Stephens, OC. A. Davis; George Straton; James Smith;
James Scrivener; Benjamin Sanderson; Susanna Smith; Jeremiah
String; John Smith, OC. G. Payne; Newberry Stegdon; Lemuel
Susart; Samuel State, OC. J. Cesher; John Stephenson; Samuel
Sevier; John Skinner; Joshua Smith; William Tally; Shadrick
Wen; Edward Tucker, OC. H. Martin; Esrim Tipton; Geo. Tally;
Bennet Tilley; James Turner, jr.; Tarkin Tolten; Nathaniel
Teauque; Smith Turner, OC. I. Taylor; Thomas Tipton; Thomas
Thompson; Jeremiah Tanlin; James Taylor, OC. S. Miller; Dirk
Roger Todd, OC. JS. Gasper; Augustus Thrall, George Teater;
Enoch Taylor; Gilson Tuttle; John Vanhorne; Thomas Whiltey;
Isaac Varke; Jese Vincent, OC. Jn. Walch; Jacob Wortebeson;
Sampson Wright; Westley, OC. W. Wright; Israel Wilcox; James
Wiseman; Samuel Wilcolmen; Charles Wren; Jesse Whick; Joseph
Wind, OC. Jn. Walch; Benjamin Whick.

Ste. Genevieve County, Missouri, Concessions, 1766 - 1804

Name		Name	Year
Antoine Aubuchon	by	Henri Peyroux	1789
Augustin Aubuchon	by	Francisco Cruzat	1787
Jn. Bte; Beauvais	by	Zenon Trudeau	1796
Vital Beauvais	by	Francois Valle	1794
Widow Belmar	by	Zenon Trudeau	1797
Jean Phillippe Benard	by	Francois Valle	1793
Charles Bequet	by	Francois Valle	1793
Joseph Bequet & others	by	Francisco Cruzat	1797
Francois Bernier	by	Francisco Cruzat	1787
Pierre Blot	by	Charles D. Delassus	1799
Louis Bolduc and Parfait Dufour	by	Charles D. Delassus	1803
Charles Boye	by	Francois Valle	1793
John Burck	by	Francois Valle	1799
Louis Byate and Hypolite Robat	by	Zenon Trudeau	1799
John Calloway	by	Chas. D. Delassus	1799
Archibald Campster	by	Pre. D. D. Deluziere	1801
Claude Carron	by	Francis Valle	1771
Elias Cowen	by	Pre. D. D. Deluziere	1805
Andre Chevallier	by	Pre. D. D. Deluziere	1799
Joseph Chevallier	by	Chas. D. Delassus	1799

(Ste. Genevieve County, Missouri Continued)

Name		Name	Year
Jacob Chevallier	by	Chas. D. Delassus	1804
Camille Delassus	by	Chas. D. Delassus	1802
Pre. C. D. DeLassus	by	Zenon Trudeau	1798
Henry Dielle	by	Zenon Trudeau	1798
Israel Dodge	by	Pre. D. Deluziere	1800
John Dodge and his wife, Ann Keen	by	Fcois. Valle & wife	1787
Edmund Dunigan	by	Zenon Trudeau	1797
Dr. Walter Fenwick	by	Francois Valle	1800
Dennis Fool	by	Zenon Trudeau	1797
Alexis Griffard	by	Zenon Trudeau	1797
Louis Gravelle	by	Henri Peyrouz	1793
Jacques Guibourne	by	Francois Valle	1799
John Hawkins and Amos Rowark	by	Pre. D. Deluzieu	1799
William Hawthorne	by	Zenon Trudeau	1797
Jean Baptiste Janise	by	Zenon Trudeau	1804
Jean Baptiste Janise	by	Francois Valle	1800
John Johnson	by	Francois Valle	1800
Louis Caron and Chas. Robin	by	C. DeH. Delassus	1800
Conrad Kester	by	Zenon Trudeau	1798
Daniel Kippler	by	Pre. D. Deluziere	1799
Jean Baptiste Labricke	by	Henry Peyroux	1789
Antoine and Joseph Lachance	by	Francis Valle	1795
Nicholas Caillot dit Lachance	by	--- Peyroux de la C.	1787
Pierre LaChappelle	by	Francis Valle	1792
Louis Lacomble	by	Zenon Trudeau	1797
Nicholas Caillot dit Lachance	by	Zenon Trudeau	1792
Nicholas Lacomble	by	Zenon Trudeau	1792
Louis Lacroix	by	Francois Valle	1771
Nicholas Caillot dit Lachance	by	Francois Valle	1792
Andre Lalande	by	Francois Valle	1792
--- Laflueur dit Lalumdiere	by	Francois Valle	1770
Louis Lasource	by	Francisco Cruzat	1787
Pierre Lalulipe	by	Manuel Perez	1792
Jacques Laume	by	Francisco Valle	1771
Jean Marie Legrand	by	Zenon Trudeau	1793
David Logan	by	Chas. D. Delassus	1799
Joseph Loisel	by	Francisco Cruzat	1787
Thomas Maddin	by	Zenon Trudeau	1799
John Mathews	by	Pre. D. Deluziere	1800

(Ste. Genevieve County, Missouri Continued)

Name		Name	Year
Jeraume Matisse	by	Zenon Trudeau	1797
James Maxwell	by	Chas. D. Delassus	1799
John Mellvone	by	Zenon Trudeau	1797
Jean Baptiste Millet	by	Francis Valle	1792
William Morehead	by	Zenon Trudeau	1798
Alexandre Murdough	by	Pre. D. Deluziere	1803
Francois Oge	by	Henrie Peyoux	1791
Jonathan Owsley	by	Pre. D. Deluziere	1799
Etienne Paget	by	Zenon Trudeau	1797
Etienne Paget	by	Francois Valle	1797
Etienne Parent and Etienne Govro	by	Zenon Trudeau	1798
Joseph Perez	by	Francois Valle	1793
Pierre Charles Peyroux	by	Francois Valle	1792
Antoine Pratte	by	Chas. D. Delassus	1799
Henry Pratte	by	Chas. D. Delassus	1804
Jean Baptiste Pratte	by	Zenon Trudeau	1797
Pierre Auguste Pratte	by	Chas. D. Delassus	1804
John Price	by	Zenon Trudeau	1799
Thomas Riney	by	Chas. D. Delassus	1799
Louis Roberge	by	Zenon Trudeau	1798
Hypolite Robert and L. S. Buyate	by	Zenon Trudeau	1799
Jn. Capt. Placet	by	Francois Valle	1799
Charles Robin and Ls. Caron	by	Carlos Deh. Delassus	1800
Amos Rowark and J. Hawkins	by	P. de la Coudeniere	1801
Joseph Seraphin	by	Francois Valle	1792
Andrew Snoddy	by	Pre. D. Deleziere	1800
Roberts S. Slaughter	by	Zenon Trudeau	1797
Jn. Bapt. Tardif	by	Francois Valle	1771
----- Tramore	by	Francois Valle	1797
Joseph Tisserot	by	Zenon Trudeau	1798
Jas. Twyman and Wm. James	by	Francois Valle	1796
Jn. Bte. Valle	by	Zenon Trudeau	1797

Ralls County, Missouri, Delinquent Tax List, 1830.

Lewellyn Brown, Benjamin Bradley, Moses Bales, Charles F. DeLaurieri, William Brigham and Isaac Norris, Alby Easton, John R. Carter, Jacob Codington, Sary E. Easton, Nancy Gray, James Foreman, Jeremiah Grosby, Stephen Glascock, John Wash, Thomas Haden, Durrell Hubbard, John Jamison, Peter Lundele, George Markham, Joseph M'Coy, Lewis Music, Heirs of William B. Pudon, Joshua Massel, William A. Pocke, Moses Robnett, Felix Rorke, Joseph Wright.

A List of Persons Receiving Franch and Spanish Land Grants,
Land Title Registers, Located at State Archives.

Peter Abar, John Abernathie Joseph Abillet, Jacob Adams, Robert Adams, Samuel Adams, John Adkins, Thomas Ailer, John B. Aime, Christopher Aidenger, John B, Aime, Joseph Aime, Louis Aler, Antoine Baccane, Ludwell Bacon, Phillip Buccane, David Allen, Doedot Allen, John Allen, John Alley, William Alley, Baptiste Becquette, Charles Becquette, Mordecai Bell, Thomas Alley, William Alley, Eugenio Alvarez, John Barnabas, --- Amiot dit Peltier, John Anderson, Wm. Anderson, Nicholas Beaugenaux, Alexander Andrews, David Andrews, Abraham Baker, James Badeau, John B. Barselaux, Christopher Barnhart, John Andrews, Christopher Anthony, Elijah Averitt, Daniel Barton, Richard Applegate, Thomas Applegate, Michel Aquetan, Asher Bagley, Louis Baby, Henry Dodge, Auguste Chouteau, Samson Archer, Abraham Armstrong, Solomon Armstrong, Tom Broux, Wm. Brown, Aristide A. Chouteau, Francis Arnaud, Joseph Arnaud, John Ball, Fifi Beaugenaux, ---- Beauchamp, Joseph Bear, Wm. Bizet, James Arrell, David Ashbranner, Urban Ashbranner, Wm. Bates, ---- Ashbrook, Auguste Aubuchon, Joseph Aubuchon, Wm. Booner, Michel Bonneau, James Bryan, Antoine Bizet, Baptiste Aumure, Daniel Baldridge, Joseph Beachemin, Jonathan Bouis, Adam Brown, Francois Brazeau, John August, Horace Austin, S. P. Cerre, Moses Austin, Nicolas Auger, Antoine Bouis, Joseph Blay, Charles Bissonette, Charles Bonneau, James Baldridge, Louis Bear, Elias Bates, Alex Bredon, Gabriel Cerre, Andrew Chevallier, David Cole, Andrew Baker, George Ayrey, Joseph Beckett, Baptiste Baccane dit Riviere, Louis Barrada, Samuel Bridge, Jesse Bouding, Daniel Boone, Antoine Baimme, Holman Bankson, John Baird, John Basye, Asher Brown, Joseph Brazeau, Francis Bittick, Jesse Blanks, Elisha Baker, Robert Bay, Wm. Bates, J. B. Bravier, Hypolite Bolon, Daniel Bollinger, John Baptiste Becquette, David Brown, Francis Bissonette, Joseph Belan, John Bell, Miles Barefield, Jesse Baker, Nathan Boone, Louis Aubuchon, Handel Barks, Nathaniel Bassett, J.B. Bouvet, Alexander Bailey, Samuel Bay, John Brooks, Peter Beevul, Wm. Boydston, John Baker, Moses Bates, Hugh Barnett, Elizabeth Chitwood, Almond Cottle, Louis Dubriel, Ezekiel Bassnett, J. B. Beauvais, Thomas L. Beers, Michel Bone, Joseph Bissonette, James Bayancour, Antoine Barrada, Jacobs Barks, John Block, St. James Beauvais, Raphael Brinsback, Louis Bourri, Francis Barume dit Batheaume, James Brown, Vital Beauvais, Antoine Bonneau, John Baker, sr., Francois Basquin, Hugh Brannon, J. Dubrielle, Francis Beatty, Daniel Bankston, James Brown, Wm. Boice, Jacob Beaugard, Joseph Baker, John Bishop, Tho. Ball, Louis Brazeau, Richard Caulk, John Byrd, Ignace Chatigny, S. Blanchet, Henry Barley, David Boyd, Timothy Belleu, Benjamin Caldwell, Christopher Clark, Benj. Delaplane, Israel Dodge, Joseph Beauchamp, Charles Bradley, Ephraim Carpenter, Joseph

(French and Spanish Land Grants Continued)
Brazeau, Milciah Baldridge, David Bollinger, sr., Alexander Clark, Thomas Baker, James Arrell, Fracis Barois, Francis M. Benoit, Charles Boyer, David Bowie, Louis Chevallier, Edward Butler, John Carpenter, Baptiste Belland, John Boli, Etienne Boyeau, Jonathan Bryan, Amos Cox, Godfrey Crow, Jacob Cotter, Pierre Chouteau, Jacques Clamorgan, Daniel Clark, Drusilla Dickson Antoine Dejarlais, John Dollac, Louis Dubois, James Bankston, Daniel Brant, Franky Bradbourn, Etienne Bannister, Charles Cardinal, David Crips, Elisha Crosby, John Connor, David Collum, Cerre Choteau, Bernard Clay, Robert Barclay, Francis Baraine, James Beatty, Vincent Bouyet, Ambrose Boles, James Boyd, Charles Bowers, Wm. Belleu, Elijah Benton, Louis Bissonette, Elijah Belsha, Daniel Brant, Jacob Boisse, James Caldwell, Joseph Chartrand, John Capehart, John Burget, John B. Challifaux, Elias Carter, Abraham Byrad, Jesse Cain, John Bollinger, Edward Bradley, Henry Cassady, Charles Chartier, Hugh Cannon, Andrew Burns, Auguste Buyron, James Cooper, J. B. Lamarche, Joseph Lewis, Antoine Lachance, John Boyd, Wm. Bradley, Louis Bolduc, Ignace Belland, Etienne Bernard, John Bollinger, jr., John Billet, Hugh McChisholm, Thompson Byrd, Thomas W. Caulk, Jean Baptiste Chartier, John Marie Cardinal, Joseph Calais, Arthur Burns, Albert Burdeaux, Thomas Chaffin, Joseph Boyer, Joseph Boice, Solomon Bodwell, Joseph Boudoin, Joseph Bogy, Henry Block, Lemuel Cheney, John B. Chandillon, Charles Castonget, Mathias Bollinger, Sophia S. Boli, Pierre Boyer, Francois Bellanger, Peter Bissonette, Waters Burrows, Wm. Burts, Archibald Campster, Francis Cailloux, John Brown, Hugh Creswell, Elias Coen, Andrew Cottle, John Cook, Charles Crabbin, Francis Couteley, Bartholomew Cousin, Manuel Blanco, Rezon Bowie, George F. Bollinger, James Carl, Wm. Campbell, Jacob Chambers, John Butler, jr., Bart Butcher, Moses Byrd, Henry Crow, James Cox, John Coontz, Andrew August Conde, Wm. Conaway, James Dobson, Elijah Dougherty, Louis Delisle, John Drouin, David Devore, Charles Fenwick, Mary Gill, John Ferry, Charles Gill, Patrick Estes, Charles Ellis, Andrew Edwards, Alexander Duclos, Pedro Dumond, Etienne Dumay, John W. Engle, Asa Farrow, Andrew Godair, George Dunn, David Green, William Hebert dit Lecomte, John Hart, Abraham Helderbrand, Purnell Howard, Archibald Huddleston, Christopher Hays, Henry Hand, John Freeman, Jeremiah Grojean, William Harris, James Hannah, Jacob Foster, Angus Gillis, Catherine Gerrard, John Fallin, Cornelius Everett, John Dumay, Isidor Dupre, Mathew Garland, Benjamin Gareau, Charles Fallenash, J. B. Belleferville, Wm. Fitzgibbon, Louis Boice, Polly Boyd, Joseph Brown, Genevieve Charleville dit Duchequette, John Caldwell, John Burk, Mary Bison, Elijah Belsha, Roland Boyd, Henry Carter, Hugh Burns, Thomas Brooks, Joseph Brant, Samuel Bradley, Daniel M. Boone, Phillip Bollinger, Julien Chouquette, Peter Chevallier, John

(French and Spanish Land Grants Continued)
John B. Belland, Peter Bellestre, Nicholas Boislevin, Henry Bollinger, Peter Belleu, Louis Boyer, Mathias Belson, Perry Brown, James Belveur, Michel Bonnon, Renna Brummet, Francis Bourapas, Julia Papin Benito, Squire Boone, Simon Brundog, Samuel Block, Peter Billet, John B. Billette, Jean Bertrand, Flanders Callaway, John Choisser, Seth Chitwood, Noel Burke, David Byles, Vincent Carrico, Charles Borme, Jesse Bouden, Widow Boudoin, Jean B. Billet, Wm. Bouilliette, Jesse Benton, Hyacith Bertheaume, Albert Berdu, Raphael Bennette, Michael Burns, Alexander Doude, Wm. Doss, Peter Deveau, Hezekiah Dickson, Charles Delauriere, James Donnelly, Charles Demoss, Hezekiah Day, James Callaway, Baptiste Champlain, Abraham Byrd, jr., Christopher Carpenter, Peter Burdeaux, Wm. Burch, Sarah Bull, Amos Byrd, William Carter, Walter Carter, Jacque Chauvin, Rene Buet, George Buchanan, Daniel Hazel, Alexander Graham John Hays, Edward Hawthorn, Jonathan Foreman, Ebenzer Folsom, Patrick Flemming, George Green, Daniel Griffith, Wm. Hamilton, Christopher Haines, Veronique Guitard, James Head, Francis Howell, Daniel Johnston, George Hoffman, Uriah Hull, Daniel Hodges, Bart Herrington, Jonathan Hubble, John Lard, Joseph Labussiere, Francois Lesieur, Phillip Lady, Joseph Lapointe, Peter Labombarde, Andrew Lalande, Andrew Kincaid, Charles Lee, Adam Martin, Charles Mercier, Wm. Meek, James Meck, Antoine Marechal, James Maxwell, Charles Mathis, Jacob Myers, Jacques Normandeau, Patrick McDuff, Archibald Morgan, Abram Musick, John O'Connor, David Murphy, Barbara Caldwell, Robert Burns, Toussaint Cerre, Joseph Challifaux, Zachariah Dowty, John Dominque, Israel Denton, Auguste Delarebaudiere, Francis Degray, Isaac Davis, Frederick Connor, Isaac Cottle, David Clark, Thomas Crispin, William Cotton, Louis Courtois, Bartholomew Courtmanche, Wm. Harris Glass, William Fullerton, John Gilmore, Wm. Ewing, David Eshborough, Hyacinth Eglise, John Greenwalt, Charles Haut, Andrew Franks, Jacques Gotiot, John Griger, Thomas Harris, George Hamilton, Benjamin James, Francis Hudson, John B. Hervieux, Frederick Hoffman, Elmsley Jones, Milton Lewis, Benjamin Lachance, Joseph Laplante, J. B. Lacroix, Peter Martin, Charles Matthews, Patrick May, Wm. Masters, Wm. North, Alex McDonald, Alexis Moreau, Alexander Murdock, Paul Primo, Alexander Patterson, Jonathan Preston, Andrew Reed, Antoine Rivierre, Joseph Roubideaux, Wm. Rose, Louis St. Aubin, Charles Sanquinette, Antoine Smith, Etienne St. Pierre, Antoine Soulard, Andrew Scott, Francis Roy, John Tucker, David Trotter, Charles Thibeault, Thomas Twentyman, Thomas Bull, Joseph Calve, John Callaway, Micajah Callaway, Robert Caldwell, John Dowlin, Antoine Dubrielle, Wm. Dickins, Charles Dejarlais, Peter Deroche, Jonathan Ditch, Wm. Cox, Wm. Crow, Gabriel Constant, James Clay, Fine Connelly, John Sutton Farror, Wm. Farnsworth, Charles Dumoss, David Edwards,

(French and Spanish Land Grants Continued)
Baptiste Godair, Micajah Harris, James Green, Jacob Greater, Charles Finley, Etienne Goret, William Hays, George Grount, Jonathan Hurley, Benjamin Jones, Ebenezer Hubble, Wm. Holmes, Domingo Huge, Michael Huckington, Antoine Janis, Adam House, Francis Hostetter, Elisha Herrington, George Henderson, John Howell, Ciril Leduc, Louis Lebeaume, Francois Langlois, John Kennedy, Anthony Keller, Marie N. Lesbois, Robert Lane, John Logan, Francis Michel, Alexis Marie, Lawrence Long, Francis Maisonville, Joseph Mason, Jacob Miller, Charles Lucas, John Losla, Hugh Moreland, Francois Moreau, Hugh Nicholas, Peter Newkirk, Samuel Pew, Andrew Patterson, Antoine Pratte, John B. Perron, Samuel Pierceall, Francis Pasquin, Etienne Papin, Aaron Quick, Peter Robert, Thomas Rose, Ezekiel Rogers, John Robertson, William Smith, Christopher Sommalt, Bernard Smith, Isidore Savoy, Jacques St. Vrain, Alexis Roy, Joseph Tucker, Charles Tayon, Alex Summers, James Stewart, David Strickland, Abner Wood, Christopher Winsor, Andrew Wilson, James Varnum, Thomas Carlin, John Butler, Boston Butcher, James Burns, jr., Henry Canour, Joseph Chartrand, jr., John F. Chatigny, John Chandler, John Chambers, Louis Cayleaux, Stephen Byrd, John B. Cartier, Amable Chartran, Francis Deroche, Louis Denoyer, Andrew Dryhead, Terence Dial, Jacob Crow, Catherine Crepan, John Colgin, Bernard Coleman, Paul Chouteau, Louis Collins, James Cunningham, Stewart Cummings, Peter Cline, James Cox, jr., James Claret, Nicholas Coontz, John Cooper, Alexander Giboney, John B. Dufour, John B. Duchassin, Francois Dupin, Robert T. Fallin, Henry Godair, Jesse Evans, David Ferrill, Antoine Gayon, John Garland, Benjamin Gardner, John Elliott, James Fenwick, James Green, George Hays, Bazil Hebert, Peter Hartle, Joseph Guenard, Benjamin Foy, Joseph Greenwalt, John Grace, Absalom Hacker, John Hawkins, Thomas Harrod, Joseph Griffin, Stephen Hancock, Richard Green, David Gray, Stephen Guibarre, Lawrence Huff, John Jones, John Johns, Wm. James, Charles Hogan, Peter Hoffman, Daniel Hubbard, Michael Horine, Louis Lajoie, Joseph Luduc, Peter Lausson, Louis Lathan, J. B. Lapierre, Baptiste Lesage, Louis Lefevre, John Krytz, Wm. Linn, James Manning, Francis Marechal, Francis Michau, Jesse Masters, John Long, Charles Logan, Daniel Littlejohn, James Mackay, Pierre Lord, Gabriel Marlow, Daniel Meredith, Peter Menard, Arthur Mellon, Michael Null, John McCormack, Thomas Neeley, Isidore Moore, Asa Musick, Daniel Mullins, Michael O'Hagan, Peter Noblesse, John Newman, John Niel, Theophilus McKinney, Jacob Mosteller, Couis Moro, George Morgan, Daniel McCay, Jacob Neal, John Pritchet, Leonard Price, John Pettit, Eustache Pelletier, Pierre Perron, Abram Parker, James Piper, Alexis Picard, Peter Philberry, James Russell, James Rogers, Anthony Randall, Joseph Riendeau, Daniel Richardson, Charles Robert, Peter Roudin, Christy Romine, Geo. N. Razin, Charles

(French and Spanish Land Grants Continued)
Roy, Fredrick Sinkler, James Samuels, John Sender, Andre Roy, Peter Saffray, Alex Samson, Ann Skinner, Andrew Snoddy, John Smith, Joseph Story, Harold Stilwell, Hughes Stephen, Helen Tayon, Antoine Trudell, Winslow Turner, Bart Tardineau, John Watts, John Watkins, Elisha Winters, John Zellifrom, Austin Young, George Cavander, Thomas W. Caulk, jr., James Burns, John Charleville, Marfaret Byrd, Kincaid Caldwell, Archibald Cainsfer, John P. Cabanne, John Draper, John Doghead, Julian Dubuque, James Derrick, Charles Deputy, Wm. Drakins, Joshua Dodson, Joseph Dube, Widow Dubrielle, J. B. Dubay, Eustache Delisle, Francis Clark, David Coonrad, Nathaniel Cook, Jacob Cullins, Auguste Chouteau, the son of Pierre Chouteau, John Clemens, John Cordell, John Crow, Joseph Fight, John Guinn, Jenkin Harris, Benj. Hardgrove, Jeannette Flora, Wm. Frazer, Simon Guerin, James Hart, Robert Harper, Forest Hancock, J. B. Hebert, Daniel Helderbrand, Thomas Howard, Felix Hubbard, Francis Janis, Francis Jacobs, Thomas Huff, Ignace Hunot, J. B. Jeffre, Robert Hinckson, John Hoff, Samuel Holmes, Louis Jones, John Horner, James Hutchins, Joseph Hubert, Cumberland James, Jacob Lens, Paul Lefevre, Joseph C. Lallifaux, Michel Lachance, Hyacinthe L'Englise, Phillip Leberge, John Lewis, Gabriel Lachance, James Lambert, Nicolas Lecompte, Benrard Layton, Antoine Lafonte, Absalom Kinnerson, Timothy Kibby, Francois Lachapelle, Nicolas Lachance, Charles Kyle, James Martin, Francois Milhomme, John Megar, Louis May, Alexander Millikin, Bapt. Lorins, Joseph Loisel, John Littlejohn, Wm. Miller, Francois Menard, Auguste Chereau, Joseph Chartrain, Joseph Charpentier, Louis Charbonneau, Edmond Chandler, John B. Gobeau, Auguste Giguiere, Humphrey Gibson, Robert Gibany, Jean Andre Escrivano, Toussaint Gendron, John Ferguson, John Fayzer, Andrew Fagot, Joseph Fuland, Ambrose Dumay, Francois Gervais, Mary Eagers, Abraham Eads, Richard Glover, Ezekill Fenwick, Joseph Genereaux, Thomas Dyal, Thomas Gilmore, John N. Shaw, Adam Sommalt, Barrane Sarpy, Robert Sloan, Ambroise Seraphin, Vital St. James, Richard Secoy, James Scott, Jesse Smith, N. Savage, Baptiste Saucier, Nathaniel Shaver, Jacob Sommalt, Richard Taylor, James Trotter, J. B. Trudeau, John Townsend, Salomon Thorn, Thomas Thompson, Bazil Valle, Henry Tucker, Joseph Tayon, Daniel Stinger, Zachariah Thorp, Isaac Thomson, Francois Valle, Ransom Thacker, Zachariah Tharp, T. Todd, Isaac Van Metre, John Wideman, Swanson Yarbrough, John Wilson, Nathaniel Warren, Hardy Ware, Jacob Wheat, Jeremiah Wray, Benito Vasquez, Isaac Weldon, James Burris, Wm. Burns, George Buchanan, Robert Buchanan, Peter Bubont, Lee Fenwick, Wm. Girty, John Duval, Antoine Gautier, George Fallis, James Gill, John Gerrard, George Germain, David Edwards, Francois Dunegant, Master Fenwick, Louis Sojourner, Elijah Smith, Jon Sip, Jeremiah Simpson, Gregoire Sarpy, Daniel Sexton, Joseph

(French and Spanish Land Grants Continued)
Henry Ryley, Gregoire Sarpy, Tilman Smith, Lawrence Snyder, Antoine Saugrain, Mathew Saucier, Nathaniel Simonds, Etienne Ste. Marie, jr., Job Self, John Starnetter, Hypolite Tirart, Francis Tayon, Isaac Thompson, Eli Strickland, Ephraim Stout, James Stephens, Michael Tucker, Peter Troge, John Townsend, Wm. Stuard, Jesse Taylor, Peter Tucker, Thomas Tucker, John Tibeau, Wm. Tarbet, Hubet Talbot, Jacob Sweeny, John Valle, Peter Valign, Robert Trotter, Wm. Vanberkelaw, Lewis Worth, Peter Van Iderstine, John Weaver, Elisha Winsor, Wm. Ward, Edward Young, M. Fitzgibbon, John Green, Robert Green, Benj. Harrison, Richard Hazel, James Hawkins, Henry Hatton, Jacob Grojean, Aaron Graham, Francis Godfrey, Augustin Gonzales, Jacques Guibourd, Charles Guildeault, David Harris, Francis Hamelin, Joseph Gravier, Alexis Griffin, Louis Grimand, John Hagan, Clement Haden, Amable Guyon, Chas. Friend, Hyacinthe Hamelin, Antoine Jeanot, John Jarrot, James Jamison, Gilbert Hodges, sr., Gabriel Hunot, Pierre Janin, William James, John James, jr., Daniel Hubble, Wm. Hughes, John Henry, Benjamin Laugherty, John D. Kerlegand, Samuel Kenyon, Francis Largeau, Clement Knott, John Lamb, Adrain Langlois, Isidora Lacroix, Louis Jordalles, Christopher Kemplar, Josiah Lee, sr., Louis Lamalice, Charles Lardoise, Molly Lewis, Peter A. Laforge, Samuel Kennedy, Isaac E. Kelly, John Lafleur, Joshua Massey, Reuben Middleton, Middleton, Chas. Meville, Antpine Meloche, John May, Edward Mathis, Joseph Mathis, Samuel Masters, John Lovel, Auguste B. Lorimier, Gabriel Long, Charles Logan, Frs. Mandall, John Baptiste Maisonville, Joseph Miles, Valentine Lorr, Baptiste Marly, Francis Mitchell, Frs. Michel, Robert Logan, Jacques Marechal, Abner Masters, Louis Lucas, Samuel Louis, Louis Lorimier, Alexander McConohon, Alexander McLain, Andrew McQuitty, James O'Carrol, George W. Morrison, Antoine Mcrin, Matthew Mullins, Charles McDermott, Morris Oath, John Null, Wm. Null, Charles McLane, James Murdock, Joseph Moreau, John McMillan, John Nusam, Arthur O'Neal, Thomas Oliver, Wm. McConnell, Charles Nielson, Henry Peyroux, Bernard Pratte, Thomas Powers, John Portel, Nicolas Plant, Jeremiah Paynish, James F. Pillar, John Pyatt, Baptiste Placet, John M. Papin, Jose Perez, Jesse Pendergrast, John Pollette, Joseph Piquet, Charles Robert, John Reguiendau, Joseph Reed, Louis Roberge, David Reece, Joseph Rivet, Seneca Rollins, Joseph Robidoux, Andrew Robertson, sr., Thomas Ring, Andrea Ramsey, Adeston Rogers, Louis Charleville, Louis Chancelier, Barn Burns, Wm. Girouard, Joseph Gerrard, Auguste Gamache, John B. Dupuy, Francis Dursey, George Gatty, Jean Bapitste Gamache, Andrew Godair, John Gibany, Isaac Fallis, Robert Estes, Wm. Easters, Pascal Dufour, John B. Placet Dugay, Bapt. Ernaud, Antoine Ganier, Leonard Faurot, James Farrow, Terence Dyal, Ebenezer Fulsom, Joseph Smith, Francois Saucier, Peter San Quartier,

(French and Spanish Land Grants Continued)
Michael Rybolt, Amable Roy, Antoine Roy, Bapt. Roy, John P. dit Lapense, Joseph Roy, Louis Roy, Peter Roy, Francis St. Cyr, Hyacinthe, Hy. St. Cyr, jr., Leon N. St. Cyr, Raphael St. James, Louis Franceway, --- St. Germain, Baptiste St. James, Bte. Ste. Maire, Etienne Ste. Marie, Francis Ste. Marie, John Ste. Marie, John Ste. Marie, Joseph Ste. Marie, Stephen Ste. Marie, James St. Vrain, --- Savane, --- Savoir, John Scarlet, Claude Scarrette, Isidore Scarrette, John N. Seeley, Guy Seely, John Scott, Charles Sexton, Joshua Sexton, Phillip Shackler, Sophia S. Shafer, Joseph Shatrow, Darius Shaw, Frs. Shaver, David Shelley, Eli Shelley, Rees Shelley, Widow Shelley, Henry Sheridan, John Sheridan, Jacob Shiler, John Sharter, Joseph Silvain, Charles Simoneau, John Adam Smith, Jeremiah Simpson, Jon Skinner, Frederick Slinker, Tho. Smith, George Smirl, James Smirl, Abram Smith, Francis Smith, Henry Smith, James Smith, Mary Smith, Peter Smith, Andrew Somalt, Robert Smith, Samuel Smith, Thomas Smith, Nicholas Thibeault, Andrew Sommalt, Chris. Commalt, jr., John Tibeau, Peter Sommalt, Gabriel Soulard, Madam Choteau, John Collins, Auguste Conde, Wm. Crafford, James Cox, Robert Cummings, John A. Crow, Charles Findley, Fine, Phillip Fine, James Finley, Joshua Fisher, Antoine Flandrin, James Flaugherty, Antoine Govreau, Miles Goforth, Sylas Fletcher, James Griffin, Ninian Hamilton, Louis Gotiot, Touissaint Friend, Joseph Guignolet, Francois Hebert, John Harvey, Benj. Helderbrand, Geo. Horn, Jonathan Hubble, jr., Jacob Jacobs, Adam Johnson, John Hunot, Louis Jiguaires, Walter Jewitt, Robert Jewitt, Thomas Huff, jr., Pierre Jordalles, John Journey, Francis Kebard, Joseph Keffer, Peter Lewis, Levi, Samuel Levin, Benard Laponte, J. B. Lamarche, Maragret Lachaisse, Ignatus Layton, John Layton, sr., John Layton, jr., Abram Keeney, Daniel Keithelie, Abram Keithelie, Jacob Kelly, Jacob Kelly, jr., Simon Kenyon, John Laibond, Pierre F. Laforge, Leonard Kemplar, Rene Kercereau, James Kerr, Paul G. Kiercereau, Rene Kiercereau, A. LeBeaume, Daniel Kieseler, David Kincaid, Peter Krytz, Edward Johnson, David Helderbrand, Isaac Helderbrand, John Helderbrand, John B. Janis, David Hensley, Samuel Hibbler, Louis Huneau, Isaac Herrington, Samuel Hinch, Joseph Hunot, David Johnston, John Janes, Joseph Hortiz, John Hoss, Sylvestre Labaddie, Raphael Lesieur, Joseph Lesieur, Auguste B. LeGrand, Pierre LaFevere, J. B. Latrimoule, Francis Lacombe, Louis Lacroix, H. Marotte, Clement Misti, Lavina Mills, James Mills, Alex Milligan, J. Miller, B. Millet, Baptiste Martigny, John Marechal, Gabriel Lord, Francois Liberge, Fred Limbaugh, jr., Joseph Mainville, Thomas Madden, John Loyed, Wm. Lowry, Acquilla Low, Francis Matien, Thomas Overstreet, Robert Owen, Germain Ouilet, John McMichel, Henry McLaughlin, Frs. Murphy, Isaac Murphy, James Murphy, Wm. Muss, John B. Mortfez, Wm. Morrison, Ewel Musick,

(Franch and Spanish Land Grants Continued)
John Dye, Wm. Dade, James Earle, John Ears, Louis Eastache, John Easton, Joseph Eatue, Jas. Edwards, Peter Edwards, John Sullens, Jeremiah Thomson,Jean Baptiste,Valle,Edward Stoker, Louis Souligny, Joseph Soumande, Jonas Sparks, John Tanhill, Joshua Tansy, Wm. Talbert, Hubert Tabot, James Swift, Thomas Spencer, Nathaniel Spilman, John Taylor, Samuel Tipton,Louis Tirard, Nicolas Tirart, Albert Tison, John B. Tison, Andrew Tocumbrood, Martin Tosh, Mary Tosh, Toussaint Tourville, N. Thibeault, Joseph Thomson, Wm. Tinnin, William Thompson, J. B. Thibeault, Matthias Vanderhider, Benj. Vandenburgh, Wm. Vantico, Charles Vallet, Francois Valliere, Louis Valliere, Moses Vannses, L. Vaschard, Samuel Watkins, Samuel Weathers, Isaac Williams, Jacob Waggoner, John Viot, Mackay Wherry, J. B. Langlois, Joseph Lachance, Joseph Legrand,Paul Laderoute, John Lavalle, Henry Laughon, John Lathan, Peter Lashaway, M. P. Leduc, Louis Martin, Bapt. Marion, Louis Marie, William Lorimier, J. B. Lorins, Peter Lovel, Francois Pacquette, Wm. Page, John Paul, Etienne Pavant, Peter Payan, Joseph Payne, Belle Peche, Antoine Peigne, Amable Patnote, Noel A. Prieur, Richard Price, Samuel Price, John price, Peter Primo, Peter Perkins, Etienne Paggett, Henry Paggett, Peter Pallardie, J. B. Placide, Louis Placide, Amable Partenais,Antoine Poirier, Francis Poilliere, Baptiste Provenchere, Amable Parkway, J. B. Pratt, John Neighbour, Peter Neal, Samuel Neal, Ira Nash, Gabriel Nicotle, James Norris, Thomas Norris,John Nusam,jr., Jacob Odum, Michael Odum, John Ogeune, Henry O'Hara, Charles nash, Wm. Mock, Norris Monday, Pierre Montardy, Benj. Myers, Alex McKinney, Allen McKinney, David McKinney,John McKinney, Robert McKinney, Wm. McHugh, Geo. McFall, M. Motier, James McKinley, Joseph Neyswanger, John McNicolson, Elias Muscik, John McNeal, Joseph McMurty, David McMultrie, Philip Robert, Josiah Quimby, Robert Quimby, Stephen Quimby, Michael Raber, Francois Racine, Louis Ride, Benj. Rose, Hypolite Robert, Jesse Rene, James Rankin, Antoine Raynal, Robert Reed, John Ridenhour, Abram Richman, John Richman, John Russell, Martin Ruggles, Solomon Ruggles, John Ruddel, Peter Godair, Joseph Fenwick, Walter Fenwick, Evin Farrow, Humphrey Gibson, jr., Thomas Gibson, William Gibson, Charles Duncaster, Parafait Dufour, Christian Feuder, Bazil Gerard, Alexis A. Fallin,J. B. Gerard, Baptiste Duvall, Darius Duncan, Charles Valle, A. Lebeaume, Ezekiel Lard, Joseph LaMarche, Joseph LaFleur, Wm. Patterson, Michel Placet, Peter Provenchere, Charles Pruitt, John Pruitt, Samuel Pruitt, Marie Ann Quebec, Joseph Murphy, James James Moore, jr., James Montgomery, Alexis Morris, Wm. Nash, jr., Charles Neylson, Thos. Musick, Alex Murdock, Frs. Moro, Francois Rivard, Maria Josepha Pinconneau Rigoche dit Rigauche, Thomas Riddick, Claibourne Rhodes,Anthony Randall, Thomas Russ, Joseph Rundeau, Daniel Rowland,Peter Roussell,

(French and Spanish Land Grants Continued)
Michael Rabor, John B. Racine, Athen Raime, F. Raime, jr., J. B. Raime, James Rally, Matthew Ramey, Andrew Ramsay, sr., Andrea Ramsay, Andrew Ramsay, jr., John Ramsay, Wm. Ramsay, Robert Ramsey, Enos Randall, Enos Randall, jr.,James Randal, John Randall, Medad Randall, Samuel Randall, Amos Rawls, Reed, Hardy Rawls, James Razin, Thomas Reed, Wm. Reed,jr.,J. B. Rouillers, Azor Rees, Dinah Martin Rees, Charles Refield, Antoine Reilke, Nicholas Revelie, Phillip Revere,Peter Rock, Baptiste Reviere, James Reynolds, John Reynolds,John Rourke, bart Richard, Ephraim Richardson, James Richardson, Augustin Rogue, John Richardson, Jesse Richardson, Ignace Rigauche, Venne Rigauche, James Riley, Thomas Riney, Daniel Ritchelet, John Robert, John Robert, jr., Louis Robert, Peter Robert, Paul Robert, John Roberts, Phil Roberts, Abram Rukman, Peter Roussell, Andrew Robertson, jr., Manuel Rocque,Geo. Roebuck, Martin Rodney, Thomas Rodney, John Rodngues, Michael Rogan, Bernard Rogan, David Rohrer, John Rogers, Lewis Rogers,Robt. Rogers, John Romine, Genevieve Rouquier, Abram Ruddel, Moses Russell, Wm. Russell, Arund Rutgers, Baptiste Duchouquette, Francis Duchouquette, Phillip Ducomb, Claude Dufois, Daniel Duggins, Joseph Dumay, Peter Dumay, James Dunkin, Wm. Dunn, Piche Dupin, Alex A. Fallin, Jacob Fallin, Jonas Fallin, Philbert Gaignon dit Laurent, Charles Gail, Hyacinth Gayon, Augustin Gamache, Peter Gayon, Peter Chouteau,Francis Clark, Henry Clark, Thomas Clark, Wm. Clark, Wm. Clark, jr., Samuel Clay, Jeremiah Clay, James Clemens, James Clemens, jr., John Clement Daniel Clinginsmith, Peter Clyne, Gabriel Cobb, Aron Colvin, Louis Coignier, Smith Collum, Francis Colman, Thomas Comstock, Hugh Connelly, J. Connelly, J. Connelly, Timothy Connelly, Patrick Connor, James Connoway, Jeremiah Connoway, Joseph Conway, Nicolas Coontz, John Corder, Baptiste Corley, Jeptha Cornelius, John Cothner, Martin Cothner,Benjamin Cox, jr., Benjamin Cox, sr., Robert Cramp, Wm. Craig,Thrs. Crely, Levin Cropper, Thomas Cropper, Ezekiel Crosby, Isaac Crosby, Ben. Crow, Louis Crow, Michel Crow, Walter Crow, Tho. Cruce, George Crump, Joseph Crutchelow, Duwalt Crutz,John Cummings, John Culbertson, Wilson Cummings, Charles Curatte, Richard Sullens, Nathan Sullens, Simon Subtil, Robert Spencer, Benj. Spencer, George Spencer, Dennis Sullivan, Phillip Sultz, J. Stedman, Andrew Summers, James Summers, John Summers, John Summers, jr., Alex Summerville, Sarah Starnettler, Francois Thibeault, Henry Stephenson, John Stephenson, John Stewart, John Stilwell, Joseph Stilwell, Joshua Stockade, Jonathan Stoker, Samuel Stoddard, Frs. Stockler, Conrad Stotler, Adam Stotler, Peter Stotler, Jos Strickland, John Strickland,Bte. Taumier, Titus Strickland, George Stringer, Samuel Strother, Benjamin Strother, Charles Tayon, jr., John Tayon, Auguste Trudell, Charles Tayon, jr., John Tayon, Joseph Tessier,Frs.

(French and Spanish Land Grants Continued)
Thibeault, John B. Thibeault, Levi Thiel, Claude Thirot,Jas. Thompson, Martin Thomas, James Thompson, jr., John Guire, Joseph Thompson, Mary Fitzgibbon, Fields Flouriont, William Flynn, Wm. Flynn, jr., Francis Foisey, Francis Foldener, T. Friend, jr., Benj. Fooy, Berg Fooy, Henry Fooy, Isaac Fooy, Elijah Ford, Francis Fortin, Michel Fortin,Jacob Foster,jr., Jacob Foster, sr., James Foster, Thomas Foster, John Frazer, Daniel Frazer, jr., Daniel Frazer, Elisha Goodrich, George Gordon, Joseph Goret, Hugh Graham, John Graham, James Gray, Augustin Grande, Charles Gratiot, Charles Gratis, John Hahn, Wm. Griffin, Peter Grount, Henry Groves, J. B. Grunard, John Gryer, John Guething, Louis Guitard, George Hacker, William Hacker, Aquila Hagan, Joseph Hagan, John Hague, Jos. Haines, Henry Hall, Robert Hall, Wm. Hancock, John Hand,Wm. Hartley, John Hawthorn, John Hargrove, Andrew Harris,Samuel Harrison, Michel Hart, Wm. Hartley,Michael Hebert, Noel Hebert, Widow Hebert, Phil Hebert, Gibert Hector, John Helderbrand, Thomas Henry, Peter Helderbrand, Hill Henry, jr., Anthony Hibernois dit Mesloche, Peter Higgins, Wm. Hinckson, Wm. Hill, Joseph Hioche, Edmund Hodges, Ebenezer Hodges, jr., Samuel Hodges, Edward Hogan, John Hogan, Francis Honore, Louis Honore, Noel Hornbeck, Felix Hoover, David Horine, John Horine, Jonathan Horsley, Thomas Horsley, Alvarez Hortiz, Newton Howell, Tho. Howell, Isaac Hostetter, Jacob Hostetter, Peter Hostetter, Michael Hubert, John A. Hunt, John W. Hunt, Joseph Hunter, Joseph Hunot, jr., Moses Hurley, Elisha Jackson, Jas. James, Stephen Jackson, Joseph Jacobs, Joseph James, Morris James, Sarah James, Joseph Jamison, William Jamison, Nicolas Janis, Louis Jennet, Benj. Johnson, John Johnson, Thomas Johnson, Wm. Johnson, George Johnston, John Johnston,Elizabeth Jones, John Jolien, Caleb Jones, Malachi Jones, Phoebe Jones, Rich. Jones, Samuel Jones, Stephen Jones, Thomas Jones, Wm. Jones, Joseph Lafernoit, George Lail, John B. Lalande, John Lalove, Auguste Langlois, John Laplante, Joseph Lapresse,Josiah Lee, jr., Louis Lardois, M. Lardoise, Absalom Link, Solomon Link, John Link, Michael Limbaugh, John Lindsay, Joab Line, John Litten, Joachim Lisa, David Logan, Matthew Logan, John Mann, Regis Loisel, Louis Lorimer, jr., Louis Louvierre, John L. Marc, J. B. Louzon, John Manning, Joseph Manning, Francois martie, Mark Manning, Didier Marchand, Louis Marchand, John Masters, Nicolas Marechal, Joseph Marie, Agnew Massey, Wm. Massey, Bapt, Mason, Henry Masters, John Masters, Richard Masters, Robert Masters, Lemuel Masters John Masters, jr., Edw. Matthews, Edward Matthews, jr., John Martien, Joseph Martien, Jacques Metot, Elias Metz, J.B. Millette, Joseph Millette, John Miller, Wm. Montgomery, John Montmenie, Bede Moore, John Moore, Joseph Moore, Nicholas Moore, Wm. Moore, J. B. Moreau, Thomas Mores, John Morgan, jr.,Solomon Morgan,

(French and Spanish Land Grants Continued)
John McRin, Joseph McRin, Pelagi McRin, Manuel G. Moro, Jos. Motard, John Murphy, Wm. Murphey, sr., Wm. Murphey, jr., Wm. Musick, John Myers, Kersiah Myers, David Myers, Robert McCay, John McClanahan, James McClean, John McConnell, Adam McCord, Eliz. McCordle, Peter McCormack, Geo. McCouklin, James McCoy, Joseph McCouklin, Alex. McCountney, James McCountney, Joseph McCourtney, Ananias McCoy, Hugh McCullough, James McCullough, James McDaniel, James McDonald, Allen McKenzie, Wm. McKim, Farquor McKensie, James McMillan, J. B. Olive, John Orain, John Ottery, Isaac Vanbibber, James Vanbibber, James Vernon, Joseph Vandenbenden, Benito Vasquez, jr., Registe Vasseur, Peter Vaughan, Louis Verdon, Rodolph Veriat, Joshua Viceroy, James Vernon, Noel Vien, Antoine Villars, Dubreuil Villars, Marie Valle Villars, Jonathan Vinyard, John Violeny, Manual Violet, Joseph Voisard, Samuel Wakeley, Andrew Walker, Noah Wall, Benjamin Walker, Joseph Wallace, Joseph Waller, John Ward, Paul Washburn, Richard Jones Waters, John Wealthy, Job Westover, Peter Weaver, Joseph Webkins, John Wedsay, George Weeland, John Weldon, Jacob Welker, Leonard Welker, Elisha Welsh, Joseph Westbrook, Richard Westbrook, Conrad Wheat, Elias Wheat, Hugh White, Robert White, John G. Whitesides, Thomas Whitley, Jeremiah Whitson, Elisha Whitaker, Aquila Wickersham, Jacob Wickersham, Jacob Wickersham, jr., Francis Wideman, Mark Wideman, Levi Wiggins, John Wilbourn, Thomas Wilbourn, John Wiley, Robert Wiley, Wm. Wiley, John Williams, James Williams, John Willgate, Jesse Williams, Tho. Williams, Theophilus Williams, George Wilson, Robert Wilson, Jonathan Wood, Samuel Wilson, Samuel Wilson, jr., Thomas Winsor, Wm. Winters, Gabriel Winters, Jacob Wise, Jonathan Wiseman, Tho. Witherington, Matthew Wishart, Christian Wolf, Michael Wolf, Thomas Wolsey, Andrew Wood, Francis Wood, Zadock Wood, Fred Woolford, James Worthington, John Worthington, Francis Wyatt, Joseph Worthington, David Yarbrough, Emelian Yosty, Amable Yon, Edward Young, Joseph Young, Morris Young, Phillip Young, Robert Young, Wm. Zanes, John Zellifrow, James Curin, Joshua Crutchelor, Isaac Devore, John Dougherty, Catherine Denoyer, Isaac Doghead, Susannah Doggett, James Douglass, Amable Dion, Wm. Palmer, Dan Paneton, Claude Paneton, Joseph Parish, John Patterson, Joseph M. Papin, Andrew Parker, Hiram Patterson, Joseph M. Papin, Benj. Patterson, Daivd Patterson, Eleazer Patterson, Robert Patterson, Joseph Peigne, Frs. Pelletier, Peter Pelky, Joseph Peigne, J. Anoit. Pelletier, J.F. Perry, John B. Pelletier, Peter Pelletier, Joseph Perkins, Edward Perry, Leni Perry, M. Perryman, Eli Pettibone, Benj. Pattit, Solomon Pettit, Sylvanus Philip, Chas. Philips, Dan. Philips, Marie Picard, Joseph Pouillot, Peter Powers, Joseph Presse, Peter A. Pratte, J. B. Pugal, James Curren, John Daney, Wm. Dabron, Abram Darst, David Darst, sr., Augustin Daudier, J.

(French and Spanish Land Grants Continued)
B. Dauphin, Rene Daudier, Chorn David, Wm. Davis, Hyacinthe Deheltre, Louis Deheltre, Henry Deille, Eloi Dejarlais, Paul Dejarlais, Camille Delassus, Joshua Delaplane, Charles D. Delassus, David Delauny, Francis Delauriere, Bapt. Delisle, Louis Delauries, Pierre Deluziere, Charles Deluziere, Benj. Demint, Jesse Demint, James Dennis, Francis Denoyer, John B. Deplacet, Fracis Derousse, Jacob Devore, Jesse Devore, Luke Devore, Lois Dickson, Charles Disuet, Gabriel Dodier, Widow Dodier, Rene Dodier, Jacob Doghead, Baptiste Domine, Joseph Donnahoe, Thomas Donnahoe, Joseph Dorian, Pierre Dorian, Wm. Dougherty, Louis Dollac, Peter Dollac, Samuel Dorsey.

Franklin County, Missouri, Tax List, 1820.

James Armstrong, John Anderson, James Anderson, John Adams, David Anderson, Edmond Anderson, Robert Anderson, Phimeas Adams, Thomas Antvobus, Phillip Bell, Thomas Brown, Mathew Burnsides, Daniel Brown, Henry Brown, Russel Brown, Mathew Blackwell, Talton Brock, Joshua Brock, John Bell, Ambrose Bowles, John Burnsides, John Daniel Bell, James Brown, Jacob Clark, Kinkade Caldwell, James Colvin, John Colvin, Andrew Caldwell, jr., Sally Crow, Mathew Caldwell, James Campbell, Robert Caldwell, David Cole, Andrew Caldwell, sr., William Campell, George Cole, Moses Croff, John Decker, Baley Dent, William Dorherty, Joseph Durham, Hiram Eastes, Elisha Eastes, Spencer Eastes, John S. Farrow, Richard Farrow, David Gall, John Gall, William Fullerton, Leonard Farrow, Wm. Hammcok, Zacheriah Hall, John Hornsurger, Samuel Hutton, Tho. Henry, Frances A. Haywood, John Henton, sr., Jacob Henton, Reuben Harrison, Josiah Harrison, Gilbert Hodge, John H. Haywood, Benjamin Hodge, William Hardin, Clayton B. Henton, Achilles Jeffries, Issac Hardin, Jobe Henton, Ephraim Jamison, Andrew King, James Kinkade, William Kid, Sylvester Lann, Vincent Lewis, William Lewis, Liedare Lewis, Lewis Mansker, Richard Richeson, Isaac Murphey, Anna Murphey, James North, Newton Pickil, George Pusley, James Parker, Gideon Richeson, Nathan Richeson, Amos, Richeson, sr., John Read, Hensly Read, David Read, Barabas Redenaure, Daniel Richeson, Amos Richeson, Wm. Osborn, Samuel Stell, Baxter Smith, John Stites, Henry Stees, Barnabas Stricklan, Benoni Sappington, Isaiah Todd, George Thompson, William Massy, Phillip Miller, Lear Maupin, George Maupin, Leades Maupin, John Morris, John Thompson, Jonathan Vineyard, Thomas Veach, John Wyatt, Henry Ware, Wm. West, John West, Joseph Welch, William Walker, Michel Alkile, Wm. Brown, Phillip Boulware, jr., George Boulware, Robert Band, James W. Brumley, Phillip Boulware, sr., William Baily, John Burchard, Mathias Baker, Robert Crawford, William Cerley, Daniel Caldwell, Daniel Cryder, Lewis Devual, William Dodds, Abraham Derrberry, Lewis Davids, Benjamin Edmonds, John Edds,

(Franklin County, Missouri Continued)
William Edds, David Edwards, John Edds, James Flat, Samuel Gibson, sr., Henry Hall, Uriah Hursk, David Hubbard, William Hughs, John Hughes, Isaac Hammer, Edward Howard, John Helton, John G. Heath and Robert A. Heath, Hugh Heatherly, Benjamin Laughlin, James Hull, Lewis Hall, James Kegans, Peter Lasua, Samuel Laughlin, Jeffrey Lively, William Laughlin, Anthony Margraves, John Laughlin, Willis Lay, David Massey, Joseph Marrow, James Miller, James Owens, William Owens, John Prior, Levi perkins, Robert Prior, William Prior, Wm. Penter, Isaac Perkins, Joseph Pinter, George Penter, jr., Samuel Roberson, John Phillips, James Parsons, Alexander Roberts, George Read, Leonard Read, Alexander Rattles, Joel Roberson, John Stevens, Thomas Shockley, James Stevens, Samuel Shobe, Edward Simonds, Benjamin Simpson, Daniel Simpson, Joel Starkey, Wm. Tacket, Jarvis Starkey, James Simpson, Beriman Tacket, John Tacket, Phillip Tacket, John Woollams, William Wyatt, Moses Wetton, Bartlett Woollams, William West, Richard Watson, John Green, Samuel Yates, Charles Arthers, James Burns, Sandford Baikus, Margaret Butler, Daniel M. Boone, George Brown, Wm. Brown, Francis Bresto, John and Alexander Bladridge, Andrew Brown, George Barton, Joseph H. Buckhart, Isaas Cressin, John Huff, Thomas Compton, Nathan Chewring, Edward Conel, Wm. Duncan, Mannen Clements, Andrew Clements, Abraham Clements, Charles Drotet, John Duncan, jr., John Duncan, sr., William Gorden, Robert Evans, Bassel Drotet, Thomas Gibson, William Gorden, David Horine, William Hart, George Henson, William Hawkins, James Harris, David Hoops, John Harris, Josiah Hibberd, John Johnson, Robert Little, Charles Lane, William Lane, Charles McGowing, Thomas Moore, Archibald McDonald, John Martin. Wm. Martin, Johnathan McClary, James and John McDonald, Benjamin Skaggs, George Snotgrass, Isaac Robinson, Sylvester Pattit, David Nowland, Seth McKee, Joseph Brown, John Skaggs, Jacob Mashack Skaggs, Moses Skaggs, David Skaggs, Robertson Stowe, Henry Skaggs, Charles Thompson, Absolem Trible, John Vest, Jesse Vanbibber, David Walden, Alexander Willard, Archibald Young, John W. Buckner, Lazarus Benton, Thomas Blare, Elijah Baker, Abraham Benton, Jemina Boyd, Robert Bay, Mathew Cole, James Caldwell, Anthony Dering, Joseph Dearrul, Jesse Enloe, Robert Duncan, Nicolas Darter, Alexander Eaff, Joseph Fisher, Benjamin Enloe, Leonard Eastwood, Benjamin Evans, William Gibson, George Fryer, John Frasier, Garland Harding, William Hearst, Jeremiah Hamilton, B. Hamilton, John Humphrey, John Pepper, Jonathan Humphrey, George Hearst, Robert Hines, John Horine, Elizabeth Hyde, John Hughes, William Hill, William Michael Thomas Johns, James Kimberlin, John Lewis, Daniel B. Moore, Anthony Larul, James Lofton, Perry Moore, Noah Pane, Bartlet Martin, James Michel, Francis Miller, James Martin, John Nichols, Newman Powns, Joseph Pisin, Robert Pepper,

(Franklin County, Missouri Continued)
James Pepper, Samuel Pepper, John Pritter, Jonathan Potts, John Richeson, James Richeson, Nathan Robinet, Samuel Short, Clabourn Sullevant, Eli Short, David Skaggs, Samuel Travis, Samuel Smith, Mark M. Sullevant, John Stanton, Wm. Steward, John Twitty, Albert Twitty, John Timmonds, Thomas Twiner, Wm. Twitty, James Woodland, Francis, Henry Whitmore, Lewis Young, John M. Young, Benjamin Alexander, Samuel Abbet, James Brown, John Anderson, Addam Baker, Benjamin Brown, John Breeding, Robert Brock, John Bird, Cabel Baily, William Bray, Samuel Cantley, James Cheak, John Breeding, sr., Elijah Breeding, John Cantley, sr., John Cantley, jr., John Chetwood, Charles Collard, William Cotes, John Davis, jr., Enoch Greenstreet, John Davis, sr., Absolem Greenstreet, William Greenstreet, James Greenstreet, jr., James Greenstreet, sr., Wm. Hensly, jr., Allen Benjamin Heatherky, William Hensley, Zacheriah Sullens, George Kelly, William Kelly, Richard Larrimore, sr., Phillip Larrimore, Richard Larrimore, jr., Robert Larrimore, Charles McManis, William Maupin, John Miller, Jesse McDonald, Peter Massey, James McDonald, Widow Purkins, John Parsons, David Purkins, John Purkins, Charles Phillips, James Snelson, Elihu H. Randolph, James Roark, Michel Roark, Joseph Reavis, Patrick Spence, John Sullens, jr., Thomas Smith, Wm. Smith, James Snelson, John Simpson, James Smith, Michel Sone, John Sullens, sr., James Shelton, Samuel Shelton, John Shelton, Jesse Thomas, John Woolery.

Cooper County, Missouri, Delinquent Tax List, 1835.

Name	Comments
Anthony Arnold	Gone to Fishing River
Thomas Arnold	Gone to Fishing River
Orville Baty	Gone to Pettis County
John Buss	Gone to Pettis County
William Bledsoe	Gone to Morgan County
James Bell	Gone to Pettis County
Matthew Coy	Gone to Lafayette County
Ruebin Clark	Gone to Cole County
Sandford Corum	Gone to Santafee
William Dallam	Gone
William Ducker	Gone to Jackson County
James Dobbins	Gone
John Denson	Gone to Cole County
Thomas Foster	Gone to Cole County
David Guthrie	Gone
John Goddnoe	Gone to Texas
Hiram Gist	Gone to Morgan County
Hezekiah Hagin	Gone to Morgan County
Hardin Hix	Gone to Morgan County
Harvy Harper	Gone to Morgan County

(Cooper County, Missouri Continued)

Name	Comments
George C. Harper	Gone to Boone County
David Johnson	Gone to Morgan County
Benjamin Kellogg	Gone to Texas
David Liles	Gone to Morgan County
Uriah Leonard	Gone to Cole County
Andrew McClure	Gone
John Nico	Gone
John H. Meadows	Gone to Cole County
John Paule	Gone to the mines
Jabez Proctor	Gone to Cole County
Joel Pointen	Gone to Texas
Francois Parzette	Gone to Pettis County
Caleb Purdin	Gone to Pettis County
John Prelly	Gone to Kentucky
Benjamin Proctor, jr.	Gone to Fayette, Indiana
Joseph Proctor	Gone to Pettis County
Benjamin Pawling	Gone
Thomas Powers	Gone
David Reed	Dead
John Smith	Gone to Pettis County
James Smith	
Joseph Stephens	Gone to Pettis County
Benjamin B. Sutton	Dead
Andrew Standly	
Elbridge G. Sanders	
Colby F. Stephens	
Howard Steward	
Zacahriah Short	Gone to Pettis County
John Shaw	Gone eastward
Hardin M. Williams	
Westly Watson	
Hiram Weedin	Gone to Saline County
Henry Woolery, jr.	Run away
James Williams	Gone to Jackson County

Ste. Genevieve County, Missouri, Bonds, Notes, & Obligations

Name	Year	Doc.	Name
William Abley	1801	Bond	Callyway's estate
Abraham Baker		Bond	Francis & Martha Doquet
John Barns	1816	Bond	Governor
T. P. Bedford	1802	Bond	Moses Austin
Louis Chamard	1771	Bond	Francis Valle
Chas. Charleville	1787	Bond	Widow Perthuis
Elias A. Elliott	1813	Bond	W. C. Carr
Ant. Deselle Duclos	1776	Bond	Jn. Datchuruet
Jean Bapt. Delisle	1784	Bond	Andre Dequire
Guiho Dekerlegand		Note	Francis Valle

(Ste. Genevieve County, Missouri Continued)

Name	Year	Doc.	Name
Honerie Carpenters	1774	Note	Lasorce minors
Aug. & Ch. Chatel	1772	Bond	Ant. Carbonneau
Auguste Chatal	1771	Bond	Antoine Guelle
Dom. Bergan dit Jn. Lours	1782	Bond	Joseph St. Aubin
Jn. Bapt. Boudeau	1775	Note	
Jean Datchurut	1784	Bond	Pre. Deguire dit Duroser
Henry Dodge	1814	Bond	Governor
Fcois. Dury	1766	Note	---- Bossern
Mich. Chauvin dit Joyeuse	1770		---- Rouquier
Guillaume Desrousses	1768	Bond	---- Cere
John Dugan	1799	Note	Me. Peyroux de Rodriquez
Ed. Dugan	1799	Note	Mrs. Booba
Edmund Dugan	1791	Note	Maria Anne Laplante
Joseph Farrell	1800	Bond	Israel Dodge
E. Fenwick	1819		J. Jackson
Jean Gomez	1799	Note	Joseph Barbeau
Joseph Tellier	1767	Note	Jean Datchuruet
Pierre Gadobert	1772		Martin Duralde
Pierre Gadobert	1772	Bond	Noel Larose
Pierre Gadobert	1772	Bond	F. Valle
Jn. Gilbert dit Lafontaine	1773	Bond	----- Dubreuil
William Gvitz	1800	Bond	James Finley
John Hawkins		Note	----- Dutton
Joseph Hunt	1828	Note	James H. Relfe
Isaac Kester	1799	Bond	Jeremia Perrel
----- Cantrel dit Filbustier	1776	Bond	Simon Hubardeau
Noel Larose		Note	Daniel Chuavin
Manuel Lespagnol		Note	Francois Langellier
Malachi Madden	1830	Note	B. Bossier
Malachi Madden	1830	Note	Bridget Hayden
Malachi Madden	1832	Note	Bart Johnson
Malachi Madden	1832	Note	Pierre Pratte
Malachi Maddin	1830	Note	Ferdinand Rosier
Pierre Messager	1776	Bond	Louis Chamard
Perthuy Perluio dit la guele pique	1766	Note	----- Leclere
Mrs. Marguerite Perthuis	1770	Bond	Joseph Segon
Mrs. Peroux		Bond	----- Price
Marianne Plante	1805	Bond	Marguerite Boyer
Louis St. Germain	1770	Bond	Jn. Gilbert
Jean Bapt. Tessier	1767	Note	Michel Placet

(Ste. Genevieve County, Missouri Contined)

Name	Year	Doc.	Name
Pierre Vereau	1773	Bond	Joseph Delor
Antoine Valliere		Bond	Jean Gilbert dit LaF.

A List of Persons Receiving Military Bounty Land for the War of 1812 in Missouri.

Charles H. Abbey, Peter Abbott, Ezekiel Ackley, William Ackman, David Adams, Henry H. Adams, Thomas Adams, William Adams, Solomon Adcock, Robt. Addis, James Agan, John Agan alis Hagan, William Agnew, Amos Aimes, John Albright, Joseph Albertson, Isreal Aldrick, Philadelphia Aldrick, John Alfred, Betty Aldridge, John Aldrige, Andrew Alexander, David Allen, Jesse Alexander, John Alexander, John C. Alexander, Quarters Alexander, Jonas Alexander, Joseph Alexander, George Algier, Letitia Alexander, Peter Allabada, Campbell Allen, Campbell Allen, Charles Y. Allen, John Allen, John R. Allen, William Allums, John S. Allen, Lewis L. Allen, Lucy Allen. Lewis L. Allen, Casper Alsaver, Adam Alter, Moses Alverson, Charles Ames, Edmund Alvis, John Amich, Andrew Ammons, Wyatt Bailey, James Anderson, John Anderson, Joseph Anderson, Bela Barney, Larkin Anderson, Nathaniel Anderson, Robert Anderson, Samuel Anderson, Shardy Anderson, Solomon Anderson, William Barron, Thomas Anderson, Jacob Andey, Brinthinger Anderw, John Banks, Charles Beam, Nicholas Beall, David Bealer, William Beache, John Beache, John Bazewell, John Baxter, Jacob D. Armstrong, James Andrew, Michael Andrews, Phinehas Andrews, William T. Barrow, Isaac N. Baxter, John G. Baumgardiner, Geo. Bateman, Bartholmew Armistead, David Baumgardiner, John Bass, Thomas Barnard, William Badger, Appleton Bailey, Isaac Bailey, Ira Barkem, Joseph Batrand, Henry Ayres, Stephen Andrews, Phl. Andrews, Mathias Angel, Aaron Anglin, George Angst, William Annadell, Heny. Annadown, John Annadown, John Aslin, Lindsey Arnold, Sarah Basford, Billings Babcock, Zachariah Arriwood, Rodman Barnes, Silas Ball, William Bailey, John Ayre, James Annibal, Jethro Babb, William Bassett, Edward Ballard, Hiram Arnold, Hardaman Anthony, Richd. Apperson, William Ashbrooke, William Bass, Francis Bass, Edward Bass, Amos Avery, Thomas Armstrong, James Basford, William Barton, Jonah Barton, Mary Arnes, Henry Babcock, Latimore Bachelor, Enoch Bailey, Isaac Baker, Fredk. Baker, Moses Baker, Susannah Baker, Abraham Bartlett, Jacob Applegate, Nicholas Applegate, Saml. Arnes, William Baker, William Baldwin, Joseph Baliff, Abner Ball, Andrew Ballard, Jonathan Banister, Samuel Arnet, John Backus, Henry Barton, Aaron Barton, John Bartlett, Saml. Arns, John Arnold, Samuel Arnett, Artemis W. Bacon, Henry Aux, William Barnett, Mary Arns, Thomas Ashbrooke, John Asherton, Solomon Barnes, Joseph Bradley, Nathan Barnhill, Henry Botts, George August, Robert Austin, Ebenezer Bacon, Jas. Boyd, Henry Box,

(Military Bounty Land Continued)
Josiah T. Askew, Erastus Barnard, James Barncastle, Jonathan Barney, Archd. B. Bates, Charles Atwell, Benjamin Atkinson, William Atkins, John Atkins, Josiah Bacon, Stephen Bacon, Wm. Bacon, Burn Barlow, William Brady, John Blankinship, William Boyles, James Bean, Joseph Bodwell, Henry Box, Charles Bower, Alexander Brackenrdige, Nicholas Biter, William Bosher, John Belcher, John Blue alias Bellow, Brumfield Biggers, Humphrey Belt, Benjamin Boyer, James Blackburn, Isaac Bosworth, Jacob Beckman, William Belstead, Uldrich Bockman, John Bland, John Bradshaw, Mansfield Braden, William B. Benson, Andrew Bowen, Frederick Blount, Jacob Bloomingdale, Samuel Bennett, Edward W. Bradford, Elizabeth Blair, James Berkwith, Reuben Bowlin, William Beardsley, William B. Boothe, Henry Bonesteel, Lewis Bowen, Lacy R. Bobo, Zachariah Burwell, James Brown, Mathew Butler, Peter Bonesteel, Saml. Brackenridge, Daniel Blevins, William Bosher, Richard Boynton, Micajah Burnett, Achilles Bruce, Alexander Brinckley, Jonathan Bean, John Boyett, Hugh Bracken, Harvey Bradley, Samuel G. Boyd, James Bonner, Robt. Bond, William Boice, William Boice, Chancy Benedict, Stephen Beard, Walter R. Basdell, Levi Bradley, Joseph Boyce, Robert Bowie, Mansfield Burrill, William A. Brownson, Hiram Burton, Abraham Burrows, Eleazor Boyce, John Bowen, James Bosworth, Thomas Booth, Eli Booth, Nathaniel Bird, John Bradley, James Birch, Lewis Belrose, Warren Benton, Burnell Bond, Thomas B. Benson, Thomas Buchannon, Solomon Boggs, Peter Bibo, Bolling Billings, Solomon Bradshaw, William Bean, John Brown, Thomas Berrian, William Bradley, William Blake, George Black, John Benson, William Brown, David Burnsides, Ezra Bush, Bayne S. Berry, Shadrack Britt, Andrew Brinthinger, Ann Burke, Calvin Bills, Daniel Birch, Richard Biddle, Amos Benedict, William Beasley, John Blacksbee, John Bosford, Jacob Brown, Charles Beasley, Samuel Buckley, Davd. Cadderman, John Bispham, John Bevans, Robert W. Beans, Jacob Brockhart, John Bonner, Evert Berger, Peter Betting, William Burman, George Burgess, Lewis Beville, John Bender, Hiram Belt, Edmund Belote, Rufus Call, Richd. Bell, Allen Blew alias Blue, Nathn. Blasdell, Isaac Beard, John Boden, David Beas, John Boern, John Beeson, John Bellow alias Blue, George Beatty, Jacob Bear, Hazen Bedel, Vevan Beck, William Bulfinch, Robert Browning, Henry Brown, Benjamin F. Button, Shadrich Briggs, William Cain, Wm. Burns, John Buckanen, Daniel Butler, George Brogdon, Andrew Burns, John Brooks, William Brinckley, Joseph Brown, John B. Burke, Francis Briston, Greenbury Brazier, Benjamin Brears, William Bryant, William Cadwell, James Buswell, Henry Bross, Timothy Clark, William Cheatham, Martin Carol, William Chamberlain, Joseph Cobb, John Crane, William Butler, Elijah Brown, John Burner, Micajah Butler, Sidney Brocket, Samuel Burns, John Burd, Leonard Bullock, Hiram Bronson, John Brewer, John Cox,

(Military Bounty Lands Continued)
George Brand, Richard Brandham, John Brant, Thomas Brazier, William Brazier, James Brerding, William Bresee, Orvis Call, Archd. Brewer, William Brian, William Bridges, Robert Briggs, Richard Briggs, James Bright, Jesse Brimer, William Brimer, Abraham E. Brown, Christian Brown, Daniel Brown, Thomas F. Britton, Jno. Brockhart, John Bryson, David Caderman, James Burner, Stephen Burk, Danl. Burbank, Stephen Bunnel, Brucer Bullard, Samuel Bulfinch, Edward Burk, Willis Burn, Joseph Burrow, James B. Brown, Mathew Brown, Mathias Brown, Robert Caldwell, Reuben Brown, Samuel Brown, Samuel R. Brown, Henry Butler, Jacob Caderman, Benjamin Cadle, John Burrows, Thomas Brown, Joshua Bryant, John Brynson, Michael Cahill, Stephen Burwell, Calvin Call, Charles Call, Ezra D. Call, Benjamin R. Christian, Henry Burkett, John Burnes, John Burruss, John S. Burton, Willand Burton, Abel Callis, David Callis, George Carter, John B. Champlain, Isaac Green Chappel, John Clark, Jesse Cochran, David P. Cobert, Stephen Cobb, Samuel Chard, Wallace Carpenter, Henry Chance, Benjamin Davis, George Day, Samuel Dayton, Abraham Dewitt, John Cunningham, Asa Edwards, Charles Floyd, John Farrell, John B. Fisher, Cornelius Evans, Thomas Charlton, Nash Calvert, Jesse Calvert, John Campbell, Benjamin Cobb, Elijah Close, Silly H. Clisby, Rueben Clarke, Torance Conner, Spencer Collins, Nathaniel Cole, Swain Cox, Thomas Dickenson, Samuel Currier, Thomas Dougherty, William Childers, John Cameron, Betsy Camp, Mary Campbell, William Campbell, Robert Campbell, Moses Canada, John Canny, Barnett Canny, Thadeus Canfield, Elijah Cantrell, Thomas Claibourne, John Cline, Henry Cline, James Clifford, George Clifford, Guy Clarke, Abner Chandler, Jacob Chandler, Daniel Cramlish, Eli Davis, Daniel Ellington, Harrison Foster, Pamelia Fletcher, Agnes Everett, James Gibson, Levi Garrett, Thomas Franklin, Thadeus Canfield, Elijah Cantrell, Ebenezer Capon, Cornelius D. Cargill, Nathanl. Capon, Jonathan Carley, James B. Carrol, Warren Cleveland, William Cowan, Jonathan Cook, Hiram Daniel, William Carley, William Carlisle, George Carlton, Thompson Carnham, John Claborn, Robt. Cissna, Elmire Caswell, Joel Denton, Daniel Davidson, Harrison Flower, Samuel Clark, John Cawley, Asa Caswell, Thomas M. Carter, Benjamin Abner Carter, Francis Carr, John Chase, Benjamin Clarkson, David Cotterman, Moses Cooper, Will Combs, Samuel Dill, Solomon English, Joel Elwell, James Carlton, John Carmedy, Thompson Carnahan, Duff Chadwell, R. B. Carpenter, Cyrus Carr, Redden Carr, Obediah Carrick, Hamilton Carrol, Daniel Carrol, James Carrol, James Crawford, Anthony Craft, Dennis Dalrymple, Daniel Earl, John Drury, John P. Gates, Hezekiah Gardiner, Alexander Furguson, Andrew Hall, John Gordon, John Hendrick, Overton Harris, Eli Lovelace, Peter Carson, Abner Carter, Andrew Clark, Solomon Ciders, Westley Christian, Stephen Cheatham, Samuel Duggins,

(Military Bounty Lands Continued)

Thomas Carty, Thomas Casey, Warren Cato, Caleb Caton, Robt. M. Caughey, Peter Caulk, Benjamin Chadwick, Ralph Chambers, Gilbert Chamberlain, Young Chamberlain, Solomon Chambliis, Zachariah Chapman, Anthony Charey, George Chavers, Kinchion Chestnut, Absolom Chrisfield, William Chrisfield, Benjamin R. Christian, Harvey Church, John K. Church, Betsey Clark, Moses M. Clanahan, Charles Clark, John M. Clark, Tho. Clark, Carpen Clarke, James Clarke, John Clarke, Parsons Clarke, William Clarke, Charles Clary, Stephen Clement, John Clerk, Thomas Cleveland, Samuel Cooksey, Danl. Coolman, Levi Cox, Andrew R. Crary, William Creamer, Silas Crawford, Jonathan Crow, Arthur Cornish, Cornelius Cooper, Thomas Cowan, Joseph Cozart, Frederick H. Countryman, Henry Crittenden, Jeremiah Connel, James A. Crowder, Bryan Cross, Henry Cronk, Samuel Deal, Julien Davis, Cornelius Davis, Archibald Davis, James Cushman, Michael Coon, Timothy Copeland, Wm. Coolman, Samuel W. Corbit, Eli Derrickson, John Cutler, John Cummings, John Crozier, Simon Corade, Isaac Cormack, Cyprean Cornish, Hiram Corwin, George Colwell, James Criddle, Jacob Creesey, Robert Crank, Solomon Craft, John Cochran, Mary Cochran, Nicholas F. Cocke, David Cookendaffer, Willis Cook, Thomas Cook, Hannah Conyers, William Corser, Watts Corwin, John Costley, Samuel Coulter, John Cottman, Ephraim Cowan, David Y. Cockran, John Crady, Jacob Deboard, George Cutting, James Crumlish, Joseph Davidson, Josiah Edwards, Richard Eaton, William Duncan, Asa Hazeltine, Henry Haskins, Chancey Cowles, Hugh Crayton, John Conyers, John Cody, Benjamin Cox, George Combs, Eli Collins, Hugh Craig, John Day, Oliver Emmerson, Peter Eller, Benjamin Fitch, Benjamin Farrington, Ignatius Gatewood, David Gilbert, William Hammond, Seth Hall, Benjamin Guinn, Joseph Hemmerly, George Heaton, James Cramlish, Philip R. Cook, John Conner, Absolem Conklin, John Coffman, Alex. J. Colbert, Aggy Cole, Aaron Crandell, Amasa Crane, Chancy Crane, Luther Crane, Wm. Davis, James Earsley, James Edington, Gideon English, Sally Crane, Ezra B. Crapo, Henry Cole, Morris Cole, Eliza Flisher, John Figg, Geo. B. Craft, William Creelay, William B. Cole, Enoch Coleby, Henry Collins, John Cook, John Colson, Eleazor M. William Dabbs, Daniel Cutler, George B. Curtis, Joseph E. Collins, George K. Cook, Paul Cook, Peter Cook, Wm. Eddy, James Dyer, William Eaty, Danl. Coleman, William Coleman, Francis Collier, Durham Collins, John Collins, Wm. Collins, Samuel Colson, Nicholas Columbex, David Conchev, Wm. Dice, Geo. Duke, William Dudley, Edward Edwards, Darius N. Cowles, Josiah Conner, Thomas Davis, John Daily, John Curry, Martin Culp, Joseph G. Dowsett, James Egelston, Stephen P. Connel, John B. Congden, Samuel Conger, George Conner, Levi Conner, Mathew Conner, Henry Conway, Hiram Coody, Austin Cook, Mary David, Mathias Dibler, Daniel Cutler, Saml. Davis, Wm. Dugan,

(Military Bounty Land Continued)

Joseph Crowder, Amos Dixon, William Diamond, Abraham Davis, Joseph Deboard, John Day, Samuel Currier, sr., Edwin Davis, Nicholas Edington, Charles Dougherty, Abraham Doty, William Donaldson, Samuel Emmons, Perry Edwards, Jesse Eason, David Davis, Charles Davis, Edmund Davis, Ephraim Davis, Jeremiah Davis, James Davis, Jacob Davis, John Davis, Frederick Denio, Lewis Davis, William C. Crowder, Simeon P. Crumb, William Cumpton, Moses Davis, Willis Davis, John Day, William Dexter, Daniel Crumlish, Joseph Crushaw, Ephraim Cummings, William Dalton, David B. Dayton, David Dearborn, Thomas R. Debnam, Jacob F. Cunningham, James Curlett, Rueben Currier, William Curry, Henry Curtis, Cyprean Cutting, Jacob Deboard, Charles Dewitt, William Degrew, Nathaniel Deland, Rochard Demony, W. G. Evans, Cyrus K. Francis, John Fraill, Francis Fontain, R. J. Head, Nathaniel Henderson, John Huff, Benjamin Howard, W. G. Hood, Rowland Denton, Joseph R. Denner, Jonathan Devaughn, Michael Daily, George Daffen, Michael Daily, Daniel Dingley, James Dishon, John Dilmore, Caleb Dill, Wilson Dickson, Wm. Dickenson, David Devore, James Deshon, Mahlon Dalrymple, Wm. R. Daniels, Heirs of James Dakin, Abiah Daman, Onis Damerson, Robert Daniel, Timothy O. Daniels, Henry Derby, James Darden, Fredk. Dauson, Daniel Davidson, John Davidson, Alfred Davis, Robert Davidson, Amasa Davis, Ananias Davis, Rebecca Edick, Ezekiel A. East, John A. Eastland, Levin Dize, Arthur Dobbin, James Dobbins, Henry Eastman, James Dow, Rock Durway, George Eaton, John R. Easton, John Fitzpatrick, John Fox, Charles I. Downing, David Doe, Henry Doinburgh, Stephen Dolby, Issac O. Donald, John Dominick, Dennis Dolph, Coleman Duncan, John Elliott, James Dougherty, Gillfield Dinally, Greenbury Finn, George L. Ferrell, Samuel Fox, John Done, John Durgen, Lewis Duncan, Lyman Dorsett, Lettice Ederty, Joseph Doneway, James Dugan, George Donoho, Clement R. Dosey, Thomas B. Dosey, Wm. Duchan, Clement R. Dossey, John Doty, Joseph Doty, Benjamin Dow, James Eckford, Elisha Edwards, Thomas T. Doty, George W. Drake, John Thomas Egelston, Dennis Dougherty, Elisha E. Elam, James Foster, James Floyd, Israel Flemming, Zachariah Ferrel, Edward Dougherty, Peter Dougherty, John Doughton, W. J. McElroy, Timothy Lucas, John Love, John Lindsey, Samuel Dowell, Jeremiah Douglass, Joseph Dowling, Peter Dowling, G. W. Martin, Peter Dowling, Jonathan Downes, James Downs, John Duboy, Lyman Dowsett, Willey Doyal, James K. Drake, Ebenezer Drennon, Aaron Dressier, Warren Driver, Elisha Dubois, James Dwell, Larkin Duett, Patrick Duffy, John C. Duke, Sullivan Dunbar, John Duncanson, Jabez Dunham, John Dunn, Jeremiah Flinn, Thomas L. Dunn, William Dunnan, Walter P. Dunnivant, John Dunton, Peleg Dunton, Elisha Edwards, Thomas Edwards, James Ekelston, John Thomas Ekelston, Jacob Ellinger, Noah Ellis, Coemad T. Elmendorf, Joseph Emery, Reuben Emmerson,

(Military Bounty Land Continued)
Emanuel Eomer, David Erskine, Joseph Erskine, Rachael Erwen, John K. Erwin, John Eamon, John E. Essleiver alias Silver, Benjamin Evans, Daniel Evans, David Evans, Henry Evans, Wm. Evans, Joseph Evans, Wright Evans, Frederick Eveland, Moses Eveland, John Everett, Philip Everett, Elisha Ewen, Matthew Ewing, John Ewen, James Ewing, Balsam Ezell, Jack Fairfield, Peter Fait, Oliver Fales, Joseph Ferguson, Thos. H. Ferguson, W. B. Farnsworth, George Farrell, Robert Farrell, William Forbes, Daniel Farry, Jacob Faulkner, Daniel Fauy, Heirs of Henry Fears, Jacob Felty, Henry Felty, Leonard Felty, James C. Ferguson, Joseph Ferguson, Thos. H. Ferguson, John Fields, John O. Ferrell, James Ferrell, George Fields, William Gage, Judah Gage, Joseph Giles, William Gates, James Fry, William Garrison, Francis Fox, William Fowler, Thomas Fowler, Henry Fountain, James Gillaspie, Seth Gerry, Jonathan Garrett, Wm. Gann, Ambrose Gail, James Gaines, John Ferrison, David Foot, louis Filluet, Leonard Finch, Jonathan Floyd, Wm. Foster, Wm. Foley, Job Fish, Francis Fisher, Frederick Fisher, Mary Ann Flemming, Conrad Fergus, Gamuel B. Fessenden, Lemuel Fisher, Jasper Gates, Philip Fry, John G. Gale, Peter Gloyd, Oliver Fletcher, Jonathan Gale, Roderick Glover, John Glenn, Martin Fisher, Asa Fisk, James Fitzgerald, Alexander Foster, George Ford, Richd. Fitzjeffery, Rees Fitzpatrick, Isaac Galligher, James Flemming, Eliza Flesher, John Flesher, Guin Fletcher, Gersham Flick, Richard Fling, John Flisher, Beldad Flower, James Floid, John Gamble, Nathan Gammell, William Hall, John Foster, Alexr. Fossett, Rodk. R. Foot, Zion Flowers, Daniel Gardiner, John G. Gardiner, Simeon Gale, Reuben Garlick, John Gibson, Ephraim Francis, George Francis, John Franklin, John Franks, Lewis Franklin, Olney Franklin, Bruet Franks, Rodney French, John French, Eleazer Frary, Benjamin Frary, Thomas French, Moses Freeman, Hugh Freighner, William Frith, Aaron Frost, Nehemiah Frost, John Fryer, Henry Fuller, John Fulton, Jonas Furgason, Larkin Furguson, Alexander Furguson, Abraham Garnett, Everard Garrett, John Garrett, Henry Garring, Peter Gates, Eleanor Garvey, Joseph Garvey, Thomas Garuin, Joseph Gatling, James Gaurtney, William D. Gentry, Thomas German, David Gettis, James Gibson, Thomas Gibson, Gilman Gilchel, John Gill, Anty, Gillegan, Sherwood Ginn, Edward Ginnings, Thomas Gladhill, Moses Gleeton, James Glisson, James Hall, William Gloster, Robert Glover, Henry Guffy, Benjamin Haines, James Grimes, Bezabiel Grandy, Zachariah Hagins, Jacob Guyer, Andrew Gregg, Frederick Goodwin, Joel Hancock, James Hammond, Samuel Grace, Lee Gordon, John Hamlett, Joshua Hawks, Samuel Hendricks, Thomas Harris, William Hanna, John Grover, Thomas Hamby, William Haden, Abraham Goble, Stephen Goble, Vincent C. Graves, Fredk. Hahn, Adam Grant, Samuel Heath, John Hart, Daniel Hughes, James Hudson, Josiah Howard, John Hunt, Jacob

(Military Bounty Land Continued)
Hall, Burley Godsey, Burton Godsey, John Godson, Warren Goff, William Hayes, John Henry, David Hart, William Harris, John Harper, Sanford Hughes, Hezekiah Hudson, John Hurley, Samuel Hill, William Jackson, Henry Jones, Nathaniel Leonard, Jacob King, John Lane, Charles McCarty, James Lindsey, James Gray, Edward C. Goggin, Eliza Golden, John Gonier, Archer Goodson, Luther Goodridge, Samuel W. Gorbit, John L. Gordon, Baziel Gore, Joseph Gorse, Thomas Gorley, John A. Gorton, Jeremiah Gove, Henry Gosman, Jacob Goulding, William Goulding, Daniel W. Gowan, Philip Gowan, Charles Gowen, Charles Gowen, Robert Gragg, Christian Gower, George Graham, James Grandy, Samuel Grapevine, James Grant, Ichabod Graves, Isaac Graves, Henry Grenwood, William Gray, Nathaniel Graham, Jonathan B. Green, Isaiah D. Green, Heirs of Martin Green, Robert Green, Uriah B. Green, William Green, Silas Greeman, Philo Gregory, Lewis Grey, William Gregory, Isaac Griffin, Patrick Griffin, John Groshong, William Griffin, Conrad Haney, James Hance, John O. Hans, Benjamin Hammond, Charles Hammock, William Hamley, Duncan Hamlett, John H. Hamilton, Haunce Hamilton, Thomas Hamblet, John Halterman, John Hallock, William Halley, John Hall, Randolph Grimes, Abraham Groesbeck, Peter W. Groesbeck, Gines Groves, Abraham Gruindike, Eldred Gulledge, Jonathan Hagins, Sarah Gulledge, Beverly Gunnell, William Guynn, John Heath, Martin Gunsalus, Joseph Gurrier, Robert Hall, Martin Hall, Joseph Hall, Joseph Hall, Joel Hall, James Hall, James S. Hall, David Hall, Patsey Halbert, Keider Hail, Wm. Hays, Stephen Hagerman, John Hagan alias Agan, James Hankerson, Eaton Harwood, Jacob Harwood, Aaron Haskins, Samuel Haskins, Mark Hathcock, Willias Hathcock, Robert Hatton, Christian L. Hauver, Isaac Hauver, Isaac O. Haverland, George Hawks, John Haydon, Jesse D. Haydon, Joshua Haymes, Ausbon Haynes, Mich. Haynes, Lawrence C. Head, Smith Heath, Thomas Heald, Thomas Harrington, Jabel Heath, Peter Heathcocke, Nathaniel Harvey, John Hankeran, George Hankins, James Hankins, James M. Hanks, John Hanna, John Hannah, James Hannon, Philip Hansell, John Hanson, John Hanup, Robert Hany, Isaac Harbenson, Jeremiah Hardison, Jeremiah Harbour, William Heaton, John Hedge, Joel Hardy, Jethro Hardee, Mitchel Hardwick, Younger Hardwick, Benjamin Hardy, Ebenr. Hardy, James Hardy, Hamlon Hargrove, Peter Harman, Amos Harper, Daniel Harper, Thomas Harper, John Henderson, Edward Hedges, Jacob Heeler, David Heeter, Edward Hartwell, Lethro Harrell, Bennett Harrelson, John Harrington, Alexander Harris, George Harris, Lucy Harris, Moses Harris, William Harris, Jane Heisey, Peter Helmes, William P. Harris, Jacob Helsley, James Helton, William Helton, James Hemphill, John Hemmingway, Robt. Hendricks, Caleb Heninger, Jas. Henry, Peter Henley, John Henley, Jonathan Henshaw, Nicholas Heter, Zacahriah Harris, Jeremiah Harrison, William Harris, Richard

(Military Bounty Land Continued)
Harrod, Winens H. Harris, Isaac Harrison, Leonard Harrison, Charles Hart, John Hartman, Wiley Harty, James Harvey, Hugh Hevitt, Nathan B. Harvey, Isaac Hester, Silas Herron, John Herron alias Harren, Patrick Kavenaugh, Zachariah Jones, Wm. Mathews, David Mason, Sherwood Martin, Richard Morris, John Parker, Joshua Overton, Alexander Patterson, William G. Orr, John Pollard, Asa Pratt, Ezra Porter, James H. Roberts, John Roach, William Rice, John D. Reed, Zacheus Richardson, Jesse Ruble, Erastus Saunders, Abraham Smith, Eleazer Stone, John Stewart, David Howard, Philemon Hurt, Henry Hurst, Leonard Hurry, Edward Howard, William Heyser, Joel Hurley, Joseph W. Hibbard, John Hoveritts, John Houston, Charles W. House, Asa Holton. Ensign Hickly, Fredrick Hickman, John Hicks, Findley Hiddleton, Elizabeth Higbee, William Higbee, Ansel Higgans, Elijah Higgins, Charles H. Hilbert, Oliver Hildreth, Henry Hill, James Hill, William Hill, William B. Hill, Frederick Hummell, Peter Hille, John Hindman, William Hines, Abraham Howe, Otis Hinsdale, James Hissam, Comfort Hix, William Hix, Joseph Hobbs, Lewis Hobbs, Nicholas Hocke, William Hodge, James Hogard, John Hogarty, Josiah Hoge, Temple Hoit, Philip Holbert, Daniel Holden, Henry Holden, John Holden, William Holloway, John Holloway, John W. Holding, John Holderfield, John Holden, John Holly, John Holman, Hugh Holmes, Solomon Holmes, James Holmes, Daniel Holt, James Holt, John Hopkins, Nathaniel Holt, Richd. Holterfield, Joseph Horn, Peter Host, William Hosack, Joseph Johnson, Bradford Jennings, Wm. Ijams, William Hyde, John Jewell, George Lee, Daniel Keith, Henry Maxfield, Charles Mann, Michael Myers, James Moore, Benjamin Miller, Samuel M. Palmer, William Oliver, David Price, John Philips, Joseph Plummer, Archibald Rutherford, John Sherron, Jonathan Howard, Reuben Howard, Henry R. Howe, John Huggs, John W. Howell, Thomas Howell, Willis Howington, James Huffy, Daniel Hubbard, Thomas Hubbard, John Hudson alias Hutson, W. McElroy, Samuel Hudson, William Hudson, Calvin Hurd, William J. Huff, William Hunter, Elijah Hunter, William Hunt, Oliver Humphreys, Adam Huffman, Jacob Huffman, James Huges, Johnson Hummer, Aaron Hughes, Anna Hughes, James Hughes, Eliphalet B. Hunt, Richd. Hughes, John K. Hughlett, Yarrett Hughlett, John Humphreys, Mathias Humphries, James Humes, Henry Hunt, Ethan Hulbert, Isaac Hulbert, Walter Hulen, Jonathan Hunt, Philip D. Hunt, Theodorick Hunt, Francis Joy, John Kane, Jonathan Jones, John Lee, Jonathan Laurence, Bartholomew Lenham, John Jackson, Thomas Jenkins, John Husah, Jesse Huskey, John Kay, Thomas Huskey, Amos Hutchin, Benjamin Johnson, Simon Jenkins, Abraham Johnson, Alexander Johnson, William Jackett, Samuel Kester, Lewis Jenks, William Jennings, Thomas Jent, William Henry Jones, John Irwin, John Huttonhow, Peter Kays, Thomas Jones, Benjamin Jacobs, Nathaniel Jordain, Solomon Johnson,

(Military Bounty Land Continued)
James Jett, Crampkin Jewell, Amasiah Johnson, Amos Johnson, Enoch Johnson, Hanna Johnson, Isaac Johnson, James Johnson, John Johnson, Jonathan O. Jonathan, Joshua Johnson, Nicholas Johnson, Samuel Johnson, William Johnson, William M. Johnson, Joseph Joiner, Charles Jones, Henry T. Jones, Jarvis Jones, John Jones, Joshua Jones, Levin Jones, Robert Jones, Robert T. P. Jones, William Jones, Wood Jones, Peter Joseph, Jacob Kene, Benjamin Jourdan, Patrick Kalvay, Ephraim Kanada, John Kavanaugh, Polly Kay, Noah Kester, Eliakim Hutchings, Henry Hutchins, Samuel Hutchinson, Saul Hutchinson, Constant Hyde, Sewall Hutchinson, Thomas Hutchinson, John Hutson, David C. Irvine, Isaac Ijams, Amaziah Ingraham, Levi Inman, Charles Irones, William Ives, James Ivey, Joseph Jacklin, Stephen L. Leforge, Gabriel Jackson, Green T. Jackson, James Jackson, Joseph Jackson, Moses Jackson, Samuel Jackson, Joseph Jay, Sheldon Jackson, Elisha Jacobs, William Jacobs, John Lea, Samuel James, William James, Gideon Jerrolld, Joseph Jasmine, Peter Jasmine, Peter Jasmyne, Thomas Jefferes, Daniel Lane, Richard Jeffers, John Jeffrey, Drury Jenkins, Hannah Jenkins. John B. Jenkins, William B. McDugell, James Nelson, Mtthew McGallaspie, Laurence Lewis, Joseph Lewis, John W. Lewis, Wm. Leach, Isaac Lewis, Henry Lewis, Elijah Lewallen, John Levi, Alexander Lester, Jacob W. Lepper, David Leonard, Frederick Lefford, George Kreps, Joseph Koile, Joseph Knowles, James Knight, Daniel Knight, John Kneeland, Bastian Kneedler, John Leeman, Sumpter Land, Joseph Land, George Lancisicus, Jacob Lancaskes, David Leonard, Alfred Leonard, Jacob Lentz, Henry Lentz, Jacob Lents, Eli Lenderman, Hiram McDonald, Alexander McFadion, Reuben Ladd, James Lafayette, George Leferry, John King, Benjamin Laird, John Laird, William Laird, John Lang, Heirs of Saml. Lake, Jesse Lakeman, Moses M. Lakin, William Lancaster, Saxton Lamphier, Michael Lampart, John F. Lambert, John Lamb, Sihon Keith, Patrick Kelly, Samuel Kendal, Samuel Kendley, Eliphalet Kennison, Samuel Keyes, Flemming Keyser, Joseph Keywood, Christopher Kilby, John Kiley, Robert Layne, William Kimble, Elijah Kimbrough, Abm. Kiner, David Kiner, Conrad King, Elizabeth King, Ignatius King, Michael Leavitt, Thos. King, Thos. G. King, William King, Hugh Kirkpatrick, William Kingrey, Moses Kitchen, Drew Kittrell, David Klipper, George Klingman, Joseph Klipper, Bastian Kneedler, William J. Lane, Joseph Leech, Richard Lee, Lydia Lee, James Lee, Harvey Lawton, Andrew Lawson, James Lawrence, James Larkin, John McAllister, Archibald Lucas, Daniel Lookingbill, Russel Larrabee, Charles Laugherty, Joseph Lark, Joseph Larencell, Robt. Lapping, William Mason, William McCrumb, Lewis McCary, Robt. Lappin, John Lappin, Micajah Lansford, Edward Lanier, John Laning, Clement Lanier, Peter Languel, Thomas Langrell,

(Military Bounty Land Continued)
Andrew Landroche alias Landroff, Pierre Landroche, Timothy Langael, Isaac Lane, Elhanah Lane, John Lyons, Thomas Lyons, Patrick Maxfield, William Martin, Joseph Morris, Stokely B. Parker, Dominick Pike, David Roach, Paschal Roberts, Mathew Robison, Benjamin Smith, Charles Shoemaker, Claiborn Scott, Nathaniel Stone, William Stearnes, David Staples, Vanlentine Thompson, Samuel Thomas, Elizabeth Taylor, Enoch Ward, John Williams, Martha White, Francis M. Young, George Williamson, Thomas Lewis, Gabriel Licose, Baker Liggett, James Lillard, Daniel Lincoln, Thomas Lincoln, Francis Lindsey, Joel Long, John Lingar, Noah Lingard, Elijah Lingo, Alpheis Linsey, Wm. Linsey, John Lishmore, Charles Liswell, Thomas Liswell, John Lockhart, Isaac Littlehale, Jacob Littlefield, Andrew Lockie, John Loftlin, John Logan, Philip Logan, Peter Loge, Pierce Lokey, Giles London, Reuben Long, James Longwith, John McCoy, Josiah Longwith, Samuel Lontz, Danl. Loomis, Samuel Loree, Philander Loomis, Samuel Louge, James Love, David Lovelace, George Lovegrove, Richard Lovering, George Lowther, William Lucas, Ashael Lucas, Wm. Luckett, James Lucky, Abner Lynch, John Lynch, William Ludlam, Daniel Luffman, Stephen Lufkin, John Lumberson, Charles D. Lumsden, James Lansford, Thomas McGee, Joseph McField, James McFee, James McFarland, Daniel McFarland, Samuel McEwen, Thomas McElliott, John McDugell, Daniel McDuff, John M. McDonald, Francis McDonald, William McCollough, Jacob Lysinzer, Robert Lytle, William Mashburn, William P. Marshall, James R. McMullen, Jesse McAnally, John McBay, Robert McAnmon alias McCammon, Jesse McAnally, James McBride, Thomas McBroom, John McCaffel, John McDade, William McCollester, Peter McDermott, Elijah McCurdy, Thos. McCall, James McCafferty, John McCallister, John McCannah, William McCreary, Isaac McCarty, John McCarty, James McClare, John McCarty, John McClary, Hally McClendon, David McConchey, Asa Mediste, David McConchey, David McCoy, Hugh McCoy, John Mcoy, Anguish McCra, John McCrea, James McCready, Corns. McCurdy, Daniel McCurdy, Tarlton Murphy, Thomas Morgan, Joshua Mills, Jacob Ostrander, Alexander Nichols, Sarah Porterfield, Miles Portico, Moses Richardson, Mathew Rhea, Phillip Russell, Job Snell, Samuel Turner, Thomas Ward, George Washington Wallace, Edward Watts, Martin C. Whitman, Samuel Wilson, John Mason, Nehemiah Messick, Caleb Merritt, James W. Merrit, Zachariah Malin, Nicholas McGenity, Charles McGiffin, Paul McGinnis, Michl. McGraw, John McGuire, Robert McGuire, James McGuyer, Reuben McHawes, Samuel McIlvain, Robert McIntire, John Mann, Abraham Maronex, Ephraim Marsh, Joseph Marsh, Edward Martin, Daniel McIntosh, Anthony McKnight, James McKain, Levi Melton, Solomon McKenna, John McKenney, Patrick McKenny, Wm. McKim, James McKinley, Michl. McKinley, David McKonoghy, William McLaughlin, James McLaughlin, John McLean, George McManing,

(Military Bounty Land Continued)
John McMillan, Salley Merrill, John McMillen, Hugh McMullen,
Neal McMullen, David McMurphy, John McNeilly, Spencer Macon,
Gideon H. Macon, Daniel McQuilkin, Andrew McWharter, William
Maddan alias Madin, Samuel Maddox, John Magee, Jacob Melvin,
Jesse H. Mallory, Mitchel Mahen, William Menard, Geo. Manes,
Abel Manchester, Samuel Mandell, Stephen Mann, Leonard Manon,
John Mansfield, James Mapes, John Marable, Agur B. Marchent,
Louis Marie, John Marks, Nathaniel Marks, Christopher Marson,
Eleanor Marstellar, Dory Martin, Elijah Martin, John Martin.
Henry Martin, James Martin, Rhodeham Martin, Samuel Martin,
Thomas Martin, Thomas Martine, David G. Mason, Laban Mason,
Willard Mastick, Samuel Matheney, Drury Mathews, Absalom
Melton, John Mathews, Thomas Mathews, Simon Mathias, Patrick
Maxfield, Levi Mattoon, Henry Maxfield, Orran Maybrray, John
Measer, Jacob Means, James Meader, Basil Medley, John Meeker,
John Melder, Peter Meloy, James Melton, Jno. Mencher alias
Minshall, John L. Meredith, John Morgan, Paul Morgan, Elijah
Morley, Westley Morr, Jacob B. Morrill, John Morrill, Daniel
Morris, David Morris, Ephraim Morris, H. J. Morris, Hezekiah
Morris, Isaish Morris, Jacob J. R. Morris, Mayhew Morris,
Morris Morris, Timothy Morris, William Morris, David Morrow,
Moses Morrison, David Morrison, Newbury Morse, Newbury Morse,
Patrick Morton, Philip Mosher, Polly Mosier, Harris Mount,
Thomas Mothershed, Thomas Mulany, Ananis Milford, William T.
Neiter, Ambrose Munday, Andrew Mundel, Samuel Murfey, Matty
Murdel, William Muroe, Samuel Murphey, William Murphey, Isaac
Murrow, Daniel Muse, Jacob Musser, Charles Myers, John Myers,
Peter Myers, Francis Metavia, Allen Miles, William Miles,
Elizabeth Miller, George Miller, Jacob Miller, James Miller,
John Miller, Rebecca Miller, Ezekiel Millikin, Alfred Moore,
Sterling T. Millikin, Aaron Millrany, Gideon Mills, James,
Menan Mills, Alexr. Milton, Robert Minott, Hugh Montgomery,
Jno. Minshall alias Mencher, Thomas Minshall, Richard Moise,
Thomas Mitchell, James Moite, John Monroe, James Montgomery,
Noble Montgomery, Richd. Montgomery, David Moon, James Moon,
John Moon, Thomas Moon, James Mooney, Allen Moore, Auguste
Moore, Hugh A. Moore, John B. Moore, Joseph Moore, Michael
Moore, Martha Moore, Thomas Moore, William Moore, Wm. Moran,
Mary Morehouse, William Morau, William Morehead, Thomas H.
Moreland, John Moreland, Timothy Moorhouse, Chs. Moorhouse,
Charles Morgan, James Morgan, James W. Morgan, Jeremiah W.
Morgan, Henry Oxley, Mary Nelson, Reuben Owings, Ephraim F.
Nichols, David Parker, James Parker, George Nix, John Otis,
James Nesbit, William Newsom, James Newton, Francis Nicholas,
John Nichols, Joseph Plumb, Stephen Pierce, Nicholas Perry,
Adolphus Preble, William L. Richards, William Rainwater, Hugh
Robinson, John H. Nichols, Elenor Osborn, Zadock Parish, John
Page, Peggy Nichols, Samuel Nichols, Noah Pain, Hugh Ormon,

(Military Bounty Land Continued)
Albert Patterson, Jeremiah Pascall, Elijah Partin, Anderson Parker, James M. Nicholson, John Nicholson, Seth Nickerson, William Nixon, John Noble, Daniel Nock, Stephen Nock, Zuriel Palmer, William P. Owens, John Owens, Evan Owens, John Colear Outerbridge, Randolph Nolan, Mordicai Nolen, Benjamin Page, Joseph Nolin, John B. Nonty, Elkiakim Norman, James Norman, James Norris, John B. Norris, William Northover, Eli Olds, John Northrap, Miles Northum, Asa Northup, David Nute, Fredk. Nowlin, Electus Oakes, William O'Bannion, Luke O'Brien, Amos Ogden, Richd. O'Brien, Thos. O'Connor, Comfort O'Diorm, John O'Neill, Mathew O'Donnell, Benjamin Odum, Patrick O'Fling, James Ogden, Orandatus Olds, Joshua Oliver, Amos Olivet, Wm. B. Oliver, Henry O'Neil, Jacob Orison, Hugh Ormon, Ebenezer Orn, Hugh R. Orr, Isaac Osburn, Wilson S. Osborne, Pharis S. Palmer, John Ostrander, Tunis Ostrander, John O'Vail, Edward Palmer, Harriet Overton, Willis Overton, Lewis Parker, James Parks, Daniel Paetzman, Ephraim Palmer, Richard Palmer, John Palmeteer alias Palmetier, David Percells, Burwell Parker, Azariah Parish, Stephen Parker, Stokely W. Parker, William Parker, Henry Parkest, Thomas Parkinson, Jacob Parnell, John Parrish, Francis Parozett, Samuel Parrish, Tho. Parrott, John Parsell, David Parsell, David Parsons, Moses Pierce, William Pierce, Simon Pierce, Jeremiah Piersoll, William Piffle, Ann Prescott, James Patterson, John Patterson, Alexr. T. Patton, Matthew Patton, David Paul, Jesse Paul, Simeon Paul, William Paxton, Agnes Payne, Benjamin D. Payne, Moses Payne, Robert A. Payne, Absolom Peace, Thomas Pead, Jeremiah Pearce, John Pease, John Peavy, Andrew Peck, Jacob Peck, Edward Pennell, Thomas Pell, Alexander Peeples, Edward Penny, Jacob Penturf, Ira Penny, John Peoples, Thomas Peoples. Lydie Perkins, John B. Ponts, Thomas Perry, William Perry, James Peters, Warner Peters, Henry Peterson, Mason Pettes, Benjamin Pettest, Hugh Porter, Heirs of Thomas Pike, George Pine, Darius C. Pinney, Joseph Pine, Charles Pitcher, James Pitt, Constant W. Price, Alexander Price, Nathan S. Prescott, Theo. B. Prentice, John Prentice, Thomas Pratt, Jesse Pratt, Ebenezer Pratt, Charles Prather, James Powers, Daniel Powers, Augustus Powell, Martin Powll, Richard Powell, Lewis Poultett, Nicholas Potter, John Pixley, Zachariah Piver, John D. Plain, Abegail Plummer, Josh Plummer, Peter Poland, Robert Pollan, Joseph Polard, Robert Pollard, Thomas Pollard, John B. Pons, Eunice Pool, Josiah Porter, Andrew Potter, Humphrey, Christian Port, John T. Ray, David Porter, William Pettigrew, Thomas Pettus, William B. Phillips, Jacob Phillips, Alvin Phelps, John S. Pevey, Zaran Phillips, William Pettigrew, Thomas Pettus, Zaran Phillips, Daniel Phinny, William Phippen, James Picett, Lester Picket, Benjamin Pickard, Augustin C. Pierce, Eliakim Pierce, Joseph Pierce, Israel Pierce, Lyman Pierce, George Reese, John Rhea,

(Military Bounty Land Continued)
Elizabeth Price, Francis Price, Hurd Price, Isom Price, John Price, Stephen Price, William Price, William Pringle, Daniel T. Puffer, Peter B. Puckett, John Prunell, John Pully, Wiley Qualls, William Pully, Stephen Purrington, Christian Purth, Thomas Puryear, Benjamin Putney, Andrew Quay, Finch Ragland, Woodson Radford, Paschal Quarles, alias Qualls, John Rampier, Edmund Rainwaters, John Rainwaters, Newson Rainwaters, John G. Randolph, William Ralph, Montice Rampier, Charles Ramsey, Henson Ramsey, Peyton Randolph, Daniel Rardon, Benjamin Ray, Aaron Ray, Mary Ratcliffe, Gardner Raymond, Gilbert Raymond, Jame Raymond, Robert Read, James Reamy, Ephraim Rector, John Rector, William Redman, David Reece, Daniel Reed, Jacob Reed, James Reed, Peter Reed, William Reed, George Reese, Elijah Reider, James Renn, Samuel Rutherford, William Revels, Danl. Reynolds, Nathaniel Reynolds, William Lund Rhea, Jesse Rice, Richard Rhode, Champion, William Rhodes, Daniel Rice, Enock Rice, Gustavus, Peter W. Rice, Thomas Rich, Meavit Richards, Edward W. Richards, John Richards, Athelson Richardson, Amos Ricker, Richoboam Richardson, Sharon Richardson, Charles B. Roberts, Chrisn. Richert, Henry Richmand, William Ricketts, Jason Ricks, John Riddle, Jacob Rider, William Ridley, Miles Riley, James D. Riley, Sarah Riley, Charles Risley, Daniel Ritter, James Roach, Samuel Roach, Dudley Robbins, Patrick Roberts, Issac Roberts, Joab Roberts, Joel Roberts, Ezekiel Russell, Josiah Roberts, Seth Roberts, John Rousseau, James Rouse, Stephen Roberts, Thomas Roberts, Walter Roberts, John Roys, Wiley Roberts, William Roberts, Caleb Robertson, David Robertson, Eli Robertson, John Robertson, Samuel Robertson, Susannah Elizabeth Robertson, William Robertson, Thomas Roy, Daniel Robinson, Gordon Robinson, James Robinson, Washington P. Robinson, John Robinson, Joseph Robinson, Robert Robinson, Patrick Robinson, William Robinson, Willis Robinson, James Robinson, Abraham Rockwell, Jeremiah Rockwell, Robt. Roddam, John H. Roden, William Rodgers, John Roe, Jeremiah T. Rogers, Evan E. Rogers, Isaac Rogers, James Rogers, Patrick Rogers, John Rogers, Thomas Rogers, Thomas P. Rogers, Abel Rogerson. Elijah Rollet, William Rollet, John Romines, Clarissa Root, Austin Root, John Root, James Roots, Thurret Rose, William Rose, James Roseberry, John Roseberry, Aaron Ross, John Ross, William Roseberry, Oliver Rosenquest, Huldah Rouviere, Ralph Rouzed, Bethuel C. Rowell, John Rowell, Abednego I. Roy, Wm. Roy, Samuel Roy, Jacob Ruble, Epaphroditus Rudder, Benjamin Runnyan, Michael Ruggles, Dewey Russell, John Rutherford, Rlisha Ryan, James Rynot, Eldad Sabin, Eliada Sabin, Oliver Sabin, Benjamin Sadler, John St. Clair, Elisha Samuels, John Salmon, John Salkeld, Antoine Salisse, Gideon Salisbury, John Saunders, Samuel Salisbury, Edward Saunders, Abel Saunders, George Sarters, Daniel Sargent, Richard Saunders, Mary Ann

(Military Bounty Land Continued)
Saunders, William   Savacool alias Savercool, Solomon Savary, Deborah Sawyer, Moses Sawyer, Moses Sherwood, Thomas Shevans, Elizabeth Shields, John Shields, Patrick Shields, John Shaw, Robert Shirley, Luther Shivers, Elijah Shockley, Ralph Shaw, John Shoemaker, Peter Shoemaker, George Shuffield, Malachi Sikes, Henry Sikely, Wiley Sikes, Charles S. Simmons, George Simmons, Thomas Simmons, Amos Simons, Benjn. Simpkins, Elijah Sims, Samuel Simpson, Lela Simpkins, Darius Simpkins, James Singleton, John Sims, Robert Singleton, Aquilla Sherrill, Andrew Slater, George Slaughter, James Slip, Catherine Smith, John E. Sliver alias Essleiver, Bryan Sloan, Christian Smith, Thomas Sloan, Elisha Smallwood, John Smart, Abner Smith, Adam Smith, Christian B. Smith, Curtis Smith, Eli Smith, Jeremiah R. Smith, Elisha Smith, George Smith, Henry Smith, Seybert C. Shelton, Hiram Smith, Jacob Smith, James Smith, John Smith, Joshua Smith, Levi Smith, Lewis Smith, Adam Sherline, Isham M. Shell, Mathias Sheran, Byrd Sheppard, Abraham Shephard, Thomas Shelby, Charles Sheffield, William Shed, Seers Shay, Stephen Shaw, Jonathan Shaw, Daniel Shaw, W. Shattuck, Jacob Shank, William Sharpe, Wilson Sharp, Robert Sharp, Abraham Sharp, David Sharp, Richard Shapleigh, Andrew Shannon, Isaac Sessions, Heirs of Ezekiel Sayles, John Scanthing, Dederick Schultze, John Schollar, John Schofield, Henry D. Schoff, Wm. Shanahan, John M. Shallenburgh, Dennis Shaft, George Shafer, W. Shadduck, William Shaddock, John A. Shackles, Merrite M. Sexton, Henry Seymour, John M. Sexton, James Sexton, Henry C. Sevier, Richard Sessums, Samuel Sergeant, James Salomon, Elijah Seely, James Searles, Lewis Sealy, Thos. Scully, John Scott, William Scott, Thomas Scott, Samuel Scott, Jas. Scott, Lemuel Scott, Benjamin Scott, Moses Smith, Thomas Smith, Ira Sommers, Thomas P. Smith, Warren Smith, William Smith, Hiram Smither, Harrison Sneed, Shadrach Snell, Adam Snider, Henry Snow, William Snodgrass, Joseph Snow, Nathn. Snow, Paul Snow, Phares Snow, William Snyder, John Sommers, Peter Sook, John Sorey, Willoughby Sorey, John Southards, Emery Souther, John Spalding, Levin Southern, Isaiah Souther, Daniel Spear, Abel Spencer, Timothy Spear, Joseph C. Spence, Daniel M. Spencer, E. P. Spencer, Joseph Spencer, Thomas Sperling, Jacob Staley, Benjamin Spikes, Moses G. Spivy, Abraham Sprague, Benjamin Sprague, Francis Springer, Jacob Springstead, James Squires, Frederick Squires, John Squires, Edward Stafford, Ann Stibbs, Jacob Staley, Anthony Stall, Hardy Stallings, John Stanley, Herbert Stallings, Nancy Stallins, W. Stallins, John Steele, Robert Stanhope, John Stanley, William Stansberry, Sylvester Stickney, James Stanton, Jesse Stanton, David Staples, Jacob Strickler, Ebenezer Strickland, John Strength, David Stout, Thomas Staples, Turner Stark, Abraham Starns, Jacob Stevens, Thomas H. Stead, Jonathan A. Stearnes, John Stiver, William

(Military Bounty Land Continued)
William Steerman, George Steen, Stephen Step, Jacob Stilts, Giles Stephens, Davis Stephens, John Stephens, John Stinson, John Stephenson, Henry Stevens, James D. Stevens, Alexander Stewart, John I. Stevens, Francis R. Stewart, Isaac Stewart, Robert Stewart, Samuel Stewart, Thomas B. Stewart, William Stewart, William Stickney, John Stileson, Nelly Stillwell, James Stocker, Abel Stockwell, William Stockwell, John Troy, Avery Stoddard, Nathan Stoddard, Berriman Stoker, Wm. Stone, Ebenr. Lock Stone, Asahel Storrs, John M. Stotts, William Straughn, James Stover, Hosea Stratten, Carmill Strickland, John Strope, John Strover, John Stull, William Sturgeon, Wm. Teal, Isiah Sugg, James Sullivan, Jos. B. Sullivan, William J. Toller, Judith Sullivan, Jethro Summer, James Sutterfield, Joseph Sutton, James Swain, David Sweeny, Nelson Sweet, Ona Stweet, Daniel Sayers, Anson Talley, Stephen Tanner, Harriot Tapscott, James Tapscott, Simeon Tasker, Elijah Tate, Irvin Taunt, Ashbell Taylor, Benjamin Taylor, Daniel W. Taylor, Eliphalet Taylor, Jacob Taylor, Jesse Taylor, John Taylor, Richard Taylor, Stephen Taylor, Thomas T. Taylor, William Taylor, Warren Taylor, Moses Teer, David Tennison, Dickinson Terry, John Tharp, Amos Thatcher, Charles Thatcher, Johnson Thomas, Honor Thayer, Calvin Thomas, James Thomas, Samuel W. Topping, John Thomas, Lewis Thomas, William Thomas, Eliza Thompson, George Thompson, Griffin Thompson, Henry Thompson, Henry J. Thompson, James Thompson, Jesse Thompson, Thomas J. Thompson, John Thompson, Joshua Thompson, Robert Thompson, Thomas Thompson, William Thompson, G. F. Thorp, James Toy, Oliver Thruston, Fredk. Tiffany, David Tilley, George Tilley, Sally Tilley, Ezra Tillorson, Deborah Timmons, John Timmons, Samuel Timmons, Daniel Tingley, Thomas Tinsbloom, Wm. Wiatt, James Tompkins, Joseph Toner, Thomas E. Totty, James Tower, Micah Towers, Edmund Town, Andrew Toy, Silas Tracy, Thomas Tracy, Joseph Travis, George Traylor, David Treal, Rosewell Tyrrell, Hugh Treighner, John Tremble, Peter Tremble, Jacob Trout, John Trumley, Benjamin Tucker, William Tucker, Larkin Turgett, Ahas Turke, Benjamin Turke, Edward Turner, Ezekiel Turner, Jesse Turner, John Turner, Joseph Turner, Thomas Tuttle, Fredk. Turnham, Joseph Twin, Elisha Utley, Littleton Underwood, John Uptergrove, William H. Upright, Henry Vager, George Uptergrove, Henry Valencourt, Peter Vanburen, Henry Van Campson, John Van Buren, Christian Van Bomble, Cornelius Van Vrankon, Jesse Vance, Robert Vance, Henry Varner, Robert Vance, Jesse Vance, Jacob Vanderbeck, Henry Varsham, Daniel Van Drewer, Garret Vanderburgh, John Van Drewer, Jno. Wade, George Vangeson, John Vannator, Isaac Van Pelt, Joshua Van Sant, Raymond Van Ville, Jacob Van Vrankon, Richard Venable, David Vaughn, Rochard Venus, Nathaniel Verrill, Jno. Waide, Memory Victory, Jesse Vincent, James Viverett, John Washam,

(Military Bounty Land Continued)
Micajah Viverett, Ezra Voluntine, Peter A. Von Hagen, John Vosburgh, Peter J. Vronan, Benjamin Wabround, George Waddle, Zacahriah Wade, Edward Wade, John F. Waggoner, Jabez Waldron, Michael Waggoner, John F. Wagner, Mark Wagnon, David V. Wait, Chechester Walker, Elisha Walker, James Walker, Jeremiah Walker, Samuel Walker, Spencer Walker, Thomas Walker, David Wall, William Walker, james Wall, Thomas Wall, William Wall, Aaron Wallace, Daniel Waller, Edward Waller, Isaac H. Waller, Sterling Waller, Bartholomew Walsh, John Walsinger, Vincent Walton, Christian G. Walther, William Waltriss, Wm. Wamack, James M. Ward, Jasper Ward, Samuel Ward, William Ward, Joel Wardwell, George Warderman, Daniel Wardrode, Daniel Wardwell, Jesse Warner, Lot Warren, Heirs of William W. Warren, Daniel Warrin, John Washam, Thomas Washbourn, Lewis Waterberry, Luke Waterman, Samuel Waterman, Nicholas Watkins, Thomas Watkins, William H. Watlington, Ansel Watson, Joseph Watson, Solomon Watson, Zariel Watson, Burgess Watts, James Watts, Charles Way, John Watts, Ruben Watts, John Wauger, Henry Waems, Henry Weathers, Isaac Weaver, Homer Webb, Joshiah Wedington, Grant Weed, Jacob Weed, John Weed, Abraham Weekly, William Willes, Edward Welch, Jacob Welch, John Welch, Mathurin Welcome, Eli West, Aaron Wells, Miles Wells, Peterson E. Wells, Armistead Whitehead, Robert Wells, David Welsh, Thos. Wesner, Reuben Wessen, Henry Wessenhunt, James West, John West, John Wiley, Nimrod S. West, Robert D. West, William West, James Weston, Thomas Westbrook, Rufus Wetherell, Jeremiah Whalen, Richard Whalen, Romanta L. Whaples, Daniel Wharf, Henry Wheeler, Lion Wheless, Jerrod Wheeler, Peter Wheeler, Martin Whelin, Chas. White, Martin Whelin, Michael Whidden, martin B. Whipple, Ira Whitaker, Thomas Whitaker, Benjamin White, Bennett White, Freeman White, George White, George W. White, Henry White, Ira White, Jacob White, John A. White, Joseph White, Robert White, William White, Daniel Whitehead, James Whitehead, Tho. Whitehead, James Whitely, Gifford G. Whitfield, John Wide, John Whitfield, Richard Whitfield, William Whitfield, Simeon A. Whitlock, Solomon Whitlow, Alvin Whitman, David Williams, Jeremiah Whitman, John Whitman, Jonathan Whitmore, Abijah R. Whitmey, Caleb Whitney, William Whitney, Joseph Whitson, John Wickwise, Joseph Whittlesey, Jonathan Whitton, Sally Wiard, David Wickard, Samuel Wickersham, Robert Wickham, Anderson Williams, Alpheus Wickwise, John Wickwise, Edward Wiggins, Charles Wilbar, Daniel Wilcox, Titus Wilder, Michael Wilds, Isaac Wiley, Jacob Wilhelm, Allen Wilkerson, George Wilkey, Andrew Wilkinson, Daniel Wilkinson, Drury C. Wilkinson, John B. Williams, Samuel Wilkinson, Henry Willey, David Williams, Elijah Williams, George Williams, Henry I. Williams, James Williams, Laban Williams, Littleberry Williams, Mary Young, Permenos Williams, Richd. Williams, Thomas Williams, Thomas

(Military Bounty Land Continued)
Williams, William Williams, George Williamson, John Wooton, James Williamson, John Williamson, Lucinda Williamson, John Wills, Thomas Williamson, Jonan. Willis, Joseph Willis, John Wilson, Abraham Wilson, Alexander Wilson, David Wilson, Asa C. Wood, Gilbert Wilson, Giles Wilson, Jonathan Wilson, Lee Wood, Moses Wilson, Robert Wilson, Thomas Wilson, William Wilson, Nathn. Winslow, William Wirtz, Daniel Wiswell, David Wood, Isaac Wood, John B. Wood, John L. Wood, William Wood, Lewis Woodbanks, Israel Woodbury, Aaron Woodcock, Jonathan Woods, Allen Wooden, Curtis Woods, Jeptha Woods, Silas Woods, Ziba Woods, Charles Woodward, John Wooten, Daniel Worden, John Worsham, John Worley, William Wray, Caleb Wright, John Wright, Charles Wright, Christopher W. Wright, Jacob Wright, James Wright, John E. Wright, Martin Wright, Chas. Wyhte, William Wyatt, James Wyatt, Samuel W. Wright, William Yearns, Nathaniel Wright, Ambrose Yancey, Benjamin Yarbrough, George Young, John Yeaty, Benjamin Yarney, Isham Young, John Young, Levy Young, Martin Young, Frederick Zimmerman.

New Madrid County, Missouri, Delinquent Tax List, 1830.

Jacob Myers, Antoine Grimelen, Joseph Leduc, Joseph Hunt, sr., Joseph Michel, Hezaieth Gayon, Joseph L. Grand, Peter Nollepe, John Viet, Frances Lefluer, Joseph Generoux, Peter Derbigany, Rochard J. Waters, John B. Clive, Robert McCay, John D. Asine, Jacob Myers, Alexander Sampson, James Farris, Felix A. LaForge, Rusell Myers, Francis Howards, Henry Logo, Louis Loyourner, Zachariah Sharp, Richd. J. Waters, Martin Coons, Thos. and Elisha Windsor, Francis Hudson, Wm. Bacon, Joseph Gravier, Henry Master.

Cooper County, Missouri, Tax List, 1819.

David Adams, James Alexander, Iasieuz Braffie, Robert C. Boyo, James Anderman, Joseph Biller, Samuel Bary, Aquilla Banksan, Sarah Banksan, David Burris, Jeptha Billingsly, Realy Baley, Hugh Brown, Reidley Bailey, Jeremiah Clay, Wm. Bartell, Stephen Cole, Abraham Collett, Hannah Cole, Robert P. Clarke, Leven Cropper, Frederick Carrviex, Wm. Chambers, Christopher Cartan, Roddon Cole, Rochard W. Cummings, John Catham, William Cooper, John Creamer, James Dunwady, Samuel B. Davis, Isaac Davis, D. Robert Dawson, Isaac Ellis, Henry Estis, William Edwards, Thomas Estes, Peter Estis, Littlebury Estis, Joel Estis, Amini Ervine, John Evans, Julieus Emmans, David Fine, James Farris, James Fulkenson, William Frazier, Samuel Forbes, Asa Findlay, Humphrey Gibson, William Gibson, Duff Green, John Gabriel, Henry Gasper, George C. Hunt, Wm. Hays, Michael Hornback, Benjamin Hickeson, Joseph Hill, John Hassell, Silvester Hall, George Hamman, John Inglish, James James, Charles Inglish, William Jack, William Ish, Wm. Jobe,

(Cooper County, Missouri Continued)
John Kelly, William Kelly, Alexander Kellbreath, James Lame, William Kinchelow, Joel Lee, Byrd Lockhart, William Lillard, John Lillard, Thomas Love, Bazeleel W. Levin, William Moore, David McPhartan, John Riddle, Samuel Reavis, Edwin Reavis, Joseph Robinson, John Roberts, Joseph Stephens, Thomas Smila, Peter Stephens, Elisha Spitha, Lewis Switler, Wm. Stephens, George C. Sildey, Robert Stone, Joseph Smith, Peyton Thomas, James Turner, David Trotter, Gabriel Titsworth, Wm. White, George Tampkins, Daniel Tilman, Anthony Thomas, John Turner, Notley Thomas· George Tennel, Stephen Turley, Isiah Vivian, Thomas Ward, John Wood, Paul Whitley, Joseph Westbrook, Wm. White, Richard Westbrook, Robert Wallace, William Wolfscale.

Lincoln County, Missouri, Delinquent Tax List, 1835.

Name	Comments
Rolin Ham	Left the state
John Martin	Under age
Beckim May	Went to Illinois
James Rhodes	Moved
Jacob Harper	Left the state
Margaret Haws	No sutch person (sic)
William Brown	Left the state
Forbus Gordon	Dead
Samuel Shirky	Not the correct name
Toby Hill	Drown
Jacob Capps	Went to Illinois
Charles Dulany	Went to Virginia
Orval Cottle	Went to the mines
John Ward	Drunk
Hiram Segrass	Came to the state in Nov.
Robert Briant	Cannot locate
Joseph Collard	Went to Illinois
Daniel Carney	Ran away
William Dudley	Went to the mines
Elisha Dennis	Cannot locate
Hiram Hall	Sleeps in two diff. places
William Gordon, sr.	Dead
Jonathan Smith	Dead
Thomas Smithers	Poor
Nicholas Ludy	Went to the mines
William McDonald	
Jonah Moffit	No longer in the county
Stephen Mangle	Gone
Jo. or Joseph May	Gone
Josiah Parker	Gone
Stephen Smith	Will not pay
Abraham Campbell	Moved
Valentine Purdom	Moved

(Lincoln County, Missouri Continued)

Name	Comments
William N. McFarlin	Cannot find him
James Springston	Went to the mines
Jesse Smith	Cannot find him
William Grochauer	Went to the mines
Thomas Graves	Cannot locate
Letty Itson	Cannot locate
Abraham Kelly	Cannot locate
Jefferson Kirkum	Cannot locate

Pardon Papers, Secretary of State, 1837 - 1839.

Name	Date
Wilson Edison	December 18, 1837
Benj. P. Major	December 25, 1837
Hyram S. Wells	December 15, 1837
Willis Arman	January 22, 1838
James Brown	July 17, 1838
---- Cayton	November 30, 1838
Francis M. Dillon	January 27, 1838
Henry Horst	February 15, 1838
Edwin Hunting	May 4, 1838
Edgar Keys	April 20, 1838
James Layman	November 12, 1838
George Manning	February 27, 1838
Spencer Nortin	February 19, 1838
Hiram S. Wells	April 2, 1838
William O. Blanton	July 10, 1839
Richard Foster	July 10, 1839
William Hildebrand	August 17, 1839
Samuel Hyman	October 15, 1839
Mat - slave of Tho. Latimar	February 16, 1839
John C. Reevers	September 23, 1839
Allen Watson	September 23, 1839

St. Francois County, Missouri, Tax List, 1830.

Name	Orig. Claimant	Acres
Andrew Corbin		
Wm. H. Andrews	Wm. H. Andrews	154
John Baker	Andrew Baker	255
Wilson Barry	Wilson Barry	80
Isaac Baker	Andrew Baker	247
Isaac Baker	Thomas Ally	340
Isaac Baker	Jn. Hannatin	200
Isaac Baker	Henry Baggett	255
Samuel Brown	Samuel Brown	80
George Barnsback	Jn. Andrews	340
George Barnsback	Abn. Eady	42
Jn. Bequtte, sr.	Jn. B. Valle	118

(St. Francois County, Missouri Continued)

Name	Orig. Claimant	Acres
Wm. Blackwell	Nathaniel Cook	74
Wm. Blackwell	William Holmes	76
Alexander Byrd	Hardin Wilson	74
Alexander Byrd	Jonah Johnson	24
Thos. E. Burnham	William Murphy	93
Nathan Bequette	Wm. Patterson	85
Joseph Bogy, jr.		
Jonathan Brownden		
Bengn. Burnham	Wm. Murphy	76
Frank W. Braley	Jesse M. Yarlind	80
John Blanton	John Duff	80
John Boyer	Sarah Murphy	76
John Boyer	David Murphy	85
John Boyer	Jo. & Jn. Kennedy	33
Mathew Cunningham	Jas. Cunningham	96
Robert Chapman	Robert Chapman	160
Isaac Cunningham	Jas. Cunningham	155
Bengn. Crump	Bengn. Crump	108
Jas. Cunningham	Jas. Cunningham, sr.	150
George Cardin	Josiah Johnson	40
Eleazer Clay	Eleazer Clay	240
Jno. Cobb	Wm. C. Greenup	80
Jas. Caldwill	Nathl. Cook	162
Jas. Caldwill	Wm. Holmes	16
Jas. Caldwill	Robt. F. Friend	235
Jas. Caldwill	Jas. Caldwill	88
Chas. Cunningham	Jas. Cunningham, sr.	80
James Clark	Jos. Murphey	160
Mark Dent	Mark Dent	160
John Dent	Jno. Dent	80
Thomas Doggins	Isaac Doggins	184
Ganon Estes	Ganon Estes	160
Ganon Estes	Ezekiel Estes	185
John Estes	Robert Estes	190
William Evans	John Ally	210
William Evans	Sarah Murphey	140
Ovey Estes	Robert Estes	50
Nich. L. Flemming		
Henry Fory	Ezekiel Estes	270
A. Goza and Jas. Austin	Jno. August	275
Michl. Goza	Sarah Darnation	320
Jas. H. Griffin	Andrew Baker	10
Louis Griffin	Austin Sims	80
Joseph Liverau	Joseph Liverau	80
Aaron Lambeth	Jacob Mostellior	150
Tousaint Larkaint	Tousaint Larkaint	40
Ama. Larkaint	Tousaint Larkaint	40

(St. Francois County, Missouri Continued)

Name	Orig. Claimant	Acres
William Mitchele	Jas. Cunningham	160
Hardy M'Cormack	Peter P. M'Cormack	107
Isaac Mitchel, jr.	Isaac Mitchel, sr.	80
Isaac Mitchel, sr.	Isaac Mitchel, sr.	188
David Murphy	David Murphy	288
Delilah Martin	Robt. Estes	50
Thos. Madison	Thos. Madison	80
Jacob Mosteller	Jacob Mosteller	340
Richard Murphey	David Murphy	85
Archibald McHenry	Archibald McHenry	60
Elam McHenry	Archibald McHenry	66
Peter P. McCormack	Peter McCormick	92
George Marks	George Marks	80
Wm. Murphy	Sarah Murphy	82
John M'Farlan	John M'Farlan	126
Jn. Murphy	William Murphy	180
George Magahan	Abraham Eudis	468
Rubin McFarland	Rubin McFarland	127
John McKee	Jacob Doggette	160
John McKee	John McKee	250
Wm. Murphy, sr.	Wm. Murphy, sr.	330
Hiram Markin	Hiram Markin	80
James McFarland	James Davis	150
George Madison	Elias Even	100
Davis F. Marks	Michael Hart	226
Davis F. Marks	Davis F. Marks	124
Davis F. Marks	John Burnham	20
Alexander McCoy	Abraham Parker	290
Alexander McCoy	Henry Porter	15
James McCoy	Abraham Parker	190
Dubart Murphy, sr.	David Murphy	200
Wm. D. Murphy	Jacob Mosteller	150
Jno. B. Pratte	Jno. B. Pratte, jr.	680
Henry Posten	Henry Posten	160
Henry Posten	Abraham Parker	10
Henry Posten	Saml. Peanall	160
Jno. Pelons		
William Porter	William Porter	110
David Pinkston	William Patterson	160
Henry Potis	William Patterson	80
James Perry	Wm. Montgomery	10
James Perry	Wm. Ally	156
Leonard Parker	Robert Estes	100
Geo. W. Robinson	Seth H. Robinson	80
Jno. B. Robinson	Jno. B. Robinson	80
John Robinson	John Robinson	160
Pamelia Ross	Israel Johnson	19

(St. Francois County, Missouri Continued)

Name	Orig. Claimant	Acres
Pamelia Ross	Hardin Wilson	6
Jas. S. Ray	John Baker	280
Jas. S. Ray	Wm. S. Ally	99
William Smith	William Brady	80
Lewis Sims	Lewis Sims	80
Elijah Sibasin	George Sebastian	40
George Sebastian	George Sebastian	209
William Shaw	William Shaw	63
William Shaw	Joseph Griffith	40
Wm. Spradling	Jacob Doggette	160
Mathias Stegal	Etienne Coin	145
Jas. M. Smith	William Holmes	190
Jas. M. Smith	Robert F. Friend	112
Jas. M. Smith	Saml. Kinkaid	80
George Taylor	George Taylor	160
Thomas Tarpley	John Perry	80
Samuel Vance	Jonathan Starks	160
Jas. Williams, sr.	Jas. Williams, sr.	80
William Wiser	Elias Coen	137
Frederick Woolford		

Patriotic War Contributions, Spanish Government, 1799, taken from the Cuban Papers.

Contributors	Residence	Rank
Don Pierre Charles de Hault Delassus de Luziere	Nouvelle Bourbon	Commander
Israel Dodge	"	Planter
David Sterling	Bois Brule	"
Antoine Lachance	Nouvelle Bourbon	Carpenter
Paul Deguire	"	Planter
Joseph Teserot	"	"
Jaque Tomson	Bois Brule	"
Jerome Matis	Nouvelle Bourbon	"
Louis Tommelier	"	"
Samuel Bridge	Aux Salines	Cooper
Noel Hornebek	"	Saltmaker
David Clark	Bois Brule	Planter
Joseph Boice	"	"
Jaque Doyson	"	"
Joseph Lachance	Nouvelle Bourbon	Carpenter
Pierre Chevallier	"	Planter
Gabriel Lachance	"	"
Francois Lachance	"	"
Louis Deguire	"	"
Alexis Griffard	"	Saltmaker
Joseph Cuture	"	Planter
Guillaume Hellay	Aux Salines	Cooper

(Patriotic War Contributions Continued)

Contributors	Residence	Rank
Hipolitte Bolon	Aux Salines	Translator
Jaque Burnes	Bois Brule	Planter
Jean Duval	Aux Salines	Saltmaker
Jean Callaven	"	Saltmaker
Benjamin Cox	"	Planter
Jean Donahue	"	"
Guillaume Strother	"	"
Benjamin Walker	Bois Brule	"
Louis Coyteux	"	"
Francois Clark	"	"
Jonas Nusam	"	"
Michel Burnes	"	"
Jean Hunkis	Aux Salines	Saltmaker
Jaque Farel	"	"
Jaque Meleane	"	Planter
Jean Robert McLaughlin	Bois Brule	"
Joseph Donahan	"	"
Joseph Eustin	Aux Salines	"
Jeremie Perelle	"	Saltmaker
Jean Hartlor	"	"
Guillaume Moore	"	Planter
Henres Turther	Bois Brule	"
Guillaume Burney	"	"
Guillaume Roberst	"	"
Benny Burnes	"	"
Jaque Davis	"	"
Elias Coen	"	"
Daniel Meredith	"	Gunsmith
Jean Grenaval	"	Planter
Tomas Donahue	"	"
Andres Cox	"	"
Gabes Sanborn	Aux Salines	Merchant
Tomas Fenwick	"	"
Isaac Packaret	"	"
Israel Danton	"	Saltmaker
Tomas Hart	"	Cooper
Bengamin Spincer	"	Saltmaker
Guillaume Casvan	"	"
Jean Paul	"	Baker
Augustin Heen	"	Saltmaker
David Rohzer	"	"
Jesa Helay	Nouvelle Bourbon	Planter
Joseph Gimes	Riv. au Vases	"
Guillaume Murphy, sr.	Riv. St. Fran.	"
Heran Gearem	"	"
Salomon Georges	"	"
Guillaume Reed	"	"

(Patriotic War Contributions Continued)
Name	Residence	Rank
Tomas Maddin	Big Swamp	Planter
J. Florver	Riv. au Vaes	"

Washington County, Missouri, Delinquent Tax List, 1830.
Ameline Harriet, Austin Baker, A. W. Hudspeth, Wm. Haynes, Andrew Henry, Samuel Hughes, Mathey McPike, Joseph Rayburn, Peter Martin, Nathan Parker, Amos Shook, George F. Strother, Samuel Staples.

Petition to Congress for the establishment of an Academy, St. Charles County, December 12, 1817, Vol. XV, Carter's Papers.
Haile Talbot, Andrew Frust, William Ramsay, jr., William T. Lamme, James Ruhterford, H. B. Lane, Daniel Gossin, Thos. Edmonds, Jenkin Williams, John P. Scott, Joseph Moody, Geo. Avery, Nathaniel Taque, Joseph Johnston, Frazer Ward, Isaac Bledsoe, Jacob Groome, Huston Reynold, John Rumsy, Joseph Martin, Benj. Sharp, Mordcai Morgan, Saml. Morris, Absalom Hays, Andrew McWilliams, William Ramsey, Benjamin James, John Davis, Anthony Wyatt, Joseph Le Baron, John Young, Thomas Talbot.

Litigations, Ste. Genevieve County, Missouri.

Name	Name	Case	Year
Ezekiel Abel	vs. Wm. Girty	Salt Furnace	1803
Ezekiel Abel	vs. Jas. Murdock	Oxen	1803
Charles Aime	vs. J. Bte. Tetrau	Crops	1796
Philomen Askew	vs. Nic. LaPlante	Debt	1809
Joseph Aubin	vs. ---- Gabobert	Debt	1771
Pierre Aubuchon	vs. Mrs. Gabobert	Negro	1771
---- Aufreret	vs. --- Tellier	Debt	1775
Moses Austin	vs. Nath. Mullens	Lead	1799
Moses Austin	vs. Robt. Greer	Debt	1799
Moses Austin	vs. Bart. & Mich. Boucher	Debt	1802
Jean Andre Avy	vs. Pas. Datchemendy	Debt	1800
Francois Azau	vs. --- Morel	Debt	1791
Abraham Baker & Wife, Wid. Ja. Daguet	vs. Murphy	Debt	1804
---- Barbier	vs. Dugan	Debt	1799
---- Barbier	vs. Jer. Perelle	Pirouge	1798
Etienne Barre	vs. Wm. Derousel	Hogs	1776
Wididow C. Millet Barsalou	vs. --- Harrison	Negro	1789
J. B. Beauvais	vs. Fredk. Custer	Debt	1798
J. B. Beauvais	vs. Walter Fenwick	Debt	1800
Marguerite Beauvais	vs. ??????		
Widow Bentley	vs. ??????		1789

(Litigations, Ste. Genevieve County, Missouri Continued)

Name	Name	Case	Year
Vital Beauvais	vs. Jacq. Mercier	Cattle	1798
T. P. Bedford	vs. Hy. Jennings	Debt	1801
T. P. Bedford	vs. David Porer	Debt	1801
T. Bentley	vs. Jos. Maison	Personalty	1775
Baptiste Bequette	vs. Augn. Bartot	Curch	1794
Jn. Bapt. Bequette	vs. S. Hubardeau	Assault	1789
Francois Bernier	vs. ---- Dobbie	Debt	1771
Carlos Bizet	vs. Louis Delaurier	Debt	1776
Daniel Blouin	vs. His Creditors	Debt	1773
Helen Blouin, wife of Michael Antaya	vs. Daniel Duff	Debt	1789
Joseph Bobards	vs. Isaiah Packard	Debt	1800
Louis Bolduc	vs. Charles Charleville	Debt	1792
Louis Bolduc	vs. Joseph Gerard	Debt	1789
Louis Bolduc	vs. ---- Malveau	Debt	1770
Hypolite Bolon	vs. Israel Dodge	Libel	1796
Hypolite Bolon	vs. Wm. McIntosh	Testimony	1790
Louis Boucher	vs. Mme. Griffard	Repairs	1779
John Boyce	vs. Fcois. Clark, Jas. & Benj. Cox	Debt	1803
Pierre Boyer	vs. Estate of Silv. Philibustier	Cantrel dit Engages	1777
Michael Burns	vs. William james	Cattle	1799
Nicholas Briedbach	vs. --- Bellemare	Debt	1771
---- Bruner	vs. --- De Gimes	?????	1797
Louis Canae dit Marquis	vs. Creditors		1775
Silvestre Cantrel dit Filibustier	vs. --- Kennedy	Debt	1771
--- Carpentier	vs. Ant. Janis	Debt	1768
E. Carpentier and R. Boyd	vs. John Price	Debt	1800
William C. Carr	vs. Gregoire Jr. & Pratte	Debt	1828
---- Carpentier	vs. --- Goudon	Wood	1776
Slivi Francois Cartabona	vs. Benito Basquez	Boat	1776
Gabriel Cerre	vs. Wm. Lecomte & Pre. Leclere	Debt	1786
Gabriel Cerre	vs. Wm. Lecomter & Pre. Leclere	Debt	1782
Louis Chamard	vs. Gibert dit Lafontaine	Debt	1771
Louis Chamard	vs. Jn. Datchurut	Debt	1769
Louis Chamard	vs. Jos. Second	Debt	1774
Louis Chamard	vs. Jn. Ble. Mentas	Debt	1777

(Litigations, Ste. Genevieve County, Missouri Continued)

Name	Name	Case	Year
Francois Clark	vs. Jos. Boyce	Wagon	1797
Jacques Clamorgan	vs. Dupont & Gacard	Debt	1800
Me. Chs. Charleville	vs. Hugh Howard	Slaves	1788
Francois Clark	vs. Jn. Marie Le Grand	Debt	1799
John Coffee	vs. Me. Peyroux	Salt	1801
James Cooper	vs. Thos. Bedford	Wages	1801
James Cooper	vs. Thos. Bedford	Debt	1803
Pierre Couder.	vs. ---- Messager	Note	1771
William Cowan	vs. James Ferrell	Pigs	1800
William Cowan	vs. Benj. Spencer & P. Lafleur	Furnace	1801
William Cowan	vs. Jas. Ferrell	Salt	1799
Louis Coyteux	vs. Fredk. Custer	Debt	1798
Louis Coyteux	vs. Mich. Lasource	Indians	1793
Benjamin Cox	vs. Jos. Boyce	Horses	1803
Jean Datchurut	vs. Louis Chamard	Debt	1788
Jean Datchurut	vs. ---- Fauche	Protest	1767
Jean Datchurut	vs. Louis Chamard	Debt	1770
Jean Datchurut	vs. --- Delorier	Note	1789
Jean Datchurut	vs. Estate of Meziere Hubardeau	Debt	1771
Jean Datchurut	vs. Math. Kennedy	Debt	1771
Jean Datchurut	vs. Barteya Leblanc	Note	1771
Eliz. D'Acherutte	vs. Ant. Aubuchon	***	
*** Free Negress claiming Ant. Aub. to be the father of her ten children			1798
Joseph Davidson	vs. ---- Alombi		1801
Julien Choquet	vs. ---- Deroussel	Oxen	1772
Jacques Clamorgan	vs. ---- Decelle	Debt	1800
--- Debruisseau	vs. ---- Blouin	Papers	1771
Jn. Bapt. Deguire	vs. ---- Bellemare	Debt	1770
Jn. Bapt. Deguire	vs. Louis St. Jean	Debt	1770
Camille Delassus	vs. Jacob Daguet	Concession	1802
---- Delorier	vs. Augustin Bertau	Debt	1775
Fremon Delaurier	vs. Francois Lalumandiere	Lead/Debt	1798
Fremon Delaurier	vs. Peter Flora	Oxen	1800
Louis Delorier	vs. Jac. Boyer, jr.	Tobacco	1779
Louis Delorier	vs. Silv. Cantrel dit Filibustier	Note	1779
Louis Delorier	vs. J. Clamorgan	Lead	1784
--- Derousel	vs. --- Ls. Lacroix	Cattle	????
Israel Dodge	vs. Hypolite Bolton	Threat	1796
Israel Dodge	vs. Jn. Callowan	Salt	1800
Israel Dodge	vs. Wm. Cowan	Debt	1800
Israel Dodge	vs. Decelle Duclos	Note	1801

(Litigations, St. Genevieve County, Missouri Continued)

Name	Name	Case	Year
Israel Dodge	vs. Jos. Fenwick	Debt	1795
Israel Dodge	vs. Geo. A. Hamilton	Debt	1778
Israel Dodge	vs. Mr. & Mrs. Lyon	Debt	1803
Israel Dodge	vs. Guiho de Kerlegan	Land	1802
Israel Dodge	vs. Fcois. Comparet & bro.	Contract	1793
John Dodge	vs. Pre. Cornover	Debt	1789
Israel Dodge	vs. John Smith	Debt	1803
John Dodge	vs. Lardner Clark	Debt	1788
Joseph Donohue	vs. --- Dugand	Salt	1799
--- Drouart	vs. --- Lafontaine	Note	1771
Joseph Dubord	vs. Jos. Tellier	Debt	1777
Louis Dubreuil	vs. Jn. Gibert	Debt	1775
Wid. Duchouquet	vs. Mrs. Gadobert	Slaves	1771
Antoine Duclos	vs. Michel LeCheval	Canoe	1779
Alexandre Duclos	vs. Amable Macon	Debt	1802
Mrs. Duff	vs. Thos. Allen	Assualt/Child	1800
Louis Defresne	vs. --- Carpentier	Def. of Char.	1770
James Dunn	vs. --- Barhart	Debt	1798
James Dunn	vs. Francois Clark	Debt	1798
--- Easton	vs. Jas. Maxwell		????
Philipe Fainer	vs. Andre Fainer, (Brother)		1782
James Farrel	vs. Neal Hornbeck	Furnace	1800
---- Pauche	vs. Ant. Janis		1768
---- Pauche	vs. ---- Viviat		1766
James Fenwick	vs. Israel Dodge	Debt	1798
Samuel Filson	vs. Jeremiah Perel		1799
Samuel Filson	vs. Thomas Wilson		1799
James Finley	vs. John Duff	Slave	1800
William Finley	vs. Wm. Girty and Widow Duff		1800
Pierre Pouche	vs. Jacq. and Pre. Laderoute	Debt	1766
Pre. Gadobert	vs. --- Labastide	Theft/Slaves	1771
Pierre Gadobert	vs. --- Lafontaine	Debt	1770
Pierre Gadobert	vs. Noel Larose	Debt	1772
Mrs. Gadobert	vs. --- Catalon	Debt	1769
Joseph Gerard	vs. Nicolas Boyer	Cow	1784
Joseph Gerard	vs. Dr. Samuel Thompson	Debt	1796
Jn. Gibert dit Lafontaine	vs. Pre. Gadobert	Debt	1771
Jn. Gibert dit Lafontaine	vs. Math. Kennedy	Libel	1771
John Hague	vs. Jos. Donahue	Acct.	1800

(Litigations, St. Genevieve County, Missouri Continued)

Name	vs.	Name	Case	Year
Dr. Bernard Gibkins	vs.	---- Laviolette dit Boucher	Debt	1778
Dr. Bernard Gibkins	vs.	Pre. Masset dit Picard	Debt	1777
Dr. Bernard Gibkins	vs.	--- Witmer	Note	1771
--- Gibert dit Lafontaine	vs.	Jn. Langlois dit Duval	Debt	1771
--- Girouard	vs.	Decelle Duclos	Note	1797
--- Girouard.	vs.	Jos. Juteau	Note	1800
Thomas Hart	vs.	Jn. McLanahan	Debt	1798
John Hawkins	vs.	--- Adams	Debt	1803
William Hickman	vs.	Ls. Robitaille	Debt	1803
Neal Hornbeck	vs.	Jn. McDuff	Debt	1800
Neal Hornbeck	vs.	Wm. Cowan	Note	1800
Hugh Howard	vs.	C. Charleville	Bond	1770
Jn. Bte. Hubardeau	vs.	Jn. Bte. Fortin	Debt	1770
Jn. Bte. Hubardeau	vs.	S. Hubardeau (Brother)		1771
Simon Hubardeau	vs.	--- Beaulieu	House	1771
Simon Hubardeau	vs.	--- Lachance	Horse	1797
Simon Hubardeau	vs.	--- Laffont	Trade	1784
Simon Hubardeau	vs.	Gerard Labglois	Debt	1771
Simon Hubardeau	vs.	Jn. Mrie Pepin	Rent	1797
P. Hubert	vs.	Ls. Lorimier	Peltries	1790
Antoine Hunaud	vs.	Rev. P. Gibault	Ferry Bill	1784
Mrs. Hunaud	vs.	Ls. Courtois (Son-in-law)	Stealing	1770
Chitte. Jean Hunaud	vs.	Widow Troto	Cow	1775
Genevieve Hunaud	vs.	Ls. Courtois (Husband)	Separation	1770
William James	vs.	Michael Burns	Cattle	1799
Nicolas Jamis	vs.	Amable Partenay	Road	1793
Nicholas Jarrot	vs.	Jean Arvin	Debt	1800
Mathew Kennedy & Ls. Chamard	vs.	Jn. G. dit Lafontaine	Debt	1771
Joseph Labusciere	vs.	Jean Lagrange	Note	1766
Antoine Lachance	vs.	Nicolas Canada	Note	1800
Nicolas Lachance	vs.	Hugh Howard	Debt	1788
Joseph Lachance	vs.	John Smith	Lead	1803
Jn. Bte. Lacroix	vs.	Jn. Rice Jones & M. Austin	Bond	1801
Pierre Langlois	vs.	--- Fagot	Threat	1788
Jn. Bte. Lacroix	vs.	Ls. Chamard	Note	1771
Jn. Bte. Lafont	vs.	Joseph Tellier	Note	1776
--- Laforme	vs.	L. Largeau	Bond	1788
Jean Lafourcade	vs.	Jos. Fenwick	Ferry	1798
Jean Lafourcade	vs.	Henri Peyroux	Debt	1804

(Litigations, Ste. Genevieve County, Missouri Continued)

Name		Name	Case	Year
Nicolas Laplante	vs.	--- Bedford	Debt	1802
Pre. Lapin dit Bideau	vs.	S. Cantrel dit Filibustoer	Estate	1776
Nicolas Laplante	vs.	Alex. Dupont	Debt	1800
Noel Larose	vs.	Pre. Gadobert	Libel	1773
Regis Lasource	vs.	Pre. Masse dit Picard	Debt	1776
Francis Lecelere	vs.	--- Barre	Slaves	1771
Pierre Lecomte	vs.	Pre. Marchand		1776
Pierre Levrard	vs.	--- Bedford	Debt	1802
Jane Line	vs.	Joab Line	Debt	1803
Joab Line	vs.	Aquilla Low	Partnership	1803
Ant. Jos. Longval	vs.	---- Le May	Peltries	1788
Louis Lorimier	vs.	Trope Ricard	Partnership	1789
Francois Lumas	vs.	--- Morgan	Seizure	1800
Thomas Maddin	vs.	--- Bedford	Debt	1803
Stephen Martain	vs.	John Frank	Note	1816
Amable Mason	vs.	Alex. Duclos	Debt	1802
--- Mason dit Partenay & Bapt. Larose	vs.	Nic. Lachance	Quarrel	1795
Picard Masse	vs.	S. Filibustier	Horse	1776
Edward Matis	vs.	--- Cantrel dit Filibustier	Debt	1776
Joseph McAdams	vs.	Wm. Morehead	Debt	1799
Daniel McDuff	vs.	--- Edgar	Debt	1789
Daniel McElduff	vs.	--- Chouteau	Slave	1789
Joseph McFerron	vs.	Ps. Detchemendy	Letter	1800
William McIntosh	vs.	Jn. Price	Engage	1798
John McKee	vs.	Wm. Montgomery		1803
James McLean	vs.	Jer. Percelle	House	1799
Jacque Maxwell	vs.	Estate of Rbt. Brewster		1798
Pierre Menard	vs.	--- Fremon	Mortgage	1801
Jacques Mercier	vs.	Vital Beauvais	Livestock	1798
Laurent Metayer	vs.	Jn. Haig	Debt	1797
William Montgomery	vs.	Saml. Simmons		1800
Mrs. Montmirel	vs.	John Dodge	Fences	1793
Joseph Morancy	vs.	--- Fauche	Passport	1772
Jn. Bapt. Morel	vs.	--- Johnson	Shooting	1771
William Morehead	vs.	Jos. McAdams	Debt	1799
Widow Moro	vs.	A. Partenay	Lead/Land	1804
Joseph Motard	vs.	---- Duclos,jr.	Debt	1776
James Murdough	vs.	Ezekiel Able	Debt	1803
Jacob Neal	vs.	Calvin Adams	Debt	1799
Gabirel Nicol	vs	Israel Dodge	Whiskey	1801
Jones Nusans	vs.	Jas. Hawkins	Salt	1798
Katherine Peers	vs.	Jas. McLain	Debt	1802

(Litigations, St. Genevieve County, Missouri Countinued)

Name		Name	Case	Year
J. M. Pepin	vs.	S. Hubardeau	Oxen	1797
Jn. Marie Pepin	vs.	Pre. Daune	Engage	1796
Jeremiah Perrel	vs.	Dav. Rohrer	Debt	1801
Jeremiah Perrel	vs.	Jas. McLean	Debt	1799
Charles Peyroux	vs.	Amb. Canadien & --- Lafleur	Robbery	1792
Henri Peyroux	vs.	Ls. Bulduc	Trespass	1796
Henri Peyroux	vs.	--- Chatover	Debt	1795
Henri Peyroux & wife	vs.	--- Presse	Merchandise	1798
Henri Peyroux & wife	vs.	Jerome Perelle	Salt	1798
Wd. Marg. C. Peyroux	vs.	H. Peyroux (son)	Personalty	1794
Emanuel Picher	vs.	--- Lacroix	Salt	1771
Jean Pierre	vs.	Gilbert Dupre	Peltries	1778
Nicolas Plante	vs.	Michel Huron	Peltries	1778
Joseph Placy	vs.	--- Durcy	Debt	1777
Fcois. Poillievre	vs.	--- Dugins	Debt	1799
William Porter	vs.	Clamorgan, Loisel & Co.	Note	1799
Bernard Pratte	vs.	Manuel Blanco	Debt	1797
Bernard Pratte	vs.	Joseph Peigne	Debt	1795
Jn. Bapt. Pratte	vs.	Pre. L.Lorimier	Peltries	1788
John Price and C. Delassus, for their wives, Euphro. and Mat. Villars	vs.	Est. --- Villars (Step-Mother)		1804
John & Andre Price	vs.	Alexis Paquin	Debt	1798
John & Andre Price	vs.	--- Lione	Debt	1798
John & Andre Price	vs.	Mme. Peyroux	Debt	1799
John Price	vs.	Francois Lalumandiere	Debt	1799
John Price	vs.	Ls. Robitaille	Debt	1801
Louis Robinet	vs.	Creditors	Debt	1771
Mrs. Ls. Robitaille	vs.	Wm. Hickman	Board Bill	1803
Mrs. Ls. Robinet (Mad. Raddic, dau. Thos. R. & F. York)	vs.	Creditors	Property	1771
M. Mad. Riddic	vs.	Creditors		1771
Nicolas Paquin	vs.	Richard Winn		1798
--- Wilson	vs.	--- Perrel	Debt	1799
Thomas Wilson	vs.	Wm. Filson	Debt	1799
--- Wittman	vs.	Fcois. Alary dit Gosse	Debt	1771
Mrs. Abner Wood	vs.	Joab Strickland	Assualt	1804
Richard Waters	vs.	Wm. Cowen	Debt	1799
David Williams	vs.	--- Bard	Debt	1770
John Whitford	vs.	Fcois. Berthion	Debt	1803
Pierre Vivat	vs.	Manuel Blanco	Debt	1797
Denia Veroneau	vs.	---- Feuilletot	Debt	1770

(Litigations, St. Genevieve County, Missouri Continued)

Name	Name	Case	Year
Wid. Vero dit Tirat	vs. --- Gibault	Debt	1784
Benito Vasquez	vs. Joseph Tellier	Debt	1784
Antoine Toussaint	vs. Gibert Dupre	Peltries	1799
Joseph Tellier	vs. --- Durcy	Debt	1776
Henry Stein	vs. Ed Duigan	Debt	1799
Antoine Sculard	vs. --- Dodson	Debt	1803
John Smith	vs. Charles Ellie	Debt	1803
John Smith	vs. Israel Dodge	Debt	1803
John Smith	vs. Dav. Strickland	Debt	1803
Hy. Coleman Smith	vs. Benj. Strother	Character	1778
Jos. Seraphim & wife Isab. Billeron			1806
Fcoise. Simonneau	vs. --- Deselle	Estate	1800
Joseph Second	vs. --- Delaurier	House	1774
Joseph Scott	vs. Ore. Menard	Oxen	1798
Silvestre Sarpy	vs. Ls. Dornon	Peltries	1782

Ste. Genevieve County, Missouri, Delinquent Tax List, 1830.

Charles Belmar, Widow Belmar, Widow Bermier, Henry Dodge, Antoine Calliot, Paschal Dutchmandy, John D. Cook, William Morrison, Widow Emanuel, Francis Lacroix, Hugh Maxwell, jr., J. Bte. Lacroix, Joseph Lachance, Widow Laffleur, Michael Lachance, Pierre Srouge, Breton West, dec.

St. Ferdinand Twshp.,St. Louis County, Petition to Congress, for the Establishment of a Post Office at Florisant, Vol.XV, Carter's Papers, February 24, 1818.

Rob Brotherton, Dennis Carrico, Wm. Parker, John Strain, James Voshall, Thomas Welch, Edward Herrimand, Thomas Ward, C. James, W. R. M'Adams, Peyton Jamison, Wm. Young, Iasibaus Hubbard June, Wm. Young, Wm. Twitty, Albert G. Twitty,Robert Scott, Wm. Mason, Isaur Miles, Duritt Hubbard,Jaret Hubbard. Bar B. Harris, Elisha Patterson, M. Dunand, --- Collin, John E. Allin. Jas. Buck, Mosias Jones, Pierre Saint Ons,Tyree H. Jones, Christopher Jones,Alt. Payant, Paschal Dubriel, Henry F. Gass, Frederic Hieatt, Bonaventure Marrion, John Greene, Charles Marichal, Augte. Chouteau, M. O'Connell, Alexander Palmer, Fenton Filson, Joseph Menard, John B. Lorain, J. S. Dozer, P. James, Chs. A. Lewis, A. Stewart, Joseph M'Clung, jr., Owin Wingfield, John Patterson, E. Hubbard, sr., John C. Sullivan, Wm. Patterson, Harlen Bonham, James B. Beatty, Francois Rappieux, Benjamin Allen, David Burk, Tyree Martin, Peter Bowler, Jno. B. Creeys, sr., Charles Letour, Anderson Boles, Randolph Nolan, James Richardson, Robert Jefferies, John Humes, James Chambers, Charles Mercier, William Smith, James Smith, George Smith, Francois Teisson, John R. Twitty, Levi Smith, J. H. Scott, Richard Lanham, Moses Hieutt, John

(Petition, St. Louis County, Missouri Continued)
Seelye, Francois Lourain, Noel Bouche, Robert Jefferies,jr., Squire Sappington, David Diggs, Joseph Carns,Anderson Boles, Rus Twitty, James Cochran, Wm. McKinney, John R. Twitty, G. Dewit, Henry Scroggins, Robert Cragf, Edward Hegan, William Miller, Thomas Wittinston, Antoine Tyson, Jas. Sullivan, Wm. Richardson, David Musick, David G. Martin, John Brown, Lewis Martin. David Twittey, Hugh Fraynum, Henry Sappington, John Mussey, Abraham Niell, Francois Creelis, John Buzan, Joseph H. James, James McAlister, Wm. McMillin, Jonathan Martin, C. T. Hildebrand, John Whiteside, Wm. R. Laughlin, John Clark, Jacob Houselight, Benjamin McCoy, John Howdishell, Nathaniel Peoples, J. A. Martin, Larkin Dotey, Thos. Denton, W. Lynes, James Hunter, T. C. Trustee, Wm. Martin, David Martin, Peter Hunter, Richard Lundy, Lewis Muscik, William Nevill, David Thomas, William Thomson, David English, Andrew Hunter, John Foster, William Hunter, William Thomas, Alexander Douglass, William Douglass, Ephraim Hunter, David M. Martin, William Miller, Thomas Whiteside, Adam Martin, John Doty, Valentine Neel, Robeert M'Millin, Robert H. Martin, Peter Ellis, Peter Bryant, Mishal Fortee, James Neel, Paton Neel, Jas. McCoy, Joel L. Musick, David Musick, John Baker, James S. Douglass, James Watt, David Diggs, Abraham Ellis, G. Manard,R. Lanham, F. Sappington, Jos. Lynes, T. Jones, Chs. Jones, S. Jones, Thomas Witherington.

New Madrid Census, 1797, Taken from Cuban Papers.

Head of Household	#Women	#Sons	#Daugh.	#Slaves
Pedro Derrocher	1		1	
Ricardo Jones Waters				3
Roberto McCoy	1	1	1	
Francisco Lesieur	1		2	
Widow Rees	1			5
Josef Aranot	1	1	3	
Josef Story	1			
Jacob Miers	1	2	4	
Josef Santa Maria	1	1		
Francisco Riche Dupin	1	1		
Moises Lantforg	1	1	3	
Francisco Santa Maria	1	2	3	
Hugguer Mo. Dn. Chisholm	1	1	3	2
Phelipe Leduc				
Josef Leduc				
Widow Cirille Leduc	1			
Francois Gonnette				
Tomas Jacob	1			
Juan Arast				
Alexander Sanson	1	1		
Josef Lafanait	1	1		

(New Madrid Census Continued)

Head of Household	#Women	#Sons	#Daugh.	#Slaves
Pedro Atr. Laforge	1	2	2	
Bartolomy Tardiveau				2
Luis Vandenbenden	1			4
Henry Green				
Joseph Vandenbenden				
Pedro Lequin				
Andres Goder	1			
Juan Lavallee	1	1		2
Juan Bautista Racine	1	1	2	
Juan Bautista Dutrecuble				
Llisah Jacson			2	
James Rayen				1
Juan Pretchet		3	1	
Guillermo Mock	1			
Joseph La Plante	1		2	
Francisco Racine	1	2	3	
Juan Bautista Maisonville				
Francisco Maisonville				
Pierre Garan	1	1		
Pedro Sabourin	1	1	1	
Widow Daria	1	1	1	
Arthur Mellon				
Juan Bautista Barsaloux				
Joset Legrand				
George Wilson	1	1	1	
Carlos Bonneau	1	3	2	
Clermont (a Woman)	1	2		
Francisco Paquette	1			
Laurenzo Aveline				
Juan Thirios				
Felix Longue				
Carlos Guillbaut	1		2	
Juan Derlac	1		1	
Francisco Berthiaume				
Josef Berthiaume				
Josef Rideau	1	4	1	
Luis Brouillette	1	3		
Antoino Aubernois	1			
Estevan Santa Maria		3	2	
Isaac Thompson	1			1
Francisco Paquin	1	7		
Luis Saint Aubin	1	1	1	
Juan Simon Guerin	1	2	1	
Jacolo Adaver	1		3	
Juan Guilmore				
Andres Drybread				
Juan Drybread			1	

(New Madrid Census Continued)

Head of Household	#Women	#Sons	#Daugh.	#Slaves
Tomas Horsley				
Francisco Langlois				
Jacobo Laderoute				
Ambrosio Seraphin				
Jacobo Beaugard	1	4	3	
Pablo Laderoute	1	1		
Moises Malleat	1		2	
Juan Bautista Chartier				
Widow Soldeñer	1			
Juan Bautista Grimar				
Luis Denovon				
Samuel Dorsey				
Nicolas Auger	1			1
Josef McCourtney	1		1	
Phelipe Siebert	1	3		
Andres Wilson	1			
Jacobo Cotter		1	1	
Juan Bautista Dupuic				
Pedro Saffray				
David Gray				
De Biggis	1	1		
Widow Chartier	1	1		
Maria Cheraquise	1	1	3	
Nicolas Pedro Poirier	1	1		
Josef Michel				1
Ysidor Dapuir	1		1	
Pedro Gibault			1	
Jacobo Guilt	1			
Luis Dubois	1	2	2	
Largillon (a woman)				
Antonio Vachard	1	1		
Joseph Factto	1			
Agnes Seraphine	1			
Alexo Picard	1	3		
Ducomb (a woman)	1			
Catalina Charauone	1	1	1	
Labuilere (a woman)	1	1	1	
Martin McCormeek	1	1	2	
Jacobo Crow	1	1		
Jacobo Kerette			1	1
Francisco Desrousse			1	
Toussaint Gordes				
Boruel Breby			1	
Jales Walis				
Andres Giroult				
Juan Sommer				
Juan Bautista Chaudillon				

109

(New Madrid Census Continued)

Head of Household	#Women	#Sons	#Daugh.	#Slaves
Juan Walton				
Jacobo Mean				
Georges Onraw				
Tomas Faustismen	1	3	2	
Juan Viot dit Gascon	1	2	3	
Francisco Couteley	1	1		
Nas. Peigne	1	1	1	
Samuel Arill				
Juan Walls				
Francisco Archasubean				
Juan Bautista Gervais				
Alberto Filson				
Phelipe Louvieres				
Maney Faul	1			
Francisco Hadson	1	2	1	
George Ruddell	1	4	2	5
Juan Hornes	1			
Roberto Withe	1	2		
George M. Reagan	1	1		10
Christopher Winsor	1	2		
Juan Parkes				
David Shelby	1	6	2	
Claude Thiriet				
Jacquin Lewis	1	2	2	
Luis Metayes				
Miguel Metivee				
Roberto Opten				
Juan Bautista Langlois				
Juan Barry				
Pedro Vanidestine				
Rose Rowen				
William Murphy	1	2	2	
Daniel Rice				
William Luermes				
Tomas W. Caulk	1	3	3	
Widow Mathews	1	3	4	
Daniel Mathews				
Santiago Cavenagts	1	2	1	
Jacobo McFarlen				
Benjamin Patersomme	1	2	2	
Carlos Crabin				
Juan Lamb				
Guillermo Botton				
Jacobo M. Mollen	1			
Juan McCleland				
Tomas Crispin				
Josef Geuereis				

(New Madrid Census Continued)

Head of Household	#Women	#Sons	#Daugh.	#Slaves
Carlos Loignon	1	1		
Francisco Morin				
Aarom Graams	1	2	3	
Daniel F. Vanghaus				
Ricardo Westbrook	1	2	4	
Andres Block	1	1	2	
Pedro Vives	1	1	2	
Guillermo Dorson				
Waaling Silch	1			
Juan Stridley	1	2		
Guillermo Taylor				
Pablo Sheves				
Juan Sliter				
George Dorman	1	1		
Jacobo Parker				
Abner M. Kentocke				
Roberto Polderin				
Juan Bautista Caton				
Juan Tukes				
Joseph Lewis	1			
Guillermo Rose				
Nicolas Devores				
James Sirres				
Joseph Sincops				
Tomas Lenze				
Christopher Tipus				
Michel Murphy	1			
Widow Sampson Arches	1	2	3	
Benjamin Denunter	1	1		
Jacobo Bowen				
Juan Bautista Dubois				
Jacobo Smith	1	1		
Tomas Nuley	1	1		
Mineure Lowaros	1			
Conrad Carpetitor		2	2	
Juan Fice	1		1	
David Simple				
James Parce	1	1		
Patrick Cojidi				
Alexander Auguste Sollin				
Guillermo Bouillette			2	
Henrico Stoffle	1	1		
Luis Baby	1	2		6
Robert Roger	1			
Francisco Brown				
Nicolas Subtib				
Maria Wood	1			

(New Madrid Census Continued)

Head of Household	#Women	#Sons	#Daugh.	#Slaves
Maria Mole	1			
Francisco Michel	1	1	1	
Luis Saint Jean				
Joseph Saxton	1	2	1	
Juan Bautista Mellet	1	3	3	

Montgomery County, Missouri, Tax List, 1819.

Mathew Aga, Dennis Askron, Sampson Allen, Thomas Allen, Bethel Allen, Robert Anderson, William Apling, Lee Alexander, Presley Anderson, William Armstrong, James Anderson, Samuel Benefield, Silvester Baker, Zebediah Baker, Joseph Baker, John Burgit, sr., David Burgit, Amous Boucher, Samuel Baker, Esau Baker, George W. Boothe, Robert Baker, Jacob Baker, John Best, Isaac Best, George Bright, James Bryant, John Butler, Cornelus Burnett, Morgan Bryant, Samuel Bethel, Samuel Boon, Daniel M. Boone, Gabriel Brown, Joshua Brown, Abram R. Baily, Nathan Browning, Daniel Bane, William Brown, Andrew Brown, James Barnes, Sumner Bacon, Dabney Burnet, David Bryan, John Carter, James Bayers, Henry Bryan, James Cates, Jacob Coil, Robert Colgan, Daniel Colgan, Ransom Clifton, William Cates, jr., Joseph Callaway, Thomas Callaway, Jonathan Crow, Robert Craighead, James Cantley, Tillman Cullom, Noah Caten, Larkin T. Callaway, Jonas Caten, Harold Clark, John Comer, William Cundiff, Mark Cole, David Craig, Lewis Cundiff, Simon Creech, John Cottleman, Thomas Cannaday, Gion Cannaday, Jesse Cane, James Cannaday, Flanders Callaway, Andrew Cochran, William Carver, John Dunnica, Louis Dehoit, Thomas Duley, Howell Demoss, John Davis, Wm. H. Dunnica, George Evans, Benjamin Ellis, Jesse Evans, John Evans, Patrick Ewing, John Estes, sr., James Estes, John Estes, jr., Louis Edwards, John Faris, James Estill, Edward Ellis, John Furguson, Joshua Furguson, Antoine Faye, Charles Faye, Mark Foster, Jean Farmer, John Owings, Nicholas Foy, William Ferguson, Nathaniel Farrione, James Faris, Andrew Fourt, James K. Fryer, Benjamin Foreman, Enoch Fruit, Levi Fine, Abraham Fine, Mary Fine, Benjamin Gammon, Aaron Groom, Capt. Baptiste Gragane, Joseph Gordon, James Gordon, James Goodrich, John Gibson, William Grisham, Leonard Grigs, Jonathan Gordon, Daniel Gosen, Wiley Grigs, Jacob Groom, Samuel Grigs, Robert Graham, John Grimmeson, John Gibson, Robert Gray, Thurston Garner, Robert Galaspie, Jonathan Gordon, Jabez Ham, Jonathan Holloway, John Harriman, James Henderson, John Ham, John Hays, George Hackett, John Heath, Peter Hawn, William Hancock, David Howard, Wm. Hall, James Hughes, Absalom Hays, Thomas Hickason, Greenup Hays, Henry Hall, John Hall, David Hall, Boon Hays, James Hutton, William Hopkins, William Harris, Charles Hubbard, John House, Francis Holder, John Hawn, sr., John Hawn, jr., Joseph Hobbs,

(Montgomery County, Missouri Continued)
John Jones, Joseph Johnston, James Jackson, Benjamin James, Lewis Jones, Joshua James, James Journey, Robert Jonston, Preston King, Nathan Kouns, George King, Thomas Kitching, James Kincaid, Isaac Kent, William Kent, John Kent, John King, Hugh Logan, James Langley, Moses Langley, John Lenox, Lewis Laplant, Collect Langley, William Lenox, James Lisle, Rachel Lampkin, Isaac Langley, Isael Lomax, James Level, Wm. T. Lamme, Edward Level, Angus L. Langham, Alexander Logan, Henry Logan, William Lisle, William Logan, Dennis McGarvin, Antoine Marshall, John Messorsmith, Enoch Murrey, Andrew McWilliams, Wm. McGlochlin, Geo. Mouzzer, jr., Geo. Mouzzer, sr., Thomas Marr, Joseph Martin, Samuel Morrice, Isaac Moody, Oliver McAnin, Thomas Moor, Jeremiah Moor, Merriman Moore, John Morrow, Wm. McFarlane, Hugh McDermed, Thomas McQueen, Henry L. Mills, John McKinzey, John C. Milligan, Caleb Nix, Neill Maccan, Wm. McReynolds, Wells E. Marian, John Nixen, Mordicai Morgan, George Miller, John McKinney, Thomas Oden, Alex. McKinney, John Merchant, Hugh Nance, William Nash,jr., William Nash, sr., Jeremiah H. Neill, John Northcut, Thomas C. Owings, Micajah Ousley, Irvine J. Pitman, William Pratt, Drury R. Prichard, Jessee Philips, John Philips, Samuel Pace, James Philips, Henry Parish, James Pennington, James Price, William Patton, Jacob Patton, sr., Lemuel Price, jr., Thomas Puryear, William F. Page, William Pennington, Joseph Revard, Jacob Quick, sr., Jacob Quick, jr., Aaron Quick, Alexander Quick, Francis Roy, Louis Roy, Nicholas Raier, Baptiste Roy, Charles Rial, Josiah Rouceville, Jonathan Ramsey, Job Stark, Josiah Ramsey, sr., Josiah Ramsey, jr., Joseph Roy, Robert Reid, Samuel Reynolds, Huston Reynolds, James Reynolds, Ezra Sutton, Reuben Rider, Benjamin Rodgers, Thomas Smith, Edward Stephenson, William B. Scott, Seth Strickling, David Smith, Rudolph Shobe, Daniel Shobe, Moses Summers, James F. Sharp, Greenbury Spires, John Snethen, James Stephenson, Jacob L. Sharp, Benjamin Sharp, Thomas Smith, John M. Stotts, Joshua Stockstill, Jesse Summers, James Talbot, William Thornton, Francis Tebo, Joseph Tebo, Francis Tayon, John Tice, James Tuttle, William Tutt, William Tinsley, Haile Talbot, David J. Talbot, William F. Talbot, Thomas Talbot, Johnson Taylor, Bryant Thornhill, Nancy Tuttle, John Trimble, Francois Urnon, Peleg E. Thomas, Low Venan, Joseph Vanbibber, Asa Williams, Joseph Williams, Isaac Williams, Joseph Wiggins, John Wyatt, Anthony Wyatt, Henry E. Welch, John Wyatt, sr., John Welch, Frazier Ward, Joseph Ward, George Williams, James Whitesides, Francis Whitesides, John Ward, Aaron Watson, Jacob Zumwalt, Cornelus Williamson, Samuel Williamson, Christopher Zumwalt, Douglass Wyatt, Chester Wheeler, Charles Younger, Benjamin Young, John Young, sr., John Young, jr., Flanders Callaway, Joshua Brown.

St. Louis, Militia, 1780, Taken from the Cuban Papers.
First Company:

Name	Occupation	Born	Age
Lt. Don Augustin Chouteau			
Sub-Lt. Pedro Montardy			
1st Sgt. Nicolas Roy	Trader	France	48
2nd Sgt. Pedro Quienel	Trader	Canada	20
2nd Sgt. Luis Honore	Tailor	Ilinueses	25
1st Corp. Jos. Labuciera	Habitant	Ilinueses	24
1st Corp. Pedro Gonon	Habitant	Canada	36
1st Corp. Pedro Elias	Rower	France	36
1st Corp. Juan Pedro Porsley	Habitant	France	36
2nd Corp. Alexandro Cote	Habitant	Canada	42
2nd Corp. Bapt. Bibaren	Mason	Ilinueses	30
2nd Corp. Tomas Ubaldy	Currier	Italian	38
2nd Corp. Andres Feneti	Rower	New Orleans	34
Nicolas Lecomte	Carpenter	Canada	40
Guillermo Lecomte	Rower	Canada	36
Francisco Delorier	Blacksmith	Canada	40
Esteban Sumande	Rower	Canada	40
Joseph Sumande	Rower	Canada	25
Joseph Sanselie	Habitant	Ilinueses	30
Antonio Gotio	Rower	Canada	26
Juan Bapt. Laflanbuesa	Rower	Canada	23
Francisco Vigo	Merchant	Italian	35
Antonio Galve, sr.	Habitant	Canada	50
Antonia Galve, jr.	Rower	Ilinueses	17
Luis Potie	Habitant	Ilinueses	50
Felizberto Ganon	Habitant	France	50
Gabriel Serre	Merchant	Canada	45
Lorenzo Derroge	Storekeeper	Canada	34
Joseph Cale	Rower	Canada	36
Antonio Lahe	Rower	Canada	28
Juan Bapt. Hortez	Carpenter	France	40
Joseph Teneroso	Rower	Canada	35
Lorenzo Basedonio	Rower	France	40
Juan Luis Lacroia	Storekeeper	New Orleans	27
Juan Maria Papin	Mason	Canada	40
Juan Bapt. Sabus	Habitant	Canada	40
Francisco Verio	Mason	Canada	35
Luis Laflor	Mason	Canada	35
Ignacio Brigpohe	Trader	Canada	42
Rene de Pre	Cooper	Canada	34
Pablo Laderruta	Rower	Ilinueses	26
Antonio Ladusor	Habitant	Canada	38
Luis Lasudray	Rower	Ilinueses	38
Joseph Marchoteau	Carpenter	Ilinueses	25
Noel Brunet	Habitant	Canada	34

(St. Louis Militia, 1780, COntinued)

Name	Occupation	Born	Age
Luis Chavalie	Habitant	Canada	32
Joseph Duchene	Habitant	Canada	40
Antonio Sansy	Mason	Canada	40
Nicolas Chorret	Rower	Canada	46
Pedro Debo	Rower	Canada	26
Pedro Pepen	Rower	Canada	26
Juan Bapt. Lamarina	Rower	Canada	25
Juan Porter	Rower	Canada	30
Todos Santos Paran	Rower	Canada	30
Pedro Lerru	Rower	Canada	25
Francisco Borrosie	Habitant	Canada	33
Luis Beno	Rower	Canada	40
Juan Lepir	Rower	Canada	50
Nicolas Guion	Blacksmith	Canada	40
Luis Laret	Rower	Canada	38
Carlos Balle	Hunter	Canada	50
Pedro Vizonete	Habitant	Canada	38
Joseph Beno	Hunter	Canada	45
Andres Vequet	Rower	Ilinueses	18
Andres Vizonete	Rower	Canada	38
Juan Bapt. Probanche	Habitant	Canada	43
Anrry Orra	Habitant	Amereican	45
Joseph Marichar	Rower	Ilinueses	26
Antonio Marichar	Habitant	Ilinueses	36
Francisco Chole	Rower	Canada	28
Jacobo Marichar	Habitant	Ilinueses	40
Lorenzo Michon	Hunter	Canada	40
Joseph Ribet	Habitant	Canada	36
Amable Demarre	Rower	Canada	35
Pedro Cudorche	Merchant	France	44
Joseph Par	Canada	Canada	40
Silvestre Labadia	Trader	France	43
Bernardo Dubal	Rower	Canada	38
Joseph Papen	Merchant	Canada	36
Carlos Simono	Habitant	Canada	40
Francisco Vizonete	Habitant	Canada	50
Joseph Basor	Rower	Ilinueses	26
Basilio Basor	Rower	Ilinueses	23
Luis Vior	Hunter	Canada	40
Baptist Vizonete	Rower	Canada	34
Juan Bapt. Cambas	Carpenter	France	44
Pedro Choteau	Merchant	New Orleans	22
Joseph Caze	Rower	Ilinueses	20
Joseph Tayon	Farm Laborer	Ilinueses	28
Luis Chil	Rower	France	25
Juan Pablo Tembal	Merchant	France	43
Luis Rover	Habitant	Ilinueses	38

(St. Louis Militia, 1780, Continued)

Name	Occupation	Born	Age
Francisco Corno	Rower	Canada	43
Baptista Cantara	Hunter	Canada	38
Pedro Bernie	Rower	Canada	30
Pedro Sorret	Carpenter	Canada	35
Joseph Labrose	Habitant	Canada	43
Joseph Verdon	Carpenter	Canada	46
Luis Dubroy	Habitant	Canada	38
Pedro Durbois	Rower	Canada	28
Luis Fallar	Rower	Canada	30
Alexandero Balle	Hunter	Canada	33
Juan Probo	Hunter	Canada	36
Alexandro Michon	Hunter	Canada	38
Luis Mercie	Rower	Canada	44
Antonio Huder	Rower	Canada	34
Luis Chatelero	Trader	Canada	40
Salomon Paty	Hunter	American	26
Pablo Guitar	Habitant	Canada	45

Second Company:

Name	Occupation	Born	Age
Lt. DOn Luis Sanselier			
Sub-Lt. Don Carlos Tayon			
1st Sgt. Joseph Polo	Trader	France	34
2nd Sgt. Jn.Bapt. Lapierre	Blacksmith	Canada	36
2nd Sgt. Luis Otonere, sr.	Tailor	Canada	50
1st Corp. Jacobo Labe	Habitant	Ilinueses	40
1st Corp. Carlos Hot	Hunter	Canada	35
1st Corp. Ant. Belpecher	Habitant	Ilinueses	40
1st Corp. Carolos Roy	Habitant	Ilinueses	26
2nd Corp. Pedro Bofrer	Tailor	Canada	35
2nd Corp. Andres Dupuy	Tailor	Canada	26
2nd Corp. Francisco Honore	Tailor	Ilinueses	17
2nd Corp. Ant. Venzan	Trader	France	28
Nicolas Daniel	Hunter	Canada	38
Pedro Plancha	Caulker	France	43
Joseph Tibo	Rower	Canada	38
Pedro Peltie	Habitant	Canada	33
Miguel Lamy	Habitant	Canada	50
Enrique Duchoquete	Habitant	Ilinueses	20
Joseph Peron	Rower	France	30
Alexandro Luese	Habitant	Ilinueses	30
Francisco Duchoquete	Habitant	Ilinueses	17
Bapt. Moro	Rower	Canada	26
Juan Boduen	Rower	Ilinueses	18
Jacobo Lasablonera	Habitant	Canada	38
Carlos Chanrrion	Rower	Ilinueses	43
Pedro Roy	Blacksmith	Canada	45
Todos Santos Lorrose	Rower	Ilinueses	18

(St. Louis Militia, 1780, Continued)

Name	Occupation	Born	Age
Nicolas Bogeneau	Habitant	Ilinueses	38
Jacobo Tabo	Habitant	Canada	36
Simon Cuzot	Habitant	New Orleans	30
Joseph Lapierre	Habitant	Canada	25
Antonio Lusere	Carpenter	Canada	44
Luis Crepo	Habitant	Canada	27
Juan Gilver	Potter	France	48
Joseph Jirar	Rower	Canada	33
Joseph Chartŕan	Habitant	Canada	38
Joseph Rubidu	Shoemaker	Canada	36
Francisco Porten	Rower	Ilinueses	25
Pedro Belhumor	Rower	Canada	30
Francisco Grene	Rower	Canada	50
Pedro Jonca	Rower	Canada	36
Nicolas Lacomble	Cooper	Canada	42
Gregorio Guiersero	Habitant	Ilinueses	28
Baptista Lorenzo	Currier	Canada	36
Pedro Cuzote	Rower	New Orleans	22
Luis Lemez	Shoemaker	New Orleans	30
Joseph Larduera	Rower	Canada	33
Jacobo Larduera	Rower	Canada	28
Antonio Larduera	Rower	Canada	24
Luis Larduera	Rower	Canada	20
Luis Brunet	Hunter	Canada	45
Antonio Brunet	Hunter	Canada	18
Joseph Cote	Rower	New Orleans	17
Pablo Canpo	Rower	Canada	35
Baptista Pety	Rower	Canada	40
Luis Marcil	Rower	Canada	40
Baptista Dujo	Habitant	Canada	40
Joseph Fache	Hunter	Canada	38
Juan Luis Derruen	Habitant	Canada	50
Gaspar Rubio	Merchant	France	50
Juan Baptista Derruen	Rower	Canada	18
Estevan Derruen	Rower	Canada	20
Antonio Rivera	Habitant	Ilinueses	50
Baptista Rivera	Rower	Ilinueses	26
Phelipe Rivera	Rower	Ilinueses	18
Esteban Beron	Rower	France	50
Agustin Hever	Hunter	Ilinueses	44
Francisco Marichar	Habitant	Ilinueses	34
Joseph Ortiz	Merchant	Spain	34
Joseph Beancur	Rower	Canada	43
Bapt. Humet	Rower	Canada	38
Pedro Ganon	Mason	Canada	40
Juan Bapt. Brucieras	Rower	Canada	35
Guiery Denoye	Habitant	Canada	46

(St. Louis Militia, 1780, Continued)

Name	Occupation	Born	Age
Francisco Villars	Rower	Canada	30
Luis Breda	Shoemaker	Ilinueses	24
Francisco Bernie	Rower	Canada	30
Gabriel Dodie	Habitant	Ilinueses	48
Agustin Dodie	Rower	Ilinueses	23
Baptista Henete	Rower	Ilinueses	28
Pedro Bequete	Rower	Ilinueses	43
Gabriel Bequete	Rower	Ilinueses	22
Luis Bulrry	Rope-maker	France	46
Lorenzo Ride	Rower	Ilinueses	24
Luis Boduen	Habitant	Canada	30
Antonio San Francisco	Rower	Ilinueses	25
Baptista Trudo	Rower	Canada	35
Luis Huno	Rower	Ilinueses	25
Luis Ride	Habitant	Canada	50
Guillermo Leconte	Habitant	Canada	46
Joseph Leconte	Rower	Ilinueses	18
Amable Guion	Rower	Ilinueses	16
Juan Martiny	Trader	Canada	50
Joseph Ribar	Trader	Canada	50
Joseph Berge	Hunter	Canada	48
Pedro Dechene	Trader	Canada	36
Juan Casa Noba	Rower	France	50
Francisco Caida	Trader	France	40
Joseph Tesier	Rower	Canada	35
Juan Baptista Labreche	Rower	Canada	34
Carlos Sanguinete	Merchant	Canada	43
Joachim Roy	Carpenter	Canada	38
Francisco Barrera	Baker	France	43
Luis Fache	Rower	France	50
Isaac Tros	Rower	American	36
Andres Fidecharme	Rower	France	45
Antino Lajoy	Habitant	Ilinueses	18

St. Louis County, Missouri, Tax List, 1805.

August Chouteau, Charles Gratiot, Edward Kelly, Nicholas Bougeneau, John Flemming, M. P. Leduc, Louis Delisle, Calvin Adams, Simon Woods, Antoine Sulard, Ph. Watkins, Manuel Lisa, Francy Nois, Theres Bezare, --- Claymorgan, --- Zandt, Bapt. Ferar Tibo, John Dorroin, Louis Labaum, John Connor, Joseph Hortiz, Louis Brazo, Joseph Hortiz, John B. Tetrodusham, F. M. Benway, Louis Ammell, Lora Reed, Piere Getard, B. Easton, Joseph Lasoire, Regis Vassuer, Jack Chovin, Bapt. Marlie, M. Joseph Hebeau, Jack Chovin, Amable Flamo, Eugo. Alvarez, John B. Ladusir, --- Landerville, Leonar Lafond, Louis Lamond, John Bapt. Trudo, Bates Dushucate, Francy Lebarge, Louis Bodoin, Francy Lebarge, Charles Sanguinet, Charles Sanguinet, Philip

(St. Louis County, Missouri Continued)
Biviar, --- Bissonet, Louis Boisi, Antoine Riviere, Margaret Flandron, Joseph Bazel Bisonet, Francy Duchouquet, Antoine Vansan, Alence Lalonel, --- Crane, --- Dogan, Joseph Sigan, John Bapt. Tisson, --- Baribana, Baptes Belford, John Tiyon, Frances Tiyon, Joseph Lalois, Charles Simeno, Benard Pratte, Francy Valvey, --- Parisien, --- Vital, Michael Lamot, John B. Hortiz, Tarant St. Cyr, Tarant St. Cyr, --- Lacompte, John Taylor, --- Kenal, Bapt. Labo, --- Rankin, --- Malanphy, Mme. Chouteau, Benito Pantoin, sr., D. Deloney, Paul Menard, Wm. Dubroil, E. Yostee, Benoit Vazquez, Gabriel Becht, Francis Masso, --- Duchequet, Joseph Charleville, Dominique Huges, Benito Pantoin, sr., McNair Denny, Joseph Hebert, John Biggs, Louis Cayou, Francis Cayou, Eustach Cayou, Marie Labostie, Le Cin (a free negro), Ther (a free negro), --- Datcherut, Wm. Sulivan, Janet, Reaman, Isaac Darniel, Samuel Solomon, John Hankinson, Joseph M. Lanahan, Thomas F. Reddic, Paul Gatar, Alexan Bushso, Francis Chenelle, Louis Gatar, Michel Alender, --- Frazer, Harry Chouquet, Bapt. Boilier, Charl. Laddois, Paul Robert, Antoine Besda, Amable Fertre, Pier Delastergut, Julian McLaine, Joseph Menar, George Shultz, Christ. Shultz, Gabriel Uno, Cahrles Busson, Henry Delourie, Joseph Labade, Michel Marley, J. Bte. Provencher, John L. Provencher, Madam Morrin, Charles Buisonet, Campbell Mattock, Dr. Saugraine, Pier Chouteau, Pascal Cayriou, Patric Lee, John Michum, Mme. Bichar, Francy dit Saugrin, Baptist Charleville, Bapt. Papin, John M. Papin, Robert Westcoat, Samuel Neusen, August Ledon, Joseph Robedoux, Joseph Robedoux, Petit John, Francois Roy, John Coons, Ph. Delor, Chs. Robert, Auguste Langlois, Louis Courtois, Courtois, jr., Julian Chouquet, Louis Motie, Bpt. Gamash, Peter Vallier, August Gamash, Louis Maerd, Michael Teso, J. Bapt. Lajaye.

<u>The Following Persons Petitioned Congress to Approve Their New Madrid Land Titles, Relief for Earthquakes, December 30, 1818, Carter's Papers, Vol. XV.</u>

Peter A. Laforge, Joseph Pain, Josiah Thompson, -- Paman, Peter Painin, Saml. Black, --- Lefever, Jno. B. Sallie, Katy Shawnee, Marie Pheraquille, Elisha Jackson, --- Amelin, John Bigne, Pierre Perrin, Andre Racine, Louis Toussant, Francois Riene, --- Denoyer, --- Mallet, --- Chillard, Charles Boneau, --- Mallet, --- Denilly, Thomas Powers, David Gray, Francois Decomb, Peter Dubigny, Charles Anoth, Elisha Jackson, Arthur Miller, Charles Boneau, Stephen St. Mary, Josef L'Amoureux, Jacob Myers, Antoine Gamlin, Francois Riene, Thomas Jacobs, Simon Jacoba, --- Lafleur, Francis B. St. Mary, James Gill, --- St. Antoine, Paul Putneuf, K. St. P. Servant, Francois Paquin, Joseph Rondeau, Francois Pasquin, John Niot, Francois Galen, James Adams, Jam. Hunot J. Bayard, Etienne St. May,

(Petition to Congress)
Grand Jean, Joseph Lesiur, Joseph Lewis, Josef Maisonville, Nicholas Pierre, Henry Peyroux, Charles Gilbault, Jean St. May, Joseph St. May, --- Runby, Peter Francis Laforge, Josef Michel, John Brigne, Francois Nachette, Hyacinthe Bathiaume, John B. Carter, Louis Denoyer, Antonio Denoyer, Charles St. May, Thomas Fowler, Francois Contly, L. St. Paul Lalime, P. F. Laforge, Antoine Nachette, Lewanna Gill, John Niott, Geo. Wilson, Louise Gamlin, Rosela Gamlin, Hipolte St. John, Josef Garet, Joseph Genereux, Pierre Gavian, Louis Jirard, Jacob Myers, Paul Laderoute, Nicholas Auger, Nicholas Hebert, Jean Derlean, --- Blandeau, Pierre Peron, P. A. Laforge, David Devore.

Platte County, Missouri, Personal Property Tax List, 1839.

James A. Anthony, Cromwell Ashby, Samuel Austin, Solomon Allen, David Allen, Isaac Allen, Jeremiah Atkins, Williamson Atterbury, Samuel Adamson, Thomas Adams, Levi Adamson, James Atterbury, Thomas Atterbury, Joseph Alfry, Robert Allen, John Artman, Reuben Arnold, Thomas M. Aull, Isaac Archer, Samuel Allen, Jesse R. Allen, Robt. Anderson, Thomas Allen, Jacob Anderson, Wm. Anderson, Joel Albright, William B. Allman, Sterling Ashworth, David D. Ashworth, Bethel Allen, Moses Allen, James Arter, Joseph Atkins, David Anderson, Martin T. Berry, James Anderson, John Allen, William Asher, Washington Funderbark, Jacob Adamson, Geo. W. Anderson, W. B. Aldman, Manasseth Beth, James Bird, Bane Baldon, William Bane, Milton Brown, John Bryant, D. G. Deauchamp, Isaac Blanton, Jackson Butts, Martin Baldwin, M. Bryan, Henry Bradley, Henry Butts, John B. Bounds, Joseph Baker, William Bell, Edwin Bedford, Henry F. Bark, Joseph Britian, Lewis W. Bell, William Baley, Caleb Baley, Philip Bolwar, Wesley Baker, Cyrus Barnes, John Baker, Sidney Brooks, Perry Bales, Sampson Butler, Lossen Baker, David Bell, Thomas Beegle, James Beegle, Wm. Beegle, Henry Brail, Green H. Barnes, R. P. Beauchamp, Randal Baker, David Brown, Isham Baber, David Braton, James Belienr, John Delienr, sr., Micajah Belienr, Henry Barnes, John Boilston, John Barge, Nathaniel Boilston, Thomas Boilston, Hugh Brown, John Bywaters, Joseph Blakly, James Brown, Hugh Brown, Nancy Baits, Jackson Baits, Andrew Baker, John R. Buchanan, Calvin Brown, John Brown, Harrison Brown, G. W. Brunett, John Bane, James Brooks, Gotham Brown, John Bigham, James W. Bigham, B. C. Brown, Elisha Barnes, William Best, Moses Barnes, Elisha Brown, Felix G. Bush, Elisha Brown, Abner Bayarth, Delania Boland, Chiles Bennett, William Boland, Benj. Boland, Henry Barker, Ezekiel Blanton, William D. Boland, William Bennett, Lewis Burnes, Elias Barker, John Barker, Micajah Brown, John Brink, Martin Buff, Carr Baley, Michael Bird, Samuel Brown, John E. Brown, Jordan Babaer, William Bird, Stephen Bedwell,

(Platte County, Missouri Continued)
Andrew Brown, Richard Bickerstall, Thomas Blankenship, James Butler, Sylvester Blankenship, William Banta, William Butler, Isaac Barnes, Abram Barton, James Brasfield, Willis Bledsoe, James H. Berry, Moses Boilston, Addison Bruton, L. F. Brown, William Brown, sr., William Brown, jr., Archibald Brown, B. C. Brown, Sarchel C. Bawn, Adam Brown, Gray B. Brown, Stephen Beauchamp, Squire Babcock, Joel Blanton, John Bowlwar, David Borden, William Borden, Adam Cristison, Andrew Campbell, Eli Casey, Daniel Clary, Daniel Carey, Berry Carwood, Beaufort Carpenter, James Canter, James Coleman, Gabriel Clark, John B. Collier, Mathias Cline, Abraham Cline, Joseph Cox, Allen Crook, William Chance, R. Church, John P. Cincaid, William Cox, Archibald Campbell, James Cox, Jacob Cox, William Clay, Abraham Collett, Johnson Clay, Beery Creek, George W. Cannon, Joseph I. Cannon, W. M. Carter, Lacy Carter, Wakefield Coks, Wiley Cooper, Henry Cooper, Robert Cain, David Carson, Joseph W. Coks, Rev. James W. Coks, Washington Campbell, Jonathan Carpenter, Willis Cartwright, James Cartwright, John Cooper, Isaac Cartwright, Samuel Cannon, Jonathan Carpenter, James Collins, Alexander Cannon, Patrick Cooper, John Cooper, Rbt. Cooper, John Downing, Elias Davis, Williamson Donaldson, I. I. Draper, Truman Day, Thomas Dye, Flemmonds Drummons, Abner Dean, Bartlett Dean, Francis Dean, Edward P. Duncan, William A. Dunn, Frederick Dean, Daurbin Donell, James Dyer, Thomas Duncan, Davis Duncan, Washington Duncan, John Dyer, James Derland, Dury Duncan, Wade Davis, Madison Draice, Wm. Dull, Jackson Draice, John S. Davis, John Deacon, G. P. Dorriss, Washington Dyer, Joseph Davis, James M. Davis, James Duncan, James Dougherty, John Dunigan, George Dyle, Preston Dunlay, Allen Davis, Benjamin Davis, Lott Drummons, Archibald Elliot, Robert Davis, Thomas Edwards, Elisha J. Edwards, Isaac J. Edwards, Isaac M. C. Ellis, Thomas F. Ellis, John Elloitt, Benjamin F. English, Robert T. Evins, Thomas H. Evins, John H. Evins, John Eldrige. John Eaton, Joseph Elder, Isaac Eads, William Ellington, Doctor Ellis, Joseph Elder, John Eaton, Jesse Eads, Solomon Eads, Moses Eads, Charles Early, James Flannery, sr., W. M. English, William Fox, John F. Fry, Jacob Foreman, Mathias Frickle, James Fulkerson, George Funderbark, George W. Ford, Levi Fowler, Elisha Francis, George Ferguson, Neeley Frame, Sasil Fewgett, John M. Foris, Ezekiel Fugett, John W. Foris, William Fulton, James Fox, Allen Furgerson, Samuel Finley, William A. Fox, Andrew Foster, Thomas Fields, Levi Fields, Benjamin Fields, Hiram Ferrel, Thomas Farmer, Ansom Farmer, M. D. Faylor, Ambrose Foster, Absolom Fickle, John Fleming, Samuel Ford, William M. Fox, Jesse Gibson, Wm. Gibson, James Gibson, Jesse Fleming, James Flannery, sr., A. Gordon, Abner Fickle, Alvey Graves, Philip E. Gill, Robert P. Gillan, Jesse Gillum, Riley Gregg, Jacob Guyer, John Greene,

(Platte County, Missouri Continued)
John Gillan, David Gladden, Harmon Glasscock, John K. Gyle, Isaac W. Gibson, Stephen Gibbs, Daniel Grober, Elisha Green, Jackson Gann, Caswell R. Gray, David Gregg, James H. Gribble, Benjamin Green, George W. Gason, Charles Gray, Thornton Gann, James Gray, Silas Glem, Gregg Gafferson, James Gregg, Henry Gunn, David Gunn, John Grooms, James Griffeth, Rebecca Gunn, Andrew Henson, William M. Hayes, John Hendricks, Alison Hill, Daniel Hunsaker, Isaac Hunsaker, Joseph Hunsaker, William E. Henson. Robert Haston, John Herron, John Hognight, Jefferson Harris, Gideon Harson, B. M. Hughes, Orum Hulet, James Hull, Charles Hungerford, Anna Hungerford, Benjamin Holland, Thomas L. Holland, Robert W. Holland, Nathaniel Holland, Samuel Hoy, Derman Henderson, John Henderson, Thomas Harrington, James Holeman, W. B. Hungerford, Joseph Henderson, Giles Henderson, Miles Harrington, Slyvester Hunt, William Huffman, Alfred W. Hughes, William Huffman, Jacob Hayes, S. C. Hayes, David R. Holt, D. R. Hayes, Enoch Howard, James Halford, John Harris, John Howard, Elisha Hatley, Solomon Hater, Thomas Henderson, John Higgans, Jonathan Hincher, Archibald Hill, James Hamlin, George Hunter, Adam Hornback, Henry Hamlin, Peter Hendricks, David Hamilton, Mathias M. Hughes, Philomon Higgins, Josiah Higgins, Jacob Higgins, William Hardey, James Henshaw, Henry Her, Richard Her, Jacob Her, William Indicott, William Ish, Richard B. Indicott, William Jack, sr., Stephen Johnston, Wm. Jack, jr., Alfred Jack, David Johnston, Jefferson Jones, F. B. Jones, Lewis Johnson, Benjamin Johnson, Edward Johnson, Beremore Johnson, David James, Stephen Jones, Henry Jones, Barbara Johnson, Henry James, James C. Jordan, William S. Jones, John E. Jetson, John H. Johnson, Daniel Jackson, Wallis Jackson, James Jackson, jr., James Johnson, Brooking Jeffers, Uptiam Jenkins, Moses Jennings, Leanded, William Kavinan, Benjamin Kuykendall, William Kincaid, James Kaye, Johnson Kimsey, Harvey Kincaid, James Kincaid, James C. Key, Thomas A. Key, James Kimsey, John F. Kimsey, George P. Kaye, Miles Keyton, Daniel King, Abner Kaye, John Kimsey, William Little, Alois Kimsey, Caleb Lowns, John Lewis, L.L. Leonard, William Lovelady, James Lovelady, sr., Thomas Lovelady, Levi Lawler, James Lynch, Isaac Lesch, Isaac F. Lewis, Robert F. Logan, Moses Lovelady, Adam J. Lucus, Richard Linville, John Lewis, Byran Lewis, William Lewis, sr., James Lindsay, Marcus Lipcomb, Abraham Linville, Jackson W. Lee, John Larker, Jesse Lively, William Lockhart, John Long, Willis Long, Isaac Lebo, Thomas Landley. John Lewis, Jesse Lewis, Slone Lewis, Isaac Lewis, John Liggett, Joseph Lynch, John Lynch, James Mobley, John Linville, Granville Linville, Harrison Linville, Simon W. Levendy, Joseph Monneyham, William Monneyham, Greenfield Matthews, Ervin Monneyham, John S. Malott, Patton Murphey, Charles Mullins, Anthony Mahan, Jesse McCall, Isaac Moody,

(Platte County, Missouri Continued)
Jonathan Mosure, Nimrod McCracken, Jesse Moore, John Morin, Thomas Marchael, Anderson McFall, Matthias Maston, Felix G. Mulligan, L. W. McManus, Jonathan Mitchell, Charles Mucey, David McCollum, George McAfee, John Marsh, John McCarty, W. S. May, Jesse Morin, Silas May, George Martin, Isaac Miller, William McBride, Jacob McKissick, John Martin, David McGee, Henry Matheney, Robert McCracken, James Miller, John Miller, Jacob Milihan, William Moore, Samuel McGown, Anson McCracken, John McCord, Albert W. Mason, William McGuire, Wm. Malotte, Abraham Miller, Joseph Martin, Den Meddlin, Thomas McClair, George McClair, James McClair, William McClair, N. P. Owen, Samuel T. Mason, Richard McMahon, James McMahon, J. H. Owen, Samuel McAdow, George B. McAdow, Robert B. Mitchell, William Manian, John McClair, Woodson Manian, George Martin, Wesley McCollom, James C. Meens, John Miller, Jackson McCollom, A. J. Markwell, David S. McWilliams, Jesse Morras, Joseph Moore, Houston McFarland, William S. Murphey, Sandy H. Moreland, J. M. Marchael, Elisha Morgan, John F. McWhirter, Jesse Masse, Elisha Morgan, Sandy H. Moreland, Alexander McDonald, Daniel Moreland, John H. Meador, John McClarey, Thomas Malott, Wm. Martin, Nathaniel Mann, Hugh McCafferty, Samuel McCafferty, Edward McFerson, Nicholas McFerson, Benjamin Moncus, William Martin, Franklin Martin, Harden Martin, Zadock Martin, Jesse Masse, Joseph Martin, Bright Martin, William McCray, William Masse, Frederick Marshall, Joshua Noland, Hosea Norris, Wm. Nave, Gabriel Nilson, Daniel Night, Abner Norris, Thomas H. Noble, C. C. Nichles, James Nichles, Abner Morris, Daniel Night, Isaac Norman, Nicholas Noland, Obed Noland, William Newman, John Noland, Joel Noland, Aaron Owen, Timothy Owen, E. C. O'Keef, John R. Owen, M. N. Owen, J. H. Owen, William O'Vanion, Isham Owen, Henry D. Oden, John Packwood, William Packwood, P. W. Pearson, William Praiter, David Poor, Ervin Parrott, William Peters, James Pennington, Hezekiah Porter, Enoch Patrick, John Pace, Harrison Pinkston, Thomas M. Page, Henderson Pinkston, Levi Pilkinton, Robert Patton, Daniel K. Parker, James Parker, L. M. Pittman, Reuben Pigg, William Pearson, Berry Pitcher, Hiram Pitcher, Henry F. Powers, Jacob Pitts, Robert Pearson, Foniley Price, Samuel Phillips, Wilson Potter, Bentley Potter, Amos Riley, Benjamin Robertson, R.M. Robertson, Thomas Ring, Henry Renick, Riley Ramsey, Daniel Reed, John Ramset, Abraham Risk, Robert Renick, John Routh, George W. Renick, Mallon Renick, J. C. Robertson, Jeremiah Rose, James Rutledge, David Rutledge, John P. Rogers, James B. Riggs, Charles Robertson, William Robertson, James Roup, William Roup, Robert Ross, Garrison Reed, John Rummons, John Rouo, Alexander Russell, Samuel Ross, David Roup, Anderson Rogers, James M. Rogers, John Rogers, Sidney Ray, Russell Rogers, F. M. Randolph, William Rolston, William M. Sutton,

(Platte County, Missouri Continued)
Elijah Shepherd, William Slawn, Benjamin Stanton, Jonathan Smith, Buford Stanton, Jonathan Scaggs, Joseph Shannon, John Stillwell, William Sharp, Nicholas Sharp, Alfred Sanders, George Smith, William Shafer, Isaac Stobaugh, James Smith, John Seers, John M. Savage, Jonathan Shaw, Joseph Still, Job St. John, George Stallcup, James Sanders, John C. Statt, D. A. Sutton, Isaac Stoats, Samuel Surney, Wayman St. Clair, Eli Shepherd, Medcalf Smith, William St. John, Jeremiah Stanford, Zephaniah St. John, John Sipes, Jeremiah Spratt, Thomas K. Simpson, James Spratt, George Southard, Reuben Shackleford, Henry Sharp, Daniel Sharp, George Sharp, John P. Smith, Mrs. Nancy Smith, Doctor Smith, James Simpson, Richard Smith, Wm. Simpson, Robert Stone, William G. Smith, James Simpson, Bird Speerlock, James R. Shepard, Jonathan Shepard, Lewis Scott, Benjamin Smith, Joseph Swanson, Jacob Swops, James B. Smith, Gishum Springer, George Springer, P. B. Solomon, R. P. Wood, Samuel Stitt, Absalom Smith, Josiah Thorp, William Tate, John B. Terry, Nathan Thorn, Joseph Todd, jr., Isaac Thomas, David Thomas, Joseph Thomas, William Turnhill, S. B. Taylor, John Thornburg, Silas Tribble, Joseph Todd, sr., Reuben B. Tilley, John Tincher, Daniel Thomas, John Trapp, John M. Tate, Robert Todd, William Todd, sr., John Todd, Anderson Tribble, Thomas Turner, William Todd, jr., Andrew Thompson, John Timberlick, Thomas Tawson, John W. Taylor, Boston Temple, James Thorpe, Terry Trapp, Mrs. Lydia Tebbs, Squire B. Thorp, John Tipton, Albert Tipton, Jonathan Todd, Dudley Tribble, William Usry, Henry Underhill, Wesley Vaughn, Barrel Vaughn, David Vaughn, Joseph Vilatt, Jesse Vineyard, John W. Vineyard, Benjamin Van Meter, Thomas M. Ward, Charles Wills, Edward Wilcox, W. J. Winwright, Ellis Williams J. W. B. Winn, James White, J. B. Wilson, David Woody, Dalin Williams, James Wilson, James Wood, Stephen Wills, Wim. Walker, James Wills, Harvey White, James Walters, Elijah Whitton, Wm. Wilson, Nathaniel Wice, Joseph B. Wells, Dudley Wells, Rich. Walker, Andrew Welch, Zachhariah Warner, Hiram, Hall L. Wilkerson, Samuel Walker, Jeremiah Wilson, John H. Winston, Joseph Winston, David M. Williams, Jacob Younts, Washington Yates, John Young, Jesse Yocum, William Young, Rufus Young, John E. Young, Benjamin Yocum, Joshua Yates, Leroy Yates, Abel Yates, William Yates, Thomas H. Yates.

Petition to Congress to Establish a Postal Route, St. Michel, Ste. Genevieve County, Missouri, Carter's Papers, Vol. XV, March 10, 1818.
Merril Lanson, A. Bird, Jno. Robinson, R. B. Griffith, J. Robinson, Wm. Sims, John Arnes, Jonathan Hembley, John Smith, John Barnes, Jonathan Hembey, John Callaway, Robert Crawford, Moses Bates, Saml. Campbell, Peter Callaway, Thomas Crawford,

(Petition to Congress)
Thomas Thorson, John Burdett, Wm. Shaw, Wm. Benett, Thomas Craddock, Jacob Stephens, Gabriel J. Stephens, Wm. Stephens, G. W. Callaway, Wm. Edgar, Thomas Griggs, Thompson Crawford, Thomas Cooper, John Pinkerton, Joseph Lubby, Jonathan Isom, Moses Baird, Jas. Moore.

Spanish Census Cape Girardeau, 1803, Taken from the Cuban Papers.

Note: There were no ages stated concerning the classes.

Name	Males			Females		
	1st	2nd	3rd	1st	2nd	3rd
Louis Lorimier	2	4		1	2	
Bartholomew Cousin		1				
Pierre Godair		2		2	2	
Solomon Thorn	1	1	1	2	1	
Benjamin Goodwin	1		1		1	
Andrew Ramsey	1	3	1	2		1
Andrew Ramsey	2	1			1	
Alexander Parish	3	1		1	1	
William Boner		1		2	1	
Samuel Bradley		1	1	2	1	1
Tmothy Connelly	3	1			1	
Mrs. Alex Guibony	2	2		2	2	
Jeremiah Simpson	4	3		1	2	
Abraham Byrd, sr.	3	3		1	1	
Jacob Jacobs		1				
John Weaver	1	1		1	2	
James Cox	2	8	1	3	2	1
Simeon Kenyon	1	1		2	1	
Jeremiah Thompson		1			1	
John Thompson		1			1	
Elizabeth Thompson	1				1	
Samuel Randal		2			1	
Mrs. Samuel Randal	3				1	
Enos Randal	1		1		3	
Moses Hurley	2	1		1	1	
Joseph Thompson		4			2	
Joseph Worthington		2		2	1	
Samuel Strother	1	1			1	
William Strother	1	1		1	1	
Benjamin Hatgrove		3		1	1	
Matthew Hubble	2	3		2		
Daniel Hubble	1	1			1	
Ithmar Hubble	2	2		3	1	
Jonathan Hubble		1			1	
Horace Austin		1			1	

(Spanish Census, Cape Girardeau Continued)

Name	Males			Females		
	1st	2nd	3rd	1st	2nd	3rd
Martin Rodney	1	3		1	1	
Jacob Foster	2	1	1		1	1
Jacob Foster		1			1	
William Murphy	2	3	1		1	
James Caruthers		1		1	1	
Renna Brummit	1	2		4	3	
John Drybread		1	1	2	3	
Joseph Fyght	1	1			1	
John Losta	2	1		1	1	
Andrew Franks	2	2	1	2	1	1
Allen McKenzie	2	1		1	1	
Mrs. Walter Burrows	1	1		1	1	
John Burrows		1			1	
John Summers		2	1			1
John Summers		1		3	1	
Andrew Summers		1			1	
Modad Randal	2	1			1	
James Randal	1	1			1	
Anthony Randal	1	1		1	1	
Hugh Cresswell	2	1		1	1	
Joseph Waller	2	1		1	1	
James Dowty	3	1			1	
William Williams	1	1			1	
Isaac Williams		1			1	
Mrs. Dixon					1	1
Enos Randal	1	1			1	
John Abernathy	1	4		3	1	
Lewis Eustache	2	1		4	1	
Thomas Bull	2	1		2	1	
William Daugherty		2		2	1	
Elijah Daugherty		1			1	
Jesse Cain	2	1		1	1	
Robert Green	1	3		3	4.	
Lewis Latham		1		3	1	
Mrs. James Miller	3			1	2	
Daniel Brant		2			1	
Jonathan Foreman	1	4		2	3	
James Arrell	1	1		1	1	
Henry Sharadin	1	2		1	4	
Henry Hand		3		1	1	
Lewis Dixon	2	1		3	1	
Gilbert Hector	3	1		2	1	
Chistopher Hays	1	1	1	2	3	
George Hays	1	1			1	
Samuel Pew	5	1		1	1	
Charles Fallenash	2	1		1	1	

(Spanish Census, Cape Girardeau Continued)

Name	Males			Females		
	1st	2nd	3rd	1st	2nd	3rd
Hezekiah Dixon		1		1	1	
Elijah Wittaker	2	1		2	2	
Benijah Laugherty		1		5	1	
Hugh Connelly		2		2	2	
James Cooper		1			1	
David Patterson		2			2	
John Patterson	1	1		2	1	
James Boyd		2			3	
John Magee		2		2	1	
William Hill	4	4		1	1	
Stephen Byrd	1	1		2	1	
Jonathan Buys	2	1		2	1	
Jeptha Cornelius	3	2		2	2	
Amos Byrd		1	1		1	
Abraham Byrd, jr.	1	1				
John Byrd	3	1		4		
Isaac Kelly	2	1			1	
Joseph Young		1			1	
Philip Young		1			1	
John McCarty	1	2		3	1	
Josiah Lee			1			
Josiah Lee	1	1			1	
William Russell	2	1		1	1	
Charles Demoss	1	1		2	1	
Morris Young	1	1		1	1	
Michael O'Hogan						
John Freeman	2	1		1	2	
George F. Bollinger				1		
Daniel Clingingsmith	4			1	1	
Joseph Nyswonger		2			2	
Joseph Baker	1	1			1	
John Probst		3		4	4	
Jeremiah Banish		1	1	1	2	1
David Bollinger	1	4		3	2	
Philip Bolinger	2	3			4	
Mrs. Slinker		1		5	3	
Peter Cryts	1	1		3	2	
Conrad Strother	1	1		2	2	
Adam Strother	1	1		3	1	
Joseph Worthington	2	1		1	2	
Peter Strother	2	1		3	1	
George Grount	1	1			1	
Peter Grount	1	1		4	3	
Mathias Bollinger	4	1		3	1	
Henry Bollinger		1			1	
John Bollinger	2	3			3	

(Spanish Census, Cape Girardeau Continued)

Name	Males			Females		
	1st	2nd	3rd	1st	2nd	3rd
William Bollinger		1		1	1	
Daniel Ashabranner	1	1		1	1	
John Hoss	4	2		1	4	
Leonard Welker		3	1	2		
William Flanaing		1			1	
Cgristopher Aidinger		1		1	1	
Valentine Lorr		1				
Peter Hardell	3	1		2	1	
Jacob Caruther		3	1		4	1
Fred Limbach, jr.	2	1		2	3	
Handel Barks	3	1		2	1	
Jacob Barks		1		1		
John Miller	4	5		1	3	
John Guething		1				
James McMillen		1			1	
Martin Cotner		2			2	
Tillman Smith	1	4		2	2	
Ephraim Stout	3	4		2	1	
Jacob Kelley	2	1	1	1	1	
John Latham	1	2		1	1	
Ezekiel Block	2	2		4	1	
Andeston Rodgers	3	2		3	1	
David McMultrie	1	1			1	
Frederick Slinker	2	1		3	1	
William Smith		3		2	3	
John Hays		1			1	
Francois Berthluame	1	2			1	
Robard Meredith		1				
George Cayender		1			1	
Charles Friend	4	4		3	2	
Thomas Wellborn	2	3		4	4	
William Ross	2	2		2	1	
Edmund Hogan	5	1		4	1	
William Smith	1	2		2	4	
Daniel Sexton	1	1			1	
Lemuel Cheney		1				
James Curvin	3	1		2	1	
Stephen Quimby		2				
Robert Quimby	2	1			1	
Mrs. Williamson	3				1	
Robert Lane	1	2		3		
Jesse Bowden	1	1		1	1	
Alexander Milliken	1	2		1	1	
Charles Findley	1	1		2	1	
Jacob Lene	2	1		2	1	
John Loved	1	1		2	2	

(Spanish Census, Cape Girardeau Continued)

Name	Males			Females		
	1st	2nd	3rd	1st	2nd	3rd
Thomas Woolsey	1	1		3	1	
Abraham Randal		1			1	
Terence Dyal		1			1	
Alexander Bailie		1			1	
Charles Lucas	2	2		1	2	
Joseph Magee	3	2		2	1	
Thomas Norris	1	1		3	1	
Curtis Wellborn	3	3		2	1	
James Wellborn		1			1	
Jonathan Wellborn	2	1		2	1	
John Powlin	1	1		3	1	
Jacob Welker	1	1			1	

<u>Memorials for Governor Wilkinson, December 1805, Vol. XIII., Carter's Papers.</u>

 <u>Ste. Genevieve</u>: Pierre Abar, Charles Archanbeaux, Wm. H. Ashley, Francois Aubuchon, Francois Auguste, Pierre Aubuchon, P. Aubuchon, Thomas Baer, Joseph Bare, Raphael Bauvais, J.S. G. Bauvais, Louis Bauyer, Bte. Bequet, sr., Bte. Bequet, jr., Francois Bernier, James Berry, John Birk, Manuel Blanco, Cola Cocent, Joseph Blay, Joseph Bogy, Louis Bolduc, David Clark, Alex Coleman, Jacob Bonne, Joseph Boyer, Jh. Boyer, Baptiste Dufour, Joseph Dufour, Louis Dufour, Parfait Dufour, Joseph Donnohue, Louis Govro, sr., Louis Govro, jr., Michel Govro, Pierre Govro, Antoine Govoro, Bazile Mesplay, John O'Daniel, John Patterson, Jno. Paul, Etien Quienelle, George Seaburd, Oliver Taylor, John Wells, Jacob Wise, Antoine Buate, Josiah Ellis, Anrie Govort, Francis Grande, Joseph Grenon, Christian Hunter, J. Bre. Hubardeau, Antoinne Guelle, Jph. Guelle, D. L. Johnson, Edward Johnson, Timothy Kelly, Absalom Kinnison, Dominique Legrand, Jacque Lemoine, John Limberick, Abraham Newfield, Charles McDernitt, Alexander McConnochi, Ambroise Placet, William Pope, Charles Rochefort, John Seely, William Russ, Armant Tellier, Baz. Valle, Julien Trote, Ate. Cerre, Saml. Bridge, Duff Chadwell, Ambroiz Caraphen, William Dunn, Ed Gibson, S. De Kerlezand, Alexander Dechee, Charles Henry, John Hawkins, James Hunter, William James, P. Leuvard, James McLean, Francois Mannish, Js. Maxwell, Pierre Mesplais, Bte. Moro, Bte. Moro, jr., Joseph Moro, Mathew Mullins, Francois Roussin, Joseph Belete Pere, Robt. Rairdon, Bte. Pratte, J. B. Pratte, John Price, John Perio, Jean Bte. Taumier, James W. Wright, James Young, Francois Cahot, Batites Caos, Andrie Chantilon, Antoine Chenete, Pl. Detchemendy, Fs. Dielle, Flynn, sr., Wm. Flynn, jr., Jean Gagnon, Henry Dodge, Israel Dodge, Bte. Janis, sr., Bte. Janis, jr., Francois Janis, L. Lector, Rowland Keown, Johan Klein, Pierre Lechaple, Louis

(Memorials, Ste. Genevieve District Continued)
Lafours, Frans. Langellier, Bte. La Plante, French Strother, Charles Patten, John Patten, Ambroise Placet, Bte. Placet, Louis Placide, Hippolite Robert, Paul Robert, Josphe Renger, Jacob Reed, Vital St. Gem, Berthelemis St. Gemme, Beauvais St. Gemme, John Seely, B. Strother, William Strother, Louis Villenave, Rob. Sprigg, Jacque Winston, Charles Vallee, Benj. Walker, Francois Thibult, Joseph Tesserau, Michel Griffard, J. Guibourd, Vainsan Lafoise, Louis Lacroy. Auguste Obuchon, Charles Obojez, Amable Patnode, James Moore, sr., James Moore, jr., Joseph Miles.

St. Charles: Louis Lorain, Joh. McDonald, Louis Mercelle, Louis Menare, Jh. Marye, Bt. Mareche, Ant. Marechalle, John McMickle, John North, H. O'Neill, Batite Palor, Glai Panlon, Bate Gour, Allen Greenstreet, Eunock Greenstreet, Bt. Gresa, James Greenstreet, William Greenstreet, F. Guenneville, Bt. LeBaus, Joseph Hainds, William Hays, Charles Hebert, Patrise Honor, Francois Honore, Francis Howell, John Howell, Thomas Howell, George Huffman, George Huffman, jr., Piater Huffman, Pe. Janis, Louis Jeans, Daniel Little John, James Jones, F. Lesieur, Moses Kenney, John Kerr, Daniel Kethley, Pier Troge, Timothy Kibby, Pole Lacrois, Pierre LaCroixe, Jh. Laglois, Bt. Lajeunessee, Michelle Lamonte, Jn. La Plante, T. Whitley, Bte. Las Croix, Nicau La Saille, Gabriel Latrielle, Charles Laverdure, Andre Le, jr., --- Leclere, Alexy Le Conte, James Lewis, Simons Lepage, Francois Liberge, Charles Valle, John Walker, Pascalle Vale, James Van Bibber, Alexy Visin, Joseph Voisare, Augustin Villon, Bartholume Woolooms, Andrew Zumwalt, Bartholume Woolooms, jr., John Woolooms, Etien. Pepins. William Steward, John Simpson, Thomas Smith, Francois Smyth, Michael Squire, John Sullons, jr. John Scott, H. Savoye, Bt. Savoy, Jh. Saurino, Charles Tayon, Charles Tayon, Louis Tayon, Bt. De Nouie, Louis Chambirs, Ml. Chele Pitre, William Clark, Bt. Dant, Auguste Clemens, Bateas Cluka, Fra. Cois Golin, Fran. Cois Presans, Bte. Cote, Aexi. Cote, --- Cotte, D. Eshbough, Oliver Cottle, Warren Cottle, Piere Couravie, Abraham Darst, J. Marie Courtois, Godfrey Crow, Pier Danielle, David Darst, Jon. Day, Louis Denoie, Matthew Devenport, Francois Duquette, Peter Ditsler, Joshua Dodson, Fs. Dorlac, Louis Gau, Baptiste Dousirs, Baptise Dousirs, jr., Jh. Du Boy, Pier Du Boy, John Baldridge, William Dunn, Louis Duquet, Charles Fabrire, Biel Farnsworth, William Farnsworth, Jacques Fitteau, Louis Biore, Antoine Gautie, Joseph Gervais, Anguis Gillis, Moses Burbank, Francois Ambroise, Pier Bisonssnaite, Antoin Becain, J. Mary Besaunte, Bt. Bequiette, Charles Cadinalle, Carbonneaux, J. Marie Cardinalie, Bt. Bruguere, Pery Brown, Pier Boutans, Ga. Mabane Brielle, John Bell, Francois Beau, James Boldridge, Joseph Basile Beau.

St. Ferdinand: Baptiste Bacane, Baptiste Billeau, Francois

(Memorials, St. Ferdinand District Continued)
Dunegan, Ant. Gauder, Fs. Delaurier, Bte. Delisle, Charles Degerlais, Paul Dejarlai, Juste. Dehetre, Bapte. Creti,Andre Peltier, Francois Chinel, --- Collin, Ante. Senecal, Joseph Rapieux, Pierre Payant, Amable Wimet, Fs. Tibeau,Jh. Tibeau, Toussaint Tourville, Augte. Trudelle, Louis Lirette, Pierre Boure, Joseph Calvai, Benja. James, Durrett Hubbard, Bapte. Lorens, Ante. Malette, Lnt. Milice, Ensaigne Milice, Lis. Ouvre, Jh. Obuchon.

St. Louis: John Litle, John Little, John Little-John, A. Nerut, James Lockhart, William Loder, Matthew Logan, John Long, William L. Long, John Long, sr., Mathew Lord, William McConnell, John McConnell, Lewis Lorimier, Bte. Lousigman,J. Michau, sr., Peter Lovel, Peter Lovel, jr., John Lovel, John Low, Charles Lucas, Friederich Lundige, Peter McCalister,Uri Musick, Alexander McCartney, Daniel McCay, Robert McCay, Eli Musick, John McCollough, Adam T. McCord, Peter McCormack, M. Michaels, George McCown, Alexander McCoy, Annanias McCoy, E. Parkson, James S. McDaniel, James McDaniel, Joshua McDonald, Edward McDonaugh, George McFall, John McFarson,Thom. McKibb, William McGlaughlan, James McGregor, Alex McKinney, Robert McKinney, David McKinney, John McKinney, Theo. McKinnon, Fs. Moque, Allen McKinze, John McKullum, John McLaughlan, Jacob Myers, John R. McLaughlin, James L. McLaughlin, John Newman, Thomas McLaughlin, John McMurry, Joseph McMurtry, Anthony C. Parmer, Thomas Maddin, Baptiste Maisonville, John Manly, M. P. Leduc, Alexis Marie, Bonadventure Marion, Lewis Martin, David Marten, Adam Marten, Moses Martin, Thomas Mason, John May, William Mass, Lemuel Masters, Samuel Masters, Priestley Myers, Henry Masters, Allen Mathews, Edward Mathews, Edward Mathews, jr., Charles Mathews, Joseph Mathews, John Mathews, Jeraume Matise, James Meek, Samuel Meek, Louis Menard, sr., Joseph Menard, David Merdel, Danl. Merideth,Troper Mesplais, Rowling Meredith, Joseph Michel, Jacob Mier, James Mitchel, Isaac Miller, John Miller, Francois Milliet, John B. Mire, James F. Mitchell, Daniel Mollens, Green Mollens, Am. Guyon, James Moore, Nicolas Moore, Richard Moore, William Moore, A. Burns, James Moore, sr., Bede Moore, William Moorhead, Louis Moque, Michel Morain, Thomas Morgan, Louis Morin, Adam Null, Daniel B. More, Curtis Morris, Thomas Morris,John Mullanphy, Arthur Mullin, Alexander Murdough, Jas. Murdough,Asa Musick, Isaac Murphy, John Murphy, Joseph Murphy, Richard Murphy,Edi Musick, David Murphy, William Murphy, William Murphy,Abraham Musick, Frans. Murphy, Ephraim Musick, James Musick, Charles Nelson, Lewis Musick, Thos. Roy Musick, Gabriel Nicole, Jn. Wm. Buttner, Joseph Neuschwanger, sr., Joseph Neuschwanger, jr., Peter Boblesse, John North, jr., William North, William Null, Michael Null, Aug. Obuchon, Antoine Obuchon, James Y. Oclarrel, Michel Odom, Alperd Oliver, Johannes Opelhatt, J.

(Memorials, St. Louis District Continued)
--- Orleans dit Lapointe, Jean Bte. Ortes, Robert Owins, A. Johnston, Henry Paget, William Palmer, Joseph Papin, Jonah Parke, Charles Parker, Thomas Parker, Amable Partnay,William Paterson, Eleazer Paterson, Jh. Girrard, William Girty, John Bt. Gobeau, Andre Goder, Henry Goder, Charles Godfray, John Godfray, Peter Godier, James Goforth, Miles Goforth, Henry Graf, Alexander Graham, Hugh Graham, Samuel Graham, Hezekiah P. Harris, Pierre Graimnard, Henry Grass, Charles Gratiot,J. Gravier, William Gray, John Greene, John Greenewault,Michael Grefore, Alexi Grefore, Louis Jos. Grenon, sr., Gne. Hunot, Frans. Grenon, Daniel Greter, Jeremiah Grogon, Mills Hull, Aquilla Haggin, Joseph Haggin, Peter Hahn, Friederich Hahn, Lorins Hallabert, Jeremiah Hamilton, Ninian B. Hamilton, Jh. Hortiz, Henry Hand, William Hand, John Hankinson, Jonathan Hubbell, Saml. Hanna, Enos Hannah, John C. Harbison, Bryson Hard, John Hankinson, jr., Isick Harington, John E. Hartt, Lanard Harris, Micajah Harris, Johannes Has,Richard Hawkins, Clement Hayden, Larkins Hays, Jurnel Hayward, Joseph Hebert, Jh. Hebert, Gilbert Hector, John Hendrickson,John Henderson, Thomas Henry, Davis Hensley, William Hensley, John Hensley, Willis Hensley, Barthomee Herington, John Herington, Samuel Herington, William Herington, Samuel Hibler, William Hibler, Samuel Higenbottom, Thomas Higginbotham, Jonathan Hubble, W. B. Lacroix, Joseph Lacroix, Christen T. Hilderbrand, David Holly, Daniel Hilderbrand, Samuel Hinch, jr., Solomon Huitt, David Hilerbrand, Isaac Hilerbrand, John Hilerbrand,Jonathan Hilerbrand, Daniel Hodges, Ebenezer Hodges, Gilbert Hodges, David Holley, Samuel Holmes, William Holmes, Thomas Hooper, George Horn, John Horn, Joseph Horn, Thomas Horsley, Durritt Hubbard, Fs. Hortiz, Daniel Hubbard, Mathew Huble, Joseph Hunot, John Hudges, John Hurley, Jonathan Hurley, John Leek, Moses Hurley, Josiah Hunter, Joseph Hunter, Joshua Hunter,C. Land James, James James, James James, Morris James, Benjamin James, John James, William Jameson, John Janes, Janes, Green Jewitt, Louis Jeans, Francois Jaque, James Jewitt, Benjamin Johnston, David Johnson, John Johns, George Johnston, Thomas Johnston, William Johnston, Emsley Jones, John Jones, Samuel Jones, Stephen Jones, William Jones, William Jones, Marshel Jons, Roger Kaygle, Daniel Keehely, Francis Keennen, James Keeth, John G. Keennen, Edward Kelley, John Kelly, Jaduthun Kendall, Charles Kilas, David Kinkaid, Matthew Kinkaid, Jas. Kinked, James Kirkendoll, Francis Kishler, Clement Knott, Joseph Labbe, Joseph Lachance, F. S. Lachance, Patrick Lee, G. L. Lachance, Ame. Lachance, Nicholas Lachance, John Link, Michele Lachance, Joseph Lachance, Nicola Lachans, Francois Langleenway, --- Lacombe, Bernard Laffont, Bapt. Laflower, Antoine Lafont, Pierre Antoine Laforge, Pierre F. Laforge,M. C. Stats, George Lail, William Laird, Lrt. Lajoye,John Land,

(Memorials, St. Louis District Continued)
G. L. Lachance, Ame. Lachance, Nicholas Lachance, Ignatious Layton, Michele Lachance, Joseph Lachance, John Lewis, Hugh Lewis, Joseph Lewis, Francois Lesieur, Louis Lemonde, Joseph Legrand, Louis Lemonde, Henry Leek, Nicolas Lecomte, Francois Latour, Nicolas Lecomte, Pierre Latieure, John Latham, Noel Lasiserae, Ant. Lassell, Louis Larcohe, Joseph Laprise, Jos. Laplant, Hartley Lanham, --- Lalumendier, Ezekiel Able, Jer. Able, Robert Adams, sr., Robert Adams, jr., Samuel Adams, L. Brazeaux, Samuel Adams, David Alexander, Jehu Allen, Robert Allen, Thomas Allen, John Alley, Thomas Alley, William Alley, John Amery, Michel Amoreux, John Anderson, David Andrew, Jn. Boshow, Thomas Applegate, Abm. Armstrong, Jesse Arnow, James Arrel, Jesse Arriva, Jesse Arway, George Ashbrook, Toussaint Cerre, John Atkins, John Aubenheuser, John August, Abraham Baker, John Autrey, Louis Baby, Andre Backar, Ludwell Bacon, David Bailey, Henry Baker, John Baker, Joseph Baker, Thomas Baker, John Ball, Holeman Bankson, Antoine Baranda, John Bte. Barsaloux, Pierre Baribeau, Francois Barrans, William Bates, Vitale Bauvais, Robert Bay, Samuel Bay, John Bayly, Alexander Carson, John Beare, Gimiain Beauvais, Hatter Becker, Charles Belange, Mordeca Bell, Philip Bell, William Bellew, Charles Belamre, Mathias Belsons, Gabriel Bequet, Pea Berdon, Louis Bernier, John Berry, Thomas L. Bevis, Anton Bird, Jan Bire, John Black, James Black, William Black, Peron Blanch, Jesse Blanks, William Blount, Jacques Bodouen, Charles Bogenou, P. L. Cerre, Nicolas Bogenou, sr., Nicolas Bogenou, John Bogy, Vital Bogenou, Louis Boisse, John Boldey, Daniel Boldridge, Daniel Bollinger, Etienne Bolduc, Johannes Bollinger, Joseph Bombardier, Charles Bonneau, Michel Mono, Daniel Boone, An. Vincent Bouis, Js. Boyd, Royland Boyd, Louis Brada William Bradburn, James Brady, Joseph Brant, Jh. Brazeaux, D'Hustache Caillou, Mabane Brielle, Js. Brineke, Mathias Brinley, John Brooks, James Brooks, Mark Brooks, Adam Brown, Barney Brown, Eleas Brown, George Brown, John Brown, Jehu Brown, Luallen Brown, Robert Brown, William Brown, Joseph Browne, Jonathan Bryan, James Bryan, David Bryan, Jh. Buissonnet, John Burk, Daywalt, John Burgitt, Hugh Burney, Arthur Burns, J.W. Cayse, Barney Burns, James Burnes, Michael Burns, John Busby, Wm. Burns, Micager Byrd, Moses Byrne, --- Cabanne, Louis Caillou, Arthur Call, James Callaway, John Callaway, David Calwell, William Cambell, James Canady, Joph. Caraphen, Thomas Carlin, Jonas Carl, Johan Carrico, Vincent Carrico, Uriah Chandwick, John Carson, Friedria Casselring, Moses Cavett, James Clay, Louis Chabonneau, Benjamin Terry, Joseph Tesserau, Robert G. Waters, Michel Tesson, Noel Tesson, Chl. Thebaut, Levi Theel, Clabourn Thomas, James Thomas, Mark Thomas, Isaac Thompson, James Thompson, Jerimiah Thomson, Thomas Tomson, Bte. Tibeau, William Thomason, Jean Baptiste Tison, --- Tonnellier, John Towsend, John Baptist Towsan, David Troter, James Troter, J.

(Memorials, St. Louis District Continued)
Jacob Chambers, John Chambers, Robert Chapman, Walter Crow, Robert Chapman, Grimot Charpentier, Joseph Charpantier, John Crow, Baptiste Chartier, Amable Chartran, James Cheek, Henry Choquet, William Cheek, James Cheek, P. Chevallier, Jonathan Foreman, Andre Chevallier, Henry Choquet, John Easr, Jullien Choquet, Augte. Chouteau, Pre. Chouteau, Wm. Christy, James Connor, Louis Denogines, Joshua Edwards, Charles Gill, James Clemmens, Jeremiah Clay, Thomas Clarke, Francis Clark, jr., J. Clamormorgan, Bernard Cisselle, Eleenor Clemmons, Stewart Clemmons, Elias Coen, Bernard Coleman, James Colevan, Robert Commens, Jeremiah Conaway, William Conaway, Gabriel Constu, Martin Coons, John Cooper, Thomas Cooper, Hiram Cordell, Ira Cottle, John Coleman, Aron Colvin, James Colvin, Frederick Conner, John Conner, William Connor, Nathaniel Cook, Thomson Craford, Elam Cotton, John Counts, Louis Courtois, jr., John Cox, Louis Courtois, sr., William Cox, Moses Crafts, James Crage, Peter Craig, James Crawford, David Crips, John Daniel, David Crips, Jean Crochet, William Croford, Hezekiah Crosby, Benjamin Crow, Henry Crow, Lewis Crow, Godfrey Crow, Michael Crow, Daniel Crump, Robert Crump, John Culberson, Baptiste Gamache, John Cummens, --- De Flammand, John Dailey, Antoine Dauren, David Davis, James Davis, John Davis, Luke Decker, --- De Gagne, --- Degrosilliere, Andre Deguire, Jess Demint, Francois Deguire, Louis Deguire, Paul Deguire, Baptise Degur, Auguste Delariboudoais, Pre. De Lassus De Luziere, William Eads, Camille Delassus, D. Delaunay, Trophet Delor, Benjamin Deming, Charles Demoss, Andrew Deniston, Antoine Denoyer, J. V. Garnier, Jn. Denoyer, Louis Denoyer, Michell Derchaut, F. Fournier, Isaac Dovore, Jacob Devore, Luke Devore, Alexander Fisher, Robert DeWitt, Walter Dewitt, Lewis Dickson, William Drinnen, Pierre Didier, William Dillon, Mikel Dodd, Terence Doyle, Josiah Dodge, Thomas Dodge, Isaac Doggett, Thomas S. Rodney, Zephaniah Sappington, George Smith, Joseph Sinkler, William Seely, Fredrick Price, Daniel Richardson, Richard Everitt, John Dominick, John Donnohue, Thomas Donnohue, Jessy Dooling, Saml. Dorsey, James Dotson, Joseph Doubleday, James Dowty, John Dowty, Antoine Dubreuil, Bte. Duchouquet, Henri Duchouquet, Antoine Duclos, Bte. Duiguire, Joseph Dumay, John Duval, Pierre Dumay, Pier Due Per, Louis Dupres, Senna Duval, Thomas Eads, Matthew Eads, Ledford Eastridge, James Farris, William Eastridge, Zekiel Eastridge, Philip Eignet, Charles Ellis, Petter Ellis, Julius Emmons, Robert Estis, David Fine, Barnet Estus, John Estus, Patrick Estus, Jesse Evans, Elijah Evens, Stephen Evens, David Everitt, Edward Everitt, William Everitt, William Ewing, George Fallis, William Farnsworth, James Farris, John Ferry, David Fine, Samuel Flint, Abraham Sharp, Daniel Foreman, John Foreman, Jona. Forman, Jeremiah W. Still, David Forril, Michel Fortin, James Foster, Nicolas

(Memorials, St. Louis District Continued)

Gaisdanas, Jacob Friend, Hugh Fulton, John Furgeson, Auguste Gamache, Pierre Gamelin, William Garner, Pierre Garoux, Chs. Glasson, Joseph Gerrard, John Giboney, Jesse Gibson, Samuel Gilbert, Tousant Gilleaugh, John Gilmore, Jacob Gipson, Ben Shell, Uphry Gipson, William Gipson, Umphry Gipson, Elisha Patterson, Eliazer Patterson, John Patten, Samuel Patterson, William Patterson, John Patton, Jno. Pauley, David Roberts, Samuel Pearshall, Jeremiah Peirceall, John Perio, Frederich Shahler, Pier Perlaise, Joseph Perodot, Jeran Perrau, James A. Sturgus, Bt: Petie, Lee Pettet, Eli Pettibone, Wm. Smith, Solomon Pettit, Samuel Pew, Alexr. Phillips, John Phillips, Charles Phillips, Bte. Pichet, James Pillars, John Pillars, James Piper, Jph. Plasi, Paul Pourneuf, Biron Pratte, Jacob Price, Bd. Pratte, Bt. Prele, Pascalle Presans, George Price, Koonrod Price, Augustin Price, Michael Price, Reese Shelby, Risdon H. Price, James Priest, Louis Provenche, Batis. Pujot, Provenchere, George Pussley, Tunas Quick, Michell Quisnelle, James Ramey, Mathew Ramey, Andrew Ramsey, Alexander Sampson, Andrew Ramsey, jr., James Ramsey, John Ramsey, Saml. Randal, William Ramsey, sr., William Ramsey, jr., Robert Ramsey, Ad. Rugers, James Tallet, Joshua Tanzy, Levy Tansy, Bapt. Tebou, Abraham Randall, Anthony Randall, Enos Randol, James Randol, Thomas Rareden, sr., John Rareden, Amos Rawls, Hardy Rawls, John Reaves, Hardy Rawls, Andrew C. Reed, Joseph Reed, John Reynolds, Nicholaus Teich, Jesse Taylor, Richard Taylor, Jon Smitch, Joseph Reed, Robert Reed, William Reed, Paul Robert, Thomas Remey, Anointe Reynal, sr., Antoine Reynal, jr., James Richardson, Claiborne Rhodes, Joseph Richard, Jesse Richards, John Richards, Larkin Richardson, James Richoson, John Ward, John Rickman, Hennery Ridenour, Charles Reid, Abijah Rigdon, Thomas Rinoy, John Risher, Amos Ritchason, Jh. Rivare, Louis Roberge, Philipe Rivierre, Charles Robert, Phi. Robert, John Robertson, Philip Shuler, Jacob Shook, Joseph Shandy, Edward Robertson, Andrew Robertson, sr., John Robertson, jr., John R. Robertson, William Robertson, Joseph Robidoux, Louis St. Jean, William Robinson, Andrew Robison, John Robison, Peter Rock, Martin Rodney, Bernard Rogan, Ezekiel Rogers, Samuel Rogers, Pre. Roi, Christy Romine, John Romine, M. A. Roque, Robert Ross, Stephen Ross, Amos Rourk, John Rourke, Julien Roy, Ralph Rowzee, Louis Roy, Francois Roye, Abraham Ruddell, George Ruddell, John Ruddell, Ralph Rowzee, Louis Roy, Paul Sabourn, Thomas Russ, Colas St. Andre, Jean At. Andre, Louis St. Garmin, Haisinthe St. Cyr, Bourbon Sainte Marie, Etienne Sainte Marie, Etienne St. Pierre, Joseph Saloir, Richard Sapenton, Gre. Sarpy, Mth. Saucier, Mth. Saucier, jr., James Scott, Christopher Schultz, Wm. Savage, Andrew Scot, Joseph Seigun, James Scruggs, Jonas Seely, Edward Selans, David D. Wentzell, Daniel Walder, Francis Wideman, Geo. Shannon, John

(Memorials, St. Louis District Continued)
Sinkler, Nathl. Simonds, George Sibley, John Simson, Charles Simms, William Sinklar, Isidor Skerrett, George Smirl, John Smirl, Thomas Smirl, John Smith, John Smith, sr.,John Smith, jr., Barney Smith, Robert Smith, Samuel Smith, Marton Somes, Lewis Sojouner, Antoine Soulard, Nele Spears, Jesse Taylor, William Spence, William Spurgin, John Starnater, Adw. Woods, And. Steele, George Statelar, Thomas Steerman, Peter Stern, John Stephenson, Daniel Stainbeck, John Steward, Christopher Zeumwalt, jr., Joshua Stockstill, Joab Strickland, Daniel Stringer, James Stuert, Jno. Summers, Jesse Taylor, Josephus Tucker, Richard Taylor, George Taylor, Samuel Taylor, Martin Woods, Jean Baptiste Tison, Christopher Zeumwalt, sr., Peter Zeumwalt, John Zeumwalt, Jacob Zeumwalt, Adam Zeumwalt, John Yont, --- Tonnellier, John Townsend, John Baptiste Towsan, J. Bte. Truteau, John Tucker, Joseph Tucker, Antoin Vachare, Peter Tucker, Thomas Twentyman, Fcois. Bte. Valle, Frederick Woolford, Bte. Valle, John B. Valle, Frois. Valle, J. Bte. Valle, Fcois Valois, Benj. L. Vanamburgh, Moses Vance, Henry Velker, Jh. Vanden Bunden, Daniel Vaughan, Jas. Vernon, John Wadkins, Antne. Villars, Thomas Vinens, William Virdian, Wm. Woodlan, Isaac Votars, Abraham Waigle, Lurat Walder, Maurice Williams, Laken Walker, Geo. Wallis, Nathel. Waring, William Williams, Paul Washbourn, jr., Richd. Jones Waters, Jonathan Wiseman, Thos. Waters, John Weaver, James Welborn, William Wood, Ilijo Welch, Robt. Wescott, Job Westover, Jacob Wheat, Conrad Wheat, sr., Conrad Wheat, jr., Joseph White, Jonithen Wilson, Conrad Wheaton, Thomas Whitside, Paul Whitley, Jacob Wickerham, Jacob Wickerham, jr., Quillar Wickerham, John Wideman, Mark Wideman, George Wieland, James Williams, John Wilson, Samuel Wilson, Andrew Wilson, Joseph Williams,Martin Woods, Francis Woods, Zadock Woods, Joseph Williams, Isaac Williams, Lewis Williams, John Williams, sr., John Williams, Thos. Williams, William Williams, Micager Williams, Emilian Yostie, Wm. Winchester, Owen Wingfield, Abner Wood, Thomas Worthington, Jona. Wood, John Worthington, Jacob Yont, Thos. Wright, Henry Yont, Edward Young, Lewis Young, McKey Young.

Callaway County, Missouri, Tax List, 1823.

Joseph Aud, Elisha Archer, Archabald Allen, Bethell Allen, William Anderson, Shadrack Alvis, Charles Allen, Wm. Adams, Charles Allen, Sampson Allen, Dennis Arskren, Morris Baker, John Burt, George Burt, Thomas Brooks, James T. Brown, John Burkett, sr., John Bennett, James Brooks, Berryman Beadles, Martin Baker, John Baker, William M. Baker, Azle Barns, John B. Bragg, Isaac Black, Felix Brown, John Burkett, jr., Geo. Bartley, Henry Brite, Lawrence Biggs, Henry Burt, dec., John L. Boone, Samuel Boone, Jacob Baker, Thomas H. Baker, Robert Baker, Esau Baker, George Bradford, Samuel Bethell, Mordecai

(Callaway County, Missouri Continued)
Bell, Daniel   Brown, Aaron G. Bennett, William Bryant, Henry Baker, Silvester, Zebediah   Baker, George   W. Boothe, David Burkett, Joseph P. Callaway, James Coats' heirs, John Coats, Bosman   Clifton, John Coons, Robt. Wm. Criswell, Wm. Coats', sr., Alberth Carruth, Mark Cunningham, Isaac Chanier, Samuel Crockett, Daniel   Colgan, Solomon Craghead, John Charlton, Robert Craghead, Jonathan Crow, Joseph Callaway,Rich. Crump, William   Coats, sr., Robert Colgan, Fayette Collins, William Clendinnen, John Conger, Daniel   Clendinnen, William   Coats, jr., John Dunnica, Nathaniel Duly, Mary Darling,Abner Davis, Thomas   Denton, John Duncan, Samuel Crockett, Gabriel Davis, John Dyer, Robert Dunlap, David Dunlap, James Dunlap,Stephen C. Davis, Jonathan Davis, Charles Dougherty, George   Dillon, Robert   Davis, Edward   S. Ellis, Abraham Ellis, James Estel, William Edwards, Matthew   Edwards, Wm. Edwards, John   Estel, John Estes, Robert A. Ewing, John Evans, George Evans, James T. Guthery, Rebecca Ferguson, John Ferguson, Isaac Graheart, John Gibson, Jane Farmer, Nicholas Fia, Wm. Grant, Benjamin Goodrich, Israel B. Grant, William Griffin,Torkle Galbreath, William Grissinn, Baptist Grason, Joseph Gordon,John C. Ham, James Gordon, Leonard Garmon, Irvine O. Hockaday, Richard N. Humphreys, James Humphreys, Collett Haynes, John Hays, Henry Harper, Thomas Hatton, William Hicks, Wm. Henderson,James M. C. Huddson, Paul Herryford, John Herryford, David Henderson, Jesse Henderson, James Henderson, Abner Holt, Tho. Harrison, sr., Abner Holt, Hiram Holt, Thomas   Harrison, jr., Jonathan Hollaway, John Hamilton, Thomas Harper, John Hughart, Samuel Humphreys, Robert Humphreys, Richard Humphrey, John Hamblin, Thomas Harris, Peter Harris, Henry Hall, George Hirsh, Rufus Hornbuckle, Absalom Hollaway, William Hornbuckle, Adam Hope, Thomas   Hornbuckle, Isaac   Jefferson, John JOnes, Wm. Jones, Stephen Jones, Joseph Inks, Moses Joiner, Thomas   Kitchings, Isaiah King, Thomas King, Nathan Kany, George King, Asahail Lomax, Cullin Langley, Moses Langley, jr.,John Langley, sr., Moses Langley, sr., James Langley, Louis Laplant, Wm. Lenox, George Lankim, Patrick Lawler, Thomas G. Lee, John Lee,Isaac Langley, Andrew Lockhart, William Luca, Samuel T. Moore, Wm. Martin, Enoch Murry, Abraham Miller, Samuel   Miller, William Miller, Hugh Menix, Silus Melton, James McKinney, Henry May, Wlliam McCormick, James R. McCutchon, Wharton R. Moore, John Martin, Robert   Moore, Francis   McDonald, Daniel McLaughlin, William McLaughlin, Thomas McQueen, Stephen Monselle, Peter McKenna, Gabriel May, James Nevins, John Nevins, Henry Neil, Joseph Nevins, John Newsom, Robert Newsom, Caleb Nix, Arthur Neill, Anderson Newcom, James Nicholas, Nancy Nance, William Nash, Ira Nash, William Owen, Hans Hatton, Aaron Quick, John Pratt, Silas B. Pugh, Charles Poewel, Orestes Prince, Hiram Pare, Daniel Prince, Wm. Pratt, John Phillips, James Rippee,

(Callaway County, Missouri Continued)
James Phillips, Polly Parker, Andrew R. Phillips, Bazel Rose, sr., Bazel Rose, jr., James Rose, Josiah Ramsay, jr., Richard Runnels, Josiah Ramsay, sr., Allen Ramsay, Joseph Roy, John A. Robinson, Mary Rutherford, Samuel Rhodes, Noah Robinson, George Rhodes, Henry Rhodes, James Riggins, Robert Read, Asa and Jos. Williams, Bryant Roark, Thomas Rankin, Francis Roy, Nicholas Royer, Josiah Rounsaville, Thomas Ragsdale, Baptist Roy, Lewis Roy, Simon Riggs, Jonathan Ramsay, Jeffrey Sitton, John Read, Samuel Stiles, John D. Stokes, John M. Smith, Wm. B. Scott, Thomas P. Stephens, Elijah Stephens, John Stuart, Dudley Simmons, Willis W. Snell, Samuel Still, John Sitton, Ezra Sitton, Joseph T. Sitton, Foster Simpson, Jesse Scholl, Selby Simpson, James Shannon, John Shobe, Thomas Smith, John Salsbury, David Steriger, Joel Tipton, Thomas Tucker, Jesse Thompson, Malinda Thompson, William Thompson, Joseph Tebeau, John H. Thomson, John Taylor, Robert Taylor, Elisha Thomas, Solomon Thomas, Lewis B. Thomas, Martin G. Turner, Christo. Zumwalt, jr., Francis Tyon, Daniel Vincent, James Vanbibber, Irvine Vanbibber, Joseph Vanbibber, Lewis Vincennes, Payton Williams, William Wallace, John Wilfrey, David Walker, John Ward, Samuel Williams, Zachariah Wood, Wynkoop Warner, James Wilson, Charles Ward, William Williams, Patrick Ward, Jacob Zumwalt, Francis Wadley, Benjamin Young, Wm. Younger, Jacob Zumwalt, dec., Charles Younger, Benj. Young, Peter Zumwalt, Christo. Zumwalt, James Zevely.

Perry County, Missouri, Delinquent Tax List, 1830.
    Ezekiel Able, J. Farquhar, Joseph Fenwick, Clement Haden, Joseph Hagan, George A. Hamilton, John Hays, James Hutchins.

Oaths of Allegiance, New Madrid, 1793 - 1795, Taken from the Cuban Papers.

Name	Date
Christoval Roque Marco	April 7, 1793
Pierre Duncan	April 7, 1793
Jose Hunot	April 7, 1793
Francisco Cayole	April 7, 1793
Nicolas Esclieu	April 7, 1793
Jean Baptista Moyso	April 7, 1793
Benjamin Miller	April 7, 1793
Jose Casagrande	April 7, 1793
Enoche Bodevell	April 7, 1793
George Ungu	April 7, 1793
B. Tardiveau	December 15, 1793
Andy Goder	July 28, 1794
Baptista Gandron	July 28, 1794
Marc Ravel	July 28, 1794
Ettiene Pasar	July 28, 1794

(Oaths of Allegiance, New Madrid Continued)

Name	Date
Juan de Baptista	May 14, 1793
David Gray	May 14, 1793
Bartolome Rodriguez	May 14, 1793
Pere Gibault	December 23, 1793
John Summers	November 28, 1794
George Vilson	January 23, 1794
Jacob Bogan	January 23, 1794
Juan Collins	January 23, 1794
James Longwell	January 23, 1794
John Walde	January 23, 1794
Cornelius Lecon	January 23, 1794
James M. Miller	January 23, 1794
Joseph Bogard	January 23, 1794
Juan Masedt	May 27, 1793
Pedro Droullard	May 27, 1793
Joseph Tovonson	May 31, 1793
Stephen Burk	June 18, 1793
B--- M'Laughlin	June 18, 1793
Ph-- Boyle	June 18, 1793
Joan Gill	June 24, 1793
Patrick Laughlin	June 24, 1793
G-- Junnex	June 24, 1793
Johann Klein	June 26, 1793
Jose Barbier	June 26, 1793
Noel Antoine Prieur	June 26, 1793
Philip Ducomb	June 26, 1793
Lucas Despeentreaux	June 26, 1793
P. Menaro	February 5, 1794
L. Vandeneud	February 5, 1794
Michael More	July 18, 1794
J. Cruzel	February 11, 1794
Dec- Martinas	February 11, 1794
Joseph McCourtney	July 18, 1794
Pedro Gren	February 18, 1794
John Davis	March 31, 1794
F. Resmemier	April 8, 1794
Juan Ducille	April 8, 1794
Francois Xavier Tousney	April 9, 1794
Frank Smith	April 12, 1794
Felix J. Sons	April 5, 1794
Francis Torance	April 5, 1794
Johann Wieffermullir	June 30, 1794
George Buru	June 30, 1794
Louis Marquet	April 9, 1794
George Rams	April 9, 1794
Joan Combe	April 9, 1794
Francois Caperon	November 28, 1794

(Oaths of Allegiance, New Madrid Continued)

Name	Date
Alexis Tuiret	November 28, 1794
Charles Tela	November 28, 1794
William Pillsnoth	November 28, 1794
A. Breard	November 28, 1794
Samuel Lloyd, jr.	April 12, 1795
Guillamo Woodes	December 20, 1794
Joseph McCourtney	January 9, 1795
Charles Campbel	January 16, 1795
F. Birin	January 17, 1795
Cornelius Seily	July 30, 1794
Michael Ryan	August 25, 1794
James O'Bune	August 25, 1794
Samuel Hill	August 25, 1794
Jan Frison	January 25, 1795
J. Buzenet	January 25, 1795
George Ruddell	February 27, 1795
Robert Ushara	February 27, 1795
Ysidoro Dupuy	February 16, 1795
Luis Girard	February 16, 1795
Pascual Green	February 16, 1795
John Witt	February 16, 1795
Samuel Reed	February 16, 1795
Tomas Fuentiment	February 16, 1795
Benjamin Green	February 16, 1795
Jacoba Cro	February 16, 1795
Ysack Cro	February 16, 1795
David White	February 16, 1795
Matthew M'Cornis	February 16, 1795
Jacobo Reume	February 16, 1795
Luis Banceloux	February 16, 1795
Jose Bergenon	February 16, 1795
Guillaume Duggan	March 21, 1795
James Mace	March 21, 1795
Peter Johnson	March 21, 1795
Philipe Engel	April 19, 1795
Henry Wert	April 19, 1795
Francisco Bruiet	April 24, 1795
Juan Baptista Latuche	April 24, 1795
Pedro Dragon	April 24, 1795
Pedro Lataille	April 24, 1795
David Lendroy	April 24, 1795
Ysidore Sherrette	May 7, 1795
James Johnson	May 7, 1795
W. Mesnor	May 18, 1795
Ysaiah Pachara	May 18, 1795
Jehiel Stodeland	May 18, 1795
Luis Heki	May 18, 1795

(Oaths of Allegiance, New Madrid, Continued)

Name	Date
William M. Fray	July 21, 1795
David Shelby	July 21, 1795
John Alley	July 21, 1795
Miguel Burnes	July 21, 1795
Thomas Ally	July 21, 1795
George Shiro	July 21, 1795
William Ally	July 21, 1795
Baranabas Burns	July 21, 1795
William Bogard	July 21, 1795
James Trary	July 21, 1795
Andrew Cose	July 21, 1795
James Burns	July 21, 1795
Juan Ridvell	July 21, 1795
Basilio Bougard	July 21, 1795
Samuel Parker	July 21, 1795
Antonio Houton	December 13, 1795
John Hernes	December 13, 1795
Juan Nicholas	December 13, 1795
George Ope	December 13, 1795
John Trang	December 13, 1795
Pierre Gueruge	December 13, 1795

St. Charles County, Missouri, Petition to Congress for the establishment of a post office at Louisiana, Vol.XV, Carter's Papers, January 22, 1819.

John Hymers, George D. Strothers, M. Robison, John Valier, John Conway, Thos. P. Ross, Robert Anderson, Andrew Russel, Obediah Dickerson, James Johnson, Samuel Kean, Moses Kelly, John Johnson, John Campbell, Willis Mitchell, John Wamsley, Dixon Porter, Robert Muir, Charles Smith, John M'Cune, Wm. L. Moss, William P. Holliday, William Bless, William Onstat, Wm. Drake, Rob Hemphill, Levi Very, Jno. Basye, James Hatfield, Marshall Parks, John Clements, John Ortner, Jesse M'Cormick, John Jordan, James Kenney, John Shwimmer, James Crider, John F. Thrasher, James Finley, David Garnsey, Lewis Swarms, John P. W. Morris, Isaac Ash, Callaway Parrish, Jas. McWilliams, James Venable, Jeremiah Claton, Isaac Hosstetter, Bannister Gregory, Samuel Keithly, Solomon Fisher, James McNew, John Hostetter, Richard Matsen, Enoch Matsen, Jacob Dennis, Thos. Foris, Reubin Pakes, Henry Robinson, James Pearce, Archibald Clayton, Gordin Jenens, Jacob Hames, John Pursell, Harrison Boothe, Jacob Onstatt, Joseph Wright, John Scandlin, Nathan Watson, Ziney Hayden, Henry Budd, Jesse Barret, Ely Hackson, Thomas Norton, Thos. Chrouch, Wm. Crouch, Adam Fisher, John Scott, George Fisher, Peyton Matsen, John Brown, Joshua Ely, James Pierce, Wm. Cuningham, Thos. Ely, Benjamin Ely, Jacob Gromer, John Simes, Starke Simes, John Williams, Thos. Dods,

(Petition to Congress, St. Charles County Continued)
Sam Watson, sr., William McConnell, William R. Pickens, John Hatfield, William Boothe, Barthm. Lenham, James Orr, Barthm. Lenham, John Robinson, John Venables, Fountain Conway, Isaac Orr, James Smith, Cyrus L. Watson, James Watson, John Bryson, William Fullerton, James R. Watson, James Culbertson, Joseph Carroll, Edward Byers, Joshua Bishop, Reuben Parks.

Callaway County, Missouri, Non-Resident Tax List, 1823.

Andrew Armstrong, Moses Allen, William H. Ashley, William Apling, Peter Bass, James Beatie, Nathan Boone, John Brown, James H. Benson, Lawrence Bass, Jonathan Bryant, John Bell, Philip Bell, John Bartley, Thomas H. Benton, Taylor Berry, Simon Black, Ludwell Bacon, Reben Bacon, Lancston Bacon, Eli B. Clemson, James Craig, Milton Clevelnad, John Clark, Isaac Clark, Tilman Cullins, Amos Clark, Joseph Crow, Samuel Dyer, Pierre Chouteau, John Decker, Robert D. Dawson, Peter Ellis, Samuel Ewing, Jesse Elder, John Taylor, Dabner Finly, John Finly, Henry Gray, John Gray, Presley Gray, Squire B. Grant, John Henthorn, Patrick Haynes, Andrew Hunter, John S. Hardy, William Heiskell, Barnabus Harris' heirs, John Howdeshell, Lewis Hirne, Frederick Hiatt, Charles Hemstead, John Morris, Samuel Hammond, John King, Charles Lucas, dec., Wm. Sientz, William T. Lamme. August Langham, Elias S. Langham, Sharrach Mosely, August Langham, Matthew McDonald, Christo. Monicle, Philip Miller, Jesse Masters, James Marrs, John Miller, John Smith, Stephen Neill, James North, Risdon H. Price, Benjamin Sharp, John Robinson, William Rector, Elias Rector, Rochard Tegard, David B. Stith, Thomas A. Smith, George Sexton, Amos Stoddard's heirs, Jaconias Singleton, John Trevilion, Roger N. Todd, James Thompson, Stephen R. Wiggins, James E. Welch, David Zumwalt, James Whitesides.

Letters at the Post Office on December 31, 1822, Franklin County, Missouri, Missouri Intelligencer, Vol. IV, No. 23.

Per John T. Cleveland, pm.: Anna Anderson, John Braly, John Burton, James H. Benson, Pemberton Bridges, Wm. Clark, Alfred Basye, Obadiah Babbitt, Zachariah Benson, Rosannah Driscoll, Joseph Cockrill, George Chrisman, Thomas Collins, Wm. Clarkston, Charles Carroll, Charles Calloway, William Doty, James Depra, Tramell Ewing, Paris Ellison, George S. Foster, William Fisher, Armstead Grundy, James Greenstreet, Gordon, Freerick Greenleaf, Joseph Gill, Richard Gibbs, John S. Gillett, Nathan Glasgow, Hugh Garton, John C. Gordon, Ann Harl, Joshua Harris, Wm. Hawkins, Jonathan Hopkins, James Hines, George Hughes, Samuel Hibbard, Archibald Huddleston, Patsey Hurt, Benjamin Holliday, Alexander Johnson, Enoch Job, Richard Jacks, Robert Jones, Dabney Johnson, John Kelly, Peyton Jamison, Benjamin Johnson, Maj. D. Ketchum, William

(Letters at Post Office, Franklin Co., Missouri Continued)
W. Kavanuagh, John Kelly, J. C. Ludlow, Sally Lockhart, Byrd Lockhart, Joseph Legget, John M'Daniel, Fontain Marr, Angus M'Phail, William Miers, Jonathan Marney, Jacob Maggart, John M'Donald, Thomas Minns, John Mines, Lydia M'Corkle, Robert M'Gavock, Col. Samuel M'Clure, Phebe Noland, George Parris, Garrison Patrick, Sylvester Pattie, Phebe Noland, Catherine Small, George Parris, Adam Peisinger, Robert Peneival, Jesse Patterson, Wm. L. Robinson, Michael Robb, James Richardson, James Ray, Thomas Ridgeway, James Reddy, Samuel Robertson, Nathan Roberts, Robert Rings, Benj. H. Reeves, John Rawlins, Esther Rawlins, Stephen Stemans, Giles M. Samuel, Catherine Small, Capt. G. Stapleton, Nero. M. Thompson, William Tharp, Ephraim Thompson, George Thompson, Capt. J. Thompson, George Teford, Dodson Thorp, Stephen Trigg, Obadiah Tindall, Robert White, John Wilboit, Thomas Winn, John Wilson, Adam Wilson, John Wilkinson, Charley, James Wiseman, Elijah Whiton, Uriah Williams, Robert White, John Wallace, Robert Yancey, Finds Yenen.

Persons listed in the receipts and expeditures of Callaway County from December 10, 1821 to December 10, 1822, Missouri Intelligencer, January 14, 1823, Vol. IV, No. 24.

Jabez Hahn, Green Lee, J. M. Boone, Wm. Tumblinson, James Brooks, L. F. Collins, Leonard Garmand, Robert Moore, John Langley, D. M'Laughlin, Collet Langley, Samuel Baker, Henry Brite, I. O. Hockaday, Patrick Ewing, William M'Laughlin, Samuel Miller, Wynhoop Warner, Stephen C. Dorriss, Adam Hope, Josiah Ramsey, George Hirst, J. B. Bragg, --- Boone, William Blois, --- Creamer, --- Creamer, James Nevins, Thomas Hatton, James Humphries, Henry May, Jeffery Sillon, Paul Herriford, Enoch Fruit, Benjamin Young, Herrald Clark, Samuel T. Moore, Peter Zumwall, Beston Callahan, Nathan Kouns, Harvey Colgan, P. M. Dillon, Robert Taylor, A. Miller.

Johnson County, Missouri, Delinquent Tax List, 1838.

Jeremiah Lightner, Robert Thaxton, Samuel Wilson, Joseph Campbell, Silas Bones, Hughes Bradley, Benjamin Briham, John R. Gallaspie, Charles Warnich, Adam Crous, Miles Williams, John Cully, Jacob Coffman, Jonathan Dunham, Allison Frizell, Leonard H. Renick, Allen Warick (sic), Allen Warnick (sic), Bud Warnick.

Chariton County, Missouri, Tax List, 1830.

Solomon Adcock, Amos Aines, John Albright, John Allen, J. S. Allison, John Allison, Israel Aldrick's heirs, Edw. Alves, James Anderson, Nathaniel Anderson, Hardeman Anthony, Hiram Arnold's heirs, Nicholas Applegate, Charles Atwell, William Bailey, Bartholomew Armstead, Zackariah Arriwood, Samuel G.

(Chariton County, Missouri Continued)
Boyd, Henry Aux, Henry Ayers, jr., David Baker, Love Baker, Israel Baker's heirs, David Baker, Silas Ball, Wm. Barnes, Solomon Barnes, John Banister, James Barry, James B. Bates, James S. Bayless, John Belcher, Hiram Belt's heirs, Joshua Berry, George Black, John Blackless, Henry Blano, Mansfield Braden, Jesse Blocker, John Boden, Burnett Bond, Wm. Boyce, Robert Bond, John Bowen, Thomas Bradley, N. Branson's heirs, Benjamin Brears, John Brewer, James Bright, Shadrick Briggs, Samuel Brown, Wm. Bryant, Leonard Bullock, Geo. Burges, Wm. B. Burr, James Buswell, Samuel Butts, Wm. Caldwell, Charles Canole, Jesse Calvery, Martin Carroll, John Carter, Ebenezer Catterlin, Mark Carter, Asa Caswell's heirs, Ralph Chambers, Absalom Chrisfield, James Clark, John Clark, John Cline, Wm. Curry, David Clipper's heirs, David Cochran, Geo. Coit, John Coleman, Henry Cole, Morris Cole, David Coltet, Geo. Connor, Benj. Coleman, Nicholas Columbia, Timothy Copeland, Anthony Craft, Levi Cox, Cy Cornish's heirs, E. Coursalt, Geo. Craig, Amasa Crane, Silas Crawford, Wm. Creeley, Jacob Cresscey, W. F. Currin, Bryant Cross, Joseph Crowder, Wm. C. Crowder, D. and Charles Daniel, Charles Currote, John Curry, Wm. Doolin, Henry B. Curtis, John Daney, Hiram Daniel, Robert Day, Moses Davis, Mathew Daniel, Timothy Daniels, Edwin Davis, Samuel Dayton, John Deal, James H. Dearing, John Deboard, Frederick Dennis, Robert Desha, Alonzo Dickens, Amos Dickson, Stephen Donohoe,S, Smith,Samuel Dorsey,Daniel Dougherty, Ezekiel A. East, James Dougherty, Michael Dousoman, Daniel Dover, John Embersa, Charles Downing, James Downs, Thomas Duley, James Earsley, W. H. Duly, Richard Dunony, Bernard Durton, Jacob Ellinger, Wm. Early, Wm. Eddy, Conrad Elmundorff, Greenbury Gaither, Samuel Emmons, David Elliott, Gideon English, John Even, Emanuel Eomer, Wright Evans, Henry Evans, M. T. Ewing, Robert A. Ewing, Henry Evans, John O. Farrell, Amos Ferris, Joseph Ferguson's heirs, Laken Ferguson, Patrick Fling, John Frail, Jersham Filcher, Jeremiah Flinn, Henry Fountain, Wm. Francis, Francis Fountain, Aleney Franklin, Benjamin Fray's heirs, Moses Freeman, Judah Gage, Simon Gall,Curtis Gilbert, Roger L. Gamble, John Gardner's heirs, John Garrett, James Gibson, R. Gaskey, James Gilson, Moses Gleeton, Frederick Goodwin, Edward Goggin, Tousant Godair, jr., Robert Gragg, Wm. Green, Isaac Griffin, Patrick Griffin, Ira Grover, Lewis Guyor, James Grundy's heirs, Wm. Hague, James Haggard, Joel Hall, Daniel Hall, Robert Halton, Martin Hall, Moses Harris, Thomas Hambett, Thomas Hamby, Benj. Hammond, Joshua Haymel, Johnston Hammett, Jeremiah Harbison, John Hemmingway, Elbert Hedgeman, Wm. Hays, Peter Helmes, James Hemphill, Richard Hughes, James Hemphill, Jesse Henderliter, John Henley, Wm. Henderson, Simon Hensley, Charles Highy, James Hill, Garrett Hughete, Wm. Hilton, W. Hitch, Wm. Hite, Hiram Holt, Hiram

(Chariton County, Missouri Continued)
Holt, Benj. Howard, David Howard, James Hudson, John Hughes, Jabez Hunter, John Huston, Thomas Hutson, James Jackson, Wm. Jones, Benj. Jacobs, Joseph James, Samuel James, Christopher Kelly, Harrison Johnson, Jonathan Johnson's heirs, Ephraim Kennedy, Robert Johnson, Jarvis Jones, Peter Justus, James Keyete, Joseph Keywood, Elisha Kimbers, Jonas Kingrey, John King's heirs, Jeremiah Kingsberry, Bastian Kneedler, Samuel Lear, Henry Knock, Robert Lapping, Joseph Lapoint, William B. Phillips, Allen Latham, Wm. Lawrence, Charles Laugherty, Audrey Lawson, Baker Liggett, Abner Linch, Peter Lindell, Francis Lindsley, Jacob Littlefield, Peter Look, C. McClove, Thaddus Loomes, James Lunsford, Benj. Lucroft, Thomas Lyons, jr., Jacob Lysinger, Thomas McCalla, John McCallister, Lewis McCary, Robert McCoy, Wm. McCrumb, Francis McDonald, Audrey McDowell, Geo. McGunnigle, Andre McIntire, Patrick McKenny, Robert McMemory, James McMullen, John McNelly, Asa Northup, Joseph Magagnus, Zach Mallen, Abner Martin, Thomas Martin, John L. Martin, Zach Martin, David G. Mason, Wm. Mathews, Simon Mathias, Levi Matton, John Maxwell, John Measor, Aron Milbramy, James Miller, John Miller, Absalom Milton, Walter Mitchell, Jacob Moore, James Moore, Thomas Moore, Wm. Morris, Daniel Morris' heirs, Richard Morris, Joseph Mount, Stephen Munn, Samuel Murphy, Wm. Murphy, James Neshit, Wm. Newsom, Seth Nickerson, Electus Oakes, Wm. Oliver, Wilson Osborn, John Otis, John Overby, John Owens, Robert Owens, John Page, jr., Zadock Parish, Addison Parker, Aobert Patrick, David C. Penny, Spencer Pettis, Daniel Phinney, Ezekiel Pierce, John Pollard, Charles Pitcher, James Pitts, Joshua Plummer, Ezra Porter, Robert Poland, Nath. Prescott's heirs, John Pully, Jeremiah Pursall, John Rainwater, Henson Ramsay, Thomas Ray, John Rainwater, Jonathan Ramsay, Nathan Rainwater, Wharton Rector, Thomas F. Reddick, Wm. Redmond, Peter Reed, Bennett Riley, Wm. Ralph, Amos Ricker, Elijah Rider, Charles Risby, Samuel Roach, John Robertson, Seth Robertson, W. Robertson, Wiley Roberts, Joseph Robinson, James Rose, Elijah Seeley, Bethell C. Rowell, Wm. and Fred Rowlen, Samuel Rutherford, Saul Rutherford, Elijah Samuels, Edward Sanders, Benjamin Shirtliff, Richard Sanders, Joseph Schoval, Starr Scotland, John Scott, Thomas Scully, Dederick Scultz, Luther Shovers, J. B. Sexton, Andrew Shannon, Richard Shapleigh, John Shaw, Adam Sherline, Moses Sherwood, Charles Shumaker, John Weed, Charles Shumaker, Charles Simmons, Thomas Simmons, Charles Simons, Rueben Sipton, Samuel Saytor, Andrew Sleator, Hiram Smith, Jacob Smith, James Smith, John Smith, Richard Smith, Levi Smith, Thomas A. Smith, Warren Smith, Thomas Sperling, Francis Springer, John St. Clair, John Stanley, Wm. Stokes' estate, Oran Stone, Asahel Storrs, John Stover, Wm. Stuart, Joseph Strong, Thomas B. Stuart, John L. Sutton, Asa Wood,

(Chariton County, Missouri Continued)

Geo. Taylor, John Taylor, Stephen Taylor, Johnson Thomas, Nathan Thompson, Robert Thompson, Joseph Toner, Henry Vager, Robert Thompson, Michael Towers, Jesse Townsend, Littleton Underwood, C. C. Traline, Samuel D. Vanderbeck, John Varek's heirs, Chester Walker, David Wall, John Wanger, Edw. Watts, Daniel Wardon, Robert Watson, Grant Weed, John Welch, Wm. West, Alphonso Wetmore, Daniel Wharff's heirs, Samuel Wiggin, Anthony Wheeler, Ira White, Jacob White, Joseph White, John Wide, Martin B. Whipple, Gilbert Whitefield, George Young, Richard Whitefield, David Wickerd, Saul Wiggin, Wm. Wyatt, Daniel Williams, Henry T. Williams, James William, Humphrey Williamson, George Williams, Wm. Williams, John Wilson, E. R. Worthington, David Wood, Aaron Woodcock, Robert Wilson, John Wirt, Henry Withers, Caleb Wright, Martin Young.

Benton County, Missouri, Marks and Brands, 1839.

Name	Township	Date
Stephen A. Howser	Lindsey	April 26, 1839
Thomas H. Alexander	Montgomery	July 6, 1839
Lewarth Alexander	Alexander	July 7, 1839
Sarah Powell	Alexander	July 7, 1839
John Machlin	Lindsey	July 17, 1839
Elias Hughes	Lindsey	July 29, 1839
Adamson Cornwall	Lindsey	July 29, 1839
William Roberts	Alexander	August 5, 1839
John W. Brown	Lindsey	August 5, 1839
Thomas Moon	Williams	August 12, 1839
William Thurston	Williams	August 14, 1839
John C. Lusk	Alexander	August 19, 1839
Isaac H. Lusk	Alexander	August 19, 1839
Ezekiel Williams	Williams	August 21, 1839
Wesley Johnson	Cole	October 18, 1839
Elijah Doty	Alexander	October 18, 1839
William Lusk	Alexander	November 4, 1839
Hosea Powers	Williams	November 4, 1839

Henry County, Missouri, Bethel Baptist Church Cemetery, Bethehem Township, Located about five miles southeast of Clinton.

Name	Born	Died
Louisa Boles	November 6, 1813	December 5, 1882
Eliza A. Carter, wife of G. C. Carter	November 23, 1833	January 24, 1891
John Chapman	March 25, 1832	September 16, 1899
Hugh Franklin Charles	December 1, 1820	June 4, 1880
Alfred M. Chiles	January 26, 1817	August 10, 1875
J. D. Cox	January 10, 1820	August 20, 1883
Solomon Hendrix	June 19, 1832	October 19, 1873

(Henry County, Missouri Continued)

Name	Born	Died
Campbell Herst	April 11, 1807	May 17, 18?
*Margaret T. Devine	1818	1869
*Native of Ireland		
#Sarah M. Herst	December 1, 1812	May 3, 1879
#Wife of Campbell Herst		
James Huey	October 7, 1814	December 20, 1890
John G. Hunt	April 9, 1824	June 26, 1881
@Frances Jones	December 2, 1827	December 9, 1897
@Wife of G. T. Jones		
Dixon Kirk	1790	October 9, 1856
Berryman Knight	February 13, 1811	July 13, 1875
David Lee	February 9, 1789	October 22, 1875
James Lee	December 26, 1801	March 10, 1894
$Naomi Lee	August 8, 1802	September 22, 1873
$Wife of Jas. Lee		
¢Ann C. Levy	September 4, 1814	February 5, 1857
¢Wife of Parker Levy		
Henry A. Levy	October 16, 1838	May 17, 1859
Parker Levy	May 14, 1804	December 11, 1875
Marion G. Lockridge	January 15, 1838	December 2, 1865
Joshua Major	October 5, 1812	February 19, 1888
%Martha C. Martin	July 28, 1819	October 8, 1879
%Wife of Wm. Martin		
E. W. Miller	1827	December 1, 1881
Edith F. Pogue	April 2, 1828	August 16, 1884
Jacob Richter	July 17, 1819	November 24, 1881
&Sarah M. Rickett	July 22, 1839	April 4, 1875
&Wife of T. A. Rickett		
+Ann Robertson	December 12, 1810	September 26, 1872
+Wife of Robert R. Robertson		
Robert Robertson	March 4, 1820	July 8, 1859
*Isabel Shankland	December 29, 1806	February 17, 1869
*Relict of James H. Shankland		
#Jinnie Shankland	March 15, 1837	March 15, 1867
#Wife of W. L. Shankland		
John Slavens	June 2, 1800	December 10, 1881
John Slavens	December 28, 1798	February 16, 1865
Rueben Slavens	September 27, 1825	September 26, 1891
@Mary Smith	May 12, 1806	July 9, 1880
@Wife of James Smith		
Smith Stephenson	1829	1872
Nancy Stricklin	September 1, 1826	October 13, 1876
James Ward	April 12, 1835	January 29, 1899
$David B. Watson	January 19, 1837	November 22, 1870
$Husband of Adaline Watson		
Basil Woods	August 19, 1805	December 29, 1861
Rev. James Woods	January 16, 1807	September 11, 1872

(Henry County, Missouri Continued)

Name	Born	Died
*Cornelius William	June 2, 1807	February 24, 1876
*He was a Mason.		
#Eliza A. Woods	September 28, 1805	December 27, 1874
#Wife of Rev. James Woods		

Ray County, Missouri, A List of Persons in the Receipts and Expenditures for December 18, 1821 to February 3, 1823, The Missouri Intelligencer, February 25, 1823, Vol. IV, No. 30.

Timothy Riggs, Isaac Martin, Jas. Snowden, Elisha Camron, William B. Martin, Jonathan T. Burch, John Shields, William L. Black, William L. Smith, Wright Cunningham, Daniel Dewall, John Stone, John Thornton, John Harris.

Ray County, Missouri, Tax List, 1830.

Wm. Agnew, James Allen, Thomas and Fred Allen, John Fryer, Benjamin Alkinson, Samuel Anderson, Love Baker, David Doe, Aaron Barton, James Basford, Hazen Bedell, Wm. Davis, Thomas Bentley, Taylor Berry's heirs, Daniel Blevins, Jacob Brown, James Brown's heirs, Wm. Burrow's heirs, John Burrows, John Cook, Barrett Canny, John Carmody's heirs, Wm. Evans, Henry Carroll, Barrett Canny, Thomas Casey, Parsons Clark, Warren Cleveland, Geo. Clipper's heirs, Henry Collins, Henry Cook, Wm. R. Daniels, Geo. Davenport, Thomas Davis, Wm. Garrison, Thomas Davis, John Davis, Caleb Dill's heirs, Nathaniel Holt, Daniel Dingley, Michael Dousman, Peter and Joseph Dowling, John Doboy, Wm. Dougan, Wm. Dudley, Samuel Duggins, Charles W. House, James Fitzgerrard, Richard Fling, Charles R. Hall, Anthony Gilligan, James Foster, Francis Fox, George Francis, Ephraim Francis, Rueben Gardick, Andrew Godair, James Holt, Burton Godsey, Christian Gowen, Absalom Hacker, Joseph Hall, James Janks, Charles Haney, James Head, John Hendricks, Adam Huffman, Joseph Hemmerly, Ethan Hulbert's heirs, Alexander McFadden, Moses Jackson, Sheldon Jackson, John Jones, Peter Lindell, Amasiah Johnson, John Kay's heirs, Saul Keith, Wm. Leach, Barry Langford, Michael Leavitt, John Leeman, Elijah Lenzo, Nathaniel Leonard, Robert Lytle, Samuel McEwin, John McLean, Charles McGriffin, Geo. McGunnigle, Mayberry Morris' heirs, John McLester, Charles Mann, Elijah Martin, Mordecai Nolen, John Martin, John Mason, John Meeker, David Morrow, Hugh Moore, Talton Murphy, Wm. Neiter, James Newton, Zacheus Richardson, James Newton. Randolph Nolen, John Ovail, French Ragland, Alex Peeples, Stephen Pierce, Dominick Pike, Hiram Pool's heirs, Hugh Porter, Wm. Price, Hugh Robinson, Thomas F. Rogers, John Ray, John Romain, Wm. Roseberry, Wm. Russell, John D. Scoff, Benjamin Shirtliff, Samuel Simpson, Thomas Sloan, James Smith, Thomas A. Smith, Paul Snow's heirs, John Stewart, Antoine Soulard' heirs, Stephen Step, Wm. Stickney,

(Ray County, Missouri Continued)
Silvester Stickney, Nathan Stoddard, Warren Taylor, Henry T. Williams, John Thomas, Daniel Tingley, Geo. Uptergrod, Henry Varner, Nathaniel Verille, Jeremiah Walker, Jonathan Wood, Bart. Walsh, Wm. Warren's heirs, John Williams, Charles Way, Abijah Whitney, Charles Wilbar, Geo. Wikey, Joseph Willis.

Howard County, Missouri, Licenses, November 2, 1816, Missouri Gazette.

Price Arnold, Alexander Bell, N. Cole, I. W. Feller, John Ish, Harper C. Davis, Thomas Gray, Alexander Lucas.

Chariton County, Missouri, Letters at the Post Office, Vol. IV., No. 26, Missouri Gazette, January 28, 1823.

S. D. Looney, a.p.m.: John Allen, A. Armstrong, Alexander Bogart, David Baley, Daniel Bouie, F. H. Bradford, William P. Buchanan, James Campbell, John Cross, J. Cunningham, John Welch, Elsey Eppler, Perry Erickson, Samuel Farest, Simon Foot, Richard Frestoe, Esther Findlay, Joseph Gibson, Thomas Griffin, Harman Gray, Peyton Hurt, Charles Harrington, J. E. Hukees, John Harrison, Joseph Hughs, Peter Kerkehall, J. S. Ludlow, Salem Luden, Andrew Means, Stephen Maud, Daniel M'Daniel, Wiley Martin, Jane Morin, William Probesk, Joseph Robinson, --- Palmer, John Shruggs, Richard Samuel, Roland Sutton, Rivenson Steals, Thomas Shackleford, --- Thornton, Joseph Vance, W. N. Wickliffe, Henry Wilkison, Geo. Williams, Robert Wilsere, James Wilkinson.

Randolph County, Missouri, Tax List, 1830.

Wm. Agnew, Charles Allen, Love Baker, James Barnes, James Beach, Henry Blevin, N. Branson, John B. Clark, Ruben Nelson, Alexander Colbert, James Collins' heirs, John Collins, Terry Dickerson, Michael Dousman, Henry Eppler, John Gillet, John S. Gilbert, Greenburry Fenn, Robert A. Ewing, Hawkins Harris, Stephen Glascock, Lee Gordon, John Hannah, John Harris, John McCrary, Jeremiah Harris, James Harryford, Hiram Holt, Isaac Lewis, George Latham, Joseph McCain, Isaac McCarty, Anderson McDowell, John McCrary, Geo. McGunnigle, Hugh Mead, Ambrose Mundy, Elijah Mosely, Wm. Morehead's heirs, Wm. Miles, G. W. Martin's heirs, James Murphy, Hugh R. Orr, Jacob Ostrander, Mary E. Pindell, Jonathan Ramsay, Wharton Rector, Benjamin Shirtliff, Daniel Rardon, Israel B. Read, Thomas Robinson, Henry Rogers, Isham Sexton, Charles Simmons, John Welch, Wm. Stanberry, Estate of William Stokes, John H. Stone, Robert D. West, Dickerson Terry, Hugh Treighner, George Ward, Benj. Watwood, Henry Weans, Joseph Whitson, Geo. Woodward.

Franklin County, Missouri, Delinquent Tax List, 1830.

David Adams, Robert Barthy, J. C. Brown, Nicholas Brown,

(Franklin County, Missouri Continued)
James Burns, Thomas Caulk, Charles Clarkson, Charles Haskill, Tarlton Goe, Phenton Goss, John Nickles, John Ruddle, Thomas Wethington, John Wickam, John Young, Lewis Young.

Cooper County, Missouri, Delinquent Tax List, 1826.
John Adams, Wm. Adams, Abraham Barnes, G. Burnnett, John Dunlap, --- Canote, J. Hickman, C. Lucas, Israel B. Read, E. Smith, Robert Wallace, Jason Whiting, Wm. Sprig.

Howard County, Missouri, Delinquent Tax List, 1830.
James Alcorn, Fred Bainbrick, Ira Barbee, Samuel Beatie, Frank Bradbourn, John B. Clark, Fisher Coleman, S. B. Craig, Perrin Cooley, Joseph Cooper, Janny Cooper's heirs, John T. Craig, Stewart Cummings, Francis Derouse, Daniel Durbin, Wm. Monroe, Francis Drinkard, James Douglas, Henry Earthman, Wm. Maupin, Joseph Frazier, Coleman Fisher, Edward Good, Amable Guyon, Willis Green, John Green, Robert A. Heath, Wm. Lamme, Robert Hancock, Wright Hill, James Hickman, Alfred Johnson, Elisha Jackson, Nathaniel Hutchinson, Francois Langlois, Wm. Pipes, Peter Labourboard, John Link, Raphael Lessieur, John Lovell, John Matthews, Robert M. Morris, Joseph Mitchell, Wm. Nash, Francis Millette, Ira Nash, Antoine Naschard, Eustache Peltier, Robert Payne, Benj. H. Reenes, Charles Simmons, Ely Shelby, Wm. Scott, John Scott, Benj. Staff, Louis St. Aubin, Jonathan Smith, John Thompson, Geo. Thompson, Ransom Thacker, Daniel Stringer, Thomas Vaughn, James White, Robert Wash, Henry T. Williams.

Ste. Genevieve County, Missouri, Licenses, Missouri Herald, August 13, 1819.
Michael Amoreau, Simon Block, sr., Peter Dagguit, Charles Ellis, Peter Frasure, Mich. Mecho, Adam Rissinger, Ann Wilson.

St. Louis County, Missouri, Delinquent Tax List, 1830.
C. Agniel, J. Baker, Elias Barcroft, Moses Bates, Joseph Beyelle, J. W. Bayse, Thomas Biddle, Francis Bissonette, Wm. Scholters, John D. Bolland, Nicholas Bougenoux, Louis Breda, Anthony Bouis, John Bringlas, John Bright, Julien Chouquette, Richard Chitwood, David and Darling Cherry, Wm. Channon, Wm. C. Carr, Colet Carmon, --- Carsner, Edw. Coleman, Elizabeth Kard, Pierre Chouteau, Madam Chouteau, Gabriel Dodier, Rufus Easton, Pierre Chouteau, Madam Chouteau, Marc Hardy, Gabriel Dodier, Catharine Dodge, John B. Dechamp, James Keyte, Geo. C. Fraizer, Susannah Duncan, Francis Dorlac, Jeanette Flores, Gabriel Garish, Geo. Gooding, Charles Gratiott, Paul Guitard, Lawrence Haffe, Jeremiah Hamilton, Wm. Hawkins, Widow Hebert, Dennis Higgins, Nicholas Jannis, Jeanette (free negro), John Smith, Peter Lassuente, Richard Lanham, Angus Lanham, Joseph

(St. Louis County, Missouri Continued)
Keifer, Leclede Legust, Widow Alexix Leland,Michael Liminio, David Loignard, Lawrence Long, James McCoy, Matthias McGirk, Arthur Melon, James Mainville, John Markeakus,Philip Monday, Wm. Miller, --- Motard, Francis Moreau's heirs,Risdon Price, Andrew Murphy, Henry Peroux, Spencer Pettis, Solomon Rogers, Peter Rock, James Roubidoux, Wm. Russell, John Sanders, Geo. C. Sibley, Benjamin Terry, John Watkins, William Waters, Wm. Ryan.

Cooper County, Missouri, Delinquent Tax List, 1827.

J. Alexander, Abraham Barnes, David barton, Taylor Berry, Jacob Chisum, T. P. Copes, John Douglas,C. Lucas' heirs, J. Miller, N. Ragland, Isreal B. Read,Wm. Sprig,Robert Wallace.

Gasconade County, Missouri, Delinquent Tax List, 1826.

James Clay, Geo. Collier, P. M. Dillon, Isreal B. Dodge, Wm. Thompson.

St. Charles County, Missouri, Delinquent Tax List, 1830.

Frances Allen, Lewis Barada, Etienne Bernard, Ettienne Bienvenu, Charles Boi, Daniel Boon, jr., Charles Cardinal, James Carr, Paschat Cerre, Gabriel Cerre, Augustus Chouteau, Pierre Chouteau, Jacques Claymorgan, Auguste Clement, David Walyer's heirs, Joseph Conders, David Conrod, John Cook, J. Farquhar, John Coons, Isaac Cottle, Sylvanus Cottle, Paul Coynoyer, Christian Dennis, Baptiste Dechamp,Abraham Duma, Thomas Fallis, Geo. Eoff, Isaac Fulkerson, Auguste Felteaux, Lewis Goe, Peter Ganau, Joseph Gravlin, sr., --- Hempstead, Robert A. Heath, Wm. Hays' heirs, Lewis Hunot, John Jones, Lewis Hunot, Isaac Hostetter, Francis Hostteter, Alexander Hill, Malcomb Henry, Louis Janett, L. James, Simon Lapage, David Kichelie, Joseph Lorse, Francis Longrel, James Piper, Francis Longrel, Charles Lefevre, Auguste Lefevre, Antoinne Reynol, Alexis Lefevre, Antoine LeClair, Henry McLaughlin, Wm. McConnell, Thomas Means, Charles Marten, Alexis Marai, James Mackay, --- Motard, Baptiste Morin, Francis Moquez, Spencer, Pettis, Louis Pajol, Madame Bapt. Pajol, Antoinne Reynol, Pierre Pallardi, Mary A. Quebeck, Patrice Roy, Louis Roy, Julian Roy, Antoinne Reynol, jr., W. C. Sampson, Joseph St. Mary, Hyancith St. Cyr, Antoine Soulard's heirs, Matthew Soucier, Charles Soucier, Francis Soucier, John Tayon, Peter Zomwalt, Barnabas Thornhill, Charles Tayon, Andrew Walker, James Vandendendum, Hugh White, Mack Wherry, Walker Wright, John Welty, Christian Wolf.

Chariton County, Missouri, Tax List, 1827.

Grant Allen, David Baker, Love Baker, James Barry, Fanny Berry, Joshua Berry, M. Bennett, R. Benam, J. M. Bell, Amos

(Chariton County, Missouri Continued)
Bruce, J. R. Caldwell, P. Carnay, J. Cotterlin, H. Clay, D. E. Cuyler, Wm. Curry, J. J. Crittenden, E. Coursalt, Jacob Delster, J. Cooper, A. Dickinson, Robert D. Dawson, Thomas Duley, John Dunlap, R. J. Davis, Michael Dousman, Robert A. Ewing, A. H. Evans, J. Emmons, Nehemiah Eastman, John Harvey, J. P. Fulkerson, Henry Fitts, E. Griffin, L. Gregnon, Hiram Holt, A. Graves, G. Hayes, D. Hubbard, H. Howland, Thomas A. Smith, W. L. Hite, J. W. Hickman's heirs, Henry Lariter, F. Loring, J. Laffton, Peter Lindell, H. B. Laterwhite, Robert McMennony, Geo. McGunnigle, John McDowell, John L. Martin, Abner Martin, Joseph Magagnus, John McNairy, J. Miller, J.M. Millington, Thomas Newton, J. Newman, M. Nathan, A. Pierce, W. G. Pettus, Spencer Pettis, R. Peck, Isreal B. Read, John Ramsay, H. Rodgers, Geo. Robinson, Abram Richwell, D. Rice, C. Skinner, Benjamin Shirtliff, J. B. Sexton, John Taylor, John Scott, Joseph Schoval, J. Southett, Joseph Strong, John L. Sutton, Oran Stone, John W. Ursher, John Wyche, Henry T. Williams, S. Woodson, Parker Williams, John Wyche.

Macon County, Missouri, Marks and Brands, 1837 - 1839.

Name	Date
John Walker	May 19, 1837
Richard West	May 20, 1837
James Holloway	May 20, 1837
Thomas Williams	May 25, 1837
Hiram Summers	May 25, 1837
Edward Stewart	April 9, 1837
William Stewart	April 9, 1837
George W. Green	April 13, 1837
William Garrett	April 13, 1837
Neley Anders	April 13, 1837
Felix Baker	April 13, 1837
John S. Cullum	April 13, 1837
George Cain	April 22, 1837
Joseph J. Morrow	May 30, 1837
William J. Morrow	May 30, 1837
James Cain	April 12, 1837
Tyre Dabney	April 13, 1837
Mancel Garrett, jr.	April 13, 1837
Enoch Griffin	April 13, 1837
Isaac Gross	April 13, 1837
Lewis Gilstrap	May 30, 1837
Hezekiah and J.C. Gartwell	April 19, 1837
Henry Hinds	April 13, 1837
Micajah Hull	April 24, 1837
Clem Hutchison	April 13, 1837
William Johns	April 13, 1837
Enoch Johnson	May 10, 1837

(Macon County, Missouri Continued)

Name	Date
Absalom Lewis	April 13, 1837
Jefferson Morrow	April 13, 1837
Joseph Ownsbey	April 13, 1837
Hiram Reed	April 24, 1837
William Roberts	April 22 , 1837
Howel Rose	May 8, 1837
James Richardson	May 13, 1837
Thomas J. Rice	May 13, 1837
Samuel H. Rice	May 13, 1837
Johnson Summers	April 13, 1837
Francis Taylor	April 22, 1837
James Taylor	April 22, 1837
William Williams	April 22, 1837
John Williams	May 8, 1837
Haden L. Rutherford	June 21, 1837
Alexander Gooding	June 2, 1837
Canaday Ownsbey	June 3, 1837
Abraham Morris	June 10, 1837
Nathaniel Richardson	June 12, 1837
James Philips	June 12, 1837
Abraham Dale	June 12, 1837
Adelis Finney	June 15, 1837
Sanfred Murley	June 15, 1837
Mark Dunn	August 2, 1837
Mancil Garret, sr.	August 3, 1837
John Cain	August 17, 1837
James Clifton	August 17, 1837
Martin S. Garrett	August 17, 1837
John Larthrop	August 18, 1837
David Williams	October 12, 1837
William Huckaby	October 12, 1837
James Myers	August 18, 1837
John Miller	October 30, 1837
John Summers	November 10, 1837
Patten Martin	November 16, 1837
David Young	December 26, 1837
Stephen T. Smith	January 9, 1838
John S. Morris	January 15, 1838
John Gross	December 6, 1837
Moses Summers	November 26, 1837
James H. Ray	March 5, 1838
John W. Beall	May 23, 1838
William Brassfield	April 9, 1838
Abner Vickery	April 12, 1838
Benjamin Martin	April 12, 1838
Robert M. Myers	April 12, 1838
James B. Wiggins	May 7, 1838

(Macon County, Missouri Continued)

Name	Date
William Stanfield	May 12, 1838
Samuel Stanfield	May 12, 1838
Nathaniel Dabney	May 25, 1838
James G. Montgomery	July 15, 1838
Charles Butter and Benj. Rose	September 12, 1838
William Saling	October 30, 1838
Columbus J. Sloan	October 30, 1838
Charles W. Cooper	November 3, 1838
John Holman	November 3, 1838
James Griffin	January 20, 1839
Isaac Gooding	January 30, 1839
John Griffin	January 20, 1839
William Griffin	January 20, 1839
Allen Jones	February 16, 1839
Philip Dale	February 16, 1839
Shelton Cross	February 18, 1839
Andrew Milsap	February 18, 1839
Henry Harris	February 18, 1839
William B. Hall	March 20, 1839
John Davis	April 30, 1839
Nathaniel Floyd	April 1, 1839
Jebel Dabney	April 1, 1839
Jehorah Marsh	April 15, 1839
William Burris	April 15, 1839
Jefferson Fair	April 15, 1839
Robert C. Armstrong	April 24, 1839
Joel Kay	May 13, 1839
Rindol Mott	May 21, 1839
George W. Mullian	June 11, 1839
Walter Thompson	June 13, 1839
William Brammer	July 31, 1839
James Thelum	April 10, 1839
Voluntine Cook	September 7, 1839
George B. Cook	August 17, 1839
Simon Woodward	August 29, 1839
Andrew Hood	August 30, 1839
Lorenzo Miller	September 21, 1839
John J. Miller	September 21, 1839
Elias Fletcher	September 24, 1839
John Beard	October 12, 1839

<u>Jefferson County, Missouri, Delinqent Tax List, 1830.</u>

Antoine Calliot, James Cockrell, Walter Dewitt, Wm. Estes, Henry DeWitt, Joseph Dinelly, Walter Fenwick, Walter Jewitt, John Henderson, Luke Lawless, Mathias McGirk, James Peppers, Wm. Russell, John Shannon, John Watkins, Robert Wash, Simon Woods, John Williams, sr.

Osage County, Missouri, Old St. Joseph Cemetery, Westphalia.

Name	Born	Died
Mary Bode	Aug. 28, 1812	Jun. 8, 1898
Anton Schmieder	Apr. 25, 1809	Oct. 1, 1896
Gasper Vogel	Nov. 11, 1829	Nov. 20, 1896
John Thora	Apr. 19, 1810	Nov. 20, 1896
Antona Schwarzelthal	Dec. 6, 1830	Jan. 9, 1897
Anton Schwazendahl	Apr. 11, 1820	Dec. 13, 1896
Charles Werner	Jan. 1, 1827	May 7, 1897
Johanna Borgmeyer	Oct. 11, 1832	May 10, 1892
Anna B. Castrop	Jun. 12, 1811	Oct. 3, 1897
Maria Anna Brunner	Mar. 17, 1831	Oct. 22, 1898
*Christina Luecke	Jun. 19, 1829	Dec. 11, 1893
*frau von Wm.		
Henry Bexton	Aug. 18, 1811	Feb. 1, 1894
Wm. Lueke	Feb. 24, 1811	Jul. 29, 1894
Carolina Bernsmeyer	Mar. 25, 1824	Nov. 19, 1894
Anna Maria Hoer	Nov. 11, 1810	Apr. 6, 1885
Joseph Stegman	Oct. 30, 1829	Sep. 27, 1895
Bernadim Castrop Koester	Dec. 6, 1822	Dec. 26, 1893
Theodore L. Schmitz	Oct. 26, 1823	Dec. 31, 1890
Maria G. Schmitz	Nov. 22, 1831	Jan. 7, 1891
Gertrud Fectle	Apr. 8, 1823	Mar. 27, 1891
Whilham Werstorff	Mar. 9, 1834	Aug. 4, 1891
Joseph Borgmeyer	Jun. 11, 1820	Aug. 6, 1891
Christana Lueke	Feb. 22, 1812	Nov. 4, 1891
Joseph Goelner	Mar. 1, 1816	Jan. 4, 1892
H. Heinrich Holterman	Apr. 4, 1834	Nov. 15, 1886
Johann Hundepohl	Mar. 15, 1826	Dec. 2, 1886
Joseph Meyerpeter	Sep. 23, 1809	Jan. 10, 1887
Gerhard Hilkemeyer	Apr. 8, 1808	Jan. 18, 1887
A.M. Gertrude Morfield, witteve von J. George	Jan. 13, 1820	Jan. 27, 1887
Theresia Lebbert	Oct. 21, 1826	Mar. 19, 1883
Anna Rademacher	Nov. 14, 1815	May 1, 1888
Frank Hazeboeck	Nov. 1, 1807	May 8, 1889
Joseph Kuesterstephan	Sep. 8, 1828	Mar. 10, 1884
Maria Schroder	Jul. 15, 1803	Nov. 16, 1885
Bernhard Meluis	Nov. 12, 1821	Oct. 12, 1886
Johanna Radmacher	Mar. 4, 1836	Sep. 1, 1886
Margaretta Huthman	Oct. 28, 1805	Dec. 1, 1886
Maria Hertmann	Apr. 4, 1836	Jan. 18, 1882
Margartom Plassmeyer	Feb. 17, 1837	Feb. 13, 1882
Frank Berhorst	Mar. 6, 1794	Jun. 11, 1883
Maria Behorst	Mar. 1, 1798	Dec. 24, 1882
Conrad Castrop	Dec. 18, 1807	Feb. 7, 1883
Carl Holtschneider	Oct. 9, 1816	May 13, 1883
Christina Bode	Mar. 10, 1821	Nov. 19, 1883
Mary Gertrude Thora	Dec. 8, 1809	Dec. 26, 1883

(Osage County, Missouri Continued)

Name	Born	Died
J. Bernard Bode	Mar. 13, 1808	Feb. 16, 1879
Stephen Johannasmeyer	Nov. 26, 1821	Jul. 27, 1879
Heinrick Bexten	Nov. 2, 1821	Jan. 22, 1880
J. Hermann Knuever	Nov. 24, 1790	Nov. 31, 1875
Maria Nackle	Apr. 27, 1802	Jan. 19, 1876
Joseph Nacke	Sep. 23, 1806	Nov. 22, 1887
Rosina Alhusa, relict of G. Herman	Jul. 20, 1820	Mar. 9, 1876
Christina Bandtenies	Mar. 25, 1808	Aug. 12, 1876
Angela Anna Maria Bertels, frau von Fraz nee Schreve	Sep. 15, 1807	Oct. 13, 1876
Heinrich Stegman	Dec. 11, 1835	Feb. 3, 1877
Bernard Temmon	Jun. 22, 1832	Feb. 3, 1877
Anna Maria Winkelman, wife of Henrich	Jul. 2, 1802	Oct. 1, 1823
Anna G. Fechtel, wittwe of Hermann	Apr. 2, 1809	Sep. 23, 1873
Anna Maria Heckemeier, wife of Gasper (b. Westphalen Prussia)	Sep. 29, 1820	Jan. 11, 1873
Gasper Heckemeir	Mar. 21, 1821	Jan. 15, 1873
Gerhard H. Wessling	Jan. 18, 1803	Jan. 21, 1874
Hermann Winkleman	Nov. 29, 1830	Apr. 11, 1872
Heinrich Dickneite	Jan. 10, 1819	Sep. 8, 1871
Elizabeth Walters	Nov. 17, 1808	Oct. 18, 1870
Johann B. Walters	Sep. 29, 1808	Dec. 13, 1864
Conrad Schulte	Dec. 15, 1809	Dec. 5, 1871
Fraz Lueke	Sep. 20, 1808	Jul. 19, 1868
Annie Temmen	1789	May 12, 1870
Maria Adrain	Nov. 29, 1830	Jan. 8, 1867
Stephen Borgmeyer	May 16, 1829	Nov. 16, 1866
George J. Morfeld	Mar. 13, 1817	Jan. 19, 1864
John H. Fechtel	Nov. 9, 1796	May 3, 1865
Gerhard Winkelman	Jul. 1, 1833	Mar. 24, 1865
Anton Fechtel	Sep. 5, 1817	Oct. 1, 1864
Bernard Holterman	Mar. 19, 1837	Oct. 4, 1865
Annam E. Wessing	Nov. 8, 1802	Nov. 16, 1865
Christine Boessen	Aug. 2, 1787	Jan. 12, 1866
Anna Adelheit Lindenbusch	Oct. 7, 1823	Apr. 21, 1863
Hermaronia Hunaephol	Jan. --, 1811	Jan. 19, 1864
Maria G. Adrain	Aug. 18, 1794	Aug. 17, 1864
George Fennewald	Feb. 8, 1801	Mar. 24, 1859
Henrich Weistorf	Mar. 24, 1837	Feb. 1, 1862
Anton Barton	Jul. 30, 1809	Jun. 15, 1853
Maria Clara Bode, wife of Bernard	Mar. 10, 1810	Apr. 29, 1858
Heinrich Heckemeir	Aug. 6, 1796	Jun. 19, 1858
Heinrich Poepping	Dec. 31, 1807	Nov. 24, 1852

(Osage County, Missouri Continued)

Name	Born	Died
Anna Angela Kunolt, wife of H. Kunolt	1819	1852
Henry Kunolt	Feb. 28, 1834	Sep. 25, 1867
Heinrich Porth	Oct. 13, 1830	Dec. 30, 1862

Henry County, Missouri, Bear Creek Chapel Cemetery, four miles south of LaDue, Mo.

Name	Born	Died
Mary K. Collier	1829	1873
B. F. Gashman	Oct. 29, 1838	Nov. 19, 1894
Martha Hayden, wife of James Hayden	Mar. 7, 1827	Mar. 31, 1895
*James Hayden	---	Mar. 2, 1891
* age: 73 years, 11 months, 11 days.		
David Inman	Mar. 16, 1817	Mar. 12, 1885
George W. Keep (Mason)	Nov. 26, 1829	Sep. 23, 1872
George Munich	Feb. 9, 1822	Mar. 9, 1899
Elizabeth Munich, wife of George Munich, (no date)		
Ann Mollet	1817	1896
Lucy Renfro	Nov. 13, 1813	Feb. 9, 1886
Jas. C. Sisson	Dec. 25, 1820	Jan. 14, 1880
Ellis Smith	1821	1899
William T. Strickler	Dec. 24, 1823	Jan. 18, 1864

St. Charles County, Missouri, Tax List, 1817.

James H. Audrain, John Armstrong, Patsy Anderson, Dennis Askins, John Anderson, Ebenezer Ayres, Reachal Allen, George W. Atchinson, William Adams, Jonathan Bryan, William Bladwin, David Bryan, Henry Bryan, John P. Burgate, James Baldridge, John Burgate, Robert Baldridge, Robert W. Baldridge, William Bess, Leman Barker, Jeremiah Beck, John Barker, David Boyd, Martin Bradbury, David Baldridge, John Bess, Samuel Bethwish, Ahab. Born, Hugh Baniss, James Brams, Author Brams, Thomas Buchannon, Cliad (sic) Burhalis, Jenett Burkebd, John Bryson, Thomas Blankenship, William Brice, Moses Banks, Thomas Brown, Amos Burdoine, Randolph Biggs, Atcienne Barnard, John Boone, William Burkeloe, Thomas Brown, Nathan Boone, Joseph Bryan, Anthony Bledsoe, Whitfield Brvadas, Mary Brown, John Beard, Timothy Brown, Jacob Biddle, Joseph Baugh, Antoine Berbona, Griffith Brown, Thomas Brooks, Joseph Baugh, Henry Brown, John Brown, John Beard, Stephen Best, Joseph Buchinin, John Bert, Joseph Beatty, Isaac Bert, Daniel Boone, Thomas Bowen, Pierre Berdeau, Antoine Berdeau, Bapriest Busziere, Joseph Bepouste, Taylor Berry, Louis Berdeau, Joseph Brown, James Clay, Sussanah Bussnetti, Francis Callaway, Larkin Callaway, Jesse Cain, John B. Carter, Jonas Caton, Jesse Caton, Noah

(St. Charles County, Missouri Continued)
Caton, William Crow, Warren Cottle, Jacob Coons, Louis Crow, John Castleman, Joseph Collard, William Craig, Joseph Canns, Nancy Callaway, John Castlier, Thomas Chambers, James Clark, Christopher Clark, Elijah Callard, Chisty Callaway, Edward Cout, Joseph Cout, Stephen Cout, Hugh Cummins, Spencer Clay, Zachariah Callaway, Archibald Chiton, Isaac Cout, Patience Castleman, Bosman Clifton, Abram Cumminger, Sylvenius Coute, Ira Coute, John B. Callaway, Henry Crow, Michael Crow, Henry Crow, Jonathan Crow, William Cashou, Joseph Callara, Ruebin Cara, James Callaway's heirs, James Canilery, George Chapman, Oliver, Mary Ann Cleuienne, John Coulliux, Stephen Clewir, Jacob Criel, Abraham Pettor Climme, Daniel K. Colgan, Pierre Connayer, Augustin Chouteau, Gabriel Cevie, dec., Jean Mary Carliene, Louis Coniyer, Peter Carbinoe, Peter Choteau, John Cumer, Almond Coutle, Richard Caulk, Simon Cousol, William Jn. Churty, John Cumer, Simon Cousol, John Collier, Nicholas Coons, Daniel Colgan, sr., John H. Coons, Andre Coute, John Davise, William Daugherty, Samuel Davise, Samuel Darson, Wm. Denny, Zechiel Downing, Daniel Draper, Jacob Denison, Louis Dergy, Charles Denny, Andrew Downing, Thomas Dozie, Joseph Dastime, Andrienne Deleule, Joshua Dodson's heirs, David Danst, Isaac Danse, Abram Danse, Joseph Dubois, Thomas Daxy, David Daloney, Charles F. Delauviere, C. D. Dallassus, Bapt. Dolack, Auguste Dolack, Charles F. Delauviere, David Evans, Mary Duquelle, John Ewing, Samuel Ewing, Alexander Ellison, Andrew Edwards, Benjamin Edmons, John Isaac Ewing, Noah Jn. Ebow, Jesse Evens, jr., Joseph Evens, Patrick Ewing, Rufus Easton, Duncan Edwards, Jesse Evan, Charles Elara, Anarru Fort, Thomas Forman, Thomas Fugette, Burt Farnsworth, Josiah Fluger, Joshua Fisher, James L. Flaugherty, John Ferry, John Furguson, Isaac Faulkerson, James Frazier, Jane Fanner, John Frazier, Auguste Fecteau's heirs, Nicholas Faye, Angus Gills, William Farnsworth, Thomas Fallis, Joshua Furguson, Timothy Flint, Jonathan Gudin, William Gudin, John Gibson, Jeremiah Gushing, Joseph Gibson, Jacob Gushing, Thomas Gilmore, John Gabby, Guian Gibson, Samuel Gibson, William Guirn, Samuel Gushing, Fursden Gentle, George Gally, Jacob Guons, James F. Guire, Sam. Griffin's heirs, John Green, Robert Green Daniel Griffith, James Green, John B. Grazier, Benjamin German, Hugh Griffith, John Gibson, Antoinne Guyaudin, Joseph Garcia, Asa Griffith, Elisha Goodrick's heirs, Charles Gabearth, William K. Hancock, James Hutton, James Hughes, Luke Holdin, William Haskins, Paul Harpole, Benjamin Hurt, Charles Hubbard, Hugh Henry, Isaac Hatfield, John Hunter, Thomas Hampton, William Houashall, Joseph Houashall, Jesse Hughes, Jacob Hammes, R. and John G. Heith, Isaac Hostetter, Christain Hostetter, Wm. Hays, Francis Howell, Jacob Haun, John Haun, Newton Howell, John House, James Head, Boone Hays, William Hays' heirs, A.

(St. Charles County, Missouri Continued)
and Green Hutchings, Thomas Howell, Leonard Harde, Joseph Head, Francis Howell, Henry Haverstick, Samuel D. Holmes, Aron Hutchings, Francis Honoire, Nathan Haird, Alexander Hise, George Hofman, Joseph Hainds, Daniel Hays, Jabes Ham, Jonathan Hilleway, Peter Hofman, George Hofman, John C. Ham, Mackaham Henry Henry Hight, Daniel Hubbard, Thomas Kennedy, Edward Hempstead, Stuart Huran Edward Hempstead and Pratt Pernace, Christopher Hutchins, Larkin Hancock's heirs, Wm. D. Hardin, Stuart Hempstead, William Jemison, Benjamin James, John Jones, Joseph Jenks, Jonathan Jones, Joshua Jones, Geo. Jemeron (sic), John Jerdon, Peter Journey, Joseph Johnston, Mary Johnston, Robert Johnston, Joseph Jereseoui (sic), John Johnston, James Journey, Daniel Johnston, John Jacob, David Kingcade, Antonie James, William Keathly, Philip Keller, Wm. Kent, Thomas Kennedy, James Kennedy, Isaac Kent, Lydia King, Abram Kennedy, Richard Kerr, Joseph Keathly, Samuel Keathly, Charles Kirkpatrick, Laurence Hillebau, Abram Keathy's heirs, James Kerr's heirs, James W. Kerr, Daniel Kissler's heirs, John King, Michael Kennedy, Wallis Kirkpatrick, John Kenny, Joseph Kenny, Osborne Knott, Wm. Kirkpatrick, Wm. F. Lamme, William Logan, Hugh Logan, Hugh Liles, William Liles, James Liles, Robert Liles, John Lindsay, William Linn's heirs, H. F. Michan, Samuel H. Lewis, James Lewis, Even Lamasters, Wm. Lammes, Isaac Lamaster, Benjamin Lamaster, David Lamaster, Joseph Leanoiex, Francis Lameious (sic), Mary Lamarsh, Hugh McLaird, Gabriel Lattinary, Syvester Labbaddie, Patrick Lee, --ridann Lee L'Saleaun, William Marshall, Aron McWaters, John Marshal, Robert McKenney, David McKenney, Alexander M'Kinny, John M'Kinniy, Alexander M'Kinney, jr., William McCoy, Hugh McCoy, Robert McMann, David Marriole, Enoch Matson, Thomas Macky, John Macky, James Macky, John Macky, jr., Wm. Martin, Thomas Macky, William M'Clain, William M'Canna, John M'Mick, Robert M'Canna, Zachariah Moore, John M'Coy, Daniel M'Coy, Polette Myette, Charles Markham, John B. Marten, Wm. Miles, Alexander McCullough, James McNough, John C. Milligan, John M'Connald, Gabriel Marten, William M'Laughlin, Joseph Moody, William M'Farlin, William M'Hughs, sr., Seth Millington, John Noor, David McKay, Joseph Move, Mathias M'Clark, Alexander McKaire, Jesse Mondon, Alexander M'Clain, Elijah Matterson, Mathew M'Cormack, Brady M'Knight, Reubin Norr, Jacob Norr, Wiley Norman, Thomas Norton, John T. Nash, Mary Nourr, John Oden, William Nash, Charlotte Nourr, Thomas Oden, Drury R. Prichard, John Owens, Jesse Owens, John Onstill, Nathaniel Overall, Person Overall, John Pitman, Green Priest, William Petty, Elizabeth Price, Kederick Price, Makem Pusell, David Peter, Francis Prauer, N. Prauir's heirs, Ephraim Purkins, Robert Purst, Samuel Price, Justus Post, Joseph Phillipson, Peter Provinchere, William Palmer, Joseph Poveau, Richard B.

(St. Charles County, Missouri Continued)
Pilman, Mary Paushase, Robert Pendergrass, Louis Patelle, Francis Prepeau, Joseph Pappan, Mary Patin, Dwine Pitman, Justus Post, Jacob Pullen, B. Preshall, Peter R. Pioteray, Wm. Phillips, Henry Parrish, Martin Parmer, P. Pera, Peter Qubeck, Jacob Quick, Alexander Quick, P. Quarles, Isiadore Ribideau, William Russell, James Reynolds, Ruebin Rider, Wm. Ramsay, Jonathan Riggs, Henry Ridenhaus, Henry Robertson, William Rollings, Claiborne Rhoades, John Robertson, Antoine Roy, Leon Rutgers, Simon Roy, Edward Rear, Patrick Roy, John B. Roy, Francis Roy, Fabian Roy, James Richards, Charles Roy, Alexander Roy, James Roy, John B. Roy, Charles Reid, Joseph Roy, Joseph Renvace, Louis Renvace, Robert Rird, Welcome A. Robins, Francis Robins, Moses Robins, Thadias Robins, Proper Rollens, Antoine Raynold, Antoine Raynold, jr., James Rin's estate, Thomas F. Redic, Benjamin Sharp, James Sharp, Moses Summers, William Stuart, Robert Spence, John Shum, Lawence B. Stelen, Job B. Starks, James Shall, James Stanley, Samuel Scouts, Moses Sappington, Robert Stuart, James Starks, Lydia Spears, Starks Simes, John Simes, Henry Smith, John Smith, Thomas Spencer, William Smith, Henry Smith, Thomas Spencer, Daniel Smith, Robert Smith, Hezekiah Smith, Louis Sancilare, James Smith, Mathias Sauciere, James Sauiar, Antoine Seouce, Antoine Suacole, Gerard Smiercer, Thomas Stephenson, Joseph Summa, Andrew Smith, Thomas Smith, Louis Sancilare, Leonard Stamp, George Smilioer, Joshua Stogstetter, Ante. Saucese, William Tharp, Albert Teason, Nathaniel Tucker, Miles Turner, Giles Thompson, Ruebin Thornhill, Brent Thornhill, Winslow Tinner, jr., Winslow Tinner, Widow Tharker, James Temptation, Abram Thomas, William Torbot, James Talbot, William Talbot, Christopher Talbot, Hair Talbot, Thomas Talbot, Louis Trim, Nathaniel Teason, William Thompson, Charles Tyson, Joseph Tyson, Joseph Voisard, John Venables, Isaac Vinbitter, Peter Venseau, Benito Vasques, Louis Vincent, Lander Veach, James Vanbibber, Allen B. Williams, jr., Anthony Wyate, P. Welden, Leven Williams, Zadock Woods, Allen B. Williams, John Watts, Thomas Williams, Job Williams, Jean Welss, John Watson, John Wyatt, David Watson, Samuel Watson, Joseph Walls, Jonathan heirs, William Worten, Francis Wygate, John Wadkins, Joseph Yardley, Paul Whittery, Amos Wheeler, Wherry Wacky, Solomon Yakin, John Young, John Yarnell, Andrew Zumatt, Jacob Zumatt, Adam Zumatt, jr., David Zumatt, Henry Zumatt, John Zumatt, Adam Zumatt, sr., Andrew Zumatt, jr., Geo. Zumatt, Christopher Zumatt, John Zumatt, jr., Geo. Zumatt, Adam Zumatt, jr., John Zumatt, sr.

Nathan Boones's Co., July 13, 1812, Carter's Papers, Vol.XIV.

Name	Rank	Appointment Date
Nathan Boone	Captain	

(Nathan Bonne's Company Continued)

Name	Rank	Appointment Date
Wm. T. Lamme	First Lieu.	
David McNair	Sec. Lieu	
J. W. Boone	Sgt.	June 18, 1812
David Bowling	Sgt.	June 18, 1812
James Clark	Sgt.	June 18, 1812
James Huff	Sgt.	June 18, 1812
Lowry T. Hampton	Corp.	June 18, 1812
Evan LeMasters	Corp.	June 18, 1812
Moors Burbanks	Corp.	June 18, 1812
Enoch Carmack	Corp.	June 18, 1812
Thomas McNair	Trumpeter	June 18, 1812
William Hooper	Private	June 18, 1812
Anderson Chase	Private	June 18, 1812
John Huff	Private	June 18, 1812
Robert Brown	Private	June 18, 1812
Thomas Piper	Private	June 18, 1812
Jesse Hetford	Private	June 18, 1812
Milton Lewis	Private	June 18, 1812
Samuel Vanburkels	Private	June 18, 1812
Israel Massey	Private	June 18, 1812
Job Williams	Private	June 18, 1812
Ezekiel McNair	Private	June 18, 1812
Nathan Barney	Private	June 18, 1812
William Burns	Private	June 18, 1812
Job Stark	Private	June 18, 1812
Hartley Sappington	Private	June 18, 1812
David LeMasters	Private	June 18, 1812
William Landers	Private	June 18, 1812
William Paris	Private	June 18, 1812
George H. Jackson	Private	June 18, 1812
Jesse Vanbibber	Private	June 18, 1812
William Jameson	Private	June 18, 1812
John Ramsey	Private	June 18, 1812
William Wolfe	Private	June 18, 1812
William Crow	Private	June 18, 1812
Joseph Mitchell	Private	June 18, 1812
William Tomkins	Private	June 18, 1812
Peter Holderman	Private	June 18, 1812
Morgan Bryan	Private	June 18, 1812
William Miller	Private	June 18, 1812
William Keithley	Private	June 18, 1812
Ira Slaton	Private	June 18, 1812
Joel Nolan	Private	June 18, 1812
Benjamin LeMasters	Private	June 18, 1812
David Philips	Private	June 18, 1812
James Tygart	Private	June 18, 1812
Peter Pugh	Private	June 18, 1812

(Nathan Boone's Company Continued)

Name	Rank	Appointment Date
John Lewis	Private	June 18, 1812
John Sappington	Private	June 18, 1812
Bryson O'Hara	Private	June 18, 1812
William McHan	Private	June 18, 1812
Thomas Massey	Private	June 18, 1812
Thomas Reynolds	Private	June 18, 1812
John McCoy	Private	June 18, 1812
Elisha Moore	Private	June 18, 1812
George Burns	Private	June 18, 1812
John Ewing	Private	June 18, 1812
Lewis Jones	Private	June 18, 1812
Jonathan Stouchmen	Private	June 19, 1812
John M. Barr	Private	June 19, 1812
William Wells	Private	June 19, 1812
Daniel McHugh	Private	June 19, 1812
Samuel Shaw	Private	June 26, 1812
Dabney Burnett	Private	June 26, 1812
Jonathan Crow	Private	June 26, 1812
Peter Massey	Private	June 27, 1812
Benona Sappington	Private	June 18, 1812
Archibald McDonald	Private	June 19, 1812
William Bays	Private	July 1, 1812
William Ewing	Private	July 1, 1812

Ralls County, Missouri, Delinquent Tax List, 1826.

Davis Riggs, Wm. Biggs, Stephen Burts, Samuel Cane, Geo. Collier, S. Cheatwood, Walter Conway, Finley Dabney, Isaac Green, Edw. Davis, -- Ewing's heirs, E. Easton, R. Graham, Stephen Glascock, Fanny Gilbert, Archibald Gamble, Edward Latimore, John McKey, D. McCoy, Wait Lowery, Type Martin, P. Manchester, John Mackey, jr., James Murphy, J. Murphy, John Milam, David Porter, Milton Robert, Geo. W. Stone, Robert Wallace, Brigham Williams.

Henry County, Missouri, Tebo Township, Three and one-half miles east of Shawnee Mound.

Name	Born	Died
G. T. Woolfolk	Jan. 19, 1804	Jul. 28, 1862
Isaac Wise	Jan. 11, 1818	Oct. 30, 1887
James Wiley	1803	Jan. 30, 1875
Eliza Wiley	Dec. 15, 1819	Jan. 30, 1875
W.A. Robertson	Jun. 17, 1818	Feb. 24, 1899
Adaline Roberston	May 22, 1836	Jun. 5, 1895

Johnson County, Missouri, Delinquent Tax List, 1836.

James Adams, James Arnold, Nancy Anderson, Geo. Bradshaw, Jacob Arterman, John H. Cowan, George W. Douglas, John Kelly,

(Johnson County, Missouri Continued)
Thomas J. Duncan, John Demaster, James R. Duncan, Abraham Davis, Henry Davis, William Ford, Drucella Hayslip, William Lynch, Lewis Jones, John A. Lewis, Benjamin Mathew, James D. Oglesby, Andrew Patrick, Joel Riddle, L. H. Renick, Thomas W. Tablo, John Stall, John Sears, William Thortom, William T. Hoas, George Wade, Josiah Trebble, Jesse Cox, Isaac Cox.

St. Louis County, Missouri, Marriage Contracts in the Deed Index which were executed under the Spanish Government, 1766 to 1804.

Groom	Bride	Year
Hunau Toussaint	Mary Ste. Beujenon	1766
Louis Marchdeau	*Veronique Panisse *(Widow Panisse)	1766
Paul Kierenau	Marie Josephile Michel	1766
Francis Moreau	Catharine Marechal	1767
Pierre Rougeau	Therese Herbert	1767
Pierre Laceroux	Helen Larche	1767
Jn. Bte. Pamahe	Charolotte Lowners	1767
Lefevre Deserusseau	Marg. Laferme	1768
Alexis Cottle	Elizabeth Dodie	1768
Nicholas Barsadoux	Madeline Lepage	1768
Jn. Bte. Durant	Marie Josephte Marcheteau	1768
Philibert Pagnon	Mary Newby	1769
Antoine Sansouiery	Mary Frce. Visvarenne	1769
Jn. Bte. Lavor	*Louise Laduvantage *(Widow)	1769
Nicholas F. Dion	Therese Heriuex	1769
Joseph Mainville dit Decherse	Ann Chancellier	1770
Jn. Sale dit Lafore	Mary Roz Videlsan	1770
Joseph Simmoneau	Mary Pieart	1771
Joseph Labrosse	Thereze Louvieve	1771
Jacques Lasablonieu	Helen Beauqenon	1771
Louis Bissonet	Genevieve Routieu	1771
Charles Chauvel Dubreuil	Susan Santos	1772
Joseph Chancellier	Elizabeth Bequent	1772
Louis Marcheleau	Angelique Metivier	1772
Valentin	Jeanette (free colored)	1773
Simon Coussot	Mary Therese Dodier	1774
Gregouier Kiencerseau	Madeline S. Francois	1774
Jn. Bt. Benoni Dufaut	Mary A. Roussillet Laroche	1774
Charles Bizet	Marie Pepin LaChance	1774
Francis Hebert	Madeline Leroy	1774
Antoine Martin dit Ladouever	Marie E. Marchel	1774

(St. Louis County, Missouri Continued)

Groom	Bride	Year
Louis Dubrevel	Mary Ann Laroche	1776
Silvester Labbudie	Pelagie Chouteau	1776
Francisco Dunegan	Mary Catharine Langoumois	1776
Martin Dunvalde	Mary Josephte Perrault	1776
Jn. Bte. Petit	Therese Charron	1776
Jn. Bte. Vifvarenne	Genevieve Cardinal	1777
Gaspar Fr. Roubleu	Marie A. Laferme	1777
Clement Delor	Angelique Martin	1779
Charles Leroy	Susan Dodier	1779
Charles Lanquinet	Marie A. Conde	1779
Ignace LaRoche	Marie Louise Chouteau	1779
Guillaume Herbet Lecombe	Margaret Blondeau	1780
Joseph Hortiz	Margaret Bequette	1780
Joseph Lapierre	Rosalie Oliver	1780
Louis Barada	Marie Bequet	1781
Jn. Bte. Provenche	*Marie Pepin *(Widow Bizete)	1781
Joseph Tayon	Mary Berger	1781
Francois Fostin	Rosalie Kienceveu	1781
Charles Gratiot	Victoire Chouteau	1781
Jacques Noise	Therese Beaugenau	1781
Louis Letoumeau	Marie Bisonet	1781
Francois Cailhol	Madeloine Deloc	1781
Joseph Robidou	Catharine Rollet dit Laderoule	1782
Louis Bunnenu	Catharine Nicole Lisbois	1782
Joseph Louins	*Catharine Rosier *(Widow Barada)	1782
Gabriel Bequet	Mary L. F. Francois	1782
Jn. Bte. Hortes	Elizabeth Barada	1782
Louis Chancelier	Mary L. Deschamp	1782
Philip Fine	Mary Newby	1782
Antoine Vincent	Mary Rouett	1782
Eigenio Alvarez	Josephite Crepeau	1782
Hyaceinthe Civs	Helen Herbert	1783
Emelien Yosty	Thetiste Durand	1783
Peter Chouteau	Pelagie Kiererau	1783
Amable Puion	Reine Felicite Robert	1783
Antonio Revinal	Mary Tousant	1784
Michelalexio Marie	Mary Rose Delor	1784
Francois Dorlac	Einable Lalande	1785
Pierre Charrette	Mary Jte. Kiencerau	1786
Henry Duchouquent	Felicite L. Felip	1786
Antoine Potie	Elizabeth Bequet	1786
Joseph Desatellis	Therese Mainville	1787
Baptiste Benan	Catharine Lalande	1788
Jn. Bentura Collell	Constance Conde	1788

(St. Louis County, Missouri Continued)

Groom	Bride	Year
Louis Beaudouin	Mary Tesson Honore	1789
Eugene Dorsievre	Mary Nicole Lesbois	1789
Pierre Gagnon	Helen Mainville	1789
Michel Quenal	Mary Louise Jourdain	1790
Louis Bonpart	Celeste Duchoquet	1790
Louis Blanchet	Angelique Lauvagesse	1790
Hyacinthe Dehere	Frse. Normandeau	1791
Pierre Chalifoux	Victoire Coussot	1792
Jn. Bte. Prevost	Angelique Lauvagesse	1792
Pierre Chouteau	Brigitte Laucier	1794
Francois Volois	Julie Beauqenou	1794
Francois Drouin	Catharine Pougat	1794
Joseph Cordaivr	Angeline Roch	1794
Pierre Ladouceur	Angelique Bissonent	1794
Bernard Pratte	Emilie Labbadie	1794
Philip Fine	Celeste Bolaille	1794
Antoine Soulard	Julie Cerre	1795
Antoine Flandrin	Maragaret Barada	1795
Antoine Entienne Baccane	Charlotte Roche	1795
Bte. Bricaut dit LaMarche	Louise LaLande	1795
Tousaint Jacques Lebeau	Marie LaFrenaie	1795
Louis Boissy	Marie Bisette	1795
Jn. Bte. Vien	Euphrasinie Hunaue	1795
Pierre Bordeaux	Therese Petite	1795
Joseph Rive	Marianne Olivie	1796
Jacque M. F. Vrain Delassus	Felicite Dubreul	1796
Antoine Barada	Elizabeth Tesson Honore	1796
Alexander Bellessime	Josephte Robidou	1796
Joseph Lufrenait	Margaret Purcelliy	1796
Jn. Bte. Lebeau	Mary J. Alverez Hortis	1796
Julien Roy	Reine Guilgaut	1797
Louis Honore	Catharine Rivet	1797
Louis Corgnard	Julie Vasques	1797
Pascal Leon Cerre	Therese Lamy	1797
Fr. Levige alias Leplante	Marie Malet	1797
Jn. Gates	Genevieve Morin	1797
George Lehoulse	Victorie Tesson	1797
Patrick Lee	Constance Conde	1797
Joseph Chareville	Victoire Verdon	1797
Charles Robert	Jeanne Courtois	1797
Pierre Berge	Josephte Mayet	1797
Gregoire Lanpy	Pelaqie Labladie	1797
Antoine Rencontre	Marie Brazeaux	1798
Fremon Delaunere	Celeste Dubreuit	1799
Jn. Bte. Girard	Josepht Rivette	1799
Francois Dunegant	Eugenie Jarret	1799

(St. Louis County, Missouri Continued)

Groom	Bride	Year
Pierre Payant	Elizabeth C---	1799
Jacques Ljenesse	Helen Vacheur	1799
Jn. B. Bravier dit Ceril	Elizabeth Rie	1800
Michel Rolel dit Laderoule	Joste. Morisaux	1800
Joseph Herbert	Victoire A. Hortiz	1801
Philip Rivierreud Bacanne	Marianne Liberge	1802
Auguste LeFevre	Felicite Vayancour	1802
Michel Valle	Francoise Lueyeuse	1802
Louis Courlois	Marie Louise Menard	1802
Mary P. Ledue	Margaret Papin	1802
Christoval Shoulse	Elizabeth Honore	1803
Louis Beset	Euphrosine Trudeau	1803
Peter Thoeclse	Marie R. Dunequant	1803
Pierre Boling	Marie Duneqant	1803
Andre Pilier	Euphbrine Gayne	1803
Michel Herbet	Marie Ursule Rapieux	1803
F. Cevienes	Marie Beadouin	1803
Pierre Rousselle	Francoise Gainet	1803
Dominque Huge	Mary R. Porcelly	1803
Pierre Provenchere	Marie Gen. Rutgers	1803
Francois I. Labrosse	Sally Russell	1804
Henry Delauvier	Helen Bissonnett	1804
Israel Dodge	Catharine Camp	1804
Joseph Fayet	Felicite Marechal	1804
Francois Doyn	Pelagie LaPlante	1804
Joseph Thibault	Mary Louise Vincennes	1804
Louis Jn. Vincennes	Elizabeth Deves	1804
Joseph Rousseau	Margaret Hortiz	1804

Steamboat Disaster, Missouri Intelligencer, March 23, 1823, Vol. IV, No. 34.

On February 8th the steamboat "Tennessee" sank. These persons died: M. J. Nouvel, Lexington, Kentucky; Mr. Pool, Baltimore; Mr. Maybin, Philadelphia; Mr. Carothes,Tennessee; Geo. Sanders, Lexington, Kentucky; Samuel Cooper, Kentucky; David Knaw, Kentucky; John Steward; John Kipler;Mrs. Mansker and child; Mr. Terley; James Bradford; negro Henry.

Washington County, Missouri, Grand Jury Members, Missouri Intelligencer, August 20, 1819.

B. J. Thompson, Foreman; John Sloss; Samuel P. Browne; Abraham Brinker; Benrard Coleman; William Henderson; Thomas Hurst; Benjamin Imboden; Amos Minks; James H. Mantsey; John Scott, jr.; James F. Perry; John Stuart.

Chariton County, Missouri, Delinquent Tax List, 1829.

Daniel Ashley, Love Baker, Abraham Barnes, James Bogg, J.

(Chariton County, Missouri Continued)
M. Bell, John Baden, W. R. Boothe, N. Branson's heirs, John Coy, H. Brown, J. Coleman, B. C. Cooper, D. Coulter's heirs, E. Coursalt, George Craig, J.J. Crittendon, D. E. Cuyler, M. Dillingham, Michael Dousman, Thomas Duley, W. F. Dunnica, J. Elston, Robert A. Ewing, Patrick Fling, J. P. Fulkerson, J. B. Grant, Joseph Gill, Job Goodall, Wm. Grant, John Halbert, Patrick Griffin, Moses Harris, G. Hayes, Robert Hays, F. Hix, W. Hobby, Hiram Holt, W. G. Hood, Howland, Wm. Jones, Peter Justus, James Keyte, Jere Kingsberry, M. Lambert, Jonathan Ramsay, Peter Lindell, John McDowell, Geo. McGunnigle, John McNairy, Robert McMennoy, J. McCausland, Joseph Magagnus, Stephen Man, Abner Martin, John L. Martin, Gabriel Maupin, John Maxwell, John Moore, Robert Owens, Nath. Patton, Geo. Robinson, Israel B. Read, Jonathan Ramsay, Spencer Pettis, Samuel Rutherford, Saul Rutherford, Joseph Schoval, James Sipple, J. B. Sexton, Benjamin Shirliff, N. Smith, Thomas A. Smith, Oran Stone, Asahel Storrs, Joseph Strong, H. Vanphal, J. C. Sullivan, John L. Sutton, J. M. Thurston, T. Turner, Jesse Townsend, James Whitesides, Henry T. Williams, Parker Williams.

St. Francois County, Missouri, Marriages Listed in Deed Book A, 1819 - 1835.

Groom	Bride	Date
*Richard Murphy	*Sarah Murphy	Jan. 10, 1819
(Both are from Ste. Genevieve County)		
Joseph McFarland	Polly McFarland	Jul. 4, 1822
John Sissel	Charlotte Faught	Dec. 8, 1822
James Monteer	Delilah Estes	Dec. 19, 1822
James Younger	Rachel Murphy	Feb. 2, 1823
Martin Stegall	Nancy Jones	Apr. 6, 1823
Robert Blackwell	Catherine Rayburn	Apr. 10, 1823
Solomon Griffin	Clarysa Hays	Jul. 18, 1823
George Wilson	Nancy Cunningham	May 11, 1823
Joseph Monteer	Elizabeth Estes	May 25, 1823
George Dill	Ann McCormack	Sep. 27, 1823
Joseph F. Hurry	Nancy Cunningham	Dec. 7, 1823
David Evans	Katharine Windes	Dec. 17, 1823
Peter McCormick	Eliza Alexander	Mar. 25, 1824
John Murphy	Betsy Robinson	Apr. 11, 1824
Isaac N. Davis	Malinda Gillispy	May 9, 1824
John Cunninghaam	Sarah Bain	Mar. 21, 1824
Frank M. Braly	Elizabeth Madison	Jul. 19, 1825
Josephus Kennedy	Rachael Griffith	May 29, 1825
Jacob Nisong	Letty Sims	Apr. 3, 1825
Moses Cunningham	Huldah Starks	Jul. 24, 1825
George Madison	Eliz. McFarland	Oct. 16, 1825
Nathaniel Gilbert	Eliz. Stafford	Dec. 14, 1825

(St. Francois County, Missouri Continued)

Groom	Bride	Date
William Wilson	Temperance Murphy	Sep. 25, 1825
George Shoemaker	Mary Peyton	Sep. 26, 1825
*Joseph Brutte	Polly Paterick	Sep. 25, 1825

*(married at the house of Caleb Patrick, Perry Twnshp.)

Groom	Bride	Date
Robert Hayes	Margaret Starks	Jan. 29, 1826
George Stamm, sr.	Mary Delany	Jan. 13, 1823
Jacob Cunningham	Sally Thompson	Feb. 22, 1826
Luke Davis	Nancy McKee	Feb. 19, 1826
#John C. Scott	Louisanney Fisher	May 23, 1826

#(The groom is from Washington County. The marriage took place at the home of George Day. Witnesses were John F. Mudd, George Day, Vincent B. Miller, John Cobb, G. W. H. Coulton, and James Farquhar.)

Groom	Bride	Date
Milton Latimer	Susan Kinsworthy	Jun. 19, 1826
William Waterman	Anne Lewis	May 24, 1826
@Nathan Linson	Susannah Keith	Jul. 30, 1826

@(Groom from Washington County. Bride from St. Francois)

Groom	Bride	Date
Philip Davis	Rachel Herrod	Aug. 31, 1826
William Andrews	Eliz. Parshall	Mar. 22, 1827
*Jacob Anderson	Margaret Duff	Apr. 15, 1827

*(Groom From Gasconade County. Bride from St. Francois.)

Groom	Bride	Date
James Marlow	Jane Doren	Mar. 1, 1827
Joseph Still	Emily Estes	Feb. 22, 1827
George Crump	Betsy Aramen	Jun. 28, 1827
William Doggett	Nancy Armon	Jun. 28, 1827
John Sago	Sally Crump	Jul. 19, 1827
Joshua Richardson	Polly Stafford	Oct. 28, 1827
+Henry Hampton	Mary Frey	Jul. 19, 1827

+(Married at the home of Gainim Estes)

Groom	Bride	Date
William Grisom	Sarah Mosley	Sep. 25, 1827
Lewis Cannon	Nancy Rods	Mar. 19, 1828
Nathan Becket	Rode Patterson	Feb. 10, 1828
Joseph Brown	Reziah Ragland	Feb. 10, 1828
Thomas Parrick	Lucy Marlow	Jul. 13, 1828
xJames Hickcock	Malinda Gosa	Dec. 1, 1828

x(Bride was underage, but had parental consent)

Groom	Bride	Date
Charles Hiccocks	Mariah Hill	Nov. 15, 1828
$David Murphy, jr.	Elviry Whitinburg	Feb. 5, 1829

$(Married in St. Francois Twnshp.)

Groom	Bride	Date
¢Antwn. Barry	Salle Webb	Nov. 1, 1827

¢(Married at the home of Alexander Gavens, Perry Twnshp)

Groom	Bride	Date
John B. Robinson	Sarah M. Rownels	Sep. 13, 1828
Francois Deguer	Sophia McFarland	Dec. 20, 1827
Charles B. Cunningham	Lucy Wilson	Feb. 26, 1829
William Murphy	Mrs. Frances Johns	Mar. 12, 1829
Eli Halbert	Frances Shirrel	Dec. 11, 1828
Isaac Rogers	Mahala Brown	Oct. 26, 1828

(St. Francois County, Missouri Continued)

Groom	Bride	Date
Thomas Madison	Caroline Griffith	Jan. 3, 1830
James Conellay	Susan Maria Spradling	Nov. 23, 1829
William Cooper	Mariah Lewis	Mar. 18, 1830
David Flied	Susanah Roade	Feb. 2, 1831
James Keith	Catherine Manning	May 8, 1831
William Madison	Sarah M. Taylor	Apr. 14, 1831
*Francis Deguire	Eliza McFarland	Nov. 28, 1830

*(Groom is from Madison County. The bride is the daughter of John McFarland)

Groom	Bride	Date
#Ransom Cartee	Martha Bounds	Jul. 3, 1831

#(Married at the home of Jesse Bounds, Pendleton Twnshp)

Groom	Bride	Date
Hezekiah W. Horton	Elizabeth Bradshaw	Jul. 19, 1831
John V. Henderson	Elizabeth O'Haver	Oct. 21, 1829
James Clay	Polly Ann Spradling	Jun. 25, 1831
Pleasant G. Keith	Clarinda Baker	Aug. 18, 1831
Thomas McKee	Rhoda ---	Jan. 20, 1831
Thomas Tapley	Patty Cole	Sep. 21, 1830
Samuel B. Herrod	Harriet Smith	Dec. 11, 1831
George Santee	Eliz. Sebastian	Sep. 21, 1830
Moses Baker	Polly W. Walker	Nov. 3, 1831
Robert Wiger	Annie Hull	May 26, 1832
xHenry Banister, jr.	Margaret Hill	Jun. 27, 1832

x(Margaret Hill was a widow. Married at the home of James Gunter, sr.)

Groom	Bride	Date
@John Delanny	Tempy Banister	Aug. 26, 1832

@(Bride is underage. Her mother Widow Nancy Banister gave her consent)

Groom	Bride	Date
David H. Murphy	Lucretia Cundiff	Aug. 26, 1832
L. M. Kennett	Martha Boyce	Sep. 15, 1832
Wm. Sutton	Hannah Duff	Nov. 8, 1832
Allen Williams	Charlotte Williams	Nov. 1, 1832
George Pettit	Elizabeth Shaw	Jul. 10, 1832
Silas Freeman	Epsey Marlow	Dec. 27, 1830
*Samuel Byington	Emily Breassie	Nov. 15, 1832

*(Groom from Ste. Genevieve Co., Bride from St. Fran.)

Groom	Bride	Date
Philip G. Long	Isabella Murphy	Jan. 15, 1833
Rolly Turley	Lucinda Smith	Mar. 12, 1833
&Webster Jamison	Nancy Peyton	Feb. 22, 1833

&(Groom underage)

Groom	Bride	Date
Peter Torick	Eliz. M. Jones	Jan. 10, 1833
Mark Renfro	Cynthia Murphy	Jul. 4, 1833
+John B. Brinker	Sarah Murphy	Dec. 31, 1833

+(Groom from Washington Co. Bride from St. Francois)

Groom	Bride	Date
William Mitchell	Polly McKee	Mar. 21, 1833
Josiah Holbert	Amy Kinsworthy	Jul. 7, 1833

(St. Francois County, Missouri Continued)

Groom	Bride	Date
Joseph McFarland	Polly Eliza *McFarland	Jan. 12, 1834

*There is another marriage with the same names in 1822.

xJoseph Perkins	Mrs. Emily Lacey	Jan. 26, 1834

x(Groom from Madison County. Bride from St. Francois.)

@Abijah W. Hudspeth	Sarah Gray	Oct. 30, 1833

@(Groom from Washington. Bride from St. Francois)

Shepply Wilburn	Eliz. Bressie	Jan. 20, 1834
John H. Vance	Sally Vance	Mar. 25, 1834
@Perry Moore	Nancy Clay	Jan. 13, 1834

@(Groom from Washington County and his parents are dec. His brother Wm. Moore acting as guardian gave consent)

Walton Alexander	Isabella Taylor	Feb. 2, 1834
James Mitchell	Elizabeth McKee	Mar. 20, 1834
John Kennedy	Ann Cayce	May 8, 1834
#Joseph Holt	Mary Cunningham	Nov. 2, 1834

#(Groom from Washington County. Bride from St. Francois)

Steven Quarles	Annette Cross	Aug. 7, 1834
Jesse McIlvain	Meekey Smith	Apr. 17, 1834
Peter Brickey	Mary Wizor	Nov. 9, 1834
William Wood	Laura Byington	Apr. 2, 1835
&John Stuts	Orpah Greenstreet	Oct. 7, 1834

&(Married at the home of John Stuts, Perry Twnshp.)

*William J. Allen	Sucky Abernathy	Mar. 26, 1835

*(Bride is the widow of Uriah Abernaty and the daughter of James Holbert. Groom from Madison County)

Joseph Carver	Martha Cunningham	Jan. 22, 1835
William M. Cruneleton	Eliza Jane Cole	Jan. 15, 1835
Alexander Gittar	Fanny Edwards	Feb. 5, 1835
Lewis Dent	Eliza Ann Simms	Jan. 8, 1835
Richard C. Poston	Martha Hill	Jan. 22, 1835
$Orvile E. McIlvain	Minerva A. Baker	Jan. 22, 1835

$(Groom from Washington County. Bride from St. Francois)

Isaac Baker	Rachel McKee	Jan. 22, 1835
Nathan Holbart	+Eunice Kinworthy	May 10, 1835

+(Bride daughter of Joshua Kinswrothy)

James D. Matkins	Martha Dorse	Jul. 9, 1835
James Gunter	Peggy Banister	Jun. 21, 1835
Robert Cleveland	&Mrs. Frances McGlandin, widow	Oct. 30, 1834

&(Groom from Washington County. Bride from St. Francois)

Willis Armon	Susanna Mosteller	Mar. 15, 1835
Elam McHenry	Nancy Poston	Jan. 18, 1827
Abraham Ringer	Barbary Norwine	Oct. 13, 1827

Cape Girardeau, Missouri, Tax List, 1822.

Thomas Adams, Christian Albright, John Albright, William I. Albright, Daniel Abernathy, Daniel Abraham, Joseph Baker,

(Cape Girardeau County, Missouri Continued)
Henry Ashebramer, Daniel Boucher, Henry Bollinger, Thomas Brady, John Boucher, John Bollinger, Henry Bollinger (son of Nathaniel), Moses Baily, Peter Boucher, William Bolen, John Baker, Andrew Bollinger, David Bollinger, John Bess, Peter Bess, John Baily, Martin Bess, Michael Bess, Michael Bess, Peter Baker, Jacob Bess, George Barey, Henry Baker, William Bollinger, Hiram Barey, Aron Bollinger, Elizabeth Bollinger, George Bollinger (son of Daniel), Jacob Barks, Morgan Byrne, Geo. Bollinger, sr., John Coon, Peter Critz, jr.,Joel Critz, Daniel Crater, Devault Cook, John Caldwell, Peter Critz, Hay Helm, David G. Caldwell, Daniel Critz, Moses Critz, John L. Conrod, Jacob Critz, Adam Clingsmith, Abraham Conesker, John Critz, Andrew Cosner, Randolph Cheek, Jacob Cook, jr., John Dack, George Cook, William Crowder, David Davault, Robert Dishay, James Duncan, Jacob Davault, Mary Deck, Isaac Deck, Andrew Davault, James Eaker, Christopher Edinger,Hiram Esks, Phillip Eigert, Christopher Eaker, jr., Christian Eaker,John Eaker, Henry Eaker, Joseph Eaker, --- Gross, Martin Gurtner, Isaac Gregory, Peter Goodwin, David Ground, Jacob Gross,John Hahn, Peter Gross, Peter Hahn, Elizabeth Harth, Jacob Harks, Simon Harker (adm. of P. Harker, dec.), Enoch Hudson, Jacob Hasty, Ephraim Hunt, Daniel Harly, Henry Hahn, Daniel Hahn, John Hostotter, Frederick Hagger, Hilgard Hicks, Adam Hoss, Daniel Harke, Simon Hartel, Henry Hostotler, John Howel,John Hendricks, Widow Hubble, John Hariman, Philip Hahn, William Hendricks, Peter Houck, James Irwin, Lewis Irwin, Elizabeth Johnson, Isaac Johnson, Jacob James, David Johnson, Constant Johnson, John Josahowter, Daniel Josahowter, Henry Kinder, Daniel Klingsmith, Elizabeth Kinder, Henry I. Kinder, Conrod Kinder, Jasmitton B. Kimmsont, Jacob Kinder, Cemson Kythies, David Kinder, Adam Kinder, Conrod Kinder, jr., Isaac Lack, Henry Limbaugh, Daniel Limbaugh, George Lastley,Simon Louis, Margaret Laget, Daniel Kinder, Isham Lucy, Joseph Lincoln, John Lorance, Jacob Limbaugh, George Lambert, D.B. Lincecum, Frederick Limbaugh, Stephen Malon, Jonathan Molan, Stephen Mayfield, John Master, Samuel McMinn, Nicholas Miller, Thos. P. McKelvey, John Miller, sr., John Miller, jr., John May, Nicholas Miller, Thos. P. McKelvey, Daniel Masters, Joseph Niswanger, jr., David McHaven, David Masker, John C. Miller, George Miller, Joseph Niswanger, sr., Henry Noble, Ethelebd Rivel, Moses Norman, John Oaks, Jacob Propst, John Peringer, John Perkins, Daniel Propst, John Peringer, John Perkins, Daniel Propst, John Polk, Isaac Rwel, David Rwel, John Rose, John Rasher, Samuel Rhodes, Daniel Rhoads, Jacob Rooks, M.P. Ringer, George Rhodes, Christopher Rhoads, Thomas Rhyme, Ann Rwel, Samuel Ramsey, William Revil, Macajah Rivel, Frederick Russ, Frederick Roors, Buswell Rwel, Henry Sifford, Samuel Sifford, David Stephens, Barnet Snider, Charles Saxton, John

(Cape Girardeau County, Missouri Continued)
Snider, Christopher Scarbourough, Philip Smith, Daniel Smith, Daniel Stinkard, Benj. Stevens, Robert H. Steed, David Shell, Isaac Snider, George Stroup, Benjamin Shell, George Snider, Christain Scabaugh, jr., William Sifford, Jacob Sifford, Geo. Simon (Adm. Zn. Snider, dec.), Gasper Simon, Gasper Shell, Jacob Srumm, Joseph Srumm, Michael Smith, Daniel Smith, John Smith, Polly Swell, Christian Scabaugh, sr., William Smith, Peter Scabaugh, Joseph Scabaugh, Emmauel Scabaugh, Nicholas Shaum, Andrew Stroup, Mary Stateler, Henry Smith, Alexander Strother, Mary Stateler, (adm. of Peter Stateler, dec.), Wm. Timmin, Thomas Shaman, Lewis Sifford, Azarich Timmin, George Tanqusley, Charles Tanqusley, Vanlentine Underwood, Samuel Virgo, Thomas Viley, William Wilson, John G. Wilson, Winston Wart, John Wilson, Ezekiel Ward, James Wilson, Samuel Welch, Abraham Witeman, John C. Williams, Martin Wilfong, Lorance Younce, Martin Wilfong, (adm. Christian Gross), John Wood, James Wilson, John B. Wheeler, Maria Yount, Marry Young, John Yount, Jesse Yount, Adolph Yoder, William Young, Henry Yount, B. W. Allen, Batter Abernathy, Jeremiah Able, Edward Archer, Batter Abernathy, Scott Abernathy, Joah Aberenathy, Joseph Abernathy, Thomas Atwell, Stephen Byrd, jr., Matthew Borein, Moses Byrd, Elias Barber, Levi Bennett, William A. Bull, D. F. Steinbeck, Thomas Bull, David Bollinger, Benjamin Bacon, John Byrd, (guard. for Nancy Byrd), Benjamin Brown, William Steinbeck, John Brown, John Byrd, Kilsey Boren, Eli Shelby, James Summers, Nicholas Swirs, D.F. Steinbeck for V. Miller, Alex Summers, James Smith, Jesse Story, Isaac Thomas, Joseph Thompson, Asa Tivers, Thomas Baker, Joseph Vandenburgh, John C. Watson, D.H. Whipple, Nelson D. Walling, Richard Walker, Joseph Whitney, Charles Wall, John Akin, Larkin Abernathy, Jeremiah Abernathy, Sol. H. Armour, Susannah Abernathy, B. W. Allen, David Armour, Harly D. Abernathy, Jeremiah Able, Batter Abernathy, Joab Abernathy, Edward Archer, William A. Bull, Thomas Atwell, Stephen Byrd, jr., Matthew Boren, Moses Byrd, Elias Barber, Levi Bennett, Levi Bennett, Thomas Bull, David Bollinger, William Droom, Benjanin Brown, John Brown, John Byrd, Kilsey Boren, Abraham Byrd, Henry Bollinger, John Byrd, William Byrd, Andrew Burns, George Bullit, A. Bravery, Alex. Buckner, David W. Brant, Wesley Byrs, Benjamin Boyce, Stephen Bacon, Thomas Blair, Stephen Byrd, Stephen Byrd for E. Love, John Blair, James Brooks, Daniel Bollinger, Francis Blair, Rozin L. Bishop, Matthew Bolinger, John Brown, Hundel Barks, Jonathan Buis, Jacob Bessy, David Bollinger, William Cox, R. H. Curtteo, David Gritz, Samuel A. Campbell, Daniel Clippard, Philip Cricks, James Crawford, Jacob Croker, Jacob Craks for Saml. Crader, Jacob Croker, Daniel Critz, William Creath, Conrod Cottman, Robert Cowen, Betsey Campbell by Wm. Charles, N. Creath, David Criswell, David Campbell, Ephriam

(Cape Girardeau County, Missouri Continued)
Critz, Jacob Clopeter, Jonathan Chandler, Hugh Criswell, J. B. Davis, George Cavenor, Jacob Cotner, George Cotner, Jones Cupples, Ephraim R. Conrod, Saml. Cupples, Giles S. Cowhead, Ephabit Coborn, John Davis, (Adm. of Samuel Hams), Daniel Davis, Z.B. Davis, Jacob Delph, John Long Daniel,G.W. Davis, James Davis, Elijah Daugherty, William Daugherty, Hiram C. Davis, James Dowty, John Daugherty, R. Daugherty, John Dunn, Peter Poremus, Henry Droore, Isaac Drorre, John Dilwood, Wm. Fishbeck, John Davenport, G.W. Davis for David Davis, Andrew Dunlap, Ruth Dunn, Samuel G. Dunn, Philip Dare by I. Erwin, James Evans, James Eakins, David Evans, James Edison, George Frickle, Jacob Fulbright, Wm. Frazier, Joseph Freizel, Allen Gochom, C. P. Fulmwider, Joseph Frizel, (exc. Jos. Seawell), E. Flinn, Mitchel Flemming, Thomas W. Graves,Christian Gaks, Thomas W. Graves, (adm. of Wm. Coersam, dec.), James Goza, David Green, Hiram Gilleland by E. Suly, Fielding Glascock, John Gibney, Robert Green, Scarlet Glascock, John Glascock, Peter R. Garrett, Joseph Duffy, John Hays, Joshua Hail, John Gilleland by I. McWilliams, John Hays for Christopher Hay's heirs, Thomas Hail, James Hendnoock, Jacob Hetherbrand, John Houk, Henry Howard, Isikieh Howard, Gilbert Hector, Robert H. Henderson for Matthew Henderson, Matthew Handlin, John Horrill, Peter Huncle, Robt. H. Henderson, William Hector, Thomas Howard, Samuel Hector, Michael Hogan, Edward Hale, Abraham Harmicks, Sarah Hays, (adm. of George Hays, dec.), John Hilderman, Jacob Horse, Ebenezer Hubble, Thomas Hubble, Peter Hubble, Jesse Hail, Daniel Hilderbrand, Henry Hatten, John Hoose, Elizabeth Horse, Francis Horse, Josiah Hunter, Milton Harris, Daniel Hickman, Abraham Hughes, Lewis Hope, Cyrus Henderson, John Higgins, R.W. Harris, Oliver Harris, Richd. P. Harris, O.B. Harris, Saml. Hughes, Isaac Jetten, Johnathan Johnson, William Jones, John Johnson, John Judson, sr., Theodore Jones, Jacob Kance, James Kymian, Daniel Link, John G. Love, John G. Love and A. B. Neely, Samuel Lockhart, William Long, Michael LaMaster, Wm. P. Lacey, Josiah Lee, John Link, Alexander Little, Rachel Laugherty, I. McFarland, George Meaizo, R.S. McFarland, Isaac Miller, William McGwin, Nathan McCarty for William McCarty, George Morrough, Joshua McDonald, William McGwin, (adm. Edward McGwin),James Medlby, Jos. Meolby, Ezekiel Muncy, William McClain, Thomas Miller, John Martin, Joseph Miller, Drury Massey, John McComb, John McKinsey, Edward McDurmitt, Abram Manning, Thomas Neal, Levi Norman by P. Gitz, Abaham Newfield, Nathan Notions, Richard B. Newlock, Isaac Notions, John Oliver, Price Parrish, John Payne, jr., John Patterson, jr., David Pew, Clara Byrd, Wm. Patterson, John Prim, Andrew Price, William Polk, Samuel Pew, Robert Patterson, (adm. of David Patterson, dec.), John Propst, George Prowher, Robert Patterson, Thomas Priest,John

(Cape Girardeau County, Missouri Continued)
Queen, James Russell, Thomas S. Ramsey, Michael Rodney, Wm. Reed, Thomas Ramsey, (guard. for T.J. and Polly Ramsey),Wm. Russell, Thomas Rice, Johnson Ramsey, Martin Rodney, Russell Roy, John Rodney, James Russell, Burrel Roberts,Martin Rine, John Raton, Hugh P. Rogers, Henry Rodes, William Rosneau, Edmund Rutler, Lineas B. Subbitt, Adam Stoker, Jacob Sexton, Ruth Sullinger, (adm. of James Stanford), Henry Steel, Henry Steel, Henry Shram, James Stevenson, Frederick Shram, Robert Smith, jr., John Smith, David Self, Levi Sides, David Smith, Frederick Stockard, Jacob Seapouch, Adam Seapouch, Joseph Shultz, John Sheppard, Joseph Shultz, Isaac Sheppard, Thomas Subblett, Frederick Shram, William Sewel, George H. Scripps, Washington Sterritt, Henry Shaner, James Step, James Starn, Henry Steel, (exc. R. Steel, dec.), Ezekiel Seely, Benjamin Thompson, Mark Shultz, Philip Self, David Shultz, Richard S. Thompson, James Thompson, Royal Thompson, Michael Thorn, Eli Umberfield, Lewis Tash's heirs, Martin Thomas, S. Vincent, Thomas Vest, Nathan Vanhorn, Daniel Will, Abraham Will, John Wright, James Wilkinson, N.W. Watkins, Philip Wire, Nicholas Whitelow, Sally Welker, John Wright, John F. Whitledge, Wm. B. Wallace, Henry Walker, James Wallace, Levy Wire, William Wallace, Jacob Welty, James B. Wilson, John Wilson, William Whittenbaugh, John Wesky, Benjamin Wilson, John P. Wright, John Wallace, Francis Wilson, Stephen Warfield, James Block, Philip Young, John Zillefrow, Thomas Byrne, John Baldwin, James Bennett, William Baldwin, Isaac Brewer, William Broom, Killiam Corner, Samuel Croley, John Cooley, Abraham Cross, --- Campbell, Elias Davis, Asa Foster, William Fuget, Titman Gibson, Moore Haney, William Hatson, Martin Horner, Wilson Kelso, Enoch Larriba, Martin B. Lawrence, David McKensie, Jesse Parker, William B. Lawrence, John Ramsey, John Ross, Johnson Strong, Robert Smith, Timonthy Shaw, William Tyler, Isaac Thompson, Robert Trother, John Wiley, Mathew Wiley, James Wiley.

<u>Johnson County,Missouri,Brethren Cemetery,Approximately one mile south of Warrensburg.</u>

Name	Born	Died
Catharine Hershey	Nov. 25, 1817	Jun. 8, 1897
John Hershey	Mar. 26, 1820	Aug. 6, 1896
Barbara Leary	Sep. 9, 1811	Jan. 7, 1898
William Matthews	Oct. 5, 1812	Feb. 15, 1899
Newton L. Murphy	Sep. 22, 1822	Aug. 25, 1893
H. J. Ruthraff	Oct. 21, 1832	Apr. 17, 1894

<u>Franklin County, Missouri,Missouri Intelligencer,Letters at the Post Office, April 1, 1823, Vol. 4, No. 35.</u>

J. T. Cleveland, a.p.m.: John Adams, Robert Ash, Nicholas

(Franklin County, Missouri Continued)
Amick, William Atteberry, Amy Ammick, Thomas Alexander, J.
or B. Burns, Thomas Alsop, Caleb G. Anderson, William Burk,
Susannah Brown, John and Thomas Bradly, Joseph Burr, James
J. Byrns, Obadiah Babbitt, Henry Bry, Elias Bancroft, Alfred
Baysye, Edward Ballen, Richard Brannin, John Bird, Charles
C. Beatty, George Burnet, Thomas Bradly, Shadrick Cluk, Geo.
Chapman, Charles Carrol, Thomas Cofer, Benjamin Cooper, Maj.
Alexander Cummings, David Doyle, Alfred A. Coats, Wm. Clark,
Tilmon Clark, Jerry Crowley, Robert Cooper, Robert Castle,
Thomas Copher, Nathan Clampet, Col. Benj. Chambers, George S.
Foster, Wm. Datson, Samuel Dent, John Duncan, Abraham Dale,
Henry or Thomas Frazer, William Fisher, David Feland, James
Fulkerson, John Feland, George Frakas, Martin Gibson, Rueben
Gentry, James O. Goether, Robert Gragg, William Grubb, Elias
Elston, Harmon Gragg, John Eween, Wm. J. E. Ewing, William H.
Head, Thomas Embree, Philip Edwards, Henry Earthman, James
Elams, Slias Enjart, Mrs. Docia Garner, John C. Gordon, Frye
Harris, Willis E. Green, Thomas Grant, Willis Grimes, Thomas
Harris Jabez Hubbard, Joseph Hughes, B.F. Hickox, Wm. Huse,
Joseph Huston, Wm. Heath, William H. Head, Samuel Harrison,
Richard Hines, John Harrison, Thomas Hardeman, James Hawkins,
Thomas Harrington, John Hardeman, Jonas Hay, Michael Hinch,
Michael Hornback, Andrew Johnson, James Johnson, John Kelly,
Richard Johnson, George Jinkenson, John Jackson, Nancy and
Susan Jackson, James Jackson, Sarah Johnson, Hiram Little,
William Lillard, Daniel Lay, Ewen M'Lain, Mr. Marly, Charles
M'Lean, Samuel M'Clure, Andrew M'Quitty, Abel Marly, Daniel
M'Kaller, Elisha M'Daniel, Thomas Morgan Cornelius Maupin,
George Masters, John P. Morris, Baily Marshall, John M'Gee,
Andrew S. M'Girk, James Moren, James Moberly, Niley Martin,
James M'Gee, Richard Mitchell, Isaac Martin, James Murphy, W.
H. Means, Benjamin Morgan, Daniel Munro, Squire Nichols, John
and Robert Newsom, Henry Owens, Iqnatius P. Owen, Elizabeth
Parker, Thomas Perry, John S. Patton, Andrew Polk, William
Poor, Lemon Parker, Robert Patrick, Wm. W. Payne, Zachariah
Short, John Patton, Willis Parks, Daniel Rector, Cornelius
Ringo, Charles Robertson, Owing Rawlins, Ester Rawlins, Wm.
L. Robinson, Absalom Renshaw, Col. Benj. H. Reeves, Samuel
Ringo, James Reed, John C. Rochester, Robert Ringo, Jackson
Smily, James Riddick, James Reavis, James Stinson, Peletiah
Scribner, Ann Sandford, John Steepton, John Silvers, Henry
Simpson, John Sneed or Hazel Tetson, Henry Smith, Harrison
Stapleton, Daniel Storms, George Stapleton, Uriel Sebree,
David Sleater, Isaac D. SKelton, Elisha Stanley, Col. Philip
Trammel, John Terrell, Lucius, William Tooms, Christopher
Trigg, Stephen Trigg, Asa Q. Thompson, Robin Thrasher, James
Taylor, Elijah and Joseph Wisdom, D. Workman, Samuel Wharton,
Caleb Weeden, Justinian Williams, Nathaniel Walker, Wm. Wilson,

(Franklin County, Missouri Countinued)
Wm. Ward, James West, Finds Yersen, Rbt. Yancy, Geo. Yount.

St. Francois County, Missouri, Delinquent Tax List, 1830.
John August, Wm. Russell, Vincent Simpson, J. Westoner.

Dissolved Partnerships, Missouri Republican, St. Louis County.

Partner	Partner	Issue
David Gay	Elisha S. Beebee	Mar. 19, 1823
Wm. McGunnegle	William Hill	Oct. 14, 1823
Jonas Newman	Thomas Newman	Mar. 23, 1824
Henry Reily	Arthur Ingram	Jun. 24, 1824
Hugh Richards	Tracy & Wahrendorff	Nov. 7, 1824
William Glasgow	John Niven	Mar. 2, 1826
Andrew Burt	Bernard Green	Sep. 14, 1826
William Skinner	William Smith	May 31, 1827
Samuel Willet	William R. Grimsley	Jun. 10, 1828
John Tatem	John Perr	Aug. 12, 1828
W. A. Beard	John Salmon	Nov. 18, 1828
Hiram Alexander	Thomas Ficklin	Feb. 10, 1829
Thomas Andrews	Joseph Liggett	Mar. 17, 1829
Philip Cassilly	Henry Johnson	Mar. 31, 1829
W. A. Beard	John Lee	May 19, 1829
John A. Irvine	B. F. Payne	Aug. 4, 1829
Joseph Walton	Archibald Orme	Feb. 16, 1830
Isaac Dyer	Jesse H. Rogers	Mar. 23, 1830
Jacob V. D. Stout	Thomas Williams	Apr. 6, 1830
William Starr	R. T. McKenny	Apr. 13, 1830
Joel Campbell	William R. Turpin	Apr. 13, 1830
Augustus Bowles	William P. Maddox	Aug. 10, 1830
George Collier	Peter & Jos. Powell	Oct. 12, 1830
Elias Bates	John W. Honey	Mar. 22, 1831
William R. Grimsley	Wm. A. Lynch	Apr. 19, 1831
Edwin Draper	Hampton Weed	May 24, 1831
A.W. Vanleer	----	Jul. 26, 1831
Robert D. Sutton	----	Sep. 20, 1831
Thomas Barnett	J.T. Ivers	Nov. 8, 1831
Dr. C. Campbell	Dr. J. Woolfolk	Aug. 28, 1832
Joseph Bates	Stewart McKee and and Robert Cathart	Sep. 4, 1832
Silas Drake	Curtis Skinner	Oct. 27, 1829
John Cleveland	Nathaniel Potter	May 10, 1834
John Boyd	Thomas Graham	Nov. 6, 1832
Jared W. Folger	Martin Robinson	Aug. 21, 1832
John Riggin	--- Marshall	Nov. 13, 1832
Samuel Veacock	Wm. Morrison	Dec. 11, 1832

Boone County, Missouri, Delinquent Tax List, 1830.
Wm. Adams, Luke Bellefuille, Taylor Berry's heirs, Joseph

(Boone County, Missouri Continued)
Bozarth, G.E. Branham, Christopher Buckhart, S. Craig, Larkin Craig, Thomas Duley, James Dunn, Wm. Edwards, Wm. Ferguson, Abraham Foley, Seth Gerry, Benj. Gooden, Samuel Grapevine, David Gray, James Gray, F.W.S. Grayson, Wm. Grisham, Jacob Guyer, Clayton Hart, Thomas Hart, Hawkins Harvie, William S. Hatch, Benj. Hays, Robert Jones, James King, Mathew Kinkead, Ceril Leduc, Wm. Leintz, Raphael Lessieur, John J. Lowry, P. H. McBride, John McDonald, Charles McIntire, Enoch McKinney, Stephen McKinney, Benj. Mothershed, Ira Nash, William Pratt, Joshua Newbrough, Harvey Pritchet, John Rochester, William Sprigg, Thomas Story, John Sullens, Enoch Turner, James West, Nathan Turner, John B. Wallace, Boone Pike, Thomas Waters, John Williams, Thomas Williams, Jacob Wiseman, Jacob Wyan, Benj. Young.

Johnson County, Missouri, Hocker Cemetery, seven miles north of Knob Noster on J Road.

Name	Born	Died
Wm. S. Elder	1834	1891
George B. Estes	1838	1880
Amanda W. Huff, wife of M. E. Huff	May 16, 1816	Feb. 1, 1881
Mary J. Nace, wife of J. H. Nace	Jul. 15, 1838	Mar. 6, 1884
Charles G. Oglesby	Apr. 1, 1835	----
Elizabeth F. Oglesby, wife of Chas. G.	May 19, 1836	Nov. 20, 1891
*J. P. Oglesby	---	Sep. 24, 1885
*(Age: 54 years, 3 months, 19 days)		
Mary Jane T. Oglesby	Feb. 10, 1839	Dec. 23, 1862
John Robinson	Mar. 26, 1812	Oct. 16, 1886
Joseph Robinson	#Jan. 28, 1766	Dec. 12, 1841
#(Born: Guilford County, North Carolina)		
@Mary Margaret Robinson	Feb. 25, 1839	Nov. 29, 1858
@(Dau. of J. and Ja. Robinson)		
Susan Senor, consort of S. Senor	Jan. 2, 1811	Jun. 15, 1848
Elizabeth Tivis	Sep. 5, 1833	Aug. 13, 1893
Silas Tivis	May 12, 1825	May 30, 1894
Milton W. Tyler	Feb. 28, 1812	Sep. 6, 1892
Martha E. Williams, wife of Thomas D. Cash	May 22, 1839	Mar. 27, 1866

Ralls County, Missouri, Licenses, December 6, 1821, St. Chas. Missourian.

Phillip Sargent, John E. Allen, Stephen Glascock, Lewis Kinney, Richard W. Jones, Joshua Massey, Joseph Wright.

Gasconade County, Missouri, Tax List, 1828.

Thomas Apling, John Adams, Benjamin Allen, James Arthur,

(Gasconade County, Missouri Continued)
Barnabas Arthur, William Arthur, Jacob Anderson, Andrew Cox, Samuel Abbot, Michael Alkire, John Breeding, Adam Bradford, Isaac Bradford, John Baldridge, Alexander Baldridge, Joshua H. Buckhart, William Bradford, William Baker, Isaac Brown, William Bradford, William Baker, James Bates, Matthew Bates, James Boyd, Samuel Brown, Nancy Brown, Moses Brown, Jeremiah Brown, William Bowles, James Benton, Abram Benton, Alexander Castleman, Abel Benton, James Ball, Elijah Benton, Frederick Barbarick, Mark Benton, Jesse Benton, Mark Benton, sr., John Blize, Wilbourn Britton, Frankey Britton, Bedford Britton, William Britton, Mathias Baker, Jesse Ballew, Robert Clinton, Alfred S. Bone, William Bumpass, Thomas Bittick, James Burns, Samuel Burchard, Thomas Basket, Willis O. Bryant, Frederich Capehartt, William Bell, Margaret Butler, Joseph Butler, Wm. Brown, Sanford Baccus, Hugh Bartlett, John Burchard, George Burchard, Elijah Breeding, George Boulware, James Collens, Thomas Bales, Frances Carman, Gabriel Chinoweth, John Coyl, William Cornelius, Alexander Coppedge, George Coppedge, Geo. Cole, John Carter, Zandy Carter, Washington Carter, Jonathan Clinton, Jonathan Cane, James Campbell, Moses Campbell, John Capehartt, Thomas M. Casebolt, Jacob Casebolt, James Coyle, Mannen Clement, William Clement, Andrew Clement, Joshua Cox, Abram Clement, Daniel Crider, sr., Joseph Crider, Mary Cox, Daniel Crider, jr., Henry Cowen, Thomas Cox, William Cason, Lindsey Coppedge, William Coppedge, Dianna Coyl, Seth Cason, Immanuel Case, Nancy Caldwell, Pemborter Cason, John Dunlap, Edmond Cason, Nicholes Clark, Stephen Combs, William Carely, John Costly, James Carely, Henry Carely, David Davis, Thomas Capehartt, Isaac Christman, Stephen Christman, Henry Duncan, Bazeel Drolett, William Christman, Bazeel Drolett, Harrison Davis, John Decoursey, Joseph Dickson, Isaac Davis, Stanmore Nobles, Farmer Doyl, Lewis David, John Duncan, sr., Leonard Eastwood, William Gillaspy, John Duncan, jr., Bowls Duncan, Samuel Duncan, John Duncan, Thomas Dulon, William Dodds, Wm. Montgomery, Ledford Eastis, Jesse Evans, George Evans, James Eastis, Hugh Eastis, Nancy Eades, Benjamin Eades, John Lamb, Peggy Flatt, Nelson Grogan, John Givens, Thomas Gibson, John Gibson, James Gillaspy, Alfred Givens, Samuel Glover, James Glasgow, Abraham Gibson, James Gibson, Samuel Gibson, James Harrison, John Grady, Battest Grassaw, Patience Howard, John Honsinger, Joseph Holbert, Newel Hayden, Thomas Hightower, Charles Helm, Peter Hobaugh, William E. Hawkins, John Lewis, Bartlett Harris, George Hinson, John Humphrey, Acra B. Hurt, John Honsinger, jr., Joseph Hays, Jonathan Humphrey, Ezekiel Hinchy, Joel Humphrey, John Hinchy, Uriah Hinchy, Alexander Hill, Audrey Hobaugh, John Hobaugh, sr., Henry Holder, John Martin, George Hill, Bilberry Hinchy, David Hoops, Nathaniel McKean, David Hoops, jr., Jonathan Holloway, William Morris,

(Gasconade County, Missouri Continued)
George Hoops, Jacob Halloway, Hugh Hetherly, William Hughs, John Huffman, Jooseph Hughs, Henry Hall, Drury Hall, John Hughs, John Howard, Henry Hull, William Howard, Robert Law, William Howard, sr., Willis Hensly, Willis Hensly, sr., Dull Johnson, James Inglis, James Johnson, William Jordon, Thomas Johnson, Susannah Jamison, Luke Jefferson, James Jett, John Lewis, sr., William James, William Jarvis, John Johns, Lewis Letney, Samuel King, Obadiah Key, George Kitchens, Zephiniah Nobles, Hardy Keene, Barney Lowe, James Landsell, Camarro C. Lane, James Luster, William Laughlin, John Laughlin, Jeffery Lively, Benjamin Laughlin, Jesse Lively, Anthony Larue, John Mercer, David J. Long, Charles Lane, James Loftin, Merriman Loftin, David Lenox, William Laughlin, Lewis Leplant, James Newberry, Paul McDenoway, Battest McDenoway, James Massie, Luisong McDenoway, Lewis McDehat, Francis McDenoway, William Morrison, Charles Miscal, John McFerson, Stephen Mason, John Ormsby, Hiram Morrison, James Massie, Samuel Massie, William Miller, Macaijah Morris, Ellis Matlock, Abner Starret, John Montgomery, Thomas Matlock, Reuben Melton, Robert Montgomery, Bryant McClenden, Walter Maxey, Katherine McGee, George M. Perry, Bryant McClenden, William Margrave, Anthony Margrave, Joseph M. Morrow, William Massay, David Massay, John Strain, Tarlton Massay, David Massay, jr., Gideon P. Norman, Spencer O'Neal, Merit Nobles, Richard Nobles, Aaron Night, Nicholas Ownsbay, Henry Ormsby, William Owens, William Parker, Samuel Woods, John Pettis, Stephen Pettis, George Poynter, Jeremiah Potts, Thomas Patterson, Asa Pinnell, Newman Pounds, William Truesdall, Levi Perkins, John Poyter, Robert Pryor, William Pryor, James Parsons, David Perkins, Hiram Perkins, William Reed, John Pryor, Daniel Pryor, Joanah Poynter, John Scott, Jesse Patterson, John Patterson, Phillip Patterson, Ephraim Perkins, John Phillips, Isaac Perkins, Alexander Patterson, Cyrus Patterson, Robert Patterson, Charles Rail, jr., James Renfro, Charles Rail, sr., Amos Reed, Mary Reed, Elizabeth Shobe, John E. Robertson, Amos Richardson, jr., E.W. Waldo, Amos Richardson, sr., Hiram Robertson, Robert Rollins, Joel Robertson, Leonard Reed, jr., Leonard Reed, Washington Revis, Alexander Rattles, Bartlett Renfro, Thomas Robertson, James Roark, William Roark, William Robertson, Thomas Roark, Otis Turner, Fountain Self, Jacob Snowden, Henry Stuart, William Shivers, James Stuart, Jacob Stuart, James Skaggs, James D. Watkins, Parmer Sinclair, William Spear, Reuben Sparks, John Timmons, James Stark, Josiah Stills, Aaron Spann, Wm. West, Thomas Stark, Charles Stuart, Andrew Skaggs, John Stevens, Henry Skaggs, John Skaggs, Mark Sullivant, John Wilson, Joel Starkey, James Snodgrass, George Snodgrass, Isaiah Shockley, James Snelson, Thomas Shockley, Daniel Shockley, Davis Waldo, James Sullivant, Moses Simpson, Daniel Simpson, James Wyatt,

(Gasconade County, Missouri Continued)
Samuel Shobe, Solomon Shode, Robert Shode, Uriah Shockley, Job Throckmortin, George Tifore, William Twitty, John Turpin, Josiah Tigert, Samuel Travis, William Tanzy, Thomas Taylor, William Tuckett, Phillip Tuckett, John Tuckett, John Wyatt, John and Reuben Vest, Reuben Vaughan, John B. Waldó, James Wright, John Williamson, James Williamson, James Wilson, Rola Williams, sr., Willis Nelson, Elias Williams, Peter Walters, Greenberry Williams, Nancy Watson, Wm. Ware, Edward Watson, Robert Wright, Moses Welton, Lewis Welton, Joseph Waldo.

Henry County, Missouri, Mt. Olivet Baptist Church Cemetery, Springfield Township, eight miles south of Winsor.

Name	Born	Died
Mary R. Atwell, wife of James Atwell	Jan. 2, 1816	Mar. 18, 1898
Charles Bettison	Mar. 7, 1820	Sep. 11, 1878
Lindsey Bowman	Sep. 4, 1808	May 15, 1880
Elizabeth Carter, wife of John Carter	Nov. 8, 1834	May 1, 1878
John Carter	Feb.10, 1832	Feb. 1, 1897
William A. Carter	Feb.28, 1839	Nov. 6, 1899
Phillip Cecil	Sep.14, 1821	Mar. 13, 1895
Chastain Cock	Jun.22, 1793	1883
Martha Cock, wife of Thomas G. Cook	1828	Feb. 6, 1865
Thomas G. Cock, son of Chastain Cock	Apr.14, 1824	Dec. 11, 1897
Sarah Collins	Died age 25-dau. Wm. Collins	
Ann Edwards	May 15, 1811	Nov. 23, 1893
---mity Gray	Jan.17, 1817	Jan. 8, 1889
Mary A. Gray, wife of Wm. A. Gray	Jun.27, 1835	Jun. 10, 1875
Caroline W. Greife, wife of F.C. Greife	Jun.16, 1826	May 25, 1897
George H. Gresham	Aug. 5, 1833	Nov. 9, 1898
Lucy Jane Harvey, wife of Abner Harvey	Oct.22, 1821	Mar. 17, 1867
Martin Harvey	Dec.10, 1792	Aug. 8, 1869
Elizabeth H. Jordan, wife of Wm. Jordan	Nov.14, 1816	May 28, 1860
William Jordan	Jul.17, 1819	Oct. 21, 1871
Amanda Journey	Jun. 9, 1828	Feb. 17, 1892
John Journey	Mar. 27, 1820	Aug. 20, 1892
Lewis N. Mantonya	Jun.28, 1818	Jan. 14, 1889
George R. Martin	Apr.10, 1812	Jul. 28, 1892
B. G. Parker	Dec.12, 1809	Mar. 10, 1866
Susanna Parker	Jun.20, 1815	Aug. 15, 1862
Levi Robinson (Mason)	Jul. 2, 1839	Feb. 15, 1895

(Henry County, Missouri Continued)

Name	Born	Died
James P. Thomas	Apr. 19, 1837	Mar. 30, 1873
George Spring (Mason)	Dec. 29, 1839	Feb. 26, 1888
Mandley T. Smith	Dec. 12, 1806	Mar. 19, 1892
Lucinda A. Shipp, wife of T. Shipp	Apr. 11, 1830	Dec. 2, 1895
John P. Trolinger	Feb. 7, 1835	Jan. 25, 1885
Tilitha Tullis	Oct. 11, 1816	Jun. 22, 1894
William Turner	Feb. 23, 1831	May 5, 1899
Eliza A. Wetzel, wife of S. F. Wetzel	May 2, 1822	Dec. 24, 1877
S. F. Wetzel (Mason)	Oct. 27, 1818	Oct. 23, 1878
J. A. Willcockson	Mar. 16, 1822	Jan. 2, 1887
George W. Young	Apr. 18, 1819	Oct. 22, 1899
Jane Young, wife of G. W. Young	Oct. 25, 1824	Feb. 26, 1872

Howard County, Missouri, Licenses, Missouri Intelligencer, November 26, 1822.

Price Arnold, George Craig, Jeremiah Driscoll, E. O'Hare, Robert Hood.

St. Louis County, Missouri, Licenses, May 29, 1822, Missouri Gazette.

John Armetage, Alexander Bellissime, John B. Boffee, H.W. Woodbridge, Auguste Deroucher, Jabez Faris, William Fittre, Phineas Johnson, William Kennedy, John Knight, John Lombar, Louis Marly, M. Molony, C. Osbern, Gabriel Philibar, Simon Philipin, Frances Pourier, Job Shearman, John Thornton, Louis Trudeau, Esther Walsh.

Cape Girardeau County, Missouri, Estrays, Missouri Gazette.
(1) William Bolon has taken up a bay mare valued at the sum of $22.50. (I) Mar. 3, 1819, (JP) Barnet Snider.
(2) Daniel Bullinger, German Township, has taken up a brown horse appraised at a value of $16 by Abraham Crites and Andrew Stroup. (I) Feb. 12, 1814), (JP) Wm. Tinnin.
(3) Abraham Hughs, Byrd Township, has taken up a gelding. The gelding was valued at $25. (I) Apr. 6, 1816, (JP) James Russell.
(4) Samuel Hinch, Cape Girardeau Township, has taken up a sorrel horse. The animal was appraised at $25 by Charles G. Ellis and Erasmus Ellis. (I) Jun. 27, 1812.
(5) Jacob Koonrod, German Township, has taken up a brown mare appraised at $25. (I) Jul. 15, 1815, (JP) William Tinnin.
(6) Andrew Burns, has taken up a grey filly. The filly's

(Cape Girardeau County, Missouri Continued)
value was appraised at $25 by Drurey Bishop and James Patterson. (I) Nov. 22, 1817, (JP) James Russell.

(7) Charles Wall has taken up a sorrel horse. The value of the animal was appraised at $30 by Josiah Hunter and Wm. Lloyd. (I) Jun. 29, 1816, (JP) Enoch Evans.

(8) Moses Byrd, Byrd Township, took up a chestnut horse. (I) Mar. 11, 1815, (JP) John Davis.

(9) Jacob Campbell took up a bay mare valued at $25. (I) Feb. 22, 1812, (JP) John Davis.

(10) Hutson Farmer, Byrd Township, took up a bay mare. The mare was given an appraised value of $25 by William Ferguson and Benjamin Akin. (I) Mar. 27, 1818, (JP) John Akin.

(11) Andrew Giboney, Cape Girardeau Township, has taken up a sorrel colt. (I) Oct. 28, 1815, (JP) Enoch Evans.

(12) Ezekiel Hill, Cape Girardeau Township, has taken up a colt. The colt's value was appraised at $25 by Wm. Hill and Washington Abernathie. (I) May 5, 1815.

(13) James Blunt, German Township, has taken up a black mare. The mare was appraised at a value of $17 by Samuel Ramsey and James L. Fortuneberry. (JP) Thomas Newberry, (I) Apr. 20, 1816.

(14) David McCheskey, Cape Girardeau Township, has taken up a white horse. The horse was appraised at $40 by John Harbinson and Char--- Glasscock. (I) Jun. 25, 1814.

(15) James Blunt, Byrd Township, has taken up a chestnut horse. The horse was valued at $10 by Leavin Watkins and Ezekiel Hill. (I) Sep. 28, 1816, (JP) John Akins.

(16) William Bridge has taken up a brown horse. (JP) James Russell, (I) Aug. 16, 1816.

(17) William Myres has taken up a sorrel horse. The horse was valued at $18 by John Lee and Sampson Furr. He also reported a second animal which was appraised by Stephen Myers and John Hawley. (I) Feb. 25, 1815.

(18) Anthony Randol, Cape Girardeau Township, has taken up a colt. The colt was given a value of $25 by Richard Walter and John Massie. (I) Apr. 29, 1815, (JP) John Abernathie.

(19) Jacob Conrod, German Township, took up a strawberry roan mare. The mare was appraised at a value of $25 by Henry Slagle and Jacob J. James. (I) Apr. 10, 1818, (JP) John B. Wheeler.

(20) Peter Crites, Byrd Township, has taken up a bay mare. (I) Oct. 28, 1815, (JP) John Davis.

(21) James Ellis, Cape Girardeau Township, has taken up a gray mare. The mare was valued at $37.50 by James Cox and Daniel Stout. (I) Nov. 9, 1816, (JP) G. Henderson.

(Cape Girardeau County, Missouri Continued)
- (22) William Crecroft, Byrd Township, has taken up a black mare. The mare was appraised at $30 by Thomas W. Graves and Lewis W. Mensker. (I) Jan. 23, 1818, (JP) John Akin.
- (23) Jonathan Buis, Byrd Township, took a bay horse. The horse was valued at $30. (I) Dec. 12, 182, (JP) John Davis.
- (24) Jacob Fortuneberry, Cape Girardeau Township, took up a black mare. The mare was appraised at $25 by James and Alexander Somers. (I) Jul. 16, 1814, (JP) John H. Madison.
- (25) William Galleher, Cape Girardeau Township, has taken up a bay horse. The horse was appraised at $45 by Parish Green and Isaac Williams. (I) May, 10, 1817, (JP) G. Henderson.
- (26) Peter Grunt, German Township, has taken up a roan mare. (I) Jul. 27, 1816, (JP) Wm. Tinnin.
- (27) Guilbert Hector, Byrd Township, has taken up three steers. The cattle were appraised at $35 by Samuel Pew and James Goza. (I) Mar. 27, 1818, (JP) Zenas Priest.
- (28) Uriah Hinch has taken up a brown mare. The mare was given an appraised value of $25 by William Garner and William J. Stephenson. (I) Aug. 13, 1814.
- (29) Andrew Ramsey, sr. has taken up a bay horse. The horse was appraised at a value of $30 by Joel Witt and Erasmus Elliott. (I) Oct. 1, 1814.
- (30) James G. Miller has taken up a bay mare. The mare was valued att $10. (I) Oct. 15, 1814,(JP) Wm. Kelso.
- (31) James McFaddin, St. Francois Township, has taken up a sorrel mare. (I) Sep. 19, 1812, (JP) Jacob Kelly.
- (32) David Johnson, Cape Girardeau Township, has taken up a gray colt. The colt was at appraised at a value of $20 by James Randell and Mathew Osar. He also had a bay mare valued at $25 by Isaac Worley and Alexander S. Scott. (I) May, 5, 1815.
- (33) John Wilson, St. Francois Township, has taken up a sorrel mare. (I) Nov. 12, 1812, (JP) Jacob Kelly.
- (34) Daniel Welty, Byrd Township, has taken up a brown gelding. (I) Mar. 9, 1816, (JP) James Russell.
- (35) Jacob Taylor has taken up a bay horse. (JP) James Russel, (I) Aug. 16, 1817.
- (36) Anthony Street, St. Francois Township, has taken up a sorrel mare. (I) July 17, 1813, (JP) Jacob Kelly.
- (37) James Stephen, Byrd Township, has taken up a sorrel mare. The mare was appraised at $40 by Joel Blount and Wm. Wilkerson. (I) Nov. 8, 1817, (JP) John Akin.
- (38) Edward Spear has taken up a sorrel mare. The mare was

(Cape Girardeau County, Missouri Continued)
valued at $30 by Joseph Randol and Jacob Giles.
(I) Mar. 13, 1813.

(39) Jacob Shepard, Byrd Township, has taken up two horses valued at $65. (I) Jul. 19, 1817, (JP) John Akin.

(40) Abraham How, German Township, took up a bay mare. The mare was appraised at a value of $30 by Jacob Yount and John Yount. (I) Feb. 12, 1814.

(41) William Kelso, Tywapity Township, taken up a sorrel mare. The mare was given an appraised value of $45 by Tho. Millis and Levi Wolverton. (I) Jun. 23, 1819, (JP) G. Henderson.

(42) Charles Mathews, Tywapity Township, has taken up a bay horse. The horse was valued at $55 by Wm. Smith and Jeffe Jeffre. (I) Sep. 5, 1812, (JP) Wm. Kelso.

(43) John Miller, German Township, has taken up a milk-and-cider spotted horse. (I) Mar. 12, 1814.

(44) Joseph Patterson, St. Francois Township, has taken up a sorrel horse. The horse was appraised at a value of $30 by Joseph and Horatio Parish. (I) Aug. 28, 1818, (JP) Ezekiel Rubottom.

(45) Medad Randol has taken up a black mare. An appraised value of $15 was given by Levi Wolverton and John Roche. He also had a bay horse that was valued at $15 by Michael Mulien and Saml. Miller. (I) Mar. 1, 1817, (JP) G. Henderson.

(48) John Sanders, St. Francois Township, taken taken up a dapple-gray horse. The horse was given an appraised value of $25 by Ransom Bettis and David Reese. (I) Apr. 24, 1818, (JP) Ezekiel Rubottom.

(49) Michael Shell, Byrd Township, took up a brown mare. (I) Jul. 19, 1817, (JP) John Akin.

(50) Miles Williams, German Township, has taken up a black mare. John Miller and Thomas Bolling appraised the mare at a value of $30. (I) Apr. 24, 1818, (JP) John P. Wheeler.

(51) James Ellison has taken up a brown horse. The horse was valued at $25.(I) May 19, 1819.,(JP) Jas. Russel.

(52) James McFarland, St. Francois Township, has taken up a roan mare. (I) May 1, 1818, (JP) William Shaw.

(53) Andrew Ramsey, the son of John Ramsey, Cape Girardeau Township, has taken up a bay mare. The mare was given an appraised value of $30 by Thomas English and Moses Byrne. (I) Sep. 24, 1814, (JP) Enoch Evans.

(54) Daniel Robertson, German Township, has taken up a bay mare. The mare was valued at 25 by John Miller and Richard Cato. (I) Jan. 30, 1818, (JP) John Wheeler.

(55) Michael Rodney, Byrd Township, has taken up a bay horse. David Holley and Anthony Randol appraised the

(Cape Girardeau County, Missouri Continued)
at $25. (I) Nov. 22, 1817, (JP) John Akin.
(56) Thomas Rodney has taken up a gray horse. The horse was appraised by Charles E. Ellis and John Hall.
(I) Jul. 18, 1811, (JP) Enoch Evans.
(57) William Smith took up two horse.

New Madrid County, Missouri, Licenses, February 15, 1817, Missouri Gazette.
William Bacon, Upton Butler, John LaValle, Robert McGay, Wiley Silmon, Robert G. Watson, Felicite Valle.

Cape Girardeau County, Missouri, Licenses, Independent Patriot, December 8, 1821.
Robert Smith, Simon Block, Charles G. Ellis, Joseph Thiler, Nathan Van Horn, John Rodd.

Pike County, Missouri, Licenses, December 6, 1821, St. Charles Missourian.
John E. Allen, G. W. Bright, Uriah J. Devore, John Pruit, C. C. Tribue.

Callaway County, Missouri, Delinquent Tax List, 1830.
Jacob Apperson, Andrew Armstrong, Wm. Ashley, Wm. Bryant, Liburn Boggs, Bapt. Duchouquette, Peter Ellis, Wm. Gardner, Levi James, Wm. Leintz, P.H. McBride, Wm. McKinn, Nancy Moore, Wm. Masters, John Newsom, Prior Quarles, Jonathan Ramsay, John Scott, Jas. Snowden, Simon Sutile, Jas. Trimble, Benoni Wills.

St. Louis County, Missouri, Wills and Testaments executed under the Spanish Government in the Deed Reocrds for 1776 - 1834.
Francoise Crely Trudel, 1798; Felicite Vial Panneton, 1798; Joseph Brazeau, 1798, Proven in 1810; Therese Brazeau, 1798; Anoitne Morin, 1798; Marianne Gierome Dufaux, 1798; Francis Corneau, 1799; Andre Boucant dit Fitzsame, 1799; Catharine Giarce Cerre, 1800; John Watkins, 1799; Sophia Cherfer Bolay, 1800; Jn. Jarrett, 1801; Louis Bonpart alias LaFleur, 1801; Joseph Herbet Lecomde, 1801; Isabel Lalande Delille, 1801; Joseph Loiselle, 1801; Susanna LaFleur, 1801; Jacinte Roy, 1801; Margaret Vasseur, 1801; Jn. Bt. Dufaux, 1801; Louis Lormier, 1801; Joseph Molard, 1802; Charles Lanquinet, 1803; A. Rutgere, 1803; Charles Bienvenu Delile, 1803; Jeanette Forchet, 1803; Todos Santos Buciat, 1803; .Francisco Barrera, 1803; Maragaret Bay, 1803; James Richardson, 1803; Genevieve Roulier, 1804; Antoine Reithe, 1802; John Young, 1802.

Lincoln County, Missouri, Delinquent Tax, 1830.
Jabish Bell, Louis Brazeau, Wm. Brown, Arthur Burris, S.

(Lincoln County, Missouri Continued)
M. Dean, John Castleman, Augustus Chouteau, E. Collard, Paul Chouteau, Pierre Chouteau, James Cochran, Simon Creach, John Crouch, Joseph Collard, Michael Crowsyer, Widow Dubreville, John Duvall, John Green, Robert Green, Nathan Head, Matthew Johnson, Moses Kenny, Louis Labeau, Hugh Liles, Paul Primo, Dedier Merchand, Quinton Moore, James Morrison, Robert Wash, Cerre Tousant, John Ruland, Wm. Russell, Nathaniel Simonds, Jeremiah Simpkins, Albert Tesen, Samuel Wells.

Franklin County, Missouri, Estrays, Missouri Gazette.

(1) Phineas Adams, St. John Township, has taken up a steer and a cow with calf. The cattle were valued at $35 by E. Decker and Ephraim Jameson. (JP) Henry Brown, (I) Jan. 10, 1821.

(2) James Marquess, Meramec Township, has taken up a bay horse. Bartlet Martin, Wiley Pinnell, and John Harty appraised the horse at $30. (JP) Wm. Spencer, (I) Mar. 15, 1820.

(3) Philip Boulware has taken up a roan horse. A value of $20 was given by James Steward and Saml. Duncan. (JP) John Woolams, (I) Aug. 18, 1819.

(4) John Pepper, on the Galvy, has taken up a bay horse. (JP) Daniel B. Moore, (I) Feb. 2, 1820.

(5) Robert Pepper, Meramec Township, has taken up a sorrel horse. Tho. Julius and James Caldwell give the horse an appraised value of $35. (JP) D. B. Moore, (I) Jan. 10, 1821.

(6) James Colvin, St. John Township, has taken up a yellow bay mare. The mare was appraised at a value of $50 by Russell Brown and Lewis W. Mansker. Isaac Murphy, clerk,(I) Oct. 20, 1819,(JP) David Edwards.

(7) George Pursley, St. John Township, took up a mare appraised at $20 by Thomas Henry, Henry Ware, and Louis Mansker. (JP) Henry Brown, (I) Oct. 25, 1820.

(8) John Davis, Boeuff Township, has taken up a black gelding. The gelding was valued at $40 by Allan Greenstreet, Enoch Greenstreet, and John Woolery. (JP) Jos. Reavis, (I) May 17, 1820.

(9) Lewis Mansker, St. John Township, has taken up a brown horse. The horse was appraised at $40 by Wm. Havard and John Jamerison. (I) Jul. 14, 1819, (JP) David Edwards.

(10) John Perkens, Beouff Township, has taken up a gray horse. The appraisal was made by James Brown and James Snelson. (JP) Jas. Reavis, (I) Aug. 23, 1820.

(11) William Hensley, Beouff Township, has taken up a sorrel gelding. John Woolery and Wm. Cotes valued the gelding at $60.(JP)Jos. Reavis,(I)Feb. 21,1821.

(Franklin County, Missouri Continued)
- (12) John West has taken up a sorrel mare. The mare was valued at $10 by Chas. Welsh and Wm. Lewis. (JP) David Edwards, (I) Aug. 4, 1819.
- (13) Moses Whitmore, Meramec Township, has taken up an iron-gray mare. Henry Whitmore, Philip McCade, and T. Murguys valued the mare at $30. (I) Mar.15,1820.

St. Charles County, Missouri, Estrays, Missouri Republican.

- (1) James Brumbfield, Femme Osage Township, has taken up a sorrel horse. The horse was valued at $33.33 by John Boone and Andrew Stapp. (JP) Arch. Shobe, (I) May 31, 1827.
- (2) Asa Griffith, Portage des Sioux Township, has taken up a sorrel horse. Edw. George and Robt. Cresswell appraised the horse at $50. (JP) Joseph Sumner, (I) Jun. 1, 1830.
- (3) Thomas H. Kelly, Dardenne Township, has taken up a sorrel mare. The mare was appraised at $35 by Lazarus McFall and Louis Strong. (I) Dec. 16, 1828, (JP) Green Hutchings.
- (4) Solomon Alkire, Femme Osage Township, has taken up a black mare. The mare was appraised at $20 by Cyrus Carter, Abraham Shobe and Nicholas Fisher. (I) Dec. 27, 1831, (JP) Th. Hopkins.
- (5) George Allen, Femme Osage Township, has taken up a black mare. Joseph Lynn and Henry A. H. Russell valued the mare at $35. (I) Jun. 29, 1830, (JP) Moses Bigelow.
- (6) Evin Lemasters, St. Charles Township, has taken up a dapple gray mare. The mare was valued at $30 by James Goodrich and John Oliver. (JP) James Green, (I) Jul. 10, 1832.
- (7) Richard B. Puttman, Dardenne Township, has taken up a sorrel horse. The horse was appraised at $45 by Alden Farnsworth and John Pittman. (JP) Biel Farnsworth, (I) Jul. 2, 1823.
- (8) Moors B. Banks, Cuivre Township, has taken up two mares. Benjamin Comegys and Francis Day appraised the animals at $45. (I) Mar. 2, 1830, (JP) James H. Audrain.
- (9) At Shabonsin Sylvester Baraden, St. Chas. Township, took up a white mare. The mare was appraised by Toussaint Brunel and Etienne Kennel at $25. (JP) John Slater, (I) Apr. 2, 1823.
- (10) Adam Cluck, Femme Osage Township, took up a sorrel horse. Elijah Bryan, John Mason, and Charles McLee Ferris valued the horse at $30. (I) Jun. 2, 1829, (JP) Moses Bigelow.

(St. Charles County, Missouri Continued)
- (11) Allen Turnbow, Dardenne Township, has taken up a bay mare. John Pittman and Allen Farnsworth valued the mare at $30.(I) Aug.27,1823,(JP)Biel Farnsworth
- (12) James Silvey, Femme Osage Township, has taken up a sorrel mare. John W. Dodson and James B. Brumfield valued the mare at $60. (I) Sep. 25, 1832, (JP)Tho. Hopkins.
- (13) Peter Smelser, Portage des Sioux Township, took up a brown mule. The mule was given an appraisal of $17 by John Daivis and John Palmer. (JP) Francis Lesieur, (I) Oct. 16, 1832.
- (14) George Chapman, Femme Osage Township, took up a yellow sorrel mare. The mare was valued at $18 by Malachi Baldridge and Joseph Baugh. (JP)John Smith, (I) Jun. 15, 1826.
- (15) Benjamin Teters, Dardenne Township, has taken up a sorrel mare colt. The colt was given an appraised value of $10 by Christopher Woolf and Wm. Teters. (JP) Green Hutchings, (I) Dec, 29, 1829.
- (16) Lewallen Turnbough, St. Charles Township, took up a yellow sorrel mare. Alonzo Robinson and Lewis Gurno appraised at the mare at $25. (I) Apr. 10, 1832, (JP) Montgomery Perry.

<u>Howard County, Missouri, Petitioners to Congress, Absence of Registrar's Office, Carter's Papers, Vol. XV, Dec. 23, 1819.</u>
Gray Bynum, Augustus Storrs, John J. Lowry, J.W. Scudder, William V. Rector, Thomas Tilman, William F. Simmons, James D. Miller, R. Gentry, J. H. McKensie, N. Hutchinson, Thomas Litchworth, Augustus Evans, Nathl. Patten, jr., Jacob Gregg, Jno. Means, Lewis Ress, G. M. Alsop, John C. Mitchell, Chas. French, J. Rice, Bernard O'Neill, Floyd Rawls, Hsle. Barnes, Jas. H. Hutchison, Laban Garrett, William L. Scott, William Brown, John Costa, Wm. J. Henderson, J. S. Burckhart, Elijah Iles, John Love, James C. Ludlow, Waddy T. Currin, Jonathan R. Standley, David Magill, Abraham Groom, Caleb Magill, John Hall, James Laughlin, David Reavis, Williams Woods, William O. Short, G. W. Bartlett, D. M'Kensie, William Howard, David Floyd, Burton Lawless, Thomas Edwards, Robt. Moderwell, John Witt, Richard Samuel, James G. Smith, Lemon Parker, Absolem Ream, Herod Corum, Amos Rees, James Henry, Joerid Morrison, George Bellas, R. Prichard, Little B. Hunt, D. P. Boggs, Harrison G. Rogers, James Chitwood, Anthy. Owsley, Robert W. Rankin, Chs. D. Jeanneres, David Bryant, P.W. Thompson, John A. Maths, Samuel A. Brown, Charles Callaway, Achrey B. Hurt, Edward Irwin, John Homan, Jedson Hazel, Daniel Tolson, Saml. McCorell, William Taylor, William Andrews, William Taylor, Ben Holliday, jr., E. R. Bradley, Charles P. Tooley, Hillard

(Howard County, Missouri Continued)
Fowler, James Barnes, John Martin, William Brown, L.F. Mare, John Wilson, William Thorpe, jr. Simon, H. Wolfort, Lemon Coy, J. C. Kerr, Wm. D. Swearingen, David Doyle, Wm. Lycett, Daniel Munro, Robert Jones, Presley Samuel, John Blay, James Riggins, H. L. Boon, Wm. C. Bailie, Marcus Williams, Samuel Harrison, Thomas Bradley, Thos. G. Eldridge,Thomas Woodness, Charles Vanostrownd, Michael Rice, Joel Burnam, Manon Duren, John Moor, A. Goodding, Aaron Anders, David Williams, Cooley Whitney, Robert Johnson, Jesse Denn, G. P. Ross, John Wood, Hiram Corum, John Simmer, Peter Holoweaugh, John Fitzgerald, Hiram Reed, Peter Elder, John McClelland, Stephen Tait, John O'Hara, Gabriel Bailey, James D. ---, Thomas G. Jones, James Dickson, Meshath Smith, Levi H. Jones, John Berry, Andrew M. Poage, William Haydon, Andrew McGirk, John Gray, Christopher Monical, jr., William Ward, John G. Phillips, Joel Jones, A. Riley, Mark Arnold, William Grubbs, Isaac C. Snedecor, Jonas Casner, George Crump, Levi Taylor, Clayton Hern, F.K. Whitt, James G. Montgomery, William Jones, Andrew Tiffen, Loverance Evans, Reubin Bailey, James Taylor, William Ramsey, Ezekiel Howard, John Stewart, James Cresap, Daniel Durbin, Robert P. Clark, Josiah Bones, James Miller, Segre B. Dale, Enoch Fox, David Wilson, Robert Poage, John Poage, Thomas Dale, Samuel Burnet, Jesse Richardson, Elmore Thomson, Peter Kuykendall, Elmore Thomson, Fieldin Wilhite, John Bicets, Watts D. Ewin, John Bicets, James Ketchum, Wm. Calvert, William Bicets, Wm. Johnston, Joel Herm, James Richards, John Stephenson, John R. Bicets, Benjamin Kelly, James Taylor, Joseph Taylor, John Stone, Silas Richardson, Robert Dale, Richard Chaney, Joseph Austin, Robert Hinkson, Robert Y. Fowler, Edwards Davis, Wad. H. Whitney, George Amick, Amos Richardson, Pink Hudson, Joseph Whitney, Joseph Davis, Jordan Sisemore, John Grayham, Francis Reding, James D. Whitesitt, John Elson, James Cooly, William Ferguson,William Bowers, Obediah Bounds, James Son, John Whitesitt, Solomon Cattron, Lazarus Wilcox, Williamson H. Curtis, Phineas Clarke, Henry T. Browne, Bennett Clarke, Andrew Feland, Christopher Trigg, James Brown, James Davis, Stephen Trigg, jr., John B. Clarke, Ignatius P. Owen, Samuel Evans, George Tally, Benjamin Hardin, Andrew Polk, William L. Black, Jeil King, George Potter, Mike Box, Ephraim Marsh, William Johnson, Russell Reynolds, William Dodson, Shadrach Taylor, John Sallady, John Bowman, Michael Son, Christopher Jones, Stanley G. Morgan, Philip Turner, Philip Owens, John W. Rawlins, William Ramsey, James Bounds, sr., John Burns, Samuel Foster, James Bounds, William Fix, Thomas Foster, Wm. D. Wilson. John Steel, Fields Tramell, Bennett H. Clarke, John Shaw, Nevo. M. Thompsom, Alanson Worker, Wm. Callahan, Henry Corkle, Davis Mcgee, Richard Smith, Peyton R. Hayden, James Goforth, Nicholas Kavanaugh, George Rhodes, Wm. Black,

(Howard County, Missouri Continued)
Hyseam Bosorth, John Belcher, William Corum, John M. Belcher, Aquilla Barnes, Daniel Crump, Dennis Callahan, Wm. Irving, Henry Rodes, Foster Sappington, Hiram Bryant, Elisha Todd, John B. Wallace, James Palmatary, Garland Collins, William Bartlett, Asa Morgan, William Potter, John Moreland, David Bowers, John D. Ewing, Peter R. Bowley, John Roberts, William Burk, John W. Erwin.

Macon County, Missouri, Marriage Records, 1837 - 1839.

Groom	Bride	Date
Joseph P. Owenby	Nancy Garrett	Apr. 20, 1837
Thomas J. Dabney	Cassandra Walker	May 21, 1837
Alex. Shawner	Narcissa Kerby	May 13, 1837
Aaron Gee	Margaret Moore	Jul. 22, 1837
Joseph Stewart	Mary McHadden	Aug. 3, 1837
Thomas Clifton	Rebecca Lesley	Aug. 18, 1837
Allen Fletcher	C. Ann Hatfield	Aug. 17, 1837
Lloyd H. Coulter	Emelia Cannon	Nov. 9, 1837
Thomas Tuggle	Ann Coulter	Oct. 31, 1837
Abraham Smoot	Lucinda Bozarth	Dec. 24, 1837
Joseph Cooley	Elizabeth Locke	Jan. 15, 1838
Smith Gipson	Catherine Banning	Apr. 5, 1838
John Griffin	Margaret Ann Murley	Apr. 1, 1838
Richard Fulcher	Catharine Floyd	Feb. 22, 1838
Juliann Cochran	Eliza L. Fletcher	May 17, 1838
John Smoot	Catharine Griffin	Apr. 19, 1838
Matthew Hally	Kitty Payton	Jul. 26, 1838
Stephen P. Skinner	Eliza Burton	Apr. 22, 1838
Soloman Whiskinman	Rachel Lundy	Jan. 3, 1839
Thomas Hancock	Pusena Bemos	Mar. 4, 1839
James Hancock	Martha O. James	Mar. 21, 1839
John Bennett	Roda Evans	Apr. 11, 1839
James Adkin	Susan Kerhan	Jul. 9, 1839
William Ross	Caroline Leestin	Aug. 6, 1839
Othneal Bachin	Permelia Montgomery	May 31, 1839
Henry Winkler	Orvetta Ashbell	Aug. 6, 1839
Martin Postin	Polly Litteral	Aug. 5, 1839
Jas. Staunton Buchanan	Lucinas Rosson	Jun. 26, 1839
Charles D. Cooper	Diadama Blankenship	Jun. 10, 1839
Henry Foster	Manerva Montgomery	1839 (sic)
James Griffin	Tabitha Murley	Oct. 2, 1838
Andrew Summers	Melissa Shoemaker	Oct. 24, 1838
William Cook	Elizabeth Wiggins	Dec. 9, 1838
Vestal W. Mason	--- Prather	Dec. 19, 1838
Aaron Andrews	Mildred Barnes	Dec. 24, 1838
Hamilton Glenn	Sarah Drinkard	Nov. 24, 1838
James Lyons	Nancy Rice	Jun. 28, 1838
Liggett S. Saling	Mary Ann Rigsby	Jan. 8, 1838

(Macon County, Missouri Continued)

Groom	Bride	Date
John W. Gulyen	Poline Stowe	Jan. 12, 1838
Amond Boyer	Priscilla Jackson	Nov. 14, 1839
William Morrow	Louanna Summers	Sep. 10, 1839
John Waren	Docia Mills	Sep. 1, 1839
Robert Mayers	Louisanna Blanstel	Jan. 26, 1839
Isaac Gilstrap	Elizabeth King	Jun. 18, 1839

Pike County, Missouri, Delinquent Tax List, 1830.

Joseph B. Brown, Stephen Byrd, Walter Caldwell, Charles Delassus, Geo. Davenport, John Cummings, Wm. Foreman, Aaron Garnsey, Solomon Giddings' heirs, Wm. Grayson, Wm. Hempstead, Charles Hempstead, Ezra Hunt, Jonathan Hurley, James Johnson, Josiah McClanahan, Spencer Pettus, Andrew Russell, Sam. A. Toombs, Madam Sarpy, Samuel Wells, Solomon Yokem.

Benton County, Missouri, Marriage Records, 1839.

Groom	Bride	Date
John Graham, jr.	Unice Tabor	May 1, 1839
Cabel Crews	Sally Graham	May 2, 1839
Nathan B. Jecurett	Ann Eliza Graham	May 30, 1839
John Jarrell	Eliz. Ann Dawson	Mar. 31, 1839
Peter Fry	Sally Gemerson	Feb. 15, 1839
John McCaul	Sally Casey	Feb. 24, 1839
Abner Holt	Elizabeth Berry	Feb. 28, 1839
William Sally	Emily Bowles	Aug. 13, 1839
John Porter	Mary Crabtree	Jul. 14, 1839
Milton W. Glover	Elizabeth Osburn	Oct. 15, 1839
Enoch C. Remingham	Jane Risley	Nov. 7, 1839
Bayley Elder	Elizabeth Goings	Nov. 7, 1839
Jacob S. Rice	Margaret Ford	Dec. 26, 1839
Smith Morris	Margaret Ann Mordoc	Oct. 16, 1839
George H. Blanton	Eliza Warren	Oct. 10, 1839
James A. Brown	Emily C. Staley	Dec. 24, 1839

Lawrence County, Missouri, Estrays, Missouri Gazette.

(1) David Black, Spring River Township, has taken up a bay horse. Joseph Hardin and Jonathan Magness appraised the horse at $30. (I) Sep. 13, 1817.

(2) Joseph Hardin, Spring River Township, took up a black horse. The horse was appraised at $25 by John Miller and Essex Harris. (I) Sep. 11, 1818, (JP) Richard Searcy.

(3) Micajah Harris, Columbia Township, on the Current River, has taken up a bay mare. (I) Dec. 16, 1815, (JP) William Russel.

(4) Richard Perkins, David Township, has taken up a black mare. The mare was appraised at $55 by James

(Lawrence County, Missouri Continued)
Kadu, Jonathan Comstock and Andrew Smith. (JP)Chas. Hatcher, (I) Aug. 4, 1819.

Franklin County, Missouri, Marriage Records, 1819 - 1839.

Groom	Bride	Date
William Hamac	Dammeous Richardson	Mar. 21, 1819
Hyram Easters	Lucy Richardson	Apr. 15, 1819
John Anderson	Jane Ward	Apr. 24, 1820
David Stites	Sarah Murphy	Apr. 9, 1820
Isaac Moody	Rebecca Gain	Jun. 4, 1820
James Greenstreet, jr.	Sarah Kelly	Mar. 14, 1821
*William Mitchell	Mary Pound	Mar. 29, 1821
*(of Mermack Township)		
Adam Baker	Susannah Aairs	Feb. 24, 1822
Aaron Richardson	Nancy Brown	Jan. 10, 1822
Richard Richardson	Jincy Brock	Aug. 9, 1822
William Bell	Polly Armstrong	Jun. 6, 1822
Elisha Brock	Winna Hinton	Jan. 23, 1822
John Burch	Margaret Sappington	Apr. 9, 1822
John Byrnsides	Betsy Hinton	Mar. 2, 1822
Baxter Smith	Jane Laremore	Oct. 10, 1822
Seth Chitwood	Lucinda Caldwell	Dec. 26, 1822
Philip Miller	Lucy McIntre	Jan. 30, 1823
Elias Gibson	Ester Hears	Aug. 7, 1823
Ostew Clark	Anny Collins	Sep. 26, 1823
Aaron Short	Mariah Wall	Oct. 4, 1823
James Smith	Jinsy Ramsy	Feb. 1, 1824
Elijah Halsy	Polly Moore	Feb. 22, 1824
John Armstrong	Polly Farar	May 27, 1824
William Henderick	Mildred Dodson	Mar. 30, 1825
James Glasgow	Elizabeth Groff	Jun. 12, 1825
MIcajah Caldwell	Lucretia Daugherty	Dec. 20, 1824
Kinkead Caldwell	*Mary Clark	Mar. 25, 1824
*(Widow of Samuel Clark, Illinois)		
William Wyatt	Elizabeth Burnsides	Sep. 18, 1825
Edmond Hodges	Jane Durham	Dec. 8, 1825
Samuel W. Holland	Sarah S. Colman	Nov. 21, 1825
Durret H. Jamison	Elizabeth Ausburn	Dec. 29, 1825
Morris West	Elizabeth Davis	Dec. 25, 1825
Thomas Evans	Ann Moore	Feb. 2, 1825
Dolphin Wells	Nancy Carsel	Dec. 11, 1825
Jeremiah Hamilton	Elizabeth Fisher	*Mar. 13, 1821
*(Marriage recorded Feb. 14, 1826)		
William Stites	Polly Perkins	Mar. 25, 1826
Martin Lane	Jane Caldwell	Mar. 23, 1826
Robert Baty	Lavina Dent	Apr. 5, 1826
John Baley	Mrs. Nancy Smith	Apr. 20, 1826

(Franklin County, Missouri Continued)

Groom	Bride	Date
William Brown	Betsy Brown	Mar. 26, 1826
Levi Tansy	Nancy Mitchell	Mar. 5, 1826
James G. Murphy	Cynthia Parsley	Apr. 6, 1826
John Johnston	Polly Bacon	May 10, 1826
Mathew T. W. Benton	Nancy Skaggs	Mar. 23, 1826
John W. Thompson	Polly Campbell	Apr. 13, 1826
Press Rule	Judith Stanton	May 18, 1826
John Welch	Jetdida Craft	Apr. 6, 1826
George Kincade	Mary Thompson	Apr. 18, 1826
Peter Sullens	Sinthy Pepper	May 22, 1826
Josiah Dent	Polly Jameson	Jun. 12, 1826
Thomas Groff	Elizabeth Harrison	Jul. 2, 1826
Jacob Gall	Roxana Hurt	Sep. 7, 1826
Scudder Smyth	Elizabeth Miller	Oct. 8, 1826
Wilson D. Hurt	Judith Barnes	Dec. 28, 1826
Abraham Freeman *(Washington County)	*Nancy Deen	Nov. 16, 1826
Samuel Conn	Melinda Wheeler	Jan. 14, 1827
Drury Hall	Anny Greenstreet	Mar. 2, 1827
William Jarvis	Laney Boalding	Jan. 21, 1827
Joseph Short	Jensey Boyd	Feb. 4, 1827
Oliver L. Wheeland	Melinda Prather	Feb. 11, 1827
Daniel Prather	Nancy Short	Mar. 15, 1827
Robert Wall	Mary Cole	Mar. 6, 1827
Erasmus Kinneman	Winneford Brock	Jun. 10, 1827
Joseph Crider	Priscillia Reed	Sep. 14, 1827
Mathew Blackwell *(Widow of Joshua Tansy)	*Margaret Tansy	Dec. 25, 1827
Thomas Burros *(Widow of Mathew Byrnsides)	*Ann Byrnsides	Jun. 24, 1827
Allen Greenstreet	Elizabeth Laremore	May 25, 1827
James Williams	Susannah Pepper	Aug. 21, 1827
Jefferson Miller	Hannah Simpson	Sep. 9, 1827
Leory Clark Boring	Polly Hulsy	Sep. 4, 1827
*James Evans (of Jefferson County)	Mrs. Sally Whitmore	Sep. 11, 1827
Benjamin Harris	Lucinda McKinny	Aug. 2, 1827
James Greenstreet	Margaret Smith	Nov. 15, 1827
John Greenstreet	Zippy Laremore	Nov. 15, 1827
James Laremore	Orpha Greenstreet	Nov. 29, 1827
Phineas James	Rhodian Delany	Dec. 6, 1827
Jesse McDonald *(Recorded Aug. 20, 1821)	Polly R. Caldwell	*Nov. 6, 1817
David Gall	Mary McDonald	Dec. 23, 1827
Henry Howard	Annis Nanse	Feb. 12, 1828
Masters Campbell	Sarah Armstrong	Feb. 21, 1828
George Barns	Eliz. Williamson	Mar. 6, 1828

(Franklin County, Missouri Continued)

Groom	Bride	Date
Lewis Maupin	Mary Salyers	Sep. 7, 1828
*John Brown	Rebecca Adams	Mar. 20, 1828

  *(Witnesses: Buril B. Adams, Edmund F. Brown, Jas. Barns)

Robert Brook	Marietta Rice	Oct. 11, 1828
Walker P. Brown	Susan Jefferies	Dec. 5, 1828
*Cuthbert S. Jefferies	Susannah Williamson	Sep. 13, 1827

  *(Witnesses: E. F. Brown and Buril B. Adams)

*Henry Dixon	Sarah A --	May 1, 1828

  *(Witnesses: John Pursley and Clement Brown)

*Robert Colvin	Elizabeth Cole	Apr. 10, 1828

  *(Witnesses: Rbt. Boles, John Parsly, and John B. Brown)

*Edward Bacon	Eliza Hart	Aug. 31, 1828

  *(of St. Louis County)

David Steregill	Emily Patton	Sep. 2, 1828
Kinkead Caldwell	Polly Cantty	Aug. 10, 1828
John Whitmore	Elisa Williams	Dec. 25, 1828
Alva Caldwell	Rachel Decker	Jan. 29, 1829
*Reuben Harrison	Elizabeth Boring	Feb. 26, 1829

  *(Witnesses: Sion S. Pritchett and Jesse Pritchett)

Darius Jott	Margaret Adams	Nov. 29, 1828
Marshall Duncan	Sally King	Jan. 4, 1829
James M. Cortney	Charlotte Twitty	Feb. 19, 1829
Samuel Crow	Polly Jarvis	Jan. 29, 1829
Jeremiah Hamilton	Martha Mitchell	*Jan. 5, 1810

  *(Marriage Recorded Feb. 3, 1829)

Joel Stites	Catharine Decker	May 4, 1829
Dison Johnston	Malinda Dent	May 4, 1829
Jefferson Sullins	Margaret Crow	Mar. 19, 1829
John Narce	Elizabeth Simons	Apr. 29, 1829
Edmund Doyel	Betsy Fryer	Jan. 22, 1829
Daniel Childers	Elizabeth Adams	May 12, 1829
James Heatherly	Sarah Maupin	Apr. 27, 1829
Richard Fryer	Eliza Ann Oldham	Jul. 5, 1829
Thomas F. Clayton	Nancy K. Rule	Aug. 3, 1829
Samuel West	Nancy Pointer	Sep. 4, 1829
Leonard Heatherly	Sally Brown	Aug. 20, 1829
Clayton Richardson	Nancy Adams	Nov. 1, 1829
Zabidea Shelton	Lavina Miller	Oct. 11, 1829
John Guinns	Catherine Smyth	Oct. 25, 1829
Gilford Hurt	Sarah McKinney	Aug. 13, 1829
John Todd	Betsy Gall	Oct. 15, 1829
Amos Maupin	Rebecca Heatherly	*Apr. 24, 1828

  *(Marriage Recorded Jan. 1, 1830)

John Bell, jr.	Almedea Farrar	Mar. 4, 1830
William Van	Arrabella Williams	Dec. 27, 1829
Thomas Johnson	Jane Lubbastose	Jan. 21, 1830
Samuel Green	Sarah Van	Dec. 24, 1829

(Franklin County, Missouri Countinued)

Groom	Bride	Date
Henry Carrington	Spicy Childers	Jan. 17, 1830
Short Caldwell	Joanna Williams	Feb. 25, 1830
Joseph Davis	Jane Scribner	Apr. 1, 1830
George Adams	Polly Childers	Mar. 23, 1830
John Gall	Eliz. McWilliams	Apr. 15, 1830
Wilson C. McEven	Nancy Easter	Apr. 29, 1830
*Samuel W. Holland	Martha Jeffres	Apr. 26, 1830

*(Witnesses: Akillis Jeffres, sr., Henry Brown)

Groom	Bride	Date
John Matthews	Elizabeth Butler	Jun. 20, 1830
James McBride	Mahala Miller	Jun. 20, 1830
Samuel Johns	Louisa Robnett	May 27, 1830
*Edward Read	Rebecca Colvin	Jul. 15, 1830

*(Witnesses: John Adams and John Colvin)

Groom	Bride	Date
--- Johns	Hannah Lasly	Sep. 12, 1830
William Beatty	Nancy Richardson	Jul. 11, 1830
Henry Ware	Rosanna Johns	Apr. 29, 1830
Benjamin Wyatt	Nancy Simpson	Sep. 16, 1830
David Edwards	Euphema Rule	Sep. 30, 1830
*John E. Braley	Susannah Moutry	Sep. 21, 1830

*(of Crawford County)

Groom	Bride	Date
Allen Twitty	Patsy Cowis	Jul. 29, 1830
--- Huffman	Sarah Childers	Jul. 18, 1830
Harrison Vaughn	Polly Tansy	Jul. 29, 1830
William Parks	Polly Stites	Aug. 4, 1830
Henry McCann	Polly Caldwell	Sep. 23, 1830
John Caldwell	Louisa Douglass	Oct. 26, 1830
Perrin Farrar	Adaline Clark	Jan. 20, 1831
Jesse A. Parker	Salle Bay	Dec. 26, 1830
Armstead Elam	Eliza Ann Rhodes	Jan. 31, 1831
*James McDonald	Jane Caldwell	Jan. 9, 1831

*(Witnesses: George Mitchell and Samuel Rule)

Groom	Bride	Date
Thomas Ward	Mahala Horne	Mar. 14, 1831
David Hail	Narsisse Peen	*July 17, 1833

*(Marriage Recorded Jul. 22, 1833)

Groom	Bride	Date
Rebey Vaughan	Polly Wall	Jan. 13, 1831
Anderson Vaughn	Lucy Brock	Feb. 10, 1831
Martin Blize	Helary Brown	Apr. 21, 1831
John Blize	Evelina Coulter	May 9, 1830
Henry Hall	Nancy Self	Sep. 30, 1830
Joseph Davis	Jane Scribner	Apr. 2, 1830
Lewis Redding	Lydia Ivers	May 28, 1830
William Gibson	Nancy Tansey	Apr. 26, 1831
Dr. Elijah D. McLean	Judith Rule	Jun. 23, 1831
Samuel Shelton	Prudy Miller	Jan. 25, 1831
Jacob Clark	Phebe Whelman	Jul. 19, 1831
Caldwell Brynsides	Salina Campbell	Sep. 22, 1831
Alvin P. Williams	Elizabeth Armet	Aug. 21, 1831

(Franklin County, Missouri Continued)

Groom	Bride	Date
Daniel Crafts	Margaret Fisher	Oct. 13, 1831
*Jonathan Crow	Mary Zumwalt	Oct. 4, 1831
*(Both are from St. Charles County)		
Reuben Sterut	Ruthy Mincher	May 8, 1831
John E. Davis	Clementie Campbell	Aug. 25, 1831
Benjamin Miller	Sally Jamison	Dec. 4, 1831
John Daugherty	Margaret Wilson	Dec. 4, 1831
Caleb Johns	Nancy Woodland	Nov. 24, 1831
James Price	Elizabeth Decker	Jul. 4, 1832
David Hilderbrand	Polly Parker	Nov. 11, 1831
Joseph Williams	Rachael Laramore	May 15, 1832
Hosea Brown	Ellen Fackler	Feb. 1, 1833
James Hickill	Matilda West	Feb. 10, 1833
Moses Whitmore	Nancy Wheeler	Nov. 30, 1832
Lewis Collins	Jane Pound	Feb. 18, 1833
Daniel Moore	Elizabeth Adams	Feb. 24, 1833
William Reed	Elizabeth Ridenhour	Sep. 30, 1832
Allen W. Brown	Frances H. Brown	Jan. 14, 1833
William P. Roberts	Mary Goode	Jan. 31, 1833
John B. Brown	Martha Adams	Feb. 7, 1833
Henry Groff	Harriet Pinkleton	Feb. 15, 1833
Thomas M. Rogers	I. James	Mar. 3, 1833
George Thompson	Elcey Greenstreet	Feb. 8, 1833
*William Ramsy	Malinda Collins	Apr. 11, 1833
*(of Crawford County)		
William Renphroe	Lucy Reeves	Oct. 15, 1832
Garrett David	Eve Shookman	Aug. 25, 1832
Hiram McKee	Nancy Truesdell	May 21, 1833
William R. Dougherty	Easter E. Luckey	Jun. 13, 1833
Wilson Park	Nancy Frazier	Jul. 6, 1833
Eben Ferril	Mrs. Lucy Richy	Jun. 7, 1833
David Hail	Narcisa Peen	Jul. 17, 1833
Edward Cazy	Lydia Redmond	Jul. 25, 1833
Lemuel Hensly	Elizabeth Morgan	Jul. 27, 1833
Mack H. Goode	Paulina A. Brown	Aug. 1, 1833
Levi Woolsy	Maranda Wall	Jan. 29, 1832
Lewis Frasier	Susannah Skinner	Jan. 10, 1833
Richard Skinner	Ann Eliza Dent	Mar. 1, 1833
John Wathinton	Sarah Twitty	Jun. 21, 1833
William Cooper	Mary Williams	Jul. 18, 1833
John Null	Lucey Hyet	Nov. 4, 1833
Solomon Drace	Comfort Osborn	Nov. 25, 1833
Achilles Jeffries	Elizabeth Bell	Mar. 14, 1833
Winsen Campbell	Margaret Morris	Dec. 5, 1833
Thomas B. Armstrong	Nancy J. Harris	Dec. 12, 1833
Elisha Harbour	Elizabeth Reeves	Dec. 12, 1833
Benjamin Enloe	Isabella Wisdom	Sep. 29, 1833

(Franklin County, Missouri Continued)

Groom	Bride	Date
James Baily	Senia Maupin	Jul. 8, 1832
James Brown	Rebecca Plummer	Nov. 5, 1832
Lewis Ramsy	Elizabeth Hetherly	Aug. 22, 1833
John Alder	Frances Rogers	Jul. 13, 1833
Rolin Hinton	Elizabeth Brammel	Aug. 29, 1833
John D. Hensly	Mary Sullens	Sep. 5, 1833
Thomas Childers	Polly Hinton	Nov. 28, 1831
Baxter Estis	Senna Brown	Jul. 27, 1832
John Brown	Nancy Richardson	Sep. 1, 1831
Isaiah Todd	Elizabeth Prather	Jan. 7, 1833
William Dollarhide	Martha Holt	Jan. 23, 1834
Thomas Johns	Agnes Boyd	Jan. 9, 1834
Richard Brown	Mrs. Jemina Turner	Feb. 9, 1834
George Miller	Sarah Huffman	Nov. 1, 1832
Joseph Fowler	Mahala Huffman	Aug. 12, 1832
Daniel Maupin	Rebecca Nix	Nov. 11, 1832
James Huffman	Jane Smyth	Nov. 18, 1832
John Brown	Nancy Richardson	Feb. 20, 1834
David Hinton	Rebbecca Sullens	Mar. 13, 1834
Robert Harrison	Mary Susan North	Jan. 1, 1834
*Ambrose H. Posey	Eliz. Ann Southworth	Jun. 29, 1834

*(Groom late of Georgia. Bride late of Tennessee and now residing in Crawford County)

Thomas Bay	Nancy James	Mar. 23, 1834
Henry Adams	Sally Huffman	Jul. 14, 1834
George Cooper	Levena Parks	Jul. 30, 1834
William Prather	Hetty Bay	May 8, 1834
Charles R. Todd	Ester Fisher	Sep. 15, 1833
John Sumpter	Malinda Prather	May 29, 1834
Samuel Vaughn	Emily Hornie	Jan. 2, 1834
John Hilderbrand	Susy Parker	Dec. 10, 1833
Numan Bay	Nancy Johns	Feb. 20, 1834
Henry Skaggs	Elizabeth Momon	Jun. 29, 1834
Samuel Wilson	Jane E. Anderson	Aug. 21, 1834
John L. Morris	Permelia K. Hinkle	Oct. 16, 1834
Adam Zumalt	Mahala Jaks	Oct. 12, 1834
William Spencer	Hannah Croft	Oct. 26, 1834
David H. Bishop	Mary A. Park	Dec. 20, 1834
*Joseph Crane	Cassea Sullivan	Oct. 26, 1833

*(Groom of Crawford County.)

William T. North	Mary Ann Owens	Dec. 8, 1834
James Murdock	Lydia Belt	Jan. 6, 1835
*Flavins J. North	Francis C. Goode	Nov. 27, 1834

*(Witnesses: M.H. Goode and Edward Goode)

Henry Brown	Elizabeth E. Jones	Jan. 8, 1835
Elamuel Boyd	Lydia Johns	Jan. 18, 1835
Joseph Hull	Constincy Alley	Dec. 18, 1834

(Franklin County, Missouri Continued)

Groom	Bride	Date
Jonathan Compton	Annis Dollarhide	Feb. 5, 1835
Alton Horine	Sary Shuffield	Nov. 20, 1834
Thomas Boyd	Mary Clifton	Nov. 20, 1834
John Simpson	Sarah Enloe	Jan. 15, 1835
Jesse Harris	Susan Medlock	Jan. 23, 1835
William Blackwell	Sary Gavner	Aug. 14, 1834
John Richardson	Britanny Multon	Mar. 6, 1835
Robert M. Combs	Polly White	Mar. 8, 1835
Lewis Davis	Dicy Morris	Aug. 8, 1834
Lewis Terry	Catrean Armen	Mar. 17, 1835
John Suther	Sarah Cane	Jan. 25, 1835
John Call	Sarah McCourtney	Dec. 25, 1834
William North	Nancy Williamson	Feb. 19, 1835
William Wrangler	Katherine Buddamen	Feb. 1, 1835
Alexander D. Clark	Sarah Morris	Jan. 15, 1835
Prsely McWilliams	Eliza Jane McCoy	Apr. 9, 1836
Henry P. Steel	Sarah Walker	Apr. 26, 1835
John A. Ramsey	Maraine Miller	Aug. 14, 1834
Adam Russell	Avena Barmell	Feb. 19, 1835
John Phillips	Elizabeth Bailey	Jul. 20, 1835

(Witnesses: Moses Maupin and Russell Frarris)

John R. Twitty	Elvia Patton	Jul. 22, 1835
Uriel Baily	Jane Mosely	Mar. 13, 1835

(Witnesses: George Mitchell and James Baily)

Perry Cahill	Katherine Triplett	Aug. 9, 1835
John Q. Bridges	Marthy Rutherford	Jun. 21, 1835
Griffith Stoner	Jaming Williams	Jul. 12, 1835
Clayborn Jackson	Nancy Vaughn	Jul. 16, 1835
Frederick Dings	Ida Stein	Jul. 18, 1835
John Tenell	Amanda Richey	Oct. 5, 1835
John Patton	Margaret Maupin	Oct. 8, 1835
James H. Jones	Ann Roades	Aug. 20, 1835
Luster Barnes	Margary Shourne	Nov. 8, 1835
Jackson Hammock	Polly Brown	.Nov. 5, 1835

(Witnesses: Jesse Brown and Miss Frances Spars)

John Lintacund	Sarah Caldwell	Oct. 25, 1835
Lewis Greenstreet	Nancy Davis	Dec. 31, 1835

(Witnesses: Wm. Hannock and Absolom Greenstreet. The wedding took place at the home of Elizabeth Davis)

Julius Emmons	Levisey Robinett	Nov. 1, 1835
Joshua Pinkston	Polly McKinney	Nov. 2, 1835
William Skinner	Marinda Richardson	Dec. 6, 1835
Samuel Beatty	Patience Kelly	Dec. 3, 1835
Job Hinton	Nancy Terry	Mar. 22, 1836
John S. White	Martha I. Barney	Mar. 16, 1836
John Lack	Martha A. Crowder	Jan. 13, 1836
Isaac Stoner	Nancy J. Roberts	Feb. 21, 1836

(Franklin County, Missouri Continued)

Groom	Bride	Date
William King	Polly Young	Jan. 31, 1836
Francis Miller	Fany Phillips	Mar. 20, 1836
W. McAfee	Mrs. Fine Perkins	Feb. 28, 1836
(Marriage performed at the home of William Perkins)		
William Crow	Susannah Patton	Apr. 17, 1836
John Breeding	Mrs. Elender Greenstreet	May 31, 1836
William Adams	Elizabeth Hyatt	Jul. 17, 1836
Johnson Childers	Margaret Blare	Jan. 20, 1836
William Pointer	Mary Jones	Feb. 25, 1836
Francis Conway	Nancy Burtin	Jun. 16, 1836
John W. Farmer	Mary Casey	Jul. 17, 1836
James B. Southworth	Exony Reocrd	Jul. 23, 1836
Thomas L. Cofer	Charity Ann Whitmire	Jul. 31, 1836
Daniel B. Moor	Mrs. Celia Tate	Jul. 17, 1836
Stanford Whitworth	Vineel Dunkin	Dec. 10, 1835
Solomon Colvin	Mary Ann Gardner	Dec. 17, 1835
Jesse Zumwalt	Nancy Grider	Aug. 25, 1836
Daniel Penrod	Queen Short	Aug. 16, 1836
Jesse Walker Blair	Emeline Sullivante	Aug. 11, 1836
James B. Braley	Minerva Enloe	Aug. 23, 1836
Thomas Estes	Rody Farmer	Oct. 27, 1836
William G. Adams	*Celia Baily	Nov. 3, 1836
*(Bride is the daughter of Caleb Baily)		
Afgey Shelton	Nancy Shooms	Oct. 14, 1836
Joseph Bay	Emily Parker	Nov. 24, 1836
William Loftin	Mrs. Sally Robinett	Jan. 12, 1837
Henry Childers	Elizabeth Maupin	Nov. 1, 1831
William Johnson	Sally Stockston	Dec. 8, 1836
Jacob Wallis	Katharine Rice	Nov. 2, 1836
G. W. McCullough	---	Feb. 2, 1837
Moses Maupin	Nancy Patton	Dec. 18, 1836
(Witnesses: Benjamin Perkins and George Patton)		
John S. Ridenhour	Isabel Hiliard	Jan. 21, 1837
John Franklin	Ann Conner	Mar. 1, 1837
David Parker	Sarah Lefton	Jan. 2, 1837
Henry Woodcock	Minerva Wittington	Jan. 3, 1837
James Brown	Elizabeth Blair	Mar. 9, 1837
Joseph R. Harden	Mary Ann Murphy	Mar. 9, 1837
Thomas Stapleton	Elizabeth Spencer	Mar. 2, 1837
Asa Scott	Polly Pepper	Nov. 3, 1836
John Pepper	Lucinda Wilson	Nov. 21, 1836
John Harden	Rachel Hyatt	Dec. 25, 1836
William C. Chiles	Martha Jones	Feb. 2, 1837
Henry Dingas	Elizabeth Ferguson	Jan. 19, 1837
Calvin Waldo	Francis North	Jan. 12, 1837
Felix Taylor	Rebecca Nickols	Mar. 23, 1837

(Franklin County, Missouri Continued)

Groom	Bride	Date
Francis Beckman	Mary Eliz. Musiack	May 4, 1837
John D. Enloe	Drusilla Tailor	Feb. 9, 1837
Adolphus Kriger	Emelie Rathge	Apr. 15, 1837
Robert Stapleton	Melinda Bradburry	Apr. 9, 1837
John Triplett	Sarah J. Buckner	May 7, 1837
Hiram Estes	Penina Farmer	May 8, 1837
George W. Johns	Nancy J. Prichett	Apr. 30, 1837
Harris Colvin	Susan Steel	Jun. 8, 1837
Wilson D. Hurt	Mary J. Jefferies	Jun. 8, 1837
James Bell	Susan A. Vest	May 28, 1837
Osborne Halen	Eliza Jones	Apr. 13, 1837
Silvester Reed	Elizabeth Ware	Jul. 19, 1837
William Greenstreet	*Elizabeth Anderson	Aug. 27, 1837

*(Bride the daughter of John Anderson)

Groom	Bride	Date
Adam Dillinger	Mary Fraser	June 8, 1837
Jacob Decker	Betty Withington	Aug. 17, 1837
Isaiah T. Murphy	Rebecca Clark	Aug. 26, 1837
Adolph Franklinburg	Maria Engel Huvelmeyer	Sep. 15, 1837
Nathl. Hampton Parker	Elizabeth Johns	Jul. 9, 1837

(Bride the daughter of Thomas Johns)

Groom	Bride	Date
Ephraim Perkins	Olive Smith	Aug. 6, 1837
Jonathan W. Jones	Marietta Musick	Aug. 27, 1837
John Duncan	Elizabeth Duncan	Oct. 13, 1837
Rev. John Monroe	*Mrs. Sarah S. Stewart	Sep. 26, 1837

*(Bride from Ohio)

Groom	Bride	Date
William Watson	Marry Ann Blanton	Sep. 26, 1837
Isaac Courtley	Polly Simpson	Sep. 22, 1837

(Bride the daughter of John Simpson)

Groom	Bride	Date
William Blackwell	Mary Armstead	Aug. 13, 1837
Charles C. Kanada	Sarah A. Jones	Aug. 28, 1837
James North	Mary F. Martin	Aug. 11, 1837
Robert Bellups	Paulina Davidson	Aug. 14, 1837
James Ferrell	Mary C. Billups	Nov. 2, 1837
Nelson Withinton	Rebeckah Decker	Sep. 17, 1837
George Bates	Elizabeth Bacon	Nov. 2, 1837
James Burchfield	Harriet Sullivant	Sep. 3, 1837
Samuel Grooms	Betsy Ann Posey	Dec. 26, 1837
Martin Johnson	Comfort Drace	Dec. 26, 1837
John H. Stogdon	Louisianna Caldwell	Jan. 3, 1838
Henry Link	Sally C. Philips	Dec. 21, 1837
John Lewis Cantley	Elizabeth Caldwell	Dec. 17, 1837
John Davis	Susan Laremore	Jan. 22, 1838
Pinkney Laremore	Ann Cheek	Jan. 4, 1838
Daniel Hammuston	Frederica Depenn	Nov. 18, 1837
Wiley Johnson	Caroline Johnson	Nov. 30, 1837
Samuel L. Drace	Minery Farrar	Jan. 4, 1838

(Franklin County, Missouri Continued)

Groom	Bride	Date
Thompson Rogers	Clarissa Hodges	Nov. 21, 1837
Samuel P. Phillips	Nancy Robertson	Jan. 13, 1838
(Bride is the daughter of James Robertson)		
John Brown	Charlitte Williamson	Dec. 14, 1847
Thomas Baly	Hilda Gobel	Feb. 25, 1838
(Witnesses: Williams G. Brown and Wm. Baily)		
Richard R. Jones	Eliza C. Chambers	Feb. 22, 1838
Samuel W. Short	Jemima Dollarhide	Mar. 29, 1838
William Brown	Eliz. Withington	Jan. 11, 1838
James B. Simpson	Polly Cantly	Feb. 22, 1838
(Bride is the daughter of John Cantly)		
William Hensley	Lucinda Cantly	Feb. 22, 1838
(Bride is the daughter of John Cantly)		
Alexander Orchard	Elizabeth Ramsey	Sep. 28, 1837
Elijah Adams, jr.	Sarah Michel	Nov. 14, 1837
Harvey Campbell	Ann Elliot Armstrong	Nov. 23, 1837
Daniel Richardson	Dorcas Dougherty	Jan. 25, 1838
James P. Caldwell	Ann Caldwell	May 6, 1838
Jesse Blackwell	Mary White	Sep. 10, 1837
James H. Ellis	Mary Ann Thomas	May 7, 1838
James Hendrick	Leah Maupin	May 7, 1838
Charles H. Mann	Magadorah McWilliams	Apr. 26, 1838
Samuel Beecher	Margaret Jane Smith	Mar. 29, 1838
Hyrum Osborne	Drusilla Sappington	Feb. 14, 1838
David Cooper	Mary Rion Richardson	Mar. 15, 1838
Charles Morten	Cyntha Walls	Apr. 10, 1838
William Montgomery	Elizabeth Shaban	Jan. 7, 1838
Samuel Harris	Ann A. Thomas	Mar. 27, 1838
Ambrose Twitty	Sarah Booke	Jul. 12, 1838
Jahon McFarland Deaver	Mary Bennett Hughes	Mar. 29, 1838
John Shelton	Nancy Doggett	May 3, 1838
John B. Wolsey	Martha Renfro	Jun. 23, 1838
George W. Boyd	Mahala Thornhill	Aug. 23, 1838
(Witnesses: Martin Alexander and Thomas Boyd)		
John Hodges	Martha Jamison	Aug. 9, 1838
John Henory Hadbrink	Ann Mary Ameling	Jun. 30, 1838
Elisha Lowell	Lucy Jones	*--- 14, 1838
*(Marriage Date recorded Sep. 8, 1838)		
William L. Margrave	Matilda Decker	Aug. 16, 1838
Forest G. Desper	Sarah Jones	Aug. 24, 1838
William G. Piper	Sarah R. Butler	Jul. 4, 1838
Samuel Hutton	Elizabeth Adams	Aug. 7, 1838
James Stites	Mary Mosbey	Sep. 20, 1838
(Groom was a minor. Consent given by Jefferson Sullins)		
William Ely Bray	Elizabeth Philips	Sep. 6, 1838
Leonard Hetherly	Elizabeth Ogden	Sep. 6, 1838
John Thurman	Margaret Cantley	Jul. 29, 1838

(Franklin County, Missouri Continued)

Groom	Bride	Date
Nathaniel Hinkle	Eleanor N. Butts	Aug. 28, 1838
James Bay	Rosannah Cole	Oct. 3, 1838
John F. Mense	Sarah S. Owens	Oct. 10, 1838
Thomas Duncan	Nancy Musick	Oct. 11, 1838

(Witnesses: Robert Duncan and Wm. Cole)

Benjamin Heatherly	Rhoda Kelly	Oct. 14, 1838
Hubbard Simpson	Sarah Greenstreet	Oct. 28, 1838

(Witnesses: Martin Crow and Rebecca Sullens)

George Vanlin	Sarah Terry	Oct. 28, 1838
John Wall	Lorinda Moor	Aug. 27, 1838
Charles Kannada	Lucy Williamson	Sep. 15, 1838
Michael Shuckman	*Mrs. Eliz. Brown	Dec. 4, 1838

*(Wid. of Frederick Brown, dec. and dau. of Geo. Miller)

Henry Duff	Ruth Braley	Dec. 6, 1838
John Pulaim	Zeznlda Hodges	Nov. 15, 1838
Benjamin Horine	Louizanna Jones	Dec. 27, 1838
*Henry Sipes	Mary Ann Stites	Oct. 25, 1838

(Both were minors. Groom had the consent of Wm. Crow)

William J. Thompson	Susan E. Wood	Dec. 13, 1838
James M. Booker	Amanda Gregory	Jan. 3, 1839

(Witnesses: Reper Gregory and Levi Primm)

John Maupin	Polly Ann Taylor	Nov. 18, 1838

(Wedding was held at the home of John Taylor. Dudley Parks and Martin G. Crow were present.)

Charles Osterwald	Mary Miller	Dec. 6, 1838

(Witness: William James)

Ira Minchels	Isabel Decker	Jan. 17, 1839
Ambrose Chuning	Elizabeth Bell	Jan. 3, 1839
Thomas Anderson	Letha Foeguson	Dec. 6, 1838
William Harris	Emily McEntire	Nov. 1, 1838
William Cowherd	Eliza Owens	Nov. 22, 1838
James Spaon	Eliza Tansy	Nov. 28, 1838
John Bay	Fedelia King	Dec. 20, 1838
Perry Cahill	Rebecca Rice	Feb. 10, 1839
Gustavus B. Horner	Elizabeth Kelly	Mar. 4, 1839
James Stuart	Sarah Decker	Mar. 21, 1839

(Witnesses: Calbourn Henderson and Elizabeth, his wife)

John Decker, jr.	Luticia Macculla	Mar. 24, 1839

(Witnesses: Nelson Withington and Abyah Steel)

John Jamison	Margaret Hodges	Feb. 6, 1839
Ross Crow	Nancy Tyre	Aug. 25, 1838
William Enloe	Rebecca Gasperson	Dec. 15, 1838
Anthony Enloe	Lucretia Tailor	Dec. 25, 1838
William Whitmire	Catharine Wheter	Feb. 7, 1839
Frederick Meyer	Catharine W. Meass	Apr. 22, 1839
William Y. Lickery	Sally Waddube (sic)	Jun. 20, 1838
Garnett Cooper	Elizabeth Brown	Mar. 21, 1839

(Franklin County, Missouri Continued)

Groom	Bride	Date
John V. Dotsel	Elizabeth M. Rattle Mueller	May 14, 1839
Leonard Rattle Mueller	Barbara Hambiter	May 14, 1839
Washington T. Brammel	Martha F. Butts	Feb. 14, 1839
Robert Brown	Judith Burton	Mar. 21, 1839
William P. Lowright	Mary E. Crowder	Mar. 5, 1839
Alexander Daniels	Elizabeth B. Sowell	Mar. 2, 1839
Peter Parent	Mary Ann Frazier	May 5, 1839

(Witnesses: F. Hamilton and Jackson M. Williams. The wedding was at the home of John Gale. jr.)

Zacahriah Reed	Susan Richardson	Mar. 31, 1839

(Witnesses: Benoni Sappington, Fielding Sappington and Daniel Hinton)

John Bay	Cath. J. Christwell	May 19, 1839

(Wedding was at the home of James Christwell)

Jesse Short	Rebecca Lewis	Mar. 31, 1839
William Friar	Winneford Griffith	Apr. 21, 1839
Anderson Parks	Susannah Stites	May 9, 1839
James A. Robertson	Susannah Perkins	May 26, 1839
Harris Bledsoe	Malinda Hamilton	Aug. 8, 1839
Henry Stophel	Juliann Leuwekamp	Aug. 7, 1839
William Thornhill	Sarah Ann Jones	Aug. 22, 1839

(Witnesses: John L. Hamilton and Charles A. Kannada)

Martin G. Crow	Jane Jump	Jul. 25, 1839

(Witnesses: Cpt. John L. Hamilton and Miss Nancy Mosley. Bride is the daughter of Capt. Samuel Jump.)

Jonathan Hutton	Levina Gordon	Jul. 25, 1839
John H. Laughnberg	Lotta Wehr	Sep. 5, 1839
Madison Hendrick	Nancy Brown	Oct. 3, 1839
Julius Emmens	Susannah Hethbran	Sep. 26, 1839
William Pounds	Margery White	Sep. 26, 1839
Thomas Pierce	Kesziah Napper	Oct. 13, 1839
Hugh Nevit	Mrs. J. Saults	Aug. 6, 1839
David E. Bell	Nancy R. Campbell	Sep. 26, 1839
Jesse C. Hull	Mahala Drace	Sep. 26, 1839
John Fitzwater	Nancy McCourtney	Aug. 23, 1839
Niman Hamilton	Eleanor Williams	Sep. 5, 1839
Clayton Blackwell	Malinda Blankenship	Aug. 25, 1839
John Truesdell	Elizabeth Ebenns	Oct. 10, 1839
Aaron Short	Harriet King	Oct. 7, 1839
John L. Strothmann	Katherine Apins	Nov. 13, 1839
William Pointer	Elizabeth Tony	Dec. 14, 1839
Thomas Roberts	Tabitha H. Crowden	Nov. 26, 1839
Jacob Johnson	Mary Ann Davidson	Nov. 14, 1839
Samuel Davidson	America A. Billups	Oct. 3, 1839
Henson Stephens	Elizabeth Gasperson	Apr. 10, 1839
Thomas Standefer	Jane Queny Penrod	Sep. 28, 1839

(Franklin County, Missouri Continued)

Groom	Bride	Date
David H. Bishop	Susann B. Stephens	Dec. 26, 1839
William M. Helm	Martha Brown	Dec. 19, 1839

(Witnesses: Geo. Mitchell and John Gregory)

Montgomery County, Missouri, Tax List, 1823.

Isaac Ammiman, William Armstrong, John B. Ammons, Leland Allen, James Autroleus, Robert Arnold, James Alfred, William Appling, Presley Anderson, James Anderson, Bryan Alexander, Lee Alexander, Michael Alexander, Charles Alexander, William Boss, John Butler, Benjamin Butcher, Morgan Bryan, David G. Cockrain, Nathan Browning, Joshua G. Brown, Widow Elizabeth Bryan, Dabney Burnet, James Barnes, Thomas Bowen, John Best, Daniel Bane, Walter Ballard, Francis J. Beaver, Isaac Best, George Bright, Ambrose Bush, Thomas P. G. Briggs, Samuel L. Daugherty, Alphonso Boon, William Brown, John Baker, George Bast, Silvester Baker for Diza Johnston, dec., Isaac Clark, Silvester and John Baker, Jesse B. Boon, Estate of N. Boon, dec., Willis Bryan, William Brown, Joseph Brown, William L. Burch, Larkin G. Carter, George Chandler, William Chandler, George Chandler, Tilman Cullom, Beston Callahan, Grove Cook, George W. Clendenning, Noah Caton, John Carter, Jesse Caton, Flanders Calloway, Larkin Calloway, Everet Check, Jesse Cox, George Clay, John Creech, Thomas Chambers, James Chambers, Isaac Chandler, Jesse Cain, Andrew Cochran, Jacob Cail, Adam or Samuel Cobb, Burton Cook, James Cantley, Benjamin Ellis, Burton Cook, James Cantley, William Candruff, Henry Clanton, Richard Candruff, John A. Crawford, Martha Cole, John Craig, Philip Cobb, Cyenius Cox, Drury Clanton, John Carver, Jonas Caton, Francis Danniel, John H. Dutton, John Davis, Joseph Edmonson, Jacob Darst, James Davis, Cale Diggs, Alexander Davidson, Abraham Davidson, Thomas Dozier, William Elston, Lewis Edward, Moses Edward, James Erwin, John Erwin, William Gee, Jacob Ellis, James Ellis, James Ellis, sr., John Johns, Janet Endin, Jonathan Eliston, John Ferguson, Francis Foust, Richard Fitzhugh, Daniel Farrer, Edward Ford, Abraham Fine, Levy and Widow Fine, William Frazare, Robert Gray, Jonathan Gordon, Daniel Graves, Robert Graham, Samuel Griggs, Michael Glass, John Griggs, Arron Grooms, Frederick Griswold, Joseph Gray, Jacob Grooms, Benjamin Gammon, Philip Glover, William Hancick, John P. Glover, sr., James Glover, Jabez Ham, James Hutton, Nathaniel Hart, John Haun, sr., Jacob Haun, Absalom Hays, Francis Holder, Charles Hubbard, David Hubbard, Howel Newton, Jno. heirs, Joseph House, Joseph Hays, William Hale, Tice Haun, John Haun, jr., John Hill, Robert Hunter, Andrew Hunter, Peter Hunter, James Hunter, Edward Hardister, David Howard, Thomas Hickerson, Daniel Hale, Cornelius Howard, Wm. Kent, Andrew Howard, Mather Hopkins, William Hopkins, Isaac

(Montgomery County, Missouri Continued)

Hopkins, Joseph Homesley, Thomas G. Hancock, Joseph Howard, James Hughes, Lewis Jones, Thomas Jones, William James, John Kent, Benjamin James, Joshua James, James Journey, Robert Job, Abner Johnson, Robert Johnson, Joseph Johnson, Thomas Kennedy, John Johnson, John King, Thomas Kennedy, Alexander Pursingle, Gayon Kennedy, Amos Kibble, William Knox, Robert Kent, Isaac Kent, James Kennedy, James Leawell, Daniel Linn, William Lamme, William Logan, Hugh Lisle, James Lisle, John Lizenby, William Lisle, William Langford, John Land, Samuel Mornice, Henry· Logan, Daniel Lark, Alexander Logan, William McGaugh, Edward Leawall, George Laurence, John Merchant, Wm. M'Farland, Widow Ludey Moody, Oliver McEwin, Patton M'Gaugh, Andrew McWilliams, William M'Connel, Wells E. Marion, George Mouzer, jr., Matthew M'Gaugh, Hugh M'Dermond, jr., Jeremiah H. Neile, Hugh M'Dermond, sr., Mathais M'Ginhin, Hugh Newt, Thomas Moor, Ezekiel M'Carty, Dennis M'Garvin, James Moody, Mordicai Morgan, John C. Milligan, John Morrow, Asa Mannon, Benoni M'Clure, Alexander M'Kinney, William Martin, Matthew Nettle, John Northent, Thomas Oden, Jacob Oden, John Owings, Thomas Owings, Micajah Ousley, Micajah Ousley adm. of Jas. Stephens, dec., Irwin L. Pilman, James Pennington, Thomas G. Puryear, Enoch Perkins, Norman Pringle, Hiram Pain, James B. Patton, James Patton, Jacob Patton, sr., Widow Mary Patton, Henry Parish, Samuel A. Pace, Martin Pugh, James Powel, John Pates, David Peweter, William Patton, Dabney Peths, William Quick, Jacob Patton of Bear Creek, John Preston, David Reed, Rueben P. Pugh, Lemuel Price, James Price, Jacob Quick, sr., Thomas Ouick, Alexander Quick, Jacob Quick, jr., Jacob Quick of Wild Cat Creek, Joseph Rhyme, John Hill, Benjamin Rogers, Jesse Retter, Benjamin Rogers of Smith Creek, Stephen Yates, John Richardson, Turner Roundtree, Samuel Reynolds, Hamilton Smith, John Reynolds, James Reynolds, George Reynolds, Peter Rock, Newton Rider, Benjamin Rowe, Moses Summers, Charles D. Wright, Jesse Summers, Allen Summers, David Smith, James M. Taylor, Darling and Senddler Smith, Joshua Stagsdill, David Shearman, Benjamin Sharp, James F. Sharp, John Sneathan, Job Stark, Widow Milly Stephenson, Henry Sally, Dugliss Wyatt, Abraham Smith, Moses Smith, Seth Strichling, Willis Shelton, jacob Spies, John Stone, Thomas Smith, Jeremiah Smith, John Stewart, Stewart Slaven, Thomas Slaven, John Tice, Johnson Taylor, John Skinner, sr., Francis Skinner, William Skinner, Jacob L. Sharp, John Thompson, James Talbot, Richard Wright, Christopher Talbert, Peter E. Thomas,Widow Elizabeth Thomas, Hail Talbot, Thomas Talbot, William Talbot, Brian Thornhill, David Talbot, Nicholas M. Tuttle, John Trimble, Wm. Tribble, Isaac Vanbibber, John Wyatt, sr., Chester Wheeler,John Wade, Henry E. Welch, John Welsh, Caleb Williams, George Williams, Joseph and William Ward, Anthony Wyatt, John Ward, Cornelius

(Montgomery County, Missouri Continued)
Williamson, Anthony Wyatt, John Ward, --- Frazerwood, Elijah Wray, John Wyatt, adm. of Jas. Wyatt, Elias Weddle, Andrew Zumwalt, Adam Zumwalt, John Willaby, Robert Weddle, Charles Wells, Olby Williams, Samuel Williamson, Frances Whitesides, James Whiteside, Aaron H. Young, John Young.

St. Louis County, Missouri, Estrays, Missouri Gazette.

(1) Ignatius Anderson, St. Ferdinand Township, took up a sorrel horse. The horse was appraised at $25 by Alex. McCloud and Jas. B. Edwards.(I) Feb. 3, 1816.
(2) James C. Curry, Bonhomme Township, has taken up a brown horse. Uri Musick and Francis Donoho valued the horse at $75. (I) Nov. 24, 1819, (JP) John S. Ball.
(3) Thomas Dozier, St. Ferdinand Township, has taken up a sorrel mare. The appraised value of the mare was given as $30 by Philip Turner and John Burk. (I) Oct. 7, 1815.
(4) John B. Stone has taken up a black mare. Nicholas Stephenson and Thomas Dozier appraised the value of the mare at $12.(I)Aug. 9, 1817,(JP) T.D. Stephens.
(5) Reuben Sullens, Bonhomme Township, has taken up two barrows, five sows and nine pigs. The hogs were valued at $28 by Richard Sullens and Samuel Harris. (I) Feb. 13, 1817, (JP) J. H. Burckhart.
(6) Benjamin Quick, Joachim Township, has taken up a black horse. The appraised value of the horse was given at $25 by Geo. and Jos. Sipp.(I)Jun. 8, 1816.
(7) William Osborn, Pt. Labadie Township, has taken up sorrel mare. Thomas Henry and Elisha Kimbro were the appraisers. (I)Mar. 20, 1818,(JP)John Burchard.
(8) George Nesbit, Bonhomme Township, offers a reward for the return of his strayed mare.(I)Apr. 14,1816.
(9) John Ogles, Joachim Township, took up a bay horse. Claiborne Thomas and Isam Ogles appraised the horse at $25. (I) Feb. 27, 1818, (JP) B. Johnston.
(10) Charles Merceer, St. Ferdinand Township, has taken up a bay horse. The horse was valued at $60 by Fenton F. Goss and Chas. Moreau. (I) Apr. 4, 1821, (JP) A. Stewart.
(11) Stephen Maddox, River des Peres, has taken up a sorrel horse. (I) Oct. 11, 1817, (JP) Thomas Sappington.
(12) William Long has taken up two gray horse. Thomas Fitzwater and John Lewis appraised both animals. (I) Jan. 29, 1816.
(13) George King, Bonhomme Township, took up a sorrel horse. (I) Apr. 26, 1817, (JP) Andrew Kinkead.

(St. Louis County, Missouri Continued)
- (14) Robert Criswell, St. Ferdinand Township, has taken up a sorrel horse. The horse was valued at $80. (I) Aug. 2, 1817, (JP) R. Chitwood.
- (15) George Cox, Joachim Township, has taken up a bay horse. (I) Apr. 11, 1812, (JP) J. Rankin.
- (16) Randolph Hoverstock, Joachim, Township, has taken up two horses. The animals were appraised by James Dowling and George Cox. (I) Mar. 15, 1815.
- (17) Henry Steel, Pt. Labadie Township, taken taken up a bay horse. John Morris and and William Lewis valued the horse at $30. (I) Jul. 24, 1818, (JP) John Burchard.
- (18) William Williams on Sandy Creek, Joachim Township, has taken up a sorrel mare. (I) Nov. 9, 1816, (JP) Benjamin Johnston.
- (19) Ed Wells offered a $4 reward for the return of his strayed horse. (I) Aug. 13, 1814.
- (20) Samuel Watson, sr., Bonhomme Township, has taken up a bay horse. (I) Nov. 9, 1816, (JP) Andrew Kinkead.
- (21) Dodsan Thorp, Bonhomme Township, took up a chestnut sorrel mare. The mare was appraised at a value of $25 by Richard Stephenson and Henry Moore . (I) Sep. 29, 1819.
- (22) John L. Smith, St. Ferdinand Township, has taken up a bay mare. (I) Oct. 31, 1810, (JP) John Allen.
- (23) Jacob Seelye, St. Ferdinand Township, has taken up a bay horse. Asa Carrico and Josiah Mills valued the horse at $27.50. (I) Nov. 29, 1817, (JP) S. Magill.
- (24) Joel Rowley has taken up up a bay horse valued at $22.50. The appraisers were Abraham Ellis and Green Dewitt. (I) Jan. 11, 1817, (JP) S. Magill.
- (25) Elias Metz has taken up a brown mare. (JP) John Allen, (I) Feb. 11, 1816.
- (26) John Simpson, Labadie Township, has taken up three horses. (JP) William Dodds, (I) Oct. 29, 1814.
- (27) Sherrel G. Swain, St. Ferdinand Township, has taken up a gray horse. The horse was appraised at $26 by John W. Angle and Elias Metz. (I) Jan. 9, 1811.
- (28) William Hensley, Labadie Township, has taken up a mare and two colts. (I) Apr. 9, 1814, (JP) William Dodds.
- (29) William Harrison, Joachim Township, has taken up a sorrel horse. Thomas Keatly and John Baily have appraised the animal at $27.50. (I) Nov. 29, 1817, (JP) -- Bowles.
- (30) Richard Gentry, Bonhomme Township, has taken up a bay horse. The horse was appraised at a value of

(St. Louis County, Missouri Countinued)

$40 by George Mock, Ezekiel Ferrall, and Robert Ferrall. (I) Feb. 20, 1818, (JP) Gabriel Long.

(31) James Foster, Joachim Township, has taken up a gray mare. The mare's value was appraised at $25 by Clab. Thomas and Rich. Hendrickson.(I)Apr.10, 1818.

(32) George Farris took up a bay horse. (JP) Gabriel Long, (I) Jan. 6, 1816.

(33) Francis Denoyer, Joachim Township, has taken up a bay horse. (I) Dec. 14, 1816, (JP) Caleb Bowles.

(34) James Colvin, Pt. Labadie Township, has taken up a bay mare. David Edwards and Peter Zumwalt valued the mare at $30. (I) Oct. 26, 1816, (JP) John Burchard.

(35) John Cole has taken up a mare and a stud colt. Wm. Cole and James Pepper appraised the animals. (I) Jun. 3, 1815, (JP) William Long.

(36) William Clinton, Joachim Township, has taken up a bay horse. The horse was given an appraised value of $30 by Isaac Evans, James Povne and Francis Watts. (I) Jan. 3, 1818, (JP) J. McCullock.

(37) Joshua H. Burkhart, St. Ferdinand Township, has taken up a sorrel horse. The appraisers were Jacob Mertz and Nathaniel Sullivan. (I) Jan. 11, 1812.

(38) Adam Brown, on the Grand Glaize, Joachim Township, has taken up a bay horse. The horse was valued at $25 by John Stephens and Wm. Riggs.(I) Aug.24,1816.

(39) Ambrose Bowles, Pt. Labadie Township, has taken up a horse. The horse was valued at $15 by Michael Crow and Peter Zumwalt. (I) Sep. 16, 1815, (JP)Luke Decker.

(40) Jacob Boas living about eight miles above St. Louis offers a reward for the return of a strayed horse. (I) Jan. 6, 1816.

(41) A sorrel mare was taken up by Wren Benton, Joachim Township. (I) Aug. 13, 1814.

(42) Samuel Stul, St. Ferdinand Township, has taken up a bay horse. Benj. Jones and Thos. Whitesides valued the horse at $20. (I) Jan. 10, 1821, (JP) Wm. Hunt.

(43) Louis Williams, Bonhomme Township, has taken up two mare and a stud. (I) May 4, 1816, (JP) Daniel B. Moore.

(44) John Wiseman, Bonhomme Township, has taken up a bay horse. A. Kinkead valued the animal at $27. (I) Dec. 30, 1815.

(45) John Zumwalt, Femme Osage Township, has taken up a bay horse. Abraham Darst and John Mazer valued the horse at $27. (I)Nov. 22,1817,(JP)John B. Callaway.

(46) Adam J. Whitesides, St. Ferdinand Township, took up

(St. Louis County, Missouri Continued)
bay horse. (I) Apr. 23, 1814.
(47) Lewis Williams, Big River Township, has taken up a bay mare. Ferguson Haile and Wm. Paxton appraised the mare at $40. (I) Nov. 2, 1816, (JP) William H. Andrews.
(48) Abraham Welsh, St. Louis Township, has taken up a black horse. The horse was appraised at $40 by John Nailer, David Hughes, and James Morel. (JP) F. M. Guyol, (I) Feb. 6, 1818.
(49) Jabez Warner, Joachim Township, has taken up a bay horse. The horse was appraised at $18 by Joseph Andrews, Joseph Hocks, and John McKean. (JP) James Rankin, (I) Apr. 18, 1812.
(50) Meshack Walton, Bonhomme Township, has taken up a bay mare. Andrew Kincaid was the appraiser. (I) July 22, 1815.
(51) John C. Sullivan, St. Ferdinand Township, has taken up a steer. The steer was valued at $9 by William Massey and John Doggett. (I) Apr. 20, 1816.
(52) Amos Steel accuses Wm. Edminson Wright of stealing a sorrel mare from St. Louis.
(53) Harrison Sartain, on the Grand Glaize, has taken up a mare and colt. Johnson Harrison and Frederick Holmes were the appraisers. (I) Sep. 22, 1819.
(54) Michael Reilley, on the River des Peres, has taken up a bay mare. The mare was appraised at $20 by William Esdale and Matthew Molony. (I) Feb. 9, 1820.
(55) William Purkins, Pt. Labadie Township, has taken up a mare and colt. The animals were valued at $30 by William Spencer and John Nickles. (I) May 25, 1816.
(56) Perry Moore, Joachim Township, has taken up a bay horse. (I) Jun. 1, 1816, (JP) James McCullock.
(57) Tyree Martin, St. Ferdinand Township, has taken up an iron-gray horse. The horse was valued at $22.50 by Wm. R. McAdams and John Jamison. (JP) S. Magill, (I) Feb. 20, 1818.
(58) Daniel M. McLaughlin, Joachim Township, took up a sorrel horse. The horse was appraised at $40 by George Sipp and Enos McDonald. (I) Sep. 13, 1817, (JP) Caleb Bowles.
(59) Michael McKee, Joachim Township, took up a roan horse. The horse was appraised at $25 by Thomas Blair, John W. Burns and Francis Miller. (JP) J.S. McCullock, (I) Oct. 23, 1818.
(60) John W. McGirk has taken up a bay mare. The mare was appraised by Josiah Todd, Francis Cooper and Phillip Miller. (I) Jul. 23, 1814.
(61) William McCully, Bonhomme Township, has taken up a

(St. Louis County, Missouri Continued)
bay horse. The value of the horse was appraised at $8 by John Johns and and David Hartt. (JP)Daniel B. Moore, (I) May 4, 1816.

(62) A dark sorrel mare was taken up William Bates. The mare was assigned a value by Joseph Andrews and G. E. Wilson. (I) Aug. 16, 1820, (I) J. Rankin.

(63) Nicholas Belcour, living on the River des Peres, has taken up a dark sorrel mare. The seven year old animal was valued at $40 by Starling Nuckolas and Julius Emmonds. (I) Oct. 2, 1818, (JP) Augustus Storrs.

(64) Clayton Hinton, Labadie Township, took up a bay horse. (I) Apr. 4, 1812, (JP) James Stephens.

(65) At Pt. Labadie Township, Benjamin Heatherly took up a bay horse. The horse was given a value of $22.50 by Zachariah Sullens and Thomas Reynolds. (I) Aug. 31, 1816.

(66) A three year old sorrel mare was took up by William Hamilton, Bonhomme Township. The mare's appraisal of $26 was made by Edward Young, Alex. McCourtney, and George Staught. (I) Nov. 13, 1818, (JP) Gabriel Long.

(67) Victer Hab offers a $15 reward for the return of a strayed mare. (I) Feb. 2, 1820.

(68) William Graham, Joachim Township, has taken up a bright bay mare. (I) Jul. 3, 1813, (JP) James McCollock.

(69) A dark bay horse was taken up by Samuel Gilbert, St. Ferdinand Township. The horse's appraisal of $50 was made by Isaac E. Robertson and Amos Wheeler. (I) Mar. 8, 1817.

(70) A bay horse was taken up by William Dowing, Bonhomme Township. The horse's value of $25 was given by John Kinkaid and Samuel Hibler. (I) Feb. 26, 1814.

(71) Francis Deroin took up a bay horse valued at $40. (I) Dec. 4, 1813.

(72) George Horine, Joachim Township, offers a reward of $10 for a stray horse. (I) Oct. 12, 1816.

(73) A five year old bay mare was taken up by Ephraim Jamison, Pt. Labadie Township. Elisha Kimbra and Thomas Hany valued the mare at $30. (JP) John Burchard. (I) Jan. 30, 1818.

(74) Near Morgan's Saline on the Meramec, Thomas Keetly's bay horse was stolen or strayed. A reward of $10 is offered for its safe return.

(75) Near McDonald's Horse Mill, James W. Lewis took up a bay horse. Joseph Doughty and Robert Martin were the appraisers. (I)Dec. 9, 1819,(JP)Tho. R. Musick.

(St. Louis County, Missouri Continued)
- (76) Zaccheus Moore, living on the Meramec, has taken up a sorrel horse. (I) Jun. 30, 1819, (JP) Thomas Sappington.
- (77) Robert Ramsay, St. Louis Township, has taken up a bay mare. (I) Oct. 10, 1812.
- (78) An eleven year old sorrel horse was taken up by Leonard Reed, Bonhomme Township. The horse's value was appraised at $30.50 by John Withington and John Young. (I) Aug. 1, 1817, (JP) Daniel B. Moore.
- (79) Jacob Seelye, St. Ferdinand Township, has taken up two horses. The appraisers were A. V. Carr, John McDowell, and Ch. Stewart. (I) Jun. 23, 1819, (JP) A. Stewart.
- (80) A nine year old black horse was taken up by Jacob Shoults, Joachim Township. The horse was appraised at $40 by Levi Teal and George Sipp. (JP) Caleb Bowles, (I) Apr. 27, 1816.
- (81) George Smirl, Joachim Township, has taken up a bay horse. The appraisers were by Hugh McCullocl and Francis Walls. (I)Jul. 11, 1811,(JP)Jas. McCullock.
- (82) John Bacon has taken up two horse. George Faris and and Thomas Keely were the appraisers. (JP) Absalom E. Hunt, (I) Sep. 22, 1819.
- (83) John Cole, Bonhomme Township, has taken up a sorrel horse. The horse was appraised at $25 by Joseph Neill and William Cole. (I) Dec. 18, 1822, (JP) Hartley Lanham.
- (84) William Erinnes has taken up two mares. The animals were valued at $50 by William Williams and St. Amant Michau. (I) Oct. 20, 1819, (JP) J. Rankin.
- (85) Patsey Barton, Bonhomme, has taken up a roan horse. The horse was appraised at $35 by Uri Musick and David McDowell. (I) Feb. 9, 1820, John S. Ball,clk.
- (86) Sefronia Chauvin, Bonhomme Township, has taken up a brown gelding. The gelding's value was ssigned at $45 by Henry Walton and David Musick. (JP) John S. Ball, (I) Jan. 9, 1822.
- (87) Living on the Mermac, David Cornwall has taken up a pair of oxen. The oxen were valued at $30 by El. Beebe and Stephen Mapes. (I) Dec. 30, 1815.
- (88) In St. Ferdinand Township, William Denny has taken up a bay horse. The horse was appraised at $30 by Samuel Gilbert and John McGee. (I) Mar. 15, 1817.
- (89) Nathaniel Bacon, Bonhomme Township, has taken up a black mare. The mare was valued at $10 by Michael Sin and John Miller. (I) Apr. 10, 1818, (JP)Gabriel Long.
- (90) Gabriel Constant, Carondelet, has taken up a horse.

(St. Louis County, Missouri Continued)
Philip Rocheblave and Robert Patton appraised the horse at $18. (I) Mar. 1, 1817.

(91) Joseph Ink has taken up a horse. (I) Feb. 11, 1815, (JP) Biel Farnsworth.

(92) Benjamin James took up an eight year old strawberry roan horse. The horse was appraised at $52.50 at Ephraim Musick, Robert Musick and Thomas Withinton. (I) Oct. 8, 1814.

(93) Thomas Keatly, Joachim Township, has taken up a sorrel horse. The horse was appraised at $45 by George Sip and Joseph Sip. (I) Mar. 22, 1817,(JP)C. Bowles.

(94) Benjamin Johnston, jr., living on Little Rock Creek in Joachim Township, has taken up a sorrel horse. The appraised value of the horse was set at $45 by Wm. Moss and David Bryant. (I) Aug. 20, 1814, (JP) B. Johnston, sr.

(95) Absalom Link, living on Fee Fee Creek, has taken up a bay mare. John Graham and Peter Jump appraised the mare at $60. (I) Oct. 28, 1815.

(96) Antoine Lucier, at Carondelet, took up a sorrel mare. The mare was appraised by Paulet de Gardin and Francois Clement. (I) Nov. 23, 1816, (JP) J. Charless.

(97) James McCormack has taken up a gray mare. The mare was appraised at $25 by Hugh McCormick and Elihu Strockland. (I) Apr. 25, 1821, (JP) Orsanius J. Belknap.

(98) Theophilus McKinnon, Bonhomme Township, has taken up a mare and two colts. The animals were valued at $40 by Langston Bacon and James Richey. Another five year old mare mare was appraised at $20 by George Farris and James Richey. (I) Apr. 22, 1815.

(99) Joseph Menard found a stray horse on the Meremack near Saline. (I) Aug. 2, 1810.

(100) John Pepper, Bonhomme Township, has taken up a bay horse. (I) Jan. 31, 1821, (JP) Hartley Lanham.

(101) Margaret Quick, living a Carey's Saline, St. Louis Township,has taken up a red sorrel mare about eight or nine years old. (I) Nov. 8, 1820, (JP) Thomas Sappington.

(102) William M. Fullerton, Pt. Labadie Township, has taken up a bay horse. The appraisers were Kinkead Caldwell and Hugh Barclay. (I) Jul. 24, 1818, (JP) John Burchard.

(103) David Bailey on the Merrimac has taken up a white horse about seventeen years old. The horse was valued at $20. (I)Aug. 2, 1817,(JP)Tho. Sappington.

(St. Louis County, Missouri Continued)
- (104) Langston Bacon has taken up a bay horse. The horse valued at $8. (I) Feb. 3, 1816, (JP) Gabriel Long.
- (105) John Caldwell, living at Gravois, has taken up a sorrel mare. (I) Oct. 25, 1817,(JP)Tho. Sappington.
- (106) William Baxley, living at Musick's Horse Mill, is offering a reward of $15 for the return of a stray horse. (I) Sep. 25, 1818.
- (107) James Glenn, living on the Mattese, has taken up a gray horse. (I) Jul. 10, 1818, (JP) T. Sappington.
- (108) Jonathan Helderbrand has taken up a bay horse. The horse was appraised at $30 by John McGee and Joshua Blair. (I) May 4, 186.
- (109) Elizabeth Horn, near the mouth of the Merrimack, has taken up some cattle. (I) Jan. 15, 1819, (JP)T. Sappington.
- (110) Robert Jeffries, St. Ferdinand Township, has taken a black mare. David Deggs, Green Dewitt, and William Jamison give the mare an appraised value of $25. (I) Jun. 1, 1816.
- (111) Benjamin Johnston, jr., Joachim Township, has taken up a sorrel horse. (I) Jun. 3, 1815, (JP)J. Rankin.
- (112) John Johns, Joachim Township, has taken up a five year old sorrel mare. The mare was appraised at $25 by Thomas Johns, Henry Scogins and Daniel G. More. (I) Aug. 17, 1816.
- (113) James Kegans has taken up a gray horse. The horse was appraised at $25 by James McDonald and James Stark. (I) Sep. 13, 1817, (JP) Jesse McDonald.
- (114) Gabriel Long, Bonhomme Township, has taken up a bay gelding. (I) Jan. 18, 1812, (JP) Richard Caulk.
- (115) Richard Low, on the Grand Glaize, has taken up a bay horse. (I) Jun. 30, 1819, (JP) Tho. Sappington.
- (116) Archibald McDonald, St. Ferdinand Township, took up a bay mare. The mare was valued at $40 by Lewis Musick, Barnabas Harris and Richard Sappinton. (I) Jan. 18, 1812.
- (117) John W. McGirk, on the St. John River, Labadie Township, has taken up a bay mare. The appraisers were James Brown, Hartley Sappington and Josiah Todd. Oct. 31, 1812.
- (118) William Myres, St. Ferdinand Township, took up two horse. The appraisers were Alexander Ellison and Sampson Furr. (I) Nov. 30, 1816.
- (119) Lafayette de Ramsey, Joachim Township, has taken up six year old sorrel mare. (I) Dec. 2, 1819, (JP) James McCullock.
- (120) Joel Rowley, near Bellefontaine, took up a seven year old brown horse. The horse was appraised at a

(St. Louis County, Missouri Continued)
value of $22 by George Kelly and Jonas Miles.
(I) Feb. 3, 1816.

(121) Samuel Bay, on Fee Fee Creek, has taken up a seven year old brown mare. Samuel Webster, Tincher Trusty and Josiah S. Maley appraised the mare at $7.
(I) Aug. 9, 1817, (JP) Thomas Musick.

(122) Daniel Bell, Bonhomme Township, has taken up an eight year old bay horse. The value of the horse given at $30 by Nathaniel Bacon and Francis Wadley.
(I) Mar. 10, 1819, (JP) William Long.

(123) John C. Benedict, Joachim Township, has taken up a sorrel mare. (I) Oct. 21, 1815, (JP) J. Rankin.

(124) James Benton, Big Rover Township, has taken up a three year old iron-gray mare. (I) Dec. 18, 1813, (JP) James McCollock.

(125) Near Lafon's Lick on the Grand Glaize, Josiah Bowen is offering a reward of $5 for the safe return of a large bay horse. (I) Dec. 25, 1813.

(126) John Breeding, Pt. Labadie Township, has taken up a bay horse. The appraisers were William Greenstreet and John Nickles. (I)Nov. 2, 1816,(JP)James Kegans.

(127) Jacques Brunette, St. Louis Township, has taken up a six year old black mare. The mare was given an appraised value of $25 by Alexander McClound and George Shultz. (I) Jan. 27, 1816.

(128) Robert Buchanan has taken up a bay mare. The mare was assigned a value of $35 by Thomas Lee and John Bailey. (I) Feb. 8, 1817.

(129) Robert Emerson, St. Ferdinand Township, has taken up a black and white spotted cow. The cow's value was appraised at $13 by George Kelly and Nathan Ramsey. (I) Jan. 27, 1816.

(130) Thomas Williams, Joachim Township, has taken up a five year old dun horse. The horse was given a value of $35. (I) Apr. 26, 1817,(JP)Benj. Johnston.

(131) Nicholas Long, Bonhomme Township, has taken up a six year old bay mare. James Long, Eben Terril, and Moses Bonham appraised the mare at $40.
(I) Oct. 27, 1819.

(132) John Wentel Engel, St. Ferdinand Township, took up a bay horse. The animal was appraised at $27 by Benjamin Quick and James Quick. (I) Apr. 4, 1812.

(133) At the mouth of the Mermac, Melsor Fine took up a bay horse. (I) Jan. 19, 1820, (JP) C. Bowles.

(134) Phillip Fine has taken up a six or seven year old bay mare and a ten year old brown horse. The value of both animals together was set at $35. (JP)Thomas Sappington, (I) Mar. 7, 1821.

(St. Louis County, Missouri Continued)
- (135) Archibald Harbison, on the Meramac, has taken up a gray horse. (I) Jul. 5, 1820, (JP) Tho. Sappington.
- (136) Benjamin Heatherly has taken up a bay mare. Simon Bacon, John Sullen and Caleb Baley appraised the horse at $22.50. (I) Jan. 1, 1819, (JP)J. McDonald.
- (137) Jonathan Helderbrand, on the Merrimac, has taken up a bay horse. (I) Oct. 19, 1816, (JP) J. Rankin.
- (138) Eliz. Horn has taken up two horse. (I)Apr. 14,1819, (JP) T. Sappington.
- (139) Edward Horryman, St. Ferdinand Township, has taken up a bay mare. The mare was appraised at $21 by Green Dewitt and Wm. Jemison. (I) Feb. 15, 1817, (JP) S. Magill.
- (140) Joseph James, St. Ferdinand Township, has taken up a bay horse. The horse was appraised at $10 by John Burk and John Porter. (I) Feb. 10, 1816.
- (141) Hugh Jameson, on the Gravois, has taken up a sorrel chestnut horse. (I) Dec. 15, 1819, (JP) Thomas Sappington.
- (142) Theophilus McKinnon has taken up two mares. The appraisers were Edward Young, Richard Gentry, and James Ritchie. (I) Apr. 24, 1818, (JP)Gabirel Long.
- (143) Andrew McQuitty, Bonhomme Township, has taken up four horses. (I) Mar. 26, 1814, (JP) Gabriel Long.
- (144) Henry Walton took up a bay horse on the road from St. Louis to St. Charles. Joseph Walton and Tincher Trusty valued the horse at $25. (I) Nov. 23, 1816, (JP) Thomas Musick.
- (145) Andrew McQuitty took up a five year old bay horse. The horse was appraised at $50 by Thomas Cunningham and Thomas Lewis. (I) Jan. 27, 1816.

Platte County, Missouri, Marriages, 1838 - 1839..

Groom	Bride	Date
John A. Ewell	Eliza Hounshell	Mar. 21, 1839
James Drake	Jane Mullikin	May 16, 1839
Jesse Yocum	Sarah Jane Finch	Feb. 7, 1839
John Burgin	Sally Ann Holladay	May 26, 1839
William T. Huffman	Martha Smith	Jan. 10, 1839
Edward Johnson	Margaret Routh	Jan. 8, 1839
George W. Smith	Sally Gentry	Dec. 27, 1838
Simon H. Wilson	Matilda Collier	Apr. 10, 1839
William N. Borden	Martha Adamson	May 15, 1839
Albert T. Norman	Minerva S. Hays	Feb. 26, 1839
Benjamin R. Morton	Sarah Jane Hunt	Jun. 13, 1839
Thomas Whitehead	Eliz. Rebecca Dowel	Mar. 21, 1839
Anthony Armenter	Polly Biddy	Jun. 23, 1839
Richard Walker	Elizabeth Hamilton	Jul. 27, 1839

(Platte County, Missouri Continued)

Groom	Bride	Date
Alexander Holkenburgh	Abigale Cargale	May 15, 1839
Joshua D. Armstrong	Elizabeth Boilston	Jun. 27, 1839
Alvis Kimsey	Casey Simpson	May 29, 1839
Benjamin F. Simpson	Eliza Jane Wisdom	May 28, 1839
William C. Bolton	Nancy Ann Canady	May 19, 1839
Joseph Harley	Rhoda Lewis	May 30, 1839
David Hunt	Ann Todd	Aug. 1, 1839
William J. Martin	Harriett Crobarger	Aug. 22, 1839
John Kirkpatrick	Jane Mainer	Sep. 4, 1839
Ransom Butler	Eliza Ann Elkins	Oct. 29, 1839
*John Younger	Polly Johnson	Sep. 17, 1839

*(Groom of Buchanan County.)

Groom	Bride	Date
John R. Clarke	Mary Collet	Oct. 8, 1839
Levi Pilkington	Margaret Jones	Aug. 25, 1839
Samuel T. Mason	Susannah Burns	Sep. 18, 1839
William Moore	Elizabeth Wilson	Jul. 4, 1839
Elijah Flanry	Tabitha Brook	Oct. 3, 1839
William S. Murphy	Nancy Jones	Sep. 10, 1839
James Lot Drummonds	Sarah Williams	Nov. 6, 1839
John Cox	Sarah Ann Mathews	Oct. 9, 1839
James Smith	Eliza Daniel	Aug. 17, 1839
Harrison Groves	Sary Ann McLain	Sep. 3, 1839
Henry Ammons	Isabel Johnson	Nov. 8, 1839
Charles B. McMillan	Mary Jane Hunter	Nov. 3, 1839
Drewry Fletcher	Eliza E. Yates	Sep. 5, 1839
Jacob Baker	Mahala Shackleford	Dec. 17, 1839
Colby Findley	Sarah Hensley	Sep. 16, 1839
Elisy Allen	Charlotte Givins	Nov. 28, 1839
Peter Coppenbarger	Nancy Mathis	Dec. 12, 1839
Jonathan Owen	Elizabeth Murphy	Dec. 5, 1839
Richard Jacks	Catherina Powell	Oct. 17, 1839
Rich. Bohannon Endicott	Disa Cartwright	Aug. 13, 1839
Henry Watts	Nancy G. Wilson	Jul. 11, 1839
Wilson Linn	Serelda Pearson	Dec. 4, 1839
Pinkston W. Pearson	Eliza Ann Lewis	Jul. 22, 1839
John H. Winston	Elizabeth Tibbs	Dec. 4, 1839
Andrew J. Gilliam	Sarah F. Clay	Dec. 12, 1839

Supporters of the Louisiana Academy, Carter's Papers, Vol. XIV, July 29, 1807.

Walter Fenwick, John Scott, Aaron Elliot, E. Fenwick, B. C. Farrar, Joseph Spencer, jr., Thos. Fenwick, Joseph Brown, George Bullit, John Hawkins, Thomas Oliver, Joshua Penniman, Otho Shrader, Francis Valle, A. Bird, Piere Faloner, Josiah Millard, John Valle, Robert Wescott, John McArthur, William Mathers, John H. Weber, Daniel Vaughn, Henry Pinkley, John A. Jones, Abraham Newfield, J. Donnahue, Andrew Henry, John

(Supporters of the Louisiana Academy Continued)
Perry, William Bates, A. McNair, John B.C. Lucas, Jh. Vital, Thos. F. Reddick, J.V. Garnier, Joseph Tucker,William James, William Hinksen, Gideon W. Treat, John Stuart, Elisha Ellis, John Whittlesey, Wm. Montgomery, Nat. Pope, John Donnahue, --- Pratt, J.S.J. Bauvais, Joseph Pratt, Pierre Daquet, Aug. Chouteau, Anri Dills, M. Gorouard, L. Buat, Widow Moreau, J. Range, J.M. LaGrand, Widow Parent, J. Bossiere, John Pauley, P. Detchmondy, Edward Cheatham, William Strother, William H. Ashley, John Burk, H. Dodge, Robert Hinkson, J. Austin, E. Hempstead, Will. C. Carr, Frederick Bates, Rufus Easton, J. Bte. Valle, Jno. Campbell, Michael Jones, Elias Bates, Danl. Phelps, Richard J. Bibb, Jas. Bryan, Dudley R. Tinker, Jos. Boring, Nathl. Cook, Robert Terry, --- Lalemendier, Amable Partoney, Widow Valle, Julien Ratte, F. Leclere, A. Obichon, T. Tomier, F. Janis, Widow Bolduc, E. Bolduc, P. Range, L. Lasous, James Maxwell.

<u>Runaway Spouses, Slaves and Bad Debts, St. Louis Missouri Gazette.</u>

My wife Polly has eloped from my bed without just cause. I will no longer be responsible for any of her debts. Thomas Beaver. (I) Aug. 17, 1808.

My wife Lucinda has absconded from my bed without just cause. I will not pay any debts of her contracting. John Brownson, Fort Osage. (I) Sep. 12, 1811.

I wish to inform the public, that I will not pay a note of hand given to Joseph Moore. (I) Jun. 21, 1810.

Reward $50. A negro man that is the property of Josiah McClanahan has ranaway. He goes by the name of Shibboleth. Brookens Cole. (I) May 18, 1816.

My wife Emily has left my bed and board without just cause. I will no longer pay any debts of her contracting. Paulet DeJardin. (I) Jan. 2, 1822.

I wish to forewarn the public that I will not pay a note given to Michael Dod, Illinois Territory, in 1810. James Fugate. (I) Aug. 24, 1816.

I wish to forewarn the public against trading for or taking assignments against a note given to Joshua Davis. I will not pay said note. (I) Jul. 28, 1819.

My wife Elizabeth has absconded from my bed and board without just cause. I will no longer pay any debts of her contracting. John Keithley, St. Charles (I) Dec. 1, 1819.

Margaret McGinnis wishes to hear from anyone that may have information regarding her husband Edward. She believes that he may be somewhere near the Ohio River.(I)Jun. 5,1821.

My wife Sarah has left my bed without just cause. I will no longer by responsible for debts of her contracting. Chas. Menees, St. Charles. (I) Aug. 2, 1808.

(Runaway Spouses, Slaves and Bad Debts Continued)

Will all those indebted, please come forward and settle your account. David Musick. (I) Aug. 9, 1810.

Reward One Cent. My apprentice Andrew Murphy has runaway. John Chandler, Potosi. (I) May 18, 1816.

I wish to foreward the public against taking assignments against or accepting a bond given to Jacob Boyse. Said bond was fraudulently obtained and I will no pay. Francis Pelham. (I) Jul. 11, 1812.

The goods, debts and porperty of the firm of Catherwood & Rankin are hereby assigned to Robert Rankin. Hugh Rankin. (I) Aug. 9, 1820.

Andrew Henry, Ste. Genevieve, has filed suit to foreclose on a mortgage payable by Amos Roark. (I) Dec. 21, 1808.

John Seelye claims bankruptcy. (I) Jul. 17, 1813.

My wife Doratha has left my bed without just cause.I will no longer be responsible for debts of her contracting. Saml. Smiley. (I) Dec. 6, 1817.

My negress Sukey has runaway from me at Ste. Genevieve. I believe that she will head for either Natchez or Kentucky. Nathaniel Sullivan, St. Louis. (I) Oct. 3, 1811.

James B. Thompson claims bankruptcy. (I) Jun. 27, 1821.

There is a reward of $10 offered for the return of my runaway negro Lewis. W. Tharp. (I) Dec. 28, 1816.

Melvin Vinings claims bankruptcy. (I) Nov. 1, 1817.

Will those indebts, please come forward and settle their accounts. John Ward. (I) Dec. 30, 1815.

I wish to inform the public against trading for or taking assignments against a note given to John and William Bown for some property of the Grand Osage. They did not own said property. James Williams. (I) May 3, 1817.

James Wright claims bankruptcy. (I) Jan. 23, 1818.

I wish to warn the public against accepting notes from my wife Sally as she took them without my permission. Calvin Adams. (I) Jun. 21, 1810.

Coonrod Ashman claims bankruptcy. (I) Sep. 13, 1820.

I wish to forewarn the public against accepting a note given to Beaty and Adam Johns for land on the St. Francois River. I will not pay said note. Jos. Beaty.(I)Sep.27,1817.

Jacques Baunou claims bankruptcy. (I) May 9, 1812.

Claude Boyer of Washinton County wishes to inform the public that he is bankrupt. (I) Sep. 2, 1815.

I wish all my debtors to come forward and pay as I am going to Kentucky to purchase leather. John A. Bright. (I) Feb, 15, 1812.

Sebastian Butcher, Ste. Genevieve, has filed suit againt Henry Peterson to foreclose on a mortgage. (I) Nov. 5, 1814.

Will all those indebted, please come foreward and settle their accounts. George Casner. (I) 27, 1818.

(Runaway Spouses, Slaves and Bad Debts Continued)

My wife Nancy has left my bed without just cause. I will not pay her debts. Dr. Solomon Cesner. (I) Jun. 17, 1815.

John Cummins claims bankruptcy. (I) May 10, 1817.

I will no longer pay any debts contracted by my wife Mary as she has left my bed and board without just cause. J. Glass, Bellefontaine. (I) Aug. 5, 1811.

Lewis Newell claims bankruptcy. (I) Jul. 25, 1821.

P. Pemberton claims bankruptcy. (I) Aug. 4, 1819.

Will all my debtors, please come forward and pay as I am leaving the territory. C. M. Price, (I) May 25, 1816.

William Risley claims bankruptcy. (I) Feb. 10, 1819.

I wish to forewarn the public against trading for a note given to Robert Shackleford. I will not pay said note. John Gudgins, New Madrid. (I) Mar. 9, 1816.

Randall Allis claims bankruptcy. (I) Aor. 25, 1821.

I want to forewarn the public against accepting note given to Henry Robison, St. Charles. He obtained said notes in a fraudulent, low and dirty manner. James Beatty. (I) May 22, 1813.

John Rogers, Ste. Genevieve County, claims bankruptcy. (I) Apr. 19, 1817.

I. Septlivres claims bankruptcy. (I) Jun. 30, 1813.

Will all my debtors, please come forward and settle their accounts. Christian Smith. (I) Oct. 5, 1816.

Francois Aroite claims bankruptcy. (I) May 9, 1812.

William Blair claims bankruptcy. He will meet with his creditors at the home of Solomon Dally, Mine-a-Breton. (I) Oct. 15, 1814.

George W. Ferguson claims bankruptcy. (I) Sept. 13, 1820.

My wife Mary has left my bed without just cause. I will not pay any debts of her making. Angis Gillis.(I)Apr.27,1816.

John Howard, Ste. Genevieve went bankrupt.(I)May 28,1814.

My wife Lercille Ornooce has left my bed without just cause. I will no longer be held responsible for her debts. Joseph Leman. (I) Jul. 28, 1819.

Robert McClelan went bankrupt. (I) May 29, 1813.

David H. Nolan claims bankruptcy. (I) Aug. 22, 1821.

Michael Roberts went bankrupt. (I) Sep. 23, 1820.

There is a reward offered for the return of my two runaway negroes Harry and Anthony. A.Rutgers.(I)Aug.22,1811.

I am seeking information on Daniel Fobes, who went to New Orleans from Alabama in 1819. Moses Smith. (I) Jun. 5, 1821.

John P. Adenne, Ste. Genevieve, claims bankruptcy. (I) Nov. 28, 1810.

There is a reward of $10 offered for the return of my negro boy Levi. Alexander Alleson. (I) Jun. 8, 1816.

Alexis Bruno, St. Louis, went bankrupt. (I) Oct. 11,1810.

Joseph Hebert claims bankruptcy. (I) May 9, 1812.

(Runaway Spouses, Slaves and Bad Debts Continued)

John McFarlane went bankrupt. (I) Jun. 13, 1812.

My wife Catherine has left my bed without just cause. I will no longer be responsible for debts of her contracting. John Meara. (I) Apr. 11, 1821.

Alfred Moor claims bankruptcy. (I) Sep. 13, 1820.

I am leaving St. Louis for a period of two years. I ask that all my creditors, please come foreward and settle their accounts. Charles Nolen. (I) Aug. 5, 1815.

Laurent Ride claims bankruptcy. (I) Oct. 8, 1814.

James Steen went bankrupt. (I) Oct. 19, 1816.

My wife Nelly has left my bed without just cause. I will no longer be repsonsible for debts of her contracting. Wm. Thomson. (I) Mar. 8, 1809.

J. Jones claims bankruptcy. (I) Feb. 14, 1821.

Larking P. Richardson, Bonhomme Township, wishes to inform the public against accepting or trading for a note given to Ignatius Anderson. (I) Mar. 1, 1817.

Antoine Roy claims bankruptcy. (I) Jun. 27, 1812.

Joseph Seigvion went bankrupt. (I) Oct. 16, 1813.

My wife Rebecca has left my bed without just cause. I will not be responsible for debts of her contracting. James Anderson. (I) May 30, 1811.

Moses Austin claims bankruptcy. (I) Mar. 15, 1820.

Pierre Bourdeau went bankrupt. (I) Aug. 3, 1816.

My accounts are in the hands of Caleb, Cox & Co. Samuel G. J. DeCamp. (I) Oct. 30, 1822.

Phineas Bartlett claims bankruptcy. (I) Jul. 5, 1820.

I want to forewarn the public against accepting a note given to Hart Fellows. I will not pay said note. Joseph Johnson. (I) Dec. 12, 1821.

Thomas J. McGuire claims bankruptcy. (I) May 12, 1819.

I want to forewarn the public against trading for a note given to Stephen Mires. Samuel Hodges. (I) Sep. 30, 1815.

Charles A. Hinkley went bankrupt. (I) Jun. 27, 1821.

I have a saddle and bridle in my possession which were found in the possession of the thief that stole my horse. Will the owners of these items, please come forward. David Hughes. (I) May 26, 1819.

Godfrey Beaujenoie went bankrupt. (I) Sep. 13, 1820.

The is a reward for the return of my runaway apprentice James Moore. George Gromes. (I) Oct. 10, 1812.

Raudolph Haverstick claims bankruptcy. (I) Jan. 30, 1813.

I want to inform the public, that I have left St. Louis without paying my debts. Jacob Hinkle. (I) Nov. 30, 1808.

I want to inform the public that I will not pay a note given to Aaron Criss. P. Bartlett. (I) Oct. 15, 1814.

Leroy Elliott claims bankruptcy. (I) May 2, 1812.

Archibald Huden went bankrupt. (I) May 5, 1819.

(Runaway Spouses, Slaves and Bad Debts Continued)

I want to forewarn the public against accepting a note given to James Coleman of Kentucky. I will not pay said note. Peter Journey. (I) Jan. 24, 1811.

Benjamin LaChance claims bankruptcy. (I) Dec. 22, 1819.

I wish to inform the public not to trade or accept a note given to Rosanna Nash, St. Ferdinand Township, St. Louis Co. John Angle, sr. (I) Mar. 13, 1813.

Jacques Feilteau, St. Charles County, claims bankruptcy. (I) Sep. 4, 1818.

Joseph Kaufman went bankrupt. (I) Jul. 25, 1821.

I want to forewarn the public against taking assignments or accepting for a note given to John McKinney, Bourbon Co., Kentucky. Philip Bell. (I) Dec. 14, 1816.

Paul Bezel went bankrupt. (I) Jun. 23, 1809.

My wife Nancy has left my bed without just cause. I will not be responsible for any debts of her making. Toussaint Couzeneau. (I) Nov. 20, 1822.

In St. Charles, Jos. Bievenu went bankrupt. (I) Jun. 14, 1809.

My apprentice John Cusake has runaway. He squints and is a very turbulent person. There is a reward offered for his return. J. Bouju. (I) May 8, 1818.

Robert Faris claims bankruptcy. (I) Sep. 29, 1819.

I believe that Richard Davis stole my negro woman Ginny. However some of my friends say that Richard Davis was lying about the matter. Eramus Ellis. (I) May 24, 1809.

Jonathan Hill went bankrupt. (I) May 24, 1820.

My wife Elizabeth has left my bed without just cause. She absconded with her half-brother from Ste. Genevieve, John Robinson. I will no longer be responsible for any debts of her contracting. Michael Hart. (I) Jan. 31, 1821.

John Hayward went bankrupt. (I) Jun. 26, 1818.

Francois Jourdan dit Labross went bankrupt. (I) Dec. 1, 1819.

I am planning to leave the country for some time. I have left my accounts in the hands of Josiah Millard. I give him clear acquittance and mutual dissolve and power to collect all notes and accounts. John H. McGinnis. (I) Oct. 5, 1808.

William H. Mosher went bankrupt. (I) Mar. 27, 1818.

Lavina Richardson is listed as a pauper on the Howard County expenses. (I) Nov. 27, 1818.

Jas. Scott, Ste. Genevieve went bankrupt. (I) Jul. 18, 1812.

Will all those indebted, please come forward and settle theirs accounts. William Shannon. (I) Aug. 16, 1810.

Resin Webster claims bankruptcy. (I) Jun. 25, 1810.

T.P. Williams went bankrupt. (I) Oct. 11, 1820.

William Janes went bankrupt. (I) Jul. 19, 1820.

I am not responsible for the expenses of the land and grist mill owned in partnership with John McCane. Adam Brown. (I) Feb. 15, 1815.

(Runaway Spouses, Slaves and Bad Debts Continued)

A parcel containing due bills and money was stolen from the subscriber. One of the bills was in favor of my brother Bernard. Patrick McGinn. (I) Aug. 2, 1820.

Nathan Mills claims bankruptcy. (I) Jan. 31, 1821.

I want to testify that Lydia Hensly willingly signed a note to William Thompson. Stephen Best. (I) Apr. 20, 1816.

Antoine Bizette went bankrupt. (I) Mar. 12, 1814.

I am leaving on October the 10th. Will all my creditors please present their bills. James C. Cummins.(I)Sep.11,1822.

Francis Deroin claims bankruptcy. (I) Jul. 12, 1820.

John Rice lost a note which was given to Nicholas Vail by Thomas English. (I) Jan. 23, 1822.

My wife Phoebe alias Smith has left my bed and board. I will no longer be responsible for debts of her contracting. John Grist. (I) Dec. 15, 1819.

Benjamin Jaquis went bankrupt. (I) Aug. 22, 1821.

My wife Mary has left my bed without just cause. I will not pay her debts. Joel Lassiter. (I) Jun. 15, 1816.

James McCoy claims bankruptcy. (I) Mar. 27, 1818.

Will all those indebted to the firm of Bates & McDonald, please come forward and pay. William McDonald, Herculaneum, surviving partner. (I) Oct. 23, 1822.

Joseph Nevett went bankrupt. (I) Jul. 25, 1821.

I wish to forewarn the public against paying John C. Potter any monies due Potter & Phelan until the affairs of the firm are settled. James C. Phelan. (I) Jul. 14, 1819.

Joshua Blair claims bankruptcy. (I) Aug. 9, 1809.

I want to forewarn the public against trading for a note in the amount of $400 to be paid in horses, given by me to George H. Daugherty. Unless compelled by law, I will not pay said note. John Bloom. (I) Nov. 30, 1808.

William Brown claimed bankruptcy. (I) Feb. 4, 1815.

Fleming Cox went bankrupt. (I) Aug. 8, 1812.

My wife Mary Ann has left me without just cause. I will not pay any debts of her contracting. Isaac Cottle, Lower Cuivre Township, St. Charles County. (I) Apr. 17, 1818.

Paul M. Gebert went bankrupt. (I) Jul. 25, 1821.

John P. Gates claims bankruptcy. (I) Apr. 13, 1816.

I want to testify that Lydia Hensly willingly signed a note to William Thompson. Sinclair Griffin. (I) Apr.20,1816.

John Hawthorn,Ste. Genevieve is insolvent.(I)Sep.13,1810.

Pierre Kenish went bankrupt. (I) Mar. 14, 1812.

Calis Montardy claims bankruptcy. (I) Jun. 23, 1819.

Benjamin Plank went bankrupt. (I) Jul. 19, 1817.

I am seeking information on my two runaway slaves. Wm. Rayan, Washington County. (I) Feb. 22, 1817.

Louis Roy claims bankruptcy. (I) Jul. 25, 1821.

John B. N. Smith went bankrupt. (I) Jul. 25, 1821.

(Runaway Spouses, Slaves and Bad Debts Continued)

My wife Ester has left me without just cause. I will not be responsible for her debts. Frederick Weber.(I)Jul.2,1814.

Amos Williams went bankrupt. (I) Nov. 1, 1817.

The is a reward offered for the return of my apprentice Amant Biron. J. Bouju, Potosi. (I) Nov. 2, 1816.

George Casner wants to inform the public that he is now insolvent. (I) Apr. 2, 1813.

Nicholas Sipher went bankrupt. (I) Mar. 15, 1817.

I want to forewarn the public against taking assignments or trading for a note given by me to James Dotson. I will not pay said note. Wm. Boron, St. Charles. (I) Jun. 2,1819.

John Dooling, Ste. Genevieve, wants to inform the public that he is now insolvent. (I) Jul. 9, 1814.

My wife Nancy has left me without just cause. I will not be responsible for her debts. John Edds, Byrge Crk.,Missouri Territory. (I) Jan. 11, 1817.

E. Fenwick went bankrupt. (I) Jun. 20, 1812.

Thomas Fryer claims bankruptcy. (I) Nov. 1, 1820.

Jonathan Ditch, late of Murfreeboro, Tennessee, alleges that Aaron Gilleland absconded from Kentucky with another man's wife. (I) Dec. 7, 1816.

Aaron Gilleland denies the charge made by Jonathan Ditch. (I) Dec. 7, 1816.

Joseph Grondin went bankrupt. (I) May 9, 1812.

John F. M. Heath, of Ste. Genevieve, wants to inform the public that he is now bankrupt. (I) Feb. 2, 1812.

My wife Elizabeth has left my bed without just cause. I will not pay her debts. (I) Joseph Hogan.(I)Feb. 20, 1829.

James Leslie claims bankruptcy. (I) Aug. 28, 1818.

J. McClenahan,St. Charles,went bankrupt.(I)Apr. 29,1815.

I want to inform the public against trusting my son Owen as he is under age. Michael McKenna. (I) May 24, 1820.

Elias Mills went bankrupt. (I) Jun. 14, 1810.

Fergus Moorhead went bankrupt. (I) Apr. 18, 1812.

My wife Hannah has left me and I will not pay her debts. William Patterson. (I) May 15, 1818.

Thomas Peebels went bankrupt. (I) Oct. 18, 1817.

James Pollard claims bankruptcy. (I) Jun. 18, 1814.

I want to forewarn the public against trading for land purchased by my son Thomas Johnson, jr. He used money and property that belong to his father Tho. Johnson., sr. Tho. Johnson, sr. (I) Aug. 28, 1818.

George Kenney went bankrupt. (I) Nov. 6, 1818.

Louis Lavanture claims bankruptcy. (I) May 9, 1812.

I advise buyers of lots in the town of Monroe not to pay Jacob Luckworth more than one-half the amount due. Isaac Galland. (I) Aug. 2, 1820.

N. H. Moore went bankrupt. (I) Jan. 19, 1820.

(Runaway Spouses, Slaves and Bad Debts)
Woodson Radford went bankrupt. (I) Jul. 19, 1820.
Elijah Smith went bankrupt. (I) Nov. 14, 1812.

Barry County, Missouri, Marriages, 1837 - 1839.

Groom	Bride	Date
James Smoot	Nancy Arnold	Feb. 19, 1837
George Nettle	Hannah Belshar	May 3, 1837
William Brackee	Eliza Vance	Jun. 6, 1837
Thomas Grayham	Ann Lewis	Sep. 24, 1837
John Gambell	Phenize Pallen	Sep. 7, 1837
Jacob Walton	Sophia Jinkins	Aug. 21, 1837
Anthony Anderson	Susan Evans	Aug. 18, 1837
Thomas Morse	Nancy Carleton	Aug. 31, 1837
J.C.A. Cunther	Mary Miller	Oct. 5, 1837
James M. Williams	Artela Barker	Jul. 18, 1837
William Stone	Elizabeth Sinnett	Sep. 28, 1837
Franklin Marrs	Julianna Havens	Oct. 5, 1837
Henry C. Brener	Martha Thereman	Oct. 1, 1837
J. D. Hillhouse	Nancy Gibson	Sep. 14, 1837
Nicholas W. Brownen	Mary E. Hudson	Oct. 19, 1837
R. Wisemant	Matilda Rosebury	Dec. 5, 1837
Joel H. Petty	Penelope Haddock	Dec. 7, 1837
William Brackeen	Harriet Winters	Dec. 7, 1837
Jacob Lee	Elizabeth Mills	Jan. 11, 1838
Henry Borden	Sally Price	Oct. 26, 1837
William Sherrer	Rebecca Spuegeon	Mar. 26, 1838
Robert McGehee	Eliza Bray	Mar. 25, 1838
Jonathan Billingsley	Mary Powers	Mar. 27, 1838
Joseph Carry	Mary Cerly	Jan. 7, 1838
Andrew J. Mars	Martha Danly	Oct. 10, 1837
Joel Cerley	Mary Blevins	Feb. 8, 1838
Claiborn Duvall	Harriet Miller	Mar. 25, 1838
William Reason	Matilda Norris	Jan. 28, 1838
James Hoffman	Jane Stephenspn	Feb. 25, 1838
Jacob Boiler	Ireney Scott	Jan. 31, 1838
George Beckett	Eliza Evans	Dec. 31, 1837
John Mulkey	Mary Evans	Dec. 19, 1837
John P. Ozburn	Agnes Pliver	Jan. 29, 1838
Henry Grindstaff	Abby Beckett	Feb. 15, 1838
Moes Powers	Jain Boyd	Mar. 4, 1838
Benjamin Jennings	Lucinda Jennings	Apr. 2, 1838
James Rolls	Martha Woods	May 21, 1838
Newberry Stockton	Sally Mills	Jul. 2, 1838
Abner H. Wilson	Lucy McFarland	Jul. 4, 1838
Richard Kelly	Eliza Smith	May 27, 1838
Spencer Williams	Dianna Makum	Dec. 20, 1837
William Sparlin	Susan Lee	Jun. 7, 1838
John Buzzard	Jane Spergin	Jul. 19, 1838

(Barry County, Missouri Continued)

Groom	Bride	Date
Moses I. Baker	Amanda Malugan	Jul. 22, 1838
Benjamin Sparlin	Ann Twitty	May 24, 1838
Daniel W. Craft	Eliza Prewitt	Oct. 11, 1838
George McWhaley	Mary Vivion	Dec. 7, 1837
Robert Gillock	Sarah Harper	Aug. 20, 1838
William Underhill	Catherine Mayhan	Sep. 6, 1838
Alexander McKenny	Marthy Mayhan	Sep. 17, 1838
Aaron Allen	Eliza White	Aug. 2, 1838
Thomas Nicholas	Mrs. Jane Hall	Nov. 3, 1838
Henry H. Zachary	Sarah J. Jones	Nov. 15, 1838
George Carver	Polly Bedinger	Nov. 39, 1838
Joseph Dennison	Lucinda Vermillon	Oct. 18, 1838
Abner Holloman	Permealia Dale	Dec. 27, 1838
Jonathan E. Danforth	Precilla Price	Dec. 19, 1838
John Hash	Millia Elkins	Jan. 10, 1839
Silbern K. Lee	Fanny Estes	Dec. 6, 1838
Jackson Jones	Rebecca Jones	Jan. 17, 1839
Benjamin Carpenter	Matilda Underwood	Feb. --, 1839
John Mills	Jane Pennington	Nov. 29, 1838
Samuel K. Duvatt	Celina McFarland	Dec. 25, 1838
David Taylor	Eliza Packwood	Dec. 23, 1838
John Lemmons	Spice South	Dec. 10, 1838
James G. Short	Susan Taylor	Feb. 13, 1839
William Landers	Nancy Hoover	Feb. 26, 1839
Lambert Bearden	Reaulah Gore	Feb. 17, 1839
Daniel Hutchison	Alvira Tilmon	Jan. 22, 1839
John Ingram	Verbina A. Brown	Mar. 12, 1839
Henry Stinnett	Melinda Brown	Jul. 13, 1839
Winford P. Townsend	Susan Buchanan	Aug. 2, 1839
John Isbell	Nancy Wormington	May 30, 1839
James C. Winston	Margaret W. Duncan	Oct. 10, 1839
John Allen	Emeline White	Oct. 17, 1839
David Look	Nancy Carter	Sep. 22, 1839
James Sexton	Sarah Faucher	Oct. 9, 1839

Ste. Genevieve County, Missouri, Estrays, Missouri Gazette.
   (1) William Montgomery, Big River Township, has taken up a gray horse. William Ally, Wm. Poston, and Wm. M. Perry appraised the horse at a value of $30. (I) Aug. 3, 1816.
   (2) John Burdet, St. Michael's Township, has taken up a bay mare. (JP) Jos. Moore. (I) Aug. 14, 1818.
   (3) Alexander Caldwell, St. Francois Township, took up a bay horse. (JP) William Shaw, (I) Jan. 2, 1818.
   (4) Robert Chapman, Big River Township, has taken up a bay mare valued at $25 by H.C. Anderson and Rawson Alley. (JP) Wm. Andrews, (I) Oct. 30, 1818.

(Ste. Genevieve County, Missouri Continued)
- (5) Isaac Cunningham, St. Francois Township, has taken up a sorrel horse. The horse was appraised at $35 by James Henderson and James Talent. (JP) Davis F. Marks, (I) Aug. 16, 1820.
- (6) John F. Dant, Clinque Homme Township, has taken up two horse. (JP) James Moore, (I) Jun. 29, 1816.
- (7) William Davis, Belleview Township, has taken up two colts. The appraisers were Abraham Richmond, James Huitt and Samuel Henderson. (JP) Josiah H. Bell, (I) Aug. 21, 1813.
- (8) John Eigelberger, living in Ruth Bottom, Plattin Township, has taken up a sorrel mare. The mare was appraised at $30 by James and Hardy McCormack. (JP) Peter McCormack, (I) Mar. 15, 1817.
- (9) Ezekiel Fenwick has taken up a bay horse. The horse was appraised at $10 by Thomas Dodge, Joel Waters, and John B. Janis. (I) Dec. 18, 1813.
- (10) William James, River Av Vase, has taken up two bay horses. (JP) Thomas Oliver, (I) Aug. 10, 1816.
- (11) Jesse Murphy, St. Michael Township, has taken up a bay mare. The mare was appraised at $40 by Samuel Halstead, Benj. Mabry and Isaac Burham. (JP) Laken Walker, (I) May 28, 1814.
- (12) Ezekiel Fenwick has taken up an eight year old bay horse. The animal was valued at $50 by John Scott, Louis Laffours and Joal Waters. (I) Aug. 6, 1814.
- (13) John Geather, Clinq Homme Township, has taken up a sorrel horse. (JP) Joseph Donnohue, (I) Sep. 25, 1813.
- (14) John Gilmore, Platin Township, has taken up a seven year old sorrel horse. The horse was appraised at $60 by Wm. Alexander and John A. Stugus. (JP) Peter P. McCormack, (I) Oct. 11, 1817.
- (15) John Tigert, St. Michael's Township, has taken up a strawberry roan horse. (I) Aug. 14, 1818, (JP) Jos. Moore.
- (16) John Thurston, Ste. Genevieve Township, has taken up a bay mare. The mare was valued at $20 by Wm. Cousins and Anthony O'Neil. (I) Jul. 24, 1818, (I) T. Oliver.
- (17) James Strickland, Plattin Township, has taken up a bay horse. The horse was valued at $20 by James McCormack and Godfrey Isaacs. (I) Jun. 29, 1816.
- (18) Moses Scott took up a bay horse. The appraisers were James Robison, Samuel Henderson and James Huitt. (I) Aug. 21, 1813, (I) J. H. Bell.
- (19) John Roberson, St. Michael Township, has taken up two horses. The horses were appraised by David Murphy and John Burnham. (I) Sep. 5, 1815.

Lincoln County, Missouri, Licenses, St. Charles Missourian, July 8, 1820.

Almond Cottle, tavern; Christopher Clark, tavern; Uriah J. Devore, merchant; Cary Duncan, merchant; Richard Fentum, merchant; John Geiger, merchant; David Laird, tavern; Joshua N. Robbins, merchant; Pros. K. Robbins, merchant; Henry Smith, peddler.

Franklin County, Missouri, Estrays, Beacon.
(1) William H. Anderson, John's Township, has taken up a black mare. The mare was valued at $30 by Joseph Jamison. (JP) W. Bray, (I) Apr. 13, 1829.
(2) Benjamin Coleman, Merrimac Township, has taken up a bay horse. The horse was appraised at a value of $23 by John Wickerham and Aaron Cook. (JP) John Stewart, (I) Dec. 9, 1830.
(3) William Drenon, Merrimac Township, has taken up a brown horse. Jonathan Drenon and Samuel Wilson appraised the horse at a value of $25. (JP) John Stewart, (I) Apr. 7, 1831.
(4) Philip Martin, St. John's Township, has taken up two colts. Nathan Richardson and Isaac McCormick valued the animals at $35. (I) Mar. 17, 1813, (JP) Wm. G. Owens.

Gasconade County, Missouri, Estrays, Beacon.
(1) Owen Shockley, Bowleware Township, has taken up a twelve year old brown mare. The mare was appraised at $35 by Joel Starkey and John J. Wyatt. (JP) Wm. Bumpass, (I) May 24, 1832.
(2) James Renfro took up a three year old bay mare. The mare was appraised at $30 by B. D. Yates and Uriah Shockley. (JP) Samuel Borchard, (I) Dec. 15, 1831.

Lincoln County, Missori, Estrays, Beacon.
(1) Wiley Hines, Monore Township, has taken up a three year old bay mare. The mare was appraised at $29 by A. C. Inman and Simon Stephens. (JP) Freeland Rese, (I) Jul. 1, 1830.
(2) R. Greene, of Troy, has taken up two horses. Jordan Sallee and John B. Stone valued the animals at $80. (JP) Charles Wheeler, (I) Jun. 16, 1831.
(3) Rinshun Robertson, Monroe Township, has taken up a bay filly. James Flemming and James Simpson valued the filly at $15. (JP) M. Nichols,(I)Nov. 24, 1832.
(4) Henry Evans, Benford Township, has taken up a three year old gray filly. The filly was valued at $20 by John Clark and Joseph House. (I) Nov. 11, 1830, (JP) Charles Wheeler.

(Lincoln County, Missouri Continued)
(5) Jeremiah Beck, Bedford Township, has taken up a gray mare. The appraisers were Isaac Litton and Jos. W. Gibson. (JP) Tho. Armstrong,(I)Dec.2, 1830.

Ray County, Missouri, Delinquent Tax List, 1826.

I. R. Allen, Berry S. Bayse, G. A. Bird, John Brooks, W. Caldwell, P. Cross, E. Davis, S. Dexter, Michael Dousman, J. W. Dolittle, Asa Griffith, Charles R. Hall, John Harvey, Jas. Jenkins, Chas. Johnson, T. Lewis, R. Little, Geo. McGunnigle, P. Manchester, H. Middleton, J. Miller, J.B. Morris, Charles Peck.

Moniteau County, Missouri, Advent United Church of Chirst Cemetery.

Name	Born	Died
John J. Blank	Feb. 12, 1819	Jan. 28, 1892
Margretha S. Wachter	Feb. 4, 1817	Nov. 18, 1898
Maria Katharine Burge	1808	Mar. 18, 1872
Margaretha Schaaf	Apr. 12, 1811	Mar. 12, 1868
Katharine Ziesler	Mar. 18, 1787	Oct. 24, 1867
Barbara Wolfrum	Nov. 5, 1804	Oct. 1, 1867
Johann Paulus Griesbach	Sep. 25, 1802	Dec. 12, 1865
Herman Knopker	Apr. --, 1807	Jan. 25, 1865
*Mary Herknleben		Jul. 22, 1830

*(age 22 years, 2 months, 12 days at time of death)

Name	Born	Died
Michael Gentzsch	Apr. 5, 1805	---
Nichaus Hofman	1818	Aug. 24, 1854
Anna M. Geminden	1801	Aug. 2, 1861
Jacob von Geminden	Aug. 15, 1795	Jan. 4, 1855
Ludwig Schaaf	Dec. 16, 1838	Jan. 25, 1858
Catharina Schaaf	Mar. 20, 1813	Mar. 26, 1858
John C. Wolfrum	Nov. 14, 1805	Sep. 9, 1863
Henry Bauer	1790	Jan. 8, 1875
John W. Schuster	May 2, 1833	Mar. 25, 1898
Anna Heinrich	Aug. 17, 1837	Apr. 2, 1880
Johann Griesbach	Sep. 25, 1831	May 31, 1882
Heinrich Dietzel	Feb. 3, 1814	Feb. --, 1886
George P. Krausz	Feb. 11, 1825	Oct. 4, 1893
Hanna L. Sperber	Jul. 24, 1813	Aug. 27, 1893
John F. Herfurth	1833	1892
John H. Rodel	Feb. 23, 1807	Jun. 25, 1894
Anna S. Robel	Apr. 5, 1808	Nov. 6, 1889
Johanna Dietzel	Mar. 16, 1821	Oct. 8, 1888
Karl Hoepfinger	Sep. 20, 1839	Aug. 2, 1895
Hans P. Matti	1823	1897

Johnson County, Missouri, Licenses, 1836.

James A. Gallagher, merchant and grocer; William H. and

(Johnson County, Missouri Continued)
and A. Tombs, grocer; J. H. Beatier, merchant; John Evans, grocer, Guyn Dudley, grocer.

Cole County, Missouri, Estrays, Missouri Intelligencer.
(1) William Newman, Moreau Township, has taken up a four year old sorrel mare. Edward Carter and Henry Sailing appraised the mare at $20. (JP)Hugh Gartin, (I) Jul. 29, 1825.
(2) John J. Clark, Moreau Township, has taken up a brown mare. The mare was appraised at a value of $8 by James Claybrook and Silas Charlton. (JP)Drury Davis, (I) Nov. 18, 1823.
(3) John Inglish, Moniteau Township, has taken up a bay horse. Jonathan Martin, John Williams and Abraham Kenny valued the animal at $55. (I) May 19, 1826, (JP) James Maupin.
(4) Jesse Eads, Montiteau Township, has taken up a two year old black mare. The mare was appraised at a value of $26.50 by John Miller and Thomas Murray. (JP) Joseph Inglish, (I) Jan. 7, 1823.

Ralls County, Missouri, Estrays, Missouri Intelligencer.
(1) Ezra Fox, Union Township, has taken up two horses. Both animals were valued at $40 by Elliott Willborn and Jordan Sizemore. (I) Jan. 29, 1831, (JP) Jacob Whittenburgh.
(2) William Atterberry, Union Township, has taken up an iron-gray mare. The mare was appraised at $25 by John M. Burton and Thomas Kelly. (I) Feb. 27, 1829, (JP) John Burton.
(3) William Brooks, Union Township, took up a sorrel mare valued at $30. The appraisers were Elijah Shanklin and Joseph Davis. (I) Aug. 12, 1825, (JP) John Burton.
(4) James Chitwood has taken up a black horse about ten or twelve years old. The horse was valued at $50 by Elizure D. Webster and Wm. Greathouse. (JP) Wm. Forman, (I) Apr. 30, 1831.
(5) William Patrick, Salt River Township, has taken up a bay colt. The colt was appraised at $25 by James Ivy and Richard Bryant. (I) Mar. 26, 1831, (JP) Wm. Bybee.
(6) James B. Reavis, Salt River Township, has taken up an eight year old bay horse. The horse was valued at $50 by Ben Davis and Ezra Fox. (I)Dec. 11,1830, (JP) Wm. Bybee.
(7) James Fugate, Spencer Township, has taken up a chestnut sorrel mare. The mare was appraised at a

(Ralls County, Missouri Continued)

value of $24 by Jas. Underwood and Solomon Onstott. (JP) Peter Grant, (I) Aug. 13, 1831.

(8) Robert Gary, Spencer Township, has taken up a gray mare. The mare was appraised at $47.50 by John G. Clarke and Aru Lanicle. (I) Jun. 18, 1831,(JP)Ralph D. Briscoe.

(9) David Onstott, Salt River Township, has taken up a roan mare. The mare was valued at $40 by Jonathan Abbay and Adam Utterback. (I) Aug. 13, 1831, (JP) Peter Grant.

(10) Nathaniel Riggs, Salt River Township, has taken up an iron-gray filly. The filly was appraised at $25 by Jonathan Abbay and Tinselley Lee. (JP)Wm. Bybee, (I) Mar. 26, 1831.

(11) Solomon Onstott, Spencer Township, has taken up an iron-gray mare. James Fugate and James Underwood valued the mare at $24. (I) Aug. 13, 1831,(JP)Peter Grant.

(12) George Saling, Union Township, has taken up a red roan filly. (I) Jan. 11, 1828, (JP) Henry Martin.

(13) David E. Sloan, Union Township, has taken up a bay mare. The mare was appraised at $40 by James Fox and George Fraker. (I)Feb. 5, 1830,(JP)John Burton.

(14) Jordan Sizemore, Union Township, has taken up a gray horse. The horse was apprasied at $40 by Ezra Fox and Robert Swinney. (I) Aug. 23, 1827, (JP)John Burton.

(15) Jacob Whittenburgh, Union Township, has taken up a mare. The mare was valued at $30 by Ezra Fox and Jordan Sizemore. (I) Aug. 15, 1828,(JP)John Burton.

<u>Callaway County, Missouri, Estrays, Missouri Intelligencer.</u>

(1) Thomas Davis, Cote sans Dessein Township, has taken up a sorrel mare. The mare is about ten to eleven years old and was appraised at $30 by Henry Harper and Hugh H. McGary. (I) Sep. 29, 1832, (JP) Robert Davis.

(2) Henry Moxly, Nine-Mile-Prairie Township, has taken up a roan horse. The horse was appraised at $40 by James Lawrence and David Kennaday. (I)May 21, 1826, (JP) Thomas Harrison.

(3) James Moore, Fulton Township, has taken up a sorrel horse. The horse was valued at $25 by Wm. Smart and Felix G. Nichols. (I) Jul. 31, 1830, (JP) Wm. Armstrong.

(4) Isaac P. Howe, Cedar Township, has taken up a three year old horse valued at $25 by Rbt. McKamey and Jas. Henderson. (I)Mar. 10, 1832,(JP)Horace Sheley.

(Callaway County, Missouri Continued)
- (5) Matthew Agee, Aux Vasse Township, has taken up a roan horse. The horse was valued at $18 by John Coats and A. Lomax. (I) Sep. 16, 1825, (JP) Bethel Allen.
- (6) Willis W. Snell, Nine-Mile-Township, has taken up a sorrel mare. The mare was valued at $25 by Larkin and Sherwood Maddox. (I) Mar. 17, 1832, (JP) Arch. Allen.
- (7) Thomas Harrison, sr., has taken up a sorrel mare. The mare was valued at $22.50 by Thomas Harrison, jr. and Wm. McCormack. (I) Nov. 20, 1830, (JP) A. Allen.
- (8) James Basket, Bourbon Township, took up a sorrel horse. The horse was valued at $45 by Austin White and Thomas Ferree. (I) Jun. 18, 1831, (JP) Isaac Black.
- (9) William Bryant, living on Cedar Creek in Cote sans Dessein Township, has taken up a bay horse. The horse was appraised at $30 by Jeremiah King and John Stokes. (I) Jan. 7, 1823, (JP) Adam Hope.
- (10) George Burt, Nine-Mile-Praire Township, has taken up an iron-gray mare. The mare was valued at $15 by John G. Galbreath and Caleb Berry. (I)Aug. 27,1831.
- (11) Lewis Day, Nine-Mile-Praire Township, has taken up a bay colt. The colt was valued at $20 by Daniel Nolley and James D. Fisher. (I) Mar. 17, 1832, (JP) Wm. Armstrong.
- (12) Samuel Dyer, Nine-Mile-Township, has taken up a black mare. The mare was appraised at $27 by Isham Douglass and Daniel Henderson. (I) Aug. 12, 1825, (JP) Thomas Harrison.
- (13) William B. Garret, Aux Vasse Township, has taken up a bay horse. The horse was appraised at $22.50 by Thomas Kitchings and James Shannon. (I)Dec. 8,1832, (JP) James Stewart.
- (14) Samuel T. Guthrie, Round Praire Township, has taken up a bay mare. The mare was appraised at $15 by Robert Criswell and Joseph Nevins. (I)May 29, 1824, (JP) Joseph Nevins.
- (15) Andrew Hamilton, Nile-Mile-Township, has taken up a sorrel horse. The horse was valued at $40 by John Guy and Nat Craig. (I) Jul. 23, 1831, (JP)Archibald Allen.
- (16) Joel Haynes, Bourbon Township, has taken up a black mare at $25 by Tho. P. Stephens and David McClain. (I) Sep. 29, 1832, (JP) Isaac Black.
- (17) John Lorton, Nine-Mile-Praire Township, has taken up two horses. The animals were appraised by Wm.

(Callaway County, Missouri Continued)
Boyes and Alfred Petty. (I) Mar. 10, 1832, (JP)John K. Barry.

(18) William McCormack, Nine-Mile-Praire Township, has taken up a gray horse. The horse was appraised at $20 by George Burt and Isaac Tate. (I)Nov. 6, 1830, (JP) Archibald Allen.

(19) Peter Mason has taken up a four year old bay horse. The horse was appraised at $20 by Mordecai Bell and Stephen Jones. (I) Jan. 7, 1832, (JP) Geo. Bartley.

(20) Thomas Moxley, Nine-Mile-Praire Township, has taken up a black filly. The filly was valued at $25 by Henry Moxley and John Todd. (I) Jun. 19, 1830, (JP) John K. Berry.

(21) Jesse D. Oldham, Nine-Mile-Praire Township, took up a mule colt. The colt was valued at $12 by Mason Hughes and Thos. Harrison, sr. (I) Mar. 10, 1832, (JP) A. Allen.

(22) James Toney has taken up a sorrel mare. The mare was appraised at $30 by John Bartley and Henry Holman. (I) Jul. 23, 1831, (JP) George Bartley.

(23) Daniel Vinston, Round Praire Township, has taken up strawberry roan mare. Mark Cunningham and John M. Smith was valued at $40. (I) Nov. 11, 1823,(JP)Jas. Nevins.

(24) Roger Wigginton, Bourbon Township, took up a bay mare. The mare was valued at $40 by Mark S. Renfro and John D. Ridgway. (I) Sep. 17, 1831, (JP) Isaac Black.

(25) John Willingham, Bourbon Township, has taken up a bay filly. The appraisers were John Kilgore and Isham Kilgore. (I) Mar. 6, 1829, (JP) Isaac Black.

(26) Christopher Winscott, Bourbon Township, has taken up a seven year old bay horse. John C. Kilgore and Isham Kilgore appraised the horse at $45. (JP)Arch. Allen, (I) Oct. 30, 1830.

Moniteau County, Missouri, German Methodist Church Cemtery.

Name	Born	Died
Elias J. Berger	1808	Sep. 2, 1845
Elizabeth Berger	May 21, 1831	Jun. 25, 1898
Jacob Bodamer	Mar. 19, 1821	Nov. 6, 1863
Frederick Bodamer	Nov. 18, 1838	Mar. 10, 1861
Johann Drechsee	Feb. 2, 1782	Dec. 30, 1846
Anna Drechsee	Apr. 6, 1772	Aug. 2, 1846

St. Louis County, Missouri, Petitioners from Carondelet, Protection of Commons, Carter's Papers,Vol.VX,Jan. 8, 1817.

Fcois. Bocher, Ant. Barada, sr., Ant. Barada, jr., Amable

(St. Louis County, Missouri Continued)
Chartarn, jr., Jacqueres Brunet, Louis Denoye,Ch. Valle,jr., Hyacinte Pizon, Nicholas Gais, Pre Lapreche, Julien Choquet, Louis Menard, sr., Tregit Delor, Gabriel Constant,Jh. Young, Fcois. Fournie, Amable Chartran, Jh. Denoyer,Chles. Vachard, Paul Rober, Hinri Choquet, Ls. Constant, Paul Porneuf,Benoit Mauchal, Leone Marechal, Jacque Maillo, Pitre South,Jn. Bte. Menard, Leon Constant, Augustin Bourbonne, Ls. Menard, Inri Roy, Fcois. Gotier, Ls. Valle, Ls. Courtois, Ante. Choquet, Augte. Gamache, Chles. Rober, Ambrose Constant, Fcois. Roy, Antre. Luisser, Gabriel Constant, Alexis Marie, Pre. Marie, Antne. Dorwaer, --- Gotier.

Randolph County, Missouri, Estrays, Missouri Intelligencer.
(1) Daniel Hunt, Salt Spring, has taken up a seven year old sorrel mare. John D. Reed and Elisha McDaniel appraised the horse at $20. (I) Jul. 10, 1829, (JP) Blandamin Smith.
(2) Peter Blanset, Sugar Creek Township, has taken up a bay filly. A.G. and Wm. S. Cochran valued the filly at $28. (I) Feb. 5, 1831, (JP) Joseph Gooding.
(3) Samuel Hardin has taken up a brown horse that was appraised at $25 by Josiah Davis and George Watts. (I) Dec. 25, 1829, (JP) Benjamin Hardin.
(4) Charles Hatfield, Salt Spring Township, has taken up a sorrel mare. The mare was appraised at $10 by Jas. Wells, Jas. Cooley and Tho. Sears.(JP)Blandamin Smith, (I) Apr. 17, 1829.

Pike County, Missouri, Delinquent Tax List, 1829.
Joseph B. Brown, Jacob Coontz,John Cummings, Wm. Foreman, Peter Grimard, Ezra Hunt, Jonathan Hurley, Peter Labourin, Josiah McClanahan, John Miller,Peter Provonchier,Mdm. Sarpy, -- Shaw, Sam A. Toombs.

Cooper County, Missouri, Estrays, Missouri Intelligencer.
(1) William Gibson, Saline Township, has taken up a mule that was appraised at $27.50 by David Lilley and William Houx. (I) Dec. 21, 1827, (JP) Levin Cropper.
(2) Leven Cropper, Boonville Township, has taken up two mares. The mares are appraised at $55 by James Farris and John Calvert. (I) May 16, 1828,(JP)David Adams.
(3) Henry Hatfield, Coleneck Township, has taken up a strawberry roan horse. The horse was valued at $30 by James L. Collins and Nimrod Rector.(JP) John Dade, (I) Dec. 19, 1828.
(4) Herman E. Bedstrup, Cold Neck Township, has taken

(Cooper County, Missouri Continued)

a dapple gray gelding. The horse was appraised at $40 by Samuel Gibbs and George Cathey. (JP) William Briant, (I) Jun. 2, 1826.

(5) Caleb Fisher, Clear Creek Township, has taken up a bay horse. The horse was valued at $20 by James Harper and Mansfield. (I) May 26, 1826, (JP) Robert Steel.

(6) John Rice, Clear Clear Township, has taken up a bay mare appraised at $20 by Mansfield Hatfield and Hugh Allison, (I) Sep. 24, 1824, (JP) John Briscoe.

(7) Stephen Rogers has taken up a black mare valued at $25 by Elijah Anderson and Robert Rogers. (JP)Saml. Kelsay, (I) Jul. 3, 1829.

(8) John M. Savage, Boonville Township, has taken up a brown filly. The filly was appraised at $25 by Peter Fleming and Joseph Chambers. (I) Nov. 3, 1832., (JP) George Crawford.

(9) Robert Sconce, Salt Spring Township, has taken up a sorrel mare appraised at $37.50 by John Weldon and Abraham Dule. (I) Jan. 18, 1827, (JP) James Wells.

(10) Harmon Smelser, Lamie Township, has taken up a six year old sorrel horse. The horse was appraised at $50 by Stephen Turley and John Fisher. (JP) Samuel Turley, (I) May 2, 1828.

(11) Andrew Wallace, Clear Creek, has taken up a sorrel horse valued at $10 by James S. Hutchison and John Hutchison. (I) Mar. 4, 1823, (JP) John Briscoe.

(12) Abner Weaver, Clear Creek Township, has taken up a black mare. The mare was valued at $45 by Abraham Fisher and Alexander Hatfield. (I) Aug. 14, 1829, (JP) R. B. Harris.

St. Louis County, Missouri, Spanish Census, 1791, Taken from the Cuban Papers.

Name	No. Men	No. Women
Dn. Augustin Chouteau	4	4
Josepf Tallon	8	1
Alexo Marie	3	2
Widow Maria Chouteau	1	1
Widow Maria Bisonete	3	2
Dn. Silvestre Labadia	5	4
Jose Maria Papin	6	6
Dn. Gasper Rpbieu	4	1
Dn. Benito Vazquez	6	4
Dn. Santiago Chauvin	6	4
Dn. Luis Dubreuil	3	8
Dn. Antonio Reilhe	2	3
Juan. Bapt. Provenche	7	3

(St. Louis County, Missouri Continued)

Name	No. Men	No. Women
Widow Madama De Rouen	9	3
Luis Laflor	3	2
Carlos Simoneau	2	2
Antonio Vincent	7	2
Luis Brazeau	6	4
Juana Bisonet	4	5
Augustin Roque	5	4
Emilian Yosty	4	1
Luis Delorier	1	
Juan Maria Papin	3	4
Lorenzo Durocher	2	2
Widow Mada Rogoche	1	1
Juan Bapt. Hortez	3	4
Dn. Gebriel Cerre	14	4
Don Pedro Chouteau	4	2
Josef Brazeau	2	2
Jacinto Sansir	9	4
Antonio Dehetre	3	2
Juan Bapt. Tiron	3	2
Dn. Santiago Clemorgan	1	
Widow Madama Dupuis	1	2
Jose Lapierre	1	2
Nicolas Lecompte	6	4
Jose Lemonie	4	1
Pedro Gagnon	2	2
Josef Memville	2	2
Josef Desotel	2	2
Luis Chevalier	2	2
Josef Sorrel	7	4
Josef Labroza	3	1
Dn. Antonio Reynal	5	2
Dn. Carlos Sanguinet	4	4
Josef Rinz	1	
Pedro Ricard	1	3
Pedro Chornete	2	1
Amable Guion	3	2
Franco Barrera	1	3
Juan Bapt. Sale	3	2
Pablo Guitard	6	1
Josef Dabadia	1	
Dn. Ventura Collett	1	1
Guillermo Lecompte	6	3
Josef Mobidou	9	1
Luis Boris	2	
Gabriel Dodier	3	4
Dn. Gregorio Sarpy	1	
Alexo Lalande	1	2

(St. Louis County, Missouri Continued)

Name	No. Men	No. Women
Alexo Lalande	1	2
Josef Rotard	2	
Josef Verdon	2	
Augustin Dodier	4	1
Regis Vasor	3	2
Juan Bapt. Bequet	2	
Josef Boduen	3	2
Jose Chorrete	5	3
Josef Liberge	3	2
Josef Bachar	5	2
Madama Verdon	1	3
Carlos Delisla	4	5
Juan Couns	1	1
Felipe Fain	3	
Dn. Carlos Gratiot	1	5
Josef Hebert	5	2
Pedro Peri	1	
Widow Campel	1	4
Denis Cabana	2	
Juan Bapt. Lorens	2	1
Juan Bapt. Dufaut	3	3
Pedro Quenel	4	2
Nicolas Bochenou	9	3
Antonio Bachar	3	1
Dn. Carlos Tallon	7	2
Widow Madama Bachar	2	2
Pedro Dumont	5	5
Josef Hortez	6	6
Franco Decari	3	
Widow Madama Porcelly	5	3
Pedro Roy	4	1
Felipe Riviera	3	4
Julian Roy	5	3
Luis Delisla	5	1
Joaquin Roy	4	1
Lucas Marly	7	2
Eugenio Alvarez	2	4
Josef Roy	2	2
Luis Barada	2	4
Dn. Pedro Mointardy	3	1
Luis Chillere	2	2
Josef Vige	2	1
Dn. Pedro Devolsey	2	
Santiago Loiselle	2	4
Antonio Moren	8	5
Antonio Pelletier	4	3
Dn. Luis Beletre	5	6

(St. Louis County, Missouri Continued)

Name	No. Men	No. Women
Juan Trudeau	4	3
Joesf Tallon, (son)	5	3
Franco Dorlac	2	3
Widow Mada. Lamy	8	3
Widow Madama Brazeau	3	4
Luis Honore	2	1
Bapt. Lacroix	2	1
Carlos Levielle	(2 free negro male, 1 free negro female)	
Neptuno	(3 free negro male, 2 free negro female)	
Widow Juana	(3 free negro male, 3 free negro female)	
Franco Borrosier	6	5
Todos Santos Parent	1	
Uberto Tabeau	2	1
Antonio Mariscal	7	2
Pedro Couder	3	
Antonio Rivera	5	1
Luis Reineau	1	
Franco Delorier	3	1
Juan Bapt. Delisla	4	5
Carlos Mercier	2	1
Juan Bapt. de Cote	3	
Franco Mariscal	1	6
Antonio River, (father)	6	2
Pedro Menar	2	3
Claudio Panton	1	1
Juan Bapt. Primor	4	4
Enrique Boteler	2	1
Amable Gagnier	5	4
Jose Calve	4	
Juan Bapt. Lachassa	2	1
Jose Lamere	3	2
Luis Dubreuil	2	4
Santiago Tabeau	1	2
Manuel Bruner	1	
Franco Moreau	4	4
Pedro de Vau	1	1
Josef Sangerman	2	2
Jose Boduen	2	2
Jose Boduen	2	2
Franco Charleville	5	3

Boone County, Missouri, Estrays, Missouri Intelligencer.
(1) John Grayum, Perce Township, has taken up a sorrel mare. The mare was appraised at $27.50 by Pierce Ward and Wm. Gaslin. (I) Aug. 10, 1826, (JP) John Anderson.
(2) Hugh French has taken up a roan filly. The filly

(Boone County, Missouri Continued)

was valued at $20 by Geo. Tally and David Wilson. (I) May 12, 1826, (JP) James E. Fenton.

(3) Isaiah Austin, Cedar Township, has taken up a bay mare. Jonathan Pace and Wilton Rucker appraised the mare at $20. (I) Dec. 8, 1832, (JP)Jas. Harris.

(4) William Bawgh, Rocky Fork Township, has taken up a bay mare. (I) Sep. 23, 1825, (JP) Jesse Turner.

(5) Allen Coats, Perce Township, has taken up a three year old dark bay mare. Thomas Ginnins and Henry Coats valued the mare at $20. (I) Apr. 16, 1831, (JP) John Corlew.

(6) Simeon Coppage, Missouri Township, has taken up a ten year old black horse. Richard Jones and Landon Snell valued the horse at $25. (I) Apr. 7, 1832, (JP) J. W. Hickam.

(7) Thomas Crowson, Columbia Township, has taken up six year old sorrel mare. The mare was valued at $25 by James Sutton and A.W. Turner. (I) Mar. 24, 1832, (JP) Warren Woodson.

(8) John B. Dennis, Missouri Township, has taken up a bay horse. The horse was appraised at $50 by John Williamson and James Hopper. (I) Jun. 23, 1832, (JP) Dabney Pettis.

(9) Thomas Densman, Rocky Fork Township, has taken up a bay horse. The horse was appraised at $25 by Ammon Hicks and Wm. Dun. (I) Feb. 25, 1823.

(10) Alexander Ellington, Missouri Township, has taken up a bay mare. R.M. Hatton and Stephen G. Evans valued the mare at $30. (I) Jun. 30, 1832,(JP) John Henderson.

(11) Elijah Foley, Missouri Township, has taken up a four year old bay horse. The horse was appraised at $18 by William Harris and Wm. S. Burch. (JP)John Henderson, (I) Aug. 12, 1825.

(12) Thorton Hames, Cedar Township, has taken up a black mare. John McDow and James Sullens have valued the mare at $37. (I) Jun. 2, 1826, (JP)John Henderson.

(13) Charles M. Hayes, Columbia Township, has taken up a three year old bay mare. Elisha McClelland and James Richardson valued the mare at $30. (JP)Warren Woodson, (I) Nov. 3, 1832.

(14) Robert Hinston, Columbia Township, has taken up a six year old sorrel mare. The mare was valued at $60 by John Cary and Tho. Maupin. (I)Sep. 4, 1824.

(15) William Jones, sr., Missouri Township, has taken up a chestnut sorrel mare. The mare was appraised at $40 by John Gray and William Jones. (JP) John Henderson, (I) Jun. 16, 1826.

(Boone County, Missouri Countinued)
- (16) William McClain, Columbia Township, has taken up a black mare. The mare was valued at $25 by Robert Lemon and Daniel King. (I) Jan. 11, 1828, (JP)Jesse T. Wood.
- (17) William McDow, Cedar Township, has taken up a colt. The colt was appraised at $13 by Reyben Hume and Peyton Collier. (I) Mar. 17, 1832,(JP)James Harris.
- (18) Foster Martin, Cedar Township, has taken up a six year old gray horse. The horse was valued at $30 by Mosias Jones and Mark Sappington. (JP) Tyre Martin. (I) Sep. 17, 1831.
- (19) Walter Maxey, Cedar Township, has taken up several horses. The appraisers were Jas. Bradley and Jacob Billet. (I) Apr. 26, 1825, (JP) James Callaway.
- (20) Daniel Mourning, Columbia Township, has taken up an eight year old sorrel horse. The horse was valued at $50 by Wm. Wright and Joseph Renfro. (JP) James Barnes, (I) Jun. 25, 1831.
- (21) Robert Nelson, Columbia Township, has taken up an iron-gray mare. The mare was appraised at $25 by Samuel Shaw and James A. Jameson. (I) Dec. 8, 1832, (JP) William Martin.
- (22) James Nichols, Missouri Township, has taken up an iron-gray filly. The filly was appraised at $25 by Ezekiel Hickam and Cornelius Lynch.(JP)J.W. Hickam, (I) Jul. 23, 1831.
- (23) Anthony Owsley, Missouri Township, has taken up an iron-gray horse. The horse was valued at $40 by John Austin and John Williamson. (I) Jan. 7, 1832, (JP) Dabney Pettis.
- (24) John Parker, Columbia Township, has taken up an iron-gray horse. The horse was appraised at $50 by John Jamison and Durrett Hubbard. (I) May 21, 1831, (JP) Warren Woodson.
- (25) Macam Purcell, Rocky Fork Township, has taken up two mares. The mares were appraised at $70 by Henry Cave, jr. and Zadock Riggs, jr. (JP) Silas Riggs, (I) Aug. 4, 1832.
- (26) William Ramsay, sr., Cedar Township, has taken up a bay horse. The horse was appraised at $27.50 by Richard Lanham and Josias Jones. (I) Aug. 12, 1823, (JP) Tyre Martin.
- (27) Reuben Riggs, Rocky Fork Township, has taken up a mare and colt. The appraisers were James Turner, Enich Turner and William Toalson.(I) Jan. 21, 1823, (JP) James R. Abernathy.
- (28) Joseph Robnett, Cedar Township, has taken up a four year old bay mare. The mare was appraised at $35

(Boone County, Missouri Continued)

by Pleasant Ribnett and Theodore Beavin. (JP) Wm. Shields, (I) Jun. 5, 1830.

(29) William Scott, Missouri Township, has taken up a sorrel horse. Benjamin Watson and Charles B. Hatton appraised the horse at $24. (I) Feb. 5, 1824, (JP) John Henderson.

(30) George Sexton, Persia Township, has taken up a ten year old bay mare. The mare was appraised at $40 by Reuben Elliott and Fielding White. (JP) Tyre Harris, (I) Jun. 16, 1832.

(31) Josiah Short, Perce Township, has taken up a sorrel horse appraised at $25 by John Short and David Gentry. (I) Dec. 4, 1824, (JP) Tyre Harris.

(32) Edward Snow, Persia Township, has taken up a sorrel filly valued at $30 by Brinsley Barnes and Reason Johnson. (I) Nov. 3, 1832, (JP) Robt. Scholling.

(33) Peter Stice, Rocky Fork Township, has taken up a bay mare. The mare was appraised at $5 by Daniel Colgan and Charles Norwood. (I) Jun. 3, 1824, (JP) John C. Gordon.

(34) Gilpin Tuttle, Cedar Township, has taken up a black horse. The horse was valued at $20 by James Dunn and Jas. Harris. (I) May 1, 1829,(JP)Jas. Callaway.

(35) John Wilborn, Columbia Township, has taken up a bay horse. The horse was valued at $35 by Wm. Grisham and John Mayo. (I) Aug. 10, 1826,(JP) P.H. McBride.

INDEX

- A -

----, Anthony (negro) 219 Clermont (a woman) 108 Ducomb (a woman) 109 Ginny (negro) 221 Harry (negro) 219 Henry (negro) 166 James D 189 Jeanette (free negro) 150 163 Juana 237 Labuilere (a woman) 109 Largillon (a woman) 109 Le Cin (free negro) 119 Levi (negro) 219 Lewis (negro) 218 Marie Jeanette (free negro) 42 Neptuno 237 Rhoda 169 Sarah A 194 Shibboleth (negro) 217 Since (free negro) 32 Sukey (negro) 218 Ther (free negro) 119
----QUEST, 40
AAIRS, 192
ABAR, 60 129
ABARE, 9
ABBAY, 230
ABBET, 73
ABBEY, 76
ABBOT, 178
ABBOTT, 76
ABEL, 1 99
ABERENATHY, 172
ABERNATHIE, 60 182
ABERNATHY, 126 170 172 239
ABILLET, 60
ABINGTON, 8 9
ABIT, 37
ABLE, 104 133 138 172
ABLEY, 74
ABRAHAM, 53 170
ACKLEY, 76
ACKMAN, 76
ACLARE, 9
ADAIR, 53
ADAMS, 1-3 9 38 46 53-55 60 71 76 92 103 104 118-120 133 136 149 150 157 162 170 174 176 177 186 194-197 199 201 218 233
ADAMSON, 120 215
ADAVER, 108
ADCOCK, 52 76 143
ADDIS, 76
ADENNE, 219
ADINSON, 53
ADKIN, 190
ADKINS, 38 60
ADRAIN, 156
AELDEN, 21
AGA, 112
AGAN, 76 82
AGEE, 231
AGIN, 53
AGNEW, 76 148 149
AGNIEL, 150
AHART, 9
AIDENGER, 60
AIDINGER, 128
AIKMON, 2
AILER, 60
AIME, 60 99
AIMES, 76
AINES, 143
AKERMAN, 46
AKIN, 172 182-185
AKINS, 52 182
AKLEMAUCT, 9
ALARY, 48 105
ALBERTSON, 76
ALBRIGHT, 76 120 143 170
ALCORN, 150
ALDER, 197

ALDMAN, 120
ALDRICK, 76 143
ALDRIDGE, 9 76
ALENDER, 119
ALER, 60
ALEXABDER, 53
ALEXANDER, ii 1 3 9 47 73 76
  92 112 133 146 151 167 170
  175 176 201 204 226
ALEXIX, 151
ALFORD, 43 44 53
ALFRED, 76 204
ALFRY, 120
ALGIER, 76
ALKILE, 71
ALKINSON, 148
ALKIRE, 9 178 187
ALLABADA, 76
ALLCORN, 2
ALLEN, 1 2 8 9 25 38 53 60 76
  102 106 112 120 133 136 142
  143 148 149 151 157 170 172
  177 185 187 204 207 216 225
  228 231 232
ALLESON, 219
ALLEY, 60 133 141 197 225
ALLIN, 106
ALLIS, 219
ALLISON, 143 234
ALLMAN, 120
ALLUMS, 76
ALLY, 94-97 225
ALOMBI, 101
ALSAVER, 76
ALSOP, 175 188
ALTER, 76
ALTHUSA, 156
ALVAREZ, 60 118 164 236
ALVENER, 9
ALVERSON, 76
ALVES, 143
ALVIS, 76 136
AMBROISE, 130
AMELIN, 119
AMELING, 201
AMERY, 133
AMES, 76
AMICH, 76
AMICK, 175 189
AMMELL, 118
AMMICK, 175

AMMIMAN, 204
AMMONS, 76 204 216
AMOIT, 60
AMOREAU, 1500
AMOREUX, 133
AMOS, 9
ANDERMAN, 92
ANDERS, 152 189
ANDERSON, 2 3 9 38 46 52 53 60
  71 73 76 112 120 133 136 141-
  143 148 157 162 168 175 178
  192 197 200 202 204 206 220
  224 225 227 234 237
ANDEY, 76
ANDREW, 76 133
ANDREWS, 46 60 76 94 168 176
  188 190 209 210 225
ANGEL, 76
ANGLE, 207 221
ANGST, 76
ANNADELL, 76
ANNADOWN, 76
ANNIBAL, 76
ANOTH, 119
ANTATA, 48
ANTAYA, 49 100
ANTHONY, 53 60 76 120 143
ANTVOBUS, 71
APINS, 203
APLING, 142 177
APLINNG, 112
APPERSON, 76 185
APPLEGATE, 60 76 133 143
APPLETON, 9
APPLING, 204
AQUETAN, 60
ARAMEN, 168
ARANOT, 107
ARAST, 107
ARCHAMBRA, 1
ARCHANBEAUX, 129
ARCHASUBEAN, 110
ARCHER, 60 120 136 172
ARCHES, 111
ARDOUIN, 50
ARILL, 110
ARMAN, 94
ARMEN, 198
ARMENTER, 215
ARMET, 195
ARMETAGE, 181

ARMISTEAD, 76
ARMON, 168 170
ARMOUR, 172
ARMSTEAD, 143 200
ARMSTRONG, 7 60 71 76 112 133 142 149 154 157 185 192 193 196 201 204 216 228 230 231
ARNAUD, 60
ARNES, 76 124
ARNET, 76
ARNETT, 76
ARNOLD, 1 44 73 76 120 143 149 162 181 189 204 224
ARNOW, 133
ARNS, 76
AROITE, 219
ARREL, 133
ARRELL, 60 61 126
ARRIVA, 133
ARRIWOOD, 76 143
ARSKREN, 136
ARTER, 120
ARTERBERRY, 7
ARTERMAN, 162
ARTHERS, 72
ARTHUR, 177 178
ARTMAN, 120
ARVIN, 103
ARWAY, 133
ASH, 141 174
ASHABRANNER, 128
ASHBELL, 190
ASHBRANNER, 60
ASHBROOK, 60 133
ASHBROOKE, 76
ASHBY, 46 120
ASHEBRAMER, 171
ASHECRAFT, 2
ASHER, 120
ASHERTON, 76
ASHLEY, 9 129 142 166 185 217
ASHMAN, 218
ASHWORTH, 120
ASINE, 92
ASKEW, 77 99
ASKINS, 53 157
ASKRON, 112
ASLIN, 76
ATCHINSON, 157
ATKINS, 77 120 133
ATKINSON, 77

ATTEBERRY, 175
ATTERBERRY, 1 229
ATTERBURY, 120
ATWELL, 77 143 172 180
AUBENHEUSER, 133
AUBERNOIS, 108
AUBIN, 99
AUBUCHON, 49-51 57 60 99 101 129
AUBURY, 9
AUD, 136
AUDRAIN, 9 157 187
AUFRERET, 99
AUGER, 60 109 120
AUGUST, 60 76 95 133
AUGUSTE, 129
AULL, 120
AUMURE, 60
AUSBURN, 192
AUSTIN, 1-4 49 50 53 60 74 76 95 99 103 120 125 189 217 220 238 239
AUTREY, 133
AUTROLEUS, 204
AUX, 76 144
AVELINE, 108
AVERETT, 38
AVERITT, 60
AVERY, 76 99
AVY, 99
AYERS, 144
AYRE, 76
AYRES, 76 157
AYREY, 60
AZAU, 99

- B -

B--RKS, 53
BABAER, 120
BABB, 76
BABBITT, 142 175
BABCOCK, 76 121
BABER, 24 120
BABY, 60 111 133
BACANNE, 166
BACCANE, 60 165
BACCUS, 178
BACHAR, 236
BACHELOR, 76
BACHIN, 190

BACKAR, 133
BACKUS, 46 76
BACON, 60 76 77 92 112 133 142
  172 185 193 194 200 211-215
BADEAU, 60
BADEN, 167
BADGER, 76
BAER, 129
BAGGETT, 94
BAGLEY, 60
BAGWELL, 7 37
BAIKUS, 72
BAILEY, 60 76 92 133 143 189
  198 212 214
BAILIE, 46 129 189
BAILY, 71 73 112 171 197-199
  201 207
BAIMME, 60
BAIN, 167
BAINBECK, 46
BAINBRICK, 150
BAIR, 53
BAIRD, 60 125
BAITMAN, 38
BAITS, 120
BAKER, 11 12 43 44 46 53 60 61
  71-74 76 94 95 97 99 107 112
  120 127 133 136 137 143 144
  148-152 166 169 170-172 178
  192 204 216 225
BAKERBREAD, 11
BALDON, 120
BALDRIDGE, 10 11 19 23 60 61
  130 157 178 188
BALDWIN, 10 76 120 174
BALES, 8 59 120 178
BALEY, 92 120 149 192 215
BALIFF, 76
BALINGER, 4
BALL, 10 46 53 60 76 133 144
  178 206 211
BALLARD, 4 76 204
BALLE, 115 116
BALLEN, 175
BALLEW, 178
BALLINGER, 53
BALLOLEW, 4
BALMORE, 1
BALY, 201
BAMISCO, 53
BANCELOUX, 140

BANCROFT, 38 175
BAND, 71
BANDTENIES, 156
BANE, 112 120 204
BANERS, 53
BANGS, 10
BANISH, 127
BANISS, 157
BANISTER, 76 144 169 170
BANKS, 10 46 76 157 187
BANKSAN, 92
BANKSON, 60 133
BANKSTON, 60 61
BANNING, 190
BANNISTER, 61
BANT, 130
BANTA, 121
BAPTIST, 26
BARADA, 10 19 24 31 35 42 151
  164 165 232 236
BARADEN, 187
BARADIE, 11 17
BARAINE, 61
BARANDA, 133
BARBARICK, 178
BARBEAU, 75
BARBEE, 150
BARBER, 37 172
BARBIER, 99 139
BARCLAY, 2 53 61 212
BARCROFT, 150
BARD, 105
BARE, 129
BAREFIELD, 60
BAREY, 171
BARGE, 120
BARGER, 4 53
BARGOR, 53
BARHART, 102
BARIBANA, 119
BARIBEAU, 133
BARK, 120
BARKEM, 76
BARKER, 3 120 157 224
BARKETT, 53
BARKS, 3 60 128 171 172
BARLEY, 60
BARLOW, 77
BARMELL, 198
BARNABAS, 60
BARNARD, 76 77 157

BARNCASTLE, 77
BARNES, 1-4 11 44-46 53 54 56 76 112 120 121 124 144 149-151 166 188-190 193 198 204 239 240
BARNETT, 1-3 37 46 53 54 60 76 176
BARNEY, 48 76 77 161 198
BARNHART, 60
BARNHILL, 76
BARNS, 74 136 193 194
BARNSBACK, 94
BARNY, 53
BAROIS, 61
BARON, 40 41
BARR, 162
BARRA, 12
BARRADA, 60
BARRANS, 133
BARRE, 99 104
BARRERA, 118 185 235
BARRET, 141
BARRIER, 11
BARRON, 40 76
BARROW, 76
BARRY, 94 110 144 151 168 232
BARSADOUX, 163
BARSALOU, 99
BARSALOUX, 41 49 108 133
BARSELAUX, 60
BARTELL, 92
BARTHY, 149
BARTLESON, 38
BARTLETT, 76 178 188 190 220
BARTLEY, 136 142 232
BARTON, 2 37 53 60 72 76 121 148 151 156 211
BARTOT, 100
BARUME, 60
BARY, 92
BASDELL, 77
BASEDONIO, 114
BASFORD, 76 148
BASKET, 178 231
BASOR, 115
BASQUEZ, 100
BASQUIN, 60
BASS, 3 4 10 43 44 53 54 76 142
BASSETT, 60 76
BASSNETT, 60
BAST, 204

BASYE, 60 141 142
BATEMAN, 76
BATES, 9 52 53 60 77 124 133 144 150 176 178 200 210 217 222
BATHCER, 53
BATHEAUME, 60
BATHIAUME, 120
BATO, 1
BATRAND, 76
BATT, 12
BATTESTON, 53
BATTLERTON, 53
BATY, 46 73 192
BAUCHE, 40
BAUER, 228
BAUGH, 10 12 53 157 188
BAUGHAN, 28
BAUGI, 49
BAULEY, 3
BAUMGARDINER, 76
BAUNOU, 218
BAUVAIS, 129 133 217
BAUYER, 129
BAWGH, 238
BAWN, 121
BAXLEY, 213
BAXTER, 2 8 38 76
BAY, 60 72 133 185 195 197 199 202 203 214
BAYANCOUR, 60
BAYARD, 119
BAYARTH, 120
BAYERS, 112
BAYLESS, 144
BAYLEY, 10 11
BAYLY, 33 133
BAYS, 1 162
BAYSE, 150 228
BAYSYE, 175
BAZEWELL, 76
BAZUS, 53
BEACH, 149
BEACHE, 76
BEACHEMIN, 60
BEADLES, 136
BEAFIELD, 38
BEALER, 76
BEALL, 76 153
BEAM, 76
BEAN, 77

BEANCUR, 117
BEANS, 77
BEAR, 60 77
BEARD, 77 154 157 176
BEARDEN, 225
BEARDSLEY, 77
BEARE, 133
BEAS, 77
BEASLEY, 45 77
BEATIE, 4 142 150
BEATIER, 229
BEATTY, 60 61 77 106 157 175 195 198 219
BEATY, 38 46 52 53 218
BEAU, 130
BEAU----, 40
BEAUCHAM, 9
BEAUCHAMP, 14 16 60 120 121
BEAUDIRUM, 43
BEAUDOIN, 42
BEAUDOUIN, 42 165 166
BEAUGARD, 60 109
BEAUGENAU, 164
BEAUGENAUX, 60
BEAUGENOU, 165
BEAUJENOIE, 220
BEAULIEU, 103
BEAUMAN, 1
BEAUONOUIS, 1
BEAUQENON, 163
BEAUVAI, 1
BEAUVAIS, 1 48-50 57 60 99 100 104 133
BEAVER, 204 217
BEAVIN, 240
BEAZLEY, 3 43
BEAZLY, 53
BECAIN, 130
BECANE, 130
BECHETTS, 37
BECHT, 119
BECK, 46 77 157 228
BECKEL, 1
BECKER, 133
BECKET, 1 168
BECKETT, 53 60 224
BECKMAN, 77 200
BECQUETTE, 60
BEDDOW, 10
BEDEL, 77
BEDELL, 148

BEDFORD, 74 100 101 104 120
BEDINGER, 225
BEDLER, 11
BEDSTRUP, 233
BEDWELL, 120
BEEBE, 211
BEEBEE, 176
BEECHER, 201
BEEGLE, 120
BEERS, 60
BEESON, 77
BEEVUL, 60
BEHORST, 155
BELAMRE, 133
BELAN, 60
BELANGE, 133
BELCHER, 3 4 53 77 144 190
BELCOUR, 210
BELESTRE, 40
BELETRE, 236
BELFORD, 119
BELHUMOR, 117
BELIENR, 120
BELISTE, 41
BELKNAP, 212
BELL, 33 46 47 60 71 73 77 120 130 133 137 142 149 151 167 178 185 192 194 196 200 202 203 214 221 226 232
BELLAND, 26 61 62
BELLANGER, 61
BELLAS, 2 188
BELLEFERVILLE, 61
BELLEFUILLE, 176
BELLEMARE, 100 101
BELLESSIME, 165
BELLESTRE, 62
BELLEU, 60-62
BELLEW, 133
BELLISSIME, 181
BELLONCOURT, 18
BELLOND, 10 22
BELLOR, 28
BELLOW, 77
BELLUPS, 200
BELMAR, 57 106
BELOTE, 77
BELPECHER, 116
BELROSE, 77
BELSHA, 61
BELSHAR, 224

BELSON, 62
BELSONS, 133
BELSTEAD, 77
BELT, 77 144 197
BELVEUR, 62
BELVINS, 53
BEMOS, 190
BENADICT, 10
BENAM, 151
BENAN, 164
BENARD, 41 57
BENDER, 12 77
BENDICK, 12
BENEDICT, 2 77 214
BENEFIELD, 112
BENETT, 53 125
BENITO, 62
BENNER, 12
BENNET, 3 53
BENNETT, 52 53 77 120 136 137 151 172 174 190
BENNETTE, 62
BENNOM, 1
BENO, 115
BENOIST, 43
BENOIT, 61
BENSON, 2 46 47 77 142
BENTLEY, 99 100 148
BENTON, 61 62 72 77 142 178 193 208 214
BENWAY, 118
BEOKITS, 4
BEPOUSTE, 157
BEQUENT, 163
BEQUET, 50 57 129 133 164 236
BEQUETE, 118
BEQUETTE, 95 100 164
BEQUIETTE, 130
BEQUTTE, 94
BERBONA, 157
BERDEAU, 157
BERDON, 133
BERDU, 62
BERGAN, 75
BERGE, 118 165
BERGENON, 140
BERGER, 40 77 164 232
BERHORST, 155
BERKWITH, 77
BERMAN, 52
BERMIER, 106

BERNARD, 10 11 17 29 36 40 61 151
BERNIE, 116 118
BERNIER, 50 57 100 129 133
BERNSMEYER, 155
BERNUM, 11
BERON, 117
BEROUDE, 40
BERRIAN, 77
BERRY, 1-4 45 46 53 77 120 121 129 133 142 144 148 151 157 176 189 191 231 232
BERRYMAN, 48
BERT, 157
BERTAU, 101
BERTELS, 156
BERTHEAUME, 62
BERTHIAUME, 108
BERTHION, 105
BERTHLUAME, 128
BERTHOL, 11
BERTRAND, 62
BESAUNTE, 130
BESDA, 119
BESET, 166
BESS, 48 157 171
BESSY, 172
BEST, 2 11 38 112 120 157 204 222
BESTEN, 156
BESTON, 4
BETES, 53
BETH, 120
BETHEL, 112
BETHELL, 136
BETHWISH, 157
BETTING, 77
BETTIS, 184
BETTISON, 180
BETTLE, 53
BEURBON, 12
BEVAMAN, 11
BEVANS, 77
BEVERLEY, 11
BEVILLE, 77
BEVIS, 133
BEXTON, 155
BEYELLE, 150
BEZARE, 118
BEZEL, 221
BIBAREN, 114

BIBB, 53 217
BIBO, 77
BICETS, 189
BICHAR, 119
BICKERSTALL, 121
BICKNELL, 1
BIDDICK, 4
BIDDLE, 77 150 157
BIDDY, 215
BIDEAU, 104
BIDICKS, 4
BIENVENU, 151
BIEVENU, 221
BIGALOW, 9
BIGELOW, 187
BIGGERS, 77
BIGGIS, 109
BIGGS, 11 20 22 119 136 157 162
BIGHAM, 120
BIGNE, 119
BILLEAU, 130
BILLER, 92
BILLERON, 51 106
BILLET, 61 62 239
BILLETTE, 62
BILLINGS, 77
BILLINGSLEY, 224
BILLINGSLY, 92
BILLS, 77
BILLUPS, 200 203
BINGHAM, 28
BINKSTON, 56
BINNS, 46
BIORE, 130
BIRCH, 77
BIRD, 8 11 55 73 77 120 124 133 175 216 228
BIRDSONG, 40
BIRE, 133
BIRIN, 140
BIRK, 129
BIRON, 223
BISETTE, 165
BISHOP, 37 46 60 142 172 182 197 204
BISON, 61
BISONET, 119 164 235
BISONETE, 234
BISONETT, 36
BISONSSNAITE, 130
BISPHAM, 77

BISSONENT, 165
BISSONET, 41 119 163
BISSONETTE, 60 61 150
BISSONNETT, 166
BISSWELL, 38
BISWELL, 37 53
BITER, 77
BITTICK, 60 178
BITTLE, 4
BIUAT, 1
BIVIAR, 119
BIZET, 40 41 60 100 163
BIZETE, 164
BIZETTE, 222
BIZEWELL, 3
BIZWELL, 3
BLACK, 10 38 53 54 77 119 133 136 142 144 148 189 191 231 232
BLACKBURN, 3 4 53 77
BLACKFORTH, 11
BLACKLESS, 144
BLACKMAN, 12
BLACKSBEE, 77
BLACKWELL, 71 95 167 193 198 200 201 203
BLADRIDGE, 72
BLADWIN, 157
BLAIR, 77 172 199 209 213 219 222
BLAKE, 77
BLAKEY, 7
BLAKLY, 120
BLANCH, 133
BLANCHET, 60 165
BLANCHETT, 32
BLANCO, 61 105 129
BLAND, 77
BLANDEAU, 120
BLANK, 228
BLANKENSHIP, 121 157 190 203
BLANKINSHIP, 77
BLANKS, 60 133
BLANO, 144
BLANSET, 233
BLANSTEL, 191
BLANTON, 94 95 120 121 191 200
BLARE, 72 199
BLASDELL, 77
BLAXEN, 11

BLAY, 60 129 189
BLEAMER, 12
BLEDSO, 37
BLEDSOE, 3 4 53 73 99 121 157 203
BLESS, 141
BLEVIN, 149
BLEVINS, 53 77 148 224
BLEW, 77
BLIN, 41
BLIZE, 178 195
BLOCK, 60-62 111 128 150 174 185
BLOCKER, 2 144
BLOIS, 143
BLONDEAU, 40 164
BLOOM, 222
BLOOMINGDALE, 77
BLOT, 57
BLOUIN, 100 101
BLOUNT, 77 133 183
BLUCHER, 12
BLUE, 77
BLUNT, 182
BLUSTER, 10
BOALDING, 193
BOAS, 208
BOBARDS, 100
BOBBINRATH, 11
BOBLESSE, 131
BOBO, 77
BOCHENOU, 236
BOCHER, 232
BOCKMAN, 77
BODAMER, 232
BODE, 155 156
BODEN, 77 144
BODEVELL, 138
BODOIN, 118
BODOUEN, 133
BODUEN, 116 118 236 237
BODWELL, 61 77
BOERN, 77
BOESSEN, 156
BOFFEE, 181
BOFRER, 116
BOGAN, 139
BOGARD, 139 141
BOGART, 38 149
BOGENEAU, 117
BOGENOU, 133

BOGG, 166
BOGGS, 77 185 188
BOGY, 61 95 129 133
BOI, 151
BOICE, 60 61 77 97
BOID, 4
BOILE, 11
BOILER, 224
BOILIER, 119
BOILSTON, 120 121 216
BOIS, 41
BOISI, 119
BOISLEVIN, 62
BOISSE, 61 133
BOISSY, 42 165
BOLAILLE, 165
BOLAND, 120
BOLAY, 185
BOLDENE, 1
BOLDEY, 133
BOLDRIDGE, 130 133
BOLDUA, 1
BOLDUC, 1 48-51 57 61 100 129 133 217
BOLEN, 171
BOLER, 3
BOLES, 61 106 107 146 194
BOLI, 61
BOLING, 166
BOLINGER, 127 172
BOLLAND, 150
BOLLING, 184
BOLLINGER, 38 60-62 127 128 133 171 172
BOLLS, 46
BOLON, 43 60 98 100 181
BOLTON, 101 216
BOLWAR, 120
BOMBARDIER, 133
BOND, 77 144
BONDURANT, 45
BONE, 60 178
BONEAU, 119
BONER, 125
BONES, 143 189
BONESTEEL, 77
BONHAM, 18 106 214
BONNE, 129
BONNEAU, 60 108 133
BONNER, 77
BONNON, 62

BONPART, 165 185
BOOBA, 75
BOOKE, 201
BOOKER, 202
BOON, 4 12 14 33 112 151 189 204
BOONE, 12 60-62 72 112 133 136 142 143 157 160 161 187
BOONER, 60
BOOS, 4
BOOTH, 77
BOOTHE, 77 112 137 141 142 167
BORCHARD, 227
BORDEAUX, 165
BORDEN, 121 215 224
BOREIN, 172
BOREN, 172
BORGER, 53
BORGMEYER, 155 156
BORING, 193 194 217
BORIS, 235
BORK, 1
BORME, 62
BORN, 157
BORON, 223
BORROSIE, 115
BORROSIER, 237
BOSAH, 10
BOSFORD, 77
BOSHER, 77
BOSHETT, 11
BOSHMA, 10
BOSHMAN, 11
BOSHOW, 133
BOSORTH, 190
BOSS, 204
BOSSERN, 75
BOSSIER, 75
BOSSIERE, 217
BOSWELL, 11 46
BOSWORTH, 77
BOTELER, 237
BOTTOM, 226
BOTTON, 110
BOTTS, 1 46 76
BOUCANT, 185
BOUCHE, 40 107
BOUCHENU, 41
BOUCHER, 99 100 103 112 171
BOUDEAU, 75
BOUDEN, 62

BOUDING, 60
BOUDOIN, 61 62
BOUGARD, 141
BOUGENEAU, 118
BOUGENOUUX, 150
BOUIE, 149
BOUILLETTE, 111
BOUILLIETTE, 62
BOUIS, 42 43 60 133 150
BOUJU, 221 223
BOULWARE, 8 71 178 186
BOUNDS, 3 120 169 189
BOURAPAS, 62
BOURBONNE, 233
BOURDEAU, 220
BOURE, 131
BOURGUIGNON, 49 51
BOURNE, 8
BOURRI, 60
BOURY, 41
BOUTANS, 130
BOUVET, 42 60
BOUYET, 61
BOVAUSHECTER, 31
BOVETT, 32
BOVICK, 53
BOWDEN, 128
BOWEN, 77 111 144 157 204 214
BOWER, 77
BOWERS, 61 189 190
BOWIE, 61 77
BOWLER, 106
BOWLES, 10 11 71 176 178 191 207-209 211 212 214
BOWLEY, 190
BOWLIN, 77
BOWLING, 44 161
BOWLS, 8
BOWLWAR, 121
BOWMAN, 180 189
BOWN, 218
BOX, 7 76 77 189
BOYCE, 37 77 100 101 144 169 172
BOYD, 9 10 48 52 53 60 61 72 76 77 100 127 133 144 157 176 178 193 197 198 201 224
BOYDSTON, 60
BOYE, 57
BOYEAU, 61
BOYER, 11 32 40 61 62 75 77 95

BOYER (continued)
  100-102 129 191 218
BOYES, 232
BOYETT, 77
BOYEZ, 4
BOYL, 52
BOYLE, 139
BOYLES, 77
BOYNTON, 77
BOYO, 92
BOYSE, 218
BOZARTH, 8 177 190
BOZER, 2
BRACKEE, 224
BRACKEEN, 224
BRACKEN, 77
BRACKENRDIGE, 77
BRACKENRIDGE, 77
BRADBOURN, 61 150
BRADBURN, 133
BRADBURRY, 200
BRADBURY, 1 157
BRADEN, 77 144
BRADFORD, 38 46 77 136 149 166 178
BRADLEY, 1 2 7 8 46 59 60 61 76 77 120 125 143 144 188 189 239
BRADLY, 53 175
BRADSHAW, 1 77 162 169
BRADY, 10 53 77 97 133 171
BRAFFIE, 92
BRAGG, 136 143
BRAIL, 120
BRAL, 56
BRALEY, 95 195 199 202
BRALY, 142 167
BRAMMEL, 197 203
BRAMMER, 154
BRAMS, 157
BRAND, 78
BRANDHAM, 78
BRANHAM, 44 177
BRANNAN, 52
BRANNIN, 175
BRANNON, 1 60
BRANSON, 144 149 167
BRANT, 8 61 78 126 133 172
BRANTINE, 10
BRASFIELD, 121
BRASHER, 2

BRASSFIELD, 46 153
BRATON, 120
BRAVERY, 172
BRAVIER, 60 166
BRAY, 73 201 224 227
BRAZEAU, 42 60 61 185 235 237
BRAZEAUX, 133 165
BRAZIER, 77 78
BRAZO, 118
BREARD, 140
BREARS, 77 144
BREASSIE, 169
BREBY, 109
BREDA, 118 150
BREDON, 60
BREEDING, 73 178 199 214
BRENER, 224
BRENT, 1
BRERDING, 78
BRESEE, 78
BRESSIE, 170
BRESTO, 72
BREWER, 38 46 77 78 144 174
BREWSTER, 104
BRIAN, 78
BRIANT, 4 93 234
BRICAUT, 165
BRICE, 157
BRICKEY, 170
BRIDGE, 60 97 129 182
BRIDGES, 78 142 198
BRIEDBACH, 100
BRIELLE, 130 133
BRIGGS, 77 78 144 204
BRIGHAM, 59
BRIGHT, 78 112 144 150 185 204 218
BRIGNE, 120
BRIGPOHE, 114
BRIHAM, 143
BRIMER, 78
BRINCKLEY, 77
BRINEKE, 133
BRINGLAS, 150
BRINK, 4 53 120
BRINKER, 166 169
BRINKLEY, 77
BRINLEY, 133
BRINNAGAN, 53
BRINSBACK, 60
BRINTHINGER, 77

BRISCOE, 230 234
BRISTON, 77
BRITE, 136 143
BRITIAN, 120
BRITT, 77
BRITTON, 78 178
BROCK, 2 71 73 192 193 195
BROCKET, 77
BROCKHART, 77 78
BROGDON, 77
BRONSON, 77
BROOK, 194 216
BROOKS, 38 46 53 60 61 77 120
  133 136 143 157 172 228 229
BROOKSHIRE, 40
BROOM, 174
BROSS, 77
BROTHERTON, 106
BROUILLETTE, 108
BROUSTEE, 49
BROUX, 60
BROWDER, 46
BROWLEY, 2
BROWN, 2 4 8 9 11 33 37 38 46
  53 59 60-62 71-73 77 78 92-94
  107 111-113 120 121 130 133
  136 137 141 142 144 146 148
  149 157 161 167 168 172 175
  178 185 186 188 189 191-199
  201-204 208 213 216 221 222
  225 233
BROWNDEN, 95
BROWNE, 133 166 189
BROWNEN, 224
BROWNING, 11 77 112 204
BROWNSON, 77 217
BRUCE, 7 77 152
BRUCIERAS, 117
BRUER, 8
BRUGUERE, 130
BRUIET, 140
BRUIN, 10 12
BRUMBFIELD, 187
BRUMFIELD, 12 188
BRUMLEY, 71
BRUMMET, 62
BRUMMIT, 126
BRUNDOG, 62
BRUNEL, 187
BRUNELL, 10
BRUNER, 3 53 100 237

BRUNET, 114 117
BRUNETT, 120
BRUNETTE, 214
BRUNNER, 155
BRUNO, 219
BRUSIER, 10
BRUTON, 121
BRUTTE, 168
BRUXIE, 16
BRVADAS, 157
BRY, 175
BRYAN, 12 53 60 61 112 120 133
  157 161 187 204 217
BRYANT, 2 12 53 77 78 107 112
  120 137 142 144 178 185 188
  190 212 229 231
BRYD, 53
BRYNSIDES, 195
BRYNSON, 78
BRYSON, 78 142 157
BUAT, 217
BUATE, 129
BUBONT, 64
BUCHANAN, 38 62 64 120 149
  190 214 225
BUCHANNON, 53 77 157
BUCHININ, 157
BUCIAT, 185
BUCK, 106
BUCKANEN, 77
BUCKER, 53
BUCKHART, 72 177 178
BUCKLEY, 12 77
BUCKNER, 72 172 200
BUCKNOLD, 4
BUCKRIDGE, 38
BUCLOUS, 1
BUDD, 141
BUDDAMEN, 198
BUET, 40 62
BUETT, 26 32
BUFF, 120
BUFFREY, 9
BUFORD, 53
BUICH, 1
BUILE, 3
BUIS, 172 183
BUISONET, 119
BUISSONNET, 133
BULDUC, 105
BULFINCH, 77 78

BULL, 62 126 172
BULLARD, 53 78
BULLINGER, 181
BULLIT, 172 216
BULLOCK, 77 144
BULRRY, 118 .
BUMPASS, 178 227
BUNDEN, 136
BUNNEL, 78
BUNNENU, 164
BURBANK, 78 130
BURBANKS, 161
BURCH, 40 53 55 62 148 192 204 238
BURCHARD, 71 178 206-208 210 212
BURCHEART, 46
BURCHEARTT, 46
BURCHFIELD, 200
BURCK, 57
BURCKHART, 188 206
BURD, 77
BURDEAUX, 61 62
BURDET, 225
BURDETT, 125
BURDINE, 4
BURDO, 10
BURDOINE, 157
BURDYNE, 10
BURGATE, 157
BURGE, 228
BURGES, 144
BURGESS, 77
BURGET, 61
BURGIN, 215
BURGIT, 112
BURGITT, 133
BURHALIS, 157
BURHAM, 226
BURK, 53 61 78 106 133 139 175 190 206 215 217
BURKE, 7 45 49 62 77
BURKEBD, 157
BURKELOE, 157
BURKENMASTER, 12
BURKETT, 38 78 136 137
BURKHART, 208
BURLESON, 2
BURLESTON, 4
BURMAN, 77
BURN, 78

BURNAM, 189
BURNER, 77 78
BURNES, 78 98 120 133 141
BURNET, 112 175 189 204 233
BURNETT, 4 48 53 77 112 162
BURNEY, 47 52 98 133
BURNHAM, 95 96 226
BURNNETT, 150
BURNS, 38 53 61-65 72 77 100 103 131 133 141 150 161 162 172 175 178 181 189 209 216
BURNSIDES, 71 77 192
BURR, 144 175
BURRICE, 1
BURRILL, 77
BURRIS, 2 40 64 92 154 185
BURROS, 193
BURROW, 78
BURROWS, 61 77 78 126 148
BURRUSS, 78
BURSON, 47
BURT, 136 176 231 232
BURTIN, 199
BURTON, 46 77 78 142 190 203 229 230
BURTS, 61 162
BURU, 139
BURWELL, 77 78
BUSBY, 133
BUSH, 12 77 120 204
BUSHSO, 119
BUSS, 73
BUSSNETTI, 157
BUSSON, 119
BUSWELL, 77 144
BUSZIERE, 157
BUTCHER, 10 12 61 63 204 218
BUTLER, 1 46 61 63 72 77 78 112 120 121 178 185 195 201 204 216
BUTTER, 154
BUTTERMILK, 3 4
BUTTNER, 131
BUTTON, 77
BUTTS, 120 144 202 203
BUYATE, 59
BUYRON, 61
BUYS, 127
BUZAN, 107
BUZENET, 140
BUZZARD, 224

BYATE, 57
BYBEE, 229 230
BYERS, 142
BYINGTON, 169 170
BYLES, 62
BYNUM, 2 188
BYRAD, 61
BYRD, 60-64 95 125 127 133 172 173 182 191
BYRNE, 133 171 174 184
BYRNS, 175
BYRNSIDES, 192 193
BYRS, 172
BYWATERS, 120

- C -

C---, 166
CABANA, 236
CABANN, 43
CABANNE, 49 64 133
CABBE, 41
CABEENM, 46
CABELL, 46
CACHOL, 41
CADDERMAN, 77
CADER, 14
CADERMAN, 78
CADINALLE, 130
CADLE, 78
CADWELL, 77
CAHILL, 78 198 202
CAHOT, 129
CAIDA, 118
CAIL, 204
CAILHOL, 41 164
CAILLOT, ii 48 49 51 58
CAILLOU, 133
CAILLOUX, 61
CAIN, 61 77 121 126 152 153 157 204
CAINE, 7
CAINEY, 4
CAINSFER, 64
CALAIS, 61
CALAWAY, 14 34
CALDWELL, 4 13 52 60-62 64 71 72 78 144 152 171 178 186 191-195 198 200 201 212 213 225 228
CALDWILL, 95

CALE, 114
CALL, 77 78 133 198
CALLAHAN, 3 4 53 54 143 189 190 204
CALLARA, 158
CALLARD, 158
CALLAVEN, 98
CALLAWAY, 44 62 112 113 124 125 133 137 157 158 188 208 239 240
CALLERSON, 15
CALLEW, 4
CALLIAM, 54
CALLIOT, 106 154
CALLIS, 78
CALLOWAN, 101
CALLOWAY, 53 57 142 204
CALLYWAY, 74
CALOIRE, 42
CALVAI, 131
CALVARY, 43
CALVE, 62 237
CALVERT, 2 8 78 189 233
CALVERY, 144
CALVIN, 53
CALWELL, 133
CAMBAS, 115
CAMBEL, 19
CAMBELL, 133
CAMERON, 78
CAMERY, 54
CAMP, 78 166
CAMPBEL, 140
CAMPBELL, 2 13 14 38 46 53 61 71 78 93 121 124 141 143 149 172 174 176 178 182 193 195 196 201 203 217
CAMPEL, 236
CAMPELL, 71
CAMPSTER, 57 61
CAMRON, 38 148
CANADA, 78 103
CANADIEN, 105
CANADY, 133 216
CANAE, 100
CANDRUFF, 204
CANE, 112 162 178 198
CANELL, 13
CANFIELD, 4 78
CANILERY, 158
CANNADAY, 112

CANNON, 15 61 121 168 190
CANNS, 158
CANNY, 78 148
CANOLE, 144
CANOTE, 150
CANOUR, 63
CANPO, 117
CANTARA, 116
CANTER, 121
CANTLEY, 73 112 200 201 204
CANTLY, 201
CANTREL, 75 100 101 104
CANTRELL, 77 78
CANTTY, 194
CAOS, 129
CAP, 46
CAPEHART, 61
CAPEHARTT, 178
CAPERON, 139
CAPON, 78
CAPPS, 93
CARA, 158
CARAPHEN, 129 133
CARARTHERS, 14
CARBINOE, 158
CARBONNEAU, 75
CARBONNEAUX, 130
CARDIN, 95
CARDINAL, 24 61 151 164
CARDINALIE, 130
CARDWELL, 43
CARELL, 38
CARELY, 178
CAREY, 8 121
CARGALE, 216
CARGILL, 78
CARL, 61 133
CARLETON, 224
CARLEY, 78
CARLIENE, 158
CARLIN, 63 133
CARLISLE, 78
CARLTON, 78
CARMACK, 161
CARMAN, 178
CARMEDY, 78
CARMODY, 148
CARMON, 150
CARNAHAN, 78
CARNAY, 152
CARNEY, 54 93

CARNHAM, 78
CARNS, 107
CAROL, 77
CARON, 58 59
CAROTHES, 166
CARPENTER, 1 45 46 48 52 60-62 78 121 225
CARPENTERS, 75
CARPENTIER, 100 102
CARPETITOR, 111
CARR, 13 74 78 100 150 151 211 217
CARRICK, 78
CARRICO, 62 106 133 207
CARRINGTON, 195
CARROL, 13 78 175
CARROLL, 142 144 148
CARRON, 57
CARROT, 1
CARRUTH, 137
CARRVIEX, 92
CARRY, 224
CARSEL, 192
CARSNER, 150
CARSON, 2 4 8 78 121 133
CARTABONA, 100
CARTAN, 92
CARTEE, 169
CARTER, 2 12 13 15 53 59 61 62 78 112 120 121 144 146 157 178 180 187 204 225 229
CARTIER, 63
CARTWRIGHT, 121 216
CARTY, 79
CARUTHER, 128
CARUTHERATHERS, 14
CARUTHERS, 126
CARVER, 112 170 204 225
CARWOOD, 121
CARY, 38 238
CASAGRANDE, 138
CASE, 178
CASEBOLT, 178
CASEY, 79 121 148 191 199
CASH, 177
CASHOU, 158
CASLEY, 6
CASNER, 38 189 218 223
CASON, 178
CASSADY, 61
CASSELRING, 133

CASSILLY, 176
CASTEEL, 7
CASTELLO, 25
CASTILIO, 14
CASTLE, 175
CASTLEMAN, 158 178 186
CASTLIER, 158
CASTLIO, 14
CASTONGET, 61
CASTROP, 155
CASVAN, 98
CASWELL, 78 122 144
CATALON, 102
CATEN, 112
CATES, 46 112
CATHAM, 92
CATHART, 176
CATHERWOOD, 218
CATHEY, 2 234
CATO, 79 184
CATON, 2 79 111 157 158 204
CATTERLIN, 144
CATTRON, 189
CAUCHRUN, 14
CAUGHEY, 79
CAULK, 22 23 27 60 61 64 79 110 150 158 213
CAUTHREN, 29
CAVANDER, 64
CAVE, 3 4 43 44 53-56 239
CAVENAGTS, 110
CAVENOR, 173
CAVETT, 133
CAWLEY, 78
CAYCE, 170
CAYENDER, 128
CAYEY, 13
CAYLEAUX, 63
CAYOLE, 138
CAYOU, 119
CAYRIOU, 119
CAYSE, 133
CAYTON, 94
CAZE, 115
CAZY, 196
CECIL, 180
CEERCE, 22
CERE, 1 75
CERIL, 166
CERLEY, 71 224
CERLY, 224

CERRE, 10 36 41 42 48 60 62 100 129 133 151 165 185 235
CESHER, 57
CESNER, 219
CEVIE, 158
CEVIENES, 166
CHABONNEAU, 133
CHADWELL, 78 129
CHADWICK, 79
CHAFFIN, 61
CHAIRMUER, 13
CHALIFOUX, 165
CHALLIFAUX, 61 62
CHALTEN, 4
CHAMARD, 74 75 100 101 103
CHAMART, 40
CHAMBERLAIN, 77 79
CHAMBERS, 2 15 31 61 63 79 92 106 134 144 158 175 201 204 234
CHAMBIRS, 130
CHAMBLIIS, 79
CHAMPAIGN, 13
CHAMPION, 88
CHAMPLAIN, 62 78
CHANCE, ii 78 121
CHANCELIER, 65 164
CHANCELLIER, 163
CHANCHILLAR, 13
CHANCHILLER, 36
CHANCILLER, 36
CHANDILLER, 29
CHANDILLON, 61
CHANDLER, 63 64 78 173 204 218
CHANDWICK, 133
CHANEY, 189
CHANIER, 137
CHANNON, 150
CHANRRION, 116
CHANTILON, 129
CHAPMAN, 4 79 95 134 146 158 175 188 225
CHAPPEL, 78
CHARAUONE, 109
CHARBONNEAU, 64
CHARBRANT, 41
CHARD, 78
CHAREVILLE, 165
CHAREY, 79
CHARLES, 54 146 172
CHARLESS, 212

CHARLESVILLE, 50
CHARLESWORT, 13
CHARLEVILLE, 61 64 65 74 100 101 103 119 237
CHARLEY, 143
CHARLTON, 78 137 229
CHARPANTIER, 134
CHARPENTIER, 64 134
CHARRETTE, 164
CHARRON, 164
CHARTARN, 233
CHARTIER, 61 109 134
CHARTRAIN, 64
CHARTRAN, 9 63 117 134 233
CHARTRAND, 61 63
CHASE, 78 161
CHATAL, 75
CHATEL, 75
CHATELERO, 116
CHATIGNY, 60 63
CHATOVER, 105
CHAUDILLON, 109
CHAUVIN, 48 62 75 211 234
CHAVALIE, 115
CHAVERS, 79
CHEAK, 73
CHEANEY, 44
CHEATHAM, 77 78 217
CHEATWOOD, 162
CHECK, 204
CHEEK, 134 171 200
CHEELEY, 15
CHEELY, 12
CHEERS, 54
CHENETE, 129
CHENEY, 61 128
CHERAQUISE, 109
CHEREAU, 64
CHERRY, 150
CHESTNUT, 79
CHETWOOD, 73
CHEVALIER, 42 235
CHEVALLIER, 41 49 57 58 60 61 97 134
CHEVELLE, 119
CHEWRING, 72
CHIL, 115
CHILDERS, 78 194 195 197 199
CHILES, 146 199
CHILLARD, 119
CHILLERE, 236

CHINEL, 131
CHINN, 12
CHINOWETH, 178
CHISHOLM, 107
CHISUM, 53 151
CHITON, 158
CHITWOOD, 60 62 150 1881 192 207 229
CHOISSER, 62
CHOLE, 115
CHOQUET, 101 134 233
CHORNETE, 235
CHORRET, 115
CHORRETE, 236
CHOTEAU, 42 61 66 115 158
CHOUQUET, 119
CHOUQUETTE, 61 150
CHOUTEAU, i 2 16 20 30 36 41-43 50 60 61 63 64 68 104 106 114 118 119 134 142 150 151 158 164 165 186 217 234 235
CHOVIN, 118
CHRISFIELD, 79 144
CHRISMAN, 142
CHRISTAIN, 4 53
CHRISTIAN, 78 79
CHRISTMAN, 178
CHRISTWELL, 203
CHRISTY, 13 134
CHROUCH, 141
CHUNING, 202
CHURCH, 79 121
CHURTY, 158
CIDERS, 78
CIMINS, 1
CINCAID, 121
CISSELLE, 134
CISSNA, 78
CIVS, 164
CLABORN, 78
CLACK, 38
CLAIBOURNE, 78
CLAMORGAN, 42 43 48-51 61 101 105
CLAMORGIN, 14
CLAMORMORGAN, 134
CLAMPET, 175
CLANAHAN, 79
CLANTON, 204
CLARET, 63
CLARK, 2 7 8 14 38 40 42 46 47

CLARK (continued)
60-62 64 68 71 73 77-79 95 97
98 100-102 107 112 121 129
130 134 142-144 148-150 158
161 175 178 189 192 195 198
200 204 227 229
CLARKE, 78 79 92 134 189 216 230
CLARKIN, 54
CLARKSON, 78 150
CLARKSTON, 142
CLARMO, 13
CLARMONT, 24
CLARY, 79 121
CLATON, 141
CLAY, 9 12 15 16 21 31 61 62 68
92 95 121 133 134 151 152 157
158 169 170 204 216
CLAYBROOK, 46 229
CLAYMORGAN, 118 151
CLAYTON, 1 141 194
CLEMAN, 45
CLEMENS, 54 64 68 130
CLEMENT, 79 151 178 212
CLEMENTS, 72 141
CLEMMENS, 134
CLEMMONS, 134
CLEMORGAN, 235
CLEMSON, 142
CLENDENNEN, 40
CLENDENNING, 204
CLENDINNEN, 137
CLERMONT, 26
CLETON, 2
CLEUIENNE, 158
CLEVELAND, 78 79 142 148 170
174 176
CLEVELNAD, 142
CLEVENGER, 38
CLEWIR, 158
CLIFFORD, 78
CLIFTON, 10 112 137 153 158
190 198
CLIMME, 158
CLINE, 63 78 121 144
CLINGINGSMITH, 127
CLINGINSMITH, 68
CLINGSMITH, 171
CLINTON, 178 208
CLIPPARD, 172
CLIPPER, 144 148
CLISBY, 78

CLIVE, 92
CLOCKER, 4
CLOPETER, 173
CLOPTON, 15
CLOSE, 78
CLOUGH, 14
CLUCK, 187
CLUK, 175
CLUKA, 130
CLYNE, 68
COALTER, 12 13
COASTRAUL, 4
COATS, 44 46 137 175 231 238
COBB, 68 77 78 95 168 204
COBERT, 78
COBORN, 173
COBS, 53
COCHRAN, 4 54 78 79 107 112
144 186 190 204 233
COCK, 180
COCKE, 79
COCKRAIN, 204
COCKRAN, 44 54 79
COCKRELL, 2 46 154
COCKRILL, 142
CODINGTON, 59
COEN, 61 97 98 134
COERSAM, 173
COFER, 175 199
COFFE, 49 51
COFFEE, 101
COFFER, 4
COFFMAN, 79 143
COGDALE, 7 46
COIGNARD, 42
COIGNIER, 68
COIL, 112
COILES, 15
COIN, 97
COIT, 144
COJIDI, 111
COKS, 121
COLBERT, 79 149
COLE, 2 14 60 71 72 78 79 92
112 144 149 169 170 178 193
194 202 204 208 211 217
COLEBY, 79
COLEMAN, 53 54 63 79 121 129
134 144 150 166 167 221 227
COLEVAN, 134
COLEY, 53

COLGAN, 112 137 143 158 240
COLGEN, 34
COLGIN, 63
COLIER, 53 55
COLLARD, 73 93 158 186
COLLELL, 49 164
COLLEN, 4
COLLENS, 178
COLLET, 4 53 216
COLLETT, 41 92 121 235
COLLEY, 46
COLLIER, 12 17 38 79 121 151 157 158 162 176 215 239
COLLIN, 3 4 106 131
COLLINS, 3 12 30 38 46 53 63 66 78 79 121 137 139 142 143 148 149 180 190 192 196 233
COLLUM, 61 68
COLMAN, 192
COLSON, 79
COLTET, 144
COLUMBEX, 79
COLUMBIA, 144
COLVIN, 68 71 134 186 194 195 199 200 208
COLWELL, 79
COMBE, 139
COMBS, 78 79 178 198
COMEGYS, 12 13 20 187
COMER, 112
COMMALT, 66
COMMENS, 134
COMPARET, 102
COMPARIOS, 40
COMPTON, 72 198
COMSTOCK, 68
CONAND, 40
CONAWAY, 61 134
CONCENT, 129
CONCHEV, 79
CONDE, 61 66 164 165
CONDER, 26
CONDERS, 151
CONEL, 72
CONELLAY, 169
CONESKER, 171
CONGDEN, 79
CONGER, 79 137
CONIER, 82
CONIYER, 158
CONKLIN, 79
CONLEY, 54
CONN, 193
CONNAYER, 158
CONNEL, 79
CONNELLY, 62 68 125 127
CONNER, 47 78 79 134 199
CONNOR, 61 62 68 118 134 144
CONNOWAY, 68
CONROD, 24 151 171 173 182
CONS, 49
CONSTANT, 62 211 233
CONSTU, 134
CONTLY, 120
CONWAY, 8 68 79 141 142 162 199
CONYERS, 54 79
COODY, 79
COOK, 4 16 32 52 54 61 64 78 79 95 106 134 148 151 154 171 180 190 204 217 227
COOKE, 1
COOKENDAFFER, 79
COOKSEY, 79
COOL, 26
COOLEY, 2 53 150 174 190 233
COOLMAN, 79
COOLY, 189
COON, 79 171
COONRAD, 64
COONS, 12 13 32 92 119 134 137 151 158
COONTZ, 61 63 68 233
COOPER, 2 48 61 63 78 79 92 101 121 125 127 134 150 152 154 166 167 169 175 190 196 197 201 202 209
COOTS, 38
COPELAND, 2 54 79 144
COPES, 12 13 151
COPHEN, 44
COPHER, 175
COPLER, 54
COPPAGE, 238
COPPEAGE, 54
COPPEDGE, 178
COPPENBARGER, 216
CORADE, 79
CORAM, 52
CORBIN, 94
CORBIT, 79
CORBONO, 13 24

CORDAIVER, 165
CORDELL, 64 134
CORDER, 68
CORGNARD, 165
CORKLE, 189
CORLEN, 45
CORLEW, 37 53 54 238
CORLEY, 15 68
CORMACK, 79
CORNEAU, 185
CORNELIUS, 38 68 127 178
CORNER, 174
CORNISH, 79 144
CORNO, 116
CORNOIREN, 20
CORNOIRER, 14
CORNOVER, 102
CORNWALL, 146 211
CORSER, 79
CORTNEY, 194
CORUM, 73 188-190
CORVOIRSER, 16
CORWIN, 79
COSE, 141
COSHOW, 14
COSNER, 171
COSTA, 188
COSTLEY, 79
COSTLY, 178
COTA, 13 24
COTE, 114 117 130
COTES, 73 186
COTHNER, 68
COTNER, 128 173
COTTE, 41 130
COTTER, 61 109
COTTERLIN, 152
COTTERMAN, 78
COTTLE, 13 15 18 60-62 93 130 134 151 158 163 222 227
COTTLEMAN, 112
COTTMAN, 79 172
COTTON, 62 134
COUDENIERE, 59
COUDER, 101 237
COULLIUX, 158
COULTER, 79 167 190 195
COULTON, 168
COUNS, 236
COUNTRYMAN, 79
COUNTS, 134

COUNTZ, 42
COURAVIE, 130
COURLOIS, 166
COURSALT, 144 152 167
COURTERMACH, 13
COURTLEY, 200
COURTMANCHE, 62
COURTNEY, 14
COURTOIS, 62 103 119 130 134 165 233
COUSIN, 61 125
COUSINS, 226
COUSOL, 158
COUSSOT, 163 165
COUT, 158
COUTE, 158
COUTELEY, 61 110
COUTLE, 158
COUZENEAU, 221
COWAN, 51 78 79 101 103 162
COWEN, 57 105 172 178
COWHEAD, 173
COWHERD, 202
COWIS, 195
COWLES, 79
COX, 1 14 15 38 46 61-63 66 68 77-79 98 100 101 121 125 134 144 146 163 172 178 182 204 207 216 220 222
COY, 7 73 167 189
COYL, 53 178
COYLE, 178
COYNOYER, 151
COYTEAUX, 98
COYTEUX, 101
COZART, 79
CRABBIN, 61
CRABIN, 110
CRABTREE, 40 191
CRADDOCK, 125
CRADER, 172
CRADY, 79
CRAFFORD, 66
CRAFORD, 134
CRAFT, 78 79 144 193 225
CRAFTS, 134 196
CRAGE, 134
CRAGF, 107
CRAGG, 1
CRAGHEAD, 137
CRAIG, 2 14 46 68 79 112 134

CRAIG (continued)
  142 144 150 158 167 177 181
  204 231
CRAIGHEAD, 112
CRAKS, 172
CRAMLISH, 78 79
CRAMP, 68
CRANDELL, 79
CRANE, 77 79 119 144 197
CRANK, 79
CRAPO, 79
CRARY, 79
CRATER, 171
CRAWFORD, 46 71 78 79 124
  125 134 144 172 204 234
CRAYTON, 79
CREACH, 186
CREAMER, 79 92 143
CREAR, 45
CREASON, 2 4 37 38 53 54
CREATH, 172
CRECROFT, 183
CREECH, 19 112 204
CREEK, 38 121
CREELAY, 79
CREELEY, 144
CREELIS, 107
CREESEY, 79
CREEYS, 106
CRELY, 68
CREPAN, 63
CREPEAU, 164
CREPO, 117
CRESAP, 189
CRESSCEY, 144
CRESSIN, 72
CRESSWELL, 126 187
CRESTWAITE, 45
CRESWELL, 61
CRETI, 131
CREW, 54
CREWS, 54 191
CRICKETT, 53
CRICKS, 172
CRIDDLE, 79
CRIDER, 141 178 193
CRIEL, 158
CRIPS, 61 134
CRISPIN, 62 110
CRISS, 220
CRISTISON, 121

CRISWELL, 137 172 173 207 231
CRITES, 181 182
CRITTENDEN, 79 152
CRITTENDON, 167
CRITZ, 171-173
CRO, 140
CROBARGER, 216
CROCHET, 134
CROCKETT, 38 53 137
CROFF, 71
CROFORD, 134
CROFT, 197
CROKER, 172
CROLEY, 174
CRONK, 79
CROOK, 121
CROPPER, 2 68 92 233
CROSBEY, 30
CROSBY, 11 22 30 42 61 68 134
CROSS, 46 79 144 149 154 170
  174 228
CROUCH, 53 186
CROUS, 143
CROW, 1 9 11 13 14 15 16 21 23
  30 32 34 61-64 66 68 71 79
  109 112 130 134 137 142 158
  161 162 194 196 199 202 203
  208
CROWDEN, 203
CROWDER, 79 80 144 171 198
  203
CROWLEY, 38 175
CROWSON, 238
CROWSYER, 186
CROZIER, 79
CRUCE, 68
CRUIZ, 36
CRUMB, 80
CRUMLISH, 70 80
CRUMP, 2 3 4 37 53 68 95 134
  137 168 189 190
CRUNELETON, 170
CRUSHAW, 80
CRUTCHELOR, 70
CRUTCHELOW, 68
CRUTZ, 68
CRUZAT, 57 58
CRUZEL, 139
CRYDER, 71
CRYTS, 127
CUDORCHE, 115

CULBERSON, 134
CULBERTSON, 8 68 142
CULLINS, 64 142
CULLOM, 112 204
CULLUM, 152
CULLY, 143
CULP, 7 79
CUMER, 158
CUMINS, 38
CUMMENS, 134
CUMMINGER, 158
CUMMINGS, 63 66 68 79 80 92 150 175 191 233
CUMMINS, 13 158 219 222
CUMPTON, 80
CUNDIFF, 112 169
CUNINGHAM, 141
CUNNIGHAM, 4
CUNNINGHAAM, 167
CUNNINGHAM, 13-15 53 63 78 80 95 96 137 148 149 167 168 170 215 226 232
CUNTHER, 224
CUPPLES, 173
CURATTE, 68
CURIN, 70
CURLE, 14
CURLETT, 80
CURNETT, 46
CURRAN, 50
CURREN, 70
CURRIER, 78 80
CURRIN, 144 188
CURROTE, 144
CURRY, 53 79 80 144 152 206
CURTIS, 53 79 80 144 189
CURTTEO, 172
CURVIN, 128
CUSAKE, 221
CUSHMAN, 79
CUSSING, 54
CUSTER, 12 99 101
CUTHERIDGE, 18
CUTLER, 79
CUTTING, 79 80
CUTURE, 97
CUYLER, 152 167
CUZOT, 117
CUZOTE, 117

– D –

D'ACHERUTTE, 101
D'AMOUR, 51
D'IBERVILLE, i
DABADIA, 235
DABBS, 79
DABERG, 35
DABNEY, 152 154 162 190
DABRON, 70
DACK, 171
DADE, 67 233
DAGGUIT, 150
DAGLEY, 38
DAGUET, 99 101
DAILEY, 134
DAILY, 79 80
DAIVIS, 188
DAKIN, 80
DALE, 4 5 54 55 153 154 175 189 225
DALEY, 54
DALLAM, 73
DALLASSUS, 158
DALLY, 219
DALONEY, 158
DALRYMPLE, 78 80
DALTON, 80
DAMAN, 80
DAMERSON, 80
DANEY, 70 144
DANFORTH, 225
DANIEL, 46 55 78 80 116 134 144 173 216
DANIELLE, 130
DANIELS, 80 144 148 203
DANLY, 224
DANNIEL, 204
DANSE, 158
DANST, 158
DANT, 226
DANTON, 98
DAPUIR, 109
DAQUET, 217
DARAT, 22
DARDEN, 80
DARE, 173
DARIA, 108
DARLING, 137

DARNATION, 95
DARNIEL, 119
DARSON, 158
DARST, 9 15 28 70 130 204 208
DARTER, 72
DASTIME, 158.
DATCHEMENDY, 99
DATCHERUT, 119
DATCHEVICT, 40
DATCHURUET, 74 75
DATCHURUT, 75 100 101
DATEHERUT, 40
DATSON, 175
DAUDIER, 70 71
DAUGHERTY, 126 158 173 192 196 204 222
DAUNE, 105
DAUPHIN, 71
DAUREN, 134
DAUSON, 80
DAVAULT, 171
DAVENPORT, 148 173 191
DAVID, 16 71 79 178 196
DAVIDS, 71
DAVIDSON, 16 78-80 101 200 203 204
DAVIS, 2-5 8 12 15 16 37 38 46 52 54 57 62 71 73 78-80 92 96 98 99 112 121 134 137 139 144 148 149 152 154 162 163 167 168 173 174 178 182 183 186 189 192 195 196 198 200 204 217 221 226 228-230 233
DAVISE, 158
DAWSON, 38 45 92 142 152 191
DAXY, 158
DAY, 16 62 78-80 121 130 144 168 187 231
DAYTON, 78 80 144
DAYWALT, 133
DEACON, 121
DEAKIN, 52
DEAL, 79 144
DEAN, 38 52 121 186
DEARBORN, 80
DEARING, 144
DEARRUL, 72
DEASTER, 15
DEAUCHAMP, 120
DEAVER, 201
DEAVINGPORT, 54

DEBAPTISTA, 139
DEBNAM, 80
DEBO, 115
DEBOARD, 79 80 144
DEBRUISSEAU, 101
DECAMP, 15 220
DECARI, 236
DECELLE, 101
DECHAMP, 41 150 151
DECHEE, 129
DECHENE, 118
DECHERSE, 163
DECK, 171
DECKER, 71 134 142 186 194 196 200-202 208
DECOMB, 119
DECOTE, 237
DECOURSEY, 178
DEEN, 193
DEER, 16
DEFLAMMAND, 134
DEFOUR, 1
DEFRESNE, 102
DEGAGNE, 134
DEGARDIN, 212
DEGERLAIS, 131
DEGGS, 213
DEGRAY, 62
DEGREW, 80
DEGRIMES, 100
DEGROSILLIERE, 134
DEGUER, 168
DEGUIRE, 75 134
DEGUR, 134
DEHAULT, 97
DEHEBRE, 43
DEHELTRE, 71
DEHERE, 165
DEHETRE, 43 131 235
DEHOIT, 112
DEILLE, 71
DEIRICE, 15
DEJANATT, 54
DEJARDIN, 217
DEJARLAI, 131
DEJARLAIS, 42 43 61 62 71
DEKERLEGAN, 102
DEKERLEGAND, 74
DELAND, 80
DELANNY, 169
DELANY, 168 193

DELAPLANE, 60 71
DELAREBAUDIERE, 62
DELARIBOUDOAIS, 134
DELASSUS, 49 50 57-59 71 101 105 134 165 191
DELASTERGUT, 119
DELAUNAY, 134
DELAUNERE, 165
DELAUNY, 71
DELAURIER, 100 101 106 131
DELAURIERE, 62 71
DELAURIERI, 59
DELAURIES, 71
DELAUVIER, 166
DELAUVIERE, 158
DELEULE, 158
DELEUVIERE, 41
DELEZIERE, 59
DELIENR, 120
DELILE, 185
DELILLE, 41 185
DELINDOT, 41
DELISLA, 236 237
DELISLE, 61 64 71 74 118 131
DELLILE, 42
DELOC, 164
DELONEY, 119
DELOR, 76 119 134 164 233
DELORIER, 101 114 235 237
DELORIERS, 49
DELOURIE, 119
DELPH, 173
DELSTER, 152
DELUQUERRE, 1
DELURE, 9
DELUZIERE, 48-50 57-59 71 97 134
DELUZIEU, 58
DEMARRE, 115
DEMASTER, 163
DEMING, 134
DEMINT, 71 134
DEMONY, 80
DEMOSCOSO, i
DEMOSS, 62 112 127 134
DENEYERS, 40
DENILLY, 119
DENINELLE, 48
DENIO, 80
DENISON, 158
DENISTON, 134

DENN, 189
DENNER, 80
DENNIS, 16 71 93 141 144 151 238
DENNISON, 225
DENNY, 16 46 119 158 211
DENOGINES, 134
DENOIE, 130
DENOUIE, 130
DENOVON, 109
DENOYE, 117 233
DENOYER, 63 70 71 119 120 134 208 233
DENOYERS, 40
DENSMAN, 238
DENSON, 40 73
DENT, 71 95 170 175 192-194 196
DENTON, 62 78 80 107 137
DENUNTER, 111
DEORO, 40 49
DEPENN, 200
DEPLACET, 71
DEPRA, 142
DEPRE, 114
DEPUTY, 64
DEQUETT, 19
DEQUIRE, 49 74 97 101 169
DERAMSEY, 213
DERAWAY, 16
DERBIGANY, 92
DERBY, 80
DERCHAUT, 134
DERGY, 158
DERING, 72
DERLAC, 108
DERLAND, 121
DERLEAN, 120
DEROCHE, 62 63
DEROCHER, 10
DEROIN, 210 222
DEROSELLIERS, 41
DEROUCHER, 181
DEROUCHEY, 33
DEROUCHY, 11
DEROUEN, 235
DEROUGHY, 16
DEROUIN, 51
DEROUSE, 150
DEROUSEL, 99 101
DEROUSSE, 71

DEROUSSEL, 101
DERRBERRY, 71
DERRICK, 64
DERRICKSON, 79
DERROCHER, 107
DERROGE, 114
DERRUEN, 117
DESATELLIS, 164
DESCHAMP, 164
DESELLE, 51 106
DESERUSSEAU, 163
DESHA, 48 144
DESHON, 80
DESMET, 42
DESOTEL, 235
DESOTO, i
DESPEENTREAUX, 139
DESPER, 201
DESROUSSE, 109
DESROUSSES, 75
DETCHEMENDY, 49 104 129
DETCHMENDY, 49
DETCHMONDY, 217
DETCHURUT, 49
DETONTY, i
DEUFAU, 15
DEVAU, 237
DEVAUGHN, 80
DEVAULT, 171
DEVEAU, 62
DEVENPORT, 130
DEVES, 166
DEVINE, 147
DEVOLSEY, 236
DEVORE, 61 70 71 80 120 185 227
DEVORES, 111
DEVUAL, 71
DEWALL, 148
DEWIT, 107
DEWITT, 78 80 134 154 207 213 215
DEXTER, 80 228
DIAL, 63
DIAMOND, 80
DIBLER, 79
DICE, 79
DICKENS, 144
DICKENSON, 78 80
DICKERSON, 8 45 141 149
DICKHOUST, 15

DICKINS, 62
DICKINSON, 152
DICKNEITE, 156
DICKSON, 62 71 80 134 144 178 189
DIDIER, 42 134
DIELLE, 58 129
DIETZEL, 228
DIGGS, 107 204
DILILLE, 42
DILL, 78 80 148 167
DILLARD, 52
DILLIN, 16
DILLINGER, 200
DILLINGHAM, 167
DILLON, 4 40 54 94 134 137 143 151
DILLS, 217
DILMORE, 80
DILWOOD, 173
DINALLY, 80
DINELLY, 154
DINGAS, 199
DINGLEY, 80 148
DINGS, 198
DINWIDDY, 46
DION, 70 163
DISHAY, 171
DISHON, 80
DISUET, 71
DITCH, 62 223
DITOR, 41
DITSLER, 130
DIXEN, 4
DIXON, 48 80 126 127 194
DIZE, 80
DOBBIE, 100
DOBBIN, 80
DOBBINS, 73 80
DOBOY, 148
DOBSON, 37 38 61
DOD, 217
DODD, 54 134
DODDS, 71 178 207
DODGE, i 1 48-51 58 60 75 97 100-102 104 106 129 134 150 151 166 217 226
DODIE, 118 163
DODIER, 71 150 163 164 235 236
DODS, 141
DODSON, 64 106 130 158 188 189

DODSON (continued)
192
DOE, 80 148
DOGAN, 119
DOGGETT, 70 134 168 201 209
DOGGETTE, 96 97
DOGGINS, 95
DOGHEAD, 64 70 71
DOINBURGH, 80
DOLACK, 158
DOLBY, 80
DOLITTLE, 228
DOLLAC, 61 71
DOLLARHIDE, 197 198 201
DOLLEY, 53
DOLPH, 80
DOMINE, 71
DOMINICK, 80 134
DOMINQUE, 62
DONAHAN, 98
DONAHUE, 98 102
DONALD, 80
DONALDSON, 80 121
DONALSON, 52
DONE, 80
DONELL, 121
DONEWAY, 80
DONNAHOE, 71
DONNAHUE, 216 217
DONNELLY, 62
DONNOHUE, 129 134 226
DONOHO, 80 206
DONOHOE, 38 46 144
DONOHUE, 102
DOOLIN, 2 144
DOOLING, 134 223
DOOLY, 55
DOPHINE, 15
DOQUET, 74
DOREN, 168
DORHERTY, 71
DORIAN, 71
DORLAC, 16 41 130 150 164 237
DORMAN, 111
DORNNAY, 34
DORNON, 106
DORRISS, 121 143
DORROIN, 118
DORSAY, 15
DORSE, 170
DORSETT, 80

DORSEY, 71 109 134 144
DORSIEVRE, 165
DORSON, 111
DORWAER, 233
DOSEY, 80
DOSIER, 7
DOSS, 62
DOSSEY, 80
DOTEY, 107
DOTSEL, 203
DOTSON, 15 16 18 134 223
DOTY, 80 107 142 146
DOUAGH, 54
DOUBLEDAY, 134
DOUBLENAY, 1
DOUDE, 62
DOUGAN, 148
DOUGHERTY, 61 70 71 78 80 121
  137 144 196 201
DOUGHTON, 80
DOUGHTY, 210
DOUGLAS, 4 52 54 150 151 162
DOUGLASS, 16 43 54 70 80 107
  195 231
DOULTON, 49 51
DOUSIRS, 130
DOUSMAN, 148 149 152 167 228
DOUSOMAN, 144
DOVER, 144
DOVORE, 134
DOW, 6 80
DOWEL, 215
DOWELL, 80
DOWING, 210
DOWLIN, 62
DOWLING, 80 148 207
DOWNES, 80
DOWNING, 80 121 144 158
DOWNS, 80 144
DOWNY, 45
DOWSETT, 79 80
DOWTY, 62 126 134 173
DOXEY, 2 46
DOYAL, 80
DOYEL, 194
DOYL, 52 178
DOYLE, 134 175 189
DOYN, 166
DOYSON, 97
DOZER, 54 106
DOZIE, 158

DOZIER, 204 206
DRACE, 196 200 203
DRAGON, 140
DRAICE, 121
DRAKE, 2 16 46 48 80 141 176 215
DRAKINS, 64
DRAPER, 64 121 158 176
DRECHSEE, 232
DRENNON, 80
DRENON, 227
DRESSIER, 80
DRINKARD, 46 150 190
DRINNEN, 134
DRISCOLL, 142 181
DRIVER, 80
DROLETT, 178
DROOM, 172
DROORE, 173
DROTET, 72
DROUART, 102
DROUIN, 61 165
DROULLARD, 139
DRUMMOND, 46
DRUMMONDS, 216
DRUMMONS, 15 16 121
DRURY, 16 78
DRYBREAD, 108 126
DRYHEAD, 63
DUBAL, 115
DUBARDO, 41
DUBAUGH, 16
DUBAY, 64
DUBE, 64
DUBEAUGH, 16
DUBET, 15
DUBIGNY, 119
DUBOIS, 61 80 109 111 158
DUBORD, 102
DUBOURG, 49
DUBOY, 80 130
DUBREUIL, 75 102 134 163 234 237
DUBREUIT, 165
DUBREUL, 165
DUBREVEL, 164
DUBREVILLE, 186
DUBRIEIEL, 40
DUBRIEL, 60 106
DUBRIELLE, 60 62 64
DUBROIL, 119

DUBROY, 116
DUBRUIT, 41
DUBUC, 41
DUBUE, 41
DUBUQUE, 64
DUCHAN, 80
DUCHASSIN, 63
DUCHENE, 115
DUCHEQUET, 119
DUCHEQUETTE, 61
DUCHMAN, 33
DUCHOQUET, 165
DUCHOQUETE, 116
DUCHORIQUET, 40
DUCHOUQUENT, 164
DUCHOUQUET, 49 102 119 134
DUCHOUQUETTE, 68 185
DUCILLE, 139
DUCKER, 73
DUCLO, 41
DUCLOS, 49 51 61 74 101-104 134
DUCOMB, 68 139
DUDLEY, 79 93 148 229
DUEPER, 134
DUETT, 80
DUFAU, 42
DUFAUT, 163 236
DUFAUX, 185
DUFF, 49 95 100 102 168 169 202
DUFFY, 80 173
DUFOIS, 68
DUFOUR, 49 57 63 65 67 129
DUGAN, 2 75 79 80 99
DUGAND, 102
DUGAY, 65
DUGGAN, 140
DUGGINS, 68 78 148
DUGINS, 105
DUIGAN, 106
DUIGUIRE, 134
DUJO, 117
DUKE, 79 80
DULANY, 93
DULAY, 48
DULCOUND, 1
DULE, 234
DULEY, 5 112 144 152 167 177
DULIN, 15
DULL, 121
DULON, 178

DULY, 137 144
DUMA, 151
DUMAY, 61 64 68 134
DUMON, 42
DUMOND, 19 27 29 61
DUMONT, 236
DUMORE, 15
DUMOSS, 62
DUN, 238
DUNAND, 106
DUNBAR, 80
DUNCAN, 1 2 8 40 43 67 72 79 80 121 137 138 150 163 171 175 178 186 194 200 202 225 227
DUNCANSON, 80
DUNCASTER, 67
DUNEGAN, 131 164
DUNEGANT, 64 165
DUNEQANT, 166
DUNEQUANT, 166
DUNHAM, 80 143
DUNIGAN, 58 121
DUNKIN, 68 199
DUNLAP, 46 137 150 152 173 178
DUNLAY, 121
DUNN, 45 46 54 61 68 80 102 121 129 130 153 173 177 240
DUNNAN, 80
DUNNICA, 112 137 167
DUNNINGTON, 46
DUNNIVANT, 80
DUNONY, 144
DUNTON, 80
DUNVALDE, 164
DUNWADY, 92
DUPIN, 63 68 107
DUPLAUY, 43
DUPONT, 101 104
DUPRE, 61 105 106
DUPRES, 134
DUPUIC, 109
DUPUIS, 235
DUPUY, 65 116 140
DUQIER, 1
DUQUELLE, 158
DUQUET, 130
DUQUETT, 23 24
DUQUETTE, 16 130
DURALDE, 51 75
DURAND, 164
DURANT, 163

DURBEN, 2
DURBIN, 150 189
DURBOIS, 116
DURCY, 105 106
DUREN, 189
DUREY, 40
DURFEY, 16
DURGEN, 80
DURHAM, 71 192
DUROCHER, 41 235
DUROSER, 75
DURSEY, 65
DURTON, 144
DURWAY, 80
DURY, 75
DUSHUCATE, 118
DUSKY, 5 54
DUSTON, 46
DUTCHIMENDY, 1
DUTCHMANDY, 106
DUTRECUBLE, 108
DUTTON, 75 204
DUVAL, 64 98 103 134
DUVALDE, 41
DUVALL, 67 186 224
DUVATT, 225
DUVAUL, 38
DWELL, 80
DYAL, 64 65 129
DYE, 67 121
DYER, 79 121 137 142 176 231
DYLE, 121
DYRE, 16
DYSART, 38
DYSERT, 46

- E -

EADES, 178
EADS, 64 121 134 229
EADY, 94
EAFF, 72
EAGERS, 64
EAKER, 171
EAKINS, 173
EAMON, 81
EARL, 16 38 78
EARLE, 67
EARLY, 54 121 144
EARNES, 16
EARS, 67

EARSLEY, 79 144
EARTHMAN, 2 150 175
EASON, 80
EASR, 134
EAST, 54 80 144
EASTACHE, 67
EASTER, 195
EASTERS, 65 192
EASTES, 71
EASTIN, 8 54
EASTIS, 178
EASTLAND, 80
EASTMAN, 80 152
EASTON, 16 59 67 80 102 118 150 158 162 217
EASTRIDGE, 134
EASTWOOD, 72 178
EATON, 16 54 79 80 121
EATUE, 67
EATY, 79
EAVES, 17
EBENNS, 203
EBERT, 26
EBOW, 158
ECHART, 17
ECKFORD, 80
EDDS, 71 72 223
EDDY, 79 144
EDERTY, 80
EDGAR, 49 104 125
EDICK, 80
EDINGER, 171
EDINGTON, 79 80
EDISON, 56 94 173
EDLING, 17
EDMONDS, 71 99
EDMONDSON, 54
EDMONS, 158
EDMONSON, 204
EDMUNSON, 4
EDWARD, 204
EDWARDS, 4 12 17 27 38 46 53 54 61 62 64 67 72 78-80 92 112 121 134 137 158 170 175 177 180 186-188 195 206 208
EGELSTON, 79 80
EGLISE, 62
EIGELBERGER, 226
EIGERT, 171
EIGNET, 134
EKELSTON, 80

ELAM, 80 195
ELAMS, 175
ELARA, 158
ELCLOSH, 17
ELDER, 121 142 177 189 191
ELDRIDGE, 189
ELDRIGE, 121
ELIAS, 114
ELINGTOM, 4
ELISON, 4
ELISTON, 204
ELKINS, 216 225
ELLER, 79
ELLETT, 17
ELLICOTT, 5 38
ELLIE, 106
ELLINGER, 80 144
ELLINGTON, 45 54 78 121 238
ELLIOT, 46 54 121 216
ELLIOTT, 1 2 44 54 63 74 80 121 144 183 220 240
ELLIS, 4 40 53 54 61 80 92 107 112 121 129 134 137 142 150 181 182 185 201 204 207 217 221
ELLISON, 52 54 142 158 184 213
ELMENDORF, 80
ELMUNDORFF, 144
ELSON, 189
ELSTEN, 54
ELSTON, 54 167 175 204
ELWELL, 78
ELY, 141
EMANUEL, 106
EMARINE, 17
EMBERSA, 144
EMBREE, 175
EMERSON, 214
EMERY, 16 80
EMMANS, 92
EMMENS, 203
EMMERSON, 79 80
EMMONDS, 210
EMMONS, 80 134 144 152 198
EMOURON, 17
ENDICOTT, 216
ENDIN, 204
ENGEL, 140 214
ENGLE, 61
ENGLEHEART, 54
ENGLISH, 78 79 107 121 144 184

ENGLISH (continued)
  222
ENJART, 175
ENLOE, 72 196 198-200 202
ENSAW, 17
ENYARD, 2
EOFF, 151
EOMER, 81 144
EPPLER, 149
ERICKSON, 46 149
ERINNES, 211
ERNAUD, 65
ERNES, 17
ERSKINE, 81
ERVINE, 92
ERWEN, 81
ERWIN, 46 81 173 190 204
ESCALERA, 49
ESCLIEU, 138
ESCRIVANO, 64
ESDALE, 209
ESHAM, 54
ESHBOROUGH, 62
ESHBOUGH, 130
ESKS, 171
ESSLEIVER, 81 89
ESTEL, 137
ESTELL, 5 54
ESTES, 2 3 5 38 54 61 65 92 95
  96 112 137 154 167 168 177
  199 200 225
ESTILL, 2 112
ESTIS, 92 134 197
ESTUS, 134
ETHELL, 5 43 54
EUDIS, 96
EULENSTINE, 17
EUSTACHE, 126
EUSTIN, 98
EVAN, 158
EVANS, 1 2 37 38 54 63 72 78 80
  81 92 95 112 134 137 144 148
  152 158 167 173 178 182 184
  185 188-190 192 193 208 224
  227 229 238
EVELAND, 81
EVEN, 96 144
EVENS, 17 134 158
EVERETT, 61 78 81
EVERITT, 134
EVERSALL, 16

EVINS, 54 121
EWEEN, 175
EWELL, 215
EWEN, 81
EWIN, 189
EWING, 46 54 62 81 112 134 137
  142-144 149 152 158 162 167
  175 190
EZELL, 81

– F –

FABRIRE, 130
FACHE, 117 118
FACKLER, 196
FACTTO, 109
FADERHOUSE, 18
FAGENBURNER, 18
FAGOT, 50 64 103
FAIN, 236
FAINEN, 5
FAINER, 102
FAIR, 154
FAIRFIELD, 81
FAIT, 81
FALE, 54
FALES, 81
FALKNER, 54
FALLAR, 116
FALLENASH, 61 126
FALLIN, 61 63 67 68
FALLIS, 64 65 134 151 158
FALONER, 216
FANNER, 158
FANT, 17
FAR, 54
FARAR, 192
FARE, 18
FAREL, 50 98
FAREST, 149
FARGUHAR, 151
FARIS, 112 181 211 221
FARMER, 17 18 112 121 137 182
  199 200
FARNAX, 18
FARNESWORTH, 18 27
FARNHARM, 56
FARNSVACK, 1
FARNSWORTH, 62 81 130 134
  158 187 188 212
FARQUHAR, 138 168

FARR, 47
FARRAR, 47 194 195 200 216
FARREL, 102
FARRELL, 75 78 81 144
FARRER, 204
FARRINGTON, 79
FARRIONE, 112
FARRIS, 92 134 208 212 233
FARROR, 62
FARROT, 41
FARROW, 61 65 67 71
FARRY, 81
FARTER, 17
FAUBASH, 5
FAUCHE, 101 104
FAUCHER, 225
FAUCY, 37
FAUGHT, 167
FAUL, 110
FAULKERSON, 158
FAULKNER, 25 81
FAUROT, 65
FAUSTISMEN, 110
FAUY, 81
FAYE, 112 158
FAYET, 166
FAYLOR, 121
FAYZER, 64
FEAGAN, 8
FEARS, 81
FEATON, 54
FEAZLE, 8
FECHTEL, 156
FECKLY, 17
FECTEAU, 158
FECTLE, 155
FECTUEAU, 32
FEILTEAU, 221
FELAND, 175 189
FELIP, 164
FELLER, 149
FELLOWS, 220
FELTEAUX, 151
FELTY, 81
FENETI, 114
FENN, 149
FENNEWALD, 156
FENT, 24
FENTON, 4 43 238
FENTUM, 227

FENWICK, 49 51 58 61 63 64 67
  75 98 99 102 103 138 154 216
  223 226
FERGUS, 81
FERGUSON, 48 55 64 81 112 121
  137 144 177 182 189 199 204
  219
FERRALL, 208
FERREE, 231
FERREL, 1 17 18 80 121
FERRELL, 17 80 101 200
FERRENS, 38
FERRET, 41
FERRIL, 196
FERRILL, 2 63
FERRIS, 144 187
FERRISON, 81
FERRY, 61 134 158
FERTRE, 119
FESSENDEN, 81
FETCH, 17
FETTER, 17
FEUDER, 67
FEUILLETOT, 105
FEVIER, 54
FEWGETT, 121
FIA, 137
FICE, 111
FICETT, 17
FICKES, 44
FICKLE, 121
FICKLIN, 176
FICUS, 5
FIDECHARME, 118
FIELD, 38
FIELDS, 8 38 47 81 121
FIENCERAU, 164
FIGG, 79
FIGHT, 64
FIGITT, 2
FILBUSTIER, 75
FILCHER, 54 144
FILIBUSTIER, 100 101 104
FILIBUSTOER, 104
FILLUET, 81
FILSON, 102 105 106 110
FINCH, 54 81 215
FINDLAY, 92 149
FINDLEY, 47 48 54 66 216
FINE, 17 18 42 66 92 112 134 164

FINE (continued)
165 204 214
FINLEY, 5 8 38 44 63 66 75 102
121 141
FINLY, 142
FINN, 80
FINNEY, 5 153
FISH, 81
FISHBECK, 173
FISHER, 5 8 17 18 66 72 78 81
134 141 142 150 158 168 175
187 192 196 197 231 234
FISK, 81
FITCH, 79
FITTEAU, 130
FITTRE, 181
FITTS, 152
FITZGERALD, 81 189
FITZGERRARD, 148
FITZGIBBON, 61 65 69
FITZHUGH, 204
FITZJEFFERY, 81
FITZPATRICK, 80
FITZSAME, 185
FITZWATER, 203 206
FIX, 189
FLAHE, 54
FLAIR, 17
FLAMO, 118
FLANAING, 128
FLANDRIN, 66 165
FLANDRON, 119
FLANNERY, 121
FLANRY, 216
FLARE, 17 18
FLAT, 72
FLATT, 178
FLAUGHERTY, 17 23 66 158
FLEETWOOD, 38 47
FLEMING, 54 121 234
FLEMMING, 8 62 80 81 95 118
173 227
FLESHER, 81
FLETCHER, 2 38 66 78 81 154
190 216
FLEURI, 41
FLICK, 81
FLIED, 169
FLING, 81 144 148 167
FLINN, 80 144 173
FLINT, 134 158

FLISHER, 79 81
FLOID, 47 48 81
FLORA, 64 101
FLORES, 150
FLORVER, 99
FLOURIONT, 69
FLOWER, 78 81
FLOWERS, 81
FLOYD, 78 80 81 154 188 190
FLUGER, 158
FLYNN, 69 129
FOBES, 219
FOCKE, 18
FOEGUSON, 202
FOISEY, 69
FOKES, 54
FOLDENER, 69
FOLEY, 54 81 177 238
FOLGER, 176
FOLLIS, 19 22 29
FOLSOM, 62
FONTAIN, 80
FOOL, 58
FOOT, 47 81 149
FOOY, 69
FORBES, 46 81 92
FORCHET, 185
FORD, 17 69 81 121 163 191 204
FOREMAN, 59 62 112 121 126
134 191 233
FOREST, 46
FORICE, 54
FORIS, 121 141
FORMAN, 8 18 134 158 229
FORREST, 46
FORRIL, 134
FORT, 46 158
FORTEE, 107
FORTIN, 69 103 134
FORTNEY, 43
FORTUNA, 1
FORTUNEBERRY, 182 183
FORY, 95
FOSSETT, 81
FOSTER, 1 2 5 46 61 69 73 78 80
81 94 107 112 121 126 134 142
148 174 175 189 190 208
FOSTIN, 164
FOUNTAIN, 37 54 81 144
FOURNEIR, 134
FOURNIE, 233

FOURT, 112
FOUSHEE, 17
FOUST, 204
FOUTAIN, 4
FOWLER, 1 2 4 37 38 46 54 81 120 121 189 197
FOX, 17 47 80 81 121 148 189 229 230
FOY, 63 112
FRAIL, 144
FRAILL, 80
FRAIZER, 150
FRAKER, 230
FRAKES, 175
FRAME, 40 121
FRANCE, 18
FRANCEWAY, 66
FRANCIS, 80 81 121 144 148
FRANCOIS, 163 164
FRANCY, 119
FRANK, 104
FRANKLIN, 78 81 144 199
FRANKLINBURG, 200
FRANKS, 62 81 126
FRARRIS, 198
FRARY, 81
FRASER, 2 200
FRASIER, 72 196
FRASURE, 150
FRAY, 141 144
FRAYNOTH, 17
FRAYNUM, 107
FRAZARE, 204
FRAZER, 64 69 119 175
FRAZERWOOD, 206
FRAZIER, 21 92 150 158 173 196 203
FRAZURE, 17 18
FREEMAN, 4 5 54 61 81 127 144 169 193
FREIGHNER, 81
FREIZEL, 173
FREMON, 104
FRENCH, 4 5 81 188 237
FRESTOE, 149
FREY, 168
FRIAR, 203
FRICKLE, 121 173
FRIEND, 65 66 69 95 97 128 135
FRINKE, 54
FRISON, 140

FRITH, 81
FRIZEL, 173
FRIZELL, 143
FROST, 38 81
FRUIT, 112 143
FRUST, 99
FRY, 81 121 191
FRYE, 8
FRYER, 72 81 112 148 194 223
FUECHAN, 54
FUEGIT, 4
FUENTIMENT, 140
FUGAT, 51 54
FUGATE, 217 229 230
FUGET, 174
FUGETT, 121
FUGETTE, 158
FUGITT, 2
FULAND, 64
FULBRIGHT, 173
FULCHER, 2 4 190
FULKENSON, 92
FULKERSON, 2 4 17 18 121 151 152 167 175
FULLER, 81
FULLERTON, 62 71 142 212
FULLINGTON, 17
FULMWIDER, 173
FULSOM, 65
FULTON, 18 81 121 135
FUNDERBARK, 120 121
FURGASON, 81
FURGERSON, 46 121
FURGESON, 135
FURGSON, 54
FURGUSIN, 4
FURGUSON, 40 78 81 112 158
FURLEY, 54
FURLINE, 17
FURR, 182 213
FYGHT, 126

– G –

GABBY, 158
GABEARTH, 158
GABOBERT, 99
GABRIEL, 84 92
GACARD, 101
GADOBERT, 41 50 75 102 104
GAFFERSON, 122

GAGE, 47 81 144
GAGNIER, 237
GAGNON, 129 165 235
GAIGNON, 68
GAIL, 68 81
GAIN, 192
GAINES, 81
GAINET, 166
GAIS, 42 233
GAISDANAS, 135
GAITHER, 47 144
GAKS, 173
GALASPIE, 112
GALAWAY, 54
GALBREATH, 137 231
GALE, 1 81 203
GALEN, 119
GALL, 71 144 193-195
GALLAGHER, 228
GALLAHER, 1
GALLAND, 223
GALLASPIE, 143
GALLEHER, 183
GALLIGHER, 81
GALLY, 158
GALVE, 114
GAMACHE, 65 68 134 135 233
GAMASH, 119
GAMBELL, 224
GAMBLE, 81 144 162
GAMELIN, 135
GAMLIN, 119 120
GAMMELL, 81
GAMMON, 112 204
GANAU, 151
GANDRON, 138
GANIER, 65
GANN, 81 122
GANON, 114 117
GARCIA, 158
GARDHEAFAIR, 19
GARDICK, 148
GARDINER, 78 81
GARDNER, 8 18 63 144 185 199
GAREAU, 61
GAREN, 108
GARET, 120
GARISH, 150
GARLAND, 61 63
GARLICH, 18
GARLICK, 81

GARMAN, 18
GARMAND, 143
GARMON, 137
GARNER, 8 39 54 112 135 175 183
GARNETT, 81
GARNIER, 134 217
GARNSEY, 141 191
GAROUX, 135
GARRET, 1 153 231
GARRETT, 78 81 144 152 153 173 188 190
GARRING, 81
GARRISON, 81 148
GARTIN, 229
GARTON, 142
GARTWELL, 152
GARUIN, 81
GARVEY, 81
GARVIIN, 19
GARY, 230
GASCON, 110
GASCOU, 19
GASH, 7 8
GASHMAN, 157
GASKEY, 144
GASLIN, 237
GASON, 122
GASPER, 57 92
GASPERSON, 202 203
GASS, 106
GATA, 18
GATAR, 119
GATES, 43 78 81 165 222
GATEWOOD, 79
GATLING, 81
GATTY, 65
GAU, 130
GAUDER, 131
GAUDIN, (dedication) ii
GAUGE, 39
GAURTNEY, 81
GAUTIE, 130
GAUTIER, 64
GAUVRAUX, 48
GAUYET, 41
GAVENS, 168
GAVESTEN, 4
GAVIAN, 120
GAVIN, 54
GAVNER, 198

GAY, 46 53 176
GAYIAN, 54
GAYNE, 166
GAYON, 63 68 92
GEAREM, 98
GEATHER, 226
GEBERT, 222
GEE, 190 204
GEIGER, 227
GEMERSON, 191
GEMINDEN, 228
GENDRON, 48 51 64
GENEREAUX, 64 120
GENEROUX, 92
GENNINGS, 2
GENTLE, 158
GENTRY, 2 4 5 7 8 54 81 175 188 207 215 240
GENTZSCH, 228
GEORGE, 39 155 187
GEORGES, 98
GERARD, 20 67 100 102
GERMAIN, 43 64 75
GERMAN, 81 158
GERRARD, 61 64 65 135
GERRY, 81 177
GERVAIS, 64 110 130
GETARD, 118
GETTIS, 81
GEUEREIS, 110
GEVERO, 1
GEYER, 2
GIBANY, 64 65
GIBAULT, 49 103 106 109 139
GIBBS, 2 45 122 142 234
GIBERT, 100 102 103
GIBKINS, 103
GIBNEY, 173
GIBONEY, 63 135 182
GIBSON, 2 64 67 72 78 81 92 112 121 122 129 135 137 144 149 158 174 175 178 192 195 224 228 233
GIDDINGS, 191
GIGUIERE, 64
GILBAULT, 120
GILBERT, 26 27 30 31 75 76 79 135 144 149 162 167 210 211
GILCHEL, 81
GILES, 81 184

GILL, 18 39 61 64 81 119 120 121 134 139 142 167
GILLAM, 4
GILLAN, 121 122
GILLASPIE, 81
GILLASPY, 178
GILLEAUGH, 135
GILLEGAN, 81
GILLELAND, 173 223
GILLET, 149
GILLETT, 19 142
GILLIAM, 38 39 216
GILLIGAN, 148
GILLIS, 19 61 130 219
GILLISPY, 167
GILLIUM, 54
GILLMORE, 39
GILLOCK, 225
GILLS, 158
GILLUM, 121
GILMORE, 19 62 64 135 158 226
GILSON, 144
GILSTRAP, 152 191
GILVER, 117
GIMES, 98
GINN, 81
GINNARD, 19 29
GINNINGS, 81
GINNINS, 238
GIPSON, 135 190
GIRARD, 140 165
GIRONARD, 1
GIROUARD, 48-51 65 103
GIROULT, 109
GIRRARD, 132
GIRTY, 64 99 102 132
GIST, 73
GITTAR, 170
GITZ, 173
GIVENS, 1 19 25 35 178
GIVINS, 216
GLADDEN, 122
GLADHILL, 81
GLAIZE, 213
GLASCOCK, 59 149 162 173 177
GLASGOW, 43 54 142 176 178 192
GLASOW, 5
GLASS, 5 19 62 204 219
GLASSCOCK, 122 182

GLASSON, 135
GLEEN, 5
GLEETON, 81 144
GLEM, 122
GLEN, 54
GLENDAY, 18
GLENN, 4 81 190 213
GLISSON, 81
GLOSTER, 81
GLOVER, 64 81 178 191 204
GLOYD, 81
GOBEAU, 64 132
GOBEL, 201
GOBLE, 81
GOCHOM, 173
GODAIR, 61 63 65 67 125 144 148
GODDES, 5
GODDNOE, 73
GODEFROY, 43
GODER, 108 132 138
GODFRAY, 132
GODFREY, 19 65
GODIER, 132
GODIN, (dedication) ii
GODSEY, 82 148
GODSON, 82
GOE, 150 151
GOELNER, 155
GOETHER, 175
GOFF, 82
GOFORTH, 66 132 189
GOGGIN, 82 144
GOIN, 52
GOINGS, 191
GOKIE, 26
GOLDEN, 82
GOLDIN, 54
GOLIN, 130
GOLTERNART, 18
GOMEZ, 75
GONNETTE, 107
GONON, 114
GONZALES, 65
GOOD, 2 54 150
GOODALL, 167
GOODDING, 189
GOODE, 196 197
GOODEN, 177
GOODHUE, 54
GOODHUGH, 5
GOODIN, 38 54

GOODING, 150 153 154 233
GOODRICH, 13 18 19 35 69 112 137 187
GOODRICK, 158
GOODRIDGE, 82
GOODRO, 37
GOODSIN, 4
GOODSON, 82
GOODWIN, 7 81 125 144 171
GOOTH, 54
GORBIT, 82
GORDEN, 72
GORDES, 109
GORDON, ii 1 19 45 54 69 78 81 82 93 112 121 137 142 149 175 203 204 240
GORE, 82 225
GORET, 63 69
GORFORTH, 4
GORHAM, 47
GORLEY, 82
GOROUARD, 217
GORSE, 82
GORTEN, 54
GORTON, 82
GOSA, 168
GOSEN, 112
GOSLIN, 54
GOSMAN, 82
GOSS, 150 206
GOSSE, 105
GOSSIN, 99
GOTIER, 233
GOTIO, 114
GOTIOT, 62 66
GOUDON, 100
GOULDING, 82
GOUR, 130
GOUSTZ, 54
GOVE, 82
GOVERO, 1
GOVERS, 1
GOVORO, 129
GOVORT, 129
GOVREAU, 66
GOVRO, 59 129
GOWAN, 82
GOWEN, 148
GOWER, 82
GOZA, 95 173 183
GRAAMS, 111

GRACE, 19 63 81
GRADY, 19 178
GRAF, 132
GRAGANE, 112
GRAGG, 1 39 48 82 144 175
GRAHAM, 5 18 44 54 65 69 82 112 132 162 176 191 204 210 212
GRAHEART, 137
GRAIMNARD, 132
GRAMMONT, 50
GRAND, 92
GRANDE, 69 129
GRANDY, 81 82
GRANT, 54 81 82 137 142 167 175 230
GRANTHAM, 19
GRAPEVINE, 82 177
GRASON, 137
GRASS, 132
GRASSAW, 178
GRATCOT, 43
GRATIOT, 42 69 118 132 164 236
GRATIOTT, 150
GRATIS, 69
GRATOR, 23
GRAVELLE, 58
GRAVES, 4 47 81 82 94 121 152 173 183 204
GRAVIENE, 19
GRAVIER, 65 92 132
GRAVLIN, 151
GRAY, 2 4 5 54 59 63 69 82 109 112 119 122 132 139 142 149 170 177 180 189 204 238
GRAYHAM, 189 224
GRAYISON, 55
GRAYSON, 5 37 54 177 191
GRAYUM, 2 37 237
GRAZIER, 158
GREATER, 63
GREATHOUSE, 229
GREEMAN, 82
GREEN, 2 4 19 35 47 54 61-63 65 72 82 84 92 108 122 126 140 144 150 152 158 162 173 175 176 183 186 187 194
GREENE, 106 121 132 227
GREENEWAULT, 132
GREENLEAF, 142

GREENSTREET, 52 73 130 142 170 186 192 193 196 198-200 202 214
GREENUP, 95
GREENWALT, 62 63
GREER, 99
GREFORE, 132
GREGG, 2 81 121 122 188
GREGNON, 152
GREGOIRE, 42 100
GREGORY, 8 82 141 171 202 204
GREHIER, 41
GREIFE, 180
GREN, 139
GRENAVAL, 98
GRENE, 117
GRENON, 129 132
GRENWOOD, 82
GRESA, 130
GRESAR, 42
GRESHAM, 180
GRETER, 132
GREY, 4 82
GRIBBLE, 122
GRIDER, 199
GRIESBACH, 228
GRIFFARD, 58 97 100 130
GRIFFAY, 19
GRIFFETH, 122
GRIFFEY, 45
GRIFFIN, 19 42 47 49 50 63 65 66 69 82 95 137 144 149 152 154 158 167 190 222
GRIFFITH, 62 97 124 158 167 169 187 203 228
GRIGER, 62
GRIGGS, 19 45 125 204
GRIGS, 112
GRIMAND, 65
GRIMAR, 109
GRIMARD, 233
GRIMELEN, 92
GRIMES, 19 81 82 175
GRIMMESON, 112
GRIMSLEY, 176
GRINDSTAFF, 54 224
GRISEAU, 18
GRISHAM, 54 112 177 240
GRISOM, 168
GRISSINN, 137

GRIST, 222
GRISWOLD, 204
GRITZ, 172
GROBER, 122
GROCE, 18
GROCHAUER, 94
GROESBECK, 82
GROFF, 192 193 196
GROGAN, 178
GROGON, 132
GROJEAN, 61 65
GROMER, 141
GROMES, 220
GRONDIN, 223
GROOM, 112 188
GROOME, 99
GROOMS, 38 39 122 200 204
GROSBY, 59
GROSHON, 14
GROSHONG, 82
GROSS, 47 152 153 171 172
GROUND, 171
GROUNT, 63 69 127
GROVER, 18 81 144
GROVES, 69 82 216
GRUBB, 175
GRUBBS, 189
GRUINDIKE, 82
GRUNARD, 69
GRUNDY, 142 144
GRUNT, 183
GRYER, 69
GUDGINS, 219
GUDIN, 158
GUELLE, 51 75 129
GUENARD, 63
GUENNEVILLE, 130
GUERIN, 64 108
GUERUGE, 141
GUETHING, 69 128
GUFFY, 81
GUIBARRE, 63
GUIBONY, 125
GUIBOURD, 65 130
GUIBOURNE, 58
GUIERRE, 42
GUIERSERO, 117
GUIGNOLET, 66
GUILDEAULT, 65
GUILIGAUT, 165
GUILLBAUT, 108

GUILLOT, 41
GUILMORE, 108
GUILT, 109
GUINN, 29 64 79
GUINNARD, 19
GUINNS, 194
GUION, 115 118 235
GUIRE, 69 158
GUIRN, 158
GUITAR, 116
GUITARD, 62 69 150 235
GULLEDGE, 82
GULLET, 1
GULYEN, 191
GUNN, 122
GUNNELL, 82
GUNSALUS, 82
GUNTER, 169 170
GUONS, 158
GURNO, 188
GURRIER, 82
GURTNER, 171
GUSHING, 158
GUSTAVUS, 88
GUTARRE, 42
GUTHERIE, 18
GUTHERY, 4 137
GUTHRIE, 73 231
GUY, 231
GUYAUDIN, 158
GUYER, 81 121 177
GUYNN, 82
GUYOL, 209
GUYON, 65 131 150
GUYOR, 144
GVITZ, 75
GYYLE, 122

- H -

HAB, 210
HACHNEY, 37
HACKER, 63 69 148
HACKETT, 112
HACKSON, 141
HADBRINK, 201
HADDICK, 4
HADDOCK, 43 54 224
HADEN, 8 59 65 81 138
HADLEY, 47
HADSON, 110

HAFFE, 150
HAGAN, 65 69 76 82 138
HAGERMAN, 82
HAGGARD, 144
HAGGER, 171
HAGGIN, 132
HAGIN, 73
HAGINS, 81 82
HAGUE, 69 102 144
HAHN, 54 69 81 132 143 171
HAIG, 104
HAIL, 82 173 195 196
HAILE, 209
HAINDS, 130 159
HAINES, 62 69 81
HAIRD, 159
HAITERMAN, 82
HALBERT, 82 167 168
HALDAINE, 5
HALE, 40 173 204
HALEN, 200
HALFORD, 122
HALL, 4 5 7 20 37 39 55 69 71 72
   78 79 81 82 92 93 112 137 144
   148 154 179 185 188 193 195
   225 228
HALLABERT, 132
HALLET, 2
HALLEY, 82
HALLOCK, 82
HALLOWAY, 179
HALLY, 190
HALOCK, 54
HALPH, 44
HALSTEAD, 226
HALSY, 192
HALTEN, 4 37
HALTON, 55 56 144
HAM, 7 55 93 112 137 159 204
HAMAC, 192
HAMBITER, 203
HAMBLET, 82
HAMBLIN, 137
HAMBY, 81 144
HAMEL, 144
HAMELIN, 65
HAMES, 141 238
HAMILTON, 2 49 51 62 66 72 82
   102 122 132 137 138 150 192
   194 203 210 215 231
HAMLETT, 81 82

HAMLEY, 82
HAMLIN, 122
HAMMAN, 92
HAMMCOK, 71
HAMMER, 72
HAMMES, 158
HAMMETT, 144
HAMMOCK, 82 198
HAMMOND, 79 81 82 142 144
HAMMUSTON, 200
HAMPTON, 158 161 168
HAMS, 173
HAMSTED, 16
HANA, 54
HANCE, 82
HANCICK, 204
HANCOCK, 2 20 21 38 63 64 69
   81 112 150 158 159 190 205
HAND, 61 69 126 132
HANDLIN, 173
HANES, 21
HANEY, 82 148 174
HANKERAN, 82
HANKERSON, 82
HANKINS, 82
HANKINSON, 119 132
HANKS, 82
HANNA, 81 82 132
HANNAH, 61 82 132 149
HANNATIN, 94
HANNOCK, 198
HANNON, 8 55 82
HANS, 82
HANSELL, 82
HANSON, 82
HANUP, 82
HANY, 82 210
HAPPER, 55
HARBENSON, 82
HARBINSON, 182
HARBISON, 132 144 215
HARBOUR, 82 196
HARD, 132
HARDE, 159
HARDEE, 82
HARDELL, 128
HARDEMAN, 2 5 175
HARDEN, 199
HARDEY, 122
HARDGROVE, 64
HARDIN, 7 55 71 159 189 191 233

279

HARDING, 72
HARDISON, 82
HARDISTER, 204
HARDWICK, 82
HARDWIN, 47 48
HARDY, 55 82 142 150
HARGROVE, 69 82
HARIMAN, 171
HARINGTON, 132
HARK, 55
HARKE, 171
HARKER, 171
HARKS, 171
HARL, 142
HARLESS, 20
HARLEY, 216
HARLY, 171
HARMAN, 40 82
HARMICKS, 173
HARMON, 21 55
HARNES, 55
HARNESS, 1 21
HARNEY, 21
HAROLD, 12 21 35
HARPER, 64 73 74 82 93 137 225 230 234
HARPOLE, 158
HARRELL, 82
HARRELSON, 82
HARREN, 83
HARRIET, 99
HARRIMAN, 112
HARRINGTON, 5 82 122 149 175
HARRIS, 2 4 5 39 44 47 55 61-65 69 72 78 81-83 106 112 122 132 137 142 144 148 149 154 167 173 175 178 191 193 196 198 201 202 206 213 234 238-240
HARRISH, 55
HARRISON, 4 43 65 69 71 82 83 99 137 149 175 178 189 193 194 197 207 209 230-232
HARROD, 63 83
HARRY, 54
HARRYFORD, 149
HARRYMAN, 55
HARSON, 122
HART, 4 37 61 64 69 72 81-83 96 98 103 177 194 204 221
HARTEL, 171

HARTH, 171
HARTLE, 63
HARTLEY, 69
HARTLOR, 98
HARTMAN, 20 83
HARTON, 55
HARTT, 132 210
HARTWELL, 82
HARTY, 83 186
HARVEY, 38 66 82 83 152 180 228
HARVIE, 177
HARWOOD, 82
HAS, 132
HASH, 225
HASKILL, 150
HASKINS, 55 79 82 158
HASSEL, 2
HASSELIN, 41
HASSELL, 92
HASTON, 122
HASTY, 171
HATCH, 38 177
HATER, 122
HATFIELD, 5 141 142 158 190 233 234
HATGROVE, 125
HATHCOCK, 82
HATLEY, 122
HATSON, 174
HATTEN, 53 173
HATTON, 65 82 137 143 238 240
HAUN, 158 204
HAUPT, 21
HAUT, 62
HAUVER, 82
HAVARD, 186
HAVEDSTOCCKER, 5
HAVENS, 224
HAVENSTEADER, 5
HAVERLAND, 82
HAVERSTICK, 159 220
HAWKES, 55
HAWKINS, 7 51 52 58 59 63 65 72 75 103 104 129 132 142 150 175 178 216
HAWKS, 81 82
HAWLEY, 20 182
HAWN, 112
HAWS, 16 93
HAWTHORN, 62 69 222

HAWTHORNE, 58
HAY, 173 175
HAYDEN, 75 132 141 157 178 189
HAYDON, 82 189
HAYES, 14 21 55 82 122 152 167 168 238
HAYMES, 82
HAYNES, 12 82 99 137 142 231
HAYS, 2 7 61-63 82 92 99 112 126 128 130 132 137 138 144 151 158 159 167 173 177 178 204 215
HAYSLIP, 162
HAYWARD, 132 221
HAYWOOD, 71
HAZEBOECK, 155
HAZEL, 38 62 65 188
HAZELING, 5
HAZELTINE, 79
HEAD, 2 4 46 47 55 62 80 82 148 158 159 175 186
HEADER, 5
HEADERICK, 20
HEALD, 20 82
HEARS, 192
HEARST, 72
HEART, 20
HEARTMAN, 21
HEATH, 2 56 72 81 82 112 150 151 175 223
HEATHCOCKE, 82
HEATHER, 8
HEATHERKY, 73
HEATHERLY, 72 194 202 210 215
HEATON, 79 82
HEBBERT, 40
HEBEAU, 118
HEBERT, 11 22 34 36 40 41 50 61 63 64 66 69 119 120 130 132 150 163 219 236
HECKEMEIR, 156
HECKMAN, 48
HECTOR, 69 126 132 173 183
HEDDEN, 47
HEDGE, 82
HEDGEMAN, 144
HEDGES, 82
HEELER, 82
HEEN, 98
HEETER, 82
HEGAN, 107

HEIN, 4
HEINLER, 5
HEINRICH, 228
HEISEY, 82
HEISKELL, 142
HEITH, 158
HEKI, 140
HELAY, 98
HELDERBRAND, 61 64 66 69 213 215
HELFRECH, 21
HELLAY, 97
HELM, 171 178 204
HELMAN, 21
HELMES, 82 144
HELSLEY, 82
HELTON, 72 82
HEMBEY, 124
HEMBLEY, 124
HEMBY, 144
HEMMERLY, 79 148
HEMMINGWAY, 82 144
HEMPHILL, 82 141 144
HEMPSTEAD, 48 151 159 191 217
HEMSTEAD, 142
HENDERICK, 192
HENDERLITER, 144
HENDERSON, 39 55 63 80 82 112 122 132 137 144 154 166 169 173 182-184 188 202 226 230 231 238 240
HENDNOOCK, 173
HENDRICK, 4 21 78 201 203
HENDRICKS, 5 81 82 122 148 171
HENDRICKSON, 132 208
HENDRIX, 37 146
HENETE, 118
HENINGER, 82
HENLEY, 82 144
HENRY, 1 8 65 69 71 82 99 129 132 151 158 186 188 206 216 218
HENS, 5
HENSHAW, 82 122
HENSINGER, 55
HENSLEY, 2 7 66 73 132 144 186 201 207 216
HENSLY, 73 179 196 197 222
HENSON, 72 122
HENTHORN, 142

HENTON, 71
HER, 122
HERBERT, 163 164 166
HERBET, 166 185
HERFURTH, 228
HERIUEX, 163
HERKNLEBEN, 228
HERM, 189
HERMAN, 156
HERMANN, 156
HERN, 45 189
HERNES, 141
HERONAMUS, 47
HERR, 36
HERRIFORD, 47 143
HERRIMAND, 106
HERRINGTON, 43 47 62 63 66 132
HERROD, 168 169
HERRON, 83 122
HERRYFORD, 137
HERSHEY, 174
HERST, 147
HERTMANN, 155
HERVIEUX, 62
HESOUGHBROUGH, 55
HESSON, 4
HESTER, 83
HETER, 82
HETFORD, 161
HETHBRAN, 203
HETHERBRAND, 173
HETHERLY, 179 197 201
HEUSLEY, 4
HEVER, 117
HEVITT, 83
HEYSER, 83
HIATT, 2 38 39 142
HIBBARD, 142
HIBBERD, 72
HIBBLER, 66
HIBERNOIS, 69
HIBLER, 132 210
HICCOCKS, 168
HICKAM, 45 54 238 239
HICKASON, 112
HICKBURN, 5
HICKCOCK, 168
HICKERMIN, 5
HICKERSON, 204
HICKESON, 92
HICKILL, 196
HICKLY, 83
HICKMAN, 2 20 45 47 54 83 103 105 150 152 173
HICKMIN, 5
HICKNEY, 54
HICKOX, 175
HICKS, 2 5 44 53 55 56 83 137 171 238
HIDDLETON, 83
HIEATT, 106
HIEUTT, 106
HIGBEE, 83
HIGENBOTTOM, 132
HIGGANS, 122
HIGGINBOTHAM, 132
HIGGINS, 2 69 83 122 150 173
HIGGS, 55
HIGHT, 159
HIGHTOWER, 178
HIGHY, 144
HILBERT, 20 83
HILDEBRAND, 42 94 107
HILDERBRAND, 132 173 196 197
HILDERMAN, 173
HILDRETH, 83
HILERBRAND, 132
HILIARD, 199
HILKEMEYER, 155
HILL, 7 39 40 47 55 69 72 82 83 92 93 122 127 140 144 150 151 168-170 176 178 182 204 205 221
HILLARD, 4
HILLE, 83
HILLEBAU, 159
HILLENCAMP, 21
HILLEWAY, 159
HILLHOUSE, 224
HILTON, 144
HINCH, 2 7 56 66 132 175 181 183
HINCHER, 122
HINCHY, 178
HINCKSON, 64 69
HINDMAN, 83
HINDS, 152
HINES, 2 72 83 142 175 227
HINKESON, 54
HINKLE, 197 202 220
HINKLEY, 220

HINKSEN, 217
HINKSON, 1 189 217
HINKSTON, 5
HINSDALE, 83
HINSON, 55 178
HINSTON, 39 238
HINTON, 192 197 198 203 210
HIOCHE, 69
HIRAM, 55 124
HIRNE, 142
HIRSH, 137
HIRST, 143
HISE, 159
HISICK, 4
HISSAM, 83
HITCH, 144
HITE, 55 144 152
HITT, 44
HIX, 47 73 83 167
HIXSON, 39
HIXTON, 39
HOAS, 163
HOBAUGH, 178
HOBBS, 83 112
HOBBY, 167
HOBS, 1
HOCK, 46
HOCKADAY, 137 143
HOCKE, 83
HOCKS, 209
HODGE, 39 71 83
HODGES, 2 5 62 65 69 132 192 201 202 220
HODGET, 37
HOEPFINGER, 228
HOER, 155
HOFF, 64
HOFFMAN, 20 62 63 224
HOFMAN, 159 228
HOGAN, 63 69 128 173 223
HOGARD, 83
HOGARTY, 83
HOGE, 83
HOGNIGHT, 122
HOIT, 83
HOLBART, 170
HOLBERT, 83 169 170 178
HOLD, 38
HOLDEN, 40 83
HOLDER, 112 178 204
HOLDERFIELD, 83

HOLDERMAN, 161
HOLDIN, 158
HOLDING, 83
HOLDRA, 20
HOLDRAUGH, 20
HOLEMAN, 47 122
HOLESCLAW, 21
HOLIDAH, 5
HOLKENBURGH, 216
HOLLADAY, 215
HOLLAND, 122 192 195
HOLLAWAY, 137
HOLLEY, 132 184
HOLLIDAY, 2 141 142 188
HOLLOMAN, 225
HOLLOWAY, 2 83 112 152 178
HOLLY, 83 132
HOLMAN, 83 154 232
HOLMES, 20 55 63 64 83 95 97 132 159 209
HOLOWEAUGH, 189
HOLT, 37 83 122 137 144 145 148 149 152 167 170 191 197
HOLTEN, 5
HOLTERFIELD, 83
HOLTERMAN, 155 156
HOLTON, 5 83
HOLTSCHNEIDER, 155
HOMAN, 188
HOME, 55
HOMES, 39
HOMESLEY, 205
HONEY, 176
HONOIRE, 159
HONOR, 130
HONORE, 40 41 69 114 116 130 165 166 237
HONORY, 20
HONSINGER, 178
HOOBERRY, 37
HOOD, 80 154 167 181
HOOK, 20
HOOKING, 55
HOOPER, 132 161
HOOPS, 72 178 179
HOOSE, 173
HOOSLEY, 5
HOOVER, 69 225
HOOZER, 47
HOPE, 137 143 173 231
HOPKINS, 21 83 112 142 187 188

HOPKINS (continued) 204 205
HOPPER, 238
HORINE, 63 69 72 198 202 210
HORN, 66 83 132 213 215
HORNBACK, 92 122 175
HORNBECK, 49 69 102 103
HORNBUCKLE, 137
HORNE, 195
HORNEBEK, 97
HORNER, 64 174 202
HORNES, 110
HORNIE, 197
HORNSURGER, 71
HORRILL, 173
HORROW, 1
HORRYMAN, 215
HORSE, 173
HORSLEY, 69 109 132
HORST, 94
HORTES, 41 164
HORTEZ, 41 114 235 236
HORTIS, 132 165
HORTIZ, 49 66 69 118 119 132 164 166
HORTON, 169
HOSACK, 83
HOSIVINGER, 5
HOSKINS, 47
HOSPER, 21
HOSS, 66 128 171
HOSSTETTER, 141
HOST, 83
HOSTETOR, 20 21 35
HOSTETTER, 63 69 141 151 158
HOSTEY, 40
HOSTOTLER, 171
HOSTOTTER, 171
HOT, 116
HOUASHALL, 158
HOUAULT, 40
HOUCK, 171
HOUK, 173
HOUNSHELL, 215
HOUSE, 47 63 83 112 148 158 204 227
HOUSELIGHT, 107
HOUSEN, 20
HOUSTON, 54 55 83
HOUTON, 141
HOUX, 233

HOVERITTS, 83
HOVERSTOCK, 207
HOW, 184
HOWARD, 2 26 55 61 64 72 80 81 83 101 103 112 122 145 173 178 179 188 189 193 204 205 219
HOWARDS, 92
HOWDESHELL, 142
HOWDISHELL, 107
HOWE, 83 230
HOWEL, 5 19 20 21 171
HOWELL, 2 7 62 63 69 83 130 158 159
HOWINGTON, 83
HOWLAND, 152 167
HOWLIN, 20
HOWSER, 146
HOY, 122
HUBARDEAU, 48-51 75 100 101 103 105 129
HUBBARD, 2 5 48 53 54 59 63 64 72 83 106 112 131 132 152 158 159 175 204 239
HUBBELL, 132
HUBBLE, 1 62 63 65 66 125 132 171 173
HUBERDEAU, 1
HUBERT, 40 64 69 103
HUBLE, 132
HUBLEC, 1
HUCKABY, 153
HUCKINGTON, 63
HUDDLESTON, 61 142
HUDDSON, 137
HUDEN, 220
HUDER, 116
HUDGENS, 1
HUDGES, 132
HUDSON, 55 62 81-83 92 145 171 189 224
HUDSPETH, 99 170
HUE, 175
HUEY, 147
HUFF, 2 39 63 64 66 72 80 83 161 177
HUFFMAN, 8 21 30 39 45 83 122 130 148 179 195 197 215
HUFFY, 83
HUGE, 63 166
HUGES, 83 119

HUGGS, 83
HUGH, 5
HUGHART, 137
HUGHES, 1 2 5 47 55 65 72 81-83
 99 112 122 142 144-146 158
 173 175 201 205 209 220 232
HUGHETE, 144
HUGHLETT, 83
HUGHS, 55 72 149 179 181
HUGHSTON, 6
HUITT, 132 226
HUKEES, 149
HULBERT, 83 148
HULEN, 83
HULET, 122
HULKEY, 20
HULL, 62 72 122 132 152 169 179
 197 203
HULSY, 193
HUME, 54 239
HUMES, 83 106
HUMET, 117
HUMMELL, 83
HUMMER, 83
HUMPHREY, 47 72 87 137 178
HUMPHREYS, 47 83 137
HUMPHRIES, 83 143
HUN, 37
HUNAEPHOL, 156
HUNAUD, 103
HUNAUE, 165
HUNCLE, 173
HUNDEPOHL, 155
HUNDER, 42
HUNEAU, 66
HUNGERFORD, 122
HUNKIS, 98
HUNN, 20
HUNNWELL, 20
HUNO, 118
HUNOT, 46 64-66 69 132 138 151
HUNSAKER, 122
HUNSICKER, 37
HUNT, 2 19 20 47 69 75 81 83 92
 122 147 171 188 191 208 211
 215 216 233
HUNTER, 69 83 107 122 129 132
 142 145 158 173 182 204 216
HUNTING, 94
HUNTSBERRY, 8
HUNTSUCKERSEN, 37

HURARDEAU, 49
HURCULES, 21
HURD, 83
HURLEY, 63 69 82 83 125 132
 191 233
HURON, 105
HURRY, 83 167
HURSK, 72
HURST, 83 166
HURT, 83 142 149 158 178 188
 193 194 200
HUSAH, 83
HUSH, 4 55
HUSKEY, 83
HUSTON, 145 175
HUTCHEN, 18
HUTCHENS, 21
HUTCHERSON, 21
HUTCHESON, 20
HUTCHIN, 83
HUTCHINGS, 39 40 50 84 159 187
 188
HUTCHINS, 64 84 138 159
HUTCHINSON, 2 84 150 188
HUTCHISON, 152 188 225 234
HUTHMAN, 155
HUTSON, 5 55 83 84 145
HUTTON, 2 71 112 158 201 203
 204
HUTTONHOW, 83
HUVELMEYER, 200
HYATT, 199
HYDE, 72 83 84
HYET, 196
HYMAN, 94
HYMERS, 141

- I -

ICENHOUR, 22
IJAMS, 83 84
ILES, 188
ILOR, 22
IMAN, 28
IMBODEN, 166
INARD, 6
INDICOTT, 122
INGLIS, 179
INGLISH, 39 92 229
INGRAHAM, 84
INGRAM, 176 225

INK, 212
INKS, 137
INMAN, 22 84 157 227
IRONES, 84
IRONS, 39
IRVIN, 7 37
IRVINE, 8 84 176
IRVING, 190
IRWIN, 83 171 188
ISAACS, 226
ISBELL, 225
ISH, 3 92 122 149
ISICK, 132
ISOM, 125
ITSON, 94
IVERS, 176 195
IVES, 84
IVEY, 84
IVY, 229

– J –

JACK, 3 92 122
JACKETT, 83
JACKLIN, 84
JACKMAN, 47
JACKS, 39 142 216
JACKSON, 2 5 6 22 55 69 75 82-84 113 119 122 145 148 150 161 175 191 198
JACOB, 107 159
JACOBA, 119
JACOBS, 64 66 69 83 84 119 125 145
JACSON, 108
JAKS, 197
JAMEISON, 55
JAMERISON, 186
JAMES, (dedication) 1 5 6 22 39 42 59 62-65 69 84 86 92 99 100 103 106 107 113 122 129 131 132 145 151 159 171 179 182 185 190 193 196 197 202 205 212 215 217 226
JAMESON, 132 161 186 193 215 239
JAMIS, 103
JAMISEN, 5
JAMISON, 5 6 59 65 69 71 106 142 169 179 192 196 201 202 209 210 213 227 239

JANES, 66 132 221
JANET, 119
JANETT, 151
JANIE, 16 21
JANIN, 65
JANIS, 13 21 22 33 34 42 49 51 63 64 66 69 100 102 129 130 217 226
JANISE, 58
JANKS, 148
JANNETT, 11 16
JANNIS, 150
JAQUE, 132
JAQUIS, 222
JARRELL, 191
JARRET, 165
JARRETT, 33 35 185
JARROT, 65 103
JARVEY, 21
JARVIS, 179 193 194
JASMINE, 84
JASMYNE, 84
JAY, 84
JEAN, 120
JEANNERES, 188
JEANOT, 65
JEANS, 130 132
JECURETT, 191
JEFFERES, 84
JEFFERIES, 106 107 194 200
JEFFERS, 39 84 122
JEFFERSON, 137 179
JEFFERY, 55
JEFFRE, 64 184
JEFFRES, 195
JEFFREY, 84
JEFFRIES, 71 196 213
JEMERON, 159
JEMISON, 159 215
JENENS, 141
JENKINS, 50 83 84 122 228
JENKS, 83 159
JENNET, 69
JENNINGS, 55 83 100 122 224
JENSTON, 55
JENT, 83
JERDON, 159
JERESEOUI, 159
JERROLLD, 84
JETSON, 122
JETT, 84 179

JETTEN, 173
JEWELL, 55 83 84
JEWITT, 66 132 154
JIGUAIRES, 66
JINKENSON, 175
JINKINS, 22 224
JIRAR, 117
JIRARD, 120
JOB, 3 142 205
JOBE, 92
JOHANNASMEYER, 156
JOHN, 22 119 130
JOHNS, 22 63 72 132 152 168 179 195-197 200 204 210 213 218
JOHNSON, 2 21 22 25 38 52 58 66 69 72 74 75 83 84 95 96 104 122 129 132 140 141 142 145 146 148 150 152 171 173 175 176 179 181 183 186 189 191 194 199 200 203 205 215 216 220 223 228 240
JOHNSTON, 44 62 66 69 99 113 122 132 159 189 193 194 204 206 207 212-214
JOICE, 47
JOILET, i
JOINER, 84 137
JOLIEN, 69
JONATHAN, 84
JONCA, 117
JONES, 3 5 6 8 10 18 22 31 34 45 47 52 55 62-64 69 82-84 103 106 107 113 122 130 132 137 142 145 147 148 151 154 159 162 163 167 169 173 177 189 197-203 205 208 216 217 220 225 232 238 239
JONS, 132
JONSTON, 113
JORDAIN, 83
JORDALLES, 65 66
JORDAN, 122 141 180
JORDEN, 22
JORDON, 179
JOSAHOWTER, 171
JOSEPH, 84
JOTT, 22 194
JOULAND, 43
JOURDAIN, 165
JOURDAN, 84 221

JOURNEY, 66 113 159 180 205 221
JOVENEUSE, 48
JOY, 83
JOYEUSE, 75
JUDSON, 173
JUMP, 203 212
JUNE, 106
JUNEY, 22
JUNNEX, 139
JURNEY, 22 30 35
JUSSAUME, 49
JUSTIN, 55
JUSTUS, 145 167
JUTEAU, 103

- K -

KACKEL, 23
KALVAY, 84
KANADA, 84 200
KANCE, 173
KANE, 83
KANNADA, 202 203
KANY, 137
KARD, 150
KASE, 23
KASSEL, 23
KAUFMAN, 221
KAVANAUGH, 84 189
KAVANUAGH, 143
KAVENAUGH, 5 55 83
KAVINAN, 122
KAY, 83 84 148 154
KAYE, 122
KAYGLE, 132
KAYS, 83
KAYSER, 22
KEAN, 141
KEANY, 3
KEASHLER, 23
KEATH, 44
KEATHLEY, 10 11 13 16 22 23 25 29
KEATHLY, 159
KEATHY, 159
KEATLY, 207 212
KEBARD, 66
KEEHELY, 132
KEELER, 55

KEELY, 211
KEEN, 58
KEENE, 179
KEENEN, 132
KEENEY, 32 66
KEENY, 39
KEEP, 157
KEETH, 132
KEETLY, 210
KEETON, 55
KEFFER, 66
KEGANS, 72 213 214
KEIFER, 151
KEISER, 8
KEITH, 83 84 148 168 169
KEITHELIE, 66
KEITHLEY, 161 217
KEITHLY, 141
KELLBREATH, 93
KELLER, 23 63 159
KELLEY, 23 128 132
KELLOGG, 74
KELLY, 5 8 23 37 45 46 55 65 66
   73 84 93 94 118 127 129 132
   141-143 145 162 175 183 187
   189 192 198 202 214 224 229
KELOE, 55
KELSAY, 234
KELSO, 37 174 183 184
KEMPLAR, 65 66
KENAL, 119
KENDAL, 84
KENDALL, 132
KENDLEY, 84
KENDRICK, 8 47
KENE, 84
KENISH, 222
KENNADAY, 230
KENNAN, 55
KENNEDY, 63 65 95 100-103 145
   159 167 170 181 205
KENNEL, 187
KENNETT, 169
KENNEY, 130 141 223
KENNISON, 84
KENNY, 159 186 229
KENT, 113 159 204 205
KENTOCKE, 111
KENYON, 65 66 125
KEOWN, 129
KERBY, 190

KERCEREAU, 66
KERETTE, 109
KERHAN, 190
KERKEHALL, 149
KERLEGAND, 65
KERLEZAND, 129
KERR, 25 66 130 159 189
KESTER, 58 75 83 84
KETCHUM, 55 142 189
KETHLEY, 130
KEUNON, 5
KEY, 122 179
KEYES, 84
KEYETE, 145
KEYS, 94
KEYSER, 84
KEYTE, 150 167
KEYTON, 122
KEYWOOD, 84 145
KIBBAY, 14
KIBBEY, 24 37
KIBBLE, 23 205
KIBBY, 37 64 130
KIBLER, 22
KICKELIE, 151
KID, 71
KIDWILL, 23
KIENCERSEAU, 163
KIENCEVEU, 164
KIERCEREAU, 66
KIERENAU, 163
KIERERAU, 164
KIESELER, 66
KILAS, 132
KILBY, 84
KILEGORE, 5
KILEY, 84
KILGORE, 55 232
KIMBERLIN, 72
KIMBERS, 145
KIMBLE, 84
KIMBRA, 210
KIMBRO, 206
KIMBROUGH, 84
KIMMSONT, 171
KIMSEY, 122 216
KINCADE, 193
KINCAID, 62 66 113 122 209
KINCHELOE, 3 47
KINCHELOW, 93
KINDER, 171

KINER, 84
KING, 8 22 37 40 47 54 55 71 82 84 113 122 137 142 145 159 177 179 189 191 194 199 202 203 205 206 231 239
KINGCADE, 159
KINGREY, 84 145
KINGSBERRY, 145 167
KINKADE, 71
KINKAID, 55 56 97 132 210
KINKEAD, 2 177 206-208
KINKED, 132
KINNARD, 23
KINNEMAN, 193
KINNERSON, 64
KINNEY, 177
KINNISON, 129
KINSWORTHY, 168 169
KINSWROTHY, 170
KINWORTHY, 170
KIPLER, 166
KIPPLER, 58
KIRBIN, 22
KIRBY, 47
KIRK, 147
KIRKENDOLL, 132
KIRKLAND, 5 6
KIRKPATRICK, 22 52 84 159 216
KIRKUM, 94
KIRKWOOD, 6
KIRTLEY, 43
KIRUMAN, 55
KISHLER, 132
KISOR, 55
KISSLER, 159
KITCHEN, 84
KITCHENS, 179
KITCHING, 113
KITCHINGS, 137 231
KITLEY, 55
KITTREL, 84
KLEIN, 129 139
KLINGMAN, 84
KLINGSMITH, 171
KLIPPER, 84
KNAW, 166
KNEEDLER, 84 145
KNEELAND, 84
KNIGHT, 84 147 181
KNOCK, 145
KNOPKER, 228

KNOTT, 22 65 132 159
KNOWLES, 84
KNOX, 47 205
KNUEVER, 156
KOESTER, 155
KOILE, 84
KOONROD, 181
KORMES, 1
KORROW, 6
KOSK, 23
KOUNS, 143
KOURNS, 113
KOYLE, 55
KRAG, 23
KRAH, 33
KRAUSS, 56
KRAUSZ, 228
KRAY, 23
KREPS, 84
KRETTZER, 22
KRICHBAM, 23
KRIGER, 200
KROH, 14
KRUISE, 23
KRUMKEY, 23
KRUST, 23
KRYTZ, 63 66
KUESTERSTEPHAN, 155
KUNOLT, 157
KUNZE, 23
KUYKENDALL, 122 189
KYLE, 64
KYMIAN, 173
KYTHIES, 171

- L -

L'AMOUREUX, 119
L'ENGLISE, 64
L'SALEAUN, 159
LABADDIE, 66
LABADE, 119
LABADIA, 115 234
LABASTIDE, 102
LABAUM, 118
LABBADDIE, 159
LABBADIE, 41 165
LABBE, 42 132
LABBIE, 43 50
LABBUDIE, 164
LABE, 116

LABEAU, 186
LABEAUME, 32 42 49
LABERDIE, 11
LABGLOIS, 103
LABLADIE, 165
LABO, 24 119
LABODEE, 33
LABOMBARDE, 62
LABOSTIE, 119
LABOUN, 40
LABOURBOARD, 150
LABOURIN, 233
LABRAUME, 42
LABRECHE, 118
LABRESS, 40
LABRICKE, 58
LABROSE, 116
LABROSS, 221
LABROSSE, 41 163 166
LABROZA, 235
LABUCIERA, 114
LABUQIERE, 41
LABURN, 13
LABURNE, 13 14 19 22 27 29 33
LABUSCIERE, 103
LABUSSIERE, 62
LACEROUX, 163
LACEY, 10 170 173
LACHAISSE, 66
LACHANCE, ii 1 48-51 58 61 62
   64 67 97 103 104 106 132 133
   163 221
LACHANS, 132
LACHAPELLE, 64
LACHAPPELLE, 58
LACHASSA, 237
LACK, 171 198
LACKENERS, 47
LACKEY, 48
LACKLAND, 24
LACLEAR, 24
LACLEDE, 40 41
LACLERE, 1
LACOMBE, 42 66 132
LACOMBLE, 58 117
LACOMPTE, 119
LACOMTE, 50 114
LACONTA, 41
LACOURSE, 51
LACROIA, 114
LACROIS, 130

LACROIX, 24 29 58 65 66 101
   103 105 106 132 237
LACROIXE, 130
LACROSSE, 19
LACROY, 130
LADD, 84
LADDOIS, 119
LADEROULE, 164 166
LADEROUTE, 41 67 102 109 120
LADERRUTA, 114
LADOUCEUR, 165
LADOUEVER, 163
LADUQUE, 24
LADUSIR, 118
LADUSOR, 114
LADUVANTAGE, 163
LADY, 62
LAF, 76
LAFAN, 24
LAFANAIT, 107
LAFANE, 25
LAFARGE, 24 26
LAFAYETTE, 84
LAFERME, 163 164
LAFERNOIT, 69
LAFERVE, 24
LAFEVERE, 24 66
LAFEVRE, 29
LAFFLEUR, 106
LAFFONT, 49-51 103 132
LAFFOURS, 226
LAFFTON, 152
LAFLAME, 40
LAFLANBUESA, 114
LAFLEUR, 1 65 67 101 105 119
   185
LAFLOR, 114 235
LAFLOWER, 132
LAFLUER, 1
LAFLUEUR, 58
LAFOISE, 130
LAFOND, 118
LAFONT, 103 132
LAFONTAINE, 75 100 102 103
LAFONTE, 64
LAFORE, 163
LAFORGE, 33 38 65 66 92 108
   119 120 132
LAFORME, 103
LAFOURCADE, 103
LAFOURETT, 24

LAFOURS, 130
LAFRANCE, 26
LAFRANCHIN, 26
LAFRENAIE, 165
LAFVERE, 40
LAGENES, 23
LAGET, 171
LAGLOIS, 130
LAGRAND, 58 217
LAGRANGE, 103
LAHE, 114
LAIBOND, 66
LAIL, 69 132
LAIRD, 84 132 227
LAISERAIT, 42
LAJAYE, 119
LAJOIE, 63
LAJOY, 118
LAJOYE, 132
LAKE, 8 84
LAKEMAN, 84
LAKIN, 84
LALANDE, 41 58 62 69 164 165 235 236
LALEMENDIER, 217
LALIME, 120
LALLE, 41
LALLIFAUX, 64
LALOIS, 119
LALONEL, 119
LALOVE, 69
LALULIPE, 58
LALUMANDIERE, 50 51 101 105
LALUMDIERE, 58
LALUMENDIER, 133
LAMALICE, 65
LAMARCH, 16 24
LAMARCHE, 61 66 67 165
LAMARINA, 115
LAMARSH, 159
LAMASTER, 173
LAMASTERS, 23 159
LAMB, 65 84 110 178
LAMBERT, 40 64 84 167 171
LAMBETH, 95
LAMBREMENT, 40
LAME, 93
LAMEIOUS, 159
LAMERE, 237
LAMI, 41
LAMM, 3 39

LAMME, 7 44 99 113 142 150 159 161 205
LAMMER, 47
LAMMES, 159
LAMOND, 118
LAMONTAGVIE, 41
LAMONTE, 130
LAMOT, 119
LAMPART, 84
LAMPHIER, 84
LAMPHIR, 5
LAMPKIN, 113
LAMY, 41 116 165 237
LANAHAN, 119
LANCASKES, 84
LANCASTER, 84
LANCE, 39
LANCISICUS, 84
LAND, 42 43 84 132 205
LANDERS, 8 161 225
LANDERVILLE, 42 118
LANDLEY, 122
LANDROCHE, 85
LANDROFF, 85
LANDRUM, 40
LANDSELL, 179
LANE, 8 63 72 82 84 85 99 128 179 192
LANEHART, 39
LANFORD, 24
LANG, 84
LANGAEL, 85
LANGELLIER, 51 75 130
LANGFORD, 5 23 25 148 205
LANGHAM, 53 113 142
LANGLEENWAY, 132
LANGLEY, 2 113 137 143
LANGLOIS, 24 41 51 63 65 67 69 103 109 110 119 150
LANGOUMOIS, 164
LANGRELL, 84
LANGUEL, 84
LANHAM, 55 106 107 133 150 211 212 239
LANICLE, 230
LANIER, 84
LANING, 84
LANKIM, 137
LANKIN, 55
LANN, 71
LANPY, 165

LANQIUNET, 43
LANQUENET, 42
LANQUINET, 42 164 185
LANS, 42
LANSE, 42
LANSFORD, 55 84 85
LANSON, 124
LANTFORG, 107
LANTHE, 41
LANY, 39
LAPAGE, 151 163
LAPENSE, 66
LAPHSEN, 24
LAPIERRE, 42 63 116 117 164 235
LAPIN, 104
LAPLANT, 1 113 133 137
LAPLANTE, 62 69 75 99 104 108 130 166
LAPOINT, 145
LAPOINTE, 62 132
LAPONTE, 66
LAPPIN, 84
LAPPING, 84 145
LAPRECHE, 233
LAPRESSE, 69
LAPRISE, 133
LARAMORE, 196
LARCHE, 163
LARCOHE, 133
LARCROIX, 62
LARCY, 44
LARD, 62 67
LARDOIS, 69
LARDOISE, 65 69
LARDUERA, 117
LAREMORE, 192 193 200
LARENCELL, 84
LARET, 115
LARGEAU, 65 103
LARITER, 152
LARK, 84 205
LARKAINT, 95
LARKER, 122
LARKIN, 84
LARKINS, 55
LAROCHAL, 1
LAROCHE, 163 164
LAROSE, 75 102 104
LAROUGE, 1
LARPY, 42

LARRABEE, 84
LARRIBA, 174
LARRIMORE, 73
LARTHROP, 153
LARUE, 179
LARUL, 72
LARVER, 24
LASABLOIEU, 163
LASABLONERA, 116
LASAGE, 32
LASAILLE, 130
LASARGE, 24
LASCROIX, 130
LASHAWAY, 67
LASIER, 24
LASISERAE, 133
LASLY, 195
LASOIRE, 118
LASORCE, 75
LASOUECE, 50
LASOURCE, 49 50 58 101 104
LASOUS, 217
LASSAME, 1
LASSELL, 133
LASSITER, 222
LASSUENTE, 150
LASTLEY, 171
LASUA, 72
LASUDRAY, 114
LATAILLE, 140
LATERWHITE, 152
LATHAM, 126 128 133 145 149
LATHAN, 63 67
LATIEUURE, 133
LATIMAR, 94
LATIMER, 168
LATIMORE, 162
LATOUR, 133
LATRAVE, 40
LATRIELLE, 130
LATRIMOULE, 66
LATTINARY, 159
LATTRAIL, 23 24
LATUCHE, 140
LATURE, 25
LAUCIER, 165
LAUGHERTY, 65 84 127 145 173
LAUGHLIN, 5 37 55 72 107 139 179 188
LAUGHNBERG, 203
LAUGHON, 67

LAUME, 58
LAURENCE, 83 205
LAURENT, 68
LAURIN, 42
LAUSSON, 63
LAUVAGESSE, 165
LAVAC, 24
LAVALLE, 67 185
LAVALLEE, 108
LAVENTURE, 223
LAVERDURE, 130
LAVIGNE, 42
LAVIOLETTE, 103
LAVOR, 163
LAW, 179
LAWLER, 122 137
LAWLES, 55
LAWLESS, 38 44 154 188
LAWRENCE, 5 55 84 145 174 230
LAWSON, 84 145
LAWTON, 84
LAY, 72 175
LAYMAN, 94
LAYNE, 84
LAYTHAM, 8
LAYTON, 64 66 133
LE, 130
LEA, 84
LEACH, 84 148
LEAKY, 3
LEAMAR, 55
LEANDED, 122
LEANOIEX, 159
LEAR, 7 145
LEARY, 174
LEAVITT, 84 148
LEAWALL, 205
LEAWELL, 205
LEBARGE, 118
LEBARON, 99
LEBAUS, 130
LEBBERT, 155
LEBEAU, 165
LEBEAUME, 63 66 67
LEBERGE, 41 64 166
LEBLANC, 101
LEBO, 122
LEBOURE, 29
LECELERE, 104
LECHAPLE, 129
LECHEVAL, 102
LECLAIR, 151
LECLERE, 75 100 130 217
LECOMBE, 164
LECOMDE, 185
LECOMPTE, 64 235
LECOMTE, 41 42 61 100 104 133
LECOMTER, 100
LECON, 139
LECONTE, 118 130
LECTOR, 129
LEDGEWOOD, 39
LEDON, 119
LEDUC, 63 67 92 107 118 131 177
LEDUE, 166
LEE, 43 47 62 65 69 83 84 93 119 122 127 132 137 143 147 159 165 173 176 182 214 224 225 230
LEEBO, 24
LEECH, 84
LEEK, 132 133
LEEMAN, 84 148
LEEPER, 47
LEESTIN, 190
LEFERRY, 84
LEFEVER, 119
LEFEVRE, 63 64 151 166
LEFFORD, 84
LEFLUER, 92
LEFRESS, 24
LEFTON, 199
LEGGET, 143
LEGON, 41
LEGOND, 40 41
LEGONET, 41
LEGRAND, 40 66 67 101 108 129 133
LEGUST, 151
LEHOULSE, 165
LEINTZ, 177 185
LEJEUNNESSEE, 130
LELAND, 151
LELANDE, 42
LEMAN, 55 219
LEMASTERS, 161 187
LEMAY, 104
LEMEZ, 117
LEMMAN, 55
LEMMON, 37

LEMMONS, 225
LEMOINE, 129
LEMON, 239
LEMONDE, 133
LEMONIE, 235
LEMOYNE, i
LENDERMAN, 84
LENDROY, 140
LENDRUM, 40
LENE, 128
LENECAL, 42
LENHAM, 83 142
LENOX, 113 137 179
LENS, 64
LENTS, 84
LENTZ, 84
LENZE, 111
LENZO, 148
LEONARD, 82 84 122 148
LEOPOLD, 9
LEPAGE, 130
LEPIR, 115
LEPLANT, 179
LEPLANTE, 165
LEPPER, 84
LEQUIN, 108
LEROY, 163 164
LERRU, 115
LESAGE, 63
LESBOIS, 63 165
LESCH, 122
LESIEUR, 62 66 107 130 133 188
LESIUR, 120
LESLEY, 190
LESLIE, 223
LESPAGNOL, 75
LESSIEUR, 150 177
LESTER, 84
LETNEY, 179
LETOUMEAU, 164
LETOUR, 106
LEUVARD, 129
LEUWEKAMP, 203
LEVALLEAU, 50
LEVEAL, 1
LEVEL, 113
LEVELY, 72
LEVENDY, 122
LEVI, 84
LEVIELLE, 237
LEVIGE, 165

LEVIN, 93
LEVITZ, 5 6
LEVRARD, 50 104
LEVY, 147
LEWALLEN, 84
LEWIS, 6 8 13 18 19 21 23 25 27
    35 37 45 47 55 61 62 64-66 71
    72 84 85 106 110 111 120 122
    130 133 149 153 159 161-163
    168 169 178 179 187 203 206
    207 210 215 216 224 228
LIBERGE, 66 130 236
LICKERY, 202
LICOSE, 85
LIENTZ, 43 56
LIGGET, 39
LIGGETT, 85 122 145 176
LIGHTFOOT, 3 38
LIGHTNER, 143
LILES, 39 52 74 159 186
LILLARD, 85 93 175
LILLEY, 23 233
LIMBACH, 128
LIMBAUGH, 66 69 171
LIMBERICK, 129
LIMINIO, 151
LINCECUM, 171
LINCH, 145
LINCOLN, 39 85 171
LINDELL, 145 148 152 167
LINDENBUSCH, 156
LINDLEY, 128
LINDSAY, 18 69 122 159
LINDSEY, 80 82 85
LINDSLEY, 145
LINE, 69 104
LINGAR, 85
LINGARD, 85
LINGO, 85
LINK, 69 132 150 173 200 212
LINN, 63 159 205 216
LINSEY, 85
LINSON, 168
LINTACUND, 198
LINVILLE, 39 122
LIONE, 105
LIPCOMB, 122
LIPSCOMB, 6
LIQ----, 40
LIQUEST, i 40
LIQUIST, 40

LIRETTE, 131
LISA, 43 48 51 69 118
LISBOIS, 164
LISHMORE, 85
LISLE, 113 205
LISWELL, 85
LITCHWORTH, 188
LITLE, 131
LITTEN, 69
LITTERAL, 190
LITTLE, 27 54 55 72 122 131 173 175 228
LITTLEFIELD, 85 145
LITTLEHALE, 85
LITTLEJOHN, 36 63 64 131
LITTON, 228
LIVELY, 122 179
LIVERAU, 95
LIVINGSTON, 2 39
LIZENBY, 205
LJENESSE, 166
LLOYD, 140 182
LOCK, 47
LOCKE, 190
LOCKHART, 85 93 122 131 137 143 173
LOCKIE, 85
LOCKRIDGE, 147
LOCKSFORD, 5
LOCLOR, 24
LODER, 131
LODIE, 24
LOELS, 1
LOFTIN, 179 199
LOFTLIN, 85
LOFTON, 17 72
LOGAN, 25 58 63 65 69 85 113 122 131 159 205
LOGE, 85
LOGMYER, 25
LOGO, 92
LOHUA, 1
LOIGNARD, 151
LOIGNON, 111
LOISEL, 58 64 69 105
LOISELLE, 185 236
LOISET, 42
LOKEY, 85
LOLLAR, 24
LOMAX, 113 137 231
LOMBAR, 181

LONDON, 85
LONEY, 47
LONG, 3 24 55 63 65 85 122 131 151 169 173 179 206 208 210 211 213-215
LONGMIRE, 8
LONGREL, 151
LONGUE, 108
LONGVAL, 104
LONGWELL, 139
LONGWITH, 85
LONTZ, 85
LOOK, 145 225
LOOKINGBILL, 84
LOOMES, 145
LOOMIS, 85
LOONEY, 38 149
LORA, 23
LORAIN, 106 130
LORANCE, 171
LORCE, 24
LORD, 25 63 66 131
LOREE, 85
LORENE, 26
LORENS, 131 236
LORENZO, 117
LORIMER, 49 50 69
LORIMIER, 65 67 103-105 125 131
LORING, 152
LORINS, 64 67
LORMIER, 185
LORR, 65 128
LORROSE, 116
LORSE, 151
LORTON, 231
LOSLA, 63
LOSTA, 126
LOTTE, 41
LOUGE, 85
LOUINS, 164
LOUIS, 65 171
LOUIS XIV King of France, i
LOUISO, 24
LOURAIN, 107
LOURS, 75
LOUSEL, 42
LOUSIGMAN, 131
LOUVIEN, 51
LOUVIERES, 110
LOUVIERRE, 69

LOUVIEVE, 163
LOUZON, 69
LOVE, 47 80 85 93 172 173 188
LOVED, 128
LOVEGROVE, 85
LOVEL, 65 67 131
LOVELACE, 78 85
LOVELADY, 122
LOVELL, 150
LOVERING, 23 85
LOW, 24 66 104 131 213
LOWAROS, 111
LOWE, 179
LOWELL, 53 201
LOWERY, 6 162
LOWEY, 40
LOWNERS, 163
LOWNS, 122
LOWRIGHT, 203
LOWRY, 66 177 188
LOWTHER, 85
LOWTHIAN, 39
LOYED, 66
LOYOURNER, 92
LUBBASTOSE, 194
LUBBY, 125
LUCA, 137
LUCAS, 63 65 80 84 85 129 131 142 149–151 217
LUCIER, 212
LUCIUS, 175
LUCKETT, 25 85
LUCKEY, 196
LUCKWORTH, 223
LUCKY, 85
LUCROFT, 145
LUCUS, 25 122
LUCY, 171
LUDEN, 149
LUDLAM, 85
LUDLOW, 143 149 188
LUDOLF, 23
LUDUC, 63
LUDY, 93
LUECKE, 155
LUEKE, 155 156
LUERMES, 110
LUESE, 116
LUEYEUSE, 166
LUFFMAN, 85
LUFKIN, 85
LUFRENAIT, 165
LUISSER, 233
LUMAS, 104
LUMBERSON, 85
LUMSDEN, 85
LUNDELE, 59
LUNDIGE, 131
LUNDY, 107 190
LUNSFORD, 37 145
LURTON, 24
LUSBY, 24
LUSERE, 117
LUSK, 50 146
LUSTER, 40 179
LVICH, 37
LYCETT, 189
LYLIA, 55
LYNCH, 24 25 37 55 85 122 163 176 239
LYNDSAY, 23 24
LYNES, 55 107
LYNN, 187
LYNTX, 55
LYON, 39 47 102
LYONS, 85 145 190
LYSINGER, 145
LYSINZER, 85
LYSON, 6
LYTLE, 85 148

- M -

M'ADAMS, 55 106
M'BAIRD, 55
M'BIRD, 55
M'BRIDE, 6
M'CAFERTY, 7
M'CALL, 1
M'CANNA, 159
M'CARTY, 6 56 205
M'CAY, 55
M'CLAIN, 55 159
M'CLARK, 159
M'CLELLAND, 55
M'CLINTOCK, 55
M'CLUNG, 106
M'CLURE, 143 175 205
M'CONNALD, 159
M'CONNEL, 205
M'CORKLE, 143
M'CORMACK, 96 159

M'CORMICK, 141
M'CORNIS, 140
M'COY, 5 59 159
M'CUESTION, 5
M'CUNE, 141
M'DANIEL, 6 42 55 56 143 149 175
M'DERMOND, 205
M'DONALD, 43 143
M'DOW, 5 6 55
M'FARLAN, 96
M'FARLAND, 56 205
M'FARLIN, 159
M'GARVIN, 205
M'GAUGH, 205
M'GAVOCK, 143
M'GEE, 56 175
M'GILL, 7
M'GINHIN, 205
M'GIRK, 175
M'GLOCKLIN, 1
M'GUIDE, 56
M'GUIRE, 55
M'GUITTY, 56
M'HAUS, 55
M'HUGHS, 159
M'INTIRE, 5
M'KALLER, 175
M'KAY, 5
M'KENSIE, 6 188
M'KINNEY, 55 159 205
M'KINNIY, 159
M'KINNY, 159
M'KINSEY, 55
M'KNIGHT, 159
M'LAIN, 175
M'LANE, 56
M'LAUGHLIN, 42 139 143 159
M'LEAN, 175
M'MICK, 159
M'MICLE, 55
M'MILLIN, 107
M'MULLIN, 56
M'NEAL, 5
M'PHAIL, 143
M'PHERSON, 5
M'PHETERS, 55
M'QUITTY, 175
M'QUITZ, 5 6
M'SWAIN, 6
M'TRICLE, 5

M--HERS, 40
MABE, 28
MABRY, 226
MACCAN, 113
MACCULLA, 202
MACE, 140
MACEY, 55
MACHLIN, 146
MACKAY, 48 63 151
MACKEY, 3 162
MACKINTOSH, 50
MACKY, 159
MACON, 86 102
MADDAN, 86
MADDEN, 66 75
MADDIN, 58 99 104 131
MADDOX, 86 176 206 231
MADICK, 53
MADIN, 86
MADISON, 96 167 169 183
MAERD, 119
MAGAGNUS, 145 152 167
MAGAHAN, 96
MAGARD, 2
MAGEE, 8 86 127 129
MAGGART, 143
MAGILL, 39 188 207 209 215
MAGNESS, 191
MAGUIRE, 39
MAHAN, 2 8 122
MAHEN, 86
MAILLO, 233
MAINER, 216
MAINVILLE, 42 66 151 163-165
MAISON, 100
MAISONVILLE, 63 65 108 120 131
MAJOR, 94 147
MAJORES, 27
MAKUM, 224
MALANPHY, 119
MALCUM, 37
MALENKOTT, 28
MALET, 165
MALETT, 26
MALETTE, 131
MALEY, 214
MALIN, 85
MALLEAT, 109
MALLEN, 145
MALLERSON, 26

MALLET, 119
MALLORY, 86
MALON, 171
MALOTT, 39 122 123
MALOTTE, 39 123
MALUGAN, 225
MALVEAU, 41 100
MAN, 55 167
MANARD, 107
MANCHESTER, 86 162 228
MANDALL, 65
MANDELL, 86
MANES, 86
MANEY, 55
MANGLE, 93
MANIAN, 123
MANLEY, 26
MANLY, 131
MANN, 39 69 83 85 86 148 201
MANNEY, 5
MANNING, 63 69 94 169 173
MANNISH, 129
MANNON, 205
MANON, 86
MANPIN, 55
MANSFIELD, 6 86 234
MANSKER, 71 166 186
MANSON, 54
MANTONYA, 180
MANTSEY, 166
MANUEL, 1 50
MAPES, 86 211
MARABLE, 86
MARAI, 151
MARC, 69
MARCH, 3 55
MARCHAEL, 123
MARCHAND, 69 104
MARCHDEAU, 163
MARCHEL, 163
MARCHELEAU, 163
MARCHENT, 86
MARCHETEAU, 163
MARCHOTEAU, 41 114
MARCIL, 117
MARCO, 138
MARCUM, 9
MARCUS, 6
MARE, 189
MARECHAL, 62 63 65 66 69 163
 166 233

MARECHALLE, 130
MARECHE, 130
MARGRAVE, 179 201
MARGRAVES, 72
MARIAN, 113
MARICE, 27
MARICHAL, 106
MARICHAR, 115 117
MARIE, 63 67 69 86 131 164 233
 234
MARION, 67 131 205
MARISCAL, 237
MARKEAKUS, 151
MARKHAM, 59 159
MARKIN, 96
MARKLE, 8
MARKS, 86 96 226
MARKWELL, 123
MARLEY, 119
MARLIE, 118
MARLIN, 8
MARLOW, 26 63 168 169
MARLY, 65 175 181 236
MARNEY, 143
MAROIS, 48
MARONEX, 85
MAROTTE, 66
MARQUESS, 186
MARQUET, 139
MARQUETTE, i
MARQUIS, 2 100
MARR, 26 113 143
MARRIOLE, 159
MARRION, 106
MARROW, 72
MARRS, 142 224
MARS, 55 224
MARSH, 47 85 123 154 189
MARSHAL, 9 159
MARSHALL, 26 27 85 113 123
 159 175 176
MARSON, 86
MARSTELLAR, 86
MARTAIN, 104
MARTAN, 1
MARTEN, 131 151 159
MARTIE, 69
MARTIEN, 69
MARTIGNY, 41 42 66
MARTILO, 28
MARTIN, 5 7 12 27 37-39 47 49

MARTIN (continued)
   55-57 62 64 67 72 80 83 85 86
   93 96 99 106 107 113 123 131
   137 145 147-149 152 153 159
   162-164 167 173 175 178 180
   186 189 200 205 209 210 216
   227 229 230 239
MARTINAS, 139
MARTINNO, 26 27
MARTINY, 118
MARYE, 130
MASCHANEY, 25
MASCHEDA, 26
MASEDT, 139
MASHBURN, 85
MASINGILL, 39
MASKER, 171
MASON, 7 25 27 47 63 69 83-86
   104 106 123 131 145 148 157
   179 187 190 216 232
MASS, 131
MASSAY, 179
MASSE, 104 123
MASSEL, 59
MASSET, 103
MASSEY, 11 17 65 69 72 73 161
   162 173 177 209
MASSIE, 8 179 182
MASSO, 119
MASSY, 71
MASTER, 92 171
MASTERS, 62 63 65 69 131 142
   171 175 185
MASTERSON, 8
MASTICK, 86
MASTON, 123
MATHENEY, 86 123
MATHERS, 216
MATHEW, 44 163
MATHEWS, 25 27 37 58 83 86
   110 131 145 184 216
MATHIAS, 5 86 145
MATHIS, 62 65 216
MATHS, 188
MATHSTEAD, 56
MATIEN, 66
MATIS, 97 104
MATISE, 131
MATISSE, 59
MATKINS, 170
MATLOCK, 179

MATSEN, 141
MATSON, 8 159
MATTERSON, 159
MATTHEWS, 8 55 62 69 122 150
   174 195
MATTI, 228
MATTOCK, 119
MATTON, 145
MATTOON, 86
MATTOX, 47
MAUCHAL, 233
MAUD, 149
MAUPIN, 25 48 71 73 150 167
   175 194 197-199 201 202 229
   238
MAXEY, 179 239
MAXFIELD, 83 85 86
MAXWELL, 1 8 50 59 62 102 104
   106 129 145 167 217
MAY, 25 62 64 65 93 123 131 137
   143 171
MAYBERRY, 39 86
MAYBIN, 166
MAYCHETT, 25
MAYERS, 191
MAYES, 2
MAYET, 165
MAYFIELD, 171
MAYHAN, 225
MAYO, 55 240
MAYS, 5 56
MAZER, 208
MC ADAMS, 104 209
MC ADOW, 123
MC AFEE, 123 199
MC ALISTER, 107
MC ALLISTER, 84
MC ANALLY, 85
MC ANIN, 113
MC ANMON, 85
MC ARTHUR, 216
MC BAY, 85
MC BRIDE, 43 85 123 177 185
   195 240
MC BROOM, 85
MC CADE, 187
MC CAFFEL, 85
MC CAFFERTY, 85 123
MC CAIN, 149
MC CALISTER, 47 131
MC CALL, 85 122

MC CALLA, 145
MC CALLISTER, 85 145
MC CAMMON, 85
MC CANE, 221
MC CANN, 195
MC CANNAH, 85
MC CARTNEY, 131
MC CARTY, 37 82 85 123 127 149 173
MC CARY, 84 145
MC CATEE, 26
MC CAUL, 191
MC CAUSLAND, 167
MC CAUSLIN, 25
MC CAY, 63 70 92 131
MC CHESKEY, 182
MC CHISHOLM, 61
MC CLAIN, 3 47 173 231 239
MC CLAIR, 123
MC CLANAHAN, 70 191 217 233
MC CLANE, 26
MC CLARE, 85
MC CLAREY, 123
MC CLARY, 72 85
MC CLAY, 26
MC CLEAN, 70
MC CLEARNEY, 27
MC CLEARNY, 27 28
MC CLELAN, 219
MC CLELAND, 110
MC CLELLAN, 39
MC CLELLAND, 43 189 238
MC CLENAHAN, 223
MC CLENDEN, 179
MC CLENDON, 85
MC CLENLLAND, 26
MC CLENNEY, 25
MC CLOUD, 206
MC CLOUND, 214
MC CLOVE, 145
MC CLURE, 2 25 74
MC COLLESTER, 85
MC COLLOCK, 210 214
MC COLLOM, 123
MC COLLOUGH, 85 131
MC COLLUM, 47 123
MC COMB, 173
MC CONCHEY, 85
MC CONNEL, 13 25 27
MC CONNELL, 65 70 131 142 151

MC CONNOCHI, 129
MC CONOHON, 65
MC CORD, 70 123 131
MC CORDLE, 70
MC CORELL, 188
MC CORKEY, 26
MC CORMACK, 63 70 96 131 167 212 226 231 232
MC CORMEEK, 109
MC CORMICK, 137 167 227
MC COUKLIN, 70
MC COUNTNEY, 70
MC COURT, 26
MC COURTNEY, 109 139 140 198 203 210
MC COWN, 131
MC COY, 9 14 26 27 39 70 85 96 107 131 145 151 159 162 198 222
MC CRA, 85
MC CRACKEN, 123
MC CRARY, 149
MC CRAY, 39 123
MC CREA, 85
MC CREADY, 85
MC CREARY, 85
MC CRERY, 52
MC CROSKIE, 39
MC CROSKRIE, 39
MC CRUMB, 84 145
MC CULLOCK, 208 209 211 213
MC CULLOCL, 211
MC CULLOUGH, 70 159 199
MC CULLY, 209
MC CURDY, 85
MC CUTCHEN, 27 28
MC CUTCHENS, 28
MC CUTCHON, 137
MC DADE, 85
MC DANIEL, 2 8 47 70 131 233
MC DEHAT, 179
MC DENOWAY, 179
MC DERMED, 113
MC DERMONT, 27
MC DERMOTT, 65 85
MC DERNITT, 129
MC DONALD, 62 70 72 73 84 85 93 123 130 131 137 142 145 162 173 177 193 195 209 210 213 215 222
MC DONAUGH, 131

MC DONNEL, 25 26
MC DOW, 238 239
MC DOWELL, 2 145 149 152 167 211
MC DUFF, 62 85 103 104
MC DUGELL, 84 85
MC DURMITT, 173
MC ELDUFF, 104
MC ELLIOTT, 85
MC ELROY, 8 80 83
MC ELWEE, 39
MC ENTIRE, 202
MC EVEN, 195
MC EWEN, 85
MC EWIN, 148 205
MC FADDEN, 148
MC FADDIN, 183
MC FADION, 84
MC FALL, 8 27 67 123 131 187
MC FARLAND, 3 85 96 123 167-170 173 184 224 225
MC FARLANE, 113 220
MC FARLEN, 110
MC FARLIN, 94
MC FARRIS, 27
MC FARSON, 131
MC FEE, 85
MC FERRON, 104
MC FERSON, 123 179
MC FIELD, 85
MC GALLASPIE, 84
MC GARVIN, 113
MC GARY, 230
MC GAUGH, 39 205
MC GAY, 185
MC GEE, 2 39 47 85 123 179 189 211 213
MC GEHEE, 224
MC GENITY, 85
MC GIFFIN, 85
MC GINN, 222
MC GINNIS, 85 217 221
MC GIRK, 151 154 189 209 213
MC GLANDIN, 170
MC GLAUGHLAN, 131
MC GLAUGHLIN, 14 18
MC GLOCHLIN, 113
MC GOWIN, 25
MC GOWING, 72
MC GOWN, 123
MC GRAW, 85

MC GREGOR, 131
MC GRIFFIN, 148
MC GUIRE, 85 123 220
MC GUNNEGLE, 176
MC GUNNIGLE, 145 148 149 152 167 228
MC GUYR, 85
MC GWIN, 173
MC HADDEN, 190
MC HAN, 162
MC HAVEN, 171
MC HAWES, 85
MC HENRY, 96 170
MC HUGH, 67 162
MC ILVAIN, 85 170
MC INTIRE, 85 145 177
MC INTOSH, 85 100 104
MC INTRE, 192
MC KAIN, 85
MC KAIRE, 159
MC KAMEY, 230
MC KAY, 27 159
MC KEAN, 178 209
MC KEE, 72 96 104 168-170 176 196 209
MC KELLAR, 47
MC KELVEY, 171
MC KENNA, 85 137 223
MC KENNEY, 85 159
MC KENNY, 85 145 176 225
MC KENSIE, 70 174 188
MC KENZIE, 70 126
MC KEY, 162
MC KIBB, 131
MC KIM, 70 85
MC KINLEY, 67 85
MC KINN, 185
MC KINNEY, 25 63 67 107 113 131 137 177 194 198 221
MC KINNON, 131 212 215
MC KINNY, 193
MC KINSEY, 173
MC KINZE, 131
MC KINZEY, 113
MC KISSICK, 123
MC KNIGHT, 85
MC KONOGHY, 85
MC KULLUM, 131
MC LAIN, 65 104 216
MC LAINE, 119
MC LAIRD, 159

MC LAMEE, 27
MC LANAHAN, 103
MC LANE, 65
MC LAUGHLAN, 131
MC LAUGHLIN, 66 85 98 131 137 151 209
MC LEAN, 50 51 85 104 105 129 148 195
MC LESTER, 148
MC LOAD, 13
MC MAHAN, 2 3
MC MAHON, 123
MC MANING, 85
MC MANIS, 73
MC MANN, 159
MC MANUS, 123
MC MEMORY, 145
MC MENNONY, 152
MC MENNOY, 167
MC MICHEL, 66
MC MICKLE, 130
MC MILLAN, 65 70 86 216
MC MILLEN, 26 86 128
MC MILLIN, 107
MC MINN, 171
MC MITCHEL, 18
MC MITCHELL, 37
MC MULLEN, 85 86 145
MC MULTRIE, 67 128
MC MURPHY, 86
MC MURRY, 131
MC MURTRY, 131
MC MURTY, 67
MC NAIR, 161 217
MC NAIRY, 152 167
MC NEAL, 67
MC NEILLY, 86
MC NELLY, 145
MC NEW, 141
MC NICOLSON, 67
MC NIGHT, 27
MC NOUGH, 159
MC NUTT, 25 37
MC PHARTAN, 93
MC PHEETER, 43
MC PIKE, 99
MC QUEEN, 44 113 137
MC QUILKIN, 86
MC QUITTY, 2 65 215
MC RAE, 8
MC REYNOLDS, 8 113

MC RIN, 65 70
MC ROBERTS, 9 25 27
MCURVINE, 26
MC WATERS, 27 159
MC WHALEY, 225
MC WHARTER, 86
MC WILLIAMS, 8 99 113 123 141 173 195 198 201 205
MEAD, 149
MEADER, 86
MEADOR, 123
MEADOWS, 74
MEAIZO, 173
MEAN, 110
MEANS, 8 86 149 151 175 188
MEARA, 220
MEASER, 86
MEASOR, 145
MEASS, 202
MECHANT, 22
MECHO, 150
MECK, 62
MEDCALF, 28
MEDDENDORF, 26
MEDDLIN, 123
MEDISTE, 85
MEDLBY, 173
MEDLEY, 86
MEDLIN, 40
MEDLOCK, 198
MEEK, 62 131
MEEKER, 48 86 148
MEENS, 123
MEGAR, 64
MEGINNES, 26
MELDER, 86
MELEANE, 98
MELLET, 112
MELLON, 63 108
MELLVONE, 59
MELOCHE, 65
MELON, 151
MELOY, 86
MELTON, 85 86 137 179
MELUIS, 155
MELVIN, 86
MEMVILLE, 235
MENAR, 119 237
MENARD, 49 51 63 64 86 104 106 119 131 166 212 233
MENARE, 130

MENARO, 139
MENCHER, 86
MENEES, 217
MENIX, 137
MENSE, 202
MENSKER, 183.
MENTAS, 100
MEOLBY, 173
MERCEER, 206
MERCELLE, 130
MERCER, 179
MERCHAND, 186
MERCHANT, 113 205
MERCIE, 116
MERCIER, 41 62 100 104 106 237
MERDEL, 131
MEREDITH, 63 86 98 128 131
MERIDETH, 131
MERRILL, 8 86
MERRIT, 85
MERRITT, 85
MERTZ, 208
MESLOCHE, 69
MESNOR, 140
MESPLAIS, 129 131
MESPLAY, 129
MESSAGER, 75 101
MESSERSMITH, 40
MESSICK, 85
MESSORSMITH, 113
METAVIA, 86
METAYER, 104
METAYES, 110
METIVEE, 110
METIVIER, 163
METOT, 69
METZ, 42 69 207
MEVILLE, 65
MEYER, 28 202
MEYERPETER, 155
MIACAL, 26
MIBERTOWER, 7
MICHAELS, 131
MICHAN, 159
MICHAU, 63 131 211
MICHEL, 56 63 65 72 92 109 112 120 131 163 201
MICHERTOWER, 7
MICHON, 115 116
MICHUM, 119
MICK, 56

MICLENNA, 28
MIDDLEBURGER, 26
MIDDLETON, 65 228
MIER, 131
MIERS, 107 143
MILAM, 162
MILBRAMY, 145
MILES, 65 86 106 130 149 159 214
MILEU, 25
MILFORD, 86
MILHOMME, 64
MILICE, 131
MILIHAN, 123
MILLARD, 216 221
MILLER, 8 21 26-28 34 39 56 57 63 64 66 69 71-73 83 86 107 113 119 123 126 128 131 137-139 142 143 145 147 151-154 161 168 171-173 179 183 184 188 189 191-199 202 209 211 224 228 229 233
MILLES, 26
MILLET, 59 66
MILLETTE, 69 150
MILLIET, 131
MILLIGAN, 66 113 159 205
MILLIKEN, 128
MILLIKIN, 64 86
MILLINGTON, 25 152 159
MILLIS, 184
MILLRANY, 86
MILLS, 66 85 86 113 191 207 222-225
MILLSAPS, 39
MILSAP, 154
MILTON, 7 86 145
MINCHELS, 202
MINCHER, 196
MINER, 56
MINES, 143
MINKS, 166
MINNS, 143
MINOTT, 56 86
MINSHALL, 86
MINTEN, 56
MIRE, 131
MIRES, 220
MIRRA, 1
MISCAL, 179
MISSLA, 1

MISTI, 66
MISTY, 16
MITCHEL, ii 26 30 33 56 96 131
MITCHELE, 96
MITCHELL, ii 2 6 7 65 86 123
　131 141 145 150 161 169 170
　175 188 192-195 198 204
MOBERLY, 175
MOBIDOU, 235
MOBLEY, 122
MOBLY, 47
MOCK, 67 108 208
MODERWELL, 188
MOFFIT, 93
MOGINZO, 26
MOINTARDY, 236
MOISE, 86
MOITE, 86
MOLAN, 171
MOLARD, 41 42 185
MOLDY, 38
MOLE, 112
MOLETOE, 26
MOLLEN, 110
MOLLENS, 131
MOLLET, 157
MOLONY, 181 209
MOMON, 197
MONCUS, 123
MONDAY, 67 151
MONDON, 159
MONICAL, 189
MONICLE, 142
MONNEYHAM, 122
MONO, 133
MONRO, 3
MONROE, 3 39 47 86 150 200
MONSELLE, 137
MONTARDY, 40 41 67 114 222
MONTEER, 167
MONTGOMERY, 39 67 69 86 96
　104 154 178 179 189 190 201
　217 225
MONTMENIE, 69
MONTOOTH, 37
MONTTMIREL, 104
MOODY, 37 55 99 113 122 159
　192 205
MOON, 86 146
MOONEY, 86

MOOR, 17 39 113 189 199 202
　205 220
MOORDOCK, 28
MOORE, 1 26 27 37 40 47 63 67
　69 72 83 86 93 98 113 123 125
　130 131 137 143 145 148 159
　162 167 170 185 186 190 192
　196 207-211 216 217 220 223
　225 226 230
MOORHEAD, 131 223
MOORHOUSE, 86
MOQUE, 131
MOQUEZ, 151
MORAIN, 131
MORAN, 86
MORANCY, 104
MORAU, 86
MORAUX, 49 50
MORDICA, 2 56
MORDICAI, 37
MORDOC, 191
MORDOCK, 28
MORE, 131 139 213
MOREAU, 48 62 63 65 69 151 163
　206 217 237
MOREHEAD, 59 86 104 149
MOREHOUSE, 86
MOREL, 49 99 104 209
MORELAND, 63 86 123 190
MOREN, 175 236
MORES, 69
MORFELD, 156
MORFIELD, 155
MORGAN, 3 7 39 40 47 55 62 63
　69 85 86 99 104 113 123 131
　175 189 190 196 205 210
MORIN, 41 111 123 131 149 151
　165 185
MORISAUX, 166
MORLEY, 86
MORNICE, 205
MORO, 1 3 48 51 63 67 70 104
　116 129
MORR, 86
MORRAS, 123
MORRELL, 1
MORRILL, 86
MORRIN, 119
MORRIS,
MORRIS, 1 8 27 28 39 43 48 55

MORRIS (continued)
67 71 83 85 86 99 123 131 141
142 145 148 150 153 175 178
179 191 196-198 207 228
MORRISON, 1 22 47 51 52 65 66
86 106 176 179 186 188
MORRISSON, 26
MORROUGH, 173
MORROW, 47 86 113 148 152 153
179 191 205
MORSE, 47 86 224
MORTEN, 201
MORTFEZ, 66
MORTON, 8 86 215
MOSBEY, 201
MOSEBY, 48
MOSELY, 142 149 198
MOSHER, 86 221
MOSIER, 86
MOSLEY, 5 168 203
MOSS, 6 7 8 45 47 55 56 141 212
MOSTELLER, 63 96 170
MOSTELLIOR, 95
MOSURE, 123
MOTARD, 50 70 104 151
MOTHERSHED, 86 177
MOTIE, 119
MOTIER, 67
MOTT, 38 154
MOUNT, 86 145
MOURNING, 239
MOUTRY, 195
MOUZER, 205
MOUZZER, 113
MOVE, 159
MOXLEY, 232
MOXLY, 230
MOYSO, 138
MOZEE, 26
MUCEY, 123
MUDD, 168
MUELLER, 203
MUHNN, 28
MUIR, 141
MULANY, 86
MULDRO, 8
MULDROW, 8
MULIEN, 184
MULKEY, 224
MULLANPHY, 131

MULLENS, 3 99
MULLIAN, 154
MULLIGAN, 123
MULLIKIN, 215
MULLIN, 131
MULLINS, 52 55 63 65 122 129
MULTON, 198
MUNCUS, 7
MUNCY, 173
MUNDAY, 86
MUNDEL, 86
MUNDY, 149
MUNICH, 157
MUNKERS, 39
MUNKIRS, 39
MUNN, 47 145
MUNRO, 3 175 189
MURDEL, 86
MURDOCK, 28 62 65 67 99 197
MURDOUGH, 59 104 131
MURFEY, 86
MURGUYS, 187
MURLEY, 153 190
MUROE, 86
MURPEY, 71
MURPHEY, 28 55 86 95 96 122
123
MURPHY, 44 52 62 66 67 70 85
95 96 98 99 110 111 126 131
145 148 149 151 162 167-169
174 175 186 192 193 199 200
216 218 226
MURRAY, 39 229
MURREY, 113
MURROW, 86
MURRY, 137
MUSE, 86
MUSIACK, 200
MUSIC, 59
MUSICK, 43 62 63 66 67 70 107
131 200 202 206 210-215 218
MUSS, 66
MUSSER, 86
MUSSEY, 107
MYER, 28
MYERS, 62 67 70 83 86 92 119
120 131 153 182
MYETTE, 159
MYRE, 25
MYRES, 27 182 213

- N -

NACE, 177
NACHETTE, 120
NACKE, 156
NACKLE, 156
NAILER, 209
NANCE, 113 137
NANSE, 193
NAPPER, 203
NARCE, 194
NASCHARD, 150
NASH, 3 4 43 56 67 113 137 150 159 177 221
NATHAN, 152
NAVE, 123
NAYLOR, 28
NEAL, 5 56 63 67 104 173
NEALEY, 5
NEALY, 56
NEEL, 107
NEELEY, 63
NEELY, 3 173
NEIGHBOUR, 67
NEIL, 137
NEILE, 205
NEILL, 113 137 142 211
NEITER, 86 148
NELSON, 54 84 86 131 149 180 239
NERUT, 131
NESBEE, 46
NESBIT, 43 86 206
NESHIT, 145
NESHT, 56
NETHEUHEAD, 5
NETTLE, 205 224
NEUSCHWANGER, 131
NEUSEN, 119
NEVETT, 222
NEVILL, 107
NEVINS, 137 143 231 232
NEVIT, 203
NEWBAUGH, 56
NEWBERRY, 179 182
NEWBROUGH, 177
NEWBY, 163 164
NEWCOM, 137
NEWELL, 8 219
NEWFIELD, 129 173 216
NEWKIRK, 63
NEWLAND, 56
NEWLOCK, 173
NEWMAN, 39 63 123 131 152 176 229
NEWSOM, 86 137 145 175 185
NEWT, 205
NEWTON, 5 86 148 152 204
NEYLSON, 67
NEYSWANGER, 67
NIBERVILLE, 48
NICHELS, 56
NICHLES, 123
NICHOLAS, 63 86 137 141 225
NICHOLS, 39 56 72 85 86 175 227 230 239
NICHOLSON, 39 87
NICKERSON, 87 145
NICKLES, 150 209 214
NICKOLS, 199
NICO, 74
NICOL, 104
NICOLE, 131
NICOTLE, 67
NIDEVER, 40
NIEL, 63
NIELL, 107
NIELSON, 65
NIGHT, 123 179
NILSON, 123
NIOT, 119
NIOTT, 120
NIPP, 28
NISONG, 167
NISWANGER, 171
NIVEN, 176
NIX, 86 113 137 197
NIXEN, 113
NIXON, 87
NOARTH, 28
NOBA, 118
NOBLE, 3 47 87 123 171
NOBLES, 178 179
NOBLESSE, 63
NOCK, 87
NOELL, 28
NOIS, 118
NOISE, 41 42 164
NOIZE, 49
NOLAN, 87 106 161 219
NOLAND, 56 123 143
NOLEN, 56 87 148 220

NOLIN, 87
NOLLEPE, 92
NOLLEY, 231
NONTY, 87
NOOKLY, 46
NOOR, 159
NORMAN, 1 37 87 123 159 171 173 179 215
NORMANDEAU, 62 165
NORR, 159
NORRIS, 59 67 87 123 129 198 224
NORTH, 62 71 130 131 142 197-200
NORTHCUT, 45 113
NORTHENT, 205
NORTHERN, 47
NORTHOVER, 87
NORTHRAP, 87
NORTHUM, 87
NORTHUP, 87 145
NORTIN, 94
NORTON, 141 159
NORWINE, 170
NORWOOD, 240
NOTIONS, 173
NOULSON, 5
NOURR, 159
NOUVEL, 166
NOVAL, 28
NOWLAND, 72
NOWLIN, 87
NUCKLUS, 38
NUCKOLAS, 210
NULEY, 111
NULL, 63 65 131 196
NULLINS, 56
NUSAM, 65 67 98
NUSANS, 104
NUTE, 87
NUTTING, 6 39
NYSWONGER, 127

- O -

O'BANNION, 87
O'BRIEN, 87
O'BUNE, 140
O'CARROL, 65
O'CONNELL, 106
O'CONNOR, 62 87

O'DANIEL, 129
O'DIORM, 87
O'DONNELL, 87
O'FLING, 87
O'HAGAN, 63
O'HARA, 67 162 189
O'HARE, 181
O'HAVER, 169
O'HOGAN, 127
O'KEEF, 123
O'NEAL, 65 179
O'NEIL, 87 226
O'NEILL, 87 130 188
O'VAIL, 87
O'VANION, 123
OAKES, 87 145
OAKS, 171
OATH, 65
OBACHON, 1
OBESHON, 28
OBICHON, 217
OBOJEZ, 130
OBUCHON, 1 130 131
OCLARREL, 131
ODEN, 113 123 159 205
ODOM, 131
ODUM, 67 87
OFFICER, 39
OGAN, 56
OGDEN, 87 201
OGE, 59
OGEUNE, 67
OGIN, 5 6
OGLES, 206
OGLESBY, 163 177
OILPHANT, 39
OLDHAM, 194 232
OLDS, 87
OLGIE, 1
OLIVE, 70
OLIVER, 28 65 83 87 131 145 158 164 173 187 216 226
OLIVET, 87
OLIVIE, 165
ONEAL, 40
ONGEE, 28
ONRAW, 110
ONSTAT, 141
ONSTATT, 141
ONSTILL, 159
ONSTOTT, 230

OPE, 141
OPELHATT, 131
OPTEN, 110
ORAIN, 70
ORCHARD, 201
OREAR, 7
ORISON, 87
ORLEANS, 132
ORME, 176
ORMON, 86 87
ORMSBY, 179
ORN, 87
ORR, 56 83 87 142 149
ORRA, 115
ORRICH, 28
ORRICK, 19 28
ORTES, 132
ORTIZ, 117
ORTNER, 141
OSAGE, 12
OSAR, 183
OSBERN, 181
OSBORN, 39 56 71 86 145 196 206
OSBORNE, 87 201
OSBURN, 87 191
OSGOOD, 29
OSTERWALD, 202
OSTRADER, 46
OSTRANDER, 85 87 149
OTIS, 86 145
OTONERE, 116
OTTERY, 70
OTTIN, 28
OUILET, 66
OUSLEY, 56 113 205
OUTERBRIDGE, 87
OUVRE, 131
OVAIL, 148
OVERALL, 28 29 159
OVERBY, 145
OVERSTREET, 28 66
OVERTON, 83 87
OWEN, 44 66 123 137 175 189 216
OWENBY, 190
OWENS, 39 47 72 87 145 159 167 175 179 189 197 202 227
OWINGS, 86 112 113 205
OWINS, 37 132
OWNBY, 47

OWNSBAY, 179
OWNSBEY, 153
OWSLEY, 59 188 239
OXLEY, 86
OZBURN, 224

- P -

PACE, 6 56 113 123 205 238
PACHARA, 140
PACKARD, 100
PACKARET, 98
PACKWOOD, 123 225
PACQUETTE, 67
PAELY, 57
PAETZMAN, 87
PAGE, 56 67 86 87 113 123 145
PAGEL, 1
PAGET, 59 132
PAGGETT, 67
PAGNON, 163
PAIN, 86 119 205
PAININ, 119
PAIRY, 56
PAJOL, 151
PAKES, 141
PALARDA, 23
PALARDU, 26
PALLARDA, 29
PALLARDI, 151
PALLARDIE, 67
PALLEN, 224
PALLENDA, 16
PALMATARY, 190
PALMER, 28 70 83 87 106 132 149 159 188
PALMETEER, 87
PALMETIER, 87
PALOR, 130
PAMAHE, 163
PAMAN, 119
PANE, 72
PANETON, 70
PANISSE, 163
PANLON, 130
PANNETON, 185
PANTOIN, 119
PANTON, 237
PAPEN, 115
PAPIN, 41 42 63 65 70 114 119 132 166 234 235

PAPPAN, 160
PAPPIN, 33
PAQUETTE, 108
PAQUIN, 105 108 119
PAR, 115
PARAN, 115
PARAT, 56
PARCE, 111
PARE, 137
PARENT, 37 49 51 59 203 217 237
PARIS, 161
PARISH, 70 86 87 113 125 145 184 205
PARISIEN, 119
PARK, 43 45 57 196 197
PARKE, 132
PARKER, 6 56 57 63 70 71 83 85-87 93 96 99 106 111 123 132 138 141 145 174 175 179 180 188 195-197 199 200 239
PARKES, 110
PARKEST, 87
PARKINSON, 87
PARKS, 5 47 87 141 142 175 195 197 202 203
PARKSON, 131
PARKWAY, 67
PARMER, 8 131 160
PARNELL, 87
PAROZETT, 87
PARRICK, 168
PARRIS, 143
PARRISH, 8 87 141 160 173
PARROTT, 87 123
PARSELL, 87
PARSHALL, 168
PARSLEY, 193
PARSLY, 194
PARSONS, 72 73 87 179
PARTENAIS, 67
PARTENAY, 103 104
PARTIN, 87
PARTNAY, 132
PARTONEY, 217
PARZETTE, 74
PASAR, 138
PASCALL, 87
PASONT, 1
PASQUIN, 63 119
PATCHEN, 29

PATELLE, 160
PATERICK, 168
PATERSOMME, 110
PATERSON, 132
PATES, 205
PATIN, 160
PATNODE, 130
PATNOTE, 67
PATRI, 29
PATRICK, 3 123 143 145 163 168 175 229
PATTEN, 5 6 30 37 57 130 135 188
PATTERSON, 7 26 29 30 37 47 48 62 63 67 70 83 87 95 96 106 127 129 135 143 168 173 179 182 184 223
PATTIE, 143
PATTIT, 70 72
PATTON, 57 87 113 123 135 167 175 194 198 199 205 212
PATY, 116
PAUCHE, 102
PAUL, 41 67 87 98 129
PAULE, 74
PAULEY, 135 217
PAUSHASE, 160
PAVANT, 67
PAWLING, 74
PAXTON, 87 209
PAYAN, 67
PAYANT, 106 131 166
PAYNE, 5 6 56 57 67 87 150 173 175 176
PAYNES, 55
PAYNISH, 65
PAYTON, 190
PEACE, 87
PEAD, 87
PEANALL, 96
PEARCE, 29 30 87 141
PEARSHALL, 135
PEARSON, 56 123 216
PEASCOCK, 47
PEASE, 87
PEAVY, 87
PECARD, 27-29
PECHE, 67
PECK, 29 87 152 228
PEEBELS, 223
PEEBLY, 39

PEEN, 195 196
PEEPLES, 87 148
PEERS, 104
PEG, 56
PEIGNE, 67 70 105 110
PEIRCEALL, 135
PEISINGER, 143
PELHAM, 218
PELKY, 70
PELL, 87
PELLEBIERD, 42
PELLETIER, 63 70 236
PELONS, 96
PELTIE, 116
PELTIER, 60 131 150
PEMBERTON, 219
PENCE, 30
PENDERGRASS, 160
PENDERGRAST, 65
PENEIVAL, 143
PENNELL, 87
PENNIMAN, 216
PENNINGTON, 113 123 205 225
PENNY, 87 145
PENROD, 199 203
PENTE, 37
PENTER, 72
PENTURF, 87
PEOPLES, 87 107
PEPEN, 115
PEPIN, 103 105 164
PEPINS, 130
PEPPER, 72 73 186 193 199 208 212
PEPPERS, 154
PERA, 160
PERCELLE, 104
PERCELLS, 87
PERE, 129
PEREL, 102
PERELLE, 98 99 105
PEREZ, 42 58 59 65
PERI, 236
PERINGER, 171
PERIO, 129 135
PERKENS, 186
PERKINS, 5 6 37 53 67 70 72 87 170 171 179 191 192 199 200 203 205
PERLAISE, 135
PERLUIO, 75

PERNACE, 159
PERODOT, 135
PERON, 40 116 120
PEROUX, 75 151
PERR, 176
PERRAU, 135
PERRAULT, 41 164
PERREL, 75 105
PERRIALT, 41
PERRILLIARD, 50
PERRIN, 119
PERRON, 63
PERROW, 29
PERRY, 3 29 37 42 54 70 86 87 96 97 166 175 179 188 217 225
PERRYMAN, 70
PERTHUIS, 74 75
PERY, 41 42
PESLAY, 3
PETER, 159
PETERS, 87 123
PETERSON, 87 218
PETHS, 205
PETIE, 135
PETIT, 164
PETITE, 165
PETTES, 87
PETTEST, 87
PETTET, 135
PETTEY, 30
PETTIBONE, 70 135
PETTIGREW, 3 87
PETTIS, 145 151 152 167 179 238 239
PETTIT, 19 24 29 63 70 135 169
PETTUS, 87 152 191
PETTY, 30 159 224 232
PETY, 117
PEUGET, 19
PEVAULT, 40
PEVEY, 87
PEW, 63 126 135 173 183
PEWETER, 205
PEYOUX, 59
PEYROUX, 48-51 57 59 65 75 101 103 105 120
PEYROUZ, 58
PEYTON, 168 169
PHARRIS, 3
PHELAN, 222
PHELPHES, 29

PHELPS, 87 217
PHERQUILLE, 119
PHILBERRY, 63
PHILIBAR, 181
PHILIBUSTIER, 100
PHILIP, 70
PHILIPIN, 181
PHILIPS, 5 6 70 83 113 153 161 200 201
PHILLIPS, 37 45 56 57 72 73 87 123 135 137 138 145 160 179 189 198 199 201
PHILLIPSON, 159
PHINNEY, 145
PHINNY, 87
PHIPPEN, 87
PIBURN, 1 39
PICARD, 22 63 70 103 104 109
PICETT, 87
PICHER, 105
PICHET, 135
PICKARD, 87
PICKENS, 142
PICKET, 87
PICKIL, 71
PIDGEON, 7
PIEART, 163
PIERCE, 39 48 86 87 141 145 148 152 203
PIERCEALL, 63
PIERRE, 40 105 120
PIERSLEY, 34
PIERSOLL, 87
PIFFLE, 87
PIGG, 5 123
PIKE, 85 87 148 177
PILIER, 166
PILKINGTON, 216
PILKINTON, 123
PILLAR, 65
PILLARS, 135
PILLSNOTH, 140
PILMAN, 160 205
PINDELL, 149
PINE, 87
PINKERTON, 125
PINKLETON, 196
PINKLEY, 216
PINKSTON, 96 123 198
PINNELL, 179 186
PINNEY, 87

PINTER, 72
PIOTERAY, 160
PIPER, 11 29 30 63 135 151 161 201
PIPES, 3 150
PIQUET, 65
PIQUIRRES, 40
PISE, 57
PISIN, 72
PISSER, 5
PITCHER, 87 123 145
PITMAN, 14 30 113 159 160
PITRE, 130
PITT, 87
PITTES, 30
PITTIS, 30
PITTMAN, 123 187 188
PITTS, 123 145
PITZERK, 30
PITZPATRICK, 81
PIVER, 87
PIXLEY, 87
PIZON, 233
PLACET, 48 49 59 67 75 129 130
PLACETTE, 48-50
PLACI, 50
PLACIDE, 67 130
PLACY, 105
PLAIN, 87
PLANCHA, 116
PLANK, 222
PLANT, 65
PLANTE, 51 75 105
PLASI, 135
PLASSMEYER, 155
PLIVER, 224
PLUMB, 86
PLUMMER, 83 87 145 197
POAGE, 3 189
POAQUE, 6
POCKE, 59
POE, 29
POEPPING, 156
POEWEL, 137
POGUE, 39 147
POILLIERE, 67
POILLIEVRE, 105
POINSALATE, 29
POINTEN, 74
POINTER, 194 199 203
POIRIER, 67 109

POITOU, 51
POKERN, 29
POLAND, 87 145
POLARD, 87
POLDERIN, 111
POLETT, 1
POLK, 56 171 173 175 189
POLLAN, 87
POLLARD, 83 87 145 223
POLLET, 42
POLLETTE, 65
POLO, 116
PONS, 87
PONTS, 87
POOL, 40 87 148 166
POOR, 123 1755
POPE, 129 217
PORCELLY, 166 236
POREMUS, 173
PORER, 100
PORNEUF, 233
PORSLEY, 114
PORT, 87
PORTEL, 65
PORTEN, 117
PORTER, 30 39 83 87 96 105 115 123 141 145 148 162 191 215
PORTERFIELD, 85
PORTH, 157
PORTICO, 85
PORTZEY, 30
POSEVIE, 40
POSEY, 197 200
POST, 159 160
POSTEN, 96
POSTIN, 190
POSTON, 170 225
POTIE, 114 164
POTIS, 96
POTTER, 39 47 87 123 176 189 190 222
POTTS, 56 57 73 179
POUARE, 40
POUCHE, 102
POUGAT, 165
POUILLOT, 70
POULTETT, 87
POUND, 192 196
POUNDS, 179 203
POUPEL, 40
POURIER, 181

POURNEUF, 135
POVEAU, 159
POVNE, 208
POWEL, 29 205
POWELL, 87 146 176 216
POWER, 30 35
POWERS, 65 70 74 87 119 123 146 224
POWLIN, 129
POWLL, 87
POWNS, 72
POYNTER, 179
POYTER, 179
PRAITER, 123
PRATE, 56
PRATER, 1
PRATHER, 87 190 193 197
PRATT, 1 67 83 87 113 137 177 217
PRATTE, 49-51 59 63 65 70 75 96 100 105 119 129 135 165
PRAUER, 159
PRAUIR, 159
PREBLE, 86
PRECEL, 56
PRELE, 135
PRELLY, 74
PRENTICE, 87
PREOR, 29
PREPEAU, 160
PRESANS, 130 135
PRESCOTT, 87 143
PRESHALL, 160
PRESSE, 70 105
PRESTON, 29 62 205
PRETCHET, 108
PREVOST, 165
PREWIT, 39
PREWITT, 225
PRICE, 1 29 30 48-51 59 63 67 75 83 87 88 100 104 113 123 129 134 135 142 148 151 159 173 196 205 219 224 225
PRICHARD, 113 159 188
PRICOT, 13
PRIDE, 51
PRIEST, 135 159 173 183
PRIEUR, 67 139
PRIM, 173
PRIMAU, 43
PRIMM, 202

PRIMO, 62 67 186
PRIMOR, 237
PRINCE, 29 137
PRINE, 39 40
PRINGLE, 88 205
PRIOR, 20 29 72
PRITCHARD, 8
PRITCHET, 30 39 63 177
PRITCHETT, 194 200
PRITTER, 73
PROBANCHE, 115
PROBESK, 149
PROBO, 116
PROBST, 127
PROCTER, 5
PROCTOR, 3 56 74
PROFFIT, 39
PROMAU, 42 43
PROPST, 171 173
PROVENCHE, 41 135 164 234
PROVENCHER, 119
PROVENCHERE, 67 135 166
PROVINCHERE, 159
PROVONCHIER, 233
PROWELL, 45
PROWHER, 173
PRUIT, 185
PRUITT, 67
PRUNELL, 88
PRYOR, 179
PUCKETT, 88
PUDEN, 56
PUDON, 59
PUFFER, 88
PUGAL, 70
PUGH, 137 161 205
PUION, 164
PUJET, 29
PUJOI, 27
PUJOL, 24 29
PUJOT, 135
PULAIM, 202
PULLEM, 30
PULLEN, 57 160
PULLIAM, 56 57
PULLY, 88 145
PULSE, 47
PUNGEMBRE, 42
PURCELL, 45 239
PURCELLIY, 165
PURDIN, 74

PURDOM, 93
PURDON, 3
PURKINS, 73 159 209
PURRINGTON, 88
PURSALL, 145
PURSELL, 141
PURSINGLE, 205
PURSLEY, 3 34-36 186 194
PURST, 159
PURTH, 88
PURYEAR, 88 113 205
PUSELL, 159
PUSINGTON, 56
PUSLEY, 71
PUSSLEY, 135
PUTNEUF, 119
PUTNEY, 88
PUTTMAN, 187
PYATT, 65

- Q -

QUALLS, 88
QUARLES, 88 160 170 185
QUAY, 88
QUEBEC, 67
QUEBECK, 151 160
QUEEN, 174
QUENAL, 165
QUENEL, 236
QUICK, 63 113 135 137 160 205
    206 212 214
QUIENEL, 114
QUIENELLE, 129
QUIMBY, 67 128
QUINNELL, 16
QUISNELLE, 135

- R -

RABAUM, 6
RABER, 67
RABOR, 68
RACINE, 67 68 108 119
RADDIC, 105
RADEMACHER, 155
RADFORD, 88 224
RADMACHER, 155
RAGAN, 47
RAGE, 56
RAGLAND, 88 148 151 168

RAGSDALE, 138
RAIER, 113
RAIL, 179
RAIME, 68
RAINWATER, 86 145
RAINWATERS, 88
RAIRDON, 129
RALLY, 68
RALPH, 88 145
RAMEY, 58 135
RAMPIER, 88
RAMS, 139
RAMSAY, 6 53 57 68 99 138 145 149 152 160 167 185 211 239
RAMSET, 123
RAMSEY, 53 65 88 99 113 123 125 135 143 161 171 174 182-184 189 198 201 214
RAMSY, 192 196 197
RANDAL, 8 68 125 126 129 135
RANDALL, 63 67 68 135
RANDELL, 183
RANDOL, 135 182 184
RANDOLPH, 73 88 123
RANGE, 217
RANGIE, 1
RANKIN, 43 67 119 138 188 207 209-211 213-215 218
RANSEY, 6 174
RAPIEUX, 131 166
RAPPIEUX, 106
RARDON, 88 149
RAREDEN, 135
RASHAW, 30
RASHER, 171
RASSOR, 31
RATCLIFFE, 88
RATHGE, 200
RATON, 174
RATTAN, 1
RATTE, 217
RATTLES, 72 179
RAUDEN, 24
RAVEL, 138
RAWLINS, 143 175 189
RAWLS, 3 68 135 188
RAY, 87 88 97 123 143 145 148 153
RAYAN, 222
RAYBURN, 56 99 167
RAYEN, 108

RAYMOND, 88
RAYNAL, 67
RAYNOLD, 160
RAZIN, 63 68
RAZY, 56
READ, 6 71 72 88 138 149-152 167 195
READER, 37
READHORST, 31
READMAN, 30 31
READY, 6 45 56
REAGAN, 110
REAIRS, 56
REAM, 188
REAMAN, 119
REAMY, 88
REANNEY, 19 30
REAR, 160
REASON, 224
REAVES, 54 56 135
REAVIS, 52 73 93 175 186 188 229
RECTOR, 3 47 48 88 142 145 149 175 188 233
REDCOCK, 38
REDDIC, 119
REDDICK, 145 217
REDDING, 195
REDDY, 143
REDENAURE, 71
REDIC, 160
REDING, 189
REDMAN, 31 38 52 88
REDMIND, 56
REDMOND, 145 196
REECE, 3 65 88
REED, 39 56 62 65 67 68 74 83 88 98 118 123 130 135 140 145 153 174 175 179 189 193 196 200 203 205 211 233
REEDER, 31
REENES, 150
REES, 56 68 107 188
REESE, 87 88 184
REEVERS, 94
REEVES, 31 143 175 196
REFIELD, 68
REGUIENDAU, 65
REID, 113 135 160
REIDER, 88
REILHE, 234

REILKE, 68
REILLEY, 209
REILY, 176
REINEAU, 237
REITHE, 185
RELFE, 75
REMEY, 135
REMINGHAM, 191
REMMONS, 31
RENAUD, 50
RENCONTRE, 165
RENE, 67
RENFRO, 157 169 179 201 227 232 239
RENFROE, 39 57
RENGER, 130
RENICK, 123 143 163
RENJSTOFT, 31
RENN, 88
RENNARD, 31
RENNER, 22
RENPHROE, 196
RENSHAW, 175
RENVACE, 160
REOCRD, 199
RESE, 227
RESMEMIER, 139
RESS, 188
RETTER, 205
REUME, 140
REUSAU, 1
REVARD, 113
REVELIE, 68
REVELS, 88
REVERE, 68
REVIERE, 68
REVIL, 171
REVINAL, 164
REVIS, 179
REXROAD, 31
REYNAL, 135 235
REYNOL, 151
REYNOLD, 30 99
REYNOLDS, 31 39 68 88 113 135 160 162 189 205 210
REZELSSEUR, 6
RHEA, 85 87 88
RHOADES, 160 171
RHODE, 88
RHODES, 67 88 93 135 138 171 189 195

RHORER, 49
RHYME, 171 205
RIAL, 113
RIARDON, 49 51
RIBAR, 118
RIBET, 115
RIBIDEAU, 160
RIBIDOU, 42
RIBNETT, 240
RICAR, 50
RICARD, 48 50 104 235
RICE, 6 8 30 31 56 57 83 88 110 152 153 174 188-191 194 199 202 222 234
RICHARD, 68 135
RICHARDS, 3 6 31 39 56 86 88 135 160 176 189
RICHARDSON, 3 6 7 40 55 56 63 68 83 85 88 106 107 134 135 143 148 153 168 179 185 189 192 194 195 197 198 201 203 205 220 221 227 238
RICHERT, 88
RICHESON, 71 73
RICHEY, 31 198 212
RICHFIELD, 7
RICHMAN, 67
RICHMAND, 88
RICHMOND, 226
RICHOSON, 135
RICHTER, 147
RICHWELL, 152
RICHY, 39 196
RICKER, 88 145
RICKETT, 147
RICKETTS, 88
RICKMAN, 135
RICKS, 88
RIDDICK, 67 175
RIDDLE, 6 56 88 93 163
RIDE, 67 118 220
RIDEAU, 108
RIDENHAUS, 160
RIDENHOUR, 67 196 199
RIDENOUR, 135
RIDER, 88 113 145 160 205
RIDGEROVE, 56
RIDGEWAY, 3 45 143
RIDGIVARY, 6
RIDGWAY, 56 232
RIDLEY, 88

RIDVELL, 141
RIE, 166
RIENDEAU, 63
RIENE, 119
RIFFE, 39
RIGAUCHE, 67 68
RIGDON, 135
RIGGIN, 176
RIGGINS, 138 189
RIGGS, 6 7 39 40 47 48 56 57 123 138 148 160 162 208 230 239
RIGHTSMAN, 39
RIGOCHE, 67
RIGSBY, 190
RILEY, 68 88 123 145 189
RIN, 160
RINE, 174
RINEY, 59 68
RING, 65 123
RINGER, 170 171
RINGO, 31 175
RINGS, 143
RINOY, 135
RINZ, 235
RIPPEE, 137
RIRD, 160
RISBY, 145
RISHER, 135
RISK, 45 56 123
RISLEY, 88 191 219
RISSINGER, 150
RITCHASON, 135
RITCHELET, 68
RITCHEY, 8
RITCHIE, 215
RITTER, 52 88
RIVAR, 41
RIVARD, 67
RIVARE, 135
RIVE, 165
RIVEL, 171
RIVER, 237
RIVERA, 117 237
RIVET, 65 165
RIVETTE, 165
RIVIERA, 236
RIVIERE, 60 119
RIVIERRE, 62 135
ROACH, 83 85 88 145
ROADE, 169
ROADES, 198

ROARK, 73 138 179 218
ROBARDS, 56
ROBAT, 57
ROBB, 143
ROBBINS, 30 31 88 227
ROBEDOUX, 119
ROBEN, 1
ROBER, 233
ROBERGE, 59 65 135
ROBERSON, 72 226
ROBERST, 98
ROBERT, 1 41 59 63 65 67 68 119 130 135 162 164 165
ROBERTS, 3 6 39 43 68 72 83 85 88 93 135 143 145 146 153 174 190 196 198 203 219
ROBERTSON, 3 39 63 65 68 88 123 135 143 145 147 160 162 175 179 184 201 203 210 227
ROBIDOU, 42 43 164 165
ROBIDOUX, 41 65 135
ROBIEU, 41
ROBIN, 58 59
ROBINET, 48 73 105
ROBINETT, 198 199
ROBINS, 160
ROBINSON, 1 46 47 56 72 86 88 93 96 124 135 138 141-143 145 148 149 152 167 168 175 176 177 180 188 221
ROBISON, 85 135 141 219 226
ROBITAILLE, 103 105
ROBNET, 8
ROBNETT, 44 59 195 239
ROCH, 165
ROCHE, 165 184
ROCHEBLAVE, 50
ROCHEFORT, 129
ROCHELBLAVE, 212
ROCHESTER, 30 52 175 177
ROCK, 68 135 151 205
ROCKWELL, 88
ROCQUE, 68
RODD, 185
RODDAM, 88
RODEL, 228
RODEN, 88
RODES, 174 190
RODGERS, 88 113 128 152
RODNEY, 68 126 134 135 174 184 185

RODNGUES, 68
RODRIGUEZ, 139
RODRIQUEZ, 75
RODS, 168
ROE, 88
ROEBUCK, 68
ROGAN, 68 135
ROGER, 111
ROGERS, 26 34 36 40 47 56 63 65 68 88 123 135 148 149 151 168 174 176 188 196 197 201 205 219 234
ROGERSON, 88
ROGOCHE, 235
ROGUE, 68 135
ROHRER, 68 105
ROHZER, 98
ROI, 135
ROLAND, 56
ROLEL, 166
ROLET, 40 41
ROLLENS, 160
ROLLET, 88 164
ROLLIMS, 39
ROLLINGS, 160
ROLLINS, 65 179
ROLLS, 224
ROLSTON, 123
ROMAIN, 148
ROMINE, 42 63 68 135
ROMINES, 88
RONDEAU, 41 119
ROOKS, 171
ROORS, 171
ROOT, 88
ROOTS, 88
ROQUE, 42 235
RORKE, 59
ROSE, 10 62 63 67 88 111 123 138 145 153 154 171
ROSEBERRY, 88 148
ROSEBURY, 224
ROSENQUEST, 88
ROSIER, 75 164
ROSNEAU, 174
ROSS, 6 31 37 47 56 88 96 97 123 128 135 141 174 189 190
ROSSEAU, 31
ROSSON, 190
ROTARD, 236
ROUBIDEAUX, 62

ROUBIDOUX, 151
ROUBLEU, 164
ROUCE, 31
ROUCEVILLE, 113
ROUDIN, 63
ROUETT, 164
ROUGEAU, 163
ROUILLERS, 68
ROULIER, 185
ROULSON, 6
ROUNDTREE, 205
ROUNSAVILLE, 138
ROUO, 123
ROUP, 123
ROUQUIER, 68 75
ROURK, 135
ROURKE, 68 135
ROUSE, 88
ROUSSEAU, 88 166
ROUSSELL, 67 68
ROUSSELLE, 166
ROUSSIN, 129
ROUTH, 123 215
ROUTIEU, 163
ROUVENBERGACH, 31
ROUVIERE, 88
ROUZED, 88
ROVE, 28
ROVER, 115
ROWARK, 58 59
ROWE, 205
ROWELL, 88 145
ROWEN, 110
ROWLAND, 6 39 43 44 47 67
ROWLEN, 145
ROWLEY, 207 213
ROWNELS, 168
ROWZEE, 135
ROY, 17 29 31 42 43 62-64 66 88 113 114 116 118 119 135 138 151 160 165 174 185 220 222 233 236
ROYE, 135
ROYER, 138
ROYS, 88
RPBIEU, 234
RUBARDEAU, 48
RUBARDU, 30
RUBIDU, 117
RUBIO, 117
RUBLE, 83 88

RUBOTTOM, 184
RUCEN, 35
RUCKER, 238
RUDDEL, 67 68
RUDDELL, 6 135 140
RUDDER, 1 88
RUDDLE, 150
RUGERS, 135
RUGGLES, 67 88
RUHTERFORD, 99
RUKMAN, 68
RULAND, 186
RULE, 193-195
RUMMONS, 45 123
RUMSY, 99
RUNBY, 120
RUNDEAU, 67
RUNNELS, 138
RUNNYAN, 88
RUPARD, 31
RUPE, 3
RUSE, 57
RUSELL, 55-57
RUSH, 8
RUSS, 67 129 135 171
RUSSEL, 28 37 39 141 183 184 191
RUSSELL, 6 56 63 67 68 85 88 110 123 127 148 151 154 160 166 174 181-183 186 187 191 198
RUTGERE, 185
RUTGERS, 21 26 68 160 166 219
RUTHERFORD, 57 83 88 138 145 153 167 198
RUTHRAFF, 174
RUTLEDGE, 123
RUTLER, 174
RUTTER, 8
RWEL, 171
RYAN, 6 56 88 140 151
RYBOLT, 24 31 33 65
RYLEY, 65
RYNOT, 88

- S -

SABIN, 88
SABOURIN, 108
SABOURN, 135
SABUS, 114
SACK, 32 34
SADLER, 88
SAFFRAY, 64 109
SAGO, 168
SAILING, 229
ST ALBIN, 50
ST ANDRE, 135
ST ANTOINE, 119
ST AUBIN, 51 62 75 108 150
ST BEUJENON, 163
ST CLAIR, 88 124 145
ST CYR, 66 119 135 151
ST EBAU, 17
ST GARMIN, 135
ST GEM, 130
ST GEMME, 130
ST GERMAIN, 66
ST JAMES, 64 66
ST JEAN, 101 112 135
ST JOHN, 120 124
ST LOUIS, 32
ST MAIRE, 66
ST MARIE, 65 66 135
ST MARY, 119 151
ST MAY, 119 120
ST ONS, 106
ST PIERRE, 49 62 135
ST VRAIN, 50 63 66
SALE, 163 235
SALES, 48
SALING, 154 190 230
SALISBURY, 40 88
SALISSE, 88
SALKELD, 88
SALLADY, 189
SALLEE, 227
SALLIE, 119
SALLY, 191 205
SALMON, 88 176
SALOIR, 135
SALOMON, 89
SALSBURY, 138
SALYERS, 194
SAMPSON, 33 34 39 92 135 151
SAMS, 8
SAMSON, 64
SAMUE, 55
SAMUEL, 6 56 143 149 188 189
SAMUELS, 32 64 88 145
SANBORN, 98
SANCILARE, 160

SANDERS, 74 124 145 151 166 184
SANDERSON, 6 57
SANDFORD, 175
SAN FRANCISCO, 118
SANGERMAN, 237
SANGUINET, 235
SAN QUARTIER, 65
SANQUINET, 51 118
SANQUINETE, 118
SANQUINETTE, 62
SANSELIE, 114
SANSELIER, 116
SANSIR, 235
SANSON, 107
SANSOUIERY, 163
SANSY, 115
SANTA MARIA, 107 108
SANTEE, 169
SANTOS, 163
SAPENTON, 135
SAPPINGTON, 7 44 56 71 107 134 160-162 190 192 201 203 206 211-215 239
SAPPINTON, 213
SARGENT, 88 177
SARPY, 41-43 50 64 65 106 135 191 233 235
SARTAIN, 209
SARTERS, 88
SAUCESE, 160
SAUCIER, 64 65 135
SAUCIERE, 160
SAUGRAIN, 65
SAUGRAINE, 119
SAUGRIN, 119
SAUIAR, 160
SAULTS, 203
SAUNDERS, 83 88 89
SAUPE, 33
SAURINO, 130
SAVACOOL, 89
SAVAGE, 3 64 124 135 234
SAVANE, 66
SAVARY, 89
SAVERCOOL, 89
SAVOIR, 66
SAVORY, 26
SAVOY, 63 130
SAVOYE, 130
SAWYER, 89
SAXTON, 112 171
SAYERS, 90
SAYLES, 89
SAYTOR, 145
SCABAUGH, 172
SCAGGS, 124
SCANDLIN, 141
SCANTHING, 89
SCARBOUROUGH, 172
SCARLET, 66
SCARRETTE, 66
SCHAAF, 228
SCHMIEDER, 155
SCHMITZ, 155
SCHOFF, 89
SCHOFIELD, 8 89
SCHOLL, 138
SCHOLLAR, 89
SCHOLLING, 240
SCHOLTERS, 150
SCHOVAL, 145 152 167
SCHREVE, 156
SCHRODER, 155
SCHULTE, 156
SCHULTZ, 34 135
SCHULTZE, 89
SCHUSTER, 228
SCHWARZELTHAL, 155
SCHWAZENDAHL, 155
SCIDMORE, 33
SCOFF, 148
SCOGINS, 213
SCONCE, 234
SCOOBARK, 34
SCOT, 135
SCOTLAND, 145
SCOTT, 3 31-33 39 50 55 62 64 66 85 89 99 106 113 124 130 135 138 141 145 150 152 166 168 179 183 185 188 199 216 221 224 226 240
SCOUGH, 31
SCOUTS, 160
SCRIBNER, 175 195
SCRIPPS, 174
SCRIVENER, 57
SCRIVINER, 7
SCRIVNER, 6
SCROGGINS, 107
SCRUGGS, 135
SCUDDER, 188

SCULARD, 106
SCULLY, 89 145
SCULTZ, 145
SEABURD, 129
SEAGRAVES, 32
SEALY, 89
SEAPER, 56
SEAPOUCH, 174
SEARCY, 56 191
SEARLES, 89
SEARS, 47 163 233
SEATON, 6 7
SEAWELL, 173
SEBASTIAN, 97 169
SEBREE, 175
SECOND, 100 106
SECOY, 64
SECTSER, 56
SEE, 8
SEELEY, 66 145
SEELY, 89 129 130 134 135 174
SEELYE, 107 207 211 218
SEERS, 124
SEGON, 75
SEGOND, 50
SEGRASS, 93
SEIGUN, 135
SEIGVION, 220
SEILY, 140
SEIPES, 34
SELANS, 135
SELF, 65 174 179 195
SEMPLE, 47
SENDER, 64
SENECAL, 131
SENOR, 177
SEOUCE, 160
SERAPHIM, 106
SERAPHIN, 59 64 109
SERAPHINE, 109
SERGEANT, 89
SERRE, 114
SERVANT, 119
SESSIONS, 89
SESSUMS, 89
SETTLES, 8
SETTON, 48
SEVIER, 57 89
SEWEL, 174
SEXTON, 64 66 89 128 142 145
  149 152 167 174 225 240

SEYMOUR, 89
SHABAN, 201
SHACKLEFORD, 39 124 149 216
  219
SHACKLER, 66
SHACKLES, 89
SHADDOCK, 89
SHADDUCK, 89
SHAFER, 66 89 124
SHAFT, 89
SHAHLER, 135
SHALL, 160
SHALLENBURGH, 89
SHAMAN, 172
SHANAHAN, 89
SHANDY, 135
SHANER, 174
SHANK, 89
SHANKLAND, 147
SHANKLIN, 229
SHANNON, 8 32 48 89 124 135
  138 145 154 221 231
SHAPLEIGH, 89 145
SHARADIN, 126
SHARP, 89 92 99 113 124 134 142
  160 205
SHARPE, 89
SHARTER, 66
SHATROW, 66
SHATTUCK, 89
SHAUM, 172
SHAVER, 33 34 64 66
SHAW, 3 32 37 39 64 66 74 89 97
  124 125 145 162 169 174 184
  189 225 233 239
SHAWNEE, 119
SHAWNER, 190
SHAY, 89
SHEARMAN, 34 181 205
SHED, 89
SHEDICAR, 37
SHEFFIELD, 89
SHELBY, 89 110 135 141 150 172
SHELEER, 33
SHELEY, 230
SHELL, 56 89 135 172 184
SHELLEY, 66
SHELLY, 3
SHELTON, 9 25 32 33 39 56 73
  89 194 195 199 201 205
SHEPARD, 124 184

SHEPHARD, 89
SHEPHERD, 32 124
SHEPPARD, 89 174
SHERAN, 89
SHERIDAN, 66
SHERLEY, 10
SHERLINE, 89 145
SHERRER, 224
SHERRETTE, 140
SHERRILL, 89
SHERRON, 83
SHERWOOD, 89 145
SHEVANS, 89
SHEVES, 111
SHEVIL, 31
SHIELDS, 7 39 89 148 240
SHILER, 66
SHINN, 32
SHIPP, 181
SHIRKY, 93
SHIRLEY, 89
SHIRLIFF, 167
SHIRO, 141
SHIRREL, 168
SHIRTLIFF, 145 148 149 152
SHIVER, 7
SHIVERS, 89 179
SHOATS, 56
SHOBE, 33 72 113 138 179 180 187
SHOCK, 43 45 56
SHOCKLEY, 7 72 89 179 180 227
SHODE, 180
SHOEMAKER, 85 89 168 190
SHOMAKER, 31
SHOOK, 99 135
SHOOKMAN, 196
SHOOMS, 199
SHORT, 7 57 73 74 175 188 192 193 199 201 203 225 240
SHOULSE, 166
SHOULTS, 211
SHOURNE, 198
SHOVERS, 145
SHRADER, 216
SHRAM, 174
SHROER, 33
SHRUGGS, 149
SHUCKMAN, 202
SHUFFIELD, 89 198
SHULER, 135

SHULTZ, 119 174 214
SHUM, 160
SHUMAKER, 145
SHWIMMER, 141
SIBASIN, 97
SIBLEY, 32 136 151
SIDES, 174
SIEBERT, 109
SIENTZ, 142
SIFFORD, 171 172
SIGAN, 119
SIKELY, 89
SIKES, 89
SILAN, 6
SILCH, 111
SILDEY, 93
SILLON, 143
SILMON, 185
SILVAIN, 66
SILVER, 57 81
SILVERS, 3 56 57 175
SILVESTER, 137
SILVEY, 188
SIMENO, 119
SIMES, 141 160
SIMMER, 189
SIMMONEAU, 163
SIMMONS, 3 6 38 46 47 89 104 138 145 149 150 188
SIMMS, 136 170
SIMON, 172 189
SIMONDS, 30 65 72 136 186
SIMONEAU, 66 235
SIMONNEAU, 106
SIMONO, 115
SIMONS, 13 89 145 194
SIMPKINS, 89 186
SIMPLE, 111
SIMPSON, 6 31 49 50 56 64 66 72 73 89 124 125 130 138 148 175 179 193 195 198 200 201 202 207 216 227
SIMS, 6 7 44 45 56 89 95 97 124 167
SIMSON, 136
SIN, 211
SINCLAIR, 179
SINCOPS, 111
SINGLETON, 89 142
SINGMOND, 56
SINKLAR, 136

SINKLER, 64 134 136
SINNETT, 224
SIP, 64 212
SIPES, 124 202
SIPHER, 223
SIPP, 206 209 211
SIPPLE, 167
SIPTON, 145
SIRRES, 111
SISEMORE, 189
SISSEL, 167
SISSON, 157
SISTON, 53
SITTON, 138
SIZEMORE, 229 230
SKAGGS, 72 73 179 193 197
SKELTON, 175
SKETTETT, 136
SKINNER, 57 64 66 152 176 190 196 198 205
SLACK, 45
SLAGLE, 182
SLASA, 57
SLATER, 89 187
SLATON, 161
SLATOR, 32
SLAUGHTER, 59 89
SLAVE Mat, 94
SLAVEN, 205
SLAVENS, 147
SLAVIN, 45
SLAWN, 124
SLAYTER, 47
SLEATER, 175
SLEATOR, 145
SLICE, 6 56
SLINKER, 66 127 128
SLIP, 89
SLITER, 111
SLIVER, 89
SLOAN, 64 89 148 154 230
SLOCUM, 7
SLOSS, 166
SMALL, 143
SMALLWOOD, 89
SMART, 48 89 230
SMELSER, 32 33 188 234
SMELSOR, 3
SMEMURE, 33
SMIERCER, 160
SMILA, 93

SMILEY, 218
SMILIOER, 160
SMILY, 175
SMIRL, 66 136 211
SMIT, 2
SMITCH, 135
SMITH, ii 2 3 6-8 12 30-34 37 39 40 47 48 55-57 62-66 71 73 74 83 85 89 93 94 97 102 103 106 111 113 124 128 130 134-136 138 139 141 142 144 145 147 148 150 152 153 157 160 167 169 170 172 174-176 181 184 185 188 189 192 193 200 201 205 207 215 216 219 222 224 227 232 233
SMITHE, 31 33
SMITHER, 89
SMITHERS, 93
SMOOT, 190 224
SMYTH, 130 193 194 197
SNEATHAN, 205
SNEDECOR, 189
SNEED, 89 175
SNELL, 85 89 138 231 238
SNELSON, 73 179 186
SNETHEN, 113
SNIDER, 89 171 172 181
SNODDY, 59 64
SNODGRASS, 89 179
SNOTGRASS, 72
SNOW, 89 148 240
SNOWDEN, 39 148 179 185
SNYDER, 32 33 65 89
SOANE, 40
SOCIE, 11
SOCIER, 24 26 32 36
SOCTIN, 56
SOJOURNER, 64 136
SOLCIE, 56
SOLCUM, 56
SOLDENER, 109
SOLLARS, 39
SOLLIN, 111
SOLOMON, 119 124
SOMALT, 66
SOMERS, 183
SOMES, 136
SOMMALT, 63 64 66
SOMMER, 109
SOMMERS, 89

SON, 189
SONE, 73
SONOSS, 6
SONS, 139
SOOK, 89
SOREY, 89
SORREL, 235
SORRET, 116
SOUCIER, 151
SOULARD, 62 66 136 148 151 165
SOULIGNY, 67
SOUMANDE, 67
SOUTH, 225 233
SOUTHARD, 124
SOUTHARDS, 89
SOUTHER, 89
SOUTHERN, 89
SOUTHETT, 152
SOUTHWORTH, 197 199
SOUVAL, 1
SOWELL, 7 203
SPAIN, 32
SPALDING, 32 89
SPANHOUSE, 33
SPANN, 179
SPAON, 202
SPARKS, 67 179
SPARLIN, 224 225
SPARS, 198
SPEAR, 89 179 183
SPEARS, 136 160
SPEERLOCK, 124
SPENCE, 57 73 89 136 160
SPENCER, 13 32 33 49 50 56 67 68 89 101 151 160 186 197 199 209 216
SPERBER, 228
SPERGIN, 224
SPERLING, 89 145
SPICER, 39
SPIES, 205
SPIKES, 89
SPILMAN, 67
SPINCER, 98
SPIRES, 31 113
SPITHA, 93
SPIVY, 89
SPLAWN, 39 47
SPORTSMAN, 47
SPRADLING, 97 169
SPRAGUE, 89

SPRATT, 124
SPRIG, 150 151
SPRIGG, 130 177
SPRING, 181
SPRINGER, 89 124 145
SPRINGSTEAD, 89
SPRINGSTON, 94
SPUEGEON, 224
SPURGIN, 136
SQUIRE, 130
SQUIRES, 89
SROUGE, 106
SRUMM, 172
STACK, 6 57
STADLER, 56
STAFF, 150
STAFFORD, 89 167 168
STAGSDILL, 205
STAINBECK, 136
STALEY, 89 191
STALL, 89 163
STALLCUP, 124
STALLINGS, 89
STALLINS, 89
STAMM, 168
STAMP, 160
STANBERRY, 149
STANDEFER, 203
STANDLEY, 188
STANDLY, 74
STANFIELD, 47 154
STANFORD, 124 174
STANHOPE, 89
STANLEY, 7 39 89 145 160 175
STANLY, 52
STANSBERRY, 89
STANTON, 73 89 124 193
STAP, 8
STAPLES, 85 89 99
STAPLETON, 45 143 175 199 200
STAPP, 8 187
STARK, 89 113 161 179 205 213
STARKE, 44
STARKEY, 72 179 227
STARKS, 97 160 167 168
STARN, 174
STARNATER, 136
STARNETTER, 65
STARNETTLER, 68
STARNS, 89
STARR, 176

STARRET, 179
STATE, 57
STATELAR, 136
STATELER, 172
STATON, 1
STATS, 132
STATT, 124
STAUGHT, 210
STEAD, 89
STEALS, 149
STEARNES, 85 89
STEDMAN, 68
STEED, 172
STEEL, 3 30 33 48 174 189 198 200 202 207 209 234
STEELE, 89 136
STEELSMITH, 32
STEEN, 90 220
STEEPTON, 175
STEERMAN, 90 136
STEES, 71
STEFENSON, 22
STEGAL, 97
STEGALL, 167
STEGDON, 57
STEGMAN, 155 156
STEIN, 106 198
STEINBECK, 172
STELEN, 160
STELL, 71
STEMANS, 143
STEP, 90 148 174
STEPHEN, 33 64 183
STEPHENS, 6 7 39 56 57 65 74 90 93 125 138 171 203-206 208 210 227 231
STEPHENSON, 2 3 6 7 14 26 33 35 57 68 90 113 136 147 160 183 189 205-207 224
STEREGILL, 194
STERER, 32
STERIGER, 138
STERLING, 97
STERN, 47 136
STERNS, 57
STERRITT, 174
STERUT, 196
STEVENS, 7 72 89 90 172 179
STEVENSON, 174
STEWARD, 73 74 130 136 166 186
STEWART, 63 68 83 90 106 148 152 189 190 200 205 206 211 227 231
STIBBS, 89
STICE, 240
STICKNEY, 89 90 148 149
STIDE, 45
STILES, 138
STILESON, 90
STILL, 124 134 138 168
STILLS, 179
STILLWELL, 90 124
STILTS, 90
STILWELL, 64 68
STINEMILLER, 34
STINGER, 64
STINKARD, 172
STINNETT, 225
STINSON, 90 175
STIP, 45
STITES, 71 192 194 195 201-203
STITH, 142
STITT, 124
STIVER, 89
STOATS, 124
STOBAUGH, 124
STOCKADE, 68
STOCKARD, 174
STOCKER, 90
STOCKLER, 68
STOCKSLAGER, 32
STOCKSON, 6
STOCKSTILL, 113 136
STOCKSTON, 199
STOCKTON, 224
STOCKWELL, 90
STODDARD, 68 90 142 149
STODELAND, 140
STOFFLE, 111
STOGDON, 200
STOGSTETTER, 160
STOKER, 67 68 90 174
STOKES, 6 138 145 149 231
STOLEN, 56
STONE, 6 39 44 45 47 56 83 85 90 93 124 145 148 149 152 162 167 189 205 206 224 227
STONEMAN, 47
STONER, 198
STOPHEL, 203
STORMS, 175

324

STORRS, 90 145 167 188 210
STORY, 64 107 172 177
STOTLER, 68
STOTTS, 90 113
STOUCHMEN, 162
STOUT, 65 89 128 176 182
STOVE, 56
STOVER, 90 145
STOWE, 6 72 191
STRAIN, 106 179
STRANGER, 47
STRATON, 57
STRATTEN, 90
STRAUGHN, 90
STREET, 183
STRENGTH, 89
STRICHLING, 205
STRICKLAN, 71
STRICKLAND, 1 63 65 68 90 105 106 136 226
STRICKLER, 89 157
STRICKLIN, 43 147
STRICKLING, 113
STRIDLEY, 111
STRING, 57
STRINGER, 68 136 150
STROAD, 56
STROCKLAND, 212
STRODE, 7 8
STRONG, 145 152 167 174 187
STROPE, 90
STROTHER, 32 68 98 99 106 125 127 130 172 217
STROTHERS, 141
STROTHMANN, 203
STROUKHOFF, 34
STROUP, 172 181
STROVER, 90
STUARD, 33 65
STUART, 138 145 160 166 179 202 217
STUCKLIN, 7
STUERT, 136
STUGUS, 226
STUL, 208
STULL, 90
STULTSMITH, 33
STUMP, 32 33
STUPP, 32
STURD, 28 32 33
STURGEON, 57 90

STURGUS, 135
STUTS, 170
STWEET, 90
SUACOLE, 160
SUBBITT, 174
SUBBLETT, 174
SUBTIB, 111
SUBTIL, 68
SUGG, 90
SULARD, 118
SULIVAN, 119
SULIVEN, 31
SULLEN, 215
SULLENS, 56 67 68 73 177 193 197 202 206 210 238
SULLEVANT, 73
SULLINGER, 56 174
SULLINS, 6 44 194 201
SULLIVAN, 48 68 90 106 107 167 197 208 209 218
SULLIVANT, 179 200
SULLIVANTE, 199
SULLONS, 130
SULTZ, 68
SULY, 173
SUMANDE, 114
SUMMA, 160
SUMMER, 90
SUMMERS, 63 68 113 126 136 139 152 153 160 172 190 191 205
SUMMERVILLE, 68
SUMNER, 32 33 187
SUMPTER, 197
SURNEY, 124
SUSART, 57
SUTEE, 32
SUTHER, 198
SUTILE, 185
SUTTERFIELD, 90
SUTTON, 74 90 113 123 124 145 149 152 167 169 176 238
SWAIN, 90 207
SWANSON, 124
SWARMS, 141
SWATHERCUP, 33
SWEARINGEN, 189
SWEENY, 65 90
SWEET, 90
SWELL, 172
SWENDERMAN, 32 33

SWEZY, 40
SWIFT, 19 29 30 67
SWINNEY, 230
SWINNY, 38
SWIRS, 172
SWITLER, 93
SWOPS, 124
SYLVA, 33

- T -

TABEAU, 237
TABLO, 163
TABO, 117
TABOR, 191
TABOT, 67
TACKET, 72
TAGART, 35
TAGGART, 38
TAGNON, 42
TAGOT, 41
TAILLON, 41
TAILOR, 200 202
TAIT, 189
TALBERT, 6 67 205
TALBOT, 65 99 113 160 205
TALENT, 226
TALLA, 6
TALLET, 135
TALLEY, 90
TALLON, 234 236 237
TALLY, 6 57 189 238
TAMAU, 1
TAMPKINS, 93
TAMU, 1
TANHILL, 67
TANLIN, 57
TANNER, 90
TANQUSLEY, 172
TANSEY, 195
TANSY, 67 135 193 195 202
TANZY, 135 180
TAPLEY, 169
TAPSCOTT, 90
TAQUE, 99
TARART, 18
TARBET, 65
TARDIF, 59
TARDINEAU, 64
TARDIVEAU, 108 138
TARPLEY, 97

TARPY, 42
TARWATERS, 39
TASH, 174
TASKER, 90
TATE, 37 90 124 199 232
TATEM, 176
TATUM, 34
TAUMIER, 68 129
TAUNT, 90
TAWSON, 124
TAYLER, 6
TAYLOR, 225
TAYLOR, 1 3 7 8 12 14 34-36 39
    41 42 48 57 64 65 67 85 90 97
    111 113 119 124 129 135 136
    138 142 143 146 149 152 153
    169 170 175 180 183 188 189
    199 202 205
TAYO, 41
TAYON, 24 25 29 34 35 63-65 68
    113 115 116 130 151 164
TAYSON, 41
TEABEAU, 13
TEABO, 34
TEAL, 90 211
TEAQUE, 6
TEASON, 160
TEATER, 35 57
TEAUQE, 19
TEAUQUE, 57
TEBBS, 124
TEBEAU, 138
TEBO, 113
TEBOU, 135
TEER, 90
TEETER, 44
TEFORD, 143
TEGARD, 142
TEICH, 135
TEISSON, 106
TELA, 140
TELEN, 6
TELER, 56
TELFORD, 39
TELLIER, 75 99 102 103 106 129
TEMBAL, 115
TEMMEN, 156
TEMMON, 156
TEMPLE, 124
TEMPTATION, 160
TENELL, 198

TENEROSO, 114
TENGELDENE, 35
TENNEL, 93
TENNISON, 90
TERLEY, 166
TERRELL, 175
TERRIL, 48 214
TERRY, 90 124 133 149 151 198 202 217
TESEN, 186
TESERO, 1
TESEROT, 97
TESIER, 118
TESO, 119
TESSERAU, 130 133
TESSIER, 68 75
TESSON, 40 41 133 165
TETERS, 188
TETHUM, 37
TETRAU, 99
TETRODUSHAM, 118
TETSON, 175
TEUNGO, 25
TEVAULT, 39
THACKER, 64 150
THACKUM, 1
THARKER, 160
THARP, 7 48 64 90 143 160 218
THATCHER, 90
THAXTON, 143
THAYER, 90
THEBAUT, 133
THEEL, 133
THELUM, 154
THEOBALD, 51
THEREMAN, 224
THIBAULT, 166
THIBEAULT, 62 66-69
THIBULT, 130
THIEL, 69
THILER, 185
THIRIET, 110
THIRIOS, 108
THIROT, 69
THOECLSE, 166
THOMAS, 8 34 35 46 47 69 73 85 90 93 107 113 124 133 138 146 149 160 172 174 181 201 205 206 208
THOMASON, 133

THOMPSON, 3 7 35 39 52 53 57 64 65 67 69 71 72 85 90 102 108 119 124 125 133 138 142 143 146 150 151 154 160 166 168 172 174 175 188 193 196 202 205 218 222 189
THOMSON, 1 64 67 107 138 189 220
THORA, 155
THORN, 64 124 125 174
THORNBURG, 124
THORNHILL, 15 35 113 151 160 201 203 205
THORNTON, 40 113 148 149 181
THORP, 3 55 64 90 124 143 207
THORPE, 124 189
THORSON, 125
THORTOM, 163
THORTON, 7 48
THRALL, 6 57
THRASHER, 8 141 175
THROCKMORTIN, 180
THURMAN, 8 201
THURSTON, 54 90 146 167 226
TIBBS, 216
TIBEAU, 65 66 131 133
TIBO, 116 118
TICE, 113 205
TIDWELL, 1
TIFFANY, 48 90
TIFFEN, 189
TIFORE, 180
TIGERT, 180 226
TILLERY, 40
TILLEY, 57 90 124
TILLORSON, 90
TILMAN, 48 93 188
TILMON, 3 225
TIMBERLAKE, 34
TIMBERLICK, 7 124
TIME, 48
TIMMIN, 172
TIMMONDS, 73
TIMMONS, 90 179
TINCHER, 124
TINDALL, 143
TINGLEY, 90 149
TINKER, 217
TINLEY, 7
TINNER, 160

TINNIN, 67 181 183
TINSBLOOM, 90
TINSLEY, 113
TIOHALL, 7
TIPCER, 34
TIPTON, 6 7 57 67 124 138
TIPUS, 111
TIRARD, 67
TIRART, 65
TIRAT, 106
TIRON, 235
TIRRART, 67
TISDALE, 34
TISON, 67 133 136
TISSCART, 34
TISSEROT, 59
TISSON, 119
TITSWORTH, 93
TIVERS, 172
TIVIS, 177
TIYON, 119
TOALSON, 239
TOBBE, 34
TOCUMBROOD, 67
TODD, 2 3 6 54 57 64 71 124 142 190 194 197 209 213 216 232
TOLLER, 90
TOLSON, 6 188
TOLTEN, 57
TOMBS, 229
TOMIER, 217
TOMKINS, 161
TOMMELIER, 97
TOMPKINS, 90
TOMSON, 97 133
TONER, 90 146
TONEY, 232
TONIECH, 1
TONNELLIER, 133 136
TONY, 203
TOOD, 6
TOOLEY, 48 188
TOOMBS, 191 233
TOOMS, 40 175
TOPPING, 90
TORANCE, 139
TORBOT, 160
TORICK, 169
TOSH, 67
TOTTY, 90
TOULOZE, 40

TOURVILLE, 67 131
TOUSANT, 164 186
TOUSNEY, 139
TOUSSAINT, 106 163
TOUSSANT, 119
TOVONSON, 139
TOWER, 90
TOWERS, 34 90 146
TOWN, 90
TOWNSEND, 64 65 133 136 146 167 225
TOWSAN, 133 136
TOY, 90
TRACY, 90
TRALINE, 146
TRAMEL, 48
TRAMELL, 189
TRAMMEL, 175
TRAMMELL, 3
TRAMORE, 59
TRANG, 141
TRAPP, 124
TRARY, 141
TRAVIS, 3 34 73 90 180
TRAYLOR, 90
TREAL, 90
TREAT, 217
TREBBLE, 163
TREDEAU, 1
TREIGHNER, 90 149
TREMBLE, 90
TRENT, 38 48
TREVILION, 142
TRIBBLE, 37 124 205
TRIBLE, 72
TRIBUE, 185
TRIGG, 143 175 189
TRIM, 160
TRIMBLE, 113 185 205
TRIPLETT, 198 200
TRITLEY, 34
TROGE, 65 130
TROLINGER, 181
TROS, 118
TROTE, 129
TROTER, 133
TROTHER, 174
TROTO, 103
TROTTER, 3 8 40 62 64 65 93
TROUT, 90
TROY, 90

TRUDEAU, 42 43 48 50 57-59 64 166 181 237
TRUDEL, 185
TRUDELL, 43 64 68
TRUDELLE, 131
TRUDO, 118
TRUESDALL, 179
TRUESDELL, 196 203
TRUMLEY, 90
TRUSTEE, 107
TRUSTY, 214 215
TRUTEAU, 41-43 136
TUBBLE, 6
TUCKER, 1 12 28 57 62-65 90 136 138 160 217
TUCKETT, 180
TUGGLE, 190
TUIRET, 140
TUKES, 111
TULLIS, 181
TUMBLINSON, 143
TURGETT, 90
TURKE, 90
TURLEY, 3 93 169 234
TURMURE, 1
TURNAGE, 39
TURNBEAU, 34
TURNBOUGH, 188
TURNBOW, 188
TURNER, 2 3 6-8 34 39 44 45 48 55 57 64 85 90 93 124 138 160 167 177 179 181 189 197 206 238 239
TURNHAM, 90
TURNHILL, 124
TURNLEY, 34
TURPIN, 47 176 180
TURTHER, 98
TUTT, 113
TUTTLE, 6 7 53 54 57 90 113 205 240
TWENTYMAN, 62 136
TWIN, 90
TWINER, 73
TWITTEY, 107
TWITTY, 73 106 107 180 194-196 198 201 225
TWYMAN, 34 59
TYGART, 161
TYLER, 42 174 177
TYON, 138

TYRE, 202
TYRRELL, 90
TYSON, 107 160

- U -

UBALDE, 42
UBALDY, 114
UMBERFIELD, 174
UNDERHILL, 124 225
UNDERWOOD, 90 146 172 225 230
UNGU, 138
UNO, 119
UPRIGHT, 90
UPSHAW, 35
UPTERGROD, 149
UPTERGROVE, 90
URNON, 113
URSHER, 152
USHARA, 140
USRY, 124
UTLEY, 90
UTTERBACK, 230

- V -

VACHARD, 41 42 109 233
VACHARE, 136
VACHEUR, 166
VAGER, 90 146
VAIL, 222
VALANDINGHAM, 40
VALE, 130
VALENCOURT, 90
VALENTIN, 163
VALIER, 141
VALIGN, 65
VALLE, 1 48-51 57-59 64-65 67 74 94 129 130 136 166 185 216 217 233
VALLEE, 130
VALLET, 67
VALLEY, 25 32 36
VALLIER, 119
VALLIERE, 67 76
VALOIS, 136
VALVEY, 119
VAN, 194
VANAMBURGH, 136
VANBERKELAW, 65

VANBIBBER, 18 33 70 72 113 130 138 160 161 205
VANBIBER, 23
VANBOMBLE, 90
VANBUCKALOE, 53
VANBUREN, 90
VANBURKELER, 35
VANBURKELS, 161
VANCAMPSON, 90
VANCARNOP, 8
VANCE, 48 90 97 136 149 170 224
VANDENBENDEN, 70 108
VANDENBURGH, 67 172
VANDENDENDUM, 151
VANDENEUD, 139
VANDERBECK, 90 146
VANDERBURGH, 90
VANDERHIDER, 67
VANDERPOOL, 39 40
VANDERSON, 48
VANDREWER, 90
VANGESON, 90
VANGHAUS, 111
VANHORN, 174 185
VANHORNE, 57
VANIDERSTINE, 65
VANIDESTINE, 110
VANLANDINGHAM, 8
VANLEER, 176
VANLIN, 202
VANMETER, 124
VANMETRE, 64
VANNATOR, 90
VANNSES, 67
VANOSTROWND, 189
VANPELT, 90
VANPHAL, 167
VANQUINBUIN, 35
VANSAN, 119
VANSANT, 90
VANSPERKER, 35
VANTICO, 67
VANUESUR, 6
VANVILLE, 90
VANVRANKON, 90
VAREK, 146
VARKE, 57
VARNER, 90 149
VARNUM, 63
VARSHAM, 90

VASCHARD, 67
VASOR, 236
VASQUE, 41
VASQUER, 41
VASQUES, 41-43 51 160 165
VASQUEZ, 40 64 70 106
VASSER, 40
VASSEUR, 50 70 185
VASSUER, 118
VAUGHAN, 70 136 180 195
VAUGHN, 3 6 40 90 124 150 195 197 198 216
VAYANCOUR, 166
VAZQUEZ, 41 119 234
VEACH, 71 160
VEACOCK, 176
VELKER, 136
VENABLE, 90 141
VENABLES, 142 160
VENAN, 113
VENSEAU, 160
VENUS, 90
VENZAN, 116
VEQUET, 115
VERBRYCK, 8
VERDON, 70 116 165 236
VEREAU, 76
VERIAT, 70
VERILLE, 149
VERIO, 114
VERMILLON, 225
VERMYER, 35
VERNON, 70 136
VERO, 106
VERONEAU, 105
VERRILL, 90
VERY, 141
VEST, 72 174 180 200
VICEROY, 70
VICKERY, 39 40 153
VICTORY, 90
VIDELSAN, 163
VIEMAN, 1
VIEN, 70 165
VIET, 92
VIFVARENNE, 164
VIGE, 236
VIGO, 50 114
VILATT, 124
VILEY, 172
VILLARD, 50

VILLARS, 43 70 105 118 136
VILLENAVE, 130
VILLON, 130
VILSON, 139
VINBITTER, 160
VINCENNES, 43 138 166
VINCENT, 35 41 57 90 138 160
    164 174 235
VINENS, 136
VINEYARD, 71 124
VININGS, 218
VINSEN, 43
VINSTON, 232
VINYARD, 70
VIOLENY, 70
VIOLET, 70
VIOLETT, 11 14 16 34
VIONT, 35
VIOR, 115
VIOT, 67 110
VIRDIAN, 136
VIRGO, 172
VIRIAT, 50
VISIN, 130
VISVARENNE, 163
VITAL, 119 217
VIVAT, 40 48 49 105
VIVERETT, 90 91
VIVES, 111
VIVIAN, 93
VIVIAT, 50 102
VIVION, 225
VIZONETE, 115
VOGEL, 155
VOISARD, 35 70 160
VOISARE, 130
VOISE, 41
VOISZARD, 12
VOLOIS, 165
VOLUNTINE, 91
VONFRAZ, 156
VONHAGEN, 91
VOSBURGH, 91
VOSHALL, 106
VOTARS, 136
VRONAN, 91

- W -

WABROUND, 91
WACHTER, 228

WACKY, 160
WADDLE, 91
WADDUBE, 202
WADE, 90 91 163 205
WADKINS, 136 160
WADLEY, 138 214
WAEMS, 91
WAGGONER, 67 91
WAGNER, 91
WAGNON, 91
WAGNOR, 1
WAHRENDORFF, 176
WAIDE, 90
WAIGLE, 136
WAIT, 91
WAKEFIELD, 6
WAKELEY, 70
WALCH, 57
WALCHE, 36
WALDE, 139
WALDEN, 72
WALDER, 135 136
WALDO, 179 180 199
WALDRON, 91
WALIS, 109
WALKER, 6 8 21 25 33 35 36 54
    70 71 91 98 124 130 136 138
    146 149 151 152 169 172 174
    175 190 198 215 226
WALKOUSE, 7
WALKUP, 7
WALL, 47 70 91 146 172 182 192
    193 195 196 202
WALLACE, 3 36 70 85 91 93 138
    143 150 151 162 174 177 190
    234
WALLER, 70 91 126
WALLING, 172
WALLIS, 136 199
WALLS, 110 160 201 211
WALSH, 53 91 149 181
WALSINGER, 91
WALTER, 182
WALTERS, 124 156 180
WALTHER, 91
WALTON, 91 110 176 209 211
    215 224
WALTRISS, 91
WALWOOD, 48
WALYER, 151
WAMACK, 91

WAMSLEY, 141
WANGER, 146
WARD, 3 7 8 37 40 48 65 70 85 91 93 99 106 113 124 135 138 147 149 172 176 189 192 195 205 206 218 237
WARDEN, 3
WARDERMAN, 91
WARDLOW, 36
WARDON, 146
WARDRODE, 91
WARDWELL, 91
WARE, 64 71 180 186 195 200
WAREN, 191
WARFIELD, 174
WARICK, 143
WARING, 136
WARNER, 91 124 138 143 209
WARNICH, 143
WARNICK, 143
WARREN, 64 91 149 191
WARRIN, 91
WART, 172
WASH, 38 59 150 154 186
WASHAM, 90 91
WASHBOURN, 91 136
WASHBURN, 70
WATERBERRY, 91
WATERMAN, 91 168
WATERS, 70 92 105 107 133 136 151 177 226
WATHINTON, 196
WATKINS, 18 19 34 64 67 91 118 151 154 174 179 182 185
WATLINGTON, 91
WATSON, 35 36 48 72 74 91 94 113 141 142 146 147 160 172 180 185 200 207 240
WATT, 107
WATTES, 35
WATTS, 64 85 91 146 160 208 216 233
WATWOOD, 149
WAUGER, 91
WAY, 91 149
WAYNE, 7
WEALTHY, 70
WEALTY, 26
WEANS, 149
WEATHERS, 37 67 91

WEAVER, 3 65 70 91 125 136 234
WEBB, 91 168
WEBER, 216 223
WEBKINS, 70
WEBSTER, 48 214 221 229
WEDDLE, 206
WEDINGTON, 91
WEDSAY, 70
WEED, 91 145 146 176
WEEDEN, 3 175
WEEDIN, 74
WEEKLY, 91
WEELAND, 70
WEHR, 203
WEISTORF, 156
WELBORN, 136
WELCH, 3 71 91 106 113 124 136 142 146 149 172 193 205
WELCOME, 91
WELDE, 36
WELDEN, 21 30 48 160
WELDON, 21 64 70 234
WELKER, 70 128 129 174
WELLBORN, 128 129
WELLDON, 40
WELLES, 36
WELLS, 12 36 40 48 91 94 124 129 162 186 191 192 206 207 233 234
WELOT, 36
WELSH, 70 91 187 205 209
WELSS, 160
WELTON, 180
WELTY, 151 174 183
WEN, 57
WENSENVICKLES, 36
WENTZELL, 135
WENZEL, 36
WERNER, 155
WERSTORFF, 155
WERT, 140
WESCOTT, 136 216
WESKY, 174
WESNER, 91
WESSEN, 91
WESSENHUNT, 91
WESSING, 156
WESSLING, 156
WEST, 40 43 46 71 72 91 106 146

WEST (continued)
  149 152 176 177 179 187 192
  194 196
WESTBROOK, 70 91 93 111
WESTCOAT, 119
WESTLEY, 57.
WESTON, 91
WESTOVER, 70 136
WETHERELL, 91
WETHINGTON, 150
WETMORE, 36 146
WETTON, 72
WETZEL, 181
WHALEN, 91
WHALEY, 8
WHAPLES, 91
WHARF, 91
WHARFF, 146
WHARTON, 175
WHEAT, 47 64 70 136
WHEATON, 136
WHEELAND, 193
WHEELER, 91 113 146 160 172
  182 184 193 196 205 210 227
WHELESS, 91
WHELIN, 91
WHELMAN, 195
WHERRY, 67 151
WHETER, 202
WHICK, 57
WHIDDEN, 91
WHILTEY, 57
WHIPPLE, 91 146 172
WHISKINMAN, 190
WHITAKER, 70 91
WHITE, 1 7 8 36 37 48 49 51 70
  85 91 93 124 136 140 143 146
  150 151 198 201 203 225 231
  240
WHITEFIELD, 146
WHITEHEAD, 91 215
WHITELOW, 174
WHITELY, 91
WHITESIDE, 107 136 206
WHITESIDES, 42 70 113 142 167
  206 208
WHITESITT, 189
WHITFIELD, 91
WHITFORD, 105
WHITINBURG, 168
WHITING, 150
WHITLEDGE, 174
WHITLEY, 70 93 130 136
WHITLOCK, 3 40 91
WHITLOW, 91
WHITMAN, 85 91
WHITMEY, 91
WHITMIRE, 199 202
WHITMORE, 73 91 187 193 194
  196
WHITNEY, 91 149 172 189
WHITON, 143
WHITSON, 40 70 91 149
WHITT, 189
WHITTENBAUGH, 174
WHITTENBURGH, 229 230
WHITTERY, 160
WHITTLE, 36
WHITTLESEY, 91 217
WHITTON, 91 124
WHITWORTH, 199
WIARD, 91
WIATT, 90
WICE, 4 124
WICJERSHAM, 37
WICKAM, 150
WICKARD, 91
WICKERD, 146
WICKERHAM, 136 227
WICKERSHAM, 70 91
WICKHAM, 91
WICKLIFFE, 149
WICKWISE, 91
WIDE, 91 146
WIDEMAN, 64 70 135 136
WIEFFERMULLIR, 139
WIELAND, 136
WIETT, 35
WIGER, 169
WIGGENTON, 48
WIGGIN, 146
WIGGINS, 40 70 91 113 142 153
  190
WIGGINTON, 232
WIKEY, 149
WILBAR, 91 149
WILBOIT, 143
WILBORN, 240
WILBOURN, 70
WILBURN, 44 170
WILCOLMEN, 57
WILCOX, 6 7 57 91 124 189

WILDER, 91
WILDS, 91
WILEY, 70 91 162 174
WILFONG, 172
WILFREY, 138
WILHEIM, 91
WILHILL, 6
WILHITE, 44 189
WILKERSON, 15 48 91 124 183
WILKES, 6
WILKEY, 91
WILKINSON, 91 143 149 174
WILL, 7 36 174
WILLABY, 206
WILLARD, 40 72
WILLBORN, 229
WILLCOCKSON, 181
WILLES, 91
WILLET, 176
WILLEY, 91
WILLGATE, 70
WILLHYTE, 40
WILLIAM, 42 146 148
WILLIAMS, 3 7 35 36 39 40 48
    50 54-56 67 70 74 85 91 92 97
    99 105 113 124 126 136 138
    141 143 146 149 150 152-154
    160-162 167 169 172 175-177
    180 183 184 189 193-196 198
    203 205-209 211 214 216 218
    221 223 224 229
WILLIAMSON, 85 92 113 128 146
    180 193 194 198 201 202 206
    238 239
WILLINGHAM, 7 232
WILLIS, 92 124 149
WILLS, 40 92 124 185
WILLSON, 36 39 40
WILSARFIELD, 7
WILSERE, 149
WILSON, 37 48 55 63 64 70 85 92
    95 97 102 105 108 109 120 124
    136 138 143 146 150 167 168
    172 174 175 179 180 183 189
    196 197 199 210 215 216 224
    227 238
WIMET, 131
WINAGRAM, 7
WINAGRIN, 7
WINANT, 28
WINCHESTER, 136

WIND, 57
WINDES, 167
WINDSON, 7
WINDSOR, 92
WINFIELD, 37
WINGFIELD, 106 136
WINKELMAN, 156
WINKFIELD, 7
WINKLEMAN, 156
WINKLER, 190
WINN, 7 105 124 143
WINSCOT, 3
WINSCOTT, 7 43 232
WINSLOW, 92
WINSOR, 63 65 70 110
WINSTON, 124 130 216 225
WINTERBOWER, 37
WINTERS, 64 70 224
WINWRIGHT, 124
WIRE, 174
WIRT, 146
WIRTZ, 92
WISDOM, 175 196 216
WISE, 36 70 129 162
WISEMAN, 7 57 70 136 143 177
    208
WISEMANT, 224
WISER, 97
WISHART, 70
WISWELL, 92
WITEMAN, 172
WITHE, 110
WITHERINGTON, 70 107
WITHERS, 146
WITHINGTON, 200-202 211
WITHINTON, 200 212
WITMER, 103
WITT, 37 140 183 188
WITTAKER, 127
WITTINGTON, 199
WITTINSTON, 107
WITTMAN, 105
WIZOR, 170
WOLCUP, 3
WOLF, 35 36 70 151
WOLFE, 161
WOLFORT, 189
WOLFRUM, 228
WOLFSCALE, 93
WOLFSKILL, 3
WOLSEY, 70 201

WOLVERTON, 184
WOOD 3, 6 36 37 63 70 92 93 105 111 124 136 138 145 146 149 170 172 189 202 239
WOODARD, 40
WOODBANKS, 92
WOODBRIDGE, 181
WOODBURY, 92
WOODCOCK, 92 146 199
WOODEN, 92
WOODES, 36 140
WOODFOLK, 48
WOODLAN, 136
WOODLAND, 7 73 196
WOODNESS, 189
WOODROUGH, 21
WOODS, 2 3 7 25 40 45 53 55 92 118 136 147 154 160 179 188 224
WOODSON, 48 152 238 239
WOODWARD, 92 149 154
WOODY, 124
WOOLAMS, 186
WOOLERY, 73 74 186
WOOLF, 12 33 35 52 188
WOOLFOLK, 36 162 176
WOOLFORD, 70 97 136
WOOLFORK, 35
WOOLLAMS, 72
WOOLOMS, 130
WOOLSEY, 40 129
WOOLSY, 196
WOOLTON, 36
WOOTEN, 92
WOOTON, 92
WORD, 36
WORDEN, 92
WORKER, 189
WORKMAN, 175
WORLEY, 92 183
WORMINGTON, 225
WORSHAM, 92
WORTEBESON, 57
WORTEN, 160
WORTH, 65
WORTHINGTON, 70 125 127 136 146
WRANGLER, 198
WRAY, 35 64 92 206
WREN, 57

WRIGHT, 7 25 27 37 57 59 92 129 136 141 146 151 174 177 180 205 209 218 239
WYAN, 177
WYATE, 160
WYATT, 36 70–72 92 99 113 146 160 179 180 192 195 205 206 227
WYCHE, 152
WYGATE, 160
WYHTE, 92

- Y -

YAGER, 37
YAKIN, 160
YANCEY, 92 143
YANCY, 176
YARBROUGH, 64 70 92
YARDLEY, 36 160
YARLIND, 95
YARNEL, 36 37
YARNELL, 160
YARNEY, 92
YARNOLD, 37
YATES, 5 72 124 205 216 227
YEARNS, 92
YEATY, 92
YENEN, 143
YERSEN, 176
YOCUM, 124 215
YODER, 172
YOKEM, 191
YOKUM, 36
YON, 70
YONT, 136
YORK, 105
YOSTEE, 119
YOSTI, 50
YOSTIE, 136
YOSTY, 70 164 235
YOUNCE, 172
YOUNG, 3 6 36 37 64 65 70 72 73 85 91 92 99 106 113 124 127 129 136 138 143 146 150 153 160 172 174 177 181 185 199 206 210 211 215 233
YOUNGER, 113 138 167 216
YOUNT, 172 176 184
YOUNTS, 124

YOWS, 3

- Z -

ZACHARY, 225
ZANDT, 118
ZANES, 70
ZEDDIES, 37
ZELLIFROM, 64
ZELLIFROW, 70
ZEUMWALT, 136
ZEVELY, 138

ZIESLER, 228
ZILLEFROW, 174
ZIMMEREMAN, 27
ZIMMERMAN, 92
ZOMWALT, 151
ZUEMEL, 41
ZUMALT, 9 12 14 17 18 20 25 27 28 37 197
ZUMATT, 160
ZUMWALL, 143
ZUMWALT, 18 23 28 31-33 36 113 130 138 142 196 199 206 208

Paola Free Library
101 E. Peoria
Paola, KS 66071